MARTHA

"I know of no other biography of a dancer that probes so far into the living connection between the artist's life—especially the inner life—and the shape of the work. This book is an instance of the right person doing the right job at the right time."   —*New Republic*

"With this big, ambitious book, de Mille...paints some fine portraits—and regularly comes up with astute psychological insights. Her writing... is popular in its appeal and inviting to the general audience...a lively read."   —*Los Angeles Times Book Review*

"[A] persuasive analysis of the artistic persona...de Mille's portrait has an immediacy and sense of presence not likely to be equaled by any future biographer."   —*Washington Post Book World*

"Lively, elegant, opinionated writing...should delight anyone with an interest in American modern dance. This is a fine period history of dance as well as an understanding portrayal of Graham's art and the life she dedicated to it."   —*Atlantic*

"A rich tome brimming with facts, opinions, episodes, people's reminiscences, the author's memories and descriptions of dances, and, above all, with feeling—live, burning, yet wise emotions on every page."   —*New York Newsday*

"De Mille's substantial biography takes the reader in hand and tells the story of a ferociously creative powerhouse...a character larger than life in both horrible and splendid ways, whose triumphs and excesses rival the Greek myths."   —*Christian Science Monitor*

Agnes de Mille

MARTHA

Agnes de Mille—dancer, choreographer, director, lecturer, and writer—is the author of thirteen
books, including *Dance to the Piper, And
Promenade Home, Reprieve,* and *Portrait Gallery.*
Her ballets include *Fall River Legend, Three
Virgins and a Devil,* and the world-famous *Rodeo,*
and she choreographed many of Broadway's
best-known musicals, among them *Oklahoma!,
Carousel, Brigadoon, Gentlemen Prefer Blondes,*
and *Paint Your Wagon.* The recipient of numerous awards and honors, including the National
Medal of the Arts, the Kennedy Center Honors,
and the Handel Medallion, she lives in
New York City.

THE LIFE AND WORK
OF MARTHA GRAHAM

MARTHA

BY AGNES DE MILLE

VINTAGE BOOKS
A DIVISION OF RANDOM HOUSE, INC.
NEW YORK

**To the dancers who dedicated their lives
to developing the Graham technique and her
extraordinary repertoire.**

First Vintage Books Edition, October 1992

Copyright © 1956, 1991 by Agnes de Mille

All rights reserved under International and Pan-American
Copyright Conventions. Published in the United States by
Vintage Books, a division of Random House, Inc., New York,
and simultaneously in Canada by Random House of Canada
Limited, Toronto. Originally published in hardcover by
Random House, Inc., New York, in 1991.

Pages 476–77 constitute an extension of this copyright page.

Library of Congress Cataloging-in-Publication Data
De Mille, Agnes.
    Martha: the life and work of Martha Graham / by Agnes
de Mille.—1st Vintage Books ed.
        p.   cm.
    Originally published: New York: Random House, 1991.
    Includes bibliographical references and index.
    ISBN 0-679-74176-3 (pbk.)
    1. Graham, Martha.   2. Dancers—United States—
Biography.   3. Modern dance.   I. Title.
[GV1785.G7D4   1992]
792.8′028′092—dc20
[B]   92-50068
                    CIP

Manufactured in the United States of America
10 9 8 7 6 5 4 3 2 1

This is the story of a genius, of a woman who made a greater change in her art—in the idiom, in the technique, in the content, and in the point of view—than almost any other single artist who comes readily to mind.

Martha Graham has given us a body of dance technique as complex and formal as that of ballet; yet ballet has been evolving for over four hundred years, while Martha Graham produced her dance, the Graham, or so-called modern, technique, in the space of one lifetime. It is reasonable to believe that henceforth every theater dancer who is exposed to this new style will move differently because of it.

Graham has left a body of theater works and a style and technique of production comparable only to the Grand Kabuki of Japan. Yet the Grand Kabuki perfected its repertory and playing style during two hundred years, and the emperor and court of Japan sponsored and supported the development; Martha Graham made her contribution largely alone, and certainly without government aid. And she was poor.

"Her achievement is equivalent to Picasso's," I said to Mark Ryder, a pupil and company member of Graham's.

"I'm not sure I will accept him as deserving to be in her class."

I thought a minute. "I'm not sure, either," I said, then, "No, surely not. Surely no one has done as much original work on all levels."

"Would you accept Wagner?" another Graham pupil suggested.

"Maybe Wagner."

Now, these are big claims, and when they are made about supreme artists in fields other than dance, they can be substantiated by the works themselves, which can stand as confirmation. Moreover, the works of predecessors and successors stand alongside, so other artists can be studied in comparison with one another and judged. In fields other than dance we know an artist's works in perspective, as well as in historical progression.

But dance has no recorded history. It is like an accumulation of earth castings: we only know generally through residual tricks and devices, by simple patterns and manner, what the old creations were like. We never know exactly, and we never know the individual deviations which are the mark of personality. It is easy, for instance, to recognize eighteenth-century music immediately, but why Mozart was very much greater than any of his contemporaries we would never know if we had not other music to gauge by. Fortunately we do have it, and so we understand Mozart, and because of this we understand Beethoven, and after him Brahms. But who lies behind Petipa? Coralli, Perrot, Taglioni, and behind them Vestris and Noverre? Names only, and steel engravings. Where are their works? They are utterly lost. Only Bournonville survives, because of the meticulous and unbroken preservation of his work by the Royal Danish Ballet. What we have of eighteenth-century dancing is remnants only, embalmed within the port de bras and foot positions and the enchaînements of the classic ballet school technique. The dances themselves and the old style are lost.

So how is a writer to make claims about an artist of dance; how to substantiate claims of Graham's significant quality? If the reader cannot see, how will he be able to evaluate? Dancing is a visual art. It exists in physical movement in time-space. It does not exist in words. Yet it devolves upon a writer to evoke one art through the medium of another, always an unsatisfactory and uncertain undertaking. My claims about Graham's art, therefore, although based on fifty years of theatergoing and study with scholars who have re-created old forms, still are only claims based on air. And so my evaluation of Graham's contribution as an artist has to remain an impression, and a personal one.

Martha Graham has said, "There are two kinds of dancing: good and bad." Any humbug, anything fake, any compromise or flimflam incurred her bitter scorn. She was exacting in her criticism of others, certainly, and she was no less merciless with herself. Her life bore testimony to this.

One must recognize, I believe, that certain few individuals are obsessed, that they believe they are, in effect, vessels of higher forces, that they recognize themselves as such, and that they have no choice in the matter; they are taken over and used for life, for their art or vocation. Martha Graham believed she was such an instrument. She quoted Ibsen's phrase "doom eager"—which she first encountered in Robert Edmond Jones's lectures—to describe herself. As a result, she felt she must cut from her life all deep emotional involvements, all attachments, all comforts, even moments of leisure, and, beyond that, love involving family and children. She gave everything to her work, withheld nothing, kept nothing apart.

She could do this because she knew she was there to be used. There was no false modesty. The process had nothing to do with modesty. Saints do not doubt their own worth. Whatever their verbalizations, they are consumed. The power blinds them. There is no self left to be modest about. When one has experienced this communion with power, one is never the same again. One is selfless; one is wholly selfish. One can become cruelly brutal, because nothing else matters. It is that simple.

Few people outside the cloister have known this, except possibly tyrants such as Hitler or Stalin. This totality of dedication, however, was the price Graham, as a laywoman, was willing to pay. Whether or not it was a necessary price is open to question. But she clearly felt the sacrifice was necessary, and she was prepared to make it.

William Butler Yeats has said that the individual is capable of either great art or great life, but not both.

One must understand Graham's credo, her reason for dancing. Martha Graham wanted to dance, not just to have a pleasant time or to be the center of attention and attract praise, although these tempting elements entered into her plans. Graham wanted to attain goals that were quite different. She did not look upon dancing as entertainment but as an exploration, a celebration of life. It was her very reason for living, this dance which was all-important, in a sense sacrosanct, and never to be taken frivolously or used, as many professionals use their skills, for monetary gain. On the contrary, dancing was to be served and used only for an audience accepting of her austere terms.

Graham's severe attitude might have been considered pretentious, except for the quality of her work: her ideas turned out to be verities. Graham's point of view marks her apart from other theater artists, because although all gifted experts work under the imposition of iron standards, very few—indeed, only the inspired ones—think of themselves as chosen servants of a higher purpose.

"Wherever a dancer stands ready, that spot is holy ground," Martha Graham often said.

When she was done with an idea or a person, she cut that idea or person off, shedding a skin as snakes do, dropping habits, customs, loyal associations—yes, even friends. To some this appears phoenixlike; to others, reptilian. And, naturally, the rejects were not happy.

Making this terrible choice—serving work to the exclusion of all else—is a price modern women are now refusing to pay. But Martha, although outwardly the prototype of the advanced woman and a symbol of female achievement, in a sense reveals herself on deeper examination to have been among the last of the sacrificial females, a nineteenth-century victim. In any case, on these and many other accounts Martha Graham was supremely important as an artist and as a woman.

The actress Katharine Cornell spoke to me often of Graham as "One of the greatest artists in any field that America has produced in all its history." I would add, "And one of the bravest."

She was a great dancer. She was a greater choreographer, although she never wanted to choreograph, and she made this clear time after time. But since the kind of dancing she wanted to do didn't exist, she was forced to invent it.

When one studies the roster of Graham's works, one is brought up against the fact that here is a catalogue of comprehensive, lengthy, and splendid achievement. The list is long, the quality of work varied, the polish of performance unsurpassed, and it is all encompassed by one very small human being. Her immortality will rest on this—this and the splendid technique she devised, which was quite new, which has gone into the permanent dance vocabulary, and which of itself is very beautiful.

Martha always wanted to leave behind a legend, not a biography. To this end she deliberately and industriously made the way of any biographer difficult. She destroyed personal documents, letters, records, even books and articles about her wherever she found them: her letters to her mother, her letters to her lovers, old programs and reviews—all destroyed. The past was to be obliterated and reshaped according to Martha's will and by whatever testament she chose to leave. Martha, one must remember, was a perfectionist: one can understand, even sympathize with, her attitude that anything less than the ideal was to be abolished. Yet such sheer distortion of historical fact drives an historian mad. I'm reminded of the widow of a famous writer who said to me after burning all her husband's diaries, "Who'd want to see those old papers? There was nothing in them but facts."

Martha's legend was maintained, therefore, through the testament of students, whose memories were and are, of course, imperfect; and although they could probably reproduce the counts of an entire ballet, they could also be wonderfully casual about dates and sequences of events—in short, about facts.

I never studied with Graham. She wouldn't have it, exhorting—nay, commanding—me to find my own way. She thereby saved me a lot of time, since most certainly I would not have been a successful Graham pupil. I never saw a Graham working session, only show demonstrations, where she deliberately put her pupils, who were then called her "girls," on parade for expected visitors. I never saw a working rehearsal in which new ideas were forged out of sweat and air, but I have talked to fifty or more of her pupils, and I have bootlegged private classes from one of her oldest protégées. I believe I understand the Graham technique, which I, although I am a trained ballet technician, found impossible to execute. I am a choreographer and something of a dance historian with a keen sense of the meaning of movement. I believe I have a candid eye. Perhaps, therefore, I am more qualified to appraise Graham's work than someone who was molded by her, who knew no other dance language.

I knew Martha mainly as an adoring younger sister might, and worshiped her surprising and authentic gifts. I came to lean on her strength and often in the early days of our friendship begged her opinion after each of my own concerts. On occasion, I sought her nonprofessional advice. She must have liked me, yet very possibly I was also at times a burdensome nuisance in my constant pleading for advice, my talents manifesting themselves in such a comparatively frivolous manner and in such a derivative style. But she was kind and helpful, and not just on professional matters. Nevertheless, Martha maintained throughout the decorum of a quadrille and spoke always with delicacy about personal matters. In only one single instance did she make a personal confession to me. She did not indulge in girl-gossip or even reminiscences. Yet I can write about the person, Martha Graham, a woman whom I knew for fifty-eight years, and whom I loved. I can, I believe, indicate the forces and demons that drove this small, bewitching creature to her unmatched achievement. And I can portray her life and achievement in the context of the history of the dance.

After I came to know Martha Graham, I realized that hers was one of the most provocative minds I had ever encountered. She invariably spoke with absolute authority. It turns out she didn't always feel certain. "But"—as she explained to me later, giggling as she said it—"I never tell." No matter what she told or didn't tell, the works endure. Uncompromising, unblemished, her theater stands as a generic force in the culture of our time.

ACKNOWLEDGMENTS

Kate Medina first proposed the idea for this book in the late sixties. I agreed, not having the faintest idea what I was committing myself to. The writing has taken between twenty and twenty-five years. I had previously written several pieces on Martha Graham, mainly impressions and memories. These were casual, valuable only because they were fresh and personal. And I had written several volumes of my own memoirs. But in autobiographical instances I could be sure about dates because I remembered them, and if I made a mistake, I was misrepresenting only myself; a misstatement would not be apprehended or punished. But when dealing with other people's lives, one must be accurate. It is ill-advised to be careless, offhand, frivolous, or untruthful, and I discovered to my dismay that I had to name the exact source for every single statement. I had not kept careful records at the beginning, and had to go back over my material repeatedly. The book has been totally recast about seven times, during which I have made merciless use of everyone who knew Martha Graham.

Martha was always hostile to the idea of people writing about her personally, refusing to speak to them ever again if they did so, as in the case of Walter Terry and Don McDonagh. I made an initial and tentative attempt to persuade her to reminisce about her childhood. After submitting me to piercing scrutiny, she said tartly that she was going to write her own autobiography and changed the subject. No, I couldn't go to her or ask to use her files. Someone will have access to these, undoubtedly, unless Martha destroyed them, and it is within her pattern to have done so, but until the definitive, factual book appears we must rely on the memories of others. Friends and pupils have been more than helpful.

Not wanting to damage what was to me a valued relationship, I withheld publication of the book on which I had been working for nearly twenty-five years. Kate Medina and the publishers agreed to honor my wishes. Martha Graham died on April 1, 1991, thereby releasing me from our self-imposed restraint. My story ends in 1987, but nothing I projected has been contradicted by subsequent events. The four-year delay in publishing is hereby explained.

I want to thank especially:

Dancers: Patricia Birch, Dorothy Bird, John Butler, the late William Carter, Jane Dudley, Jean Erdman, Nelle Fisher, Erick Hawkins, Martha Hill, Mary Hinkson, Stuart Hodes, Pearl Lang, Charles McGraw, Sophie Maslow, May O'Donnell, Bertram Ross, Mark Ryder, Gertrude Shurr, Anna Sokolow, Paul Taylor, Glen Tetley, the late Charles Weidman, Sallie Wilson, and Ethel Winter.

Non-dancers: Harry Bernstein, Horton Foote, the late John Houseman, the late Robin Howard, Lewis Isaacs, Lucy Kroll, Nathan Kroll, Lee Leatherman, Lillian Libman, Gert Macy, Dorothy Madden, June Rhodes, Doris Rudko, and Martha Swope.

These kind people have each given me at least two interviews and some as many as fifteen, in particular, Pearl Lang, Bertram Ross, Glen Tetley, and John Butler, who corrected my manuscript as we went along.

I want to thank profoundly the late Joseph Campbell, who not only submitted to interviews for hours, but made me a gift of his analysis of the Kundalini after I had taped it.

My deep gratitude and thanks go to Robert Moulton and Robin Howard for their generosity in permitting me to quote from their material.

Mary Green typed the first ten years of the work, an arduous and painstaking labor; Denise Erica Cogan has done the second decade. This represents an heroic effort. Because of my physical disabilities and relative helplessness, the vast accumulation of paper, the corrections and adjustments, presented an unremitting challenge. The sheer legwork imposed unusual labor.

Jean-Isabel McNutt has corrected the final copy with unflagging care and enthusiasm; no detail has seemed too insignificant to her for verification, no date too elusive. She has persisted wonderfully. She has also used judgment, recognizing blocks for just what they were: dead ends. This sense of reality is unusual, and most welcome to an author.

Thanks to Laurie Platt Winfrey and Fay Torresyap at Carousel Research, who have been doggedly persistent in the hunt for photographs. Martha has been as well reproduced as any head of state. Fresh pictures are therefore a rarity. These they found.

Olga Tarnowski has been tireless in helping with the endless editorial and production tasks of seeing this book through to publication.

I wish to thank the Xerox Corporation, without whose extraordinary invention my book could not possibly have been written. I could not go to libraries or newspaper files or even open a dictionary; my assistant brought the libraries to me.

Throughout the long process, Kate Medina has been faithful and staunch, cheering me on with hearty optimism and strong praise when my spirits fainted from sheer ennui. In 1975 I suffered a massive stroke. I recovered, but never regained the use of my right side. My writing hand was lost to me forever. Medina had to wait for me to learn to write with the left hand. This took time. At one point there was a long period during which I was on the outs with Miss Graham and wished to hear no more about her, to think no more of her problems. And Medina, and her publishing house, waited quietly and attentively until I came out of the doldrums. Her staunchness, her cheeriness, and her very real appreciation of my labors—above all, her taste and discrimination—beggar thanks. I do not know how to describe my indebtedness. It is axiomatic that we became very deep friends in the process.

CONTENTS

first saw Martha Graham when she was a dance student at the Denishawn School of Dancing in Los Angeles in 1918.

Although my mother's first instinct was always to protect what she considered her daughter's "God-Given Talent" from outside influence, she nevertheless maintained a four-year flirtation with Ruth St. Denis and Ted Shawn, hovering and teasing around the Denishawn school while steadfastly refusing to enroll me. The upshot, inexplicably, was that Ruth St. Denis, almost perversely, became interested in my professional development, while her husband became Mother's devoted, lifelong friend. I grew to be a familiar of their school, and was invited to watch classes and performances, to browse in their library, and even to play about with veils and props under the gentlest of supervision. I remained throughout impervious to blandishments and at last entered Theodore Koslov's School of Imperial Russian Ballet and so was lost forever to nonballetic training.

But I did see Martha Graham working in class as a student, dancing first in groups and later as Ted Shawn's partner. Even then, one sensed that what she was doing was important, simply because she was doing it. What she did was exactly what the others did, and yet it was Graham one remembered.

I saw her again in the mid-twenties in New York. I would see her at Sunday-night dance concerts, sitting beside Louis Horst, the pianist, upstairs in the balcony, in the seats they could afford. They sat seemingly apart from the rest of the audience, looking somber, never joining in the crowd response. But even without moving, Martha became the center of attention. Everyone in the theater knew she was there.

I saw her give her own Sunday-night recital in New York in 1927 and was moderately impressed. Very ingenious, I thought.

I met Martha Graham in 1929. Martha was at the time thirty-five years old. Her lover, Louis Horst, was ten years older.

Louis and I got to know each other in October 1928, when I joined for a short time the Adolph Bolm Ballet Intime on its brief tour of mainly southern states. This tour was a lucky opportunity for me. I was just twenty-two, green to the profession, and had not yet made my professional debut.

We all knew who Louis Horst was. He accompanied all the important dance recitals in New York at that time. John Martin of *The New York Times*, the leading American dance critic, wrote in *Dance Magazine* in April 1955 when Louis received the Capezio Award:

For forty years Louis Horst has been a dominant figure in the development of American modern dance, not only directing orchestras, playing the piano and writing music for dancers, but also acting as guide and coach, scold and conscience, teacher, censor, arbiter of taste and general catalyst. When he came upon the scene, the modern dance was only a decade or so from its beginnings, and the presence of a strong mind with a progressive turn and a stubborn sense of discipline could scarcely have failed of effect.

Horst never confessed to an enthusiasm about dancing in any of its aspects. On the contrary, he invariably feigned a kind of amused contempt, as though dance were an inferior art. Yet he spent his entire working life criticizing, helping, teaching about dance, and, as Martha Graham said years later, "It doesn't matter what he says. I notice he's still around."

When I met Louis Horst in 1928 he was in Chicago supervising and conducting the music for the Ballet Intime. Ruth Page, Bolm's charming American prima ballerina, had married and departed the company the year before, and Bolm was sadly casting around for a replacement. It was not easy to find someone, because Page had been extremely pretty, vivacious, and effective, and Bolm missed her sorely. Then he hit upon the idea of having several solo dancers fill the vacancy instead of just one star. Before my professional dance debut, in December 1928, he invited me to join his company, sharing star ranking with Vera Mirova and Berenice Holmes. Bolm, the ex-Diaghilev soloist, was, of course, to be the absolute star.

Louis was a very capable conductor, as he was a fine accompanist, possessing the invaluable gift of an infallible sense of tempo—although not, alas, a similar regard for accuracy of notes. Tempo, however, was more important to the dancers. Dancers themselves often vary in tempo—through nerves, physical stamina, or emotional stress—and Louis could be counted on to give the right beat for the situation. For instance, a sluggish audience needed urging with a lively and zestful attack; a quick and alert house could be allowed to savor. But these adjustments are only effective in the hands of an artist, and Horst was that. He was, therefore, highly in demand. Although his fees were modest, his income was steady.

Louis always seemed mussy and his suits fit badly. The shock of hair that fell across his forehead was untidy and gradually grew gray with time until it was snow white. And in his face, always, was a cigar. I suppose he had to put aside the cigar when he mounted the podium to conduct, but it must have seemed unnatural and unnecessary to him, and I don't remember whether he smoked at the keyboard while playing a concert or not. Otherwise, he certainly smoked. The full, fleshy lips were held puckered as though for a kiss, thrust out in a childish pout, but usually clamped on a cigar. The long, pendulous nose; the cavernous, jutting eye sockets; the bushy, bristling eyebrows; the noble forehead—all together made for an imposing countenance in a large head. His body was tubular and ponderous, the arms long with short square hands of unusual strength: the hands of a pianist. He was slow. He rather toddled when he walked.

Louis was older than the others of our troupe—forty-four—and portly, with an eighteenth-century paunch and an eighteenth-century air, convivial and robust, snaggletoothed. He was very, very funny, tart, trenchant. Occasionally he was fastidious. His mind was sharp and his attention unswerving. He also cared wholly and devotedly about music, and often, in spite of his quips, about dancing. He flirted and teased without let up. In my case, all flirtation was antiseptic, because I found him flattering but physically unattractive. He was deeply experienced and I was virginal. Instinctively he sensed this. And I sensed that he didn't approve of my condition.

Because he was more realistic and reliable than Adolph Bolm, he was the father figure of the group.

His speech was short, wry, dry, and perfunctory, made up of pronouncements whined in a nasal voice that underlined their acerbity. His remarks often bordered on rudeness, but were always to the point, focusing on and drawing attention to the essential and cutting off triviality. Among the things he considered essential was kindness, his humor making acceptable, if not palatable, the sharper statements.

He preferred to conduct from the keyboard while playing, because, he explained, he could feel the rhythm more, and feel more completely at one with the dancers.

Our 1928 trip began in Des Moines, Iowa: we played to a moderately small audience in a very good theater. From there, the tour went steadily downhill: the audiences grew smaller and more uninterested, the press more variable, and our star and leader, Bolm, more capricious. On those few occasions when we had a full house, he danced with ebullience, if not éclat. But on the many evenings when there was a bad house he refused to dance at all. We all watched his secretary pack his costumes, dry and unused, back into the trunks, and the folding away had a mighty disheartening effect on the lot of us. Bolm had none of the Englishman's sporting feeling of noblesse oblige, none of that rot. If it was a small house, he raged and sulked, and he wouldn't dance; he wouldn't do his entrechats.

We heard about Bolm's bad humor on the train ride after the show, or at late supper. And then Bolm would start reminiscing about the golden days with Diaghilev in Paris at the premiere of *Prince Igor*, when he had danced the lead and the audience had stormed the footlights and carried him off on their shoulders to his dressing room. And women had thrown roses, and themselves, at his feet, before escorting him triumphantly to champagne suppers at Maxim's. His face shone as he told us about the past, as he looked around with benignity, tenderness, and disgust at the bedraggled little group that he was leading from one inglorious exposure to another. He was accustomed to Karsavina, Nijinsky, Pavlova, and Lopoukhova. Ah, well! He was accustomed to glory, and, mark you, it had been real glory. The impression of the first Diaghilev seasons has never been dimmed, and their effect on the theater of the world was permanent. Bolm was one of the banner leaders, but he found it impossible to live up to this standard without Fokine or Diaghilev at his side. Indeed, who could? None of the others did, either. But the memory was adrenaline to Bolm's heart, and he savored it vocally and ceaselessly.

As Bolm ranted, Louis Horst would sit nearby reading a detective story and saying nothing. Throughout the recital his expression remained phlegmatic. Later he would remark as he walked me home, "But it's past, you see."

There had been such dreary episodes on this tour. On the gorgeous, opulent stage of Carnegie Tech in Pittsburgh, a really beautiful theater, while we were warming up and standing around in our leggings and sweaters, Bolm suddenly went into a huddle with Horst. The whispering started. It became known very quickly that there was almost no audience and therefore no money to pay us. Bolm, of course, would not do his solos, but were we to do anything at all? He haughtily thought not. But the New York office advised us to go ahead, which stout-fellow attitude Louis reaffirmed.

"We've got to perform now that we're here and somebody's out front!"

Bolm was very grumpy indeed. Louis was philosophic. The performance, before a handful of people, was gloomy. No solos from the master, naturally, but taking into consideration the current state of Bolm's *Mazurka,* I'm not sure the audience was not fortunate after all.

This type of gypsying was an absolute first for me, and I had not been prepared for a road journey of one-night stands. I had brought along a small trunk-suitcase weighing a great deal and carrying fully half my wardrobe, a quite unnecessary amount. It was too heavy for any porter, which meant that when the train pulled in at the station I was left standing on the platform beside my trunk, looking desperate. Bolm would go off ahead of the group, coat thrown over his shoulders like a cape, arms unencumbered, hat at the back of his head, long hair akimbo, smiling at all possible managers and public admirers (a very few of these). I would stare wild-eyed at the retreating group. Horst, who was first of all caring, said to me the next time this happened, as he shouldered the reprehensible burden, "This is impossible! You must never, never do this again!"

"No," I replied meekly. "I'm so sorry." He then took me to the hotel, where we were naturally the last to arrive. Louis had a room reserved in his name, as did Bolm and the company manager. Neither I nor any of the ballet girls did. Those were the days when company managers overlooked such niceties as the care of the company. The orchestra had reserved rooms, and so did the stagehands, but the dancers scrabbled for the leavings. I was a dancer. We all gathered in the lobby like a flock of sparrows and attacked the desk en masse, twittering and screeching. By the time the others had cleared away there wasn't a room left for me. This happened several times. Then Louis began to push his way through the crowd, saying, "Miss de Mille is a star. I want her to have one of the best rooms." He got it for me and gave me the key, shouldered my trunk, and then said, "This is impossible. Follow me."

He did this at every stop, and once he said to me, "You must pay no attention to those girls. You've got to have your sleep and you must be treated as a soloist." The other girls didn't particularly mind: they expected this treatment and acknowledged that it was proper.

With these courtesies as an icebreaker, Louis and I became close conversational companions, especially on the Pullmans, where we connived to get away from the faded, often-told reminiscences of Bolm. He would begin expatiating on how Isadora Duncan had brought nothing new, that Fokine had already gone to all the museums and was doing excellent Greek dances before Isadora arrived in Russia. Over and over again: the glory of Diaghilev's first Paris season, the first London season, Lady Ripon, Lady Cunard, the Duchesse de Gramont, Isadora's claque, Isadora's false claims to innovation, Fokine's Greek studies long before Isadora arrived in St. Petersburg—Isadora as an imposter, Fokine as the true innovator.

"Rot!" Louis would say. "Not publicly, he wasn't." (Fokine later corroborated this in his autobiography!)

"I can't stand all of his graveyard conversations," Louis would mumble. "There's no future in it." We were young (not Louis, but he had thrown in his lot with the young) and at the beginning of our careers, and we were ready to talk about some glory of our own.

Louis, sitting in a dusty Pullman seat with me, was interested in the new glory. "It's coming," he said. "Isadora led the way and then Miss Ruth [as everyone called Ruth St. Denis] followed. And now there's Martha Graham."

"Why Martha?" I asked.

"You wait," said Louis. "It won't be long now. I don't know what she'll do—in fact, she herself doesn't know what she'll do. But it's there. We feel it, we who know her. She feels it. She's going to open new doors and venture down new ways, and it will be tremendous and there will be strength and vigor and truth and great, great beauty and power."

"You believe in her so much?"

"Totally," said Louis. "You wait and see. The others are going to seem pallid by comparison."

"Surely not Isadora and Miss Ruth?" I said.

"Miss Ruth certainly. Not Isadora, I believe."

"It must be exciting to stand alongside someone on the threshold. We all dream of that."

"We're all not going to have it," said Louis dryly. "But Martha is, and we'll be there to see, and we can share with her a little bit. It will come. In the meantime, she's very, very poor and she's totally unrecognized."

"Except by you."

"By me and several others. It's most certainly there, and I believe more is coming. I absolutely believe this."

I made no comment. Martha hadn't impressed me that much. What could I say?

Every night at the theater as we warmed up, Louis would sit disgruntled and bored, his Erle Stanley Gardner book open on his knee, and watch us in woolens and leggings doing battements and changements to warm our feet.

"It's ludicrous to think of an artist of my standing and ability practicing little fiddly finger exercises every day," he would say. (He avoided this foolishness by not practicing.) "It's ludicrous to think of a woman like Martha Graham, with her creativity, working at exercises the way a thirteen-year-old does. It's a great waste of energy and time and spiritual force. It shouldn't be tolerated."

Yet we had to practice, or we'd break our legs with the first jump. Martha had to practice because she couldn't use her thighs if she didn't. All of humanity had to practice, Martha among them. Louis, however, refused to practice; and what's more, he didn't care a jot. What he could do to the details—the finger work, for instance, of Scarlatti or Chopin—was monstrous. Well, he no longer played Chopin. "Too sentimental," he airily explained.

"Success doesn't matter," he said. "Do what you want and do it very well. You, Agnes, won't continue to do what you're doing. You'll do something else pretty soon, although this is very good, much better than Angna Enters*, who nausiapates me." (That was a new word, and I found it enchanting.) "But it's not good enough for you. You'll do something else. These other girls, these Bolm girls, are never going to do anything at all in their lives."

"You're in love with Martha," I said one night.

"Yes," said Louis, "I am. Every young artist, like a young vine, needs a wall to grow against. I am that wall for Martha. As a woman she has faults."

"Well, naturally."

Horst was Martha's wall. He was also her tyrant, someone to beat against, and she had to have a tyrant, I was to learn. It is doubtful that he gave her ideas, but he gave her a breast to pound upon. He disciplined her.

"You're killing me," he reported her as wailing more than once. "You're taking everything I have that is spontaneous from me!"

"Something better will come," he promised.

‖‖

One night, conversationally and without warning, Louis dragged me by the hair of my head right into the privacy of his bed.

It was the last night of the tour, when we were on our way back to Chicago. Louis came and leaned on the edge of my berth and said, "I've got to talk. I'll see her again soon, and I've got to talk to you."

I was sleeping in an upper berth, as all of the company did. (The members of the orchestra and the stagehands slept in lower berths. The head electrician, I believe, had a stateroom!) I looked at the green baize curtains all around, swaying with the motion of the train, thought of the many young, curious ears alert behind them, and said, "Let's go into an empty stateroom." So we took possession of the first empty space, leaving the door open and the lights off. I remember the station lights sliding by from time to time as the *ding-ding-ding* of the signals announced our arrival and departure and as Louis's sad monologue dragged on. He repeated himself quite a bit, as he obviously had told this story to others.

"It gets up to here," he said, pointing to his nostrils, "and then I just have to speak, the suffering is so unbearable." He was the Ancient

---

*Angna Enters was a dancer-pantomimist who at the time was having a great success.

Mariner compelled forever to tell his sad and unbearable tale. "Betty, my wife, and I had separated. Martha and I had a relationship that was meaningful and satisfying and she deliberately wrecked it. How could anyone leave in the evening"—presumably for her performance in the *Greenwich Village Follies* at the Winter Garden—"with every expression of tenderness and loyalty and then just not come home? How could she? And days later, when she did come back, how could she lash out at me with the cruelest and most vicious gibes about my age and weight? How could she?"

"Maybe she's learned a lesson?"

"She won't change. The leopard can't change its spots. Well, I threw her out. She humbled herself and came back on her knees. It was never quite as it had been before, though, but I took her back. Then she went on a tour to Chicago, and 'friends' "—Louis snorted—"*friends* wrote me that she'd gone back to the man. So I broke with her completely. She begged; I was adamant. There was Doris Humphrey. She made my life possible. But she wasn't Martha. No one was like Martha—a tigress, fire, tremendous!"

I really didn't know what he was talking about, but I sat in the dark, wide-eyed. The conductor poked his head in curiously.

"We'll leave soon," said Louis. "There's no other place to talk."

Louis droned on sadly through his nose. "Then I spent a year in Vienna living with a prostitute. Martha kept writing. I didn't answer. Finally I got a letter from her, really rather pathetic when you think about it, saying that she wouldn't write again until I asked her to. I never wrote." (This was not true I discovered. He kept sending her pictures of Mary Wigman, the great German modern dancer, and writing most stimulating accounts of the new German contemporary dance.) "When I came back, she was waiting for me. Now we're together, but it's not the same. I can never trust her, never again, and she does all the lovemaking, an unnatural situation. I never move toward her. I make her come to me. It's breaking her heart. It's breaking mine."

"Well, stop it."

"Never. That's how it is. I think she'd like me to marry her, to divorce Betty and marry her. But I won't. Not ever. Not now. Not after. Well, I had to tell you."

I didn't know exactly *what* he had told me. I sensed he felt a certain satisfaction in his stolid acceptance of this untidy life-pattern, in his contemplation of Martha's trapped suffering. His confession was some sort of expiation. But I found his exposure to me of Martha's anguish unattractive and shaming.

||||

When we returned to New York, I asked Louis if he would accompany me for the dance concert I planned to give in February 1929. He said he would, with pleasure and for a hundred dollars. I found him an enormous help, by far the best accompanist I had up to that time ever had. He was reasonably enthusiastic and supportive about my work. But he used our rehearsal time to admonish me to stop living with my mother, to give up comedy, to have an affair. This was not an opening gambit to offering himself. He thought people should have affairs, even if not necessarily with him. He was an aggressive, inexhaustible champion of free love. He thought very highly of George Sand.

He used to call me "the virgin-harlot" and blamed me for putting blue on my eyelids and rouge on my lips and wearing what he called "seductive" clothes, when I really meant nothing in particular. "You lead men on," he growled, "but you don't mean anything. A man knows you mean nothing by it." And in truth, as far as he was concerned, I meant nothing but affection and courtesy. However, I believe that if at any point in our relationship I had made a direct pass at Louis, he would have responded with astonishment and dismay, as indeed would I.

Above all, he wanted me to find a new dance style, to read Nietzsche, to stop practicing ballet exercises; and soon, he said, he hoped my mother would lose all her money and I would have to go to work and start teaching.

"Teach? Louis, you're out of your mind. Teach what? I barely know the rudiments of ballet technique. I have nothing of my own to teach. I don't know style. I know nothing of composition. How can I teach? I take a class every day to learn how to stand up and turn around."

"You'd find out as you went along. The rest do. Martha and Doris didn't know how to teach. They just started. Now they know. And, of course, their own work develops as they teach."

This seemed unreasonable. I had lost four years of dance training because I had gone to college and now found myself far behind my contemporaries, having to learn technique I should have mastered at fourteen. Martha and Doris Humphrey were in their mid-thirties, and had taught at Denishawn, and had been performing for more than a decade. However, reality did not curb Louis's tongue or stop his chivvy-ing. He wanted me to get out: to get away from my middle-class environment and my cozy home, away from my mother's gentle protec-tion, to get out, try my wings, get bruised, get hurt, get, for God's sake, experienced! This became a kind of crusade with him, a real campaign. I clung to my comfort and protection, although I did not know I was doing so. And I clung to my technique, the only one I knew, and what little I knew of my own aesthetics, and made my new aesthetics very, very slowly as I went along. What I had I didn't know, and I was not about to find out, starving and dirty in a friendless attic. I also was quite sure nobody would pay me five cents to teach him anything at all.

In time Louis introduced me to Martha Graham. I approached Martha at first somewhat warily. There she was, small, dark, practically famous, the basilisk, the femme fatale, the leopard woman who wouldn't change her spots and destroyed men at random! Whew! And there I was, our Edwardian girl, totally without worldly experience and cocooned still in my mother's nursery of cambric tea and childish civilities.

At the beginning, I was self-conscious with Martha; I knew too much about her intimate life to permit casual relations. But her grave, sweet dignity, her absolute fastidiousness of manner and speech, her ready courtesy, the constant revelation of her observations, and above all her unquestionable respect for work established a firm bond between us on our own terms. We had our separate friendship; soon it mattered not a whit what went on between her and anyone else.

At first I was fascinated by how she looked and what she said. In those days she wore dark colors or black, which enhanced her pallor and the stark quality of her lean body. On the stage she gave the appearance of majesty, so forceful was the intensity of her presence, so strong, clear, and defiant were her gestures. She was, in truth, almost tiny, and the men she met generally overtopped her. Edgar Wind, the art historian, always called her "the little one."

Her face was arresting: long, Oriental, with dead-white skin and a scarlet mouth, and eyes that seemed to protrude slightly but in fact did not—dark, all-absorbing, all-expressive, glowing with golden lights. Her regard was usually downcast or hooded. Martha's skull-like head with its deep-set eyes, the gaunt cheeks, the very visible teeth, and the long, well-defined jaw looked to me even then like a death's-head—until one considered the eyes. And one returned to them again and again. Her eyes flashed light.

Her hair was as straight as an Indian's, cut off abruptly just below the shoulders, and glossy dark. She wore it in different styles at different times; in many of her dances she wore it held back or loose. On the street it was often brushed sleek and knotted low on the nape of her neck. Her neck was swanlike, her head always lifted.

It was the attitude of the head—the awareness, the attention; the mouth—its mobile, sensitive lips slightly open—that made her seem like a child perceiving, receiving, attending, always receptive, as though about to be touched by a scent, a sensation, an awareness. And always the eyes saw everything, before, behind, above, through.

She spoke always in a soft, husky voice, a high, light, little-girl voice. There are some people who retain the sound of extreme youth even into old age. Martha did, unless she was angry. But, then, nobody is young or innocent when angry. Martha was impudent, sly, merry, her wicked humor flickering—dusting, and not necessarily with cruelty, over all occasions. Her humor was teasing and illuminating, and it was always very female, like the humor of Emily Dickinson or Jane Austen.

Her actual speech was elliptical and in no way logical or ordered. It is difficult to remember what Martha said, because the statements—and they were always flat statements that brooked no argument or even comment—were disjointed and had little relation to one another. But her words were so evocative, so freshly sharp and unexpected, that when she talked of dancing to her pupils, although they might not understand exactly what she had in mind, they did, as a consequence of the words, move differently and probably with the excitement of discovery. Martha cast her remarks up like flowers into the air and they fell every which way as all listeners grabbed to snatch at their loveliness. More frequently they were like a flight of darts or arrows. One was not convinced; one was impaled and stood like a Saint Sebastian, not knowing which shaft struck the heart.

What did she say? When it was over, what had she said? Sweep away the flower petals, gather up the broken shafts. Blood flowed and that was enough. Danger proved life.

artha never told me of her childhood beyond stray recollections. What I know I pieced together from other people's accounts.

Martha liked to say—and did so often to the press—that she was a sixth-generation American with a line of Scotch-Irish antecedents on both sides, and stretching on her mother's side directly back to the *Mayflower*. There was money in her background; Martha was never specific as to just how much. It is established that her paternal grandfather was fairly rich—something to do with real estate in Missouri—and that her father was born to a certain affluence and later earned a comfortable amount himself in medicine. "I was brought up with money," she said in an interview. "My father's income started the day he was born, with a trust fund. His father was an immigrant. Through all my childhood, all my education, I had no privation."

I inquired of Martha once where the original money came from, and she replied laconically, "Better not ask."

Her father, George Greenfield Graham, was born in 1856 in Washington, Pennsylvania, near Allegheny. He took a degree at the College of Physicians and Surgeons in Baltimore, specializing in mental disorders—at that time an unusual field for a young doctor to choose as his life's study. Apparently he was astute and remarkably observant; one of his special studies was the expression of emotion in human bodies, specifically the way people revealed themselves by the use of their hands and feet. Later he used to tell Martha that he could always recognize when people were lying by the tension in the deportment of their hands, and he taught her to watch for this as he did.

When he was twenty-seven, in 1883, George Graham joined the staff of the Western Pennsylvania Hospital Insane Department as one of two assistant physicians. He resigned eight years later and entered private practice, marrying Jane Beers—who was fifteen years his junior—of Butler County, Pennsylvania. They settled in Allegheny in a spacious house with a dispensary and consulting rooms on the ground floor and living quarters in the upper stories. Mrs. Beers, Jane's mother, joined them to complete the household.

On May 11, 1894, his first daughter, Martha, was born, a bright-eyed, intelligent, quick, black-haired baby. On May 15, 1896, the second girl, Mary, Titian-haired and quite beautiful, arrived, and in March 1900 Georgia, called Geordie by the family, auburn-haired and darling, the most beloved baby of all. She was, alas, to remain the baby, because a son, William, born when Martha was twelve, lived only two years and died of measles. His mother was inconsolable and grieved for far too long.

Martha's mother, Jane (nicknamed Jenny), was a small-boned, compact little wren of a woman, firmly fleshed but not fat, gentle, even cozy in her appearance. Jenny was about five feet, one inch tall, with smaller bones than Martha; Martha, while only five feet, two inches tall, was quite large-boned, although her feet were beautiful and apparently her father took great pride in them. He used to insist on her caring for her feet and bought her fine, lovely shoes. Jenny was a woman of considerable dignity and quiet charm, intelligent without being intellectual, soft-spoken always and sweet, never too demanding, although at the same time she was aware of her own worth. She was inclined to be timid and easily thrown off course by unfamiliar surroundings, except, quite remarkably, where her children were concerned, in whose behalf she could be brave, even dauntless. About her three daughters she was aggressively protective.

"My people were strict religionists," Martha said in an interview, "who felt that dancing was a sin. They frowned on all worldly pleasures. . . . My upbringing led me to fear it myself." Both parents saw that the girls went to the Presbyterian church and Sunday school. There were household prayers, Bible readings—all the religious trimmings. The young Martha was a conformer.

Into their conventional household a few weeks after Martha's birth entered an Irish girl, a patient of Dr. Graham's, Elizabeth Prendergast. She came full of gratitude, eagerness to work, Irish fun, and Irish myth. She served as maid, cook, bottle washer, nurse, religious mentor, and family entertainer. Lizzie, as she was known, saw to it that the girls heard all her yarns and warnings and songs, that they played theatrical games with her in the kitchen, and that they went to Mass frequently. The mystique of the Catholic church became an integral part of Martha's life, and it became a pervading influence. How often Lizzie took her toddlers surreptitiously into the mysterious nave, how often they lit candles, how often they watched the wonderful ceremonials with priests in holy, rich vestments go up the aisle, swinging censers and intoning in a sacred, unintelligible language is not recorded, but that it made a deep impression on one of her charges there is ample proof. Martha was saturated with the mythology, the power of the faith. Later it showed in her work.

It was remarkable that Martha's parents never forbade Lizzie to talk to the children about religion, or to recount to them the lives of the saints, or even to take them to her church, considering their own strict Presbyterian background. This was broad-minded for the time.

The doctor may have seemed a proper enough church member, but he was also provocative, stimulating, and quite fascinating as a husband and as a father, although he was also somewhat forbidding and on occasion unduly stern. He used to carry a gun on his hip wherever he went, an exaggerated gesture, one would think; but he was dealing with the insane, and in those days treatments were on the whole direct. George Graham was dark, good-looking, a highly romantic man, perhaps at times uncontrolled. Winthrop Sargeant, the music critic who later married Geordie, claims that "Martha hated him, and their relations were always strained." But I believe they must have had their moments of fantasy and pleasure together. She frequently quotes him. I never heard her quote her mother.

Doctor Graham cared for his four women, particularly his young wife, whom he frankly adored. He often carried her up to bed, Martha once told me. "And," she added dryly, "she was a well woman." As he became more affluent, he saw that his Jenny had strawberries in January and hothouse grapes and lovely special flowers and treats, and he was likewise solicitous with the girls.

He was exemplary, but later he apparently took to drink. Martha spoke of this once at an intimate moment with Bertram Ross, her partner in the fifties and early sixties, when she was comforting him about problems he was having with an alcoholic friend. "But she always spoke warmly of him," Ross added, "as loving and constantly caring."

Martha, being the oldest, was the natural tyrant, but she ruled also because of temperament and because of ability. By instinct she conducted herself like a little princess. The children wore white gloves— probably cotton—whenever they met guests or went out. (All her life Martha had what amounted to a fetish about gloves, and she even wore them throughout the days of her extreme poverty, when she could afford no other luxuries or accessories; her dress might be threadbare, but it was clean, and she wore immaculate gloves.) Whenever grown-ups came around and asked for a kiss, Martha told me, the little girl would chirp out concisely, "My father doesn't approve of kissing. It isn't sanitary. But you may kiss my hand." And with that she would extend her small, white-gloved hand.

In 1908, Mary's chronic asthma became very severe, and the family feared for her health. Bravely and solicitously, the doctor and Jenny traveled to the West Coast, at that time a six-day trip by train, to scout for a place to live that had a benign climate. They settled on Santa Barbara, and the following year the three little girls moved out there with them. Martha was fourteen; Mary was twelve; Geordie, eight. The doctor was forced to remain in Pittsburgh most of the time because he was locked into medical commitments, but he made the long trip west at regular intervals and visited his family. These long commuting visits were expensive and tiring, but he undertook them nonetheless.

Lizzie Prendergast had gone to California with them and now ran the Santa Barbara household. She was the beloved nanny whom they all turned to for everything. They lived in this land of flowers, and they flourished.

Santa Barbara in those days was the garden spot of the West Coast.

In addition to the native citizens and the residual of Spanish and Mexican people and enclaves of Japanese and Chinese, there was a floating population of migrant millionaires from the East and Middle West. Recognizing paradise when they saw it, they quickly bought up vast estates and established themselves in villas and on plantations of extraordinary beauty and legendary wealth. It was a city of easy spending. "The policy there, at that time," said Martha, "was 'buy now, pay later.' Real estate was speculated in extravagantly, and people had no thought to the future except in the loveliest and rosiest terms."

Santa Barbara itself was dominated by its mission, a very large one as missions go. Unlike others, the mission was functioning still, under the resident Franciscan monks. They kept the church and the gardens in order and could be seen, sandal-shod, in brown Franciscan robes, strolling through the box and yew hedges that separated the graves in the cemetery, working in the orange groves and among the grapevines, or praying in the mission. One could attend Mass or wander freely in the gardens and breathe the acrid, moldy graveyard smell of the yew and box mingled with the hot, sweet odor of orange and grapefruit. The bees buzzed, the mockingbirds fluted, and the bells sounded and dissolved in the dazzling, silent blue above. And under all, the persistent suserrant intonation of the ghost-voiced surf.

The town lay open, blessedly sunny, and exposed to every beneficent climactic influence. The mountains of Santa Barbara rise abruptly from the shelf on which the town is spread, precipitously high—not to the altitude of snow, but very high, with a sudden access of energy that is a challenge to everyone who looks at them. In the winter they are clothed with green and covered with pastures of wildflowers of intense beauty. The strong, succulent grass is tangled with yellow violets, brown-eyed, pale mariposa tulips, tufts and patches of bright poppies, wild onion, Chinese blue brodiea, irises, and lilies of many kinds. The eucalyptus groves cut across the grass; marking the ravines, marking the roads and streets, they stand in whispering borders, turning their scythe-shaped leaves with a harsh rattle to the sun. The olive trees are massed in a silvery haze. Wild lilac blooms right up the slopes of the foothills, pale blue, smoky, tangling into the wild sage, with an odor so penetrating, so intoxicatingly lovely as to make the spirit wild to run, to jump, to take off like an animal and roll on the earth. And all of this not far away, but just there, at the end of the street. Go in the other direction, and the road ends in an abutment with a sheer drop straight down to the great blue combers rolling in, roaring and hissing as only the Pacific breakers can, so much bigger, so much stronger than those of the Atlantic. They thunder without stopping, night and day. And then with sunset come skies that no easterner ever dreamt of, splashed with scarlet, torn with orange, green in the east, the sea darkly violet as the red ball drops. And on the edge of the world, an archipelago of lost islands can be just faintly discerned, a burning gold memory.

This is what the doctor offered the little girls, and this is what they grew up with.

What Santa Barbara did not have was any theater, music, or cultural life. Only a few of the greats stopped off between Los Angeles and San Francisco on their trips west. The natives had to make a three-hour journey south or a five-hour journey north if they wished to attend a concert. Bear in mind that this was long before radio, and gramophone records were at the time inexact and primitive. Martha never saw dancing.

Mary's asthma improved. Martha began to mature.

Martha's mother, according to Winthrop Sargeant, was a conventional woman, and she attempted to maintain an orderly, conventional household—a task made difficult by three very temperamental and variously gifted daughters. Jenny was inclined to be dominating, and Martha found she had to exercise a great deal of willpower to maintain her own independence. Jenny "was not very intelligent," added Sargeant, "definitely middle class, with real butter-and-egg taste." Geordie, bright-eyed, bonnie, and dear, the little sister worshiping Martha, clung to her mother and ventured not far, not ever far, but she tried. Geordie was adoring and subservient—"like a faithful dog," said her husband. "She was always a little sister to Martha, slavishly admiring. She was Martha's care and responsibility." But, as was inevitable, Geordie also resented the unequal relationship and was restless under it. "The trouble with Geordie," Martha said to me once, "is that she is the little sister of Martha Graham. She can't forgive that." And, as Martha said in an interview, "Mary was blond-red and gorgeous. Geordie had curly auburn hair and big beautiful eyes. And then there was little old slit-eyed me. I was not the pretty one."

Although seemingly conforming, Mary was, in truth, the only independent one. She was quite beautiful, not artistically inclined, not ambitious, and to all appearances a normal, healthy, happy girl. Martha regarded her wistfully. Mary seemed to be headed for a good life, certainly a much easier one than either of her two sisters. She was indeed unusually bright and as she grew older displayed talents that several who knew her called brilliant. She was the tallest of the three sisters, with long, beautiful legs: a lovely, lithesome girl. Martha was always somewhat envious of Mary and, according to the girls of Graham's later groups, had a certain wariness, even an antagonism, toward blondes.

The three sisters loved one another and, according to Gertrude Shurr, who studied with Martha and danced with her company in the twenties and thirties, they seemed quite close—as close as young women can be who are so different in temperament. But Winthrop Sargeant is convinced that Martha, being absorbed only in herself, was not really close to her sisters. Over the years Mary grew independent, pulled away, and struck out on her own. "Geordie remained clinging and Martha condescended to her, not with love, but with a sense of responsibility and family loyalty." After they grew up, the sisters were not really close or trusting or easily friendly. There was always a sense of rivalry, which bred a certain hostility and, in Geordie's case, distrust, even fear.

Martha was the rebel, the experimenter, the wild one. Martha was difficult, passionate, with a wicked temper. She was hard to control. In fact, she couldn't be controlled. And she was brazen, actually quite reckless. As she once put it in an interview, "My father said, 'Martha, you're like a horse that runs best on a muddy track.' My grandmother said, 'Martha, you've got a tongue that is hung in the middle.'"

Once, in Escondido, California, when she was quite young, Martha was discovered by her mother up in an oak tree trying to jump rope while standing on a branch. It was a live oak, with low and spreading limbs, but nevertheless, Martha told me dryly, "I was not allowed out for some time after that without supervision."

|||||

On one of his visits in 1911, Dr. Graham took Martha to Los Angeles (three hours by train from Santa Barbara) to see a concert given by the dancer Ruth St. Denis. This was an occasion. Quite gallantly, Dr. Graham bought Martha a bunch of violets to wear. (One could buy a very large bunch of violets for fifteen or twenty cents in those days of small Japanese truck gardens.) The gesture was romantic and grown-up, and Martha never forgot it. And she never forgot St. Denis. That day, at the Mason Opera House in Los Angeles, Martha saw a great dancer and was astonished and moved and changed.

In 1912 the doctor retired from his position at the hospital in

Pittsburgh and came west to take up residence permanently with his family. And whenever the doctor was at home he talked to Martha about the ideas that interested him the most.

All people look to facial expression and movement as indications of human feeling and intent. This is learned in early childhood and sharpened by life's experience. It is universal, common to all times and places; and as Charles Darwin pointed out in *The Expression of Emotions in Man and Animals* (1872), the basic expressions are the same no matter what the race or language. Expression has been scientifically studied only in the one hundred years since Darwin published his first great text on the subject, drawing attention to the characteristics common to both animals and men, and to the differences. Expression was not studied as an indication of mental disorders until the second part of the nineteenth century, and apparently Dr. Graham was among the vanguard of scientists who analyzed definite aberrations and the persistence of certain traits in normal people. The very young Martha became used to hearing about human expression, manner, and behavior discussed as the facets and evidence of life. Painters, novelists, and, of course, actors have always known the meaning of expression instinctively. Acting, in fact, is the reproduction of these outer clues to inner feeling, and the more accurately these are reproduced, the more lively and effective the actor. The dancer, on the other hand, searches for the meanings behind the clues—the meanings behind gesture and expression—and then reassembles them, works them into a pattern, a design or purpose: in short, a conclusion. This is creative. This the great actor does also, but it is the essential stuff of choreography.

Martha was trained from a young age to watch animals for the meaning behind their walking, nuzzling, snuffling, growling, and human beings for the counterparts of the same actions. She lived with this knowledge and these observed discoveries the whole of her life. I believe she owes this to her father. She once told me that Dr. Graham had said, "Bodies never lie." This statement had profound meaning for Martha. The eyes can be controlled, the mouth also, if more rarely (and that is why primitives cover the mouth in times of stress—an involuntary gesture). The hands, the feet, the neck are naked to observation, as well as, of course, the heartbeat. Now we have the lie detector, which is based on just this principle: The body cannot lie.

IIIII

Martha was excellent in school, particularly in writing, and because of the young girl's remarkable gifts, her English teachers hoped she would make creative literature her specialty. Martha had a remarkable feeling for words and language. In school she met several teachers who influenced her, particularly in the English department, and also a teacher who taught her to sew and to cut dresses. She found she had an aptitude for this, too, and took to the manual disciplines readily. Dr. Graham believed in outstanding higher education and wanted Martha to go to Wellesley College. Martha, however, had other inclinations: she had tasted the forbidden fruit of theatrical excitement in a couple of high school plays.

She was a fairly mature girl for her age, passionate and ambitious, although she was not yet clear for what. She was extremely interested in love. It is hard to know anything about this important period of her life, but once, when she was counseling me about my own personal troubles, she said very revealing things about young-womanhood. "There comes a time when virginity is a great burden. It impedes the development of the spirit and the development of the work. It blocks growth. One spends too much effort, too much time, too much force dealing with it, thinking about it, suffering from it. When I was young I was in love with a married man and I could not have him, and I went to my mother"—not her father, mind you—"and said to her, 'I wish to go to this man whom I love with all my heart and I want time and I want privacy and I am going to a hotel with him.' And I went." Her confession was to me startling. The honesty of it! The decisiveness of it!

Her mother must have been completely taken aback, but she said nothing and did nothing. At least she is not recorded as having made an outcry. It seems likely that she was becoming used to Martha's decisions, which were about as indefinite as naked swords. Martha went to the hotel.

Martha represented illicit love to me as a source of unequaled bliss, but that the experience was not as anticipated was indicated when she confessed once to Ted Shawn that her first sexual encounter was "traumatic." He credited much of her fierce and ungentle behavior to this fact.

On graduating from high school, Martha persuaded her parents to let her go down to Los Angeles alone to enter the Cumnock School of Expression, so she could have regular lessons in dramatics, elocution, and speech. Up to then, she had had no training in dancing at all. They let her go, alone. She was nineteen years old.

How good the Cumnock School was or what precisely it taught I cannot say, but I do know that Los Angeles at that time was something of a cultural center. It boasted two symphony orchestras, several art museums, an excellent public library, a fine community theater in Hollywood, three big universities, and an extraordinary natural history museum containing the oldest bones in the world, dug up from the La Brea tar pits. Martha liked to study animals and old things. Here was food for thought. The city was also the goal of every prominent visiting lecturer, all the touring concert artists, opera companies, and actor-managers with their repertory theaters. Besides, there was vaudeville, which in those days provided rich fare. Martha saw traveling ballet dancers, among them Anna Pavlova, who appeared at the Mason Opera House in 1915 and 1916.

IIIII

In 1914, Martha's father died of a heart condition. The family found that his estate was much smaller than they had anticipated (Martha claimed it was embezzled) and that consequently they were going to be hard up and would have to plan very, very carefully.

In 1916, after three years at Cumnock, Martha was graduated. Hearing about the new "Ruth St. Denis School of Dancing and Related Arts" in Los Angeles, she decided she must enroll. Mother Graham moved south and with Lizzie's help established the family residence in Los Angeles, very close to the school. The younger sisters went to high school. In the summer of 1916, Martha formally enrolled as a dance student at the Ruth St. Denis School of Dance and Related Arts. Louis Horst accompanied the first dance class she took.

ecause Ruth St. Denis and Ted Shawn had a profound and formative influence on our native dance in this century, the story of their marriage and working relationship must have been a lesson for and a warning to every artist, and particularly to their pupil Martha Graham. From their example, Martha learned early of the path that led to the death of all hope, the ruin of artistic integrity.

America in the 1890s was the backdrop for the development of Ruth St. Denis. The country was in the process of revolutionizing dance, and through it the theater of the Western world. But in point of fact, there was in the United States in the first two decades of this century almost no dancing at all. There was just a little bad ballet (the exceptions were the touring appearances of the Danish ballerina Adeline Genée and of the Russian Anna Pavlova), and there were vaudeville and variety entertainers.

The Americans Ruth St. Denis and Isadora Duncan were mavericks, lone individuals who achieved European successes at roughly the same time. Duncan became known for her freeform musical interpretations and her so-called Greek dances (not Greek at all, but barefoot displays in classic tunics). St. Denis became known for her re-creations of mystical Oriental rituals to Western music. Neither dealt in authentic re-creations. Duncan never pretended to be Greek. Further, she even denied she was a dancer: "If I am Greek, it is the Hellenism of Keats . . . I aim to speak the language of humanity, not the dialect of a folk." Both women were geniuses in that they discarded all the current theatrical practices and evoked genuine wonder and emotion with a simple means, the solo dancing body. They both had absolute faith that what they did would better mankind and lead people to higher spiritual levels and richer lives. They believed this to their deaths. They did not talk of success; they talked of greater emotional communication—Duncan in terms of Dionysian release, St. Denis in terms of Karma, reincarnation, the theosophic evolvement toward holiness and nirvana. Each spoke the jargon of her adopted faith, and each lived what she preached.

Duncan followed Nietzsche, Havelock Ellis, and the pagan Greeks. She appeared right at the crest of the release from Victorian sexual restraints, and she was the sensational public advertisement of women's freedom. Although she was by no means the first or the most effective feminist, she was certainly among the most flamboyant. She threw off her shoes and stockings—not the first to do so, but the most public. She threw off corsets and went around like the Pre-Raphaelites, those London bohemians who had been ridiculed by everyone, including Gilbert and Sullivan. Duncan made the front pages of the world, even while the world mocked her. And she was imitated everywhere.

After a dazzling beginning and solid acclaim on the European continent, her career went into a long decrescendo. In the drowning death of her two children she sustained terrible tragedy. She thereafter became progressively a compulsive wanton, a frenetic improviser, a beggar, an alcoholic, and a creature of desperate irresponsibility, whom no one would support and no one would hire, dragging out a marred and harried course, though not untouched by moments of glory, until her dreadful death in 1927, strangled on a scarf caught in the wheel of a car in which she was riding. She was forty-nine, a prematurely aged woman with dyed red hair and a flabby body.

When Isadora was forty—not so old, one would think—she visited Los Angeles, and a very large and intelligent audience attended her concert. Children were taken as to a shrine. What they saw, alas, was a prematurely aged and bloated woman, coarsened by terrible trials, laboring through gossamer steps and classical evocation. There was hard breathing and there were gestures from middle-aged arms. "Pure flab," said one witness. Genius still burned, but in what murk and confusion! Indeed, she had desecrated the vessel. She had thrown over discipline and training for indulgence.

"There must have been an initial and essential flaw," the playwright Edward Sheldon said to me. "She was known in Germany as '*die heilige Isadora,*' and students unhitched the horses and pulled her flower-covered carriage through the streets in worship. She was a dedicated servant and priestess to her art. Look now what she has become!"

Ruth St. Denis and June Hamilton Rhodes, Miss Ruth's business manager, went to Isadora Duncan's opening night in Los Angeles at the Mason Opera House. From their second-row center seats they were able to see every tragic detail, hear every panting breath. Miss Ruth, who had always honored Isadora and was, by report, not jealous of the other woman's more sensational fame, even writing superbly about her, had gone to the performance in high anticipation. Halfway through the program she grabbed June's arm and, tears streaming down her face, ran down the aisle, threw herself into a cab, and sobbed all the way home. The episode and performance were never mentioned between the two again.

I was taken to a matinee, and although I found Isadora fat and floppy, I remember still whole sequences of her dancing and the Gluck music she danced to and how she phrased her dance sequences to the music. And I remember that at the end she danced the six verses of "The Marseillaise." It was the Allies' anthem and we had to stand. Mother let me go out to the aisle, because otherwise I would not be able to see. Everyone wept for various reasons. I became aware that this audience was reacting quite differently from any theater or moving-picture audience I had before experienced. Nothing was happening onstage that seemed to me worthy of tears, yet they wept. Isadora wore a blood-red robe which she threw over her shoulder as she stamped to the footlights and raised her arms in the great Duncan salute, which was a call and a recognition. This was heroic and I never forgot it. No one who saw Isadora ever forgot her. "Oh, my dear," said Francis Biddle, our great attorney general, "it's worth being old now to have been young when she was."

St. Denis, Duncan's greathearted colleague, writes in her autobiography, *An Unfinished Life:* "It is difficult to find words with which to pay tribute to the indescribable genius of Isadora. I can only say briefly that she evoked in that pitifully small audience visions of the morning of the world. She was not only the spirit of true Greece in her effortless, exquisitely modulated rhythms, but she was the whole human race moving in that joy and simplicity and childlike harmony that we associate with Fra Angelico's angels dancing 'the dance of the redeemed.' "

St. Denis continues, with rare insight and judicial evaluation:

Mary Fanton Roberts [a patron of the dance who was friends with both Isadora and St. Denis] said years afterwards, "Isadora was Dionysiac and Ruth St. Denis Apollonian," meaning that Isadora possessed the ecstatic liberation of the soul, which I translated into form; and it was some of this ecstatic quality of her soul that I received on this occasion, never to lose as long as I live. In one arm's movement was all the grace of the world, in one backward flinging of her head was all nobility! . . . We can perhaps realize with greater love and understanding why Isadora was shaken from time to time by the power that coursed through her, so that her outer life was thrown out of focus and she was unable to set right the overbalanced elements of her life. . . . Her successors could not be more than a faint echo of this pure spirit of the dance.

Dance became prevalent, even rife, in America.

There was the group of barefooted Amazons under Marian Morgan, including a promising young Mexican, Ramón Somaniegos, who would become the movie star Ramón Novarro. In schools and colleges girls were dancing barefoot on the grass, and Dalcrozian Eurythmics—a system of movement based on the exact rhythm and time evaluation of each note—was being taught. The country had gone mad on music interpretation and the unfettered expression of emotion—no shoes, just blue scarves and feeling, perfectly harmless for developing adolescent glands and good for middle-aged developing pounds. Boys didn't do any of this. It made boys' skin crawl with shame. The American male's traditional scorn of dancing augmented strongly. Tap dancing was thinkable, but it was also very hard to do, and it wasn't art, like interpretive dancing. Art, though easy to do, could be sentimental and embarrassing; in short, sickening.

St. Denis was actually older than Isadora Duncan, but she began her career later. She was born Ruth Dennis in New Jersey in 1879, the daughter of Thomas Dennis, an Englishman, naturalized and a veteran of the Civil War, and Ruth Emma Dennis. Tom Dennis was a charming, directionless dreamer, led astray constantly by images of inventions and discoveries which never materialized into practical results of any kind. As time went on he deadened his disappointment and the shock of his general sense of uselessness with drink, and he became a worsening alcoholic. Ruth's mother was an extraordinary woman who as a young girl had vacillated between religious fundamentalism and free-thinking and in the interim had taken a medical degree in 1870 from the University of Michigan, an almost unheard-of achievement at that time, when medical students were subjected to sexist, segregated classes. The United States, recovering from the trauma of civil war, fermented with ideas for a better society. Ruth Dennis believed successively in a great many of them. She was married in 1878 to Tom Dennis, a marriage only by contract, since he was still legally married to someone else. And in 1879, one month after his divorce from his first wife was granted, and Ruth Emma could wed him legally, she gave birth to their daughter, barely assuring the child's legitimacy.

Because of Tom's irresponsibility, the mother was obliged to assume the role of breadwinner. She took in boarders and sold herbal medicines and farm produce, and she centered her entire life on little Ruthie, who was a bright and inventive child. A son, "Buzz," never baptized or given a proper Christian name, was born when Ruth was eight years old. He was a happy child, apparently, and bright, but more or less overlooked by the womenfolk in the family, who used him mainly for whatever useful purposes they were in need of or could devise; he was taken out of school for this reason. Young Ruth very early got accustomed to the idea of the men in her family being charming ("All the dogs and children loved Father," she wrote) but unreliable and, at bottom, worthless. The women supported the family and made the decisions. The women also bore the brunt of all sexual relationships. Because of her shadowy birth date and the nervous concealment of the circumstances, in the interests of the family reputation (at best equivocal in their rural community) Ruth, I believe, equated sex with "shame and ostracism."

Little Ruthie learned a great deal about Christian Science from her mother and from a boarder, and she learned also from her mother a great deal about the modern religious sect of Theosophy.* Her mother

*The second edition of the *Columbia Encyclopedia* defines the word: "Theosophy: Gr.-divine wisdom . . . it begins with an assumption of the essence of God, from which it deduces the essentially spiritual nature of the universe. . . . Evil may be overcome by complete absorption in the infinite. . . . The philosophy and theosophy of the Orient, . . . Vedic, Buddhist, and Brahminist literature are all charged with a mystical idea of a universal, eternal principle, basic to all life. . . . Modern theosophy draws much also discovered Delsarte and his system for analyzing gesture and taught Ruth a complete manual of exercises and positions and their meanings, which later stood her in remarkable stead.

Ruth was tall and loose-jointed, with a marked talent for acrobatics and a memorable flair for invention and mimicry. Her mother sensed she could be a real money earner. She had a glorious body, but since she was without instruction, she relied on self-discipline. Fortunately, she was blessed with extraordinary limber legs, a loose and supple spine, and a devil-may-care freedom of movement.

Ruthie first danced professionally under the humblest of conditions—in penny arcades, cheap variety shows, clubs, roof gardens, the Vaudeville Club in the Metropolitan Opera House (but not part of the opera organization), and touring road shows. She did well enough the required dancing, high kicks and swishing of ruffles and whatever undulations the dancer wished to throw in as sexual tease. From time to time she took odd jobs, including modeling evening gowns for Abraham & Straus. She finally wound up with a bit part in the stock company of the American producer and playwright Augustin Daly (1838–99). Daly's companies were known for their realistic acting style, and anticipated David Belasco. His New York stock company was internationally famous. Ruthie was scheduled for a larger part in Daly's company the following year, but Daly disobligingly died. (In another Daly company at that time, a young American dancer named Isadora Duncan, also discombobulated by the producer's death, was becoming equally discouraged and was about to leave with her family on a cattle boat for England.)

At the same time, David Belasco,* "the Wizard of Broadway," was scheduled to send his star, Mrs. Leslie Carter, to London in *Zaza*, and he needed a girl to go along who would do some dancing. Ruthie auditioned, got the job, and left hearth and home for foreign parts, alone for the first time, with some trepidation and her mother's down-

---

of its vocabulary from Indian sources. . . . To gain real spiritual knowledge and power the soul must pass through several existences [i.e., reincarnation]."

The Theosophic Institute in Hollywood, Kratona, was under the direction of Charles Warrington, whose daughter, Mary Neely Warrington, studied at Denishawn.

*David Belasco (1853–1931), American producer and playwright, became the most successful producer on Broadway from 1900 to 1920. He collaborated on his early plays with Henry de Mille, the father of William and Cecil de Mille. He broke with de Mille on his deciding to put his talents at the service of a star, Mrs. Leslie Carter. His most successful productions for her were *Zaza* (1898) and *Madame DuBarry* (1901).

right fear. Ruthie was delightfully attractive, bouncing with zest, and funny, but she was chilled at the heart with a basic maternal terror instilled long ago, and she permitted no dalliance. What is more, she wanted none, and she marveled at herself and worried not a little.

David Belasco himself made several gentle overtures in his courteous and "Oriental" style (Ruth's description), but Ruthie's cast-iron naïveté and effervescent astonishment warded off trouble from him as well as from all admirers. One of them was, of all people, Stanford White, the brilliant American architect, member of the famous New York firm of McKim, Mead and White, and the designer of many famous New York buildings. (He was shot to death by Harry Thaw for his relations with Thaw's new and beautiful wife, Evelyn Nesbit.) In typical roué-like tradition, White lent Ruth money and promised to look out for her overseas. Ruth accepted everything with gratitude and pretty thanks and gave nothing whatever in return. Taking is an art, and it is the art of the really frigid woman. White, surprisingly and gallantly, never pressed his advantage.

On her return from London, Ruth rejoined the Belasco company. She also discovered Christian Science, and this time it took firm root in her mature mind.

She went on tour with Belasco's production of *Madame DuBarry*, feeling she was on the verge of discovering she knew not what. And then in Buffalo, New York, with her pal Pat Donar, while Ruth was eating an ice-cream soda, the revelation occurred through the means of an Egyptian Deities cigarette advertisement: a woman in the position of the goddess Isis sitting beneath a stone doorway surrounded by a pool filled with what Ruthie discovered were blooming lotus flowers. Ruth St. Denis was born.

That woman, that position, that sense of mystery, the promise of peace, revelation, otherworldliness, enduring life, imagination beyond death! She had perceived what she must be—nothing less than the messenger of another, purer, more mysterious, more compelling life. Ruthie would be a goddess. This manifestly was the way to go. She had found her vocation. She was twenty-eight years old and her hair was already gray. She had no money and she had no love. But she was centered and happy, for she now knew what her dance was to be.

At the end of the tour she came home to acquaint her family with her mission. They were nonplused. She began to formulate dances— well, sort of dances. "I was at that time a kind of dancing ritualist," she wrote. There was no attempt whatever to duplicate the exact ritual or symbolism of Hindu dancing, and Ruth became quite mixed up in her Hindu theology. But she felt, as with technique, that the ideas as well as the muscular techniques were "sufficient, which adequately expresses and reveals the thought intended by the artist." She had no wish to be a museum duplicator. She understood the spirit and she reproduced that, relived it, and this was more than enough.

She invited neighbors off the street to come and see what she was doing and they, too, were nonplused, but also interested, and they offered criticism. She finally settled on music—the dances from Delibes's opera *Lakmé*. They were certainly not Hindu. They were French: tinkle-tinkle, coloratura, Opéra-Comique, and enchanting in their way, but not Hindu.

She gathered up her troupe from her wanderings in New York, and they were a tatterdemalion group of Hindus, Moslems, Buddhists, Turkish rug-merchants, students from Columbia, silk salesmen, and several plain American bums who were very glad of a warm evening and free food. After one hideous audition and rejection she went to Henry B. Harris, the owner and manager of the Hudson Theater on West Forty-fifth Street, and he agreed to put on her matinees, the first for managers, the second for an invited public.

Her professional name was evolved by Mother Dennis as she was labeling their costumes and props for the theater. David Belasco had called her "saint" in gentle mockery of her prudery. "Ruth St. Denis" made her debut at the Hudson Theater in January 1906. The costumes were designed by Brother Dennis, made by all of them in the parlor.

"What did the audience do while you changed costumes?" I heard my practical mother ask one day.

"They just sat and meditated," said Miss Ruth. "The people realized they had come to no ordinary theater show. It was to be an experience of quite another kind. They accepted it."

Most of the guests consisted of the elite of society, the very rich patronesses and women of power, J. P. Morgan's sister, Mrs. Jack Gardner of Boston (John Singer Sargent and Bernard Berenson's patron and the builder of Fenway Court, with its unmatched art collection), and the two Lewisohn sisters, Irene and Alice, who were to become artistic powers in the theater and dance worlds.

St. Denis's rewards were not financial, according to Mrs. Harris, but she did get attention from people who mattered and great enthusiasm from the artists who saw her. She was the only barefoot dancer whom Adeline Genée admired. The rest of them, Duncan and all her imitators, were not dancers at all, Genée said in an interview a few years later.

Without significant religious overtones, without the unworldliness, the intense and vibrant aura which was Ruth's particular and personal evocation, this dancing could not have cast the spell it did. It just was not interesting enough. In rhythm it was simplistic. In line it was lovely because Miss Ruth was lovely and noble in carriage. But every great lady posturing in scarves and drapes had done this throughout the nineteenth century, beginning with Emma, Lady Hamilton. The patterns were symmetrical and childish. Ruth's Indian dancing was not authentic—not in the use of the hands, never in facial expression, and least of all in rhythm and music. The music was dreadful—weak piano evocations in the Western scale like those by Charles Wakefield Cadman, banal and characterless, past bearing. But Miss Ruth said it was spiritual, and she was so convinced one found oneself believing.

In the Martha Graham Company's 1986 revival of three Denishawn solos, Miss Ruth's dance form could be seen to be a lyric, lovely, suggestive, wispy bit of plastique, without energy or real inner force of any kind. Without Miss Ruth's personality to give it verity and strength, it was nothing but a bit of decoration. But Miss Ruth not only had presence and evocation, she had certain technical tricks, including an arm ripple that was hers alone. Graham said to Jack Anderson of *The New York Times* that it was "one of the treasures of the world. It went from the spine through the entire body and it was in touch with all the vibrations of the universe."

St. Denis herself writes in her autobiography of a performance in Berlin: "It is hard to realize now, when most dancers use an arm ripple, that at this period it did not exist as a part of the dance. I was the first dancer in the Western world to use my arms in such a fashion, and the German professors' astonishment was more or less echoed by all my audiences." And in a television interview she added wryly that they thought she must have an extra joint in her arms. (She was, in fact, double-jointed, as is witnessed by her photographs.) But the secret of her power was that when she performed she worshiped, and the audience recognized this and shared with her the devotion. In the 1986 revival there was no sense of prayer or mystery or awe. None. Miss Ruth was not with us.*

Someone once asked Pavlova why she was the greatest dancer in the world. Pavlova did not dispute the appraisal but answered simply, "Because of my great sincerity." Miss Ruth, too, had great sincerity. She believed in what she was doing. The fact that what she was doing lacked sophistication and was, in fact, slightly spurious did not minimize the sincerity. It amounted to conversion, and the audience came to share the vision. She dabbled, as we have noted, in Indian ideas (as she much later dabbled in Christian ones, reincarnation, Theosophy), but she rejected in both Eastern and Western religion what displeased her—surely her privilege, though tending to blur the cutting edges of faith.

But there was more to Miss Ruth's appeal than that. The woman had enormous style. She had the elegance and discrimination of the real dancer. She could make a gesture that was complete and finished and instinctive. This ability is not based on muscles. If she put a hand out, it was put out with definition, so that it was final. It stayed put, so to speak, in the atmosphere. She was an artist of movement, and this is apparent on the old films, rickety and dreadful as they are. "There was God in her," said her pupil Charles Weidman. So if her dances were in a sense sham, they nevertheless evoked great emotions in her audience, and she projected an aura of mysticism and importance. She awoke similar responses in her students and in her beholders. That is why she left a name. What she accomplished was an impression of dedication and serenity. This was her personal magic, and combined with her sweet dignity and very real nobility, it enabled her to persuade.

|||||

Henry B. Harris offered to take her to London. There she put on her show in a series of performances similar to the Hudson Theater matinees. The Duchess of Manchester arranged for her to dance before King Edward and Mrs. Alice Keppel. Socially Miss Ruth was accepted, and that meant that popularly she had a success of sorts.

She went on to Austria. Vienna, having a taste for the exotic and

---

*But in 1987, when Martha persuaded the great Russian ballerina Maya Plisetskaya to perform *Incense* at the gala opening of her season, the magic was back and the audience was wonder-struck. These simple dances or evocations depend on supreme artistry of performance for their meaning.

foreign, had done much for those other Americans, Isadora Duncan and Maud Allan. And then on to Germany. And in these countries she became the vogue and attracted many admirers, among the intelligentsia, writers, and artists—among others the poet and librettist who collaborated with Richard Strauss, Hugo von Hoffmansthal, with whom she had an inconclusive flirtation. Her fame was established. Her studio was always a gathering place for talented, creative friends. The savants and the mystics flocked to her. St. Denis was photographed, painted, written about, philosophized about, argued about and feted. Famous photographers in France, Austria, and England found her irresistible. Albert Herter, the successful American portrait painter whose son Christian later succeeded John Foster Dulles as secretary of state, painted a stunning portrait of her in *The Peacock* (it now hangs at Jacob's Pillow), and so did the far finer American artist Robert Henri. He said she was the most perfect model in the world. Ruth was saved from going completely fey by the rather wholesome daily practice of Christian Science and by her stout Irish sense of humor. She managed to come home to the United States without emotional entanglements and thus remained her mother's true girl, a virgin free from contamination.

She wrote in her autobiography: "At that time Isadora and I, and others who had forsworn the orthodoxies of the ballet, were busy waging our war to make America accept dancing as an art. To compel it to accept the dance as an instrument of worship was something still to come."

It must be remembered that St. Denis played to a world jaded with labor convulsions, wearied with royal displays of unbounded extravagances, soul-sick with commercial and business entrapments. This was the period of Art Nouveau. Women wore their hair in tangles, ensnared with poppies. Electric-lamp shades were made to look like flower arbors, chairs like rosebushes, orange squeezers like grottoes. Everything was dyed or decorated or fringed or frayed. The Western way of life was appalling: we had mass starvation; it could be escaped in thickets of decoration.

In the East they also had mass starvation, and worse, but they had risen above all and were evolved, one heard, way beyond us. Miss Ruth was way beyond us too. She had access to swamis; *ergo,* she had access to higher planes of being.

It was with gratitude and amazement, accordingly, that women in great ostrich-plumed hats and hobble skirts, men in striped pants and choking collars, looked at a young woman who dared to dress in a simple choli and sari, step out with bare feet, put jewels in her hair and bells on her ankles, lift a bowl of incense above her head and say with absolute belief, "I am beautiful and this is the way to know God better."

Duncan bared her feet and dropped her corsets, but St. Denis bared her navel. There was a large and lovely expanse of bare Ruthie between ribcage and pelvis. "Duncan has given women freedom," Walter Terry reported her as saying, "but I am the one who separated [and here she pointed to upper and lower torso] church and state."

She had annual seasons in New York. She toured for several years and became a household name in America as well as in Europe, but she had no bank account and her audiences, although vocal, were moderate in size. And everywhere she went Mother and Brother attended, serving and guarding.

She wrote in her autobiography: "I sometimes marvel that this girl of twenty-six, with a passionate and intense nature, could have been so unawakened to the deeper physical significance of love. . . . My acceptance of Christian Science, in the way that I did, caused me to feel that my art life rested uncompromisingly on a sexless quality of mind and feeling, and that any influence on or penetrations of my love life would invade the vital center of my creative instincts and bring disaster." Despite this there were several tentative essays in amorous flirtation. "But I knew if I surrendered on any terms to this strong and subtle call I would endanger the whole quality of my art which I had been protecting so zealously . . ."

The precedent behind her was awful: in the nineteenth century no dedicated female artist—no great writers, no painters, no scientists (with the dazzling exception of Marie Curie) or doctors (with the exception of Elizabeth Blackwell)—were able or permitted to marry. The choice had to be either career or wifely duties. It could not be both, the sacrifice of either destroying the personality or human happiness. The battle of the twentieth century on the part of women has been not to get into men's lavatories or into men's changing rooms or into men's clubs but to achieve marriage and vocation and to maintain both together. This has been not just the women's position or problem; it is equally the men's, and I think until now, it has not been faced by the younger people. Young men, reared by women who have tried and succeeded a little, or not succeeded at all, have been there to see their mother's intense suffering and their father's bewilderment; they will expect to face it. It is a complete rebalancing of human relationships that is needed. There are millennia of cultural practices against any female having both career and marriage, but the desire is deep-rooted and persistent, and Miss Ruth was going to break precedent and attempt to have both.

The demonic possessiveness of Ruth's mother, the woman suffragist, the women's rights advocate, the medical graduate, the herbalist, the innovator, was what nearly all dancing-mothers show toward their daughters; it is not an uncommon trait. Where the mother has had an unfulfilled or incomplete life there is a degree of transference to the oldest child which goes beyond the borderlines of normalcy. It is avid and tyrannical. And behind every truly great female dancer there is usually this story. Sometimes there is a father, but in the case of dancers succession is usually dynastic. The Russian ballet in its Imperial days deftly avoided the problem by separating the children from both parents and training them as the servants of the state and of their art, releasing them only on graduation; not so the hapless youngsters of the West.

Ruth Dennis's mother consistently drove off every suitor. She played on her daughter's conscience and terrors: her loyalty to her family, her natural anxiety about compromising her ideals or her attention—whatever served the purpose of keeping the girl enthralled and exclusive. Ruth went along with Mama and paid deep heed to the savants and great men who advised her to guard her vestal qualities.

She wrote in her autobiography:

I realized in a vague, dimly formed way that it was only the interpretative artists who were fed and developed by emotional experiences. To me, who was essentially a creator, these experiences were profoundly and terrifyingly disturbing. They threatened my sanctuary! They set up such conflicts between the biologic woman . . . and the artist woman who drank from deeper springs than the language of the body could identify. Braffie [her Russian manager] once said to me "No, Rutie, you must not marry, because what you now give to your dancing you will give to your husband." I knew with a terrible inward agony that his words were true.

Some of Ruth's suitors were extraordinary men with great gifts to offer, and Ruth was well aware of this. But they did not wish to run the gauntlet of Ruth's cold doubt and her mother's ire. They withdrew, as any sensible suitor would.

Except Ted Shawn.

Shawn was a sometime religious student who, recovering from a slight bout of polio, had decided to turn his energies to dancing. He went the regular route of ballroom exhibitions in hotels and vaudeville. Then, in the spring of 1911, in Denver, he attended a performance of St. Denis's dances, and "found" himself "sobbing as if the soul rose out of my body when I saw the *Incense*—and never before or since have I known so true a religious experience or so poignantly a revelation of perfect beauty." He was handsome and personable. He was nineteen years old—thirteen years younger than she. He was ambitious.

He went to New York. Miss Ruth was in a melancholy and extremely receptive state of mind, poor as always and lonely and dispirited. She felt unwanted. South American dances were much in vogue at the time, and St. Denis regretfully concluded that she must include a maxixe in her program. "I allowed myself to believe either that the message that was given to me was of little value or that the world did not wish to receive it, and so instead of loyalty to my own genius, such as it is, I accepted the suggestion that my program should be bettered by this alien rhythm . . . . I sent out a call for young men dancers, not at all sure what I was going to do with one on my program. I had almost given up the idea when Ted Shawn walked into the house. . . . During that first long interview he told me a great deal about himself."

I'm sure he did. He was less alluring than the Egyptian Deities advertisement, but he turned out to be just as effective. Miss Ruth had met her doom.

They began to see each other and work together, and she was at once struck with his intense spiritual interest. She was also at once drawn to him romantically. They went on tour, Ted doing some of his own dances and some of the currently popular South American ones. "In Paducah, Kentucky," Ruth writes, "our idyl began to bloom. We took long walks into the country, he an eager boy with lovely brown eyes, awakening to this first genuine adoration; I a young woman, drinking in his adoration with the deepest gratitude. . . . I still did not believe in marriage, for myself, but I did not have the courage . . . to deny this love completely. . . ." In her letters she addressed him as "Friend of My Soul," adding, "Mother was outspoken in her objections and Brother, although nobody paid him much mind, agreed with Mother."

On their long trip across the United States, the lovers managed to snatch times of privacy in various cities, which Ruth recounts lovingly in her book. Finally there was a four-hour confrontation with her mother in Edgartown, Massachusetts, where she and Ruth had gone for a month in the summer to rest. In Ted's words, as quoted in *An Unfinished Life*: "Ruth's mother . . . had little to say about Ted. I think for the first time in her life she felt herself defeated, and a great sorrow rather than a resentment filled her heart." Ted later described his confrontation with her somewhat differently. She became, in succession, "a pathetic, broken old woman, a raging sea serpent, a roaring lion." Mother finally gave way but warned her daughter as she withdrew that "he's no weakling."

Indeed he was not, and this is probably the success of his supremacy. He was not a better thinker than Ruth, he certainly was not an equal artist, and he was not a kinder person and she had met those who were. He was damnably ambitious and he was determined to have his way, His way was to be Ruth's new career.

They were married on August 13, 1914, in a small bookshop uptown in New York kept by a Dr. Otterson, a retired minister. Ruth's brother Buzz and his wife, Emily, were witnesses to the wedding. Mother absented herself and sat alone on Riverside Drive, by the monument to the dead—the Soldiers' and Sailors' Monument.

June Hamilton Rhodes insists that Ted did not love Ruth. "Ted was incapable of loving any woman," she claims. But Ruth was the ideal person to help him to what he wanted: world fame, money, and power. He was smart and he would make her rich. He got after her.

"Nor did Ruth love him," June further declares.

I don't believe this, because I knew Miss Ruth and I saw how she suffered later at Ted's neglect and unkindness. She had, it seems, a deep and irrevocable dread of physical sex. That suited Ted. She hoped he would be tender and protective. She knew he was ambitious and clever. I believe she must have been very lonely—an unattached woman of thirty-five often is, and she was tired of traveling around without home or roots. She was probably very tired of Mother's domination.

She took the chance. It was a bad one.

"Ted destroyed Ruth," June Rhodes later declared, with mounting passion. Several of Ruth's pupils concur. But it must be recognized that Ruth also destroyed herself. One does not marry one's destroyer, or at least one doesn't stay with him unless there is a deep suicide wish.

"Her life with him was that of a trapped lion," continues June. "She was afraid of losing him because he could bring in new business. He showed her no tenderness, was critical, possessive and full of his own love affairs which always seemed to end in disaster and then there was crying, pouting and tantrums."

At first Ted had to take a subservient place among St. Denis's other assistants, as cup bearer, fan bearer, train bearer: definitely secondary. But on the honeymoon tour itself, Ted began to battle for equal billing and equal pay, and he fought with a tenacity that Ruth had never encountered before. This trauma lasted throughout their lives and twisted and bent them. It impressed her great pupils very deeply; Martha Graham and Doris Humphrey were shaped and influenced by it.

But that Ted loved Ruth at the beginning of their courtship, despite what June says, and despite his marked homosexuality (which neither he nor Ruth ever admitted publicly), cannot be overlooked. He said he revered her. Maybe so. In any case, he used her. I think I am safe in saying that without her he would not have achieved anything beyond the status of a slick and ordinary vaudevillian. With her he claimed parity, and that meant renown and the possibility of money.

Ted was a very attractive young man: personable, well and softly spoken, polite, ingratiating, informed, and fair-minded on all subjects not touching his ego; but his vanity was like an exposed organ. His antennae were out for hurts, and, seemingly without skin, he reacted instantly. Yet on casual meeting he could be enchanting, especially to rich, middle-aged ladies who might be induced to become patrons. These he treated with gallantry and imagination, and they became his devoted adherents.

Shawn, however, could not be honest with himself, and although he was generous to young dancers (he was very kind to me, both when I was a child and later when I was a young professional), his actions were limited by the essential lie behind his conduct. Shawn was a hypocrite and he thereby merits, in my opinion, harsh criticism. He could not follow the prime commandment in art, "To thine own self be true"— not exploitative, but true.

Ruth had no supporting company, only a group of miscellaneous people picked up as she traveled around. She had no school and therefore no pupils, and when one got right down to it, she had no set technique to teach. There was therefore no one at all she could call on from the outside who had been trained in what she was doing. There were ballroom dancers, refugees from ballet, interpretive dancers, soloists from vaudeville. But Ruth St. Denis demanded only sympathy and the ability to imitate.

Ted began saying that he would like to do solos while Ruth changed costumes and caught her breath: this seemed reasonable. Alas, his solos were of a very different genre from hers. Hers were mystic reproductions, evocative and imaginative; his were slick vaudeville routines, various kinds of ballroom dances, tangos, waltzes, mazurkas, or pseudodramatic pieces, the usual commercial fare, each one giving him a chance to show himself in costumes which got progressively briefer—although it could be said that his was not a particularly handsome example of male beauty, his hips being too wide, his musculature too soft, the flawless chest showing not a hair, the armpits as pristine as a maiden's. The body was close to immaculate, even if not particularly male, yet it was his and he saw it as fit to be displayed.

The major tussle began between them, for position and domination—the struggle Mother Dennis had foreseen. Poor Ruth! Poor lady! She hadn't a chance. Ted was inexhaustible.

The tour continued, with Ruth trying to bolster Ted's egotistic pride and Ted trying to establish his dominating strength.

Yet he always called her "Master," and in his first biographical book, *Ruth St. Denis: Pioneer and Prophet,* published in 1920, he refers to her as though she were his guru. But she was not his guru, she was his middle-aged wife, famous while he was unknown, sought after while he was passed by, worshiped by dancers while he was tolerated as their equal, envied only as having special and unfair privileges. In short, she was a bona fide star while he was a pretender. She was also a woman of genuine convictions; what he had were genuine ambitions.

They were together a year. Ted managed the business end of their work very well, and their profits were ten thousand dollars, virtually untaxed. That pleased Ruth. But Ted took all the money and purchased a twenty-five-year annuity for himself, leaving Ruth not one cent. This dismayed her. Edwinna Hamilton, later the resident Denishawn manager, trembling with rage, told her daughter June, the company manager, the ugly fact.

The school was founded in Los Angeles and advertised nationwide. It was to be the first academy of its kind in America. They called it Denishawn.

I t was Ted's idea to found Denishawn—to build a school for dancers that would be the founders' instrument, their perpetuation of ideals, technique, and compositions. Ruth did not particularly want a school of this kind, but Ted did, and what he wanted was done.

Ted's project was an academy such as existed nowhere on the North American continent, enrolling teenage boys and girls from everywhere and teaching them not only body discipline but elements of music, history of art, religion, and philosophy. They gathered around them savants and artists, as Miss Ruth always had in her studios wherever she had worked. It was a rather grandiose plan, but one which they made quite workable in their batik-and-bead way, and was fitted to the needs of the time.*

*It must always be borne in mind that Shawn's tape-recorded notes, which provided much of the material for this chapter, were made at the end of his life, a couple of months before his death. Although this was a time when he was very jealous of Martha's renown and the continuing

There was no immediate thought of building a performing troupe, but since Ted was a consummate businessman, he must have had a grand concept at the back of his mind of the first great American dance company. In any case, at that time their academy was unique. It had no rivals.

In 1915 they purchased three houses on a hilltop in Los Angeles on Sunset Boulevard, facing Westlake Park. The Hill Street trolley went around the bluff at the bottom, and the riders, gazing up at the roman- tic structure at the top, may have wondered about the dancing going on up there. More likely, since the Los Angeles citizens had grown accustomed to extraordinary sights, they probably did not give a thought to the hilltop establishment.

The three back yards were joined to form a continuous L-shaped area, its wooden floor covered with canvas. A long barre and mirrors extended down one side, where the piano of the music director, Louis Horst, stood. There was no real roof. Most of the year there was no rain, of course, but the subtropical sun was mighty in the afternoon! Bare feet on the scorching canvas! The outer boundaries of the yard were walled in by chicken wire, and the drop below to the trolley was abrupt, two hundred feet and immediate. The three houses were large and roomy. Out-of-town dancers slept on the premises and ate communally in the large dining room. Local students lived at home.

The dancers' working apparel was a one-piece bathing suit with a small apron for the girls; and this simple garment was stark innovation. At that time dancers wore tunics or they wore ballet dresses. The Denishawners wore bathing suits and had bare feet always, except when they went abroad, and then they wore what was known as the Denishawn sandal, very comely and comfortable footgear which was utilized by all the dancers of Los Angeles, including the ballet schools, it being the only shoe that did not torture feet but still supported the instep and held the arch and toes in, neat and attractive.

The students practiced every day. The daily practice was hard and

---

luster of Miss Ruth's early legend, and filled with great sorrow and bitterness because of the way Miss Ruth had treated him after their separation, he nevertheless probably spoke the truth as he remembered it. He had an unblemished record for being fair and factual. He had a deep respect for the written word, the record, history as he had experienced it. The curator of documents of the New York Public Library, Genevieve Oswald, believed his vocal autobiography to be truthful, as truthful as any human statement can be.

steady. Above all, the students were encouraged to read, think, and discuss. There was a library on the premises, and gardens: Westlake Park across the way provided many places for discussion and study, and also for gamboling on the green by the pond. Once a local Irish cop was summoned to stop the girls from barefoot exposure on the dew-heavy grass, but ten minutes with Irish Ruthie Dennis and a strong cup of tea elicited from him a vow to protect their rights to express themselves undisturbed, even in one-piece bathing suits.

Ruth and Ted had the imagination to hire extraordinary teachers, among them Henrietta Russell Hovey (wife of the poet Richard Hovey) who was—after the demise of the other two disciples, Genevieve Stebbins and Steele MacKaye—the only living pupil of Delsarte.

From Mrs. Hovey the Denishawners became acquainted with Delsarte's three laws—physical, emotional, and mental—and the categories in which he charted the physical, emotional, and mental properties of each member of the body: for instance, the heel of the hand was physical, the palm emotional, and the fingers mental. This intense analysis was intellectually stimulating, but how it helped a novice to move more spontaneously or intelligently I cannot say. As Delsarte himself explained, his was a system and not an art form.

Los Angeles in the first quarter of this century was enhanced by a quite considerable Chinatown, as large as that of New York, and a sizable Japantown, and to these communities came visiting actors and dancers as well as sages from the Orient. They were invited immediately to the Denishawn school to demonstrate and, with the aid of interpreters, to explain and lecture. This was remarkable firsthand knowledge, and the pupils counted themselves fortunate to be exposed to it.

Miss Ruth used to say to all her students, "If you will master to any degree the Japanese art of dance, anything else you do will be better done. For," she continued, "I know nothing, not even the ballet at its strictest, which can exceed the precisions and discipline of Japanese technique."

Isadora had said, "I have never been a dancer; I do not like any kind of dancing except, perhaps, the Japanese."

Every visiting swami (real or bogus, and southern California was a mecca for religious experimenters), including the truly great Swami Paramananda, came to the Denishawn school, paid homage to Miss Ruth, talked to her for hours, talked to her pupils. Paramananda taught them to sit absolutely still without moving for long periods of time, an enlarging and enlightening experience. All the experimenters with movement, the transcribers of movement, the analysts and codifiers of movement, lectured to pupils who sat silently in the lotus position, eagerly taking in the strange and remarkable learning.

Louis Horst, the company pianist and conductor of Miss Ruth's touring orchestra, was given charge of all her music, the arranging and the planning. He was born in Kansas City, Missouri, but had moved to San Francisco at about age nine. His schooling had been brief: he had not gone beyond the seventh grade. Louis, however, was a reader, and he was curious, and he educated himself in all the arts, being formally trained only in music. He always felt that school was for degree getting and not for information getting, and certainly not for the acquiring of skills. He therefore considered formal education to be of secondary importance. His father, a trumpeter in the San Francisco Symphony Orchestra, fortunately helped Louis to get jobs. Louis conducted and played both violin and piano wherever he could, a volume of Walter Pater frequently propped open on his music rack.

Ted and Ruth had for some reason fired their own conductor and were in desperate need of a music director. They called upon the house conductor, Horst, who had never served in this capacity for dancers, but he said he would try for ten days and would see them through their crisis. He traveled with them up the West Coast to Seattle, never having a proper rehearsal with the pickup musicians gathered together at every stop. Finally he declared he must have a rehearsal or he would quit. Miss Ruth approached him in what he described as "a crooning Irish way," and, smiling angelically, murmured, "But Mr. Horst, we think it's going beautifully." "I don't," snapped Louis. "I want the rehearsal." Within a day or two he got it. The ten days stretched to ten years, and, as John Martin later said, "pretty well altered the trend of a whole art."

Louis Horst had come down from San Francisco accompanied by his pretty young wife, Betty, a dancing-school teacher. She had red-blond hair and was charming, although she was an indifferent dancer.

Horst battled tirelessly to improve the regulation hackneyed Denishawn musical diet. Into the stale, faded musical fare he introduced the fresh, titillating accents of Satie, Debussy, and Richard Strauss. But he could not tease Shawn into accepting Stravinsky, Schoenberg, or even Scriabin, Shawn's Edwardian taste balking outright at this twentieth-century "caterwauling," (as Glen Tetley said Shawn called it). Miss Ruth, alas, tended to agree with her husband. In any case, Shawn favored the Americans MacDowell and Cadman, or, if Horst must get fancy and foreign, Cécile Chaminade, unless it was the classics; but Horst wouldn't accept Tchaikovsky. They compromised on Bach.

IIIII

Miss Ruth reserved to herself all Oriental studies, together with all philosophy and religious approaches that made them understandable. She had absorbed a deep reverence for the Hindu philosophy, as far as she in her limited way understood it. She did not read Sanskrit. She certainly did not read or speak Hindi. And some of the great writings had not been translated. (This was to come later, in the twenties.) Many of the ideas had not yet touched Western thought. Miss Ruth's classes developed into seminars in semi-philosophic, loose mystic discussion. She talked at length of the importance of Vedanta, and what dancing meant in the Orient and in ancient cultures. At the same time, she lectured on Christian Science. Miss Ruth's pupils had to acquire by a kind of aesthetic osmosis whatever they learned. Some did.

Miss Ruth would always center herself first: close her eyes, sometimes looking upward, sometimes waiting with quiet breathing until she felt absolute aplomb. And then she would speak.

Concentration is a matter of the reorganization of dynamic and spiritual powers and is therefore difficult to impart or teach. The Orientals spend their lifetime in learning how; it is not to be accomplished in dancing classes an hour at a time. Miss Ruth, however, tried. If her long moments of sitting and breathing before each dance session might have seemed pretentious and unnecessary, in reality they were periods of mental discipline, quite as vigorous as Christian Science or barre exercises. When she was warmed up, that is, spiritually ready, she delivered right out of her substance and belief. Miss Ruth at least reached through to her watchers, especially in the beginning. Her pupils tried industriously to copy her, usually with less success.

It was Miss Ruth's job to indoctrinate, leaving all physical exercises, patterns, and "steps" to Ted and the assistant teachers. She set dances; she coached in expression, dynamics, and meaning. Ruth's teaching was restricted, therefore, mainly to interviews about inner meaning.

She wrote, "I was never a good teacher. Obviously I am too deep an egoist to have that particularly unselfish attitude towards a student which is the basis of teaching genius."

And she offered no physical formulae. Students had such long, mystical talks with Miss Ruth at their practice sessions that they frequently found themselves with nothing done toward the next day's performance of demonstration pieces. The dances had to be rushed together in twenty minutes. They were frequently not very good.

Ted taught what our grandmothers called "fancy dancing," a free-form ballet—that is, ballet without the turnout and the extreme flexing of the feet and pointes and without the strain of straight knees or any of the distortions. It was a loose enlargement of Duncan's "natural" movement. Distortion was avoided—unfortunately, because distortion is the very essence of art and all dancing. Distortion is what saves ordinary rhythmic movement from being bland paddling in the air. A straight ballet leg, the tensed and sustaining pointes of ballet feet are distortion; the bent back hands of the Thai dancers, the turned-up feet of the classical Chinese, the knee squats and spins of the Cossacks, the zapateado finger snappings, heel drills, and arched spine of the Spanish Gypsies, the whirlings of the dervish—all are distortions. Distortion is the extension of effort, the prolongation or stress beyond the norm. It can be arresting or remarkable, and it can help fix the gesture in memory—yes, and in meaning, because it spells difficulty overcome, human dominance, and triumph. No successful dancing does without it.

And, in fact, what Denishawn teaching did not have was just this— any hazard overcome, any gravity defied, the muscular surprise and control which spell zest and delight. The Denishawn technique under Ted used ballet only as a free base for superimposing just about anything it chose, always bearing in mind grace and smoothness and, of course, the avoidance of effort.

Miss Ruth and Ted, but particularly Miss Ruth, made a cult of what they called "plastiques," posing and moving in scarves and costumes. There were frequently small audiences of nonprofessional admirers at these sessions. But in the case of Miss Ruth, "plastiques" involved more than just striking poses. Shutting herself up in her large studio, she worked on her own compositions, on costumes and on the movements of scarves and skirts. "Parading around before mirrors," Ted later described it to me, not very kindly.

But to Miss Ruth, costumes were themselves part of dancing. She considered clothes, scarves, and jewels to be the extension, elaboration, and punctuation of gesture, stressing and accenting what she did with her body and hands. In other words, costume was a kind of orchestration. She was very careful about texture and color, and as she danced she used material in ways that were musical and imaginative. Martha Graham was to learn from her a great deal of this skill. No costume existed apart from the dance: it never blocked the gesture or negated it but was an added element of magic, an added intensification. She saw woven material as very nearly a separate living substance, and one which she summoned as collaborator. Miss Ruth had a passion for beautiful brocades, Indian and Chinese silks, embroidered and jeweled velvet, silk chiffons. What Miss Ruth could do with a length of silk was poetic and creative, making costumes as she moved by folding, pleating, tucking. She trained her students to do likewise as an important part of their curriculum. They became masters at handling fabrics, and some of them became masters at cutting and adapting and designing. After all, the sari is just a length of beautiful cotton or silk which by the way it is tucked and folded into the belt becomes the traditional robe of the Hindu woman, her shelter, her protection, her adornment. Martha Graham was to learn all this.

Miss Ruth's costumes were not great costumes. They were flattering to her personally and they were the kind of costumes that most women love: pale chiffons, pale silks, plenty of jewels. They were wonderfully suitable to Ruth, her long body with its long torso, her high, beautiful bust, the long neck balancing an exquisite head. Offstage, Pearl Wheeler, her designer, a dancer, and a devoted member of the entourage, clothed Miss Ruth in all the good and lovely cloth from the East and the best of the West, Japanese in the kimonolike sleeves and neckline and soft belting. The head with its aura of white hair she left untouched, except very occasionally for a tight turban or a big, untrimmed shade hat. These dresses did not set fashions, but they set off Miss Ruth.

Ted, on the other hand, liked costumes with gimmicky effects, big veils, spears, paraphernalia, crowns, all kinds of crowns, but no covering, not on his body.

Ted taught American Indian dances, without informing his students of their religious or sociological background and without using their chief attributes: endurance and purpose. Anthropologists assure us that when the Indians dance for rain, the rains do in fact come, and no one sits down or takes a drink or even eats for days until this happens. Rain, of course, is difficult to organize as a climactic theatrical effect, but the smart Indians do their dances only at the beginning of the rainy season. Ted also taught a very free form of Spanish dancing, without the castanets and heel work, which are difficult, and various other folk dances, including American, without any buck or tap, which is also difficult.

Ted gave lectures on dance history and read Walter Pater, Havelock Ellis, Freud, and Nietzsche aloud to the young men after class. He sat in a Japanese kimono, with one hand on the book and the other languidly draped over the back of the chair. Up to that point the students had probably not read anything at all like this, and they were impressed. He became the father leader, the alter ego, Papa Shawn.

In that early Denishawn group there were Julanne Johnston (who in 1924 would star with Douglas Fairbanks in *The Thief of Bagdad*), Margaret Loomis (who later played the lead in several of my father's, William de Mille's, pictures and who sometimes understudied and doubled for Miss Ruth), Florence Andrews (who as Florence O'Denishawn—Ted invented the name—would star in the *Ziegfeld Follies*), Mary Hay (the daughter of a general and later the partner of Clifton Webb, then a revue star), Louise Brooks (who achieved fame for her portrayal of Lulu in G. W. Pabst's 1928 film *Pandora's Box*). There were also kibitzers who dabbled in order to achieve, if not grace, at least basic physical coordination: Dorothy and Lillian Gish, Constance and Norma Talmadge, later Ina Claire, Ruth Chatterton, Mabel Normand, Lenore Ulrich, Florence Vidor, Colleen Moore, and, much later, Myrna Loy. D. W. Griffith ordered all his leading ladies to take Denishawn classes.

Ted had installed Edwinna Hamilton as house manager and her daughter, June Hamilton Rhodes, a physical-education teacher from Illinois, as teacher of beginners. To the beginners June taught simple Maypole dances and European folk forms. June had her mother's head for business and gradually became involved in administration. She presently took over her mother's duties and became the organizer and manager of Denishawn, Miss Ruth's end of the business in particular. June distrusted Ted, and he, sensing an enemy, responded with a very healthy wariness which in time turned to intense dislike. June's loyalty to Miss Ruth was deep.

If there was nothing like the Denishawn school on the North American continent, it might be further argued that there was nothing like it anywhere in the world. To this lively, if mongrel, group on the hill, this mystic flotsam, came in 1916, during the second summer of its existence, a new pupil, Martha Graham, freshly graduated from the Cumnock School of Expression.

Jenny Graham, now widowed, was perfectly agreeable to keeping house for Martha near Denishawn, so that her oldest daughter could study dancing while the younger girls continued with high school. The Santa Barbara house was thereupon closed up, and together with Lizzie, Jenny made her temporary home in Los Angeles. When after a year she returned to Santa Barbara, it was to the old house with Lizzie, and she kept this always open and ready to receive her daughters as they and their friends came back for vacations.

Mary, the family beauty, long-limbed and svelte, visited Denishawn with Martha, and Miss Ruth cast a predatory eye on her as exactly the type of girl she wanted in her troupe. But it was Martha who wanted to dance and Martha who entered the school. Geordie desired to follow Martha, and in due course she too became a Denishawner, as eventually did Mary, but only for a very short time.

At age twenty-two, Martha found she was older than the other beginning students at Denishawn, but her extraordinary fervor and determination, her application and doggedness, compensated for any stiffness in the muscles. She absorbed everything, the way a plant takes in light. She was always on time and always attentive, using every faculty she had.

Ted Shawn tells of the first impression Martha made on her teachers:

Ruth said on first seeing her, "Totally hopeless. . . . What can I do with this? . . . Maybe Japanese?" But apparently Martha didn't move well enough to suit Ruth, or Martha herself . . . didn't in her heart want to be Japanese. . . . Ruth came to me and said, "Darling, why does a girl like that come to us? Can't she look in the mirror and see that she's hopeless?"
She was quite a few years above the average age of all the other girls in the school. Let's admit that she was homely, and Martha was overweight. I won't say exactly fat, but she was dumpy, unprepossessing.

Miss Ruth insisted that Martha was too ugly to be a Japanese maiden, so, with her breasts strapped flat, she was cast as a boy. Having been told she was ugly, Martha was also, not unnaturally, abnormally shy. Shawn said, "If there were twenty-five or thirty students, you'd always find Martha in the back of the back row, and she was always very embarrassed if she was asked to do something alone.

One day, at the end of her first year, Ted said to her, "Martha . . . you are willing to face the fact that you have a very hard row to hoe, face and figure and age. . . . You are slow, slow learning, very thorough when you get to it, but I seem to recognize in you a burning desire to dance. This I . . . bow to. This is the greatest power. . . . You've got a hard battle. I'll fight it with you."

It soon became apparent that whatever was said to Graham took root and produced a reaction of some sort, often an astonishing one.

Ted latched on to Martha's tremendous vitality and flair for acting. Here was an ego to match his own, and if she had doubts about his taste and abilities, she was, at least in the beginning, humbly reticent and responded eagerly to his suggestions. Miss Ruth must have been aware of Martha's qualities also. She was not attracted to Martha and perhaps was slightly intimidated, because although Martha was shy and deeply respectful, it was obvious that hers was a talent that could not be measured at the moment, that there were forces within her personality like those within a wild animal, forces which she could not herself yet gauge or understand. When she began to do solos her tremendous flair suddenly appeared, licking like fire at the opportunities, a flair that might very well bid for undue attention with the star's. And Miss Ruth was already having trouble enough with Ted's cancerous vanity; she did not want a female rival as well.

Martha danced in the Denishawn chorus with the other girls. There are many pictures of her standing in line as an Egyptian, as a Greek, as an Indian, and as a Spaniard.

Shawn continues: "I had created a dance with a circular skirt which was a blend of Spanish and North African that you could say was a mishmash. All right, so it was. It was good theater.* . . . Suddenly, for the first time since Martha had come to us . . . there at the back of the class she had come to life. I called her to me. 'Martha, you just outdanced everybody in the class.' She very modestly glowed. 'I know you have no money. I will work with you, give you all the time I can.' "

At this juncture Ted was asked to contribute an Arabian dance to S. M. "Roxy" Rothafel's show at his downtown theater in Los Angeles. Ted sent Martha with *Serenata Morisca,* and Martha made a hit. (Jane Sherman's *The Drama of Denishawn Dance* maintains that Betty Horst "was the first to perform this dance outside the classroom," but Shawn made no mention of Betty Horst.)

Martha learned thoroughly the lore of Denishawn, and this knowledge became her dowry to take with her wherever she went. First, the actual dance technique—pseudo-ballet, pseudo-Duncan, and pseudo-Oriental. All of this Graham later repudiated in toto, except the Oriental use of the ground (the employment of kneeling and sitting positions, for instance), and the use of fabric and costumes. What Martha really took into her soul was above all Ruth's extraordinary approach to dance itself, the centering of concentration and personality on one's highest instincts before proceeding into any exercise.

Pupils came from all over to Denishawn. There was Doris Humphrey, who had studied ballet in Chicago with Andreas Pavley and Serge Oukrainsky and had even ventured into vaudeville with them. Doris had joined the Denishawn staff as a ballet teacher the year before

---

*This was *Serenata Morisca,* which Graham was to revive and include in a suite made up of her old dances, produced in 1986. It was danced then by Terese Capucilli, and proved to be just what Shawn said: good theater—striking, dashing, picturesque— but of no real import. It is, as Ted also said, "kitsch" and a "mishmash," but it could become an exercise in straight audience appeal and vigorous delivery. He used a split kick on the right leg as an accent to start off the chain of movement, he says, but this, I believe, is inaccurate. Martha's split kick was on the left side, and she never in all her performing life varied it. Present here also are the ubiquitous Denishawn turns.

Martha came. At her audition Miss Ruth had asked Doris what she wished to do. "Teach," Doris replied. "This lovely quality must not be lost. You should dance," said Miss Ruth. "You can teach later if you want to, but you have the makings of a real artist." Doris was, at the time, slender, fragile, delicate, copper-curled. She soon was dancing in hoops and with scarves, ravishing but purely decorative, like a spray of flowers. But she had a mind. She was learning. This kind of dancing was not new. Girls have performed with hoops, garlands, wands since early court festivals.

Musical gymnastics, the contemporary Russian sports speciality, in which the acrobats perform with hoops, Indian clubs, and ribbons in charming patterns of movement while practicing the most elaborate cartwheels, somersaults, front flips, back flips, handstands, and so forth, are an elaboration on this same technique. The Russians claim it is a new art form. It is no such thing. Rather, it is an elaboration of Ted Shawn's formula. But whereas his works were to a childish degree musical and had a hint of mood, and therefore in a primitive way related to dancing, the contemporary Russians make no such pretense.

Doris Humphrey, pretty and unprovocative, was more to Miss Ruth's liking than Martha, and Doris responded very well to the mysticism and spurious intellectualism that Miss Ruth wrapped all her suggestions in. Martha was above all else a poet, and her instinct was to go to the bone, to cut through; this both the teachers, Ruth and Doris, found an extremely disquieting quality. Ted championed Martha; Miss Ruth, Doris.

There is no record of any jealousy or hostile action between the two young women, yet they must have eyed each other with appraisal. They were both enormously ambitious. They were both greatly gifted, and they had entirely different techniques, with one shared characteristic— dogged determination to mount to the top, and to be recognized universally for doing so. How soon did they know that a deadly rival stood opposite at the practice barre or walked on the stage close by? Right then, or a little later? But as time passed they were to know well enough. Martha, I believe, did not give the matter undue concern—she was so sure of her wants and her powers. Doris did compare; the comparison was forced on her by other people, with mounting and more acrid significance. She would have been the greatest American dancer except for . . . Doris's teeth sank into this bitter reservation very early, and she drank very deep of green envy, although she was far too dignified and sophisticated to give voice to it. There are those who think it eventually wrecked her health. But back then, in the Deni-shawn days, Doris was in the ascendant.

Charles Weidman came from Lincoln, Nebraska. He had seen Ruth St. Denis on one of her cross-country tours and followed her west with a letter of introduction to Louis and Betty Horst.

Weidman had an agile but untrained body, a fine sense of rhythm, and a genuine comic gift. He was more than droll; he was funny and fun to be with. Martha became very fond of him, and they were always attached. Charles's first lessons were with Doris Humphrey, who was an excellent teacher and who remained his chief guide and mentor throughout his career. He later became her partner and shared billing with her. Charles began by playing all the character bits and devising and dancing the first studies of genuine Americana on the American concert stage. He also danced with Martha, but Ted reserved first rights there.

|||||

Denishawn grew in fame, but it received no subsidies from state or business—in fact, no financial endowments of any kind—and, of course, nothing could be hoped for from the Board of Education or the government, as such ideas had not yet been implanted in America. Denishawn found itself pitifully unable to meet its costs by tuition fees alone. The company had to perform professionally, and that meant vaudeville, or sometimes appearing at moving-picture houses in "atmo-spheric prologues" for the big pictures. The Denishawners danced very frequently in Grauman's theaters. Here not only were the costs met but a small and very welcome profit turned. The intellectuals (and surely Ted and Ruth classed themselves among these) despised vaudeville, but Ted and Ruth turned to it again and again for a living.

It must always be remembered that Miss Ruth's taste and aesthetics, and Ted's, were based on a foundation of popular theater: of vaudeville, music halls, and nickel arcades. Other trimmings were superimposed. Miss Ruth had done her time in the music halls, and later with David Belasco, the arch showman of the New York theater. Ted had been a ballroom dancer. In one way this was a very solid asset, because the basic purpose of cheap theatrical entertainments was, as it always is, to entertain, to hold the attention, to convince. The means were often commonplace and vulgar, but not always. This penchant, this leaning in Ruth toward the common, was scorned by Louis Horst and the more high-minded students, but it was quite sound, except perhaps in the manner in which it was used. Much great theater has been popular theater. Mozart wrote in the popular forms of his time and was a great success. Verdi was an enormous hit in his day, the delight and joy of the common population, and it was from this that he derived his strength. When an artist loses touch with the people, as many have done, he is confessing to a lack of vitality and inner purpose. Miss Ruth instinctively knew this.

The great weakness in Miss Ruth's art was that the dance form she chose was sentimental and cloying, and sometimes even frivolous, and therefore fake. What is regrettable is that she always wrapped herself, mummified herself, as Ted did, in the pretensions of high art, high thought, high purpose, maintaining an attitude of haughty scorn toward commercial work, that is, vaudeville and moving pictures. They lived and toiled in Hollywood, where there was at that moment a popular form of entertainment growing up that eventually changed the world. It was not then great art. My father, William de Mille, one of the founders of motion-picture technique, said so himself: "We are not the real playwrights. We are craftsmen. The artists will come after us and profit by our findings. It will take a generation or two to produce them. In the meantime, this is a most extraordinary medium."

I don't think anyone gainsaid that belief except Miss Ruth and Ted Shawn. Much later, Sir Kenneth Clark stated in his TV lecture series *Civilisation* (later published in book form) that motion pictures could be considered as the only dynamic and valid art form of the twentieth century.

Ted and Ruth used work in movies to make extra money because they badly needed it, but they despised the movies, and their dancers who went into films (as Louise Brooks did) were treated with sorrowful pity. Ted claimed that what he taught was more important.

Martha Graham participated in one of Denishawn's adventures in moving pictures. Her dance was performed before Thomas Meighan, who played the Babylonian king in Cecil B. DeMille's *Male and Female* (1919), a liberal adaptation of Sir James Matthew Barrie's *The Admirable Crichton*. Martha, in a spangled skirt, bare midriff, and suitable Babylonian wig, whirled around, Denishawn style, with her hands in what Ted assumed were Babylonian positions and her body bent double, winding up squatting on the floor before the monarch, her skirt fanned out around her in a grand obeisance. She then beat a very hasty retreat as Gloria Swanson, in pearls and with an entire white peacock on her head, was carried in by six Nubian slaves. (The end of Graham's dance can be seen in the film.)

Martha's introduction to motion pictures went largely unremarked, although I was present on the occasion. Nobody paid her the slightest attention, because Gloria Swanson speedily and haughtily spurned the king's ignoble offer and descended into a pit where a live lion placed his paws, claws intact, on her naked back. The trainers stood by attentively with chairs reversed so that their legs stuck out, and there was a man with a loaded pistol. The cameras ground safely from above, and Cecil's heart swelled with pride as the brave and beautiful young girl, his "Little Fella," dared expose her flesh to laceration at his bidding. The greatest dancer in the Western hemisphere had just whirled around in front of the cameras, but who knew that or gave it the slightest thought?

It was on these commercial jaunts that Martha manifested the qualities for which she later became famous. She must have despised the work—Egyptian, Aztec, primeval—but if she was doing it, it had to be done with faith and attention. According to Charles Weidman, one night, at Grauman's Egyptian Theater, Helen McGee came back from dinner tipsy on bootleg liquor, and in a spirit of light frivolity put her bobbed wool wig (Egyptian, most likely) on backward, so that the black wool hair sat across the bridge of her nose and the nape of her neck was uncovered. Martha grew so outraged at this levity that she tore the backstage telephone out of the wall and threw it at the girl's head. This act is noteworthy not only for its physical prowess but also for the degree of passion it reveals about anything that diverted Martha's intention: good dance or bad dance, dance was what they were doing, and they *had* to do it correctly.

In Shawn's Aztec number, *Xochitl*, Martha raked the chest of her partner with her nails, drawing blood. She did this every night. Shawn recalled: "I went through the whole tour with the inside of my lower lip cut and bleeding from the rape scene, because with her two fists she battered my face as if she would break my skull. I had ahold of a wild cat." In the same dance she also bit Shawn on the knee, but this she did not do every night: the exuberance drew criticism from the boss, who was the owner of the knee.

Martha would "sail onto the stage like a young tornado," Miss Ruth wrote, "and vitalize the entire atmosphere. She worked long and thoroughly at any task that was given her, and in the end managed to give it her own coloring."

Miss Ruth did not sail; she pervaded, she penetrated like mist or fragrance.

Around the Denishawn school Martha was somber and reclusive, mixing with the other girls very little and spending no time in the idle gossip of dressing room or garden. June Hamilton Rhodes found her cold and a little forbidding, although seemingly meek. The company régisseur, a contemporary student, claims that when Martha was at Denishawn in those very early days she was even then what June Rhodes called a "bitter, unhappy woman." It may easily have seemed so. She wore her hair parted in the center and brushed smooth on either side, with buns of braids over each ear. No one ever knew what went on inside that sleek little skull, but people hesitated to cross her. June said, "Martha's little sister, Georgia, was fat, fun, very pretty. Martha was always bony, meager, with the concentration of a fanatic. Georgia had no talent, but in any case all of our interest was centered on Doris, whose really exquisite body, lovely face, and beautiful hair made her a most appealing dancer."

IIIII

Ted toured more frequently than did Ruth, with Martha and groups of various sizes. Louis Horst and an ensemble of instrumentalists accompanied. During Louis's absences from school, his duties were performed by Pauline Lawrence, a plump and pleasing person who also danced and played while conducting the orchestra, indicating the tempo with her head.

In 1917 war was declared, and when the war intensified Ted went into the army but was not sent overseas. He went to Camp Kearney, near San Diego, and his army duties did not prevent him from keeping in close touch with Ruth and the school.

Ruth was not happy. In fact, she wrote of this whole period, "I was desperately unhappy. I had a feeling of a spiritual and artistic sin. This mode of company life and program making was alien to the highest elements of my destiny." She tended, of course, to blame Ted for this. And yet in a spirit of desperate clarity she was forced to ask, "How, in the end, can we possibly hold anyone responsible for our own undeveloped visions, or undeveloped strength of character?"

After the first year in Los Angeles, in 1917 the Graham girls had moved out from Mother, who went back to Santa Barbara. Mary, seemingly the most gregarious of the three, had taken up housekeeping with what Charles Weidman termed a "strong-minded spinster" named Charlotte. Martha stayed with them, pursuing her own love affairs, according to Weidman, "always unhappy, always frustrated, and usually with older, married men." She seemingly needed to have a dominant force that would deny and curtail her, and she drew a kind of strength out of the struggle. Geordie, "wee tim'rous beastie," was allotted a cot in the corner and slept by the radiator.

Charles went to live with them. Martha used to take him into her bed, quite chastely, when she was unwell and in pain, when she had what she called "zizlums," and he would hold her in his arms for body warmth and comfort her. She called him her "long hot-water bottle." There was not a modicum of sex in these domestic comforts. I find this extraordinary: girls in the early 1900s were circumspect, if not decorous. Such behavior was bohemian in the extreme, and overt. Mother, I'm sure, was not told. Martha's friendship with Charles remained always close and affectionate.

After two years, Martha was established with Denishawn as a teacher. A couple of years was quite enough time at Denishawn to entitle a student to become a teacher and, given Martha's temperament and proclivities, to become a junior director and manager as well. In fact, when Ted came back from the army in 1918, for a time he and Martha were the only teachers. They established a working camaraderie which she never knew with Miss Ruth, who had separated from the school to work on her own pieces. Ted sold the Westlake property and settled on Grand Street to work on vaudeville acts.

The vaudeville tours of Ted and Ruth resumed. Now Ted began to manifest really extraordinary jealousy and unhappiness. When Ruth was along on tour and it was for her that the audiences cheered, the trips were frequently agonizing. Ted would shout and scream. He would lie on the floor and howl, or sit for hours at a time staring at her without speaking. It was intolerable and childish, not to be lived with. Ruth used to come to Martha, Louis Horst told me, and beg for help. "You're the only person he's scared of. You're the only person who can talk to him. Make him get up off the floor and wash his face. We've got to give a performance shortly." And Martha would enter the den of Ted's dressing room and scream at him to pull himself together. As a matter of fact, he was sufficiently frightened of her to do just that.

Martha intimidated him, in part because her temper matched his and in part because she was not in love with him. Miss Ruth was. Martha found all this extremely wearing.

The rivalry between Ted and Ruth continued. Ted devised large ballets for the two of them. In *Isis and Osiris*, both were gods, both crowned; but being Osiris, the sun, Ted perforce took the lead and top position; Isis, the moon, was naturally in attendance and subject to his whims. In *Tillers of the Soil* (1916), with the original man and woman plowing Egyptian mud, the man was naturally dominant. In *Miriam, Sister of Moses* (1919), performed at the Greek Theater in Berkeley, Ruth danced the title role, but I think Ted as Moses had the last word. Little by little the religious aspects of Denishawn dances thinned, became diffuse, and the production and paraphernalia more obtrusive, as the success grew more financially rewarding. They paid their bills. They expanded. They taught like anything. But it was at the feet of Miss Ruth that Martha and Doris and Charles sat and listened with their hearts.

IIIII

Ted began to cast an envious eye on Miss Ruth's solos. She did *The Nautch*, an Indian street dance: he'd be a beggar with a begging bowl in the corner, in revealing rags. She was the title character in *Spirit of the Sea*, lying flat on her stomach with green veils stretched to the wings, and only her haunting little face, haloed by her loosened white hair suggesting foam on a curled wave, visible in the soft green light. It was not an interesting dance but it made a startling effect, and in it Miss Ruth was poetic and lyrical. Ted wanted in. He would be a fisher-boy, bronzed, naked, and playing in ropes of seaweed with bronzed beach girls; then and only then, he urged, would the Spirit of the Sea awaken, rouse up, and drown him in her watery embrace. Ruth thought this a fairly cheap and horrid idea and she said so. Her husband would not be denied. He teased all night, every night. On tour Louis Horst, sleeping in the next bedroom, heard the begging and Ruth's weary refusals and at last, with dawn, the pitiful capitulation, Ruth's terribly tired voice saying, "Ted, let me sleep. It's six in the morning and I have two performances to give today. I don't care anymore. Let me sleep." Ted ran off and bought body make-up, and according to his notions the dance was improved. Well, he'd put sex into it, hadn't he, and drama? No one would discuss it with him; they just danced in silence. Years later, Louis Horst shook as he told me this story.

Nevertheless, Ted respected Ruth and needed her approval and would do nothing new without it. According to José Limón, Shawn once composed a solo to a piece by Richard Strauss: he lay covered with poppies on a silken couch, writhing, rising only to give vent to the accumulated passion. At the end he gathered up an armful of poppies, tossed them in a gesture of heartbreaking frustration onto a brazier of burning coals, which was the only other object besides the couch to share the scene with him. He turned at the conclusion, sweating and panting, and sat at his wife's, his "Master's," knees, looking up at her wistfully.

She was still the Master. "No, Teddy, no."

That closed that scene: the dance never had another audience.

In her autobiography, Ruth stresses that they were lovers. We will never know for certain, and it matters, because both their lives were warped by their relationship and by the overpowering effort of trying to conform to the regular marital pattern of Western Christianity. Miss Ruth was a devout Christian Scientist. Ted was an avid hedonist and a deep-rooted homosexual. He admitted to what he called recurrent bouts of "Arrow collar-itis."* In 1913–19 it was not possible to admit homosexual predilections publicly. Little by little Ted had begun to realize that he was more interested in young men than was compatible with his marriage vows. He began to collect and gather them up wherever he was. He was taken with the male Pygmalion image, it being nothing more nor less than the classic pattern of the older man and the adoring pupil, the beautiful youth.

I must assume from her lifelong conduct of short-lived relations and from what she has stated in her books that Ruth was frigid. But June Rhodes said, "The reason I have for being certain that Miss Ruth was not with Ted nor ever happy [with Ted] was her attraction to (and mutually returned by) a very big MAN. . . . He was a Socialist, a writer, and a great, wonderful, magnetic person. I was the only person who knew about it and I managed the rendezvous. He [Judge Sirica] was married and she was enslaved. I never told anyone." Quite understandably, Ruth never confessed to frigidity in so many words, but her long refusal to engage in sex, and her choice of a husband and subsequent lovers who for one reason or another were incapable of establishing a lasting, satisfying new sex relationship, would argue as much. And then

---

*At that time Arrow Collars ran full-page color advertisements in all the better magazines of the most beautiful men imaginable—all, of course, wearing Arrows.

there was her presence, which everyone who knew her acknowledges was chaste, mystic, otherworldly. June wrote to me, "She was spirited, intelligent, completely untamed and undisciplined. She had fine instincts and eloquence in her concepts. She was not sensual although she could depict sensuality."

But the poetic impression of sexual drive and the communication of real animal force are totally different matters. Ruth was an insatiable flirt with an unquenchable appetite for teasing. She had many light romances, all of which she made known to Ted. This was cruel but probably quite deliberate, and it may have been in direct retaliation for his escapades. Years later, Ted stated flatly that it was she who started the infidelities; be that as it may, it is clear that they were both unhappy and certainly unsatisfied in their union. The rift widened. In an effort to bring them closer he asked for a child; she recoiled. She was almost forty; she believed that a child would trap her. She was fighting for her artistic integrity and longed to recapture her independence and the identity of her genius.

As the duel between Ruth and Ted developed, her leading students, including those two very gifted women Martha and Doris, begged her, implored her to leave Ted. "We'll wash your floors. We'll teach your classes. We'll do your secretarial work. We'll do anything. Leave Ted!" Louis repeated this story many times. But she could not; she would not. She remained and diminished, and the others watched in horror and dismay.

In her students especially, the great fear of marriage deepened. From here on in, as long as they were a working unit, Martha, Doris, June, and above all Louis tried to protect Ruth's talent and guard its integrity. But as they tried, they grew increasingly disheartened.

"If she'd only listen to anyone besides that man," cried Louis.

"Never in our lives will a like thing happen to us," responded Martha and Doris in antiphonal chorus.

When Miss Ruth was finally willing to declare independence and accept help, the girls and Louis were fighting for their own careers as recognized solo artists. This story is not unusual, but it is important because it has to do with nationally known figures and one genuinely great talent, Martha Graham.

The contest for billing, which Ted had more than achieved in the school, began to extend to their professional performances. Billing, wrote St. Denis, is "an inevitable, terrifying symbol. . . . It is hard to overestimate the paralyzing fear that hovers over this simple business of a spot on the program, the size of the type on the *affiche,* and the allotment of publicity. . . . It is the outer gage of the rise and fall of the artist's value in the markets of the world."

More and more frequently Ted and Ruth made their vaudeville tours separately. Ted toured with a group of four or five but always including Martha. When *Xochitl* went on tour in vaudeville without either Ted or Ruth, Martha acted as company manager in addition to her role as star, and she was in charge of the company payroll. In this way she learned a great deal about the practicalities of running a theater.

The *Xochitl* tour wound up with a gala series at Sid Grauman's downtown Los Angeles million-dollar theater, four performances a day. Martha invited her family from Santa Barbara and friends to see one six-o'clock supper show for which she proposed to insert the Arabian *Serenata Morisca.* An Arabian dance in an Aztec ballet! Even Ted's gorge rose at this. "Who would know?" queried Martha—which shows what she thought of the ballet. "You would know the difference and I would know the difference," said Ted. This altercation took place on the stage-door telephone. Martha tore the instrument from the wall (a method of terminating conversations which seemed to be becoming a habit). Ted took a taxi to the theater. Martha did not do the dance.

Matters were less stormy with Miss Ruth's troupe. She traveled with her girls and a musician and, when she could, Doris, plus sometimes Pauline Lawrence, the pianist-dancer. Pauline and Doris became close friends for life, and after Doris married, Pauline had a direct hand in bringing up Doris's son, Charles Woodford, the future publisher of *Dance Horizons.*

Miss Ruth was an improviser. She disliked "steps" and would not fix or settle on any. Also, she found it difficult to remember them. On occasion she was extraordinarily communicative and moving, like any other votive priestess. At other times she was flat. According to Louis Horst, Miss Ruth's "steps" were particularly sketchy in her *Brahms's Waltz* (1922), in which she slipped around the stage in pale blue and gray chiffon and flowing white hair, often toward the end fetching up near Louis Horst's piano. "I can't think of anything else to do. I've run out. How much longer, Louis?" And he would say soothingly as he continued playing, "Once more around the stage, Miss Ruth, and spin a little. It'll be over soon."

Ted was even vaguer creatively, following the Denishawn adage, "When in doubt, whirl."

Martha eschewed improvisation. She didn't trust the Spirit to be on call, having witnessed too often its unreliability.

Doris Humphrey, meanwhile, was learning how to use mass and space and rhythm. She began to do studies for Miss Ruth that were more than partially her own and for which she got full credit—Schubert's *Unfinished Symphony* and the unaccompanied *Sonata Tragica*, the forerunner of her 1928 *Water Study*. Martha's and Doris's growing intellects, their growing invention and susceptibilities pressed Ted hard. But Miss Ruth, I believe, felt bolstered by them. However, Martha's enormous stage magnetism and mounting independent creativity made Ruth uneasy. Martha began to put bones into the movement, and her own work, at least, became sharply defined and individual.

In 1921 the Isadorables, Isadora Duncan's six adopted daughters, made an American tour with George Copeland as accompanist. When they reached Los Angeles, Martha went to see them. They usually wore wreaths of real flowers in their hair, and during this performance one of the dancer's blossoms became detached and fell on the stage, creating a real hazard. Before the next number Anna Duncan, the leader, crossed the stage quietly and, without hurry or self-consciousness, picked up the flower and carried it to the side where Copeland sat waiting at his piano. She laid the blossom on the music rack, then, again without hurry, took her place for the next solo. The audience watched, transfixed and silent, as though she were picking up a time bomb or a knife. No one stirred until she was ready to begin to dance again. Martha said she learned a very great deal from this simple transit, this unashamed act of stage housekeeping. She learned something about what stage time and stage presence meant: one did not always have to sit in the lotus position.

Both Doris and Martha were growing and stretching their choreographic sinews under Louis Horst. He found the readier pupil in Martha, who turned to him as her prime teacher and alter ego, her mentor. She was now assisting Ted in many of his short variations: coaching, shaping, and counseling—"a thankless task," according to June Rhodes.

Ted seemed impervious also to Louis's aesthetic promptings, and Miss Ruth was too wounded to respond freely. But the young Martha and the more practiced Doris listened with rapt wonder and took in what he had to say. The person who first opens up a young mind can lay claim to that soul thereafter. Horst had found in Martha an avid and devoted disciple. Martha said in a 1984 interview: "Louis brought me out. . . . He saw me as something strange and different. He schooled me in certain behavior, discipline and a deep respect for music. He introduced me to Nietzsche, Schiller, Wagner. . . . He had the most to do with shaping my early life." In another interview shortly after this, she said that "with his faith and devotion, his ferocious standards [Louis] browbeat me into a kind of courage." It was the classic case of the older, mature teacher and the young, gifted student eager for learning and slightly adoring: Abelard and Eloise.

That year, 1921, Ted organized a small company to go to New York, with Martha Graham as chief soloist and Betty May and Dorothea Bowen as supporting dancers. Louis Horst, of course, was musical director. Charles Weidman offered to come along to work as Ted's dresser, among other things, asking only his expenses. Ted agreed that Charles could serve as his dresser and also dance a solo, *Pierrot Forlorn*, and a duet, *A Dance of Job*, with Martha. They got as far as Texas and went broke, were bailed out by Ted's Aunt Kate, who sent them a thousand dollars, and continued to New York, where they lived at the Chatsworth, on West Seventy-second Street, in a great big dance studio with balconies. They lived communally and took what jobs they could to earn money to buy food. Charles, for instance, took a role in Griffith's film *Orphans of the Storm*. He can be seen as a skinny little dark nineteen-year-old boy running around in the "Carmagnole."

It was the Chatsworth studio with its informal communality that brought Martha and Louis together intimately. It was there, according to Charles, they became lovers.

Ted disapproved; it gave the school a bad name. While dancers were popularly imagined to be immoral, Ted and Ruth had been carefully circumspect—at least publicly. Furthermore, Ted, for all his wayward habits, was extremely prissy about sexual mores and was appalled at Martha's conduct, as well as at Louis Horst's for seducing her. Once, Martha told me, Ted had made up a wild, sensual dance and then informed Martha that she would not be permitted to perform it because it was "not suitable for a virgin to perform."

"How do you know I'm a virgin?" Martha demanded pertly.

Ted grabbed her by the arm and shook her hard. "Don't ever joke about sex," he admonished. "Virginity is a sacred thing."

Martha and Louis looked at each other. They realized with astonishment that Ted was serious.

Ted's attitude seemed to others hypocritical; it was, but it was himself he fooled most successfully. He went right on seeing boys, who were not so sordid, and who unquestionably yearned to be led to higher forms of life's experience.

During this time Ted was casting about desperately for ways to bring in money. He thought it might be expedient if Martha were to teach movement of some sort to department-store assistants and salesgirls, the lessons to be paid for by their employers. Ted was paying weekly salaries to Martha and to Louis, and there was no income from either of them. "This was a case where Martha could begin to earn her keep," he recalls thinking.

They met at the C. & L. Restaurant on West Seventy-second Street. (They called it "The Cheap and Lousy.")

"Martha was indignant," Ted recounts. " 'I am an artist and not a saleswoman. I refuse to compromise. It was you who taught me not to, Ted. Remember?' "

Ted lost his temper. "I thought, 'Jesus, lover of my soul'! I taught her never to compromise? I've had to compromise all my life. I've had to make do with what I had to do with. I've done the best I could, but I had to keep going. I've made compromise after compromise. I knew I was making them. I didn't pretend that it wasn't wrong. If I was to survive, I couldn't do it any better. . . . My mind went clear back to . . . when I wouldn't let her do *Serenata Morisca,* a Moorish dance, in an Aztec ballet."

Martha's answer to this was to rise abruptly. She snatched the table-cloth from under the dishes and cutlery and stormed out, Louis following, leaving Ted to settle with the manager. He succeeded in catching up with them as they were getting into a cab.

"Don't show your face to me," Ted screamed. "I don't ever want to see you again in my life, and I mean it!" And he slammed the taxi door so hard he broke the window.

Shawn departed on foot, leaving Louis to settle with the driver.

"Come nine o'clock the next morning," Ted continues, "the door opened and you never saw such a production: Martha managed to get the door open and then drop to her knees and start crawling across the floor. 'Oh, Ted, can you ever forgive me? I'm so mortified. I'm so ashamed of myself. Can you ever have the heart . . . to take me back into your love? I owe so much to you.' . . . And I said, 'Oh, for God's sake, get up and dry your tears! We'll start again fresh.' "

In this arid period of duress and little hope, Doris Humphrey, who was not with the New York troupe but working with Ruth out west, quite spontaneously offered Ted the loan of a thousand dollars from her small savings. He accepted gladly, paying her back as soon as he began working, with six percent interest.

Martha gave the lessons to the Wanamaker girls. She also agreed to audition for a role in John Murray Anderson's new *Greenwich Village Follies*. Anderson, however, was so put off by her dour appearance that he turned her down cold and even scolded Ted for submitting such a homely candidate.

While waiting in New York for something to turn up, Ted managed to interest the impresario Daniel Mayer in his work, and this extraordinarily skillful and experienced man took the company under his wing. He first proposed a short tour in England. Ted, of course, believed that he would be co-starred with his wife. But as it turned out, Ruth St. Denis was to be billed as the great attraction, supported by Ted Shawn, who was in turn supported by a small group. This was not a happy bon-voyage gift to the husband.

Ruth had a fine success on this, her return English engagement. London tends to be faithful, and Miss Ruth was feted and petted and welcomed home into the hearts of her admirers, and Ted with her, but always as an adjunct and consort.

If Ted was not happy, neither was Martha. Louis Horst had to some small degree repented his dalliance with Martha and was attempting a reconciliation with his wife, Betty. He had agreed to ask Ted for living costs only, in exchange for Ted's paying Betty Horst's fare on the English tour. So Betty was added to the troupe, to Martha's very great discomfiture.

Martha may have been, as she later termed it, "doom-eager," but psychologists have another name for it: masochistic. She was deeply hurt by Horst's apparent fickleness, and she was humiliated by Betty's presence in the position of wife. Her anguish was further intensified by Miss Ruth, who suddenly decided that Martha was gaining far too much attention and peremptorily arrogated for herself Martha's star turn—the Aztec maiden in *Xochitl*. Ruth's action was both brutal and unjust, but she was scared. She could not have more than one rival; Ted was enough.

Miss Ruth was badly miscast in *Xochitl*, and her portrayal of the savage heroine was shockingly inadequate. The part was designed for a wildcat. Miss Ruth was gentle, mystic, lyric. She resisted rough stuff.

When Ted grabbed her, expecting Martha's fighting resistance, she said loudly, "Now darling, there's no sense in being that rough," well within hearing of the audience. They both were exposed as fools.

On returning to New York, Betty Horst was dispatched home to San Francisco, where she remained, teaching for the rest of a long life. Louis paid her a small allowance. Martha and Louis sought to resume their somewhat shopworn relationship. There followed a U.S. tour, coast to coast, lasting from October to April. The status quo was maintained, except that Martha had her *Xochitl* role back. The tour ended with twelve performances at the Town Hall Theater in New York. Ted once again invited John Murray Anderson, and this time he was overwhelmed by Martha's performance. Forgetting his previous unfortunate judgment, he immediately made her an offer.

She had reached an impasse with Denishawn. Ted had nothing more to teach her, but he was still in a position of absolute authority and imposed his will in all artistic matters, while Miss Ruth stood directly in the path of Martha's professional advancement. Martha asked permission to leave. Miss Ruth claims she didn't care; Ted did, deeply, but he claims he bade her Godspeed and even gave her the rights to several of her most successful dances as a farewell present.

Martha, for her part, spurned Shawn's help, spurned his work, spurned him, denounced him frequently as a feeble artist and a broken-down hack. Ted was wounded to the heart, his pride shredded. In fact, Martha's defection caused part of Shawn's great bitterness and constituted the first wound in the flesh of the Denishawn company. She also publicly advocated free love, which Shawn considered reprehensible.

|||||

Martha took the job in 1924 with the *Greenwich Village Follies* at the Winter Garden Theater on Broadway, made a success, and was re-engaged.

In her second year of the *Follies* there was a girl in the cast who called herself Helen Tamiris (née Becker), and she and Martha established a relationship that, over the years, attained varying degrees of complexity. Because of their concurrent beginnings, Tamiris considered herself the rival, if not the equal, of Graham.

Another promising talent who achieved his first success in the *Follies* was a young composer named Cole Porter. In the sixth *Follies* (in 1925, Martha's second year) she was placed under the direction of Michio

Ito, a Japanese disciple of Delsarte. (Ito had previously coached both Ruth and Ted in several of their traditional Japanese dances, among them the *Japanese Spear Dance.*) Ito did not interfere with Martha's solo dances, merely setting them in artistic backgrounds that permitted her to repeat untrammeled her Denishawn successes, doing a pretty arrangement to the popular "Kashmiri Song" ("Pale hands I loved beside the Shalimar . . ."). It was no change from her previous mode of work, but at least she was free from Shawn's dictation.

Louis continued with the Denishawn troupe, although he maintained a close personal relationship with Martha. It was during this period that their first great quarrel occurred. Although he loved Miss Ruth, Louis decided in 1925 to leave Denishawn and strike out on his own as Martha had done. He stayed in New York, where he could be close to Martha, but they quarreled again (as he had explained to me so pungently on the train), and he left for Vienna, reputedly to continue his studies in musical composition under the Viennese masters.

He separated from Miss Ruth out of deep conviction but not without sadness. He knew she was on the downgrade, and he grieved because he cherished her, but he believed that artistically he could not afford to stay.

Louis wrote to Martha from Vienna and sent her pictures of the new Central European dancers—Laban, Wigman, Skoronel, Jooss, Leeder, Palucca. The Middle-European atmosphere was quick with change, Germany and Austria seething with excitement. Louis found the atmosphere heady, and he grew impatient to get started himself with Graham. In the meantime, through the mails, he nurtured Martha's young perception like a hothouse plant. He also wrote Miss Ruth letters that were plainly homesick. He said he felt painfully lonesome, spoke of his theory lessons at the *Akademie* as being "dry, pedagogical—but like sowing seeds. I only hope there will be some harvest." Then "Martha wrote me that you had gotten a [music] director. I do hope you miss me a little bit." The letter ends with the lines: "Your words of faith and affection helped me a lot—and you must know how grateful I felt for them. And some day I hope to bring you your tithe of the harvest."

At the end of the year he returned, forty pounds heavier from Viennese and German cuisine, and laden with books and pictures about the new Central European dancers.

Louis had been getting bored with the academic restrictions of the classical European musicians, who had certainly not kept pace with the new dancers. One morning he said to his Viennese professor, "I see that Erik Satie has died. We must all mourn for that." The professor had never heard of Erik Satie. That was enough for Louis. It was time to go home. Vienna was stultified, accepting no one in the way of composers whose names did not begin with "B": Bach, Beethoven, Brahms.

Once home, he and Martha attempted to patch up their relationship.

For Denishawn the double loss of Martha and Louis was cruel, but Ted and Ruth were too busy to mope. They were about to realize the dream of their lives: they were going to the Far East. They were, at long last, going to India.

Doris, Charles, Pauline, Geordie, and the rest of the troupe closed ranks and departed *en gala* for a tour of the Far East. Louis was replaced by Pauline Lawrence, Martha by Doris, and Geordie Graham was second to Doris, with solos of her own. Charles Weidman headed the male dancers. "He was creative, a good dancer, a fine person. Everyone loved him," wrote June Rhodes. "We had two of Ted's boys who were good-looking, fine bodies and dumb dancers. Doris, of course, was leading dancer after Miss Ruth. She kept the company in order. Ted was difficult and demanding, Miss Ruth in tears and unhappy."

The trip was more than just a tour. It was, in a sense, a triumphant homecoming. Ruth St. Denis believed she was bringing back the true meaning and beauty of Indian dancing to the great subcontinent. And it proved a memorable trip.

When they returned at the end of 1926 it was to a very hard-working but unremunerative life. Within the year they were obliged to go on tour with the *Ziegfeld Follies* in order to make up their losses. They left Doris and Charles in New York, in charge of their school. The Ziegfeld tour earned money but in a very real sense lost them caste and clouded the name they had brought back from the Orient.

In 1927 Isadora Duncan died. Two years later her autobiography, *My Life*, was published, to the astonishment and wonder of the literary world. It was a devastating book, and for Miss Ruth it had particular and terrible meaning. Duncan emerges from the pages an uncompromising artist who would endure anything, or get her friends to endure anything, rather than yield on an artistic point. In one of Duncan's periodic fits of extravagant poverty, although she needed the big sum offered, she refused to dance in Wanamaker's auditorium, disdaining for her art such a "scene of suspenders." She refused to appear in certain Continental theaters because they contained restaurants where dining might distract the spectators from her worth and value. Early on she refused, though she and her family were starving, to dance at the Berlin Wintergarten for one thousand gold marks a night because there were animal acts on the bill. During the worst of her final financial predicaments, in Paris, when few theaters were offering her anything at all, she refused to dance at the Théâtre des Champs-Elysées because it was a music hall.

Ruth had a Calvinistic conscience, believing that "debt always was and always will be a mild form of dishonesty." This was not Isadora's credo. She believed that the world owed a living to the artist, that is, the world owed it to Isadora Duncan, and not only a living but support and substantiation on the artist's own terms. She believed that anything paid her, anything at all, was only her just due. She considered the repayment of debts a bourgeois obligation to be scorned. Her creditors did not concur, nor did her poor family, which was called upon again and again to meet her bills and keep her out of jail. I remember Miss Ruth sitting on my mother's sofa and beating her fists. She was frantic.

"We paid our bills. We did not run up debts at hotels. We kept a school. We've trained and supported young artists. Isadora ran out on every situation. She would not meet any responsibilities—not even to her own children, and certainly not to her students."

But the accusations rankled. Miss Ruth had compromised. She had hobbled herself to Ted's pace, and Martha and Doris had watched this. Louis had watched it with breaking heart. Miss Ruth knew. She had reduced herself as an artist out of love for her husband, to serve his ambition and his vanity. And she was appalled at the ruin of her own life and work.

Doris and Charles had not gone on the Ziegfeld tour and in the absence of the masters maintained the Denishawn school in New York. At the conclusion of the winter of 1927 they gave their first independent concert, at which Doris showed her music visualizations, and most notably the Grieg Piano Concerto. New York dancers as well as John Martin of *The New York Times* were impressed, and Doris at last knew her own strength. She had tasted blood. When Ted returned she told him flatly that she, like Martha, would no longer follow his direction, would no longer take his advice, that, in fact, she did not respect his taste. Ted recounted this anecdote to me himself, quite candidly and fairly, not misrepresenting her in any way. He was fair—angry but not exaggerating.

The reason his students did not trust Ted was because artistically he did not know truth from falsehood. He had no standards of taste, and he slipped from style to style, borrowing whatever he thought would be successful. He was an artistic con man, but the main person he fooled was Ted. He was not a designing fraud, however; being a fraud implies knowing what the truth is and deliberately choosing a lie. Ted did not know the truth.

This second double defection, of Doris and Charles, was a bold and bitter break, and Ted had to search elsewhere for teachers and support. And so did Miss Ruth. Perhaps Doris would have stayed with Ruth, whom she respected and loved, but she could not do this without submitting to Ted's judgment, something she refused to continue to do. Charles remained by her side, echoing her sentiments. With their departure the old Denishawn ceased, in truth, to exist.

Ruth's love, too, had raveled out.

Ted began giving concerts on his own. Ruth wrote to my mother, on the Denishawn paper with the peacock in full color, begging her to go to Ted's concerts: to be "kind and gentle" and to realize that this was Teddy's first solo effort. Ruth stood by like a mother, protecting, supporting, encouraging, praying, although she was not always present because it was painful for her, and for him also. He wanted his freedom as a young man and as a young artist.

Ruth in her hurt pride and grief sought solace in religion. She agonized about Karma, about working through special trials to a higher understanding; but she was, in plain English, a bereft and outraged woman and she was a demeaned artist; she poured her heart out to close friends, one of whom was my mother, as in the following letter, undated but postmarked October 3, probably 1927.

Denishawn House
67 Stevenson Place
Van Cortlandt Park
New York City

Dear!

Thinking of you a little this blowy morning.

Love is infinite—which—interpreted—means that we can never exhaust it—never get to the end of it—never wear it out! Yes—*I* know well that it *seems* as though we do—most certainly get to the end of it—but this is the illusion. . . .

This [?] sense of loss if it can be used rightly—to teach us—that love is everywhere—ever present—ever powerful—to reveal itself—in immediate joy. . . .

I am taking my own medicine or I would not pass it on to you. If taken in the right quantities it works while you sleep. . . .

For the first time in my life I have begun to open my being to all manner of desire—love—and understanding, letting each element in relation adjust itself—according to its nature—without pressure. What T wishes to give I will try to accept—(This is, of course, the hardest of all)—what he cannot give—and here is the point—will be supplied. Divine Love—within us to be filled is complete.

This I stand on.

Will try to get to see you.

Ruth

Whether or not these are the words of a Hindu sage or of Mary Baker Eddy can be argued. They are certainly the words of one grieving woman to another. My mother, the year before, had suffered through a divorce after twenty-three years of marriage.

|||||

Now came the time of final dissolution, the final violent rending. Barton Mumaw, the chief dancer of Shawn's male group and his close personal friend, tells of the decision to destroy all the old Denishawn properties and costumes that were jointly owned. As Ted explained, these properties were not being used currently, there were no plans for their future use, and nobody wanted them, either to buy or as a gift. Mumaw, Pearl Wheeler (Denishawn's wardrobe mistress and costume designer for thirty years) and Jack Cole (who was to become famous on Broadway and in Hollywood) made a great pile of old scenery and properties at the Van Cortland Park School and threw on a generous helping of scarves and old clothes for a bonfire.

Mumaw wrote:

Ruth St. Denis and Ted Shawn stood facing this grotesque monument to their life's work. Then she turned to him and he nodded. As in the ritual of an Indian burning ghat, where the closest relative lights the cremation fire of a loved one, he paced around the periphery of the edifice, pouring kerosene from a container. He hesitated only an instant before he picked up a makeshift torch, lighted it, and flung it into the pile.

Pearl and I stood mute and motionless and apart when Miss Ruth ran to Shawn's side as the flames crackled high around the pyre. I turned away, unwilling and unable to witness their grief. Were they listening to the beautiful *Radetzky March* while the *Straussiana* linden trees burned? Could they see Martha and Doris and all the other Denishawn Dancers rise in their Grecian tunics to vanish into the grey smoke? Would they scent remembered scorched canvas? Did they bow one last time together to the roar of applause in the roar of the flames?

Through the spark-filled dusk, I saw a figure with white hair flee toward the house. A figure with bowed head walked with wooden steps toward me. Denishawn had ended.

Ted bought a farmhouse and tract of land in Lee, Massachusetts, called Jacob's Pillow, and there every summer he taught, composed, and rehearsed his company of male dancers. With time, his school and summer program expanded to include teachers in many styles and the addition of women. He was innovative in introducing locally unknown foreign talents and promising beginners. The Jacob's Pillow Summer Dance Festival outlasted the Bennington dance season and extended a marked influence on the development of American dance. It continues to do so long after Shawn's death.

IIIII

Ted spent the winters touring. He claimed he was restoring male dancing to its ancient and glorious status, and he desired to be recognized as the dean of American Dance. He was not so recognized by anyone, as it happened. He was not forgotten altogether, of course, but he was disregarded by the leading critics, overlooked by colleagues, and bypassed by all the honors. And with time he grew increasingly bitter.

Miss Ruth was remembered and honored for what she had been, but she was no longer needed, for she was no longer potent as an active force in the profession. Sometime later she simply removed herself from the New York scene and went back to Los Angeles. Mother Dennis, old and very sick, was in California, and Brother had an Oriental bazaar on Sunset Strip, selling imported Indian furniture, copper, and silks.

Ruth began dancing in churches. And some of her performances had beauty and fervor and the old fire, and the young saw her and marveled; but on the whole, her comings and goings went unremarked.* Brother

*In the early sixties, John Butler, a former dancer with Martha Graham's company, was choreographing short ballets for a public-television program called *A Lamp Unto My Feet*, shown at eight o'clock on Sunday mornings. These paid him just enough to

St. Dennis and Ted sent her money regularly, but on the whole they could not get her to settle her debts. She was always squandering their gifts on harebrained projects as though she still had money to waste. She held seances. She ceased to tread the earth and devoted herself to an entourage of unhappy, disappointed, and unsuccessful people of all sexes, mainly elderly, but all undeniably miserable. She wrapped herself in veils and thoughts of a higher plane, and she ceased to be an influence in the art world.

She was like a body on a gallows, left hanging in the weather as a warning.

---

commission the new scores he wanted for his own company. He retained very little for himself, and the dancers received minimum wage, a pittance. Ruth St. Denis, then in Los Angeles, heard about his activities and sent word that she would be more than willing to collaborate on his religious programs, and he replied that he was honored and pleased. She inquired whether he wished to know anything about her, explaining, "My right knee is no good," but adding characteristically and wryly, "but it hasn't been for the last thirty-five years." When she came to New York they arranged to meet and he went to see her at her hotel on Broadway in the West Eighties. It had once been very grand but was now shabby with decayed gentility. When she arrived she had in tow an acolyte who bore a heavy load of press books. All three progressed to a greasy-spoon restaurant on Broadway and established themselves at a none-too-clean table, on which Ruth spread out the books. And she talked and took over the premises and the environment and enveloped it in her magical aura of power and communication and delight. "Suddenly," said John, "we were no longer in a poor restaurant. We were in the Ritz. We were in a palace." He was bewitched. "I would love to have you in the Nativity and I would like you to play the older Elizabeth. The Virgin will be danced by Carmen de Lavallade."

St. Denis drew back in astonishment. She was a woman pushing eighty and she had a bad case of the shakes. "I play the Virgin always. I am the central figure."

And John realized that this was so and that the universe revolved around her as it always had and that any other idea was lèse majesté. All thought of collaboration was abandoned.

Martha Graham had reached a fateful decision in 1926, toward the end of her two-year stint in the *Greenwich Village Follies*. She had decided no longer to subsist on commercial work but to develop her own style and means of expression. Since she had no independent means of support, this meant she had to teach in order to live.

John Murray Anderson, the producer of the *Follies*, together with Robert Milton, administered a school to train performers for Anderson's shows. It was located on East Fifty-eighth Street between Park and Lexington avenues, just opposite the music branch of the New York Public Library. Martha was taken on as a teacher.

She taught the rudiments of acting, walking, wearing costumes, and stage decorum in general, which was needed for the tableaux and parades in Anderson's revues. Anderson himself taught what he called "court dancing." Martha was also invited to give the Anderson pupils morning and afternoon classes in Denishawn material, Denishawn acting exercises, East Indian dances, and plastiques. Louis, just back from Vienna, accompanied her at the piano.

Martha conducted a large part of her class seated cross-legged on a small, low table and, like Miss Ruth, wore, as a rule, an Indian silk sari, often of an orange or tawny color. The students were dressed in what were called "fleshings"—skintight garments of flesh-colored glove silk which they bought by the yard and stitched up themselves, long-sleeved, cut off at the groin, leaving legs and feet bare. Over this they sometimes draped saris, and Martha showed them how to pleat and fold the fabric to make skirts and how to throw the loose ends over their heads and shoulders.

The dressing rooms included a shower, which was at that time an unusual luxury and which the students used, strangely enough, not to wash off the sweat of the class but to wash off the grime of the city, cleansing themselves almost ritualistically as they arrived in preparation for work with Martha and for her presence. This seems unprecedented and indicates, I believe, a very special attitude that Graham's students developed toward her teaching sessions.

In the evenings she experimented with three girls in her own movement variations. These pupils were very young, in their early teens. Gertrude Shurr, a Denishawn student, asked to join them. Although she was older, she was small in stature and therefore matched up in size with the three adolescents. Gertrude Shurr danced and taught with Martha longer than anyone else. She became a member of that sturdy phalanx of young women without whom Martha could not have begun or developed her work. Gertrude told me:

I started my first lessons at Denishawn on Twenty-eighth Street. We always had a Denishawn barre and we always had center work, free ballet. Louis's classes were marvelous. [Necessity had driven Louis back to Denishawn to accompany classes and teach.] My dance teachers were Charles Weidman and Doris Humphrey. But my private lessons were always with Charles, who kept saying that I looked like Martha and that he would teach me all Martha's East Indian dances. While still at Denishawn I had begun studying with Martha secretly in her evening composition class at the Anderson school, and I was so enthusiastic that I persuaded her to start an evening class for adults. And I enticed several Denishawn pupils to join me, Geordie Graham among them. I don't believe Mr. Shawn thought this was very loyal. The work was hard. Geordie and I clung together for courage. Martha Hill, a ballet student, was also a member of that class.

When Doris and Charles left Denishawn and formed their independent school and company, they took a good percentage of the Denishawn pupils with them, I among them. Poor Papa Shawn! We all walked out. First Martha, then Doris and Charles, and Pauline Lawrence. Doris composed the *Grieg Concerto* with us, also *Life of the Bee*, based on Maeterlinck and performed to an accompaniment of buzzing sounds hummed by a chorus of combs led by Pauline Lawrence, and the *Color Harmony*, an abstraction created without any music or sound at all.

Ted and Miss Ruth split up at this point [1927], and Miss Ruth left Ted. I felt, because I had promised, that I was bound to stay with Doris while she was forming her new company. I wanted to work with Martha and I wanted to leave before the spring concert, but Louis wouldn't let me. I think I finally broke Doris's pride, but I was too young to realize what I had done. "What can Martha give you that I can't give you?" Doris asked me, and I couldn't explain. I wanted to go with Martha because Martha danced from the heart, while Doris danced entirely from the head. I used to go crying to Louis and say, "Louis, she dances without passion." And Louis said I was too young to understand.

Doris herself never understood. She was interested in abstract design and the power of design, as in music, the other time art. She had begun her choreographic experiments, one must recall, under the close tutelage of Louis Horst. She was interested in the organization of the visual dynamics, as in all space arts. She was interested, like Balanchine, in the architecture of dancing, its form, its structure. Doris was still a slight, slim wisp of a girl, with the body of an adolescent, and she displayed a pretty and agreeable aestheticism.

She had the mind of a mathematician, or a physicist, or possibly an architect, and she analyzed everything. It was not enough that a fall or a lean could be lovely. She had to explain why. Her pupil José Limón quoted her as saying, "In the resistance to gravity lie the seeds of dance. The thrill and drama come from the defiance of gravity, the moment of suspension when the body seemed to break free of its physical confines." Doris called this spectrum of movement "the arc between two deaths."

I, for one, think that—surely for the student, at least—the talking diminishes the excitement and limits the imagination. There are some things the student should be expected to grasp instinctively. However, José Limón adds, "With her low yet commanding voice and cooly serene manner, she [Doris] would teach us both theory and practice, fall and recovery, tension and relaxation, suspension, breath pulse, breath rhythm, always the breath. . . . She moved like a gazelle."

She was a smooth and facile dancer, technically without flaw, without knots or bumps, yet also quite bland, and quite boring. Her own dancing seemed to have little personality, while Martha's was electrifying. Martha concerned herself with the emotional meaning and dramatic impact of gesture, with terms of being, with emotional stress and resolution; if there was formidable mental achievement in all Doris did, there was no flame. These two artists represented valid approaches, the mental and the emotional, but in the case of Graham, choreography encompassed both. There was nothing Doris could do about it, and her heart broke.

When Gertrude Shurr announced to Doris that she was leaving, Doris excused her as understandably seeking freedom; but when Gertrude made it clear that she was leaving in order to join Martha, Doris was cut to the root. This was a matter of preference and choice. She felt repudiated and humiliated, and she never forgave either Gertrude or Martha.

|||||

Concurrently with her duties at the Anderson-Milton School, Martha also began teaching at the Eastman School of Music in Rochester, New York, where the young director Rouben Mamoulian was on the faculty. Martha taught Denishawn technique, that being what she knew, and such old Denishawn dances as she remembered. Then Ted presented a horrid surprise: he stipulated that she was to pay him five hundred dollars for the use of Denishawn exercises and dance material.

It was on this small and perverse point—Shawn's possessiveness and Martha's penury—that the birth and development of modern dance hinges.

|||||

Five hundred dollars* may not seem much for a stock-in-trade, but Martha didn't have five hundred dollars. She was living hand-to-mouth. If she had continued to have easy access to the old Denishawn way, she might never have invented a new one. It was Ted Shawn's acquisitiveness and splenetic meanness—no more, no less—that forced the creation of the new modern technique.

*Bertram Ross remarks that it is curious that this is the exact amount she later charged her students for the right, after thorough study with her, to use her material and to teach her technique elsewhere, away from her own supervision.

For more than a year, from 1925 to 1926, Martha maintained a double schedule, commuting to Rochester by overnight train and returning to New York for three days for duties which included work on Saturday and Sunday; and so she had no weekend rest. It was a back-breaking schedule that only a woman of enormous vigor and flaying will could have maintained. In spite of the fact that Martha had never wanted to teach, necessity was compelling her to do so, and for four or five hours a day. She could either do this or do commercial work, which she felt wasted her time and her spiritual resources even more than the traveling and teaching did.

During this period Martha began to form, probably unconsciously at the beginning, but gradually firmly and vocally, a ground plan for her life's work. *First,* never to become involved in any enterprise primarily for the sake of money. *Second,* to build her own company to perform her works. *Third,* to maintain a school that would train such a company. *Fourth,* to allow no one who had not trained in her teachings and style to perform her choreography. *Fifth,* to share a program with no other dance group (this meant that her works would not be performed in any other repertory).

These were bold and exclusive concepts for a lone woman without backing or a supporting organization, and they were of such risk that few other choreographers had hitherto attempted anything like them. Graham did. Not all at once, certainly, but not too slowly: within a few years they had become crystal clear. She was a loner and that was to be her trademark.

Martha and Louis were living separately. He had his studios on West Sixty-seventh Street at the Hotel des Artistes and he taught in Carnegie Hall. She lived on the top floor of a brownstone at Fifth Avenue and Twenty-eighth Street. If they did not live under the same roof, they shared much, although all this time Louis was sending money west to another woman, who had legal claims. Martha had none. Martha frequently had to borrow twenty-five or fifty cents from Louis to get through the day (subway: five cents; coffee: ten cents). He listed each item in a notebook he kept for the purpose, and when there was a concert she paid up, and they started the accounts afresh. His students have testified to this; they had even less, so the transactions seemed to them normal. Martha could have been left abandoned at any moment, just as she herself was free to leave. It was a fine liberal condition, one might say, but it was not restful and it did not provide a solid base from which to pursue the great adventure on which Martha was currently engaged: the creation of an art.

Martha's first step toward professional freedom was the opening of her own studio, independent of any school or curriculum. She moved to Carnegie Hall, studio number 819, on the sixth floor. The studio was entered from the Fifty-sixth Street side of the building. Denishawn had classes on the eighth floor, which was entered on the Fifty-seventh Street side; and in the summer they rented studio sixty-one, which was on the sixth floor, down a few steps from the eighth-floor studio. Carnegie Hall was a rabbit warren, and made no sense architecturally or spatially. One simply had to go where one was supposed to go and not stray. Oddly enough, there were no untoward encounters there between Martha and Ted.

Martha's own studio consisted of a long, narrow room with a cubicle for sleeping and dressing. There were no other comforts. She was constrained to go down the hall to the public bathroom. There being no cooking facilities, she had to eat out. Martha and Louis ate in the Automat on Fifty-seventh Street, or sometimes at the Anthropological Restaurant on Fifty-sixth Street, west of Broadway.

Martha's sister Mary lived in a rooming house above this restaurant. She had become a secretary and had turned her back on the stage and on all thought of dancing. Martha was a vegetarian at this point, possibly because she had no money for meat. She also abstained from alcohol, perhaps for the same reason. In any case, her life was disciplined and frugal, and the fact is, she didn't eat enough. Gertrude Shurr used to go to her own mother's home on Saturdays and load up on groceries, which she'd bring back to Martha and Louis.

But hungry or not, Martha was always meticulously neat and smart, hair combed and in place, never—not on any occasion—mussy. Among working dancers she was without parallel in her soigné appearance, her dress clean and mended and in order. She did her own laundry. The spare time of most young dancers is taken up with washing tights, underthings, leotards, which are nearly always drenched with sweat and have to be washed out every night, and the dancers have to do the washing. But Martha was always attractive, even stylish, whether in a sari or, later, in a white tunic and skirt, with smooth hair, as she came forward, barefooted, to start a class of what grew to be punishing discipline.

She had only a handful of dancers, six or seven. In these early classes one student, Martha Hill, used to count apprehensively the few pupils, to make sure Martha had enough to pay the hourly studio rental and pianist's fee, let alone any leftover pittance for herself. Her poverty was relentless. Louis's was milder, because he was playing for all the serious (that is, noncommercial) dancers in New York. Obviously, she could rarely go to the theater or to parties.

Then, by God, in this bare-boned, threadbare state, she decided to start her own theater!

The organization of a concert career required large investments of time, generally the whole of the artist's life, and cash, involving the family or rich patrons. The launching of such a career costs as much as rearing and presenting a racehorse, and I would say the risks were higher, the overwhelming predilection being for foreign artists. Martha had neither endowment nor manager. She had no patron. She had her savings and a tiny amount of money from her teaching. She had her courage, which was splendid; her sturdy health; and her talent, which was large.

She did find help. The managers of the *Greenwich Village Follies* as a favor allowed Martha to lease another of their theaters at cost. Frances Steloff, a dealer in theater and dance books at the Gotham Book Mart, who had never seen Graham perform but who knew Louis, at his recommendation pawned her one valuable possession, a jade necklace, and turned the thousand dollars over to the cause.

Martha and Louis took the plunge. They rented the Forty-eighth Street Theater for one evening, April 18, 1926. The program consisted of eighteen short numbers—showpieces, suitable for a revue. Louis Horst was at the piano.

Martha began by doing variations from her Denishawn roles and then moved into quite astonishing new inventions: studies of pure movement, the very essence of emotion. Her supporting cast consisted of three young women from the Eastman School who suddenly began making friends with the floor. Nobody had ever done this before—not in the West. The movement was unfolding, progressive, and lovely.

But what it had, predominantly, was an aura of importance, something no American program had shown since St. Denis's first solo afternoon. The mystery had come back.

It was obvious that Martha was a creator and a leader. On the other hand, many people disliked her work and mocked her, and the group of disapprovers included Ruth St. Denis and Ted Shawn. Shawn's reaction was totally negative. He collected all the condemning press and sent it to Martha with a letter advising her that she was going in the wrong direction, wasting her time and resources, and that she had made a profound mistake in leaving him. The letter approached abuse. Martha was quite naturally angered and hurt, but she merely sent him a wire saying: "Please give me the freedom to do what you would wish for yourself, to create in my own images, and in my own way."

"He was jealous," Martha added later. "He was jealous of anybody with real talent."

Miss Ruth also made known her disapproval. "Oh, Martha, this is dreadful," she said. "You must not do these things." And Martha later said that she replied: "I will go on doing this sort of work or whatever I wish to until the audience indicates to me that they wish me to stop."

The audience had, in fact, been sizable. To Martha's joy, and everyone else's surprise, she broke even on the concert and was able to pay back Frances Steloff. There were many dance students in the house who subsequently rushed to study with Martha, and influential members of the art-theater colony who were looking for teachers. There being no dance critic on any New York newspaper at that time (John Martin did not join *The New York Times* until 1927), music critics did the best they could, but the criticism was for the most part uninformed.

Sunday-night dance concerts had become a regular feature of the New York theatrical season, beginning in 1924 with Angna Enters, whose *Compositions in Dance Form* initiated a new school of mime. Enters was followed in 1926 by Martha Graham. These dance concerts were made up of short, unrelated pieces to piano accompaniment and were for solo figure in the case of Enters and for soloist and three assistants in the case of Graham.

In 1927 Doris Humphrey and Charles Weidman followed Graham's lead and gave a Sunday-night concert and then soon we all hurried along. Anyone who could raise a few hundred dollars tried his luck. We had to pay our own way, since no established managers would risk time or money on an American except St. Denis and maybe Shawn. Martha had been forbidden by Shawn to rely on anything she'd been taught by him. That left her with little except naked boards, her pupils, and her own body. She got to work.

I think Louis was happy despite the hardships and deprivations; he wanted a fresh start away from worn-out formulae. And in short order Martha came to believe that she wanted this too, and that the breaking away from Denishawn was voluntary. The marvel is that she had the capability to start completely afresh.

But the process was risky, and they were poor.

Also her refusal, and his, to accept the old, trite formulae posed a dilemma. Martha didn't know right off what to substitute. It meant that in rehearsal the dancers had nothing to do and simply had to wait for her to figure something out. Their legs got cold and they became dispirited, but they never became rebellious or disloyal.

When an instructor starts to teach a traditional technique, there is a known vocabulary, a known system, a known scale of controls. This applies to any dance technique. But when an inventor starts to teach something brand-new that has not been tried, it is a question of experiment, guessing, happenstance, trial, the slow—very slow—accumulation of success. Martha had to spin this new technique out of her own entrails: a way of moving the arms, a way of moving the legs with the torso, a way of breathing. She did not know how. No one had ever seen it done before. She just felt there must be some new approach.

"I remember the day I saw my first exhibit of modern paintings—my first Matisse and Gauguin, and, well, I had never seen such glory. I realized then that I wasn't mad, not crazy, but I had 'ancestors' who had walked this way before me. It has to do with, I would say, the explosion of a spirit and the defiance of tradition."

And in Chicago she had had pointed out to her a painting by Wassily Kandinsky and had been forcibly struck: it was a slash of red on a blue background. McCandlish Phillips of *The New York Times* quotes Graham: "Perhaps you might call [my work] painting with movement. It has color, it has continuance of line, it has shock, and it should have vibrancy." She told herself she would dance like that. It was clear to her, but translating it into muscles and exercises proved altogether more difficult.

It is very likely that Louis pointed out the Kandinsky painting and its relationship to her work. Louis was avant-garde in his tastes, enthusiastic about all the new artists in every field, and he hastened to share this enthusiasm first with Martha.

"Martha needed patient companionship," said Gertrude Shurr. "Many, many, many times I'd be sitting on the floor watching her dance and dance. She needed a sort of sounding board, and I must have been young enough to react immediately to whatever she did. Later she was to teach certain proven patterns easily and to demonstrate, which was pleasant for her and for us, her pupils. At least it was something we could get started on, which we could see, which would make our bodies warm and our muscles flex and start the motors turning over without enormous delay."

It is always great stimulation to the choreographer to see other dancers perform a set movement. As the dancers move, they generate ideas and suggestions. But they can't move, of course, if they don't know what is wanted, and if the choreographer doesn't know either, the dancers have to stand and wait. Martha's girls did a lot of waiting. This did not bother Martha a bit, she was not self-conscious or apologetic. Why shouldn't they wait? What else did they have to do? It was her responsibility to find the way. Never mind if it took some time. Were they bored? I don't believe this ever occurred to her.

The living Martha made, what small monies she commanded, came from her teaching. It is interesting and important to observe that she never, during the whole of this time, considered going back into the theater or attempting to get a commercial job on Broadway. She could have, because she had done so in the past, but she had turned her back on any such possibility.

In addition to composing new dances, developing a new technique for performing them, assembling and training her company, designing her costumes (she shopped for the material, cut it and sewed it herself, with the help of a sewing woman and students), tending to all her business affairs, and somehow, at the same time, earning a living, Martha was trying to put her private life into some kind of order, trying to forge something that would be enduring. Her emotional state was in tatters: she was in love with an older man who was married and who was making no effort to free himself for an enduring and satisfactory relationship with her. She was threading her way through quarrels and tensions that would have harassed a steadier spirit. She was working in constant crisis, she attempted daily to maintain her aplomb, to show love, to receive love, and to follow a routine of normal well-being and application. No wonder she always looked sad and troubled. She was. It is a wonder she could put her head down on the pillow at night.

uring the first five years of Martha's independence from a parent school, her creativity, in amount and intensity, was overwhelming. For instance, in 1926 Graham produced twenty-nine dances, an astonishing number. (I, in contrast, who considered myself a steady worker, achieved at most six or seven a year.) Martha's dances were short, but that did not lessen their difficulty. The problems of attack, impact, the establishment of atmosphere, the building of climax were not less for short pieces; perhaps, indeed, they were greater, because of the lack of time for build-up, development, preparation.

Graham's 1926 dances were not memorable, although they were good. In 1927 she turned out sixteen pieces and began to strike into a new and richer vein.

On October 16, 1927, she presented *Revolt,* to music by Arthur Honegger, her first piece of social comment, and—let me be emphatic about this—it did not advocate any given party line. She was speaking for the individual, for the outraged spirit—for her own spirit, in fact. In a sense she was like Kafka: she cried out. She would not accept formulae.

"Communists," Martha said to me scornfully at that time. "They should be demolition workers, or wrecking crews. Just give them a building to tear down, and they'll be quite happy to leave our government structures alone."

Martha stood for the outraged individual. She was herself a hurt girl, lonely and probably frightened. She advocated and practiced free love, though she wanted marriage, knowing at the same time that the man of her choice, who avowedly loved her, would not give her his troth. She was poor. She wanted to create beautiful and meaningful works, and nobody gave a damn, or not enough people did, to allow her to pay her rent. Cheap, faded, pretend ideas were seemingly what the public was satisfied with.

Her dancing grew ever more fierce, bound up, iron. She would not give way. She would break opposition. She developed a technique of hitting out and hitting in. The movement was rock-hewn. Some of it was indeed unlovely to look at and often tiring to watch. Some of it was strong and extremely expressive.

But she got attention, and the young radicals, political or aesthetic (and they were frequently the same people), began to take her up as their dancer, their voice. Her concerts started to command full houses. They were strange audiences, it is true, but full and paying and extremely enthusiastic.

In 1927 John Martin, a slender and soft-voiced man and an extremely witty redhead, was appointed by *The New York Times* as its dance critic, the first person to be hired to write exclusively on dance by any newspaper in the United States. Shortly thereafter, Mary Watkins was chosen for a similar position on the New York *Herald Tribune*. Those appointments raised dancing to a totally new status. Martin and Watkins began steadily furnishing discriminating articles which educated a hitherto unaware and unschooled public who had never thought that dancing had a history or rules or even a literature. The new critics came faithfully to the concerts, and they wrote with discernment and knowledge and real style. Their papers gave them space, as though dance counted. Gradually the public came to agree.

Both of these critics hailed Graham's work.

On October 16, 1927, along with *Revolt* and many other solos, Martha showed an exquisite mood picture called *Fragilité,* to music by

Scriabin. I was there. It is memorable after over sixty years for the physical beauty of the dancer, Martha Graham. The dance was done in half-light, with Martha standing on an elevation of two shallow, round steps, dressed in blue gauze of a moonlit translucency (I believe the material was organdy). The costume had a totally transparent bodice, so that her wonderful breasts showed through, half veiled. It was a dance of such enticement, allure, promise, and evanescence as to tease and excite with the power of dreams. She was a lost Proustian beauty.

In 1928 Graham composed six more pieces, striking out into yet newer territory. From here on, her dances were not only new compositions but the basis for the formation of a new language.

Each year, henceforth, saw the development, expansion, and strengthening of that language. *Immigrant,* performed on April 22, 1928, was a study in stark simplicity and basic human emotions. On the same program, *Poems of 1917,* with music by Leo Ornstein, employed a startling device: an open mouth and cupped, shaking hands to symbolize sound, both a call and a scream. It was a device which I some years later borrowed and made excellent use of in my ballets for *Oklahoma!,* and which has since been copied and used innumerable times by others. Martha was the inventor.

In 1929 she gave us ten pieces, including *Adolescence* to music by Hindemith. For this she wore her hair rolled under a long bob and was dressed in a simple dark smock like a French schoolgirl's pinafore, with a full skirt, white sleeves, and schoolgirl's collar. This is a child (yes, Martha at thirty-five played a child, creditably and with dignity) seated at the top of her two steps on her round platform, her legs tucked snugly under her. It was a dance of tentative gestures, feeling, sensing, investigating, attempting, withdrawing, touching her body with wonder and astonishment, with a hint of dread, the promise of pride and a very elusive overtone of delight, trying and withdrawing, venturing down the steps and back up and down and back and then finally stepping forth into freedom and facing whatever. It was almost nothing; it was everything. It was delicate; it was effective. I have remembered it for over sixty years.

Vision of the Apocalypse, a brilliant study of cartoon quality, was presented on April 14, 1929, done to Hermann Reutter's variations on a Bach chorale and introducing a larger group of dancers. This was Martha's first venture into biblical or metaphysical themes. On the same program was *Moment Rustica,* to music by Francis Poulenc.

Her first truly great composition, *Heretic* (April 14, 1929), was constructed of strong cruel attitudes struck by girls in black against the single lyric supplication of the soloist in white. The group movements were machinelike and killing, those of the soloist (Martha) soft and sustaining. The music, based on an old Breton song and arranged by de Sivry, had a repeated statement and antiphonal responses, remaining starkly simple throughout. The chorus was direct and without embellishment; the suppliant answered. Finally Martha lay broken on the ground (after one of her incredible spiral falls),* and the mass locked into its final position of destruction and closure, with antiphonal plaint played in absolute stillness. The figure no longer moved. Emptiness—non-movement—held the stage: one of the most powerful and compelling uses of stillness that we had ever witnessed.

On first seeing *Heretic,* I found myself uttering dry sobs. John Martin wrote in *The New York Times* the next day:

Couched exclusively in a modernistic idiom, her work in this medium is at once strikingly original and glowing with vitality. There is no taint of decadence about it, no touch of morbidity. . . . Because she paints so skillfully with movement, she creates dancing where literally there is none, and arrives at a conclusive answer to the criticism that modernistic dancing is static and introverted and cannot be lyrical.

Heretic employed straight lines, angular gestures, geometric formations. In this one aspect it resembled the mechanical dances in vogue at the time. In Europe particularly, every company boasted at least one or two of these imitations of machinery, which were supposed to be modern. In *Heretic,* Martha was dealing with machinelike tradition—juiceless, mindless bureaucracy and formula. What better symbol could anyone employ? Lifeless formula: this is the true meaning of the machine. Useful, perhaps, often powerful, but without intelligence, certainly without feeling.

Lamentation, presented on January 8, 1930, with music by Kodály, consisted of a remarkable series of grief-stricken postures, partly Greek,

---

*One began a spiral fall by pivoting on both feet while leaning back and contracting on bent knees, descending and turning simultaneously until the shoulders grazed the floor and one came to rest on one's back. The element of excitement was supplied by the fraction of a second during which the body was totally off balance and falling. One recovered by reversing the process, jackknifing, circling forward, and rising to stand erect.

partly Hebraic, basic and searing. The figure remained seated throughout. Occasionally a tortured foot, Martha's marvelous instep, was drawn up in anguish. Mainly the feet were planted on the ground and the body rotated and writhed. It was a figure of unending, burning woe.

Once, after seeing this dance, a woman came to Martha backstage, weeping bitterly. Some months before, the woman had witnessed her child being struck by a car and killed. She had been unable to shed a tear. *Lamentation* released the terrible restraints. "I realized," she told Martha, "that grief was a dignified and valid emotion and that I could yield to it without shame." And she mourned in Martha's arms. Martha related that this dance had on several occasions worked the same kind of catharsis.

Among the most notable aspects of *Lamentation* was the costume. Martha took a tubing of tricot, tied a string around the middle, and simply sat in it. It clung to her body and her arms and her head and made every position look as though it were carved in stone, the movement of the knees, legs, head, and arms giving the fabric its shape. The costume became not so much yardage as a sculpture by Meštrović, or possibly by Henry Moore. It was one of the great costume inventions of our time and could not have been devised without the new fabric. There was a rush of imitations, including one by Lester Horton, who was the high priest of modern dancing in California but took most of his ideas from Graham.

Other Graham dances of protest and revolution followed during the next years. Bear in mind that all these dances were done a decade before fellow travelers had discovered social protest. Later, when others were following the party line and obeying commands to do socially intended works, they tried to suck Martha into their projects, but she was long past them and doing different things. One must also remember that Martha's protest was for the individual against an unthinking society, and never against a class or a social order. She was concerned with the courage of one person in opposition to the masses, to terror, and to persecution. This constitutes a major difference, and it was major to Martha's life.

During the years 1926–30 Martha composed over sixty new dances, an achievement matched only by George Balanchine and Frederick Ashton. But whereas these two men worked within the frame of established ballet companies, using dancers assembled and trained by others, Martha had to assemble, train, and maintain her own company. And whereas ballet masters composed in an inherited language, a medium ready to hand, Martha invented her own language, new and extraordinary, unknown, and fresh. Hers is a unique contribution. James Joyce attempted the same in *Finnegans Wake,* but here, in a sense, the effort died aborning: there was never a second book in the same idiom. Martha's vocabulary and means of expression were copied, adopted, carried on, and developed by other people. It lives and constitutes an achievement Chaucerian in its scope and impact.

Among these sixty dances were masterpieces. They have not lasted, because Martha would permit no one else to do them; she chose never to repeat them, and so herself contributed to their evanescence.

||||||

In 1927 Martha moved down to a larger and much more comfortable studio on West Tenth Street. She stayed in this new setting for three years. Called the White House, it consisted of two large rooms on the second floor of a stone house with enormous windows facing the street. The parlor walls were hung with burlap, out of courtesy to the several cats that were Martha's companions and who liked to climb. There were no mirrors, and this was an innovation for a dance studio. A practice room without mirrors is a blind alley to ballet students, who cannot work without them, and will not. The advantage of mirrors is that the student corrects and disciplines the body exactly as it appears and not as he wishes it were or as he feels it might be. He sees what's there. The danger is that the dancer becomes fixed on the image and finds it impossible to focus attention on anything else, so that it is difficult sometimes for a ballet student to look at another performer, or to look toward the audience, or to look inwardly, or even to look up, and this can be fatal. I once remarked, "Many a dancer has, like Narcissus, drowned in his own image."

For this reason the Duncan dancers had used only blue curtains as wall draperies and scenery. And although Graham was trying a more difficult technique and new body postures, she also would not permit any correction except by the same inner discipline and self-knowledge.*
It wasn't until after the war, in the late forties, that Martha began to

*This discipline is analogous to the stringencies placed on her students by Lilli Lehmann, the great German soprano. She forbade her pupils to use the piano as an aid in practicing, lest by relying on the instrument for correction they weaken their inner sense of tonal pitch and lose the absolute pitch she demanded. Geraldine Farrar, Lehmann's pupil, told this to me.

place mirrors in her studios, and, amusingly enough, they came with the male dancers. But that was still a long time away.

The back room on Tenth Street contained an enormous bed and little else, but it had a private bath and cooking arrangements and was altogether more commodious than the studio at Carnegie Hall, if not so centrally located. But central to what? The heart of the modern-dance world was where Martha and Doris chose to live and work, and both of them were gravitating toward Greenwich Village.

Martha taught in this Tenth Street studio until 1930, and out of her heterogeneous group of girls, under her driving direction, in hard, disciplined technique to beat their bodies into conformity and style, she formed her Group.

Martha gave a class each afternoon for paying students, several of them older women. They paid, but not very much. Evangeline Stokowski, the wife of the famous conductor, was one; Alice Lewisohn, the founder with her sister Irene of the Neighborhood Playhouse, was another. Martha's "girls," the real dancers, were amused to watch these elegant ladies getting in and out of their corsets—garments long since abandoned by professional dancers. And Martha earned a little money by teaching under other auspices, but not very much. Her poverty remained severe.

In the evening Martha rehearsed her chosen girls.

In 1929 Anna Sokolow and Gertrude Shurr were accepted into the Group, which already contained Martha Hill. Although serving for the past two years as Martha's assistant, Gertrude had not hitherto been allowed to join as a group member because she had been a Humphrey student, and Martha ordained that Gertrude had first to prove her loyalty. Martha was a hard taskmistress, and not a little jealous of her exclusivity.

Geordie Graham was trying to be part of Martha's work, trying with all her might to keep up with her big sister. Gertrude helped by coaching her. But the Graham technique was too difficult for Geordie, who was actually terrified of it, and after a time she ran away and joined the company of Michio Ito and went on tour. All her life she wanted to be part of Martha's work and Martha's success; all her life she resented it and wanted her own success, her own individuality, and her own freedom. Geordie lived in a cleft stick and she was perpetually frightened. Yet she loved Martha and could not leave her.

The dancers Martha recruited as students were very different, in kind and age as well as in physical characteristics, from the dancers who went to ballet school. Ballet students traditionally were young, usually beginning serious study at nine or ten years of age, and working hard through their teens, as hard as a young tennis player or a young baseball player, with a devotion which left them neither time nor energy for scholastics. Indeed, they barely managed to get by the requirements of the Board of Education. When they were graduated from high school at seventeen or eighteen, they were also ready for the stage. And then they found that they must start the arduous—and, in America, uncertain and punitive—apprenticeship or job hunting, a pursuit which led them into cheap, corrupt, and often vicious environments. And when at last they succeeded in getting on the stage, it was in musicals, since in this country there was literally no other place for them; and the musicals at that time were entirely frivolous. The Metropolitan Opera Ballet was poor in quality and limited in opportunity. They didn't want that. Ballet students accordingly found no chance of expanding their interests in other arts, or going to museums, or meeting contemporaries, or conversing about anything except diets, slippers, teachers, and job opportunities. They had no time for reading; many grew up mentally stunted.

The girls who came to Martha, on the contrary, were older and often well educated. They came as mature, serious students of the dance, interested in new ideas. And although they had to work for a living, they had the time—they made the time—to read, to discuss among themselves, to go to museums, sometimes, if they were lucky, to go to concerts. They worked as hard at their chosen vocation as any professional, but always as adults, thinking and experimenting. In essence, they were an entirely different kind of person from ballet kids and had nothing to say to them. There was not only a generation gap between them, there was an intellectual gap of unbridgeable width.

IIIII

Like a nun, Martha kept to her regimen of work, with little social life or recreation. The daily schedule of developing a new technique, composing new dances, teaching beginners, teaching and coaching her chosen girls took all the day until midnight.

The practice room was plain and matched Martha's plain appearance, her hair brushed smooth and glossy, her dress now white, without ornament or scarf except for a ribbon tying back her hair. No more saris. She wore a white silk Japanese bolero knotted in front and later a white silk taffeta wraparound skirt, very smart. She would not let the girls wear black, however appropriate it would have been, because of the dirt from floor work (a good part of their time was spent rolling on the ground), and because she said black hid movement. They wore light-colored or pale-gray or tan tank suits (what we would today call leotards), which left their bare legs and feet exposed. The girls were neat. Martha insisted.

Martha's classes were serious work sessions, and when the students arrived they stood silently against the wall and waited to be directed. There were no "Good day"s and no "Good-bye"s and the only speaking was when Martha told them what she wanted. Some of the dancers had been previously exposed to Duncan classes, with chiffon and rosebuds, greetings and embraces; they preferred Graham's austerity. Martha never asked how the girls were getting on. She asked nothing about them personally; she told them nothing about herself. It sounds like lack of interest, but Martha was tuned to rehearsal pitch and already at work when they entered the room. Any relaxation lessened her creative tension. The comparison would be to a conductor who mounts his podium at rehearsals and does not exchange social greetings with the members of the orchestra—he raps on his desk for attention and lifts his baton. Dancing is much more difficult to control than music, because choreography is in the head, unproven, not charted on paper. Martha had to keep herself as tight as a fiddle string or none of the inner notes would sound. The girls knew this and never demanded more. They were there to participate in the act of creation and nothing else.

For classes she used piano accompaniments, but not known pieces and never melodies, merely percussive chords. (Doris Humphrey used a drum.) Martha's chords were arbitrary improvisations played by rehearsal hacks, and these served her well enough, although they were forlornly tiring to the ear. There was nothing here of the great chord sequences that distinguish Bach or Chopin. Martha's were just hitting sounds, sufficient to enable the dancers and the group to make the thrust and push together.

Every class began with certain basic warming-up exercises on the floor, stretching the back, the thighs, the arms, and the torso, and these floor exercises possibly constitute Graham's most beautiful contribution to dance vocabulary. They lasted forty-five minutes to an hour every day. "The drawback with them," says Mark Ryder, a student of Graham's in the forties, "is that the legs are relaxed from sitting. They are stretched, but they haven't the resilience that is needed for standing up and jumping. The feet and legs got cramped. And at class's finale [the feet and legs] must start jumping in that condition." Ballet dancers are not permitted to sit until after class, or at the very end of class. In ballet the big stretching muscles are initially tested in deep knee-flexes and in bendings to the floor, but always standing. And the big extensions are also developed standing, where weight and balance are the chief considerations.

After the floor exercises, Martha got her class up to balance and to lift their legs at the barre, and then they began to walk and to run and then to jump.

She divided the class: one-third seated, one-third standing at the barre, one-third moving and traversing the floor. Rehearsals or classes lasted (according to Gertrude Shurr) two to four hours. No one laughed, no one chatted, as dancers do, no one gossiped.

The classes during the first ten years of Martha's independent teaching, from 1926 to 1936, were not given for the sake of the students. That is, they were not a balanced set of exercises that would limber, strengthen, develop, relax, or make possible difficult known feats. They were experiments in unknown specialized controls and in new specialized mechanics of moving. Sophie Maslow says, "Whatever it was that Martha was interested in at the time was what we did. We would work at that technical problem sometimes for a whole year. That's why we had thighs like iron. And at the end of that time we may have been muscle-bound, but she had fulfilled herself as an artist, and we had some one new thing to add to our scale of movement."

As soon as any new technique was clarified, it was used in a dance— or, rather, the technique and the dance evolved together in simultaneous creation.

‖‖‖

What was this modern movement of Martha's? How was it new? In what way?

"Great creation," says George Bernard Shaw, "is not the first of its kind, but the last and the best. The final voice."

Ruth St. Denis had a solo in her early days entitled *The Yogi*, in which she sat cross-legged, the palms upturned, resting in lotus position. Her eyes were closed and she commenced by taking three big, deep breaths while she gathered her inner psychic forces. Then one hand, palm bent up at a right angle, measured the space from left shoulder to right shoulder to left shoulder and moved back down to rest on the lap, palm upturned. The other hand unhurriedly and with no evident consciousness of repetition did the same. The eyes opened and the palm went out into the sphere of body-reach. The body was soon outlined in a web of concentric stretchings and measurings. Then one leg was extended behind, the head lifted, the back arched. A crisis was reached by standing on one leg and drawing a knee up, then stepping out from the home spot. Several prayer gestures followed, drawing force beyond the visible and tangible; the feet returned to the lotus, hands palms up; the eyes closed in everlasting serenity and reserve.

This dance was not hard to do. In fact, I did it, without the choreographer's permission, as a child, in naïve theft. All the children at my school did it, taught by Miss Maud Fisher, who had no legal, ethical, or moral right to teach it. But it was important for St. Denis's pupils to do it, because it was the key to Miss Ruth's entire system.

Consciously, I believe, Martha drew on this simple flowerlike unfolding for many of her basic root positions in the floor exercises. A kind of special ritual, St. Denis's *Yogi* is a kindergarten exercise compared with Graham's floor exercises, which begin all her classes. *The Yogi* started in serenity, with closed eyes, the gathering of inner forces, and the taking in of breath.

"Where a dancer stands," says Martha, "that spot is holy ground." Martha sat. It was more basic and it was more oriented. But she did not sit in the lotus position. Martha sat with one leg opened with crooked knee before, the other open with crooked knee behind. It became known as the swastika position and it necessitated an absolutely sprung crotch, with the pelvis flat on the ground and the spine not leaning back, as would be natural, but pressed forward and erect. It is a devil of a position to maintain. Martha could do it because of her body structure and proportions. Some others couldn't—I, for instance. From this posture the dancer could with no shift of weight, in a single count, rise to a standing position, and could sit again just as quickly. Moreover, by swiveling the knees the dancer could bend forward to the ground, or backward. The torso was in a neutral position and capable of control in all directions, up or down, backward or forward, around or reverse.

Then, still seated, Martha began the exploration of space, and not only space but dynamics. Martha knew that all emotion is visible in the torso because of body chemistry and mechanics; great painters have also known this. Arch the spine and you have emotion. Joshua Reynolds claimed that extreme joy and grief had the same physical expression, and he drew on the classic masters to prove his point. The arms and face are peripheral, like the hair. It is the torso—heart, lungs, stomach, viscera, and, above all, spine—which expresses.

Martha stripped off the chassis of the body and exposed the motor. She got the gesture down not only to the muscles, which is "how," but to the juices and the electricity as well, which is "why." In attempting to do this she blotted out the face and rendered the hands dumb paws, holding them in cupped rigidity even when taking bows. This was a highly self-conscious and distracting mannerism which did, however, focus all attention and energy where she wanted it, on the torso; it stripped the dancers of hyperbole. When she had finally laid naked what she wished, she relinquished the strictures on hands, and (to everyone's relief) they returned to normal usage; they are, after all, the subtle speaking voice of the body. Bodies cannot lie, as Martha's father had taught her, and she used hands judiciously, even with awe. But she concentrated on the torso as the source of life, the motor, the work-room, the kitchen. The arms and legs might be useful for servicing or locomotion, and the head for judging and deciding; but everything, every emotion, she believed, starts or is visible in the torso first. The heart pounds, the lungs fill; and if the lungs fill there is a sharp spasm of activity in the ribs and diaphragm, since all life hangs on breath—or, rather, the diaphragm lifts and then there is breath, and with it life.

Other great dance creators have believed this. Duncan contended that life centered in the solar plexus. Fokine taught breathing as a prelude to gesture and instructed his Sylphides exactly when to inhale and when to exhale. He taught the arm pulses in the *Sylphides* mazurka on an inhalation and suspension of breath, giving them a sense of resonance. After Fokine but before Graham, von Laban and Wigman based all their gestures on the ebb and flow of movement, a kind of tidal rhythm which was controlled by breath.

Graham went further. The spasm of the diaphragm, the muscles used in coughing and laughing, were used to spark gesture. There was a shutting and downward movement and an opening and lifting of both the diaphragm and the pelvis. These spasms she called contractions, and they were visible—and this was the point—not just in the resulting effect but in what they caused the rest of the body to do. They were in themselves part of the performance. An intake of breath, in the early Graham technique, could be seen at the back of the theater.

Gertrude Shurr explained: "We were for many years making the consonant *ssss.* She'd say *'sssss,sss,'* and let out the whole breath, then ask, 'What do the shoulders do? What do the hips do? What does the spine do?' "

Nelle Fisher, a Graham student in the thirties, added: "You must think of the emotional aspects of the contraction, the fact that it proceeded from a deep emotional feeling, often pain. People have stamped on the earth for percussive effects, but I don't think they've ever used percussive accents within the body, except in dances of ecstasy, like flagellants or dervishes, where they were quite literally driving themselves into abnormal conditions."

In the Graham technique, the arms and legs moved as a result of this spasm of percussive force, like a cough, much as the thong of a whip moves because of the crack of the handle. The force of the movement passes from the pelvis and diaphragm to the extremities, neck and head. It is a device common to jazz dancing, and because of its origin low in the body it was considered sexy; it used to be known in popular Negro jargon as a bump. When it is restricted to the diaphragm, it is a hiccup. In either case it is percussive. Anna Kisselgoff wrote: "Angular, sharp and stunningly percussive, the Graham contraction always originates in what Graham calls 'the house of the pelvic truth.' While this often gives Graham's choreography an explicit sexual tension, the movement itself has broader metaphorical implications."

It is always emotional and represents the apex of effort. "Any prizefighter hits on a contraction as his fist goes forward," explains Martha. "The contraction is an enfoldment and a shock."

And in extreme contractions Martha told students to throw the head back, lift the chin, and gaze upward, the eyes "blind on the zenith."

Arms and legs, accordingly, were not lifted or lowered; they were driven in propulsion, and propulsion that was quite visible. The effect was of jerks and spasms, all transitional movement having been eliminated. It was taxing to watch and brought a minimum of kinetic pleasure. One did not watch and wish one could do these things. Little girls did not rush home and implore their mothers to buy them woolen leotards.

"Oh, don't applaud Martha," begged my own mother of me. "She might do it again!"

And when Mary Wigman came to New York I said to Mother, "I'm not going to take you. You don't like modern dancing."

"Oh, indeed I do. Wigman is smooth. She doesn't jerk. Martha jerks."

"Oh, dear," said one of my suitors. "Do you think any of these girls will be good mothers?"

Uncomfortable and taxing to behold. But the mind was jolted, and the faithful few who attended Martha's concerts came with the anticipation of having their minds jolted. Martha was dissecting—exposing the plumbing, the working engine.

The movement at first may well have been incomprehensible to most of us, even ugly, but after a while we realized that what we were watching was revitalized raw emotion made apparent. This is what the Greeks could do. This is what Shakespeare did. This is what every artist attempts. But most, of course, cannot even conceive of it, and nearly all refuse to pay the terrible price in time and effort of finding it.

Martha said in a speech in 1974 (I paraphrase): "There has been a lot of talk about contraction and release. It has become a cliché! It's very simple. The body can do two things, breathe in and breathe out, and this involves the whole body, and particularly the pelvis. Therefore, it is visceral."

Martha used breath for dynamics, certainly, but also for rhythm. She never would permit her dancers to count their music, insisting rather that they move on breath rhythm and inner pulse. She also insisted that they land on the beat, "in the center" of the rhythm—but not by counting. Musicians were driven to distraction—though not Louis. He understood.

|||||

Since of necessity Martha had to work with her own body, the type of movement she devised was what she herself could do instinctively and readily. Her point of view was that of a woman, and it remained so, although in later years she strove to make it all-embracing. Ballet technique is, in a sense, neuter, and only diverges into male and female in the virtuoso refinements, such as pointe work and jumps, the basics remaining the same for everybody—a device nearly as impersonal as the musical scale. Martha's technique lay within the span of her own creative life, a long one as dancers go, but not long enough to absorb all possible permutations and differences. It must be remembered, however, that it started with her own body and her emotions and, above all, her passion.

Martha was small, between five foot two and a half and five foot three. Her torso was long, her legs relatively short and sturdy. They were not out of proportion, but they were not the long, lean legs that characterize most dancers today. She had very strong thighs, producing an open spread of thigh (a rotation outward of the legs in what ballet dancers call turnout, a characteristic few men can achieve), a foot like a primitive, with a high instep and a long, pliant Achilles tendon. Woe to the girl with a tight one! Martha could squat without lifting her heels from the floor and rise to a standing position without swinging her weight forward and without lifting her heels from the floor. The superb arch and long Achilles tendon, as long as a Bushman's, enabled her to inch her way around the stage with the sole use of her instep and heel muscles. The balance of thigh and buttock made it possible for her to lever herself backward and downward with no loss of control, or rise on one leg with the other held straight before her in the air.

Mark Ryder explained this: "Men have a leg drive, propulsion from the legs. Females, on the other hand, have more pelvic flexibility. Martha has female physical construction, is in fact 'crotch-sprung,' and a great deal of her technique is unattainable for people not similarly built."

John Butler, one of Martha's leading men in the forties and fifties, said: "I never could do Martha's technique. They'd have had to take me to the hospital if I'd sat in some of those stretches. Also, she had a one-sided, left-leg split-kick technique, straight up on the left side, although she is right-handed."

In Graham's technique all falls are on the left side because, as she said, the weight of the heart is on the left side. Maybe so; but to this dancer it seems that it really was because her left leg and thigh were stronger and more stretched out. Whatever the reason, her dancers often have a lopsided appearance.

"There were never any right-handed kicks or falls," added Ethel Butler, who danced with Graham in the thirties and forties, "until the teachers tired and Martha finally gave in, but not for herself personally."

Martha's strong back, torso, thighs, and heels permitted her the great leverages, swings, and falls, the sudden release of arms and head, a rhapsodic cry in the body, the "Hasidic" cry. "Her torso has Oriental eloquence," said Pearl Lang.

Martha's falls, because they were not a yielding to gravity but a descent and lowering in thighs and back, became not so much a crashing down as a dissolving, a melting and sliding, a communion with the ground and then a recovery and regalvanizing. She worked on these falls for fifty years, and they grew astonishingly beautiful, varied, and complex. Combined with a wide variety of "pleadings" (a contraction, often from a prone position with the arms out in a begging or pleading position), they provide an extraordinarily rich vocabulary. "I use the fall as a springboard, not as an objective, so there is a spring up to life," she said. "I feel the ground is a spatial element, not to be resisted as in ballet, but to be used."

All of it was hard to do and punishing to the girls' bodies. The torso may perhaps have been eloquent; it certainly hurt. As a matter of fact, the constant pelvic drive, the hammering on the organs, engendered menstrual disturbances. Several of the girls had medical problems which left doctors baffled because they had never found these symptoms in a woman's body before. Nelle Fisher said that once it was suspected that she had appendicitis and a doctor who was examining her with some bewilderment said, "What is it you do? Show me an exercise." So she went into a simple contraction, the beginning of almost every Graham exercise, and he and the nurse gasped. The ridges of muscle had jumped out across her belly and loins, as hard as a wrestler's. "My God!" said the doctor. "Do you do this often?" "Every day," she replied politely. "For hours." He brought in another nurse and said, "Have you ever seen anything like that?"

There grew to be less and less respite for Martha's dancers and for her audience, even in the light pieces. She demanded of her audience the concentration needed for poetry. Every movement was so packed, so suggestive, and so seemingly split off (I am speaking in terms of movement only) that the effort to absorb the inner pattern could be exhausting. An entire evening of Graham was always a demanding experience, and yet for these same reasons, repeated viewings were in turn progressively rewarding. Ballet, on the other hand, has sought always to do what was pleasing, to mask the human impulses and mechanics, the animal or kitchen aspect of life, as unsuitable for viewing.

Martha's discoveries—or, more accurately, revealings—were new, and there were a lot of them (I have described only a few), more than in any other recorded dancer's contribution. For example, in the eighteenth century Camargo gave us the beaten jump, or entrechat; in the nineteenth, Taglioni gave us the perfection of pointe work, and Grisi the "high fish," or fall floating into her partner's arms. ("This *pas* includes a certain fall which will soon become as famous as Niagara Falls," wrote the critic Théophile Gautier.) Legnani in 1893 was the first to perform thirty-two whipped turns, or fouettés. (Lest the secret be stolen, she would not permit herself to be seen rehearsing it. A rival ballet master hid in the wings and solved the mystery.) Pavlova mastered the spin on both pointes and the "drill" on pointe (tiny shifts of weight in place, which she used with memorable effect in Fokine's *Dying Swan*. All of these are mere embellishments, invented with the extremely professional help of ballet masters who were on occasion great choreographers. None of these ornaments modified the basic stance, deportment, balance, or control. These were peripheral additions. Martha, her own master and choreographer, changed the root control, giving us a new system of balance, leverages, dynamics, and rhythm.

||||

The outstanding characteristic of all Martha's classes was always Martha's verbal evocation. Miss Ruth talked mysticism. Doris Humphrey talked aesthetics. Many teachers talked technique and pedantry. Martha talked enlightened poetry. Sometimes the explanations had very little to do with the work at hand—at least, it seemed that way—but they gave an oblique insight into what she was feeling. Her remarks were sometimes cryptic, generally brief—oh!, mercifully brief!—and often humorous, lightning quick in their revelation and lightning powerful in their striking force. Suddenly there would come the spark of recognition between teacher and pupil, and even as Martha found the unforgettable, the magic, dance phrase, she matched it with the verbal phrase, the phrase for that particular student to use as her own signature, to be her talisman, something she could identify with. This is great teaching—indeed, great creation.

One can dimly perceive the effect of Martha's remarks from the fragments in her published notebooks, but only partially. They nearly always need to be transfused by movement, which give blinding insights hitherto completely inexperienced.

Some of Martha's sayings:

"The theater was a verb before it was a noun."

"The spine is your tree of life. Respect it." Or, "Stand up. Keep your back straight. Remember that this is where the wings grow." (Martha has denied saying this, but there are many witnesses to testify that they heard her.)

"You attack dance as 'Now!' Not what it will develop into, not what I have done—[but] what I am doing."

"All that is important is this one moment in movement. Make the moment important, vital, and worth living. Do not let it slip away unnoticed and unused."

"I want it to look as if it's being done now for the first time."

"Our body is our glory, our hazard, and our care."

"There are times when it is almost necessary to feel an animal sensualness in dance. Not meaning sexy, but rather of the senses. Like completely primitive animal movements—like the MGM lion, or the way a cat walks."

"The dancer's body is the celebrant of life."

"A gesture does not exist alone in time. Be aware of where you have come from. There is a double pull before and after."

"One has to work around one's own spine. One makes a spiral around the back. The flesh and body are wrapped around the bones."

"The back of the head should be held high, not the face. For the animal brain is at the base of the head, and as dancing is animal in its source, we need to activate that part of our body."

This last observation may help the body stance. It is challenging and evocative, fascinating, even provocative. I must say that if one bore such an idea in mind while attempting to dance, one would become paralyzed, and I'm pretty certain Martha herself would agree. As though in corroboration, Martha adds, "Above all, stop intellectualizing technique and just let the body do it.

"Move!"

‖‖‖

One of Graham's early exercises was to have a student walk diagonally across the floor, bringing an arm up overhead in a loose arc (port de bras, in fifth, en haut) and saying at the same time, "This is my name." She claimed she could know all about you after that. She knew from the carriage of the head, from the lift of the chin, from the tension in the shoulders, from the freedom or constriction of the arm movement, from the force or weakness in the torso, from the gait—hesitant or sure, overconfident or lagging. She knew better from these hints than from the expression on the face, which can be controlled and disciplined. But the reading of these signs was not simple. Try it and see. Martha was as acute as a great diagnostician. She was, as she said, "an intuitive."

"Ah, now I know what you truly are," said Martha to someone who had just walked across the floor. "You have revealed yourself to me." And the pupil felt stripped not only of clothes but of skin, muscles, flesh, down to the central nerve. What did Martha know? Did Martha know more than the subject himself? Would she say? Was she right? Heavens! It was demoralizing.

||||

Martha believed that words were linked with gesture, that they were part of the same expression. She said to me once, "If you are stuck for a gesture, say the word, say the sentence. The action will come." Although she herself, as long as she danced, never spoke a word on the stage, words are a great part of her root source.

She studied words, really studied them, going through the big Oxford dictionaries for derivations, finding the original or obsolete meaning so that she would understand whence the word originated and therefore the idea behind it. And it often had to do, way back, with action, something physical. For instance, the verb "to scorn" originally was a term in archery and it meant "to miss the mark." "You can't think how learning that cheered me up," said Martha.

She took her inspiration from everything. "I used to walk up and down New York," she once said, "up and down, back and forth, and in the zoo before the lion's cage, studying his potential for violence, studying how he measured his captivity and turned on himself, until the zoo keepers began to look on me with considerable suspicion, and so, no doubt, did the lion."

Do not think that Graham's classes, because they were serious, were dour. Martha had wit and gaiety, even obstreperous fun. She got the girls laughing even as she drove them over the hurdles.

Her students were not just students; they were the Group and they improved surprisingly in caliber. As Martha began to have the luxury of making choices among students, she weeded out, and then she drilled those who remained without cease. They all grew close to one another, but never intimate—Martha was never in her life cozy.

Nevertheless, the Group came to have almost a familial quality. When costumes were to be made, they sat cross-legged on the bare floor of the studio, the dresses spread over their knees, and they sewed together. "Like a sewing bee, like a church social," said Martha Hill. When there was a birthday it was a group celebration. At Christmas time they had a party, and Hugo Bergamasco, who played the flute for Martha's performances and made bootleg wine, brought bottles of Chianti and home-made bread. Everyone contributed food and they all got tiddly together and improvised dances and Louis played the piano and they had a wonderful time. Husbands and lovers were let in on these occasions. Otherwise Louis was the sole male, lord of a delightful, adoring harem.

He was the male of the troupe, humorous, salty, paternal, equitable, compassionate, sane. Of all the advisers Martha was to have in her life—and she was to have many—he was the most sane, never lending himself to the vagaries and hysteria of spite, vanity, or paranoia. Emotionally he was clean and openhearted.

There was, however, one hard fact in their relationship: he would not marry her.

But he would serve her. He played for rehearsals and performances. He was the adviser and editor of the work, drilling the group, correcting them. Martha, in common with most choreographers, was impatient with the finicky business of keeping girls in straight lines and fussing over counts once she had indicated what she wanted. Louis's patience was endless.

"During all the hours he played for rehearsals," said Gertrude Shurr, "he'd sit at the piano, his heavy-lidded eyes drooping shut, and we thought he was asleep and not watching us with his x-ray eyes. Then suddenly we'd hear his voice: 'Martha! Gertrude has dropped her leg.' He permitted no marking or indication at rehearsals, no matter how many times we repeated. He was merciless." As the sole man, he was also catnip to them.

He brought to these group rehearsals the meticulous care which he certainly did not lavish on his own five-finger exercises. He brought a Germanic, scholarly, and exacting expertise. He became, in short, the régisseur. And he was the one—and the only one—who could discipline Martha herself into finishing her pieces, shaping them up and getting them ready for performance. He was quite practical about this. After giving her leeway for weeks, or even months, he would at last call a halt and demand decisions, which Martha, in her hysterical turmoils, did not always wish to make. The dances got done—not always finished, but done. There was a first performance. And that was thanks to Louis.

He was present at all rehearsals, and in the beginning he played for the classes. Later, when he was teaching dance composition, he played only for rehearsals, and generally only rehearsals of his own music. Louis also supervised most of Martha's business arrangements.

He had moved to the Village, to East Eleventh Street between University Place and Broadway, two short blocks from Martha.

Louis's studio, in which he worked with Anna Sokolow and other assistants, was as bare as a monk's cell; a Steinway, a couch, good Navajo rugs (Martha's floor was totally bare, in preparation for classes), Navajo masks, several kachina dolls, and always piles of music on the floor. From Germany he had brought back paintings by Paul Klee and George Grosz, and a drawing by Käthe Kollwitz, and he also owned works by the Americans Otto Karl Knaths and John Marin. His American collection was accumulated bit by bit and grew to be valuable. Over the bed hung a cartoon of Brahms, full length, playing something intricate and delicate, his hands crossed, his cigar jutting out of his beard. Louis resembled Brahms, bulky and German, gross sometimes, uncompromising as to taste, good and generous always, while aesthetically stern. All this was reflected in his living arrangements, his cell. It was an ascetic room, stripped for work. To this room came the Graham disciples and their pupils, Anna Sokolow, Gertrude Shurr, Sophie Maslow, Jane Dudley, Bill Bales, and even non-pupils like Ruth Page and Agnes de Mille. And to this room also came Nina Fonaroff, who a long time later was to become Louis's love. There Louis lived as uncelibate a life as he could arrange. The "little pink toes" were invited in.

He taught regular classes at the Neighborhood Playhouse on the Lower East Side, lecturing on choreography and dance form, and continued to do so to the end of his life. He also accompanied many dancers, including the distinguished soloists Harald Kreutzberg and Yvonne Georgi, and he composed.

His pupil Nik Krevitsky said the dance wasn't really Louis's first love: "He loved the dancers more, the female dancers especially."

And I would say he loved music more—or, rather, he found it more reliable. He didn't like men in the dance, though he was patient with them, and helpful. But women titillated him, enchanted him, replenished him, bewitched him. He couldn't have enough of them. He never grew tired of them. He loved them tenderly and devotedly and with relish, even as he teased them unmercifully. But this was a facet of flirtation. Louis always flirted.

Louis's main interest was not in composing, although he did do this very well, especially for Martha. It was not easy for Louis to write music. It had to be dragged out of him note by note. In fact, Martha used to beg the girls to go and sit with Louis and coax him into writing each section. Frequently they found they had to gossip for a considerable time before he was sufficiently relaxed to get down to the job; but when he did, it was excellent. He preferred arranging, discovering, selecting, and organizing. He found the music that was needed, and his taste was impeccable.

Martha taught her own technique in order to prepare students to dance in her choreographic work. Louis taught Martha's girls dance composition and pre-classic forms, not the true historical dance forms, which he knew only through books. Not having researched in the European libraries where the old notations are preserved, and not being conversant with the European folk forms from which all the old court dances derived, he worked to produce only approximate modern rearrangements based on the classical musical forms. There was no attempt at reproducing actual steps. The students, however, did learn structure soundly, composition in musical terms: the statement of a theme, its development, its inversion, complementary or contrasting statements, counterpoint.

"His was a basic, down-to-earth teaching," said Yuriko, Martha's first Japanese soloist. "Louis told us: 'Get the A-B-A form into your blood; but when you choreograph, forget it, and it will always be at the base of your choreographic concepts.' It was in my pieces, and it can easily be detected in Martha's early works."

Louis's courses were on the principles of development of thematic material. In improvising, the student might discover a phrase of movement which would become the theme of her dance and which would embody the essence of what she wanted to say. She would then examine it for form, always keeping it simple. Any further variations she devised would have to be generic to the first phrase, and all phrases were held short, two bars at most, amounting to only seconds of time. They were worked through with a variant and a return to the first statement, which by then had taken on richer meaning for the intervening second comment, the whole forming a miniature dance, or "étude" as he called it. The shortness of the piece meant that the idea had to be unalloyed and capable of development. As Doris Rudko, a student who worked with him for the last nine years of his life, says, "Every dance dictated its own form."

Rudko explains:

Once we'd mastered our material and craft, Louis wanted us to achieve the same spontaneity that we all want, but this time we were masters of what we were doing and we handled our material in an intelligent and directed way, quite unconsciously. Louis's courses were so tightly disciplined they ultimately gave freedom.

His whole method of work was about crafting movement and structuring dances. If the choreographer knew her material, her kernel, she would know how to proceed. It they understood the gestalt, then they'd know what the dance was about and where it must go. It implied a very delicate balance between "feel-think" and "think-feel." He cared less about what the dancer herself wanted. He was interested in the material as though it had a life of its own, all of which must unfold and proceed from the embryonic movement phrase.

Louis's method of working, throughout his life at the Neighborhood Playhouse, Bennington College, Connecticut College for Women at New London, and the Juilliard Foundation, was to give assignments (and when he gave assignments, he would hand out little packets containing pictures and musical suggestions to show the students that the same problems existed in other arts and that the greatest contemporary artists of the world in other media handle them also). And then he would set the students to working on the miniature études individually but at the same time, in a large studio under the traffic direction of an assistant. Each student was allotted a space and they all started working, paying no attention to anyone else. When two or three of them had gotten a short sequence together that seemed "ripe," so to speak, a batch of work ready for the oven, like cookies, Anna Sokolow or Doris Rudko or whoever would go down the hall to Louis's room and fetch him. And then they would all quiet down, clear the floor, and he would sit and judge each worker separately. This was nothing short of awful. The room was silent and the student was exposed, alone, and anatomized. But many of the students survived and became able choreographers and dancers.

Pearl Lang, later a pupil of Graham and Horst, said: "When the dance is composed, it creates a world that has never been before and will cease to be when the dance is finished. So, to be remembered, it must be strongly focused on to itself. Once the thematic material has been established, it is movement with a time and an energy all its own, not to be violated with extraneous movement, no matter how brilliant or attractive." Nina Fonaroff quotes Horst as saying: "Move as though you'd never moved before, as though the movement itself were being done for the first time." Nina's eyes grew wide as she spoke with the wonder of remembering.

Several advanced students of Graham and Horst, Anna Sokolow especially, were asked to give performances of their own works at

Louis's lecture-demonstrations. This is how so many of the great solo choreographers started: Anna Sokolow, Pearl Lang, Merce Cunningham, Jean Erdman, Sophie Maslow, Jane Dudley. Martha did not work with them on their compositions as Louis did. Martha stood by and wished them well. Louis shepherded them onto the stage. (It should be noted, though, that when Pearl Lang started her solo concerts with a performance of her *Dybbuk*, Martha not only attended each performance but gave Lang a thousand dollars toward the price of the score.)

With the girls, Louis was demanding; he made them redo things countless times. He was often crass, or even cruel, as when he first addressed Dorothy Bird, who had just arrived from British Columbia and stood before him in absolute ignorance and innocence. "Well, Dorothy, are you pregnant yet?" he asked. She was shocked, but her reserve was shattered and she got to work. He was always a terrible tease; pomposity and sentimentality as well as vagueness, laziness, and imprecision were eliminated from his classes. These are the dodges and refuges of the muddy-minded, and many a young student has sought the tangles of obscurity rather than make the effort to straighten out his ideas. Sometimes Louis would say abruptly, "Throw all that away and start completely over. You haven't a notion of what this is about." Once he kept Sophie Maslow standing in front of the class until she could think of a title for her dance. Sophie finally burst into tears. Even then he wouldn't let her sit down: she had to call it something. What Louis was after was a clarification of her ideas, and on reviewing the whole episode she came to realize as much. But, by God, they learned. "He was very strict," Pearl said. "I would be in tears with every class. He would criticize form; he would criticize exact musicality. The loss of one count in the modern forms of sevens or fives, those Bartók rhythms that we were forced to learn, if you missed a beat he would raise hell! Wonderful experience for a dancer! And believe me, he always saw two ways, one eye on the music and one on you."

"Louis always started by discouraging," she continued, "and waited to see if you would fight back. And if you fought hard, then he thought you were worth encouraging. I would say, 'Louis, you're destroying the idea. The inspiration is now being pushed under in counts and measures.' He'd snort and say, 'Well, if the inspiration is so weak, believe me, you can afford to get rid of it and get busy on something else.'" (This is an exact repetition of his many exhortations to the young, struggling Graham.)

Age did not mellow Horst in this respect. He never tolerated pretension or timidity, anything that wasted time or confused issues. Bertram Ross, a student in the fifties, speaks of his first adventures with Horst. He had signed up for Louis's classes in composition almost as soon as he entered the Graham school. Suddenly he felt abashed at his effrontery and asked to speak to Martha. "Does he frighten you?" she questioned. And Ross, wishing to seem manly and sophisticated, replied, "Oh, no, not that." And she said, "Well, he frightens me all right," and then Ross confessed that confronting Louis in class was a ghastly ordeal. Louis had asked for a pavane and demanded to know the title. Ross replied that it was taken from a Shakespeare sonnet, "Not Eased by Night." But he spoke softly and Louis deliberately pretended to misunderstand. "Not Easy at Night," he repeated, and he laughed and he bullyragged the boy until Bertram shouted the correct answer. Then he performed the dance, which Louis later—considerably later—admitted was excellent, a first-class example of the form. Still later he confessed, "I find you thoroughly convincing all the time, everything you do." Martha was astonished at the praise, because Louis was chary of praise always.

Jane Dudley said: "You never asked questions. You never thought of disagreeing or demanding answers. You took his word like God's and followed it obediently and that was also an important part of discipline, to subject oneself to strong limitations." Pearl Lang added: "He was devastatingly accurate in his classroom criticism, which he made acceptable with humor. His genius was to protect us against sentimentality. After all, he was fostering an aesthetic revolution in dance." And the critic John Martin stated, "It was Louis who insisted on form, structure, logical development, and absolute discipline. It was Louis who opened the door." (Here John Martin was quoting Dorothy Bird.)

Pearl Lang continued, "He used the Graham company to demonstrate his theories and essays, paying us each fifteen dollars. At the time I was waiting on table at Schrafft's. I gave the fifteen dollars back to Louis, and he said, 'Why do you want to do that?', snorting the way he did. 'Because I learned so much more by working with you than with these fifteen dollars that I feel that I owe them to you.'" (Louis repeated this story to his students for twenty years.) Pearl added: "He was marvelous. He really was the patron saint of all of us."

And truthfully he was. He huffed a great deal and played the role of a grouchy misanthrope, but Louis Horst paid the rent and bills of I don't know how many pupils, gave them his services, held their heads, buried their dead, and taught their young. He once even floated a loan to pay the Graham company's out-of-town hotel bills.

At a time when my own finances were precariously low, Louis offered me his services without pay for a concert. This was no trivial gift. It included, besides the performance of the concert, one month's rehearsal for an hour and a half to two hours a day, and editing, arranging, and copying the music—all time-consuming and responsible jobs. "How do I know," I asked him, "that you can afford to do all this?"

"Because," he snapped back, "I say so."

He could be personally sentimental, with rich German overtones. Years after he had left Denishawn, students came upon him standing at a corner in a Connecticut town gazing at a boarded-up theater with tears on his cheeks. "What's the matter, Louis?" they asked, rushing to him solicitously. "Are you in trouble?"

He shook his head. "I'm all right. It's just that I played my last concert here with Miss Ruth. Every town I go to, I visit the landmarks along our trail, and I always visit the theaters. I want to see how they are doing." Sarcastic, sardonic, crusty, critical, uncompromising Louis!

He could also quickly revert to his more normal carping. "These kids take toilet flushing for music and structureless immobility for dancing. To rebel, to be way out, is fine, but they don't know how far they can go and still be with us!" In his initial program, Paul Taylor had been revealed standing stock still center stage. There he remained unmoving until curtain fall. By way of review, Horst accorded him four inches of blank newspaper space and signed the emptiness solemnly at the bottom. The point was not lost on Taylor.

Or, in a more analytic mood: "The new dance does not depend on beautiful line, unearthly balance, or sexual titillation. The movement is abstracted to express, in aesthetic form, the drives, desires and reactions of alive human beings."

Or lyric: "An idea is touched upon in the briefest fashion, like an insect which lights briefly on a leaf before flying on to the next. It is suggestive."

He hunted out jobs for the dancers. He took them with him when he could employ them or get them employed. He undertook to keep them alive and busy—not just the beginners but the leaders, also, who were in need, Doris Humphrey and her girls as well as Martha. I think he would have given Miss Ruth help if there had been any realistic way to do so. In a practical sense he was directly responsible for the entire new development of the modern dance, quite apart from the ideological and emotional ways in which he helped organize the movement. Louis was largely responsible for the physical survival of the important creators.

|||||

Day after day, Martha confronted her paying students and the girls of her Group in the bare big rooms. They were clad in their neat singlets, she in her white skirt and bolero, which she slipped on for every demonstration. Each week there was something added to the invisible edifice they were building together. She began to have a body of work that was hers and no one else's, stamped with her personality and her beliefs, saturated with her own sweat.

She began to realize that she could rule, she could create a mystical relationship with an audience, or, alternately, that she could destroy. She had power. She grew to love the magic word: Power.

Each night after work Louis would leash Max, his dachshund, and together they would proceed west to the White House. After collecting Martha, the three walked to a neighborhood restaurant, Max waggling on a string beside them, Martha exquisitely neat in a bargain-basement costume, Louis quietly huffing and sardonic. Louis would order a Manhattan cocktail for himself and another for Martha, from which she would take only the smallest sip before pushing it over to him. These suppers were replenishing, *gemütlich*. They had fun, she and her "Luigi."

Martha was given a teaching position at the Neighborhood Playhouse in 1927; through it she was assured a steady, if modest, living and the patronage and resourceful help of the four powerful women who ran the school and who became her friends and backers for life.

The Neighborhood Playhouse had been founded at the turn of the century by several well-to-do girls who went slumming: that is, they began to concern themselves very seriously, if voluntarily, with the conditions of the poor people of New York's Lower East Side. Myra Kelly, a public school teacher and the daughter of a well-known physician, had been one of the first to call the Lower East Side to popular attention with her collections of short stories on the conditions of the Jewish slums. *Little Citizens* (1904) and *Wards of Liberty* (1907), while not equal in artistic worth, were the equivalent in content of the devastating photographs of Jacob Riis. Both Christian and Jew began to take note of the very serious situation developing in their City of Promise.

Quite apart from and outside of the civic framework, and financed by private donors, a settlement house was instigated under the direction of Lillian Wald, a social worker from Chicago who attended the New York Training School for Nurses. In 1893 she became the founder-president and organizer of public nursing at the Henry Street School Settlement, originally the Nurses' Settlement. In 1902 she organized the first school of home care, visiting nurses, and school nurses in the world. In 1908 she originated the Federal Children's Bureau, established by Congress, and still later she became a lecturer on social work at Teachers College of New York.

Out of the Henry Street Settlement came a remarkable school which was of crucial help to many splendid people, among them Henry Moskowitz, the labor arbitrator. In fact, it proved the only light in an otherwise infernal gloom. Its pupils were given an education and therefore a chance. They learned to speak English properly and they learned a trade. Teachers and sponsors were recruited from among the affluent and concerned, and from the gifted and established.

Two of these public-minded young women were sisters, Irene and Alice Lewisohn, the daughters of Leonard and Rosalie Lewisohn. Leonard Lewisohn was a founder of copper-mining concerns and the only brother of Adolph, who donated Lewisohn Stadium to the City College of New York; the stadium provided summer concerts at low cost. As a young woman, Irene became deeply interested in various social and philanthropic organizations, and she used her Echo Hill Farm, the eighty-acre camp outside New York City, to provide vacations for underprivileged children. The Lewisohn sisters inherited two million dollars each, at a time of minimal taxes, from their parents—at today's buying power, the equivalent of eight to ten million dollars. They did not spend their money frivolously. Like many of their generation, they undertook responsibilities and strove the whole of their lives to help both the unfortunate and the talented young.

Their father had been interested in the Henry Street Settlement because of Miss Wald, and this gave his daughters contact with the field of sociology. As a 1927 article in *The New Yorker* put it, "They were impressed by the fact that the charitably inclined almost without exception gave their money to meet the physical needs of the poor, but let them starve for beauty." The Lewisohn sisters intended to help supply this beauty and, incidentally, to furnish themselves with a vehicle for their own acting and directing abilities. For they were not only compassionate; they were stage-struck. Irene had been a pupil and disciple of Genevieve Stebbins. Together with the designer Aline Bernstein and Polaire Weissmann, Irene Lewisohn founded the Museum of Costume Art in 1937, donating Middle Eastern and Indian clothes. This developed into the Costume Institute at the Metropolitan Museum of Art.

In furtherance of their dream, in 1915 Irene and Alice Lewisohn founded the Neighborhood Playhouse on Grand Street. Their school differed from other dramatic academies in that it stressed equally music, dance, and drama; in this it was unique. The plays produced were not commercial and were short-lived; but some of them were very lovely, and they received a good deal of national publicity.

To the Neighborhood Playhouse school came the great English actress Ellen Terry, who read Shakespeare in robes designed by her son, Gordon Craig. When she saw on the public announcements for her performance that the entry fee was twenty-five cents, she stopped in her tracks. Alice Lewisohn, in her book about the Neighborhood Playhouse, quoted her as saying, "This is a bit much for Ellen Terry, but really not enough for William Shakespeare." Yvette Guilbert, the French chanteuse, not only gave a performance of her matchless songs but also staged a fourteenth-century French miracle play with the children, with Alice Lewisohn coaching and performing with them. Ethel Barrymore came downtown with her entire troupe, and after her the Yiddish actor Jacob Ben-Ami; the Shakespearean star Edith Wynne Mathison; Augustin Duncan, the brother of Isadora; the great German tragedian Emmanuel Reicher; the monologist Ruth Draper; the ballerina Anna Pavlova, the Hindu dancer Roshanara, and an American-Indian troupe; the theater of Mei Lan-Fang, with his classic Chinese actors and dancers; the mystic Gurdjieff; the Indian poet Rabindranath Tagore; the playwrights Lord Dunsany and John Galsworthy; theater craftsmen such as the designer Robert Edmond Jones;* and painters and sculptors who discussed their work problems.

*Robert Edmond Jones was one of the influential and powerful figures of American stage design in the first quarter of the century. He furnished the decor and costumes for many of the Theater Guild productions, including *Mourning Becomes Electra* by Eugene O'Neill. He also designed the costumes and scenery for the only ballet the Diaghilev company produced during their 1916 American tour, *Tyl Eulenspiegel,* choreographed by Vaslav Nijinsky. It was Jones who used to say to his classes, "Some of you are doomed to be artists." Martha picked up this phrase and used it many times thereafter." She also borrowed from him the phrase "doom-eager," which he had borrowed from Ibsen.

Martha borrowed from everyone, and Martha repeated, both herself and others. "I steal," said Martha. "I take what I want, but I like to think I always steal the very best."

Many of the Neighborhood Playhouse students got jobs as painter's models, which earned them a few useful dollars. Artists of every kind were glad to give their time, although the students were small in number and without money or prestige, and the building shabby. This generosity was provoked by the Lewisohn sisters' overwhelming sincerity and the importance of the motivating ideas behind the project. The visitors talked to the students and even helped out in seminars. It was an unparalleled experience for the boys and girls, and they never forgot it.

However, it must be remembered that the school had originally been a settlement-house project and was, as might be supposed, guided and administered by a social worker, Rita Morgenthau, the sister-in-law of Henry Morgenthau, Secretary of the Treasury under Roosevelt. Like the other Neighborhood Playhouse founders, Rita Morgenthau was a woman of means and a person of large vision. Her interest in the theater was chiefly as a social force and only secondarily as an art, and for those reasons she encouraged all available ethnic groups to participate: the Russians from Hester Street, the Poles from Third Avenue, the Italians from Cornelia and Canal streets, the Chinese from nearby Mott Street. They gave street pageants abounding in their own ethnic expressions, keeping the neighborhood around Grand Street eventful and lively.

The Neighborhood Playhouse closed in 1927 and was replaced by the School of the Theater in 1928. In 1929 the school moved to 139 West Fifty-sixth Street, where it remained for nearly twenty years, with its remarkable roster of teachers. It was now officially entitled "School for Arts Related to the Theater."

Alice Lewisohn traveled abroad extensively, recruiting lecturers and teachers and collecting music and costumes. Her sister Irene worked actively with Mrs. Morgenthau on maintaining and strengthening the faculty. The students were carefully chosen for talent and character; a good percentage were given working fellowships. Many, having caught the enthusiasm, continued on as teachers for decades thereafter.

The courses were planned so as to lay before the students the fundamental resources of the different arts, to correlate them, to engender a point of view in regard to the theater from its various angles as a synchronized experience. The courses endeavored to put the students more in touch with their own capacities and to give them a broader, keener vision of the theater as a whole.

It can readily be seen how this point of view fitted in with Martha's own theories. She believed in intention, in understanding and spiritual meaning before everything else. Both Graham and the school approached each problem in relation to the preparation of a particular production, but whereas Martha focused on the theatrical event, the school did not stress performing and never tried to.

The school was located on the second floor. It had dark, interconnecting rooms, so that the students had to go through the voice teacher's room to reach Martha's dance studio, and through the lavatory to reach the voice teacher. Anna Sokolow, in her companions' eyes a "tough cookie," incorrigible and sassy, always flushed the toilet as she passed through by way of salutation. Jean Rosenthal, who became one of America's leading lighting designers, studied there from 1928 to 1930.

All the students took every subject, while specializing in one, and went in groups of three or four to the art exhibits and concerts, supervised by a teacher, often Louis Horst.

The curriculum, accordingly, included dancing, music applied to movement, voice, acting, literature of the drama, psychology of plays, design, costume, stage direction, and research.

Martha was in charge of the dancing, and her early pupils—Anna Sokolow, Nelle Fisher, Dorothy Bird—served with her as assistants and demonstrators. To this small group was added, in the thirties, Jane Dudley, who said: "I was one of Martha Graham's early demonstrators, and I think I saw some of the finest teaching that she ever did, working with actors, because she had a way of working from images, and the things she chose to do in the class I always felt were really essential, like walking and the carrying of the body.

"There wasn't a lot of material, as I remember. She would determine on a class structure at the beginning of the term and she stayed with that pretty much the whole four or six weeks of our course. We'd start slowly in the first weeks. Everything was analyzed very carefully. And then, as we worked longer with her, she'd begin to increase the tempo and get an exercise that was counted in eight counts steadily faster and stronger, until it was completed in one. This took strength. The movement at that period was very strenuous, not showy, maybe, but demanding, and it took all your physical energy."

The students were taught acting by Sanford Meisner, who came, in

1935, from the Group Theater, where he had been shepherded by Harold Clurman through an acting career which included the early work of Clifford Odets. With Clurman he had worked as a director and teacher, developing the acting theories of Konstantin Stanislavski. Meisner has been called America's finest teacher of the art of acting. Mrs. Morgenthau devoutly believed he was.

Laura Elliott taught voice. A pupil of Jean de Reszke, she had been a singer of some note but had forsaken an opera career to give her services and time to groups of working artists. She was coaching several theater and opera stars when she became a staff member at the Neighborhood Playhouse. Her distinction lay in the fact that she focused her interest on movement and voice together—on movement in relation to music, that is, total simultaneous expression in the body: vocal, visual, and physical. She was intent on freeing the personality. She had a strong influence on Katharine Cornell, whom she helped with vocal problems, when, at the beginning of a meteoric career, Cornell was preparing her role in *A Bill of Divorcement*. Cornell's assistant, Gertrude Macy, quoted Laura Elliott as saying that the two most gifted women in the American theater were Martha Graham and Katharine Cornell, and it was from them that she expected a new theater to develop. All Elliott's dicta, including the statement "Everything fruitful and meaningful happens below the navel," spoke directly to Graham.

Of Laura Elliott, Dorothy Bird said: "She was a very strong lady. She used to pull out her hair in exasperation while teaching. She was so frustrated by us that she had a bald spot from pulling. She talked like Katharine Cornell, and I think she was a little jealous of Martha because Martha got all the publicity and attention." And Martha did.

Indeed, it was to Graham that the students turned for straight dramatic work, next to Laura Elliott, whether they were dancers or actors. Marian Seldes the actress said, "I learned everything I know from Graham." She also commented, "I have never thought about acting or theater or life in precisely the same ways since I first saw Martha Graham dance."

Louis taught music and dance forms. Margareth Dessoff, the daughter of Felix Otto Dessoff, conductor and pedagogue, whose pupils included Arthur Nikisch and Anton Bruckner, taught singing. She had made a distinguished name for herself with her choirs in Vienna, Germany, and London before coming to America and repeating her success. The designer Aline Bernstein taught costume design, and Robert Edmond Jones taught stagecraft.

For their student body of all but penniless and first-generation Americans, for their scholarship students off the streets, the directors of the Neighborhood Playhouse had provided a cultural exposure not to be outmatched or even equaled by any other academy in the United States and by very few universities. Martha Graham, who was to leave the greatest name of all, was at the time the least known.

Mrs. Morgenthau presided over them all, encouraging and reaffirming. "She'd say to the beginning teachers, and the veterans too," recounted Dorothy Bird:

"You will come through. I know you'll come through!" And she'd go into each classroom and sit there, a little, short body, short skirt, knees rather wide apart, stout shoes, and she'd look at Martha or whomever and she'd nod, you know, at anything they were doing, and it didn't matter if they were doing *Strike,* or *Revolution,* or Shakespeare or Sophocles, she'd nod in total approval. She was behind them a hundred percent, and she was behind the students and indeed they would come through. When I began to teach in the junior school, she said, "Now, Dorothy, I want you to understand we're not in business to find pretty blond girls and handsome boys and put them on Broadway. We're in the theater business as opposed to the Broadway business. I want you to know that the one with the glasses who is knock-kneed and has buck teeth is probably the playwright. And that one, the gangly one who is too tall and poorly coordinated, is going to do the lighting. This other one's going to be the stage manager. That one's going to be, maybe, a star. Maybe the others will be in the theater. Maybe they'll just love the theater. *You're* not going to decide what they're going to do. You just throw everything you have like grain to chickens. *Your* job is to give everything that's in your heart and in your experience. Give out."

"I truly loved that woman," Dorothy Bird concluded.

The students worked all day long and were encouraged to act as assistants and junior teachers as soon as they were able. In this way Louis and Martha acquired helpers, who were paid by the school. It was in this way, too, that Anna Sokolow came to assist Louis, and Dorothy Bird to assist Martha.

The leading characteristic of the school was that the teachers of the different disciplines shared the collaborative work: it was a joint group of great stimulation and benefit—playwrights, scene designers, costumers, composers, choreographers, actors, and pupils. They were all mutually stimulated. The air crackled.

The students who benefited from this wide spectrum of thinking included many of our most effective theater leaders. Besides the dancers, who number most of our modern-dance soloists, there were Gregory Peck, Efrem Zimbalist, Jr., Eli Wallach, and Joanne Woodward, and, as mentioned, Marian Seldes and the designer Jean Rosenthal.

The Lewisohn sisters and Mrs. Morgenthau were aided in every way—financially, administratively, and artistically—by Edith Julia Isaacs, a remarkable woman whose father was the owner of a prosperous shoe factory in Milwaukee. Her mother's family included successful stockbrokers and realtors in New York City, and Edith was the inheritor of a very considerable fortune. This she placed at the service, not of the poor young people of the city as did the Lewisohns, but of literary and dramatic criticism. She was the editor of the *Milwaukee Sentinel* in 1903. The following year she married Lewis Isaacs of New York, a young lawyer of wide aesthetic interests. (He had been a pupil of the composer Edward MacDowell at Columbia University.) Edith started the *Theater Arts Magazine* in 1918, which became *Theater Arts Monthly* in 1924. It was probably the best journal of critical and scholarly essays on the theatrical arts and news printed in English. Through it Mrs. Isaacs was instrumental in discovering and fostering Eugene O'Neill and Thornton Wilder, among others.

In her words, the magazine's policy was to "believe in the theatre as an art, an art which is its own master and which we can serve . . . a vital educational factor; and an activating force in social progress." These are fine and fancy sentiments, and they matched Miss Lewisohn's.

Martha was more direct and simple: "The theater was a verb before it was a noun."

Both points of view are helpful.

With her mind, which was brilliant, and her fervor, which was intense, and the additional fervor of her husband, who abetted her in all ways, and her money, Mrs. Isaacs was able to cement the efforts of the Lewisohns. She knew everyone in the literary world of America and England, and she was conversant with the theater personalities of the world. Her staff was headed by Kenneth McKowen, co-editor, and her assistants were Stark Young, the novelist and drama critic; John Mason Brown, the lecturer and drama critic; and Carl Carmer, the essayist and critic. Ashley Dukes of London, the playwright, man of letters, and husband of the former Dalcroze dancer and founder of the Ballet Club in London, Marie Rambert, and André Levinson, the Russian dance critic living in Paris, were regular contributors.

Part of Mrs. Isaacs's service was social. She made the Playhouse school known. She made the staff known. She introduced people to one another. Her salon was one of the best in the country. The names are the great legends: La Argentina, the greatest Spanish dancer of her day; Harald Kreutzberg, Mary Wigman and Kurt Jooss, the German modern dancers; Vicente Escudero, who excelled in Spanish gypsy and *zapateado* (heel work); Uday Shankar, who brought us the true beauty of authentic East Indian dancing; and Harriet Cohen, the English pianist, a pupil of Matthay. Mrs. Isaacs refused to serve any alcoholic beverages during Prohibition. With meticulous legality she maintained temperance. However, her cuisine was so exquisite, the talk so good, and her personality so warm and gracious that everybody came anyway and nobody complained about the missing cocktail. I remember many soirees, with Mrs. Isaacs stretched out on the chaise longue, rather like the great French salonist Madame de Staël. Mrs. Isaacs, by then in her late fifties, also weighed a great deal. She had magnificent, unforgettable dark eyes, a soft and lovely voice, and a mind of intricacy and power. She could talk. And she could listen.

Who could forget the beautiful high-ceilinged rooms, flower filled, with fires lit, and crowded with vivacious people, young and old, sober, happy voiced, talking enthusiastically and effectively about what they believed in. These were intellects and doers, the best of the theater (not music; Edith Isaacs did not concern herself particularly with music) and journalism. I remember once sitting at a small table with Mary Wigman, La Argentina, and Martha Graham. The first two were the leaders in dance for, respectively, Germany, Austria-Hungary, and Scandinavia, and Spain, South America, and Paris; the third was the leading new creator in North America, and shortly in the world. There was class here, and success. A provocative scene, with the enormous-eyed hostess recumbent in the middle or seated behind the coffee urn and sparking the conversation like a dynamo.

It was the beginning of the Depression. It was cold outside. But within those hospitable rooms, inside by the fire and among those people, one was alive with generative force.

Mrs. Isaacs threw her motherly wing around Martha, shielding her, protecting her, favoring her. Martha was always invited to these evenings, and she came whenever she could, because Mrs. Isaacs treated her as though she were her own daughter. Or, rather, as though she were recognized universally and on a par with all the most distinguished guests. Edith Isaacs put herself firmly and forever behind Martha's career.

And so did Mrs. Morgenthau, who doted on Martha, intrigued that though poor, she was always neatly and stylishly dressed and always, for any occasion outside of the classroom, wore gloves. This may have been endearing, but Rita Morgenthau was far from a fool, and she fully valued Martha's truly great qualities.

Edith Isaacs persuaded Stark Young to go to Martha's concerts. He had already seen her in the *Follies* in 1924 and 1925, but at that time had not thought her dancing worth mentioning. Mrs. Isaacs persuaded him to see Martha's newest works.

"She looks as though she were about to give birth to a cube," Young wrote. Isaacs persuaded him to go back. He began to reorganize his perceptions. She took him back yet again, and in a review published in the April 21, 1941, issue of *The New Republic,* Stark Young showed himself to be one of Martha's stoutest adherents:

Miss Martha Graham in my opinion is the most important lesson for our theatre that we now have. She has come more and more to exemplify some of our stage's chief needs and to illustrate fine possibilities where it may have deficiencies and gaps. Her work can be studied for its search after stage gesture in the largest sense, some discovered and final movement. And it can be imitated in the perpetual revision and recomposing that she does in her search for the right emphases, and the right pressure to be given them, as if she were feeling for the bones of the work's body, within the flowing articulation of the whole. The point here is not that everything we see Miss Graham do is beautiful or perfect, the point is scraping back to the design, the lyric and almost harsh resolution, to be honest toward it. This projection and this firm statement of the emphases are what the ordinary acting needs to discipline its shiftless inconsequence.

All of these women—and they were all women, and most of them Jews—loved and believed in Martha and tried to help in every way, short of making up a purse that would keep her in necessities. Graham still lacked the rudimentary aids that a professional theater worker needs—a permanent wardrobe mistress and a secretary. She was invariably asked to the ladies' parties, however, and introduced as "our greatest dancer," "the name we can count on." And at these events she met the European great with their entourages, as a cloistered nun meets princes. She was powerful as one set apart, dedicated, recognized, but was without means to mix equally on worldly terms.

|||||

Although the school did not stress performing techniques, they worked continuously at plays. Martha participated in some of the company rehearsals, and not always in roles which she later played onstage. Sophie Maslow remembered one rehearsal that taught the students much about acting. The subject was the Israelites at the Wailing Wall. Irene Lewisohn's manner of directing was to state the theme rather vaguely and encourage free improvisation. The students then all took off simultaneously, and there was a general writhing, crying, wringing of hands, and beating of breasts. It was quite lively and totally unmoving. Martha stood in their midst as a mourner, absolutely still. Inevitably it was *her* figure that everybody watched, *her* face, with its fearful acceptance, that caught everybody's breath. The other students never forgot. They had learned about economy.

Once a year the Lewisohn sisters gave a public dance concert at the Mecca Auditorium (now the New York City Center). For these they imported Nikolai Sokoloff and the entire Cleveland Symphony Orchestra, and for these few shows the sisters granted themselves the unusual luxury of closing off all the auditorium seats downstairs, placing the orchestra in the stalls, and selling to the public only balcony seats, because these had a better viewing angle for dance. This arrangement was artistically sound but financially disastrous, a proceeding of such monetary waste as to cause professional amazement and mirth up and down Broadway. The sisters Lewisohn cared not at all.

These annual dance productions were memorable in many ways. The stars of the evenings were generally Martha Graham and Charles Weidman, borrowed from his own school for these occasions. The cast was recruited each year haphazardly from various companies and rehearsed specifically for these few performances. (I was once asked to play a Tartar camel boy in *Prince Igor* but declined the role as miscasting, being a big-busted, well-hipped, hale and hearty wench of blatant sexual attributes.)

"Martha was wonderful. I loved working with her," said Charles Weidman, but he added, a trifle wickedly:

In the *Pagan Poem,* (Carl Loeffler), which was based on a bit from one of Virgil's eclogues, I was her lover who wanted to roam. I mounted a sort of pyramid. She started her incantation as the bereft woman and began running around its base in an enlarging circle, attracting him by centrifugal force, drawing him in in great spirals, and back to her. One day something happened, I don't know what. Martha started the incantation and she continued with the circles getting larger and larger, until she went right out the theater door and home. It was twenty-five minutes before the cast realized she had departed for the day. Martha was back again the next afternoon, warmed up, dressed, ready to work, no explanation.

The cast contained Maria Ouspenskaya, Ronny Johansson, and Benjamin Zemach,* among others. And a young actor was there to see what he could learn, Henry Fonda. He got somewhere, I believe. He's from Nebraska like me."

The choreography for these occasions usually evolved in committee discussions between Irene Lewisohn and the soloists. As she was always fraught with emotion and very nearly incoherent, the going could be slow, and Martha and Charles Weidman more than once decamped in the middle of the long discussions, hired themselves a hall where they could arrange their own choreography unhampered, and got down to serious work. This was true for Richard Strauss's *Ein Heldenleben,* and they did not return to Miss Irene until they had settled on some basics, such as which direction to go in and precisely when to start and when to stop.

Ein Heldenleben was their last performance together. Charles went back under Doris Humphrey's jealous eye and obediently stayed there. He was valuable to Doris. Doris looked on Martha as a devourer.

In any case, Martha's Group at this point consisted solely of girls, and she was not prepared to choreograph for men, nor did she think in terms or pieces involving men. Since leaving Ted Shawn, Martha had never danced with a man, except with Charles Weidman on tour and special occasions, not even in the *Greenwich Village Follies.* She taught men mainly at the Neighborhood Playhouse, but she did not promote them into Valhalla. Only those outstanding female talents

---

*Maris Ouspenskaya had been a charter member of Stanislavski's Moscow Art Theater and later became a character actress on Broadway and in Hollywood. Ronny Johansson was a concert dancer who had studied in Sweden and Germany. Benjamin Zemach was born in Russia and came to America with the Hebrew-language Habimah Theater, founded by his brother, Naum. In 1937 Benjamin choreographed *Pins and Needles* for the International Ladies Garment Workers Union.

who became manifest in her school classes were recruited into her Group and invited to join the select coterie of self-immolators who developed Graham's early essays on rebellion and punishment. They knew they were to be sacrificial, and they were glad to be. And they looked at Martha with the eyes of revelation.

o artist is ahead of his time. He *is* his time,"
said Martha Graham.

In my readings about the history of dancing I have never
heard of a group quite like the early modern-dance groups,
particularly the groups of Martha and Doris. They had the
fervor of a medieval religious cult and the physical energy
of the ancient Greek athletes, who were quite willing to die
in order to obtain the Marathon laurels. Not since the
Middle Ages and the years of cloistered religious have
people banded together to work with similar dedication,
faithfulness, and sacrifice. Money had nothing to do with
this sense of purpose. There was no money. Fame had little
to do with it. There was to be scant fame, and not for the
dancers, in any case. And they knew it. It was the religion,
the idea that they served. It has never happened before in
the theater, I believe, and it does not happen now. These
young women and, later, men were serving an aesthetic
idea as though it were the safety of their country or the
lives of their beloveds, and no amount of privation or

hardship shook their fidelity. One can only study the phenomenon and marvel. Certainly Martha could not have done what she did, what she felt she was destined to do, without them. They were her tool, the material of her craft, her bodyguard, her family, her means of existence, and they will prove to be in time the means of her preservation. The fact that they existed for so long as a unit and worked to such purpose is testimony to her enormous power as a personality and to the force and power of the ideas she generated.

When Martha said that she wanted to form a company of dancers using a new technique and doing new kinds of work, the cry was taken up in unexpected places and passed from enthusiast to enthusiast. And the young students gathered—from all over the United States, from all over the world, the pupils came to Martha, making their way east however they could, with barely enough money for train fare and with no money for maintenance, with not a promise—not even Martha's guarantee of sharing. They came on the bare chance of joining the group.

Martha did not advertise, and few people wrote about her, but word got out. In Seattle, Chicago, Dallas, Boston, New Orleans, Rochester, Honolulu, or across town, wherever she taught, all through the dancers' grapevine, the word got out. "Come." And they borrowed money for the trip and slaved in order to stay. This was a curious thing.

Martha began to recruit a permanent and enlarged group. Gertrude Shurr, Martha Hill, Bessie Schönberg, and Anna Sokolow were already with her.

Anna Sokolow was born in Hartford, Connecticut, of Polish parents, and brought to New York as a baby. She had gone to school at a settlement house, the Emmanuel Sisterhood. Her dance talent was marked, and the head of the settlement house decided that the girl needed better teaching. Anna, with the help of her teachers, went to the Neighborhood Playhouse, where Irene and Alice Lewisohn took a personal interest in her, admitting her to their permanent repertory company. Here Anna worked with Martha and Louis. Anna's mother, otherwise an enlightened and revolutionary woman, disapproved of Martha, of her life-style and her work, and forbade Anna to continue studying. To prevent her from attending classes, she locked Anna in the bathroom. But Anna found a way out through the window: she went down some pipes to a fire escape and ran away to Martha and the Neighborhood Playhouse school. She eventually became Louis's assistant, learning about music as she proceeded. In 1927, when she was seventeen, she first heard Bach from him and was "dumbfounded and fascinated." She asked about Tchaikovsky: "Too sentimental," Louis said. Scriabin was the only Russian music Louis tolerated. Anna asked about waltzes, polkas, mazurkas: the romantic forms, not the pre-classic forms. His reply was, "There's nothing as old as yesterday's newspaper." He was apprehensive of any of his pupils relying on the strong evocation and suggestibility of the great romantics, and therefore not finding the power of expression within themselves. "You know," he used to say, "you can take a can and put a beautiful wrapping around it, but if there's nothing in the can it's still empty." He encouraged Anna in her own creative efforts, which even then were marked. Anna was always able to satisfy Louis's assignments, and the other girls began to neglect their own pieces to assist in her demonstrations.

The life of a Martha Graham Group member was very hard indeed. Twelve of the dancers lived together, sharing a room in a loft. Anna was the smallest, and took the laundry bag to sleep in. She lived on less than a dollar a day. Of the fifteen dollars a week she got at the Neighborhood Playhouse as Louis's assistant, she gave her mother ten.

In a later group came Nelle Fisher, a pretty ballet dancer with fairy feet. Nelle spoke with warmth, with love, her face lighting up as she remembers "those days, those dear people." When Nelle Fisher joined the group in 1932, the conditions were more or less the same as they had been in the founding years. She came to Martha from Washington and Oregon. She was a bonny dancer with lovely, curly bronze hair, and a pretty doll-face, a dear little face, very unlike the other girls in the group—rather like a Nell Brinkley drawing. She bounced. Louis always called her "the up dancer."

Nelle Fisher said:

I first met Martha in the summer of 1931 in Seattle at the Cornish School. Every summer during the Neighborhood school vacation and the dog days, Martha went to Santa Barbara to spend two or three weeks with her mother. In 1930 and the following years she combined the visit with a teaching stint at the Cornish School, which helped pay for the trip west. Nellie Cornish, who was the founder of the Cornish School, always believed in bringing new and interesting people to teach. Miss Graham came to us with her long, beautiful black hair, very straight, and very white face and very red lips, wearing what looked like a bathing suit. We didn't know the word "leotard." . . . We were still wearing drapes and little pink flowing costumes.

Martha was dramatic in her appearance in class. I, of course, being a teenager, was deeply impressed by this. Louis Horst was with her, this wonderful man, and in his rather rotund appearance, he would get up sometimes and even demonstrate, his little feet and his enormous bulk doing "changements." He called me "Our Ballet Kid." . . . But when I had to turn in for Martha it was a very strange feeling altogether. We did lots of exercises with the legs in parallel position—brand new.

We—Bonnie Bird, Dorothy Bird [no relation], Beverly Bostick—got the fever. We went to the Graham exercises as if there was no tomorrow. I went alone to the Graham concerts at the Metropolitan Theater in Seattle because my family despised dancing and wouldn't go with me.

I couldn't believe what I was seeing on that stage. She was so . . . fragile and so strong and so beautiful . . . in a stark way, of course, and completely new. Right then my whole life changed. Before she left she said, "One of you is doomed to be a dancer." [Graham often said this to classes without singling out any particular girl. Each student was free to believe she was the chosen. Nelle Fisher received the stigmata.]

I followed her east and west to the Neighborhood Playhouse and was thrilled to receive twelve dollars a week, out of which I paid five dollars for sharing an apartment and eight dollars for food—cereals, tomato juice, the cheapest things we could buy. I learned how to make stews. I learned how to make chocolate pudding. I learned how to make things that were nourishing. I learned to eat oatmeal, which I had never liked, but it is filling. I lived on it, and got through the winter and it was fun. Some of the girls set up living at the Studio Club, which was safe, from my father's point of view.

It was overwhelmingly exciting to be in New York alone, but there were lots of times after I had joined the company when I thought, "How can I go on?" In the summer while Martha went west I would take whatever job I could get—in counseling, camp work, whatever—and then come back and live on my savings. We were able to, you know. Fifteen dollars a week could pay for a brownstone apartment with three girls sharing—about forty-five dollars a month all together. Today it would probably be two hundred and seventy-five each, or more.

But there were no extras, and no money for illness or accidents. It was frightening and always wearing. Finally, in despair I went to Martha. She always found time to talk to anyone who wanted to see her. . . . And I told her . . . I had to do something to make a living in order to continue.

She helped me get a job at the Radio City Music Hall while I studied with her for two years, I also got Louis's training in composition at the Playhouse. He let me take his course twice free and it was marvelous. It has always helped me. . . . I continued to study with Graham, and then she put me into her company. We got nothing at all for rehearsals, ten dollars for a concert, and we did two concerts a year. That's twenty dollars a year. We didn't expect to be paid. We almost didn't want to be, because, you know, it was complete dedication, like a sisterhood.

Dorothy Bird said:

I arrived at the Cornish School from Victoria Island concurrently with Nelle. We had come from all over: Alaska, California, Oregon, Chicago, British Columbia, and God knows where. It was expensive in those days, four dollars a lesson, but the students came. All the teachers were distinguished people. Every department was magnificent. There was an exquisite little theater, a magnificent setup for the practice room, wooden floors with springs, windows all the way around, maids, showers, and care for the students as you have never seen. This was paid for by Miss Cornish and her faithful patrons.

Martha was simple, direct, purposeful, with great authority. And Louis came bumbling after. "Call me Martha," Martha said. We were all staggered. Martha started immediately, in a great hurry, to teach us how to move, because she was going to use us in a performance of Aeschylus's *The Seven Against Thebes*. She had no ready technical exercises. She didn't have any demonstrators, so she had to show us everything herself, and she could—superbly.

I worked four and a half hours a day plus rehearsals and three classes. Oh, I came out flying, absolutely flying. We were so tired at night that we would go down to the cafeteria and sit on the tables, dangling our legs, because we couldn't rest our sore feet on the floor.

Everybody was hypnotized, absolutely magnetized by Martha. It was like a mass falling in love, but much, much more. It was more than a crush. She opened our eyes to the arts. I was on fire.

The dances were composed for a single performance and an audience of two hundred. Martha didn't care. It was the work that mattered.

And we were dancing. And we were acting and suggesting things that could not be seen but were only talked about. We were making theater.

"I'll see you in New York," Martha said.

How? Why, if Dorothy were to get a job with Childs restaurants, the management would move her gradually eastward, job by job, from location to location. But Dorothy's brothers, who had come into a small inheritance, magnanimously offered her their entire share, which gave her enough money to get on a train immediately. She arrived in New York knowing nothing about the city, including directions. She was so totally innocent and trusting that she thought it rude to shut the door of her boarding-house bedroom. The bootlegger in the next room found this provocative.

Dorothy Bird, in her rosy-cheeked, ebullient way, applied for a job. This was during the heart of the Depression. And so astonished were the prospective employers—astonished at her exuberance, her health, her patent innocence, her dairymaid presence—that she was given four jobs in one day. The first was flipping pancakes in the window of a Childs restaurant on Wall Street. By the time she found out where Wall Street was and how to get there, the job had been given away. Another was in a White Plains Show rehearsing at the Roseland studios on Broadway. She couldn't do tap on toe (tap dancing on pointe) but became so alarmed at the rather cozy suggestion of help from the dance director that she took refuge in the dressing room, where she discovered that all her money (eight dollars) had been stolen. The third job was as a hat-check girl, but she mixed up the tickets and was instantly fired. The fourth job, procured for her in despair by Gertrude Shurr, was at the Three Fold Restaurant, the dancers' haven, as a tray girl. She was told to clear the tables. She cleared them, snatching spoons from mouths and cups of unfinished coffee from hands. The management expressed dissatisfaction.

Martha became hysterical with amusement, concern, and exasperation. She persuaded Mrs. Morgenthau to give Dorothy a living scholarship of fifteen dollars a week, and Dorothy joined the troupe of apprenticed students that existed on sawdust and followed their star:

We lived about four in a room and there was a little room off into which those who had a boyfriend or a husband went about once a week for privacy. And anybody who worked brought hamburgers or spaghetti. No hot water, of course. We used to borrow a quarter for the day from each other: breakfast was fifteen cents; the subway was five cents. And we used to have soup. You'd go to these Second Avenue places where there were a lot of rolls and butter and free pickles with soup on any order. Nobody thought about getting proper meals. I don't remember the least bit of anxiety. It was very happy. The daily classes were wonderful. Anna Sokolow was there, May O'Donnell, Gertrude Shurr, Jane Dudley, Sophie Maslow, Lily Mehlman, Anita Alvarez, Bonnie Bird, Nelle Fisher, and later Pearl Lang.

What mesmerized the new students who gathered around Martha was not only the forming, extraordinary technique but Martha's point of view and attitude toward the work, her credo, which she had particularly inherited from Ruth St. Denis. Martha did not regard dancing and the theater as forms of entertainment, and certainly not as a means of making money. It was to her, as it had been to Ruth in her best days, and it must be reiterated, like a religious celebration, a service, and she felt the experience as a deep revelation of life. She was used by it, therefore, and the preparation of her body, of her concentration, and of her spirit was as quiet and dedicated a function as prayer. Further, the choice and training of her pupils, the fostering of their attitudes and their techniques, the choice of costume and props were as significant as the choice of religious vestments to a holy service, which derive their significance from hundreds of years of believing, work, and prayer. This is why in her achieved works, the atmosphere in her theater was of such intensity, the effect so shaking, that many of the beholders never recovered and were marked for life. And many of her pupils bear witness to the fact that their viewpoint toward the theater was then and thereafter changed. That is why the pupils were willing to come and work with no thought of recompense or worldly betterment. All the time she was training their bodies in muscular disciplines, she was talking to them in these terms and only in these terms.

|||||

After their day's bread-and-butter work, teaching, practicing, or waiting on tables, the girls met nightly to continue the creative work with undiminished energy. The technique constantly expanded, invading the body's immemorial habits. Martha's rehearsals were not merely repetitive ("rehearsal" in French is *"répétition"*) but essentially creative events.

Martha discovered the knee, the leg hinge. Not the bent knee used in crouching and squatting by Orientals and by certain Slavic peasants, and used by Occidentals in bowing and kneeling, but the bent knee as support, which had been outlawed with us and was abhorrent to all ballet dancers. Martha was the first to use the supporting knee as a hinge, with the body straight, straight spine lowered, balanced, and cantilevered backward—a position of danger, one instinctively feels, because the body cannot save itself from falling except by the unflinching support of the iron thigh. And it is this very sense of peril that gives excitement. There is, in fact, danger. Strong, straight back, lifted pelvis, strong thighs provide the only safety. The whole inclined structure rests on the seven inches of foot. This was new.

On the hinge of the bent knee, with the inclining torso and the weight of the extended arms as counterbalance, by rising on the toes and bending the knees further, the whole body could be lowered to the floor if desired. On this hinge, this stem, a new life could flower, floating, swimming, hovering, not aerial but semi-weightless, not like anything before, suggesting ecstasy.

Mechanically it proved an incomparable tool. The ground could be reached simply by overextending the balance and leaning back farther—and the ground not as a termination but as a new element to be explored by every part of the body. Hullo, new brothers, earthworms, eels, fishes, snakes! The earth now also was ours. Let us but find foothold and then in one count, up, the whole, swinging structure. No more folding, squatting, hunkering down, adjusting the burden of the bottom like the telescoping of an old camera apparatus. It was entirely a question of weight cantilevered backward and out on the bent knee. That simple! Unknown in 1925, now taken for granted by dancers all over the world.

Martha then discovered that the knee could be used for perambulation, for spinning, even for pirouettes. If the girls would come back the next night, they would see how. No knee pads. That was sissy. They'd toughen up. Get the knees to the earth and move. Burrow!

Never mind if it hurt, and it did. It gave an enormous addition to emotional language.

It also took its toll on the kneecaps. Nelle Fisher said, "We had no pads or anything. We didn't even wear tights. We were on bare flesh. I don't know how we stood it. I have unfortunate knees myself, and so right from the beginning it was very difficult for me. Some people *can* do these things. Very few. Martha had no trouble at all. She must have had flat knees because she still was able to do them at eighty-four."

The Graham knee work never got easier. It was virtuoso decades later, and Mark Ryder developed knee problems which remained for many years. Martha, he said, had "tables" on her knees. (Much later she was to caution her students, "Be careful of the kneecap. It is *delicate.*" She should certainly know.) In 1946, in *Dark Meadow,* the men were asked to do a pas de bourrée on their knees, carrying the girls. Mark Ryder can still do two pirouettes on his knee.

As is obvious, there was always a level of fanaticism, even masochism, in the Graham dancers. They came to be known as the "Graham Crackers," and their fanaticism held to such a degree that it kept the disciples from mentioning pain, Martha comfortably believing that if the weight of the body were held properly, the knee wouldn't bruise. Mark thought that the weight was just the same on the kneecap, whether properly held or not, on a believer or a nonbeliever. But they were, as he said, all "dedicated nuts."

The value of these new discoveries was not altogether in their own beauty and the widening of the scope of movement but in the fact that they were fresh and had no connotations, no suggestions, no reminders of other forms and other patterns. The ideas they clothed could therefore be studied for their own intrinsic worth, without relation to any derivations or inheritances.

IIIII

"It takes five years to learn to run, ten years to learn to walk, and fifteen years to stand still," Martha said.

Martha herself had no real elevation,* according to Anna Sokolow. She had a sort of spring. The great jumps and the delicate, brilliant, quick footwork Martha could not do; she left them entirely alone. And although she added some jumps later, when she had men in her group, she never used the foot in any of the ways that a ballet dancer does. Martha's jumps are poundings or strikings or wrenchings upward, not liftings or soarings. There was no frivolity of fingers or toes, and this is certainly a charming part of the scale of movement.

The permeation of emotion through gesture, the "going deep" into one's body, the projection into space beyond the reach of one's fingers—this touches on the border of the psychic, and Martha codified this wild power, tamed it within the studio. But it was there, alive, and the original girls knew it, with awe for its power.

And Martha was there to effect the transformation from muscles to emotion.

"Martha is as hard in rehearsal as her instinct tells her she dares to be," said Sophie Maslow. "It makes the dancers unhappy, but it does goad them to tremendous efforts. She's a tough girl. She drives."

"She would sometimes tongue-lash the girls," continued Nelle Fisher. "Oh, yes, she could put you down under the boards. Sometimes

---

*"Elevation" is the term applied to the ability to rise vertically and dance in the air, to jump for height rather than lateral space or distance. Very few women can match even the most mediocre male dancer and only a handful in ballet history can outjump a man in height (Taglioni, Savina, Sokolova). The term "ballon" is also used in ballet to denote lightness, aerial quality, and height in jumps.

it was beyond the point of being helpful. It was destructive. It takes a long time to get the body to move the way you want it to, and we're all so different. Her technique didn't work on my body easily because of the bone structure. I found all of this very, very difficult."

Martha wanted the gesture to push effort to its limits, to the point of extremity. She had a hatred of all complacent dances. "This doesn't tear," she would say.

"If she didn't like the degree of intensity that they were working with, she demanded it of them, *demanded,*" said Nelle Fisher. Martha demanded "divine distortion"—her phrase to indicate exaggeration beyond realistic imitation of gestures, which added emphasis and power to the idea by bringing in cartoon caricature.

At first, of course, Martha was *the* exponent of the Graham technique, *the* Graham dancer. But gradually, as more and more dancers came, with varying degrees of preparedness and ability, they brought to her new gifts of ability, all of which she absorbed and exploited. And the Graham technique changed. It changed with an enormous rapidity as her girls were deputized by her for teaching and rehearsing, the raw idiosyncrasies rubbed smooth with practice. Martha's limitations disappeared; the great dynamic discoveries passed into other, younger bodies, with larger, stronger muscular disciplines; the gestures expanded, grew easy, blended, developed, grew beautiful, grew permanent. This is the way ballet dancing developed. This is the way all dancing must develop, the changes working themselves into the language. Shakespeare is now part of everyman's speech. If Martha jerked, she was tugging on the strings of life, although her kite was out of sight in the dark.

|||||

The hours for rehearsal were not regular. Martha would say, "We'll not work tomorrow. You have the evening free." And then, quite often, they'd work through the evening anyway. This, of course, was disappointing and maddening to husbands, and Martha knew it. Yet she suited her own whim and her own feeling of readiness or unreadiness.

One of the husbands, the writer Joseph Campbell, thought that she deliberately kept changing times in order to keep the group at her beck and call. "We never knew when Jean [Erdman, his wife] was going to be called. It was like being a fireman. You know, the fire alarm rings and down you go."

Who shall say a word for the husbands of the "Graham Crackers"?

They were asked to donate their connubial contentment and accept exile without a murmur, and on the whole they did. Their women were in rehearsal every night and on weekends, for Martha rarely had less than a full complement of women, even on holidays, even on Christmas Eve. But on one New Year's Eve the husbands went on strike, stormed the studio, and dragged the women out. But only once.

Why did the men stay? They loved their wives.

Why did the girls stay?

"She was a gawd," said Anna Sokolow. And her voice shook as she said it.

The chosen girls, the girls who had seen revelations, stayed on and waited, went hungry and worked toward the next concert. Such devotees could not be fobbed off with anything shoddy. Indeed, the very meaning of their lives depended on the authenticity of Graham's work. And Martha answered the demands, and she was the only one who ever did. Later many of them tried to repeat the process in their own right elsewhere, but it wasn't the same. The godhead was not catching.

Martha's standards for herself were no less punishing; in truth, they were harder. Since she threw away all the pieces that seemed to her unfinished, never accepting the nearly right, it turned out that she threw away nine-tenths of what she worked out. The girls grew desperate because they could not keep, even for a single trial, whole minutes of beautiful dance invention: it wasn't what she wanted, it wasn't what she was after, she wouldn't have it, and she had sufficient confidence in her fecundity to be profligate.

Her standards were absolute and merciless, and her works were blessedly brief, until the composers made her expand them for their own purposes. Martha communicated in direct messages, like telegrams. The fault with most modern dancers, even the best, is overextension, and therefore tedium. Not so with Martha. She cut. She eliminated. "Like a sculptor," said John Martin, "chipping away marble. I don't want this. I don't need that." One is mindful of Diaghilev's dictum, "The hallmark of genius is elimination."

Pearl Lang remarked, "The words for Martha are succinctness and economy." But Nelle Fisher regretfully added, "What she threw out were great dances. The movement that she was experimenting with was unusually beautiful."

Nor did Martha compose everything she used. Gradually, after the girls had been with her for some years, and after they had taken the requisite courses from Louis and had appeared with him in his concert-demonstrations, she would permit them to work out alone sections which did not involve her. She would sometimes permit the company members to work up their own pieces, as she did in 1952 with Pearl Lang in the role of Death in *Canticles for Innocent Comedians.*

I remember the night when Martha had dinner with me and said afterward, "I have to go to the studio now because Pearl is working on her solo. When the door finally opens to reveal Death, what is revealed had better be pretty damned good." And off she trotted, ten-thirty at night, to work for who knows how many hours alone with her student, hunting for something adequate to convey Death. I saw the piece as it was revealed, and when the doors of the temple opened and there was a seated figure hidden behind a real flowering dogwood tree, it was indeed "pretty damned good."

But it must be remembered always that Pearl knew Martha's style and idiom intimately, had studied and performed with her exclusively for years, had taken all of Louis's courses, and had demonstrated for him, composing dances to illustrate his lectures. She was a seasoned, experienced Grahamite. Martha never allowed a beginner to have anything whatever to say; but it was in this manner, for Louis and for Martha, that many of the students learned the basics of their trade. They also tasted blood, and some of them began to yearn for independence.

When Martha accepted sections of movement they had composed, the dancers were bewitched. They came to feel that they, too, were part of the creation. And indeed they were. "When she took something of ours, it was the greatest honor that could happen," said Stuart Hodes, a leading dancer with the company from 1947 to 1958. "Choreographers these days are not afraid to take something from a dancer. Martha was not. And dancers who are contemptuous of the choreographer who takes from them don't understand how marvelous it is to work together with a choreographer who is creative and to have something of yours included.

"Very often those sections that Martha was not involved in we personally worked out ourselves. This meant, of course, that we worked in a style so homogeneous with Graham's that the work could be combined seamlessly. This is one of the reasons, I think, that these remarkably gifted women seldom developed individual styles, ones that were inherently different from their leader's."

"But make no mistake about it," said Pearl Lang, "the initiative was Martha's. The original germ idea was Martha's, and the realization hers as well. The dancers might work on the problem as an exercise or as a facet of a role. They might develop it, expand it; but she was there every second of the time, shaping, molding, modeling. Her hands were never off it, like a sculptor's. What the students did was to clarify the movement, codify it for teaching others. In this way they were of enormous help, but they were absolutely dependent on her fundamentally."

On her own solo pieces, Martha often worked alone, late at night or in the morning, since the Group members had to earn their livings and were unavailable during the day.

"Even way back then," Sophie Maslow explained, "she knew what she was working for and we all recognized her knowledge. It spoiled me for anyone else in terms of wanting to study elsewhere. It didn't seem worthwhile doing. This was the way movement meant something, the way she was moving, and those people who worked with her believed this."

When Martha entered the lonely practice hall, it was not to rehearse known gestures but to put herself at the mercy of atavistic instincts. She did not know what used her or how, but she was ready and exposed, and occasionally it happened. A kind of transubstantiation did occur.

Most members of the Group had no other dance technique and were just working girls who gave their lives and their bodies to Martha for shaping. They were intelligent and ambitious and capable of the special gift of dedication. Martha was not a religious teacher, nor was she at that time even a proven artist. The students took the incredible chance that what she was after might not be any good. But they were intelligent and perceptive and they saw that it was good.

And they recognized the fire of inspiration burning in this tormented young woman. Well, she was not so very young: she was in her late thirties. But in terms of art she was young, because she was unknowing and struggling to find a new way. They followed her, and, much more difficult, they waited. They sat on the floor while Martha thought things out, sometimes with her head in her hands, sometimes standing looking out the window, sometimes standing with her head on her breast, sometimes trying one thing, another thing, something else again, fifty minutes, an hour, whatever was needed. They didn't speak. They didn't rush around getting tea or coffee. They waited. They did not sit and watch to see what was there for them, or even how to imitate exactly, which is what ballet students do. They sat watching the development of ideas and the gradual clarification of emotion in physical terms. And they marveled.

Once in a great while they would go to the dressing room and talk. Mainly they sat and waited until she finally said, "Try this." And then they'd get up and try. Very frequently there was no music, and they would just try with their cold muscles to do what she wanted, or thought she wanted. And she was the essence of their emotional reason and they fed off her even as they feared her.

It was hard to say always where a class ended and a rehearsal began, or where the material of one differed from the material of the other. Martha's own girls, the Group, came to her every evening at around six o'clock and stayed until ten or thereabout—and there were times when she did nothing for three hours and then they would go home. And they would be back again the next night with enthusiasm and sit until she told them to get up. And if it looked fine they all were happy, and if it didn't suit she lashed out at them.

"We spent hours in that studio waiting," said Nelle Fisher, "and then she'd finally say, 'I can't do any more.' And we stopped. Maybe some of us wouldn't have done anything for an entire evening. Maybe only one or two."

And if the block continued: Hell! Anger, morbid depression, despondency, collapse!

She never explained to them what she wanted. Indeed, she very likely didn't know. She never explained the projects or the problems. She never talked. They just waited and watched. And when matters became absolutely unendurable they would go and weep on Louis's ample chest, and he would pat them on the head and take them out for a soda.

What Martha said to her pupils, as far as they were concerned, was immortal. There were no tape recorders then, and none of them took dictation. They just knew that they were in the presence of a very great teacher and artist.

With her own performance group, the ideas as well as the technique were shaped, and Martha became translucent. Sometimes she used some of the exercise material in her ballets. Sometimes she rehearsed in class some of the new ideas for her choreography. But technically as well as emotionally, invention never repeated itself or slacked off. There was a new idiom for every piece—a fresh way of maintaining balance, of controlling dynamics—so that if a dancer went away for a year, or even for a few months, as they sometimes did, on returning, that dancer would find herself in a strange land, talking an alien language. The rate of growth was bewildering, and Martha worked as hard in her tenth year as she did in her first, and in her twentieth and in her fiftieth, not just on creative pieces but on actual mechanics. There was a lot of Louis, too, in this growth, and a lot of his concepts. It was a combination. Louis was a structure fiend, and he required the same of her. She flourished under the compulsion.

|||||

Martha kept ample notes, not necessarily about dance movement—that came in experimenting—but ideas for the kinds of movements, the atmosphere, the quality, notes on quotations, observations, anything that might give her a point of attack. Because with Martha the gesture and the emotional thought which prompted it were one. But she would not make use of any idea or any impression, any fantasy, until it was a part of her visceral experience. It was to her like eating: there is the delicious morsel on the dish, inviting to see and taste, but until devoured and converted into body juices, flesh, and bone, it is not really ours. And it was only after the total ingestion of ideas that Martha felt she had the material ready to re-express. That is the difference between her and most of her followers: they have not made the material their own life experience, their own blood and flesh. When she had some of this material absorbed, she began making short scenarios, which grew longer and more detailed when she started commissioning scores and had to be specific with composers.

She always followed more or less the same schedule. She brooded over the subject for a long time, was ill at ease, had pre-birth worries. But, as she would say, she was Irish and could talk herself into a mood and get on with the work. And she was, as she also would say, "dogged by ancestral footsteps." She sat up most of the night (Martha was a night person and did a great deal of her planning and telephoning in the night) and typed scenarios, frequently settling into bed with a small typewriter, cottage cheese, Sanka. The notes were voluminous.

She started physical work always without music or sound, in silence, in order to be free from the hypnotizing audible rhythm and in order not to be seduced by melody. Knowing she was sensitive to both, she wished to train her eye for the visual rhythm, which is less readily perceived. When her pattern was sketched, she would summon Louis Horst for advice on her music, the selection of already composed pieces or the making of new ones. Only after receiving back the finished music did the real choreography begin, for the composer's finished score dictated a new compelling pattern.

Wallingford Riegger, who composed the music for the 1931 *Bacchanale*, said, "When I arrived at her studio I found to my surprise her dance group assembled and ready to perform for me the already completed dance."

As she said, "I am governed by music." There was quite often a struggle between the movement pattern already worked through and the music pattern, but in the end they were reconciled. They had to be. She found this stage of the composition invigorating, the music adding color and accent to the already established design.

Once she advised me to work without the chosen music lest I wear out the inspiration of sound and she advised that the addition of the finished score to established movement patterns would be extremely zestful to me. Many years later, thirty to be exact, she wrote to a friend that she needed a closer association between music and dance, something that went beyond intellectual association, what she called a breath association.

I am not an adept aesthetician, and I could not presume to analyze Martha's sense of design or approach toward design. But I believe she dealt with the elements as a mathematician would; the elements found in geometry, the elements found in physics, in mass, weight, direction, together with the added relationships of all to emotion. For example, a straight line rarely, if ever, occurs in nature, but it does occur in art, and it is used in art with various telling effects. Direction works similar magic. An approaching body produces one kind of emotional line, a receding or departing body another; the meeting of two forces produces visual, kinesthetic, and emotional effects, with a world of suggestibility around them like a penumbra that evokes many ideas and emotions whenever these forms are manipulated. Primitive (and basic) human relationships assume, therefore, almost mystic power. The simple maneuver of turning the face away, for example, removes personality, presence, the force of attention, relationship. Not only that, it seems to alter the relation of the individual to present time and present place, to make here-and-now other-where and other-time. It also shifts the particular personalized individuality to the general and the symbolic. This is the power of the human face and the human regard, and the meeting of the eyes is probably as magic a connection as can be made on this earth, equal to any amount of electrical shock or charge. It represents the heart of dynamism, life itself. The loss of that regard reduces all connections to nothingness and void. It erases. (It is interesting to note that with Eskimos, turning the back is a sign of death and of mourning for death.)

"Turning one's back" has become a common figure of speech. It means withholding approval, disclaiming, negating; and, in fact, in common conduct the physical turning of the back is equated with absolute negation and insult. No back is turned on a royal personage or a figure of veneration or high respect. This is linked with the loss of visual contact and regard. One cuts dead by not meeting the eyes.

We know much about emotional symbols. They have a history and a science, iconography. Those used by the medieval and Renaissance painters were understood by the scholars and artists of the time—but, more wonderful, they mean to us today spontaneously just what they meant then; they seem to be permanent. We dream, Jung tells us, in terms and symbols of classic mythology. Moreover, primitives shut away from classic learning dream in the same terms. Is it not also likely, then, that certain space relations, rhythms, and stresses have psychological significance, that some of these patterns are universal and the key to emotional response, that their deviations and modifications can be meaningful to the artist in terms of his own life experience and that these overtones are grasped by the spectator without conscious analysis?

Doctors are aware of this and utilize the knowledge in diagnosis. The significance of children's manipulation of space in writing and drawing is carefully studied, and the insane are observed for their relation to and use of walls, floor, doorways, heights, and so forth. Obviously these matters are basic to our well-being as land and air animals. And as plants will turn to sunlight or rocks or moisture according to their nature, so we bend toward or escape from spatial arrangements according to our emotional needs. In the diseased mind, the reactions are overwhelmingly overt. But look around any restaurant and see how few sane people will sit at a center table unless the sides are filled up. Yet formerly the king always dined dead center and many times in public.

The individual as a personality, then, has his own code in space and rhythm. It is evolved from his life history and from his race memory or, as Jung calls it, the collective unconscious. It is just the manipulation of these suggestions through time-space that is the material of choreography.

Take, for example, a simple daily gesture like walking forward and shaking hands. There are in this, first, the use of a separate limb common to most vertebrates, the upright position of the spine and head characteristic of man, the instinctively recognized expression of friendliness shared by all species as opposed to the instinctive expressions of fear and distrust. With animals, when approaching a friend, the hair lies flat, the ears are relaxed though alert, and all enlargements and ferocious distentions subside; breathing is normal. So with man. Heart, pulse, and lungs are easy, the eyes alert but neither distended to see danger nor contracted to pinpoint a target; the mouth is closed or smiling because no unusual demands will be made on hearing (to hear extraordinarily in times of acute danger, the mouth is opened and breathing suspends). And since no unusual effort will be demanded, the muscles neither brace nor tremble. The sum total of all this will be spelled out in the rhythm and position of the reaching hand.

But let there occur the slightest rebuff and see now what happens; hackles rise, hair bristles, lips curl to bare incisors, hearts pound, lungs fill, and on the instant all muscles prepare for attack. In ordinary intercourse, this naturally is not visible on full scale. But it needs only the slight widening of the pupil or nostril, the barest flicker of fingertip, to give the signal; the enemy has been recognized and addressed. Further subtle and meaningful modifications take over when the passage alters by the tension of a specific situation—when, for instance, someone who is often frightened of encounter meets a friend, or one who is never frightened meets someone not to be trusted, or two trusting friends meet under dreadful conditions, and so ad infinitum. Within each of these circumstances the body becomes a totally different chemical organization and yet retains the stamp of its own life habits.

It is the actor's art to mimic exactly with a full awareness of all the overtones and significances. The dancer, on the other hand, explodes the gesture to its components and reassembles them into a symbol that has connotations of what lies around and behind the fact, while the implications of rhythm and spatial design add further comment. Of course the choreographer is no more troubled by all this than is the businessman by the enormous anthropological heritage he puts into play every time he casually tips his hat.

Coleridge says of portraiture:

A good artist must imitate that which is within the thing, that which is active through form and figure, and discourses to us by symbols . . . the universal in the individual or the individuality itself—the glance and the exponent of the

indwelling power. . . . Hence a good portrait is the abstract of the personal:
it is not the likeness for actual comparison, but for recollection.

Every gesture is a portrait. Behind it lie the histories of the race and
the individual as well as the comment of the artist.

When I, as an artist, am moved, I must respond in my own instinctive way; and because I am a choreographer, I respond through my
instinctive gestures. I may come into the pattern with conviction and
the excitement of fresh experience, but this will reflect a personality
habit. It cannot be otherwise. Somehow, as in the grooves in a gramophone record, the cutting edge of my emotion follows a track played
deep into the subconscious.

There is a further personal identification in choreography because
most choreographers compose on their own bodies. Certain recurring
steps can be explained simply by the fact that the choreographer
performs these steps well and has a tendency to use them when demon-
strating. Martha Graham had a kick and a particular skip that stood
her in good stead for fifty years. The explanation is simply that her left
leg kicked straight up in a split, 180 degrees—a very spectacular feat.
The right did not; hence the single-legged pattern. (It has been very
interesting to observe over the years that Graham pupils who began by
imitating her mannerisms have gradually eliminated the physical idiosyncrasies and personal accent and maintained the great style unblemished. In *Diversion of Angels* and *Canticle for Innocent Comedians*,
Graham's personal gesture has been purified of all subjective tricks and
stands in the keeping of her disciples as impersonal and abstract as the
ballet code. It is overwhelmingly beautiful.) I am right-legged and
right-footed, and most of the sustaining and balancing work in my
choreography is done on the left leg; many of my dancers have complained bitterly. A dancer with short legs jumps in one manner, whereas
a dancer with longer ones performs the same kind of jumps in quite
another. So with composing. And identical pattern problems take on
the modification of the composer's physique as well as his character
adjustment, for it is always the choreographer who has to start the
moving, and naturally he does it his way. If there were no instrument
on which a song-writer could work except on his own voice, unquestionably his vocal restrictions would shape the melodic line.

The choreographer is also influenced by his performers. If I were to
work, let us say, with a soloist whose arms and back were the strongest
in the dance world and whose phrasing of legato lifts the most beauti-

ful, but whose footwork, on the other hand, and allegro were weaker, quite obviously my composing style would adjust to his needs. Were I to compose with a man of enormous elevation and brilliant *batterie* but less dramatic force, my approach would then be necessarily different. And it must be noted that one works with the dancers at hand. One cannot summon from outer space a dream body capable of anything—or even exactly what one wishes. In the matter of one's own body one has obviously even less choice and must make do.

These simple facts are known instinctively to everyone who manipulates bodies. Sometimes they are verbalized and taught. More often they are simply taken for granted, as they are taken for granted in daily life. But they are the very stuff, the essence, of choreography, and this was the material of Martha's craft.

After a dance had been roughed out, she asked Louis for his critical advice on the dance itself. This he gave with as great a severity as he ever used with a pupil, applying, in Martha's characterization, "his ferocious standards," uncompromising and unyielding to the point of harshness. He was her pounding board. Louis did not so much guide her as discipline her. "That is, he forced her to discipline herself," said Dorothy Bird. He insisted on eliminating all movement, no matter how intriguing, that was pulling a work awry. Stick to your basic material, he ordered. Louis knew exactly where to cut, what to preserve, above all, how to focus a piece. Martha recognized his value. He used to tease her as he teased everyone else, and in this way he made her keep a sense of proportion.

Martha, however, did not always take his criticism with grace. Once she threw a book at his face and left the room, and once she threw his dachshund, Max, at him, slamming the door, not returning for hours, and thus bringing the practice session to a decisive halt. But Louis never yielded. He saw his job as keeping her undeviating. He was disciplined, while Martha was at the mercy of wild impatience—her impatience with others, her impatience with herself. He was therefore vital to the continuation of her work, because when Martha was balked, when she reached a block, which all creative people do, she went to pieces emotionally. The girls might bring themselves to submit to her indecision and wait; *she* couldn't herself, and wouldn't. And when her nerve broke, then her temper broke, and Martha was at that point not a sane woman. It was in any language bad temper, but with the power of this demon personality and her enormous vocabulary she was monumental. She tongue-lashed the pianist, Louis, the girls. According to the composer Norman Lloyd, she even beat them with her fists, or slapped them. At the beginning of her career she used to scream and throw things frequently. Louis sometimes yelled back, but usually he just rode it out, taking action only in extremes.

"We used to watch her with alarm," said Gertrude Shurr. "There were troubles way back in the early Carnegie Hall studio days, at the beginning of her teaching. She had her tantrums because she couldn't draw out of herself all of the devils that she kept inside her. When she couldn't rid herself, cleanse herself, it was just frightful. Louis waited for the purge, when, and only when, would come her wonderful creativity."

Gertrude Shurr remembers that Edith Isaacs came several times and said, "Martha, if you don't control yourself you will never be the artist we want you to be." "But," Gertrude added, "I thought this was the way Martha had to be, because she wasn't a normal human being. She was a genius. We all knew that, and I think she knew it too. But, oh, she was so possessed! It was a sickness sometimes. And it had to come out of her. It had to come out in movement. It had to come."

Gertrude Shurr said that once when Martha was rehearsing *Portals*, to music by Carl Ruggles, she went into a black depression for four days, a depression well laced with whiskey, and the company waited outside her bedroom, in a morbid stupor, as the clock ticked and the performance date drew near. At the end of the ordeal, I was told, Martha rose from her bed and came forth. "Everything is clear now," she said placidly. They "could get on with their work."

W. Somerset Maugham wrote of Paul Gauguin in *The Moon and Sixpence*,

He was passionately striving for liberation from some power that held him. But what the power was and what line the liberation would take remained obscure. Each one of us is alone in the world. He is shut in a tower of brass, and can communicate with his fellows only by signs, and the signs have no common value, so that their sense is vague and uncertain. We seek pitifully to convey to others the treasures of our heart, but they have not the power to accept them, and so we go lonely.

Nelle Fisher added: "Sometimes the blocks lasted for days. Then she'd have a real breakdown, weeping and storming, with Louis trying to hold her head. Finally she'd rise from the dead and everything would be clear. It was pretty frightening."

It was even more frightening on the stage, just before performance day, on the brink. One night Norman Lloyd watched her, the company drawn up behind, in make-up, and Martha wailing and crying. She had slapped a girl, who was now being sick in a corner. Martha's tirade would have done justice to Victorien Sardou. She would not go on—positively could not, nothing was ready, nothing was good enough, and besides, her toe hurt her. Give back the money. Send the audience home.

The spectacle of Martha wailing in terror was unnerving, and it was particularly destructive at such a moment, just before a performance. Louis went up to her at this point, and when she would not quiet down he hit her across the face, open-handed, a great German clout, which undoubtedly was what Martha was waiting for. "Get on stage, you bitch, and dance." Martha stood before him, white and shaking, and then said with great docility, like a child, "Thank you, Louis. Now I can perform."

And the bitch got on with it and was incandescent.

Afterward Martha radiantly received the homage of Mrs. Isaacs, Mrs. Morgenthau, the Misses Lewisohn, and a growing number of her adorers. The company, of course, was in emotional tatters.

Martha Hill enjoyed Graham's rages. "What a wonderful, dramatic, foaming, tremendous exuberance of animal emotions! What a display! I used to marvel at the vigor and imagination. After it was all over Martha was totally ventilated and she could proceed with her work, and if one could just learn to enjoy the tantrum as a spectacle one remained inured and unharmed. And, of course, in the end the work continued, and it was richer for the emotional seasoning."

Paul Taylor, when he was working with her in the late fifties and early sixties, enjoyed the rages. "Feisty!" he said.

Another who found her "feisty" was the British choreographer Antony Tudor, who never worked with Martha but was associated with her on the faculty of the Juilliard School. In 1950 Martha produced a light, even trivial, solo, called *Gospel of Eve*. Tudor hastened to her dressing room afterward and said quite maliciously, "Well, Martha, I wondered when you would start to compromise!" He was answered with a prompt and swift kick in the shins. And this response intrigued him sufficiently to spread the story.

Martha used to say that the American Indians danced toward integration, the Negro toward disintegration; the Indians toward the gathering of control, the awareness of self, the Negro toward abandonment of control and release. Martha honored the Indian. She knew nothing of the Negro or his abandon, and yet it was the Negro frenzies, the voodoo rites, she permitted herself in her rages. She even deliberately sought release in those frenetic bouts of blind anger, choosing a self-perpetration of fury with which to blast the fortress of her unconscious. Behind the walls lay peace, lay gold. The trouble was that a horde of young girls was sucked into the fiery vortex with her, and only a few managed to remain flameproof.

All through these storms and hysterical outbursts Louis held steady, sardonic and kind. And Louis, however severe, was understanding with Martha. But even in these tantrums he would not tell her that a thing was good if it was not, and she came to rely on his truthfulness as on a lifeline.

|||||

They shared this enormous experience, she and her girls, but they shared little else. As has been stressed, Martha was very chary of being closely involved in their personal affairs.

"I always thought of her as part of the establishment," says Anna Sokolow. "She was an extremely proper woman in many ways and considered herself apart, passing above and beyond us. And she was sometimes very waspish. It is true she had a 'noble feeling' for all religions, but she didn't like her girls going to mosques or temples. She talked endlessly about the American folk roots, about Appalachia."

It is obvious that with a personality so commanding and mesmeric as this bewitching woman's, the studio would be awash with girl crushes and boy crushes, with emotional adhesions and fixations, unless Martha, with meticulous austerity, held herself apart. She could have become webbed with emotionalism, and many schools have been so enmeshed. But Martha held to her course of astringent, clean compassion, without involvement, and was therefore able to plot her own course with less distraction.

Had she not done so I think the school and the company would have ceased to exist, and Martha as an artist and as a woman would have become so dreadfully confused as to be rendered ineffective. It is not the strong nor the gifted pupils who seek emotional ties; it is the weak and desperate. The girls, and later the boys, thought she was cold. Better so, better so. Her strength lay in loneliness—or so she felt from the beginning.

Was she resented for her indifference? Disliked? Was she shunned for her temperance and coldness? No, she was not. I will not say she was forgiven; let me say, rather, that she was not judged. Martha was not held accountable for conduct other human beings must answer to. And no one—this is the remarkable point—blamed her.

They were proud to be her instruments. As members of the Group, many girls consented to give up their individuality in performances and to become, at first, members of a chorus, dressed in black, with hair tightly held in nets, whereas Martha wore white or colors with her glossy, dark hair loose, very feminine and lovely. Anna Sokolow is one of the few who resented the chorus uniform. And Martha always placed the tall girls around her to emphasize her own smallness.

She thought that she was entitled to ask everything; more, she quite simply believed that her pupils felt themselves privileged and proud to give up everything.

Dorothy Bird said:

I gave myself to it completely, willingly, and I for one wouldn't have given anything less. I never regretted it. I had a total experience. Martha just took our insides out and inhabited the body. She ate out the inner shell. She believed that it was all right to do so. And she said, "I have to break this one and that one and then rebuild them." And of course you can't rebuild anybody you break. She felt royal, with divine right, grace. I felt it too. That was the way it was. And as long as I was growing a little I accepted it. She always used you totally or not at all. She felt that each one of us would be glad to be used as a Johnny-one-note, and she developed each of our particular notes very beautifully. But in developing them, she did not develop that note in anyone else, so *we* couldn't grow as rounded artists. But I felt it an honor to be part of it, as she felt it was.

Martha used the adulation, but she could not afford to be encumbered by it. She was absolutely self-centered; her "enraptured selfishness," as Walter Prude, Martha's manager in the early forties, called it, isolated her. Well, she had lots to do and little time. Haughtiness was one of her tools, a necessary way of life. But to her co-workers it may often have seemed otherwise.

In spite of all this, Martha could be motherly. Patricia Birch, who came to her very young, testified to this:

In the midst of having gone through all her beautiful imagery, at the end of class she'd say to me, "Patsy, have you had your orange juice?," which was darling. It really was. And then she'd call up my parents and say, "You can't let her ride horses anymore. She's slightly bowlegged as it is." And then she'd call me and say that either I must stop riding or she was not going to continue paying much attention to me. So I stopped riding. But she cares, she cares. I think she'd like to care about all of her people. Think of the number! You know, she'd promise people things because she'd see the desperate hope in their eyes and did not want to disappoint them. . . . I really think that Martha attracts highly neurotic women. But—and this is important—she also gets a real kind of honest devotion, and she earns it.

Martha herself was a divine child, and although often treated as a baby Dalai Lama, nonetheless she remained a baby.

Martha was revealed to me as a very little girl, someone I barely knew, a vulnerable, frightened, irrational infant, when I once took her and Louis to my country home at Merriewold in the woods. There I had her under my roof for the first time and could observe her in everyday situations. I had given them separate bedrooms, as Martha wished. What was my astonishment when Martha, our lioness, our Joan of Arc, refused to let me put out her lamp after dark, preferring the danger of fire to the mystery of our spring night (we had no electricity at that time, so it was a kerosene lamp). I, who couldn't say no to my mother, who lived hemmed in with Edwardian strictures, had looked to Martha as the great blazing innovator, and I found that like a timid child she was afraid of the dark.

The next day I found she was afraid of the water, braving under-growth and turtles to walk to our destination but refusing to go out in a flat-bottomed rowboat on the placid lake. She had never learned to swim, and so we had to walk the long way around. The going was rough, and there was a certain hazard of snakes, which last circumstance I did not mention to her. Louis proceeded stolidly along over rocks and roots, muttering that the rowboat would have been easier. Nor would she entertain any thought of a swim. The lake was shallow where I invited her in, and not a bit cold, but no! God forbid, no! Louis explained to me that she had had to be all but carried onto the boat that took her on the first Shawn trip to England and that she had been close to unconsciousness with drink. Louis had deliberately gotten her drunk for courage. So afraid was she of water and the dark.

And the temper tantrums and screaming irrationalities before performance? Were these the conduct of a mature person?

Never mind. The girls didn't care. Possibly they loved her all the more for her vulnerabilities. The truth is, they fell in love with her. And with her vision.

And although from time to time every one of Martha's pupils and associates had been able to view her dispassionately and realize that she was dominated by self-interest, the magic spell always persisted. She had but to say, "Do this," and they were ready for immolation. They longed for it. With the doubt and the cool appraisal went the prayer, always present, always inmost in their hearts, that she really cared, that everything she said to them was from the innermost depths of her heart and for them alone.

And when they finally walked onstage dressed in sacks (but wonderfully cut sacks, because Martha cut them herself), they were the *Group*. They considered themselves a special breed. And they were. They were in a very true sense the chosen. They walked proud. They had been present. They had seen life happen.

What exactly did Miss Witch, Miss Demon-Rider, Miss Lady-Bully appear like on ordinary meeting? Perfectly adorable, that's what: vulnerable, girlish, childlike, with a light, husky voice which trembled with enthusiasm, and a giggle. And she was great fun to be with. She had an enormous sense of fun—sometimes raucous, but then there was the other side. She seemed to hear sounds we didn't hear and see colors beyond human vision. And she recognized instantaneously.

Martha had eyes like an animal, like an angel.

And there was her speaking mouth and the lips which breathed light and which promised everlasting continuity, and from which flowed poetic truth.

Conversations with Martha were like someone running around the house opening windows. There seemed to be one intent: air.

t had been outside of Martha's plan and her chosen pattern to share her theater with other dancers, but she had already transgressed her intentions in a rather spectacular way. In April 1930 Martha had made her first appearance as a dancer in a production associated with internationally known names. She was engaged by Léonide Massine to dance the role of the Chosen One in his version of Stravinsky's *Le Sacre du Printemps* for the League of Composers, with the Philadelphia Orchestra under the direction of Leopold Stokowski. For her interview with Massine, Martha wore a fur coat borrowed from Gertrude Shurr: " 'A star must appear in furs,' Martha had said. She had none, so she borrowed mine." The entire projected company—dancers, orchestra, and conductor—was to move, after three performances at the Philadelphia Academy of Music, to the Metropolitan Opera House for a gala showing in New York. Inasmuch as the League of Composers' annual spring performance was one of the musical highlights of the year, this would provide Martha with her first major showcase and obtain for her national and international press. These performances were also to be Martha's first experience under a choreographer other than Ted Shawn and her very first experience with a ballet choreographer.

Léonide Massine had replaced Michel Fokine in Diaghilev's company after the great impresario and Fokine had quarreled over what Fokine saw as the arbitrary pushing ahead of Vaslav Nijinsky in choreographic assignments. Fokine left in a rage and then Nijinsky married and was fired by Diaghilev, leaving him with neither male star nor choreographer. The very young Massine, with the stripling body and the enormous eyes of a starved gazelle, was chosen to fill the void.

He began composing rapidly, and while not all his early works were good, and few were lasting, he did build up a prodigious technique for rapid staging and brilliant invention. And he built up what all Russian ballet masters must have: total arrogance and the air of infallibility. He was taciturn and unsocial with the dancers, maintaining on all occasions an undeviating, almost military air of superiority. The caste system prevailed, and he was the top officer.

The initial idea for *Sacre du Printemps (Rite of Spring)* had been furnished by Nicholas Roerich, the Russian painter and archaeologist, a scholar with a passion for Russian art of the pre-Christian era. He provided the scenario and thematic plan, which was later augmented by Igor Stravinsky, the two men working as collaborators, Roerich designing all the sets and costumes as he had done for the *Polovtsian Dances* from Borodin's *Prince Igor,* one of Serge Diaghilev's first ballets to be given in Europe. Diaghilev commissioned the score, and handed it over to his lover, Vaslav Nijinsky. The score was extremely advanced, involving a dissonance never before heard: rhythms changing with every bar, counter-rhythms crossing major rhythms, several rhythms continuing at the same time.

Because Nijinsky was not adept musically and the score raised unprecedented difficulties, Marie Rambert, a student at the Dalcroze School of Eurythmics in Hellerau, outside Dresden, was retained to help him count the phrasing.

As choreographer, Nijinsky entertained drastically revolutionary ideas about the dancing style. It was to be archaic, primitive, the dancing embryonic, the very budding of dance movement. Where the classic technique called for elongated and stretched spine, lofty heads and sweeping arms, here the choreography demanded a drooping spine, enfolding arms, head engaged and turned inward, feet curled in, knees bent and also turned inward, hands closed—not as fists but as unrealized promises (Marie Rambert translated the Russian term as "fistikins")—and jumps not to carry the body into the air but to descend, hammer, and strike the earth: in short, to beat out a rhythm very like American Indians, the exact opposite of everything that ballet dancers had trained themselves all their lives to do. The performers in the 1913 group found their task obnoxious and thankless, and they forgot the steps together with the excruciating counts (which they kept in personal notebooks and studied as diligently as mathematics students) as soon as they could arrange to do so, which, as it turned out, was conveniently soon. There were only five performances at the Champs-Elysées theater, beginning on May 29; these were followed by three London performances at the Drury Lane Theatre, beginning July 11. Then the troublesome little notebooks were put away permanently. Later that year, 1913, Nijinsky went with the Diaghilev Ballet to South America, married unexpectedly, and deserted Diaghilev, who vowed never to take him back. *Sacre* was forgotten.

With time, judgment on the score has been more than reversed. Many of those who saw the 1913 version admitted that it was complicated and ineffective. Lydia Sokolova, who danced in the corps de ballet of the original production, called it "vague and rather sad." Nijinsky himself had said in rehearsal, "*Sacre* will prove a strangely interesting work; it is really the soul of nature expressed by movement to music, it is the life of the stones and the trees. There are no human beings in it. It will be danced only by the corps de ballet, for it is a thing of concrete masses, not of individual effect." Many who saw it thought it the true beginning of modern dance, with its stress on inner energy, all dynamics centering on the core of the body, the total disregard for peripheral gesture and attitude, the recoiling on self, the unborn essence. Without actually seeing the original movement it is now impossible to render judgment on this point.

There have been many versions of *Rite of Spring* since Nijinsky: Léonide Massine, Mary Wigman, Maurice Béjart, Kenneth MacMillan, Glen Tetley, John Neumeier, Hans von Manen, Martha Graham, Paul Taylor, Brian MacDonald, and Pina Bausch have all staged it. In November 1987 the Robert Joffrey company attempted to reproduce exactly the original Nijinsky version, making extensive use of the truly remarkable research by two English scholars, Millicent Hodson and Kenneth Archer. These two English dance archaeologists researched all available sources and gathered together every possible vestige of notes and graphic design. They interviewed all living witnesses of the original production, including Marie Rambert, members of the original orchestra, and members of the original corps de ballet. The resulting production met with serious and enthusiastic response.*

In 1920 *Le Sacre* was rechoreographed by Massine for Diaghilev, using Lydia Sokolova as the sacrificial maiden. Despite her stage name, this was an Englishwoman, Hilda Munnings, of vibrant personality and with an elevation unmatched by any female except, I'm told, Massine's first wife, Vera Savina (also English), and Nijinsky's sister, Bronislava Nijinska. Massine built into his *Sacre* a series of stupefying and spine-cracking leaps and falls for Sokolova, at the climax, and she ended every rehearsal in a fainting condition. She became so dizzy and weak with exhaustion from the inhuman effort that she kept track of the number of falling leaps (the music being of no help) by pressing her fingers to her palms one by one. In the finale there was a series of jetés en tournant (turning leaps); each time she landed she was to place her fists on the floor, bending back and looking up, after which she was lifted aloft, dead, as the vernal sacrifice.

On this second occasion, the Paris audience, having learned a thing or two about the music, reacted by yelling and shouting with approval. Sokolova found herself famous, though fatigued, and Massine was acclaimed as a master.

Diaghilev died in 1929, and the Ballets Russes shut down forever. Immediately after Diaghilev's death, Martha's onetime patron S. M. "Roxy" Rothafel, the enterprising motion-picture theater owner and producer, invited Massine to come to the Roxy in New York to stage a new ballet weekly and dance in it four times a day himself. Massine was offered seven hundred and fifty dollars a week—for him a fortune.

---

*Leeland Weindrich of Vancouver wrote me in May 1988 about the Joffrey company's *Rite of Spring:* "I found the piece fascinating and vexing—very dense and uncomfortable, but as thrilling to look at as a painting in action. For me the dance dynamics were so muted and ingrown, and I had hoped for cataclysmic upheaval."

Laura Shapiro wrote in *Newsweek:* " 'Sacre' is an astonishing ballet, no less so today than in 1913. Nijinsky's genius as a choreographer bursts forth here in the originality of his vision, the depths of his musicality, and the grand sense of inevitability that reigns over the whole . . ."

"The theater seemed to be shaken by an earthquake," wrote Valentine Gross, an artist who had been in the audience at the 1913 premiere. "Today we can still feel the theater shaking, as a long-dormant masterpiece returns to life and redefines the avant garde . . ." To me the new piece seemed remarkably primitive and at the same time sophisticated in that it was truly musical.

It was a great loss of prestige but it was money, and Massine needed money. His appearances were, however, in essence vaudeville, and America had yet to see any real Massine choreography. And so he was counting on *Le Sacre.*

In hiring Martha Graham, a modern dancer with no ballet technique, for Sokolova's great bravura solos, Massine was courting disaster. But Martha had a good reputation, and her appearance was right. She was taken on the advice of Evangeline Stokowski, the conductor's wife, who was studying with Martha at the time.

Martha now faced in Massine an ego and a temper quite equal to her own, and a man of very considerable professional fame who knew just what he wanted. The sessions were stormy. He accused her of stubbornly refusing to do anything he asked. She accused him of designing what was outside her technical capabilities. Of the two she was the better choreographer. He, on the other hand, was a king in his own theater and used to instantaneous and terrified obedience. They achieved a really splendid clashing of wills. Leopold Stokowski rode herd.

Martha had already resigned several times before I saw her sitting on her bed in Philadelphia, where the ballet had its premiere, a cup of cocoa in her hands. (She had invited me to share her bedroom while I was there for the opening.)

"I wouldn't have gotten out for anything in the world," she said pleasantly, her eyes bright as a vixen's. "There is no power that could have made me give it up. I think he hoped I would. I won't. But, of course, I've had to resign repeatedly."

The next day she suggested to Massine that he change the choreography. At this idea his eyes, already round as saucers, grew positively ringed with amazement, like a lemur's. And so it went, bitterly and feverishly, in private and in public.

Martha told me in Philadelphia before *Le Sacre* opened, "I don't like all of this production, but I'm going to appear in it. It's important. Besides, Stokowski thinks I'm good in the role."

The costumes and scenery were the original Nicolas Roerich designs, in which the ancient Russian peasants with wrapped-up legs and padded coats looked like sore thumbs, and Martha in her straight red dress looked forceful and appealing. The choreography was stunning (the best, in my opinion, ever to have been devised for this ballet), and the climax seemed quite adequate to the overwhelming music.

At the orchestra dress rehearsal, Stokowski presented his own form of stubbornness. The program consisted of two pieces: Arnold Schoen-berg's *Die glückliche Hand* and Stravinsky's *Le Sacre du Printemps*, separated by an intermission. Stokowski was, as everybody knew, a peacock, and when he found himself in the *répétition générale*, or final open rehearsal, with a full invited audience of important Philadelphia and New York critics, he suddenly stopped the run-through of Schoen-berg's opera. There he stood at the center of the universe, in his nimbus of untidy white-gold hair, and halted in his glory to attend to creation. Lowering his baton and silencing the singers in full cry so that they stood cooling in their sweat he meticulously and deliberately rearranged all the double basses, all the celli, all the brass, all the woodwinds, and he took about twenty minutes to do so. Had he not thought beforehand how he would seat his orchestra in the pit? Having conducted in the house for nearly twenty years, he knew the acoustics. The singers shifted their weight, moved restlessly about; the audience fidgeted and read their programs. After he had at last accomplished what he wanted, the impetus of the performance had been totally shattered.

Martha stood in the wings with blazing eyes. "If he dares stop me once I begin, if he dares . . ."

Stokie was cruel and egotistical, but he was no fool. He did not dare. Stravinsky's music proceeded in its thundering pattern, and Martha gathered momentum for her tremendous finale. Stokowski conducted superbly. Martha was hailed; small and heroic, she stood on the stage between Massine and the maestro, taking bows. She was now a recog-nized figure; she was now in the big league.

My partner at the time, Warren Leonard, was in a production of *Lysistrata* at another theater in Philadelphia, a production designed by Norman Bel Geddes, and staged by Doris Humphrey. After I returned to New York, Martha, still in Philadelphia, used to take cocoa with him. One night, as he sat on the floor of her room, Martha talked about herself.

He told me: "She was absolutely certain of her ultimate success. One day people would be 'on their knees' before her. She was going to give the world a new form of dancing. It would be recognized, it would be hailed. She would be imitated and followed and taught. She knew this. The people of the world would be 'on their knees.' "

At the time that Martha was speaking, her sole income consisted of her pittance for the four *Sacre* performances, her "indentured" salary at the Neighborhood Playhouse, and a few dollars from scattered teach-ing hours at the YMHA. She was deeply in debt. She had no engagements, no offers for the future. When the week with *Le Sacre* was up, she would return to the classes of stumbling and too-old girls and the merciless night rehearsals. No more orchestras, no more Academy of Music, no more costumes or color or scenery—just the barefooted girls in the dingy jerseys—"on their knees." Yet she had lifted her head as she said it, and her voice rang.

"And do you know," Warren said to me, "I believed her."

|||||

How did she know? What are the recipes for greatness? Or even for success?

It has been suggested that an unhappy childhood is necessary. Possibly. Yet many childhoods are unhappy without producing anything attractive, one almost-certain result being trouble in later life. It seems to me that all kinds of childhoods, good and bad, precede achievement. Statesmen, for instance, often have come from happy homes; playwrights almost invariably from broken or tumultuous ones; instrumentalists and dancers from homes dominated by the mother; dancers—women, at any rate—from frustrated mothers (and I think both mother and daughter tend to use dancing as a substitute for sex). Ballet mothers particularly tend to be dominant, excruciatingly so. Whether such a childhood is consciously unhappy is not the point. The reason for success lies elsewhere.

Nor is selfishness the explanation, as has also been suggested. Everyone is selfish. But the difference between great careerists and the rest of the world is that the artist knows while very young precisely what he or she wants and wastes no energy in diversions. He uses his selfishness to purpose, and his purpose is work. All artists—indeed, all great careerists—submit themselves, as well as their friends, to lifelong, relentless discipline, largely self-imposed and never for any reason relinquished. To serve talent, the artist may break up marriages; betray friends; neglect children, associates, and faith; disavow loyalties. Or, if it fits in with his discipline and desire, he may not. There have been very great artists who were distinguished citizens and loving family men. There are bad husbands and mean fathers who create nothing but suffering. Bad behavior can amount to haphazard vandalism. But—and this seems to me a fact—the artist has an end in view beyond temper tantrums and attention getting. He produces something, and that is more important than his own ego—or, rather, the ego and the art are fused.

What, then, is the difference between this artist's point of view and megalomania?

Talent is the difference. There is no substitute for talent. There is no approximation of or equivalent to talent, as there is none for sex. They are sui generis.

And character is the difference, by which I mean steadfastness, adherence, dogged patience, vision, inner faith, and perception. Most great talents have these characteristics built into the personality. But even very greatly gifted people may become suicidal, arranging consistent failures and "accidents," and hiding in illness as a final excuse for giving over the struggle. The healthy ones are driven without respite until they die. In this untiring race, they find their happiness. It's odd, but it's so.

Lastly, there is luck. The time must be propitious, the situation ready. The mechanical means of getting known are sometimes lacking. And sometimes there are direct misfortunes—manuscripts are burned or lost, ideas are pirated, paintings are shut away unseen, architectural plans are discarded. How much greatness lies on cutting-room floors, one can never know. These are fortunes of war. One expects to meet them. Someone loses in every victorious battle, and occasionally it is the better general. Suppose Martha at that time had developed trouble with her knees? She didn't.

But the instinct to know what is needed at a given period, to sense this well in advance, is a concomitant of real talent. In this way artists are like radar instruments, or seismographs. They are so instinctively a part of their time, so sensitively aware that what they feel is really the first intimations of popular emotion and change, that in telling their feelings they only give general warning. They alert.

In the long run, greatness makes itself apparent. This the artist and the prophet and the visionary confidently know all the time they are working, and all the time they may seem to be failing.

Lunatics, of course, feel exactly the same way.

How does a genius know he is not a lunatic? He knows.

T he thirties were diverting and lively enough to occupy anyone's attention, although the times were poor and the conditions confused. And always dancers struggled under historical disadvantages. For thousands of years dance has been considered among the most disreputable of professions, and (except for criminal activities such as thieving and the shameful trades) it has been among the most despised. As late as 1936, no dancers in England were allowed by law to rent an apartment, buy a car or a lease or engage in any business undertaking without substantial backing from a citizen in a more accepted profession. Even during the eras when the great imperial and royal ballets flourished, and there were groups of trained and recognized dance professionals who carried on the business with considerable distinction and royal recommendation, dancers were not accepted in society. Girls or boys of good birth were basically discouraged from joining their ranks or even studying their techniques. No members of the aristocracy ever dabbled in the dancer's practices, never under any circumstances. Among the participants themselves there were rigid hierarchies, and anyone who broke with the standard traditions was frowned on by the orthodox.

Accordingly, the practitioners of modern dance, who were rebels in the twenties and thirties, found themselves not only despised socially by the world at large but rejected by their own profession as well. They were disdained by the traditional ballet dancers, who viewed modern dancers as amateur technicians: they could not turn pirouettes, therefore they were unskilled, therefore as a matter of course they were shut out from all desirable positions and spoken of with scorn. The scorners did not always bother to go to see what it was they were mocking.

Nor, remarkably enough, did the modern dancers seek much comfort from one another. Instead, they waged an unceasing, internecine war, prompted entirely by their own egos and their proud determination to be themselves and not like anyone else. They gave two or three performances a year and starved in the intervals, always with intense pride and egregious self-satisfaction.

It is astonishing, but factual, that out of this group of quarreling egomaniacs came the impetus that changed the American theater, the world theater, and that put a stamp on our age. This is where the news was. This is where the energy manifested itself. For the time was the twentieth century, and the twentieth century is a century of movement. Our art forms are those that deal with movement, just as the theater of Elizabethan times was a theater of words, and the theater of the eighteenth and nineteenth centuries was a theater of music and sound. The twentieth century is a theater of sight and visual image. And the heralds, the guardians, were these tatterdemalion freaks, the "modern" dancers.

Most of them lived in Greenwich Village.

All the groups in the Village in this period—socialists, Communists, anarchists, revolutionary sociologists, champions of women's suffrage, labor reformers, child-labor antagonists, as well as innovative writers, painters, sculptors, playwrights, the new theatrical designers and organizers, the students and acolytes of each—met at their public spots, tearooms or speakeasies, and talked. Daily chatter was the stuff of living to them, the source of news, the zest. From these exchanges, pleasant or tumultuous, they derived enough stimulation to carry them through another straining or starving day. Even Eugene O'Neill, whose taciturnity was absolute, frequented the dives on Sixth Avenue and talked, or listened, to let off steam.

Only the dancers did not talk.

Hostile and competitive, ever suspicious of their colleagues, they remained aloof, working alone, eating alone, and venturing abroad only to the theaters and concert halls of midtown Manhattan. And, of course, to those schools and Y's where they were engaged to teach. Their pupils didn't mingle, it being considered a breach of faith to commune with members of a rival school.

Think of it: Martha Graham, Doris Humphrey, Charles Weidman, José Limón, Pauline Lawrence, Hanya Holm, Esther Junger, and Louis Horst all established, living, teaching, exhorting, and preaching within a few blocks of one another. These were among the few who changed the world aspect of their art, who forced and framed the modern dance in America, and they rarely met together, didn't want to meet. There was nowhere one could say, "This is where they eat." They didn't eat much, and they had not the leisure to chat. But mostly they were too self-centered to be interested in what one another thought.

They went to one another's concerts, however. They did that, all right, and they sat hawk-eyed.

And all of them despised ballet, a loathing which was heartily reciprocated.

The enmity, the hostility between the two groups—the classicists, or ballet dancers, and the moderns—did not slacken for decades, and it was maintained with overt energy. It is true that in the twenties and early thirties the ballet dancers in America had little enough to bolster them. They were not sustained by any companies. They were largely White Russian refugees, scattered individuals, and for the most part they were themselves starving. But the imperial Russians, those who had graduated from the pre-Revolutionary tsarist ballet schools, although dispersed by the Revolution, maintained pride of craft and vanity unmatched, feeling themselves to be the guardians of the holy shrine, believing as an act of faith that it was their privilege—nay, their duty—to oppose as an impostor or a fraud, or at the very best a well-meaning amateur, anyone else who moved to music. In this attitude they were rigid.

Their point of view was more than reinforced in 1933 by the first appearances in America of Colonel de Basil's (Vassili Vosskrezensky) Ballet Russe de Monte Carlo. The company's success made big money for the managers and some money for its chief choreographer, Léonide Massine. It made no money, but gained considerable glory for the members of its corps de ballet. It did, as a matter of fact, a very great deal of good for the art of dancing in this country. But it did not in any way heighten enthusiasm for things native.

The poor local upstarts were considered beyond the pale as they struggled along making no money and receiving little réclame.

"What did you think of Graham?" I asked the fourteen-year-old ballerina Tamara Toumanova in London in 1934, on her return from her first tour, the de Basil season in New York.

"Grahhm has a fine technick but no ideas. She is not interesting." And with that dictus the "baby ballerina" blindly dismissed the veteran artist, and with her the entire modern-dance movement. She was, of course, quoting her master, Massine.

In the January 1931 issue of *Dance Magazine*, Fokine wrote an article called "A Sad Art," in which he attacked Martha broadside. Louis replied in March in *Musical America*. Fokine added a rebuttal in the May 31 issue of *Dance Magazine*. This was the prelude to the face-to-face confrontation which occurred at the New School for Social Research the following winter. *Dance Magazine* had played rather a sorry role in the new modern dance movement. In December 1929, Paul Milton, its editor, had run an article called "A Dark Soul," which was a mockery and a condemnation of Martha. She went to her lawyer, Lewis Isaacs, who advised her to ignore the matter, but everybody she knew was urged to cancel subscriptions and Milton came out of the petty fracas with a rather dirty reputation.

Louis Horst wrote a biting refutation to Paul Milton, defending Graham against being called a "dark soul," ending his letter with the words: "I am always forced to tone down any effort on my part to get her the recognition that is due her."

Horst was being fair-minded. He had seen Balanchine's *Concurrence* with the Ballet Russe de Monte Carlo and found it provocative and stimulating. Fokine, on the other hand, was *not* being fair-minded. He went once to the New School to attend a lecture given by the great German modern dancer Mary Wigman, under the auspices of John Martin, *The New York Times* dance critic. Wigman spoke English hardly at all and was therefore at a disadvantage. Fokine, whose own English left something to be desired, baited and hounded her in a most unattractive manner. Subsequently, he attempted the same harassment procedure with our native champion. When Martha Graham's turn came to lecture, he proceeded to heckle and jeer as though she were a political opponent. Martha was articulate, she was born English-speaking, and it was well known that she had a temper. And although she respected Fokine for his achievements—one had to; he had been the backbone of the Diaghilev ballet, although he was now on the downgrade—she wasn't going to put up with any of his bad-mannered nonsense. She crossed the floor to stand in front of him, in very close proximity, and said loudly and clearly, "You came here to badger me. You did not come here to learn, or even to look. You came to scoff and mock and I wish you'd get out right now. Leave!" And she waited without moving until he had left the little auditorium. The audience applauded. I was a ballet student, not a modern, but I must say that as an American, I cheered at Martha's rightness of retaliation. Bully good for her! She wasn't tolerating hauteur from the fading White Russian.

In 1933 Louis Horst founded a journal devoted to modern dancing, because, he said, there was not one literate voice to speak out for the new form. Together with Winthrop Sargeant, Geordie Graham's husband, Horst started a publication called *Dance Observer*. It was dedicated to serving the needs of the modern group, in particular Martha Graham. John Martin called the magazine "the house organ." Horst edited and published the little paper, doing all the business himself and administering his staff of writers personally. It was a closed organization, fervent, cohesive, and devoted to Louis. He kept the extra copies of the magazine in his apartment, largely under his bed, which made sleeping rather lumpy, as people discovered when, in his absence, he lent the flat to students.

In 1936 I had received some remarkable letters from Ramon Reed, an English friend who wrote to me about the advent of Antony Tudor and his new ballet *Jardin aux Lilas.*

"If," my friend wrote, "the English can do this we are due for a renaissance of high order."

I suggested that he be the English correspondent of *Dance Observer;* no money was involved. The editors had no objection.

"But," I said, "you must understand that in England there are at present no modern dancers at all. It is all ballet. Reed will have to write about ballet."

"In that case," replied the editorial staff, "we do not want him or his pieces."

I said, "But it's news! This man Tudor is news."

"We do not wish to print one word about ballet."

I argued with them. "You're putting your head into the sand. If you print a dance journal you must write about what's happening."

But they said no. "Not a word about ballet. We don't think it's worth the paper it's printed on."

This, then, was the situation that dancing presented in the thirties. It consisted of relatively small and certainly nonessential groups of people, fanatical in their beliefs to the point of religious ferocity, mortally entangled in one another's fates but unwilling to cooperate in any way, yet forming a yeasty working matrix of mounting public interest.

And certainly, in any case, the dance picture in New York was more lively than it had ever been before. In the first place, New York was the mecca for performers, the place to establish a world reputation. We had all the greats in sequence, and several at the same time: the Spaniards Argentina, Argentinita, and Escudero; the Peruvian Helba Huara; as well as a gathering of lesser Latin stars. And we also had the great Germans—Harald Kreutzberg, Yvonne Georgi, Mary Wigman, the Ballets Jooss; the Orientals, Mei Lan-Fang and his troup of classical Chinese singers and dancers; from India, Uday Shankar and his company, and Ram Gopal; and the Russians, Colonel de Basil's and Serge Denham's Ballet Russe companies, sometimes the same company and sometimes bitter rivals. All interesting, all stimulating, but ultimately only embellishments, peripheral to the central interest, which consisted of our own struggling American moderns.

The high points of the year were therefore the Sunday-night dance recitals, toward which we all worked, and which we all attended.

Dance performers are more successful now, by far more affluent, and, on the whole, better. There is more good, even distinguished, dancing in New York in a single season today than there was in all of Europe ten years before the Second World War. There are currently in New York City six major resident dance companies with regular seasons, and there are several promising minor companies. All the powerful, curious, or exotic companies of the world visit. Dancing now competes in popularity with baseball and tennis as entertainment. It is news. But in the thirties each dancer staked everything on the next appearance, and the appearances were rare because they were costly.

Since we had no continuity and, as Americans, could not tour without strong management, and strong management would not take the risk, our appearances were isolated.

America is in certain ways still a colonial country, particularly in cultural attitudes, it being generally understood that what is European is older and therefore more mature and better. This does not apply to the American theater, which is vigorous, healthy, successful, and strong in its own right, but it certainly applies to music—orchestral, operatic, and instrumental—and until the Second World War it applied to dancing. The best European dancers with proven reputations were always imported to America and exploited by the great management companies. Americans were never given a comparable chance. They therefore found it almost impossible to gain experience and to acquire a reputation. The managers claimed they could not sell them, and never tried to. The natives, therefore, had little general experience, no backing, and small reputations. As a result they couldn't get publicity, and the combination of circumstances was a trap. That the American reputation was not based on inferiority I think was amply proven by the advent of Americans into musicals in the forties, when suddenly American dance gained an unprecedented popularity that, surprisingly, matched and outdid any European musical artist. In the theater vast audiences of ordinary people were introduced to American dance, and they found that they liked it very much indeed.

Few people wanted to see us, or they did not know that they wanted to. Tickets for American dance performances were priced with a $2.30 top, and box-office takes never exceeded a thousand dollars. Except for programs by Martha. Martha was the only one who could best this, and did so regularly.

While expenses were not great, compared with today they were heavy to meet. The theater could be rented for a hundred dollars—and that included light, heat, and the front-of-house staff: box office and ushers and those in charge of the technical staff (head grip, chief stagehand, head electrician, head curtain man). The management, usually Marks Levine, cost another hundred dollars, publicity (which included newspaper ads) cost about five hundred. The printing of throwaways was inexpensive, and we often did our own addressing and mailing. The stage—that is, lights and curtains—was run by a friend or by someone at the piano (often by Louis while he played). The costumes were homemade and semi-professional, simple but suitable and of inexpensive material. (Martha's budget was a dollar a dress.) Rehearsals were on our own time, which was our life-time, and in our own bedrooms, which were often our studio floors. In all, these expenses totaled around a thousand dollars—all we had, and all or more than we could make at the box office. Every penny given to an electrician was teaching money or money saved from food or winter clothes.

Our works were short, constructed like lieder or dramatic sketches, but with an eye toward the direct evocation of mood or emotion, and a perfection of form occasionally attained. Some of these solos were nothing short of stunning; I think some of the choreographers today who deal almost exclusively in patterns of multiple bodies and of longer duration would do well to study them. The examples Martha has dredged up from the debris of her past make present-day audiences gasp: *Lamentation* (1930), *Frontier* (1935), *Deep Song* (1937). But where are records we could study of her *Adolescence* (1929), *Heretic* (1929)? Since there is no notation for her early works, and there were no films until recently, the almost inevitable loss of a dance had nothing to do with its worth. All dances not in constant performance or in current repertories were lost and forgotten. Among Martha's lesser works were exquisite and always interesting compositions, but Martha set a standard for herself that was way beyond what was expected of most people. In general, choreographers, even the very greatest, achieve only a dozen first-class works in their lives.

We were generally not known, but for us, ourselves, we had excitement. There was no help: we hung by a rope over the abyss and had to pull ourselves up alone or drop into oblivion. And although the audience grew in size steadily, it was relatively small. And it was very peculiar.

Oh, those audiences! Even in the twenties Martha drew crowds of what later would be called hippies. At that time they were the intellectual elite and they looked like hell: beards and beads and homemade eccentricities; they were the teachers and writers and scientists who were going to shape our lives for the next forty years. Could anyone have known this to look at them?

These audiences used to make the average theatergoer uneasy. Of course, we all wanted better audiences and larger ones; we also wanted to be paid, we wanted help. In the twenties and thirties there was no help, no arts councils, no foundations.

Yet dancers went to each other's concerts, and we argued in the lobbies and over after-theater coffee, as at an election. We got used to feeling despised by the general public, but we also resented it. We got mad. We got to work.

Gradually there started a boiling-up of wider interest in dance. Lectures on dancing, for adult, practicing dancers, began to be given at the music branch of the New York Public Library, under the auspices of Dorothy Lawton, the librarian. Lecture-demonstrations were held at the Lexington Avenue YMHA: Louis Horst used his pupils and Martha's as demonstrators. Dance history was taught at the New School for Social Research by John Martin, with demonstrations by all the visiting stars and the ranking natives. Lectures at the Ethical Culture school on Central Park West, and even at that citadel of conservatism, Columbia University (in its McMillin Theater), modern dance aesthetics was accumulating a body of informed opinion, a history. And gradually even an audience. It was the so-called modern dancers who did the talking; the ballet enthusiasts did not seem to have much to say.

Young ballet dancers are not given to theorizing. Either they accept all that has been said for the last three hundred years, or they reject most of it. But they were too tired most of the time to argue.

|||||

The dancers of New York soon found that as a group they had political power, and they were ready to be considered as serious artists practicing a legitimate art form; they began to claim the respect due other artists. American dancers had become aware of themselves as members of a profession with a common cultural interest. This was a novel, even a new, point of view. More, they began to organize to effect legislation to correct old and troublesome abuses.

They assembled to make gestures of international courtesy.

Almost everyone participated in the general activity, even Doris Humphrey. Only Martha remained aloof. She was a self-proclaimed loner, and people let her be. She taught, she choreographed, she danced. And in doing so she made enough news for one human being. She did not mix.

For instance, she refused to join the newly formed Concert Dancers' League, organized in New York City to do battle for certain legal rights which could not be claimed individually. There was an old law on the New York State books forbidding any kind of entertainment on Sundays, including "cock fighting, bearbaiting and boxing with or without gloves." This law was invoked regularly by the Sabbath League to halt dance recitals. Of course, every moving-picture house in the big cities flouted this law, but those theaters were able to make payoffs to the police and thus remain unmolested. The dancers could not afford such luxuries, and since the dancers could rent theaters only on Sundays, they were mercilessly harassed. At this time there was considerable agitation among American publishers because certain books of acknowledged literary merit could not be published in the States or even sold in their unexpurgated form: *Lady Chatterley's Lover* by D. H. Lawrence was one such. And the major publishers of Boston and New York met in Albany to plead their case, not for pornography but for fine literary works that didn't meet the strictures of the Sabbath League. We made common cause with them, and their presence gave our arguments added weight.*

Eventually the law was revoked with the aid of Carl Carmer, editor of *Theater Arts,* who asked a very uninterested group of Upstate legislators to regard the dance "not like Salome before Herod but as David before the ark of the Lord." They didn't regard it as anything of the kind, but they permitted us to go ahead with our business. The Concert Dancers' League fell into oblivion shortly thereafter. But we had changed the law and made Sundays available to the dancers.

The Concert Dancers' League had also dabbled in social demonstrations, throwing a large and rather good party for the first visit in 1930 of Mary Wigman, to which everyone in the business came. But our contemporary leaders, Martha, Doris, Charles, and Helen Tamiris, were not asked to be photographed with the guest of honor. Wigman was invited to pose with Ted Shawn and Ruth St. Denis and other moldering personalities. The young and vigorous were outraged and made their discomfiture known. "Why those old has-beens?" Louis Horst remonstrated. "Why not the young people who are making history? Surely the leader of German dance would like to be photographed with the leader of American dance. This will make Europe think we haven't taken a step forward."

But the League had had its nose put out of joint, because none of the so-called leaders of American Dance would do anything at all to help their colleagues.

There were then very few places in which free-lance dancers could perform. By free-lance I mean any beginning individuals not managed either by Columbia Concerts or Sol Hurok or Daniel Mayer, Inc. No American dancers could get contracts with the big managerial agencies unless they could provide financial backing. And, of course, most could not. These included all the creators of the modern movement. So the

*There was one rather wry incident during this session: A representative of the Sabbath League claimed he did not wish to stop good books, just blatant pornography like the proffered mimeographed sheet, which he threw on the table and which passed from avid hand to avid hand down the long line of representatives. At the close of the meeting he asked for his paper back. It could not be found. It had been purloined.

few places that would give them foot room and allow them to sell tickets were cherished.

First and foremost was the Young Men's Hebrew Association at Lexington Avenue and Ninety-second Street, known as the "Y." There, under the direction of William Kolodney, in a small but adequate auditorium, a series of concerts was put on each winter with outstanding dancers. This one institution kept modern dance alive in New York City for twenty years, from 1927 to 1947; it is the veritable cradle of the modern-dance movement. It cannot be praised too highly for the enormous sponsoring work it provided.

The "Y" also hired dancers to teach. Doris Humphrey and Martha Graham gave regular courses to whomever would pay the very small fee. The instructor received ten dollars an hour, which was lifesaving to them and something to be counted on. The teaching, of course, also built up their audiences.

Another welcoming theater, under the management of Joseph Mann, was at the Washington Irving High School, on Irving Place. It was less well equipped than the "Y," with a less accommodating stage and a young and unsophisticated audience. It was not as influential as the "Y," but it helped, and it had annual series, the Students Dance Recitals, which were relied on by the good dancers.

It was at Sarah Lawrence College in Bronxville, just north of Manhattan, however, that dancers were hired for adequate pay, and students were seriously trained. Graduates of Sarah Lawrence were thoroughly indoctrinated with the basic artistic principles of fine choreography, fine performing, fine design, fine staging. This was altogether new in the academic world. Bessie Schönberg, a one-time pupil of Graham, was in charge of the college's dance department, and she furnished a truly proselytizing service. José Limón taught there regularly. Tamiris came. Ruth St. Denis was invited to talk, and, Schönberg explained, while she was not a very good teacher, she was a magic storyteller. Miss Ruth appeared in an electric-blue dress, with a silver belt to set off her aureole of white hair, and she mesmerized the students. In 1935 Martha Graham agreed to come once a month, sending her students to coach classes during the intervening weeks. The trip to Bronxville from Manhattan was approximately thirty-five minutes by train and not too onerous, but it was tiring and a bad break in Martha's workday. And so she rationed her time there.

Sarah Lawrence had become a real center for ideas and enthusiasms, and above all for taste. There Martha made the acquaintance of two young composers, John Cage and Norman Lloyd, who accompanied dance classes. She also met the designer Arch Lauterer, who wanted to do scenery for her dances. More important, she became acquainted with Joseph Campbell, the writer on mythological subjects and teacher of mythology, anthropology, and classical history.

All in all, if the environment and prospects around us were frightening, they were also yeasty and provocative. Above all they boded change. The whole theater was stirring. Theater tickets were low priced and therefore the general public could go. The playwrights writing then were extraordinary: Eugene O'Neill, Maxwell Anderson, Philip Barry, Samuel Behrman, Clifford Odets, Thornton Wilder, Archibald MacLeish, Elmer Rice, Lillian Hellman. Experiments even on Broadway were possible, because one could pull the curtain up on a straight play for twenty thousand dollars. Musical comedies were lavish, and while the shows were frivolous, the music was truly astonishing: Irving Berlin, Jerome Kern, Richard Rodgers, Harold Arlen, Cole Porter, Sigmund Romberg, Frank Loesser. These men created the popular music of the twentieth century. They were giants in their field. No one today is in their league.

There were, as well, wonderful designers: Lee Simonson, Donald Oenslager, Jo Mielziner, Robert Edmond Jones, Norman Bel Geddes.

If the dancers were all poor, and the conditions under which we worked were harsh, they were not too dreary. I think in certain respects the adversity may have worked to our advantage. There was no establishment, and therefore there was no protected class and no right or wrong way of doing things. Above all, there was no one to conform to. The ballet dancers scorned us, it is true—always did and always have. But they were out of work too, so their opinion was not considered very important. And just see what we got done while no one was looking!

overty continued, as did the paucity of public recognition, and that meant no support for American dancers, Martha among them. The obvious expedient of pooling resources had been avoided energetically until 1930, when four leaders of the modern dance finally joined forces in an effort to reach a sizable audience, obtain a longer exposure, and share decent advertising. They called themselves the Dance Repertory Theater, and included were Martha Graham, Doris Humphrey, Charles Weidman, and Helen Tamiris. The Dance Repertory Theater's joint arrangement enabled the soloists to perform continuously for six weeknights plus two performances on each of the Sundays framing that week—a luxury they would never have been able to afford individually. Although the other three despised Tamiris, they put up with her, since it was she who had organized the enterprise in the first place.

Tamiris (whose real name was Helen Becker), was a large-boned, muscular, beautifully proportioned athlete of unbounded vitality and gusto whom Martha had first en-

Agnes. The dachshunds have just eaten your stockings. I'm so mortified." Quivering with apology, she padded barefoot back into the front room to do an uncompromising dance about the Inquisition.

Canny old Louis! I heard Charlie Chaplin* scorning the audience's judgment once, and Oscar Hammerstein. Oscar it was who said, "The only way to make big money is to do the risky, uncommercial thing." That wasn't exactly Louis's angle. And it wasn't Oscar's either, as it turns out. But it's a good point of departure. This was the kind of talk that kept Martha Graham marching, that kept her head high, that kept her purpose straight.

Martha took care of Louis often. One time, when on a trip with me to Wilmington, Delaware, he sickened with a fearful bronchitis and at 1:00 A.M. phoned Martha in New York. Although she was giving a public performance that night, without hesitation she took the milk train down to fetch him home. He was without hesitation in asking her. And he knew she'd come.

One July a few years later Martha, Louis, and I joined forces in Gallup, New Mexico, quite by accident. Fifteen minutes after descending from the transcontinental train, The Chief, Louis had learned that there was to be an important rain dance at the Zuñi pueblo, to which the public was not invited. Louis immediately decided to go and was looking about for a car and chauffeur when I happened along with my jalopy. We went and immediately stepped into the Stone Age.

"They killed their Catholic priest nine years ago," whispered Martha, "and the church has not replaced him. This is a very fierce place— one does not trifle here. They warned an airline against sending a plane over the reservation—the airline persisted—the first plane fell."

Louis and Martha, watching the proceedings, were riveted, but we left precipitously, first because we were urged to get the hell out by the masked and dancing priests, and second because it had started, perhaps

---

*The remark was made at my mother's dinner table in the mid-twenties. The conversation went as follows:

CHAPLIN: Popularity has nothing to do with worth. Michelangelo considered himself a failure. He died a disappointed man.

DONALD OGDEN STEWART: Holy God! The Sistine Chapel! I would have died happily if I could have produced four square inches of that failure. My God!

CHAPLIN: He was disappointed. Popularity has nothing to do with worth. The reason people paid attention to Jesus Christ was because he was an outcast.

WILLIAM DE MILLE: As a student of theology, Charlie, you are probably the world's greatest comedian.

in response to the magic, to rain very hard. The trip home was forty miles long. The rain got harder; there was thunder, lightning, flash floods. Louis got pneumonia. His summer plans were spoiled, and so were Martha's. She brought him home and nursed him for weeks.

I had several experiences with Martha in various dilapidated cars; some of these adventures were quite silly.*

||||

The lovely old buildings on Central Park South were taken down on schedule. The new studio to which Martha moved was in the Village, at 46 East Ninth Street, between Broadway and University Place, one block from Wanamaker's and two blocks from where Louis was living.

I remember this studio well because I later rented a twin. There were French windows from floor to ceiling across the front and an open fireplace, good space, every inch of which Martha used for dancing or costume storage. There was a tiny kitchenette, a bathroom, and off the front room a cubicle hardly larger than a roomy closet, in which Martha placed her bed, a chest of drawers, and a rack for personal clothes and costumes. The studio was half a floor off the street and easily reachable by tired dancers. Stacks of shelves in the big room held bolts of costume material, the remnants Martha found on Fourteenth Street when she went bargain hunting with Dorothy Bird. The shelves were hidden by curtains of monk's cloth.

In October 1931, at the suggestion of Charles Weidman, I was made the fifth member of the Dance Repertory Theater. We had a season of two weeks this time, an even greater luxury. All of us, even I, had an evening alone, and we were also invited to do shorter divertissements, or so-called minor works, on one another's programs. At the end of that second season Martha and Doris pulled out, and the Dance Repertory ceased to exist. They did not like dancing with Tamiris. God knows what they thought of me. I was certainly alien. They took care never to dance with anybody else again, or indeed with each other.

Martha, for one, had no regrets. She had delivered herself of work

*I owned an old jalopy named Dodo, which Martha graced on occasion as we rode to concerts in the evening. Some jackanapes had cut a hole in the cloth roof and we were exposed to the rain, but Martha, with great verve and invention, had poked her umbrella through the slit and opened it above us, and so we drove giggling, elegant, and dry. I believe Louis was never with us on these escapades. He was far too grand to share our schoolgirlish high jinks.

and she could be well pleased with the season's result. Because she had, in plain truth, made history that season.

Primitive Mysteries had its premiere on February 2, 1931, in the Dance Repertory season given at the Craig Theatre (later called the George Abbott). Martha had worked on it with her girls for over a year before exhibiting it.

Primitive Mysteries was a study of the Virgin as a young, primitive girl and the vision of her transfiguration through death and agony. The score was by Louis Horst and it was simple and stark. Both music and ballet were faintly influenced by the American Indian ceremonial dances in the Southwest to which Louis had taken Martha on various vacations.

Louis knew a great deal about the Indians, Martha not very much, but she watched and learned. She and Louis had visited the little one-room mud churches of New Mexico. She had knelt in them beside the Indians and the Mexicans, before the *santos,* the primitive figures of Christ hanging on the cross, with raw wounds and blood painted on the poor, naked bodies. The Indians expect little mercy; they worship a God who died in torture.

Martha had also talked at length to Mary Austin, the grand old lady of the Indian country, novelist, poet, and foremost interpreter of Indian culture to the outer world.

Primitive Mysteries, a triptych, is plotless, three revelations resembling a danced mass or cantata: "Hymn to the Virgin," "Crucifixus," "Hosannah." The three separate pieces are joined (and separated) by formal entries and exits done in silence, processions of women surrounding or preceding the soloist, the Virgin figure. The dancers stalk in in dead silence, with long, reaching legs, the foot brought to the earth with heavy forcefulness, as though staking out territory; the steps stretch, claim, stretch, claim, demand a weight of body, of personality, and of presence, like that of an invading army.

The dancers in the original production of *Primitive Mysteries* were for the most part very tall and strong. In fact, Martha had particularly chosen them for their weight and force. When lighter, more delicate girls subsequently attempted to achieve the effect, the entries had little meaning beyond a stiff-legged prance. The walk is designed to be ceremonial, of growing intensity and import, until the dancers arrive at their stations.

The original dancers were rehearsed in this walk for months, every day for half a year, until they managed to get the invading, pre-emptive stalk that Martha wanted. Nor would she allow them to count. They must keep together on the beat by breathing together, and must take their signals of movement from the smallest indications of breath and reflex, until they moved as one organism with a collective mind, insect-like, a lower form of life bearing in its path the fragile treasure, the early virgin who had become the cumulative point of sacrifice.

The Virgin enters with them, but not of them, and takes her appointed place, the focal point, but not always the central one. Martha as the Virgin wore a white cotton dress cut like that of a paper doll, with large, loose sleeves and seemingly without seams, her hair hanging loose down her back, straight as a horse's tail, Indian style. All this takes place in a long and intensifying silence, until the Virgin puts out a hand. Then, and only then, comes the first sound, a single flute, the first sound of a solo flute threnody, like a young voice.

"When Louis's music began," said Dorothy Bird, "we all but cracked open with relief, because the silence had been so agonizing. That was not something to rehearse two or three times and get right. We had to live it. No ballet work could do this."

The first hymn was a paean of praise, a glorification of purity. The configurations of dancers looked wooden, childlike, drawn from ancient sources, possibly Oriental or pre-Christian or Indian, certainly not suggestive of the pretty fancies of the later Christian church. It culminated in the crowning of the heavenly blessed maiden while she sits on the ground, crouched against the spread knees of her attendant, leaning back as the woman suddenly fixes behind her head—nails, as it were—an aureole of spread fingers. It is a gesture rude and emphatic, implanting the instant splendor while stamping with each foot. The rays seem to bloom from the attendant's groin; the sudden godhead is visceral. This moment comes from Martha's deepest instinct and could not have been thought out as a matter of intellect. It is old and from the dark ground; it is secret and of the matrix material which generates original ideas.

At the conclusion of the hymn the women walk off ceremoniously, and, what is astounding, there is not anticlimax to this silent march, no diminuendo, but rather a heightening of suspense. All produced in total silence!

In total silence they re-enter, for the second part, and the Virgin takes her station at the rear of the stage. With the first piercing note she covers her face, and her attendant suddenly points on high toward the crucifixion. The two proceed forward with minuscule steps, the Virgin shielding her eyes from the awful sight.

The chorus is drawn up with waiting horror on one side, breaking out at last, at the very moment of the nailing to the wood: one by one, bent double, their hands locked behind their backs, like driven animals in a heavy-bodied circle, the whole foot hitting the ground with the impact of a blow. This is the pounding of black blood behind the eyes, the frantic heart, the ringing senses. The desperate pulse rocks on the beat and then stops as the world slips away in a final agony. The breaking down of animal life is a mighty and terrible passage. And it is final.

The third picture is a Jubilate, a paean of joy, the Assumption.

The attendants adore.

Gertrude Shurr described the rehearsals:

At the time of *Mysteries* my own father's death was calamitous for the family. I lost all sense of religion, that feeling for God, for the afterlife; then, in working with Martha, some of my faith returned. The *Mysteries* was, of course, Catholic, and there was a feeling for play which was strange for me. Martha explained the peons coming into a square and presenting their drama; the feeling of the virgin maiden for the celebration of the Queen of Heaven in the Adoration, being herself all the different phases of the Life and the Crucifixion, as in the Stations of the Cross. This was the first time I'd ever heard any of these terms, and it gave me a feeling of great warmth. I had never learned of Catholicism before in that way.

I think in presenting us with *Primitive Mysteries*, Martha really gave us a marvelous quietness that permeated the whole Group. Everyone felt it, this belief in oneness. And when I was near her, she had the mystic verity of a figure to be worshipped. When she put out her hand to bless, when she touched you [here Gertrude Shurr's eyes filled and she shook as she spoke], when she was performing, it was not Martha, it was the *other*. Even through the extension of her fingers or the gentleness of her hands—and, you know, they were rarely gentle in ordinary life—a vibration took over her being; you saw it in her face, you felt it in her body. She didn't see us, she made us become what she demanded of us by looking, if it was indeed looking. I think she brought out in us with her look or her presence more potentiality than we ever dreamt that we had. She made us feel "of the moment." We were caught up. She made magic.

Forty-eight hours before the opening of *Primitive Mysteries*, Martha went into her usual hysterical frenzy about costumes and decided that nothing hitherto planned would suit. She rushed off to Delancey Street and bought a great lot of dark-blue knit jersey, at something like nineteen cents a yard—that is, seventy-six cents a costume. She had twenty-four cents for hooks and eyes and thread and could still stay within her budget of a dollar for each dress. The entire set of costumes cost under ten dollars. The girls stitched frantically all day; Anna Sokolow used safety pins.

The first Group, the original Group, were all in simple dark-blue singlets and barefoot, their hair gathered back in snoods made from stockings. In fifty years no alterations have ever improved these costumes, except slight changes in the hang of the skirts because of action requirements.

Rehearsals under the Dance Repertory's joint arrangement were strained, and every dress rehearsal was an agony. On the midnight preceding the performance, each of the designated companies would enter the Craig Theatre to prepare for the following night's opening performance. By 11:45 P.M. the sets, pieces, and curtains of the past performance would have been struck and stacked neatly backstage against the brick walls. The plain black velvet curtains which served everyone—the concert blacks—were already hung, and then the lights were replaced and readied for adjustment and focusing, a process that would take hours . . . way into the early morning. And then, and not before, after a night's show, white with exhaustion, the dancers would be permitted onstage to practice the next night's opening—to learn about the physical proportions, distances, surfaces of the floor, to try out the new works in the new space, in the new exposures, with a strange atmosphere. They would not stop until three or four in the morning, to resume work at nine or ten, and to continue until an hour before curtain time. This meant that the performances of all new works were given in exhaustion, although they were the fruition of nine or ten months of unbroken rehearsing. A single performance which took the artist's entire bankroll was to be attempted in this state of depletion.

Such circumstances were universal to American dancers then. We expected them and we endured them. It was not good for our work and it was punitive to our bodies, but there was no choice. Empty theaters were too expensive to be opened for a single performance. If we wanted a theater we had to take one on the only night of the week it was not being used for another production, in this case the one night allotted to Martha in the Dance Repertory's week.

Accordingly, Martha and her girls entered the Craig Theatre at midnight, February 1, 1931. At about two-thirty, they walked out onto the stage and tried out the new *Primitive Mysteries*. Martha was rigid with nerves, as were the members of her troupe.

At one point she was downstage left. She backed up as planned and stepped up onto the thighs of her attendants behind her, who were forming a platform with their knees, and was so to be transported to center stage. But something went wrong with the balance, her foot slipped off the supporting thigh, she stumbled; she was caught, but she had stumbled. Her nerves shattered.

"That will do," she screamed. "That's enough. You don't care, you don't want this to be good. You don't want it to succeed. Get out of the theater. Get out of my sight. Go home. Go away." And she stamped off the stage and slammed her dressing-room door.

The cast stared at one another, white-faced. Nobody moved. Nobody made the slightest effort to leave the theater or even the stage, or to go home, although they were shaking with fatigue. After a while Louis said dispiritedly that they had better leave and he slowly clumped off in Martha's wake. They heard his plodding steps cross the backstage, go down the hallway, and into her room.

Some few dancers started tentatively to dress; the others stared at one another and waited. Finally he brought her back. Not a word was said. She did not seem surprised that they were still there, that they were waiting, that no one had defected. At rehearsal's end it was after 3:00 A.M. and some were due to travel home on the subway an hour and a half, only to return for a 9:00 A.M. run-through.

By performance time Martha was petrified. She wouldn't talk to anyone. Everything she had done in her life was focused on this single evening. This work was the essence of her belief, of her faith, and of their labors. And it was difficult and daring to attempt: a group of mostly Jewish girls performing a holy Catholic ritual.

But when the girls took the stage it was not as professional dancers; it was as an army of acolytes. Both for them and for the audience it was a spiritual experience. The original girls came to know beatification.

The audience gathered. They witnessed. When the curtain came down they rose and screamed. They gave Martha twenty-three curtain calls.

|||||

What, in fact, did the audience see that night? They saw a small woman in an untrimmed shift going through a formal ritual of walking and posing. Martha was not a virtuoso in the ordinary sense of the term. She was, of course, the master of her own technique, but the audience would mostly not have recognized its difficulty or its power. Any mediocre ballet soloist performing sixteen routine fouettés could have won hullabaloo. Martha was not beautiful, and she was certainly no longer young. What then did she have?

She had Vision.

And she had Presence.

Any star has the ability to seize and hold attention. This is a requisite, and a matter of dynamics, nervous projection, and a secure ego, the star's tools. But Martha had the rare, the nearly unique gift to fuse the outer manifestation with the inner concept: the word made flesh. Simply, she *was*. She approximated the Holy Virgin and her relationship to Christ. And before the awful concept, every man and woman in the house watching approached divine awareness.

Martha has been said by her colleagues to have achieved an actual physical vibration of directed force when working. Some even suggest she gave off heat, the heat of radiance and concentration. No one ever claimed she gave off light, but they stop just short of that assertion. For those short minutes during which Martha celebrated her ritual, Christ was crucified and the Virgin was assumpted into heaven.

Such ideas only the greatest artists in history have dared approach, and only a few approximate the concept, the vehicle nearly always failing the thought. But Martha laid her life's work as an offering before that audience. She was ready. The patterns held the idiom. The fragile cage was one with the content. It was clear, it was beautiful, it was lasting. She had produced a work of art.

And dancing as a medium had taken a step into new and hitherto forbidden realms. The only art to have been separated from religion, dance had shriveled and starved since 1295, when the Christian church by formal edict proscribed it. Martha threw open the great door.

That night, by the performance's close the dance had gained new perspectives, acquired new countries in which to move. It found itself released from what had bound it at 9:30 that same evening.

The audience had witnessed a masterpiece and they knew it. At that very moment they knew it. The theater has housed few such moments. The Elizabethans experienced them, and since then there have been several in the opera houses, but we Americans have had almost none.

The audience that night, February 2, 1931, in the Craig Theatre, under the Fifty-third Street crosstown El, had participated in the grandeur of a living art event.

When the applause finally abated, Martha, without a word, left the stage and went straight to her dressing room. There she sat speechless and shaking and waited for Louis. The girls wept in one another's arms.

Stark Young wrote in *The New Republic,* February 7, 1931, "Of *Primitive Mysteries* I can say that it is one of the few things I have ever seen in dancing where the idea, its origin, the source from which it grew, the development of its excitement and sanctity, give me a sense of baffled awe and surprise, the sense of wonder and defeat in its beautiful presence. . . . We have the sense that, whatever may have been left out, nothing has entered a composition that has not grown into it organically."

John Martin wrote in *The New York Times,* February 8, 1931, "Here is a composition which must be ranked among the choreographic masterpieces of the modern dance movement. . . . She has already touched the borderland of that mystic territory where greatness dwells. . . . At the conclusion of her *Primitive Mysteries* on Monday's program the majority of the house burst into cheers . . . the expression of a mass of people whose emotional tension found spontaneous release. . . . Its simplicity of form and its evocation of the childlike religious elevation of a primitive people never falter for a moment."

Fifty years later, on May 11, 1984, the choreographer Eliot Feld wrote in *Women's Wear Daily:* "When I saw Martha Graham's *Primitive Mysteries* at the State Theater [in the 1960s] I realized it was a great classical work, but the people who saw it fifty years ago did not think of it as classical. Classicism requires integrity of structure and purity of line: A dance is like a bridge, it has to stand up, the structure has to keep it erect, and then the movement invention can stand on that strong, sure structure."

Howard Moss wrote in *The New York Review of Books,* on April 26, 1984, that *"Primitive Mysteries* is a masterpiece that holds its own fifty years after it was created. A signature work, it is to Graham what *Serenade* is to Balanchine. The Christ story is reenacted through the figure of a young girl, a youthful Mary, undergoing the transition from girlhood to maturity. Her white costume is a communion and wedding dress in one."

|||||

If *Primitive Mysteries* was the first successful lay statement in dance of a holy event in the Western Christian church for upward of a thousand years, there have been a few since, notably José Limón's *Missa Brevis,* but Martha's was the first. Ted Shawn danced the doxology, but it was bad aesthetics and, therefore, I believe, impious, however unintentionally. Ruth St. Denis had experimented with religious statements—she even performed in the naves of churches—but hers were posturings in blue veils, altogether without blood. The saints have left us models to help our poor understanding and small skill; Martha studied the great models.

On that same evening, February 2, 1931, Martha gave the premieres of four other works—*Two Primitive Canticles* (Villa-Lobos), *Rhapsodics* (Bartók), *Bacchanale* (Wallingford Riegger), *Dolorosa* (Villa-Lobos)—and performed in additional familiar works. Martha danced in eight pieces that night.

On December 6 of the same year she gave the premiere of *Dithyrambic* (Aaron Copland). She was the first to use Copland's music in a dance concert, and she initiated the practice with a fifteen-minute solo danced to his *Piano Variations.*

Fifteen minutes is an unconscionably long time for a dance solo. The Sugar Plum Fairy's solo in *The Nutcracker,* for example, takes two and a half minutes. *The Dying Swan,* danced so often by Anna Pavlova, takes just under four minutes to perform. Martha's fifteen-minute marathon was a test, she said, to see if she could get through it. I always thought it was also a test to see if the audience could get through it! It was in *Dithyrambic* that I first saw Martha perform the astonishing feat of squatting on one foot, the heel on the floor, the other foot extended in the air straight before her, and in one count rise to a standing position on the strength of the single supporting thigh and leg. "Holy God!" I said aloud. I have never seen another dancer capable of doing this. And Jane Dudley was stunned (along with the audience) by something else in the same dance, "a series of back falls which she kept repeating over and over and over again. It was absolutely overwhelming. I never understood how she could do so many so beautifully, so easily."

|||||

That year, 1931, Martha was awarded half a Guggenheim Fellowship. She was recognized in all the important dance circles, here and abroad, as a real pioneer, the first artist among us. But as she was a dancer, not a musician or a painter, she was not entitled to a full fellowship. With her $1,500, Martha took Louis the following summer to Mexico, to study the Mayan and Aztec cultures which were being unearthed. She watched one tribal dance, ancient past date, standing beside René d'Harnoncourt, the head curator of the Museum of Modern Art, and he recalls that at the conclusion she was shaken so deeply that she toppled over in a dead faint. "She was stunned," he said. He was himself moved, but by her reaction more than by the dances.

The winter of 1931–32, Martha planned a dance series based on the Mayan residuals. It was called *Ceremonials*.

In mid-rehearsal she began to sense failure and she became inconsolable and frightened. I visited her Ninth Street studio during this time and found Louis there. Martha was lying in the little bed cubicle, speechless with worry and dismay, lacerating herself for her failure, for wasting the Guggenheim money. Louis sat helpless but doing his best to comfort her.

In my first book, *Dance to the Piper*, I put down the scene verbatim, as I remembered it.

"Now, Martha, you've got to pull yourself together," Louis droned through his nose.

There was a great deal of wheezing and huffing as he spoke. He took two breaths for every sentence. That was because he had four chests and all his mechanics seemed to get muffled down.

"You can't do this. I've seen you do this before every concert. You're a big enough artist to indulge yourself this way, to fall apart the week before and still deliver on the night. But the girls can't. They are not experienced. You destroy their morale (moan from out the woollens). You tear them down. They're not fit to perform. You cannot work your girls this hard and then dismay them. They will not be able to perform," said Louis.

There was only a snake of black hair lying outside the blanket. Without showing her face or moving, Martha whimpered. "The winter is lost. The whole winter's work is lost. I've destroyed my year. This work is no good."

"It is good, Martha," said Louis persuasively.

"It is not good. I know whether it's good or not. It is not good."

"It may not be so successful as *Mysteries*"—whimpers and thrashings—"but it has its own merits."

"I've lost the year. I've thrown away my Guggenheim Fellowship."

"One cannot always create on the same level. The Sixth Symphony followed the Fifth, but without the Sixth we would not have had the Seventh." (This was sound thinking and I stored it away for future comfort.) "One cannot know what one is leading into. Transitions are as important as achievements."

"Oh, please, please, leave me alone," begged the little voice. I ventured a very timid ministration. I felt like Elizabeth Arden approaching the Cross with a Band-Aid.

"Martha, dear. Dearest Martha, I thought it was beautiful." There was the sound of a ladylike gorge rising.

Louis got stern. He rose; he loomed, not over—that was impossible because of bulk—but near her. "Martha, now you listen to me. You haven't eaten all day. Get your clothes on and come out for some food."

Martha tossed the blanket a bit. The snake whisked from one side to the other. "Oh, please, just go away!" Then all was quiet in cold despair.

Louis got his ulster. Louis got his cap, a flat one with a visor which sat on the top of his white hair. Louis put the coat on Max, his Dackel, and leaned to pat Martha's Maedel. Louis progressed down the street displacing the winter before him. Low in the Horst umbrage cast by street lamps the dachshund wagged on the end of a string. Louis wheezed out his disapproval in a cloud of warm breath. "It's not worth it. Every concert the same. It's not worth it. She's put us all through the wringer. She destroys us."

"But, Louis," I said, pattering after and peering up and around his coat, "she is a genius." He snorted. "Would you consider working with anyone else?"

At this he stopped. He slumped down layers of himself to a thickened halt. "That's the trouble. When you get down to it, there is no other dancer."

|||||

The Mayan piece was not, as it turned out, very good. Martha could not beat herself into the conception.

That same year, 1931–32, my uncle, Cecil B. DeMille, planned a trip to Russia, taking his entire entourage. Theodore Koslov, his ballet-master-in-residence, was to act as guide.

This was a period when Russia allowed free access, and Cecil took advantage of the opportunities. The Russians wanted Cecil B. DeMille to film *War and Peace,* and he had been offered the Russian army and navy to augment the cast. Cecil demanded fifty percent of the profits, which the Russians considered exorbitant; they demurred. But Cecil went to Russia anyway.

As he came through New York on his way east, I suggested that he see our best dancer before embarking for foreign parts, where ballet played such an important role. And so Martha and the Group and Louis went up to the small Heckscher Theater and they hired the hall one morning especially for a demonstration of *Primitive Mysteries.*

They got Hugo Bergamasco to play the flute and Martha brought all the costumes. It cost her about twenty-four dollars to produce the morning, I am told, which she could not afford.

John Martin sat there in rapt wonder, as he always did before this work. He turned to me quietly and said, "I wonder what Diaghilev would have done had he seen this." Indeed, one must ask. Martha had no Diaghilev, no Aga Kahn. There was no one of power and imagination in the United States to give her a frame and to be her public voice. She had to wait for help.

Uncle Cecil sat stolidly throughout the performance, breathing rather heavily, his eyes fixed on the stage and on her. Turning to me, he said, "Her hair is just the right length. Exactly the right length. Longer or shorter would have been wrong."

This was the damnedest comment on *Primitive Mysteries* I had ever heard.

Afterward, Uncle Cecil went up onstage, with me trembling in tow, and was graciousness itself, beaming on Martha and complimenting her on her performance and remarking that he was so glad to have been helpful in her very early career, when she had danced as a slave in front of Tommy Meighan, the Babylonian king in *Male and Female*. Martha made a demure and appropriate remark and he moved away in orbit.

I had clearly been useless, and I apologized later for the expenditure of effort and money. The whole morning had been my idea. He hadn't, of course, understood a thing Martha was doing! I would have paid Martha back for her expenses, if I had had five dollars to spare.

Martha then said something quite sporting and very hopeful. "Don't worry. It's all right. We'll find the money and it will come back to me somehow, someplace. It will come back, you'll see. No effort is wasted." Resilient courage! But I'll be damned if I know how that morning's work was repaid in any way at all. Cecil and Cecil's staff were impervious to new impressions.

He returned from abroad to inform me that the Russians were the only people who knew how to dance. As I wrote to my father (Cecil's older brother, William), "Comrade DeMille has proceeded west in his Golden Locomotive, scattering love of mankind and artistic understanding all the way."

|||||

While Martha had no Diaghilev, nor Aga Kahn, she did have friends of some power and means. Mrs. Isaacs and Mrs. Morgenthau, for instance, had brought prospective patrons to all Martha's concerts, buying many tickets. Both women were the first to appear backstage, Rita Morgenthau herself closeted in the exhausted woman's dressing room, criticizing, advising, and worshiping, Edith Isaacs embracing Martha happily and then rushing home to prepare a celebrative party.

Her patrons may have given Martha two or three hundred dollars from time to time to settle pressing debts, which Martha was generally too shy to mention. But her very rich friends never said, "Martha, here is a couple of thousand dollars. Go blow it on whatever you want and relax." Of course, I think it likely that she would not have taken it.

However, for several summers in the thirties Mrs. Isaacs rented houses for Martha, the first time near Pound Ridge, in Westchester County, New York. Martha took there with her Dorothy Bird and Bonnie Bird, and they indulged in a month's vacation. None of them could really cook (although Martha could make an excellent pot roast) and none of them could drive a car. Even so, Dorothy learned to do both, practicing on living bodies. She cooked without instructions and she drove without a license, and on applying for a legal permit she delivered herself of a most unpromising test. But apparently her winsome personality won over the examining police officer, and he gave permission for her to continue to drive, adding, "You will change gears, won't you, dear? Please do." She stalled at every stoplight and, being shy, never asked directions. The cooking fared no better. But they survived, and Louis came to visit them from time to time. They worked out every day on their own and Martha rested and read difficult books and thought about difficult dances.

Then Martha went west to visit her difficult but dear mother.

In 1931, Katharine Cornell, the actress, had been taken by one of Martha's patrons to see *Primitive Mysteries*. Cornell was so moved that she determined to help Graham.

Katharine Cornell was one of the two most famous and successful actresses in America at that time (the other being Helen Hayes). Cornell had scored a remarkable series of hits, starring always and surrounding herself with splendid casts and fine productions. She never ventured into the movies, but she toured from coast to coast and was known everywhere throughout the length and breadth of the country. Of a dark, rich beauty, with a piquant and sensitive face and one of the loveliest voices of our time, she graced each production with memorable charm. In my opinion she was not a great actress, but that mattered not one whit; she was a dazzling theatrical presence.

She was rich not only by her own efforts but by heritage. Her father, a well-known doctor in his hometown of Rochester, New York, had in his spare time invented the windshield wiper, and he owned the world rights to this invention, which was fine for the theater because Cornell was wonderfully generous with her fortune. Her philanthropy and watchfulness were known throughout the performer's world and helped shape many a young talent. She established scholarships for young actors at the Neighborhood Playhouse and later at the Juilliard School. She paid for lessons with the voice expert Laura Elliot, so that young artists could study with this remarkable teacher. And it was Miss Elliot who told her that Martha Graham needed financial help.

"I believe," Cornell said to me, "that Martha is not only the greatest dancer in America but one of the greatest artists that this country has ever produced in any field, and certainly one of the great personalities and governing influences of the contemporary worldwide theater."

In 1933 Cornell's husband, Guthrie McClintic, was about to stage an adaptation of Shakespeare's poem *The Rape of Lucrece* for the history-making Comédie des Quinze production. He hired Martha ("for five hundred dollars," said Martha to me in wonder and pride) to sit beside him and tell him if he was on the right track in the staging. Then, in 1934, he hired her again at seventy-five dollars a week to create the dances for Cornell's production of *Romeo and Juliet*. Martha used her own company this time and did very charming and pretty arrangements, which were in no way memorable but were highly decorative and earned her cash. She proved her usefulness in other ways by whipping up a nightgown for Juliet's balcony scene, responding on the instant to Cornell's distress on viewing the overelaborate and expensive robe with roses at the neck provided by the designer, Jo Mielziner. Martha ran out, bought several yards of soft white crepe, and spent the entire night snipping and sewing. Cornell wore the Graham garment at the New York opening and thereafter until the close of the run.

Cornell was devoted to and admiring of Martha and undertook to pay some of her expenses. She rented the Labor Stage on West Thirty-eighth Street in New York City for an entire week and paid a salary to Gertrude Macy to act as Martha's company manager. This was the first time an American dance company had attempted such a long season. It was extremely daring of Martha. Although Gertrude Macy knew nothing of dancing, and even less of the business logistics of the trade, she learned rapidly from Louis Horst, and Cornell became a dependable source of income and replenishment for Martha. Martha was scrupulous about never abusing the actress's largesse, asking only the barest minimum, and never anything for personal expenses. She indeed remained extremely shy about asking for money. Any money she received went right into the company fund, to pay for rehearsals and musical scores. Martha kept nothing for herself, saved nothing, banked nothing.

Because she badly needed money she was to try several unfamiliar adventures in 1933.

S. L. Rothafel, who had produced Martha in Los Angeles in her Denishawn days and had brought Massine to the Roxy Theater, later built the great Radio City Music Hall, designed to show not motion pictures but live music-hall acts. He insisted on having quality dancing and quality singing. For the gala opening on December 27, 1932, Jan Peerce was there; Harald Kreutzberg, doing some of his sprightlier pieces; and Martha Graham, whom Rothafel had long felt was an extremely gifted woman and deserved greater recognition. Martha snatched at the opportunity for some real money and large exposure for her work.

At the opening performance there was also a full-sized ballet (thirty-two ballet dancers under the direction of Florence Rogge, the ballet mistress for Roxy's moving-picture house, in addition to the Rockettes, under the direction of Russell Market). Martha's piece, to music composed by Louis Horst, employed only twelve dancers, and was quite startling and wonderful. It moved much more forcefully than the ballet corps more than two-and-a-half times its size, but as far as the audience went it was totally unsuccessful. After one night Martha was fired, along with a number or other acts which had not caught on, leaving the commonplace Florence Rogge the heroine of the night. Rogge's ballet had resembled a revolving wedding cake, a pattern the audience could readily grasp. The strange and subtle rhythms of Martha's twelve girls, on the other hand, went unremarked. Flat is flat, and this was a flat bust. A few days later they were let go.

Mary Watkins of the *Herald Tribune* reported on January 8, 1933: "[Graham's] place at the tail of a bill . . . was not conducive to success. . . . Those who stayed at all until the eighteenth number, which was Miss Graham's uncompromising *Choric Dance for an Antique Greek Tragedy*, found themselves satiated to a point of indifference as to whether the performer were Miss Graham or Ray Bolger, or both together in a pas de deux. The few who were awake and in a condition to receive impressions were certainly in no mood to derive either pleasure or profit from anything which put even the lightest strain upon the intellect, if any.

"Hence the expulsion of Miss Graham and her devoted group upon the toe of somebody else's boot last Saturday week was not unexpected, even if the manner of it may have seemed somewhat brusque."

Within two months Martha used the piece as the ending for a fine and serious work, *Tragic Patterns*, subtitled "Three Choric Dances from an Antique Greek Tragedy." One can easily surmise why it was not fit for the mass audience of a vast music hall.

|||||

Then, on February 5, 1933, at the Guild Theater, Martha collaborated in an evening of ecclesiastical dances based loosely on Roman Catholic church ritual: *Six Miracle Plays*, costumed lavishly by Natalie Hays Hammond, who paid for the production. These turned out to be not particularly good, and Martha chided herself for having fallen into a rich girl's trap. She felt she had been bought to illustrate someone else's ideas and vowed never in her life to do it again.

Martha, for the only period in her adult life, had allowed desperation to lead her off the path.

|||||

The country at this time was going into deeper and deeper recession, deeper and deeper misery. The lines of men waiting for food stretched a block long. There began to be apple sellers on street corners. The frequency of vacant shop spaces grew frightening. There were cards in many shops reading PLEASE DO NOT PUT UP SIGNS NOTIFYING SPACE FOR RENT. There were beggars wherever one turned—not bums, but businessmen, middle-class people, neighbors, desperate and hungry.

Life was dreary in all our cities during those years. Day by day, month by month, we saw the unemployed standing, shuffling along, waiting for handouts, coffee, or soup. Anyone who saw those staring faces knew what the Depression meant. Anyone knew the extent of the catastrophe who witnessed a generation of girls and boys graduating from high school or college to nothing at all, slowly realizing that not ever in their lives for as long as they lived would they achieve anything for themselves. These young men and women were to bear the marks of their withered youth until death. We grew accustomed to the faces always before the restaurants, even the cheapest eateries, while we enjoyed our dollar or fifty-cent dinners. There were the wide, staring, hungry eyes, the drawn, attentive, waiting faces of the starving, men and women, children and adults, pressed against the glass, staring while we ate, while we lapped up our soup, while we dropped crumbs, while we left uneaten crusts—staring and waiting. They never were not there. On the streets, even the good streets, there were beggars wherever one turned, pleading for a dime for a cup of coffee, begging for five cents, even. They didn't have five cents for subway fare. These lines were always there. They never slackened. They never went away. "Brother, can you spare a dime?"

The highways were infested with hoboes, not bad men or dangerous men, just desperate men. Out in the country, men would do almost any chore for a meal.

On the trains crossing the continent, crossing Nebraska, Oklahoma, Kansas, and Colorado, we were advised to keep all windows sealed—not just shut, but sealed—against the brown dust that was in fact death coming in under the glass and lying in powder on every surface of the car. While outside in the murk, which lasted all day long and obscured the sun, stood the patient, doomed animals, victims, heads down, backs bent, waiting for the end. And there was no hope. This was the dust bowl, the grave of an entire country.

Against this running down, slowing up, this economic and spiritual disintegration, Martha as an artist stood up and called out, "Let's try something new!" Brave words! Brave girl!

In 1932 Franklin D. Roosevelt took office as President of the United States and everyone took heart—even the Republicans, who, although automatically hoping for a quick Democratic collapse, were sufficiently uncomfortable and frightened themselves to be willing to accept and profit by Democratic activity.

There was stirring in the stagnation. First, the President was shot but not killed, which made him a national martyr. Then he closed the banks, which, while drastic and novel, created a vacuum and forfended disaster by providing a breathing space for planning reforms—real reforms and financial help, not just a shifting of balances: real help for the sick, the aged, the jobless, and, most important, new and revolutionary, the giving of work to the able indigent. The W.P.A. (Works Progress Administration) provided occupation, recompense, and opportunity for the skilled, trained craftsmen, scientists, artists, painters, architects, writers, musicians, actors—although not yet dancers.

It was a time for change. The winds were coming. We all felt it. All the young intellectuals and the would-be thinkers and writers, all the young artists joined the radical movements and became fellow travelers, if not downright Communists. They didn't really understand what they were doing but they knew they had to do something, and it had to be different.

The pressure on Martha to join the Communist movement was extravagant. She did not join. She studied the sculptor Henry Moore, the painters Picasso and Klee. She went to the new art exhibits. She heard the new music. She read all the new poetry she could. And the direction she was to take, although not yet fully understood, was, she knew, on the way.

Life continued on the rigorous schedule Martha had set, all interest focused on the steadily growing repertory. Her personal life centered on Louis, not really satisfying while undeviatingly necessary. She relied on him, but she was tiring of frustration. "Why does Martha look so unhappy?" my mother asked Louis, with a certain knowing wickedness. "Unhappy sex life," snapped Louis, closing Mother's mouth firmly. Sex was not a word to be used in Mother's parlor. But there it was. Martha was not happy.

There was a rumor that Louis was impotent. This rumor was started, I am sorry to say, by Ted Shawn, who never forgave Horst for despising him as an artist and saying so publicly. Ted countered by challenging Horst's manhood—a charge that may have been fabricated. Yet years later, Helen Tamiris, in her vivid, enthusiastic style, asserted flatly, as a well-known fact, that in spite of all his philanderings, Louis was, indeed, impotent. She shook her mop of curls at me as she said this. Now, Tamiris has made many flat statements, only a few of them valid, and fewer still provable. She was emphatic but not always creditable.

"But," I asked her at the time of our talk, "how can you know this about Louis?"

"Oh, I know," she said in her vibrant, husky voice. "My dear, indeed I know."

"Then explain to me his enormous hold over all the young women he teaches."

"Oh, he has his little ways," said Tamiris airily. And I did not invite her to expatiate. But I can explain Louis's hold quite simply as being in his courage and fidelity and uncompromising bravery, as well as his taste and generosity. He was their father figure, their "wall."

But there was more than this, at least for his students. Marian Seldes, the actress and one-time drama student at the Neighborhood Playhouse, explained:

I was terribly attracted to him. I thought he was wonderful and I wanted to be near him. . . . Women—young girls, I suppose, particularly—found him fascinating, because he was unique. He looked terrible; he looked messy. Everything you shouldn't be, he was. . . . I couldn't wait to get to his class and do something for him. Because that would be my way of showing him how much I adored him. And do you know, I used to sit at the piano while he played for other classes and sort of snuggle around him? I mean, I can't believe it. I feel—and I know you must feel—that within every important artist there is something going on that doesn't have to be spoken. And if you are young enough when you meet someone great, it doesn't have to be explained. There are no embarrassments. You just go toward it. . . . Through the pre-classic dance forms and the beauty of what he helped us to create, there was a kind of power and strength. And the men became masculine and the women became feminine, and Louis Horst made it happen.

Louis was father, teacher, guru, and possibly dream romantic.

And years later Louis himself showed Harry Bernstein, his editor at *Dance Observer,* a letter from Martha in which she states that for her he had been "a king in bed."

That would seem to be that.

Louis had little money for any luxuries, even for a good dinner; but his penury was voluntary, unlike that of the dancers, because he was in constant demand as an accompanist and arranger. He nevertheless restricted his efforts so that he would have time for Martha, and for the Neighborhood Playhouse, and for his pupils. What kind of a private life he had, one cannot say, as he was enthralled by a sibyl who was inflamed with her own vision, an egomaniac who was also a goddess. Poor Louis! He was bound and shackled emotionally, forever, to cruelty.

And poor Martha! Poor, poor Martha! No place to call her own and nothing she could count on, except a couple of back falls. Feeble company in the evenings! She was a passionate, full-blooded woman, and unquestionably she needed a more rewarding relationship. But she was not self-pitying, and she never complained. Never once. Nor did she confide in any friend—not about her finances, not about her love affairs—never throughout her life. Except once—but that was later.

Martha was proud and conducted herself with unflawed circumspection. No one saw her weep, although Marian Graham, my accompanist, once observed her praying in St. Patrick's Cathedral with tears streaming down her cheeks. The cause of the tears was anyone's guess.

Martha much later claimed that she was not in love with Louis. "I was deeply fond of him and I believed his word. I was a child [for him]. It was like loving a child." That may be how she chose to remember the relationship. There are contemporary witnesses who remember it otherwise. I, for one, recall his agony and her (and his) recurrent distress. There was certainly nothing immature about the pain. She may well have experienced greater passion later, but her dismay and her grief that he distrusted her too much to marry her were acute.

On that trip to the woods of Merriewold, I had a chance to see Martha and Louis away from their regular environment. They seemed strangely alien and different from my neighbors. Down at the dam, Louis stood looking around at the mothers and children and family groups doing quite normal and pleasant things like swimming and taking bathing caps off and drying their hair and changing shoes. He said to me, "How astonishing it is that people still raise children! How really extraordinary when you think of all the sex that must go on to produce this!"

And then he chuckled and said, "Martha and I sometimes stand at the corner of Forty-second Street and Broadway and say, 'It's going on all the time, everywhere. Just look at it!' " Louis really seemed astonished by the domestic scenes; Martha, I think, less so. She knew, however, that none of it was for her.

We used quite frequently to have dinner with Hugo Bergamasco, Martha's flutist (and mine), who owned a brownstone house in the

West Seventies and who ran a charming restaurant in the basement. His mother did the cooking and his wife the serving. The mother and Hugo made a kind of bootleg Chianti which was potable, and this we drank for a very small price while we supped on extremely good spaghetti al dente and fine pastries. On the wall hung a splendid photograph of Martha in a skintight dress. And beside it was a picture of me in a Civil War costume with a Civil War gun (real) cocked on my shoulder. The conversation was always pleasant and laced with invectives against the ignorance of American managers, the lousy contemporary setup for artists, and the unworthiness of those who had already succeeded!

At the end of one meal Louis pushed his chair back from the table, half shut his eyes, gazed down his stomach, and gave voice to a comment on Martha's infidelity. The remark was like a bullwhip across the face. Martha went white and she lifted her regard. The golden light in her eyes danced. I continued staring and silent. "You're being," she fiercely murmured in a barely audible voice, "very unkind."

In all the time I knew Martha, this was the only inadequate statement she had ever made.

What Louis was being was loutish and brutal. Nobody spoke for a minute. Then we resumed our talk about the true function of art, and how inferior Tamiris was, while Louis, desperately gathering up the remnants of his tattered male pride and wrapping vulgarity around him like a mantle, paraded out of the situation and finally subsided, lonely but persistent, into a series of diminishing chuckles and sneers, like a pot going off the boil.

Martha linked arms with me as we went up the street. Louis followed, barely talking, dragging his dachshund, Max. Martha murmured very softly, "Of course, he began it. He started it all, the unfaithfulness."

I turned in amazement. "He did? He adores you. How could he?"

"Oh," said Martha, mostly to herself, "he can. He can."

This was not the only occasion when Louis whipped Martha's decencies from her. From time to time he would slip into sour confessions and intimacies. I've mentioned earlier ones made to me. It was hard to stop him; he leaked misery. It could happen at any time, according to his caprice and evil whim. Why did she tolerate this? I believe it was because our great lady, our tigress and heroine, was also a masochist. That is why she stood such treatment from the man she loved.

And Louis blurted out these hurtful taunts because of his pain.

I believe, too, that Louis felt he had to keep a whip over Martha by exposing her, by taunting. And young pupils—Dorothy Bird, for example, the beautiful, blond child in her little straight coat and pillbox hat—fled from one or two scenes of distraught fury when Martha raged and shouted because he refused to divorce Betty Horst. They had been hanging drapes and fussing over costume material in the studio one Sunday, with Dorothy helping, when the scene broke, and it was a terrible one. Dorothy ran into the street and sought succor from José Limón, who, by happy coincidence, was passing. Like Louis, Martha also had her point of unbearable pain.

And always the work went on.

And so did Louis's marital status. There was never to be a divorce. There were many, many girls, but no second wife. He sent Betty payments even through Martha's bitter poverty and need, and this was part of the problem, because all this time he adored Martha, every day, always, in every action. He served her, protected her, took care of her. But he would not marry her.

Nevertheless, Martha and Louis were locked into a major love affair. Although they seemed to devour each other, each of their lives was complete only with the other's brain and heart and vitality. And at the same time they both struggled for freedom. The anguish was lifelong, and although Martha tore herself away after some years, and Louis similarly toward the end of his life formed a good and loving liaison elsewhere, they tortured each other until death. In fact, they *were* married.

Martha and Louis: an institution, a strength; the union was recognized by everyone. And we all drew comfort from it. Yet Dorothy Bird maintains:

They weren't lovers, they were partners, and he was, as he always said, her pounding board. I don't think their relationship was physical. Nor did she have other lovers. I think she was totally, one hundred percent absorbed in what she was doing. She was absolutely charged with this. And I was there at nine in the morning, and I stayed until four the next morning and was almost never out of her sight. I just can't imagine that there was something going on anywhere. She was a fighting person, absorbed, focused, bent on one object. She was keeping a convent, and she would keep us there in rehearsal until eleven, twelve, one. . . . She wouldn't allow the girls' lovers or husbands to stand in her way at all, and they just had to put up with the situation. She felt the work was important, she felt *she* was important, and that she was on a par with Picasso. You can't flirt around when you're like that.

Martha's spring recital in New York was generally the last important Graham event of the year. In June the Neighborhood Playhouse closed for the summer. Martha gave a short, intensive course in her Ninth Street studio, to which out-of-town teachers began to come by the dozen, and then she went west with Louis for her season at the Cornish School in Seattle. This annual job helped pay for her visit to her mother. In 1927 Mrs. Graham had remarried, after a widowhood of thirteen years. Her new husband, Homer Duffy, was a vice president of the Bekins Moving and Storage Company. He was, according to Winthrop Sargeant, a true Kiwanis type and altogether alien to his new wife's strange daughters. They, in turn, found him unsympathetic but curbed their feelings out of consideration for their mother. They regarded him, and he them, as creatures of strange breeds. Yet they were grateful to him for taking over Jenny's financial support.

At the conclusion of the Seattle course in July, Louis usually continued on alone to the Perry-Mansfield Camp at Steamboat Springs, Colorado, and thence to Santa Fe and the Indian country; he proceeded later to Ravinia, where Ruth Page was ballet mistress of the Chicago Summer Opera.

But whatever he and Martha did in the summer, Louis spent the autumn weeks in New York, holed up in a hotel, devoting his days to the baseball season at Ebbets Field and his nights to delicious bachelor freedom, with solitary dinners and detective stories until sleep. This was his golden time, free of "little pink toes," and he would let nothing interfere with it.

Martha often said that she went to the baseball games with Louis and that she knew the players by name, and I'm sure she did and that she paid heed to whatever he told her about them. But I'm equally sure that it was an aesthetician's appreciation. She was interested in the way the bodies functioned in baseball games and in the way the body of a champion functioned as opposed to the arms and back and foot coordination of a rookie. Louis Horst, on the other hand, went to the games with the eagerness and delight of the avid American baseball fan. Scores mattered to him. About these he cared heartily, and he knew every one of them. I very much doubt that Martha did. She also attended lightweight boxing matches with him, but I cannot believe that it was of any meaning to her who won, as long as she saw the play of muscles and the expressions on the faces of the contenders.

After his baseball season, Louis would start work with Martha, who borrowed her next six months' studio rental as an advance on her

Neighborhood Playhouse salary and started the year's routine over again. She commented wryly, "A fine system!" She lived like an indentured servant.

Martha, unfortunately, had few means of emotional release. A visit to her mother was annual, filial, and obligatory, but not to be looked upon in any way as an easement or diversion. She never took vacations, not in those days. Martha did not read detective stories; in fact, she read hardly any fiction. I think that she could not let her mind play or rest enough to read for mere pleasure. She felt impelled to challenge and instruct herself with aesthetics, sociology, mythology, comparative religion, philosophy, and occasionally treatises on social problems, sparing herself little in the few moments snatched before sleep. Later, when she discovered psychoanalysis, she plunged into professional conversation without really putting herself in the hands of a doctor. It was poking and amateur prying merely, but it was titillating to her and she derived tremendous zest from it. Louis looked on all of this as an indulgence, but I believe he refused to participate. Obviously she longed for someone to talk to, to share something beyond the immediate work.

Martha was growing jaded. It must have gradually become a reality that she could not have an ordinary marriage with Louis. But did she really want marriage? Or, rather, was she infuriated by his denial and balking of her pride? When, after years of hesitation and delays, she at last consented to marry someone (not Louis), it was to face up to a situation of unbroken frustration without a possibility of real happiness or any peace. Martha could not give herself to another person any more than she could share her body with a child, as she later explained to Pearl Lang. Motherhood was to be denied her, and in this case she meant love and the risks of life, not only the physical but the emotional as well.

Martha knew subconsciously, and very likely quite clearly and consciously, too, that her first interest in life was her dancing and that she must serve this interest with her first strength. She could not be a true helpmate, a true wife, to any man. She might be, and very likely was, often the best company in the whole world, but not a wife. Nor could any man expect her to be. So she came to prefer men who were not demanding, who were not wholly men but only part-time males, and who could make way in their own psyches and interests for the greater dominating infatuation: *the work*. Again and again and again, as time went on, she chose to fall in love with a homosexual man. Intuitively she knew this was to be her pattern, and she accepted it. The question had to be always, sooner or later, whose work was to be served: his work or her work?

Writing to a friend in 1952, Martha said that she never could free herself to become "the most simple and elemental instrument for life." She always had to be in control or govern "even against nature."

Yet Martha lived in passion; it was obvious that she was always a lusty and highly sexed woman. Indeed, these qualities are as inherent in her dancing gestures as in the sexual overtones of her manner. The critic Alan Kriegsman wrote in 1984: "Graham thinks of sex as the very piquancy of the life force—even in her dances that approach 'pure' movement pieces, . . . there are always transactions between the sexes."

Every rehearsal with a man became a flirtation, every creative session a rendezvous. And although most of the men had no possible thought of anything physical with her, they nevertheless sensed the overtones and responded with electric excitement and eagerness. Even casual conversations with men were imbued with the overtones of her enormous, unresting excitement. I have yet to hear of a man who did not take fire in one way or another from a mere encounter with her. She carried on, sly and deadly, and always her fun was alternated with the wonder of revelation or the black passion of impatience. But to give away part of her life? To share any piece of her position, or her fame, or her standing, or her power? It was probably beyond her desires or capabilities. She could no more do this than could Isadora Duncan. The tragedy is that Martha did not recognize the fact early in her life and come to terms with it. It is a very hard idea to come to terms with because, in effect, it means that one weds loneliness, as a nun does, but with none of the compensations and none of the promises.

In fact, Martha repudiated her physical body. She had infrequent menstrual periods. When the event finally overtook her, she was prostrated with pain, could hardly stand, and had to resort to medical help. A doctor cousin of mine pulled her through one such ordeal and made it possible for her to get on the stage (Martha's Christian Science evidently not being equal to these wringing cramps). Several great dancers have been similarly afflicted, as though they denied their sex in the interest of work. They simply would not permit their bodies to take over every four weeks for biological purposes and be used like the earth for erosion.

I believe Martha gave virility to many men. She minded not at all if they were homosexual in their preferences. To her they were men, and as far as she was concerned they were men who held a tremendous zest for her and who were accommodating and not demanding.

When trouble came, and it always did, it rooted in power rivalry. The pretty, playful, sexual game ended. Up to a point Martha could tell herself comfortable lies, but suddenly, without warning, she faced the truth. She was a lightning conductor. She split open. There was the *eye*.

Martha preserved an unblemished reticence about her personal and family affairs. Her sister, Mary, who in 1929 had quietly pulled up stakes in New York, moved to San Francisco, and married a doctor, grew ill with cancer and died; not one of Martha's associates or pupils can remember her ever mentioning that it happened.

Accordingly, when Martha's first truly satisfactory love affair occurred, there was no discussion among the Group. Yet it occurred, and it was a changing experience.

She remarked to me in 1934 or 1935 that she had known something transforming, something new and extraordinary, and that when it happened it was "as natural as breathing."

"When Osiris was destroyed," she said, referring, I'm sure, to her recent passion, "he was scattered all over the world and his wife, Isis, reassembled him. But he lacked the essential part, until she finally brought it back to him. Then he had life and was whole. And it wasn't his head, and it wasn't his heart; it was his genitals."

About this same time she asked me if I'd read *Lady Chatterley's Lover*, by D. H. Lawrence, which was legally banned in the United States on moral grounds. She promised she could get it for me and advised me to read it. (In fact, I had read it in England.)

The experience had happened. In the mid-thirties a profound change occurred in Graham's life, in her manner and temperament, and above all in her work. Martha had known love. She mentioned the fact, but not the name involved. From others I learned that he was married: the relationship could not and did not last.

ennington College was seven years in the planning before it started formally, in 1932. Designed as a liberal-arts college for undergraduate women, Bennington had a curriculum that included all the sciences but stressed the arts. The college was set in rolling hills amid trees and meadows and with blue mountains in the distance, in the old Jennings estate opposite Mount Anthony, Vermont. The buildings consisted of a barn, a chicken coop, and a house for residents. The first year there were eighty-five female students and a disproportionately large faculty, which, to the girls' delight, boasted men. In addition, since Williams and Dartmouth colleges were just down the valley in healthy and happy proximity, the students found they had all the necessary comforts.

Robert Devon Leigh, the first president of Bennington, enlisted the aid of Martha Hill in 1931, who had since 1929 been a member of Martha Graham's Group and was also on the faculty of New York University, teaching composition and dance technique. Both Leigh and Hill wanted the best for the new institution, but how to finance it? At that time people were unsure how the school would succeed, and they were loath, in those post–stock-market-crash times, to commit a large expenditure for a new college or for the art Martha Hill loved best. Martha Hill loved Bennington also, and she advised against overextension. President Roosevelt was about to close the banks.

Martha Hill recalled: "I remember Mr. Leigh's saying about setting up the dance program, 'how much?' I said there was no way to pay an artist, he would just have to meet the going rate, which was fortunately low. So we charged what students would have to pay elsewhere for the kind of dance course we intended to offer.

"But in truth, they couldn't get similar training elsewhere, because we planned on assembling the top masters in the modern American dance field. We figured we could break even with sixty-five dance students. When the sixty-fifth registered we held a celebration; when the one-hundred-and-tenth registered we slammed the door shut."

The experiment of bringing together the leaders of a creative field in the theater—Graham, Humphrey, Weidman, Holm, Limón, Horst, and John Martin—was timely, and it was meaningful. Moreover, it was the very first of its kind anywhere. Some of the summer schools (the Cornish School in Seattle and the Perry-Mansfield Camp in Steamboat Springs, Colorado) employed teachers in the different dance techniques, but nowhere before had there been an attempt to assemble simultaneously all the founding leaders in modern dance. It was a plan fraught with dynamic and emotional hazards.

In July 1934, the first year, Martha and Louis taught at Bennington alone for a month, then stayed on two more weeks as Doris Humphrey and Charles Weidman arrived to begin. At the end of Doris's initial four weeks, Hanya Holm arrived. Each group was augmented by Bennington students, who also participated in the concerts given by the leaders and their own groups at the conclusion of each stint of teaching.

In 1935 they devised a five-year overall plan for the dance department. The second year Martha was to produce an original work, the third year Doris and Charles were to produce one, the fourth year Hanya Holm. In the fifth year, 1938, a crowning week was projected, with a concert by each on successive nights. This was to make up the first major festival of contemporary dance, and it was to gain an international reputation.

In addition to the teaching and composing by the choreographers, Louis Horst taught dance composition, Arch Lauterer taught stage design, John Cage and Norman Lloyd taught music, and John Martin taught dance criticism. For his purposes a press office was set up in the old infirmary. After every exhibition the students typed their own critical reviews at separate typewriters, as Martin waited for their copy. His wife, Louise Martin, taught acting, but here there was a difference of opinion; Louis Horst forbade his students to study with her.

"D'you know," said Louis, "John has grown very cool to me."

"I should think so," I replied tartly.

"Well, I had to forbid the students. She was very bad." He seemed genuinely surprised at her husband's resentment.

Martha already knew Joseph Campbell, who taught mythology and classical literature at Sarah Lawrence. Now she saw him daily. He was to write a remarkable series of books, including *The Masks of God, The Hero with a Thousand Faces*, and a superb critical key to James Joyce's *Finnegans Wake*. One of his students, the beautiful Jean Erdman, became a member of Martha's group and subsequently Campbell's wife.

Mrs. Leonard Elmhurst (née Whitney), an American philanthropist living in England, heard from Mrs. Isaacs about the Bennington adventure and offered money, first, to make a survey of dance in the United States (after a great expenditure it was found to be exactly what we all knew it was—financially unsatisfactory), and second, to establish scholarships. The first two scholarships were granted to Anna Sokolow and Esther Junger, an independent soloist; the next two to Pearl Lang and Merce Cunningham. These were of great benefit to the students and a help to their teachers.

Initially Bennington dance students were attached to the physical education department. Gradually students of theatrical ability began attending dance classes.

The modern-dance leaders were all on the premises, but let it not be thought for a moment that they relinquished their mutual distrust of one another or their protocol. Every day, when Hanya Holm was constrained to cross Martha's rehearsal hall to reach her own, Martha suspended all speech and action and stared until the door had closed softly on the departing heel. Hanya was, of course, unnerved by this conduct. The teachers dined at separate tables. And yet they were at least partially concurrent and together, so the students profited, viewing the elders' hostility with amusement. And the teachers themselves profited, in spite of their wariness—first, because there was a fine commingling of all kinds of artists, musicians, and designers, and second, because all those responsible for booking the college concert series across the continent were assembled there. They were given the opportunity of choosing wisely among the leading dancers, of comparing and selecting, while at the same time they were free from the limiting strictures of the three big monopolistic managements, who pressed for preference of their European clients. As a consequence, for the first time American dancers were hired to tour America nationwide, and this marked the beginning of their solvency.

Now, most happily owing to the exposure at Bennington, Martha was finally able to venture into the great continent, her own land, formerly closed to her, a land hitherto visited only by foreigners. The whole continent lay waiting, and she and her colleagues began to venture out. Wherever she went she met with acolytes and pupils who had been teaching her technique and spreading her gospel and who waited eagerly for her coming. The audiences were on the whole small, but they were sympathetic, and the enthusiasm grew and spread.

For these trips she needed more expert management than Louis could supply in his homemade way, and she needed it full time. Frances Hawkins, who had been a devoted admirer, came and worked as Martha's manager, booking her quite steadily and supplying the devoted professional help which Martha had always lacked.

Martha and the other groups were hired not only to perform but to teach and to lecture. Beyond this, and of prime importance, was the fact that many of their graduating students went on to head dance departments elsewhere. It was found that "modern" dancing could be practiced by girls and boys of college age, whereas ballet was too difficult for late beginners. Modern-dance technique, therefore, had found a profitable market, and it flourished in the college gymnasium, out of which it straightaway began to kick and stamp, demanding to be considered an art. This was a new wave for modern dance. The academics acceded, slowly but generally. The teachers and students who went on to head the dance departments of our colleges and who formed companies for experimental work all over the United States and throughout the world began in Bennington.

|||||

Martha was recognized as having made revolutionary changes in dance: in form, in subject matter, in the analysis and examination of her themes, and in the handling of the aesthetics itself. William Hogarth said, "Serious dancing is a contradiction in terms," to which Martha,

I believe, would have replied, "Any matter that is not serious is not worthy of dancing." She had a permanently youthful curiosity and approached each project with the innocence and the skepticism of a child, and with a child's bold excitement. And she demanded answers.

The essence of Martha's material, therefore, included fundamental psychology, fundamental emotion, and fundamental physical aesthetics.

She was also revolutionary in collaborative arts. There has been no other single person equally influential in so many fields—in choice of music, costumes, sets, nomenclature, and subject matter, as well as in dance technique. For instance, she was not a musician and played no instrument, yet she had an instinctive and searching feeling for music. Her choice of music set new styles.

The music Louis found for her was fresh, new, and striking, generally not heard before, and certainly not in dance concerts. She had begun first with the moderns, the well-known turn-of-the-century giants, Debussy, Ravel, Satie, Scriabin, Rachmaninoff, Cyril Scott—these were known. But then, under Louis's prodding, she started to work with the less well known Bartók, Goosens, Falla, Bloch, Hindemith, Kodály, Honegger, Ornstein, Malipiero, Prokofiev, Mompou, Harsányi, Milhaud, Poulenc, Krenek, Toch. And gradually she began using the Americans: Aaron Copland, Lehman Engel, Wallingford Riegger, Henry Cowell,* Edgard Varèse, George Antheil, Paul Nordoff, Robert McBride, Norman Lloyd, Alex North, Ray Green, Hunter Johnson, William Schuman, Norman Dello Joio, Alan Hovhaness. And always Louis Horst, whose music for her was unfailingly suitable and moving. (At that time Martha had rarely danced to the greatest modern composers of all, Stravinsky and Richard Strauss, not, I imagine, being able to afford the commissions and royalties.)

Young musicians came to hear the new music, and they came hoping and praying that Martha would use *their* music, because it was an effective way for them to get known.

Martha kept to a lean, acerbic diet of challenging, strange sounds, mainly percussive, which seldom embraced melody. It is no accident that she didn't use melody and that she avoided resolutely all the

---

*Cowell was in prison on a morals charge (for sodomy) when Martha commissioned a score from him. She had been told it would hearten him if he was given work to do, so she journeyed to San Quentin, discussed the work, and left the order. The piece, *Four Casual Developments*, had its premiere in 1934.

romantics of the nineteenth century, all the baroque and rococo composers of the eighteenth. There was nothing in her music to suggest past experience to the listener, nothing familiar to cherish, no memories to be stirred, no preconceptions to be affronted. Her music forced attention where Martha wanted it: on the gesture. She made the dancer indicate the atmosphere, the landscape, and the situation, without help.

There are great dangers in this procedure. As with anything very new, the music may not be valid of itself. The restraints and curtailments that great music imposes are dispensed with, it is true, but also all the old crutches and all the old aids and helps. One is therefore forced to take the problems raw, and they had better be solved satisfactorily and truthfully.

In truth, melody is banished at a price, for melody is an extraordinarily persuasive tool. It is a spiritual achievement and it cannot be freely discarded. With it go incalculable kindnesses, easements, endearments, and searchings. Without it the dance can seem dry, even bony, and often unlikable. It is impossible to think of the ballet without melody. The very term *enchaînement* means a linking, an eliding, a slipping from one pattern to another, all sustained and made meaningful by the melodic path. The ballet choreographers mask the primitive joinings and statements with graces—the grease, so to speak, of melody; they're made easy, smooth. In contrast, Martha wished them revealed. In Graham, they stand there like exposed skeletons or diagrams, and we see their authenticity, the verities of line and curve and angle and their shadows in time. I think for this reason Martha could not use anything but the most percussive and stringent of music, a mere intensification of movement.

|||||

As mentioned, Graham had become one of the great costume designers of all time. Here indeed she was supreme.

She worked in an opulent period in the theater, when the union costs were not great enough to rule out rich materials and handwork; yet she could not have afforded any of these, nor did she choose to. She found new materials—stretch fabrics, tricots, and elasticized synthetics—and she used them in new ways. She not only trimmed in a different way; she engineered the dresses in a brand-new fashion. She had a sense for her material that only the greatest craftsmen had, and she became as skillful in cutting as anyone in Paris—Vionnet, for instance, or Mme.

Alix. But her craft really stemmed from the way Miss Ruth used to fold material and drape it round herself. "Never be afraid of material," Martha would say. "The material knows when you are frightened and will not help."

She shopped for every yard of the costume material herself, delegating none of the hunting, or feeling and testing for texture, to others, because she could not. She designed with scissors and pins directly on the body, often with the actual material itself.

Everyone prepares for a serious effort. The surgeon gets his sleep, stays sober, and scrubs his hands. The athlete goes without sex. The priest abstains from food and drink. Prayer, fasting, precede all real celebration. The body and spirit must be cleansed to become the vessel. Dancers go to the theater hours ahead of performance time and warm up slowly, withdrawing tighter and tighter into the performer's world and cutting themselves entirely from daily life and family claims.

Graham had her own devices to prepare for performances. She could not rehearse the group more at that point or change the dance further without destroying morale. But she could change and destroy the costumes. Twenty-four hours before a premiere, Martha might rip the dresses to pieces and set about totally reworking line, cut, stitching. The girls would be pressed into service and would sit sewing all night and day. Martha finally pinned, too, with bleeding fingers. This madness persisted for years. The girls may have been indifferent seamstresses, but the costumes were all right, because Martha was there supervising. And the girls were all right, because they were spellbound. None of them had time to have nerves about themselves; they had open hysterics about the hang of their skirts.

One fact overrides all others: Martha's costumes may have started as a sedative for nerves; they ended up as masterpieces.

Onstage the girls and Martha had their own style, but they had their own daily fashion as well and became recognizable for it, a style of appearance which came to be widely known long before their work was understood. The ballet students of the thirties and forties tended to be cute and chic; the modern dancer ran to intensity, being larger boned and more heavily muscled. We always said that the modern dancers looked "Villagey," but the term is misleading. They became the national college-undergraduate type, with free-swinging full skirts, flat shoes, pullover sweaters, shawls or simple coats, babushkas, and enormous leather shoulder pouches, often containing their leotards and a towel. Now all the dancers—ballet or modern—wear designer jeans, their hair is in strings, and they look starved. But that is a characteristic of the time, not of the craft or its leaders.

||||

At first Martha couldn't be known for her stage decor because she could not afford any. She began using scenic devices in the late thirties, including mobiles by Alexander Calder. Her first true set was by Arch Lauterer; it was suggestive, economic, imaginative, aerial.

It was Isamu Noguchi's sparse molded forms, however, that were the unforgettable set contribution. Martha had met Noguchi when he came around the *Greenwich Village Follies,* and later, at her studio in Carnegie Hall, with Michio Ito. Subsequently she sat for two heads which he sculptured. She was interested in his work and in his ideas. He said he would indicate a set for her, that is, he would do set pieces that would suggest decor, rather like Klee. His set pieces not only added another dimension to the stage but introduced a style of suggestive decor that put a permanent stamp on Graham's theater. They helped to define and set off the movement and, in a totally abstract way, suggested atmosphere or location, but any location or atmosphere the viewer wished. And they were in Martha's style. Noguchi's understanding of Japanese and Chinese aesthetics, Oriental iconography and its relation to Zen Buddhism, had a profound and lasting influence on all of Graham's work. "Isamu Noguchi's vision of space and the integral meaning of his sculpture set me on a direction which sustained me throughout my career," she has said. Martha herself must have been well aware of the importance of his contribution and her deep aesthetic affiliation with it, because she made an arrangement with him to do many works for her and enjoined him from working for any other dancers. On occasion he told people, when he declined their offers, that he simply could not agree to work for others. With the exception of Merce Cunningham, his work in the theater was to be restricted to Martha Graham herself.

In an article in *The New York Times Magazine* in 1982, the art critic Michael Brenson quoted William Lieberman, the curator of modern art at the Metropolitan Museum, who said that "Noguchi gives meaning not only to place but to void," and that the sculptor's work is "a constantly evolving ritual." Brenson added that the innovations Noguchi created in his long and historic association with Graham (thirty-five works) transformed the theater and the dance which inhabited this changing cosmography. "Previously stage scenery had been primarily a painter's rather than a sculptor's art," Brenson said. Noguchi spurned the backdrop and put his sets on the stage floor itself, often on a series of planes that could be used by the dancers for their own planes of movement. Sculpture, he maintained, was important in relation to what it displaced:

This concept, that sculpture does not merely sit in space but also creates space, was appealing to Graham. . . .

"I realized," says Graham, "that he had the astringency, that everything was stripped to essentials rather than being decorative. Everything he does means something. It is not abstract except if you think of orange juice as the abstraction of an orange. . . ."

Noguchi illustrates the "shock of recognition." You recognize something that is a part of yourself. Nature, the points of the universe, the cosmic, natural forms—but not imitations of natural forms—the four points of the compass, anything you like. He's caught up in the happenings of the universe. . . .

Once his sculptures are on the stage, she regards them as living things, as active people in the drama, and she makes them an integral part of the choreographic movement.

Noguchi said, "My collaboration is a spatial division. The theater space is not just one level but extends out into the firmament. It is the sculpting of space. The space of the universe where we happen to be."

Graham continued, "Sometimes there is a friction. More than once I had to order him off the stage. . . . It was not always dulcet, you know."

Noguchi said, "For Martha [each dance] is a catharsis of her own. She goes through a kind of ritual each time. I was just her assistant with the necessary equipment, like in a hospital."

Brenson went on to explain what Noguchi and Graham created together:

Although usually Graham developed her choreography and Noguchi approached his designs from different points of view, their collaborations expressed similar intentions and ultimately evoked timeless images of the majestic universal legends. . . . I never subscribed [said Noguchi] to the idea that sculptures are just sculptures and not something that is a tool. These are symbolic or gesturely tools she was using. They were an extension of her body. It's my own approach to sculpture as being part of living, not just part of art. I don't look at art as something separate and sacrosanct. It's part of usefulness. . . . I used an interest that I already had elsewhere—the skeleton of the body.

Henceforth Graham's work had a spatial and formal appearance that was as eloquent as that appearing on any classic stage in the Orient, and one which gave rise to generations of derivations, both here and in Europe.

|||||

Martha also created a form of nomenclature. When she started, dance titles were usually French, musical, or generic, such as *La Soirée dans Grenade, Valse Triste, Scherzo.* She gradually changed to English and to the designations of psychological and emotional moods or states of mind: *Heretic, Lamentation, Four Insincerities.* Occasionally she used phrases from poetry that reflected a character's actions, or confrontation and conflict: *Deaths and Entrances, Acrobats of God.*

An entire school of choreography is embraced in this new approach to names.

About program notes she had in these years one rule: none.*

|||||

She introduced an extraordinary change in the literature surrounding the dance by encouraging sound and thoughtful criticism. When she started, there were only John Martin and Mary Watkins, both good, but too few. As she continued ceaselessly to produce works of substance, the critical evaluation grew in understanding. Today there are at least two dozen writers about dance in the United States, of superior force and intellect. Graham helped change the entire field to one of worth and probity. I do not think this mass of critical work would have existed without the revolutionary creations to summon the effort. The initial and continuing challenge was furnished by Graham. Martha therefore gave rise to a body of critical thinking merely by producing works of sufficient stature, of sufficient import, to invite—no, more, to compel—judgment of serious quality and merit.

At the same time, George Balanchine, Graham's exact contemporary, through his reliance on abstract visual design and a close relationship to the form and discipline of music, earned appraisal which was in every way equivalent to the best in music and art criticism. These two, Graham and Balanchine, brought dignity to the general atmosphere in which dance today functions.

*At that time, and for decades following, there were no notes. Later, there were to be enigmatic comments.

She was a great director and drew from her girls unmatched performances, although she seldom let them distinguish themselves in solo roles. As a bank or chorus they had no superior in the world. She was equally a brilliant teacher, even if not graphic or explicit, and therefore not an easy teacher to follow.

||||||

Yet Martha's greatest discoveries were her philosophy and aesthetics.

Jean Erdman first met Martha in the dancing class Martha taught at Sarah Lawrence College once a month. Jean remembers that Graham was all in white, her long hair fastened back with a single pin which continually came loose and had to be skewered into place with impatient jabs. At the commencement of class, after nailing her hair secure with a single thrust, Martha walked to the center of the floor and, into rapt silence, began to speak. "In movement there are certain absolute truths. This is a truth." And she did a second-position plié.

Martha was talking the basic dynamics of geometry. A plié is a bending of the weight-bearing knee; second-position plié is the feet separated and legs rotated outward, the weight evenly born by both legs, the back straight, and the torso descending directly like a plummet between the spread knees. The position is symmetrical and fundamental, a preparation for activity. Every dancer in the world knows that one must bend the knee before doing anything—walking, running, jumping. But to phrase it in this way! The dreary exercise took on the majesty of Newton's equations. This was architecture; this was science; this was, indeed, music. Jean Erdman right then became Martha's slave.

Louis was always concise and clear, Martha never; but Martha had emotional insight that transcended language and rules. Louis followed after, carefully plotting her meteoric course and explaining to students what she had done. The genius, the flash, of course, he could not explain.

What Martha and Louis were like in class is graphically described by Robert Moulton, a young drama and dance teacher on the faculty of the University of Minnesota, who took three summer courses from Graham, the first two at New London in 1951–52, the third at her studio in New York in 1953. Louis Horst alternated the teaching stints. These notes were made twenty years after the present point in our story, but although Martha's flow of images and pictures varied with time, the essence is the same: the difference lies in the fact that by 1950 Graham had assistants to help her demonstrate movement.

Moulton said:

One of the rituals I enjoy at the Graham school is the way class begins. You are in the dressing room and hear the applause of the class now ending and suddenly the cramped dressing room is doubly cramped with the two classes intermingling and you escape to the studio. You stretch and say hello and chat. The company member who is going to demonstrate for Miss G. enters, smiles, nods, gets to work. One does not talk too much to members of the company. After all, they are the chosen ones. Their manner is slightly aloof. They take their roles as disciples seriously—and why not? I am certain that some democratic souls find this offensive and are turned off. Thank God, it turns most of us on.

The accompanist may play a bit. And then, about a minute before class begins, a hush falls. Everyone sits [on the floor] facing the front of the studio, feet, soles together, in front of you. The spines straighten. As Gwendolen says in *The Importance of Being Earnest,* "The suspense is unbearable, I do hope it will last." Miss Graham enters behind you. Even if you didn't hear the door open you know she is there. You don't need eyes to feel the animal magnetism of Martha. She walks down the side of the studio, a small lady in a kimono. It is removed, folded, laid down. How we all try to read into each move the mood of the day. Does the black kimono mean we will be beaten into submission? Does the blue one mean we will all dance like gods? Is she smiling? Is she stoic? You soon learn that no amount of reading will tell you anything, because each class is built on its immediate problems. Each class begins at the beginning of dance all over again.

She sweeps the room with her eyes. There is no verbal greeting, only that look full of challenge, dignity, and no nonsense. A nod to the accompanist and we begin.

She is the Stanislavski of the dance. She is the only person who has said to me that whether or not I touch my toes is unimportant. What matters is that I do the things the *way* she wants but not to the same extent as my neighbor. The important thing is not just to contract or point a toe but to do it with a *purpose.* "Not, I want to be a dancer tomorrow, but *I am a dancer today.*" I got two miserable floor burns without even knowing it until the class was over. I talked to Louis that night and he said that all they could hope to do was slightly stir these foolish little girls. All *she* wants to accomplish is to have us know when we *are* dancing, and when we are *not.*

Today class was stopped. Obviously something was lacking in our efforts. Miss G.: "When I was in vaudeville . . ." (class titter.) "Oh, yes, I was in vaudeville with Ted Shawn! Our act used to be followed by a bird act. They were trained white cockatoos. Now, the moment they heard their music they would become frantic—they would claw at the bars of the cage, bite at the doors with their beaks, beat the sides with their wings, and cry out wildly, because they needed to get on stage to perform.

"*Birds, dammit, birds!* Now let's see you do that exercise as if you *needed* to do it!"

Miss G. doesn't like us to perspire in class. I made puddles on the floor. Temperature—ninety-five degrees, humidity—ninety-eight. Today she spotted my puddle and came over. "Do you realize that there is enough atomic power in one drop of perspiration to blow up a six-story building? Don't waste that energy!"

The ever-present contractions and releases are apt to slip from ritual to routine. Martha stepped in and changed that.

"When you contract from the floor you are in the image of a *pietà*, and the earth is the mother that cradles you."

"There is a moment between contraction and a release that must say something either of joy or of sorrow."

|||||

The following account is from 1953:

Each contraction must be a peeling away of self. Just as Ibsen has Peer Gynt peel away the layers of the onion, reciting at each layer a part of his past life, searching for his true self, you must go deeper and deeper into yourselves with each contraction. This is the only example of hidden irony I ever heard Martha use. I would venture to guess there were only two people in the room who knew the play well enough to remember that when Peer got to the center of the onion he found nothing at all!

Martha: "You must will yourself to do these things." This said while standing on one foot with the other casually up by her ear. As a dancer you would find yourself doing amazing things, but as a person one often wondered whether it was your will or hers.

Any good teacher of dance communicates with the student through touch. We were doing the Graham prance across the floor by twos. She was directly in front of me, prancing backward—on each beat of the music she slapped my chest, first forehand and then backhand, and shouted *"Lift! Lift!"* on every beat of the music. It hurt. "Lift yourself! Defy the earth!" It did hurt. "And remember to do it with gaiety!"

Evidently realizing that there was a near basket-case in the corner, Martha came over to me. "What's the matter, Bob?" It all poured out. She reached over and patted me on the head (a combination gesture of "There, there" and

"Stop being a fool"). She said, "But you see, the difference is that you can dance." . . .

Several dancers took unexcused leave on the July 4th holiday. Only eight out of forty on the floor. Everyone decided to take a long weekend. Miss G. sat us down and explained how furious she was and warned us: "On Monday stay near the edges of the room. If I happen to get carried away and scream at you it will only happen because I am so angry I will have forgotten that you were here. I cannot abide people who lack dedication. I am furious at people who mistreat their bodies by getting sunburned."

(Post July 4th holiday) Lobster-red, sunburned Marcia was banished from court for life. The cold, clear words, "Get out of the studio and I never want to see you ever again" were delivered with a tone that popes and kings would have envied. And yet it is so immediately terrifying, it couldn't be just acting. I never want to be near an atomic explosion—I have come too near today.

Yesterday she arrived at the auditorium to talk about her lecture. There I was in overalls. She is quite shy. She smiled and we went onstage. She needs softer light than most and I willingly stayed up till one o'clock setting them up. The other teachers are great but they do not shoot electricity out of their eyes. You can't see the lights around the other's eyes, nor can you see energy flow out of them. And I mean *see* it. She never tells you anything with just her mouth. No! She tells you with every fiber of her body. The voice just happens to be a part of her body.

Martha talking about falls—"You never go down and up, but from lightness to darkness and back to light again. For a moment the earth and gravity conquer the body, but it fights back and wins!"

Even technique is a sort of worship. Of course, Martha's approach makes it like chocolate-coated pills to me. When someone just says "Do a contraction" I hate it, but when she says "Do a contraction that says 'I love you,' " I can really do them. . . .

I did my pavane* for Louis and I was satisfactory except that I moved both hands and feet in the same pattern. The second dance was a galliard. I got to measure five. He stopped me. For twenty long, glorious minutes he laid my poor little galliard out weak and twitching at my feet. He did not leave it there. We picked it up together and like a jigsaw puzzle we set it straight as a pin. We made a good dance out of it. I took orders from him—he was at one end of the ballroom with the students banked behind him and I way out in the middle. He is very clever; it looked as if I had done it myself, and I guess in a way I did. Never for a moment did I lose confidence that I *could* do it. Loud

---

*The pavane and the galliard were fifteenth- and sixteenth-century dances. The pavane was rather stately and pacing, and the galliard, in 6/4 time, was very lively and jumped. Louis used all old dance forms to teach dance structure, but with no attempt to duplicate authentic steps.

applause when we finally did the full dance. He is marvelous. Nothing has given me such a lift as those twenty minutes, unless it be Martha G.

When Martha or any of her pupils talked about dancing in Martha's terms, the language merged imperceptibly and inevitably into mysticism. The lengthening of the torso, the pulling up of the leg ceased on that instant to be physical mechanics and became an exercise of emotion and inner being.

This is what gave her movement its sense of verity, its sense of purpose.

But Pearl Lang said the pupil longs for precise road-maps, longs to ask, "But Martha, on *which* foot? On *what* count?"

Martha never said.

|||||

One of the strengths of the Bennington experiment was that nothing done up in the Vermont hills was separate from the mainstream of the artists' intention. They continued working there, possibly with more quiet and more concentration than in the city, but on the same matters and in the same way. And the minute they left the peace, the country surroundings, they resumed their activities without delay.

|||||

Back in New York, in the winter, all the artists who had been at Bennington went on working ceaselessly, but quite independently. On West Sixteenth Street just off Sixth Avenue the Humphrey-Weidman group had bought an old building, which they renovated to form an enormous studio with a fairly sound lighting system, riser seats at one end, a very large performing space which extended into the audience, and curtains which could be arranged to simulate scenery. The dancers looked splendid in this deep and ample space, with the audience gazing down from the bleachers. Here were all the spacial requirements of the art, giving real depth to the performances and enough room to spread out the patterns so that they showed, as they should, as a conquest of space. The dances could breathe in this studio. Here Doris and Charles taught every day, and three or four times a year produced a program of, in some cases, historic creativity. The company, large in number and distinguished in personnel, included Sybil Shearer, Katherine Litz, Letitia Ide, William Bales, José Limón, Valerie Bettis, and the playwright Horton Foote, extraordinary performers and, like all concert dancers in New York, all largely unpaid. The members gave their time, working mainly at night.

Doris Humphrey was more catholic in her selection of music than Martha was, and more ambitious. She chose larger pieces—Bach's Passacaglia and Fugue in C Minor, Milhaud's *Orestes*, with choirs and full symphony orchestras. This was an unfortunate choice, since there was no such thing as proper theatrical amplification or tapes. Dancers had to pay all musical costs themselves. Therefore, sizable orchestras or choirs were beyond their means. For this reason, and because of questions of rights, some of Doris Humphrey's dances could never be performed at large theaters or taken on tour.

Studio performances had a regular clientele and began to attract spectators from uptown. The press coverage was always prominent, John Martin continuing to give downtown performances equal space with any first-class Broadway event.

The majority of critics and patrons came to think of Martha as the sounder and more interesting artist, and although she and Doris had been trained alike, they diverged in the unequal competition between them. There was an element wholly alien, exotic, perverse, even, in Graham's newer approach, which Doris resented. Doris became ill with crippling arthritis that forced her to leave the stage and made teaching difficult and painful. Friends thought the disease was aggravated by emotional turmoil over her professional situation and the lifelong unequal contest with Martha. The rivals probably did not see each other except by chance, even though they worked only four blocks apart.

Besides the moderns there were the ballet dancers, but they were largely Russian and at the Metropolitan Opera House. The entire balletic audience had wakened like Sleeping Beauty and had begun clamoring in its traditional frenetic manner for its favorites. Their raging noise and turbulence, quite legitimate and on the whole good fun, was considered by the moderns as not serious.

But of all the artists, Martha Graham was now generally held to be the Voice, and what she did and what she said and what her pupils did in her behalf was considered the latest and most important news.

N ow, in 1935, came the great time, the truly daring, expanding, and exploring time. Martha had naked space and privacy and she had the girls—faithful, believing, selfless, a cortege of eaglets not yet broken to wrist or harnessed, a rope of nuns aflame with the adventure.

Frontier was a dance essentially about distances. Isamu Noguchi provided two horizontal poles, the wooden bars of a rail fence that stretched behind Martha and on which she could set her back and lean. Directly behind her, center stage—center universe—were attached two ropes from each end of the poles, like the points of a compass, extending forward and upward to the portals of the theater, forming a great V. It was a sector of cosmography, simple and pure, and perhaps the most effective use of stage symbol ever seen in our theater.

Noguchi later explained: "I used a rope, nothing else. It's not the rope that is the sculpture, but it is the space which it creates that is the sculpture. It is an illusion of space. It is not flat like a painting used as a backdrop. It

is a three-dimensional perspective. It bisects the theater space. Therefore, it creates the whole box into a spatial concept. And it is in that
spatial concept that Martha moves and creates her dances. In that
sense, Martha is a sculptor herself."

At the apex of the V stood Martha, braced against the fence, gazing,
gazing patiently out over the grand circumference with the great vec-
tor-ropes stretching out to mark off this section of infinity—the pioneer
gazing with new eyes.

Leaning against the rails and facing ahead and away, Martha began.
Placing her left foot squarely on the top rail like a steadying arm, she
took three deep breaths as the trumpet called three times—that is, she
rose to half-pointe on her supporting right foot, stretching her torso and
expanding her diaphragm. She did not move her head but stood gazing
squarely out, and as the trumpet called she seemed to grow in dimension, to possess space, to become comfortable in her land, to take over.
She moved, and as she moved the solo figure appeared to approach in
a powerful perspective, measuring off the land to the horizon and back.
The steps were very simple—the strange inching along the ground
which only Martha, with her preternaturally developed feet, could
accomplish, with great speed and a kind of hopping vault, in an insect-
like progress of foreshortened perspective. Forward and across to the
opposite side, back into the distance, and again across the landscape,
in great squares, the pasture lands. The little measuring feet devour the
space and tag it.

This dance is as simple as a proposition by Euclid, and as unanswerable.

Louis Horst composed the sparse, marvelous, strange, provocative
score, with its magic use of a snare drum calling up all the mettlesome,
aggressive, and fighting instincts of a brave people. The melody was like
a lost voice, pure and haunting.

Martha designed her own dress, and it was worthy to be placed in
front of the beautiful Noguchi set. She looked in it rather like a
religious figure, a member of a lay order—a very simple frock, like the
dress of a Quaker or an Amish woman, suggesting a schoolgirl's uniform, of sand-colored stuff over a full-sleeved white blouse. It spelled
dignity, simplicity. It was of working material and without period. A
good dress.

Frontier, presented at the Guild Theater on April 28, 1935, was the
first success of Martha's great historical heritage dances. Anyone who
saw her in it can never forget the sense of wonder, of quiet, of latent

power and amazement at the sheer force and beauty of the environment she evoked, that she alone was able to evoke, the sense of everlasting distance. For this reason Pearl Lang, for one, feels that revivals of *Frontier* so often fail. Martha always had it—the latent power, the deep quiet, the deep wonder.

Lincoln Kirstein wrote in 1937: "She has in *Frontier* much of the courage of Whitman's unachieved dream, but she also has a more realistic and present spirit. By now she has presupposed the ferocious, bland, hysterical puritanism of *Act of Piety* and *Act of Judgment* which Hawthorne would have so completely recognized. She has created a kind of candid, sweeping and wind-worn liberty for her individual expression."

|||||

Mrs. Morgenthau, with the help of her brother-in-law, Henry Morgenthau, got Martha an invitation to dance at the White House for President and Mrs. Roosevelt in February 1937. Martha was to be perhaps the first dancer ever asked to perform at the White House, and certainly the first American dancer ever to be so honored.

Louis recounted the adventure to me. When they arrived he left his suitcase in his bedroom and went immediately to the East Ballroom to check on the piano and the performing space. The room did not then have a stage, so Martha was required to dance on the parquet. After the rehearsal he returned upstairs to change for dinner. (Martha intended to keep to her room before her appearance and would have supper on a tray.) Contrary to rumor, Louis was shy, and one can imagine his chagrin at seeing that his bag had been unpacked by a White House valet and that the bottle of bourbon he had secretly brought for courage now stood naked on his bed table, the brown-paper bag and newspaper in which he had wrapped it having been carefully pressed smooth and folded flat beside it, as well as the piece of string with which the parcel had been tied up. All was laid out bare, like surgical apparatus. His shame was exposed.

He went into the bathroom and surprised Elliott Roosevelt, who was in the shower and who straightaway hollered to Louis, "Just a minute and I'll vacate."

The dinner and the performance were uneventful and pleasantly successful. There is no record of exactly what transpired or of what program they gave. Martha had few light or humorous dances at this time. Which of her soul-racking pieces did she choose for the after-dinner entertainment? *Lamentation? Act of Piety?* Or the fifteen-minute marathon *Dithyrambic?* Any of these would have put the cap on any conversation!

They had decided not to stay the night as had been expected, but to get the midnight train home in order to be back for rehearsals the next day. As they arrived in the great foyer of the White House to take their leave, they discovered Eleanor Roosevelt seated at a small card table placed at the exact center of the hall, on the great seal of the United States. She sat on the eagle and quietly ordered one of those dinners Franklin deplored so heartily. The head butler, the chef, and two equerries were in attendance. Eleanor had a pencil—"Tomorrow," she said, "we'll have roast lamb, mashed potatoes, gravy, of course, peas, and . . ." She looked up and saw the departing guests. "Oh, my dears!" Jumping up from her chair, she approached them with open hands and called back over her shoulder, "Mint jelly, too."

She smiled, embracing Martha. "How kind of you to come, how very kind to have made the effort to come!" And there she was, our First Lady, comporting herself exactly like any gracious American hostess. It was a small sliver of history, and a pleasant recommendation to add to Martha's growing list of credits.

|||||

Martha did not exploit the tragedies of her times, but she was affected by them. Her answer to the Spanish Civil War was profound grief and horror for what might come after. She composed several dances in this mood, the best known being *Deep Song* and *Immediate Tragedy*, in 1937. I never saw them, because I was in London when they were performed, and she never repeated them;* but they left a deep mark on those who did see them.

John Martin wrote:

> Not since the eloquent and beautiful *Frontier* . . . has Miss Graham given us anything half so fine as *Immediate Tragedy.* Though its subject matter, dealing as it does with contemporary Spain, is removed half-way around the world from the early American milieu of *Frontier,* there is something that the two dances possess in common. Perhaps it is their spirit of dedication; perhaps it concerns also their simplicity of form and the transparent elements of which they are built. . . . This will be a moving dance long after the tragic situation

*She revived *Deep Song* for Terese Capucilli in 1988.

in Spain has been brought to a conclusion, for it has completely universalized its materials. Indeed, neither its title nor its subtitle, "Dance of Dedication," has a word to say about any specific happening or locale. It is a picture of fortitude, especially of woman's fortitude; of the acceptance of a challenge with a kind of passionate self-containment. From its emotional quality one recognizes its source rather than through any external means.

In 1935 a delegation of Nazis had visited Martha. The representatives from the government of the Third Reich invited her to appear for the United States in the forthcoming Olympics, to be held in 1936 in Berlin. They made their representation forcefully. Martha looked at them in astonishment. "But three-quarters of my group are Jewish," she said.

"Do you think," they responded, "that they will not be treated with courtesy and dignity?"

"Do you think," she replied, "that I would go to a country where they treat hundreds of thousands of their coreligionists with the brutality and cruelty you have shown Jews?"

The Germans drew up in haughty anger. "If you don't come," they said, "everybody will know about it and it will be a bad thing for you."

"If I don't come," she replied, "everybody will know why I didn't, and that will be a bad thing for you."

Martha recounted this incident to me and added gleefully that she had been placed on all the German lists for prompt attention after the happy conclusion of the contemplated war, when Germany would move into the United States and be free to eliminate undesirables.

This was, at that moment, a remote contingency. But Martha, with extraordinary bravery, faced a very real one. She was enormously successful and renowned in her own tight profession, but she was not known generally. She was poverty-stricken. She was forty-one years old. The publicity inherent in going to the Olympic games and representing our country would have catapulted her into worldwide fame and resulted in enormous financial returns. She refused this offer without a split second's hesitation, and at a time when a great proportion of Americans were turning a deaf ear to the cries from Germany and absolutely refusing to believe, first, that the dreadful reports were in any way true, and second, that Germany posed any kind of a threat to western Europe. Our hero, Charles Lindbergh, for one, was clear about this. Even Martha's close, sponsoring friend Katharine Cornell had returned from Garmisch with glowing accounts of the great rallies in

Munich and the promise that the Nazis were doing splendid things for their country and would conquer anything they wished to: that we hadn't a prayer to stand up against their war machine. Martha heard this daily for some time before she voiced her opinion. Then she spoke, and no one ever was in doubt where she stood.

In the summer of 1936 Martha returned to Bennington. Joseph Campbell told of that festival season:

The summer of '36 was a marvelous period, with the whole dance community as we knew it present, gathered together in one place for six weeks, all concentrating on one thing. Martha Graham was present, and Doris Humphrey, Hanya Holm, Charles Weidman, and José Limón, meeting every day, exchanging ideas (although certainly not often agreeing), teaching, conversing (not always politely). It was inspirational. This exchange was what we didn't get in New York. In spite of themselves, it was as profitable to the choreographers as to the students.

And there in Bennington, in this cradle of work and artistic exchange amid the green Vermont mountains, Martha made the acquaintance of a young ballet dancer, Erick Hawkins, a member of Lincoln Kirstein's Ballet Caravan.

Who was this young man, this unknown dancer, destined to make such a profound change in Martha Graham's life? And what was Ballet Caravan, this tiny, unknown company that caused such a stir in the stronghold of modern dance?

Erick Hawkins was a true American type, of Anglo-Saxon heritage. He was from Missouri, his rugged face even suggesting the faces on old coins and, some said, because of his wooden manner, cigar-store Indians. But Hawkins's almost disdainful manner was partially due to nearsightedness, which was acute although unacknowledged out of vanity. (Erick never wore glasses.)

He had been born in 1909 in Trinidad, Colorado, right on the New Mexico border. "The prophetic thing about the place of my birth," said Hawkins, "well, no, not prophetic exactly, indicative maybe, is that it is right where the Dionysian strain of the Plains Indians and the Apollonian strain of the Pueblo Indians meet, very near the pueblo of Taos. In its dances you can see some influence of the Plains Indians—a horse dance, for instance. But beyond the Taos Indians and Trinidad, south along the Rio Grande, the horse hasn't come into human consciousness at all." Does this clarify Erick's character and credentials? To him it does. The first picture he remembers is a rotogravure in the family dining room of an enormous buffalo standing braced and defiant. It impressed him and in a sense became his symbol.

While Erick was still a child his father returned to Kansas City, Missouri, and Erick found himself to be the brightest boy in the local school, well in advance of his years. Urged by his teachers, he applied for a scholarship to Harvard and was accepted. Equipped with the hundred dollars he had won in a literary contest with an essay on Thomas Jefferson, and a hundred more he had saved, he decided to go east. Since he was under age—still too young to enter Harvard—he waited a year, working at various jobs, before setting off with his bounty and driving to Cambridge, Massachusetts.

At Harvard he studied music because he wished to become a pianist, but he found most of the courses to be advanced theory and way beyond him. He had been good at Latin and so he began to interest himself in the classics, taking courses in Greek language, history, and philosophy. He was concentrating on this when, during a Christmas vacation, he happened to see Harald Kreutzberg dance in New York. He realized that in Kreutzberg and his partner, Yvonne Georgi, he was looking at the Greek ideal of physical, mental, and spiritual union. (Another impressionable student, this one a painter who attended the same concerts and whose life was likewise radically altered, was the young José Limón.)

"What Kreutzberg did reinforced what I came to believe then and always since," Hawkins recounted, "that music, bodily movement, and spirit are one; that the image of the human body and the human soul the way it was at the highest moment of Greek culture is one complete unity which we still don't have today in our culture. I have consecrated my life to this ideal. I saw it partially realized in Kreutzberg's dancing." Erick decided then and there to become a dancer.

Roger Sessions, the composer, recommended to Erick the new School of American Ballet as a good place to start his dance training, and Erick thinks that it is possible that his was the first professional check the school ever received. George Balanchine singled Hawkins out immediately as very promising, although Hawkins was older than the other students. Balanchine even placed him in a ballet, *Alma Mater*, in which Hawkins promptly got his nose broken. Mr. B. permitted Hawkins to teach, calling out during rehearsals, "Bravo, Erick!," which was highly unusual.

"My memory," Erick said, "is that Balanchine was more enthusiastically complimentary to me as a pip-squeak than to anybody else around.

It was amazing that they let a beginner teach. They used to say that I was rather good. Pierre Vladimiroff used to watch me. It was Muriel Stuart, however, who really taught me."

Stuart had been a student of Anna Pavlova, and a member of her company. She had also taken courses with Graham and had been indoctrinated; perhaps she had infected Hawkins with her new enthusiasm.

Erick did not, however, prove ready to take on solo ballet roles, although he continued to teach and stood in line to join the faculty permanently. Contemporaneously, he did time at the Metropolitan Opera Ballet and at one point found himself studying both the Stanislavski method and the faded opera-ballet rigmarole. Onstage one night at the Met in a debauch scene, he got into the spirit of the bacchic rites and disported himself with more than accustomed abandon. The leading lady's costume came unhooked and she found herself partially denuded before the audience.

"Help me!" she begged to the dancers as they passed. "Hook my bra!" Erick was the last in a line of revelers and, throwing her an archaic, joyous hand, ripped the small garment from her breast, flourishing it as he left and stripping her to the waist. "Well," he said, "this is what the dance is all about, isn't it?"

Somehow or other he got his hands on enough money to go to Salzburg for the summer and there he studied with Kreutzberg, returning in the autumn of 1936 to Balanchine. It was at this point that Lincoln Kirstein was forming his Ballet Caravan, and Hawkins went with him to Bennington.

Kirstein was an heir to the Boston Filene's department-store fortune. He had made a name for himself while at Harvard as the author of unusually good lyric verse and as the editor of a literary quarterly, *Hound & Horn*. His enthusiasm for dancing led him to make several trips to Europe, following the last footsteps of Diaghilev. Becoming enamored of the legend of Nijinsky, he determined to plant Russian genius in American soil, having small faith in American dance genius. This was only one of many biases which prevented him from being one of the really great critics of his time. As it is, his writing is vivid, lively, memorable, salty, and in some instances enlightened, but he was an enthusiast for and against, and always in the service of an emotional prejudice, allowing neither equilibrium nor regard for wider or differing views. He remained therefore always an apologist.

He believed George Balanchine to be the greatest living exponent of the dance profession and of the Russian tradition, which was for him the only worthwhile tradition. Balanchine was the Johann Sebastian Bach of choreography. Everyone else, even Frederick Ashton, was to Kirstein a pretender. Accordingly, he determined while still very young to put his life and talents at the Russian's service and to found an American ballet company in the best Russian tradition, which would be a worthy vehicle for his idol and with which Balanchine might dominate the American scene. Together with his Harvard classmate Edward M. M. Warburg, the son of the banker Felix Warburg, and Balanchine himself, Kirstein inaugurated in 1934 the American Ballet. Its first professional performances were a one-week run at the Adelphi Theater in March 1935, which was successful enough to be extended for another week. After that it went into hibernation, storing its scenery and costumes and sending its company back into the classrooms of his own school, the School of American Ballet. Balanchine defaulted temporarily to Broadway and Hollywood to earn some money, drawing on the school for recruitments.

Kirstein took a few of the most promising, very young students (Eugene Loring, Annabelle Lyon, Lew and Harold Christensen, Ruthanna Boris, Marie-Jeanne, and Erick Hawkins) into a splinter group called Ballet Caravan. They played a new and entirely special repertory, which in spite of Kirstein's preference for all things Russian boasted music by young Americans, among them Aaron Copland. The scenarios were furnished by Kirstein, the decor and costumes by young and barely known Americans, the choreography by members of the troupe, notably Loring. One formal, neoclassic work, *Show Piece*, was done by Hawkins.

The first performance of Ballet Caravan took place on July 17, 1936, in the Bennington College Armory, which had become by then the stronghold of modern dance, the fortress of the new beliefs. However, the stage at Bennington was also adequate for professional ballet, and the audience was curious. So Kirstein, who believed in his little troupe, was ready to brave any hostility and possible contempt from the moderns. Accordingly, the young ballet technicians made their debut before a coolly hostile audience, but one which was fair-minded, and the verdict was that the kids were at least professional.

At the conclusion of the first performance, to everyone's astonishment, Martha Graham went backstage and singled out the young Erick Hawkins for praise. Understandably, he was overwhelmed.

Kirstein disliked with intensity all modern dancing, or thought he did, and this manifested itself in scorn, spoken and written. "No one would think of playing the violin in an orchestra after three months practicing," he wrote in *The Nation*. "Yet the modern dancer assumes that the only requirement necessary is a desire to dance. . . . My faith in the future of the dance in America is my faith in the School of American Ballet." Lincoln had just helped to found that school. He was in a true sense, if not titularly, the head of that school. Conflict of interest apparently held no stigma in the dance world!

Even then, young Lincoln was intimidating. He was six foot one and a half inches tall, with a formidable physique, a massive brow, and a presence of burning intensity. "Lincoln builds dungeons in midair," said Ann Barzel, the critic. He had a demeanor so forbidding, so sullen, so unchangingly sour as to be menacing, and even, perhaps, dangerous. But he was invariably provocative, debonair, witty, eager, and even on occasion jolly, and he was stimulating always. In later years he grew more and more dour, more and more elusive. A simple "hello" came to equal an obituary.

I felt he didn't understand a thing about what Graham was doing and that he was deliberately shutting his eyes to her achievement. "Meet her," I begged. (This was before Bennington.) "Meet her, talk to her. Learn her purpose. Try to understand her aesthetic. Many hundreds of us think she is inspirational." Well, he didn't meet her and he remained blithely philistine, until finally the momentous confrontation occurred (exact date unrecorded). He became addicted. He hung around her studio. And with him was Erick Hawkins.

Hawkins tells of his change of allegiance from ballet and Balanchine to Graham. "I had a continuing desire to do Balanchine's work and I was right, but at the same time I knew that the range of the ballet technique would never let me develop as a man or as an American." (He didn't say "as an artist," which would have been more understandable.) "I had perfectly good instinct. I couldn't stay at the School of American Ballet. When Balanchine, by not using me in ballets, broke my heart, I realized I must move."

Erick was well into his late twenties by now. He was thoughtful, eager, and intent, interested in all things and all techniques. Professionally he felt he was ready for Martha—ready intellectually, that is, not physically. And somehow it seemed to him to be his duty as an American to go to her company. (Erick had a way of confounding his aesthetics with patriotism.)

The work with Graham proved hard. Erick's body, although strong and beautiful, was insufficiently exercised. He could not be called a trained dancer in any technique at all. He was stiff and angular and he was stubborn, both muscularly and emotionally; the alien Graham exercises were very difficult for him. However, he persisted with dogged intent—the same quality that had appealed to Balanchine. And also there was a roughness and a brutality, even savagery, in his nature that spoke to Martha, so that while she recognized his crudeness, she also recognized his power.

Into the Graham Group, into that fecund, female organization of dedicated women, Hawkins now cut with male strength and male force and sharpness. The ground he found was ready for him; he did a great harrowing.

Martha asked him to come to her rehearsals, and, unheard of before this, he came as an auditor. But presently he begged to join the company, if only in walk-ons, in the merest appearances, and to this she agreed. Very soon she invited him to dance—the lead, no less.

Louis Horst was instantly hostile to the idea. He had wanted the company (and Martha) to remain entirely female and celibate. He wanted Martha to be alone with her girls and if she needed a man, to be dependent on one only: himself.

The whole company was appalled; Erick had stepped ahead of ten-year veterans. Worse, he took charge of rehearsals and dared to instruct the classes—he, who was not as good as even the second-year girls, not nearly. He, who was inexperienced. But he was the man, and he gradually became rather haughty and extremely aggressive. He talked a great deal—and Erick was a fine talker. He asked questions all the time, the answers to which the other students, female, had worked out long ago and now took for granted. Astoundingly, he gave himself the airs of a master soloist. He would tender opinions and make decisions, and, what's more, Martha acquiesced. Martha permitted him to. This is what struck the others down. She invited his opinions. She even invited his criticisms. He took time to expatiate on opaque analyses, fact-choked digressions which ensnarled him like a straitjacket and from which he could never tear free. Succinctness may have been the name for Martha: it was not for Erick.

In 1939 the World's Fair opened in Flushing Meadow, New York, and Graham was asked to do a "Tribute to Peace" for the initial gala performance. (It was a little late to make peace demonstrations, since Hitler was at that moment marching into Poland and seizing Denmark and Norway. He had already annexed Czechoslovakia and Austria.)

Dorothy Bird was chosen by Martha to impersonate Peace. Being an idealist, she was overcome with the honor. Martha fashioned a costume for her out of yards of white material that she had handy (she always had her yardage handy), and Dorothy was ready to herald the President of the United States—Roosevelt, no less—in his limousine. At the last moment Martha decided it would be better if Erick led the troupe. "You don't mind, do you, dear? You agree with me, don't you?"

Martha took the standard from Dorothy's eager hands and gave it to Erick, together with an appropriate breechcloth. Dorothy's moment had been stolen.

It was planned that at the conclusion of Roosevelt's speech he would leave, and the parade of dancers would follow. But Erick held the standard in his hand, and as the audience stood in tribute to the President, Erick flourished his banner and started off, preceding the President. Dorothy, as instructed, had kept the dancers at bay; finally she released them in an unremarked straggle. Erick was very pleased with having served the cause of peace.

I think it safe to say that Erick was heartily resented in the company. In all the critical judgments that are quoted hereafter, jealousy must be taken into account.

Louis continued to disapprove. "This is Shawn all over again, and she swore it would never happen in her life," he moaned. But for once Louis was helpless. He was still the Jovian voice, but he had been relegated to a more distant position. Erick was in the room working and talking, and Louis was not in the room. Martha had other pianists. She was changing. And Erick had what the girls could not compete with— he had his manhood.

Sophie Maslow was one of the two or three girls in the company who got along with Hawkins. "Everyone in the company attributed whatever problems there were to Erick, and I'm not so sure it was always Erick's fault. He probably took over a great deal of responsibility for Martha. He was her whipping-boy and took the blame for all the unpleasantness."

What Erick gave Martha spiritually and emotionally was imponderable. It was plain to the girls and even to Martha herself that Erick's brutality stirred something in her. Although he was aware of the company's hostility, he was also aware that the greatest theatrical genius of his time was madly in love with him. She had waited and he had come. He was the man for her. Erick could endure company disgruntlement. Above all, he got her to think in terms of relationship to men, in terms of their way of moving, their bodies, their dynamics, their presence. He paved the way for work with other men. He immensely broadened her canvas.

He took over the running of the troupe and rehearsals. He took over the arduous drudgery of being group régisseur, a position that had hitherto been wholly Louis's responsibility. Erick undertook more and drilled more thoroughly.

But he was without tact or charm or consideration, and his arrogance remained unblemished. There was open rebellion. Martha was confronted not with an ultimatum, because that would have been impossible in the group, but with a raw dislike, an unhappiness among her girls. She withdrew most of Erick's rights as director and teacher and gave them to Sophie Maslow. Erick she reserved for coaching herself and for working with her on her own problems, a decision that served several of her interests—because Martha was falling very deeply in love and growing more obsessed by the emotion every day. But Erick wasn't, or didn't seem so to her. And Martha, the archseductress, was beside herself. According to Jane Dudley, Martha used to call up Louis and talk for hours in an agony of indecision and dismay. He was not sympathetic in any way to the liaison, and one wonders what his advice could possibly have been under the circumstances. But she reverted to a lifelong pattern and wailed on his shoulder.

Now, for the first time, Martha had a certain degree of relief from the work of training the company, and she was grateful for this and used it well. Erick gave her the freedom to work on her own solos and her own creations. When the Group had gone to Bennington in the summer of 1938, her new piece was well along and there was less frenzy and terror than there had ever been before. Martha began to savor the enormous returns of work adequately prepared and matured. She began to indulge in the well-being of artistic security. Of course she still changed things, of course she still fussed over details; but the drudgery of running the company, of the daily rehearsals, had been lightened for her, and there was another pair of shoulders, however immature and unpracticed, to take a good part of the burden.

Still, the pressure was great, as usual. What was unusual is that *American Document* was not a success at its 1938 Bennington premiere. John Martin gave it a stern notice.

The morning that Martin's review appeared in *The New York Times*, Martha publicly accosted him in the faculty dining room and tongue-lashed him for being unsympathetic, unhelpful, and wickedly hurting.

She didn't understand, she said, how he could be so cruel, knowing the persistent difficulties of time limitations and inadequate physical equipment under which she always worked.

"Thank you, John Martin, for your notice. Thank you very much." She bit out every word and spat them at him. He waited perfectly still throughout the scolding, eyes downcast. The entire faculty in the dining room held their breaths and averted their eyes. Martha continued to the end and then strode out. Up to that breakfast, Martha and John Martin had been deep and close friends. I think he thought none the less of her professionally afterward, but he was wary and they never were intimate again.

"She is a genius," he later said to me. "She will do what she wants to do and what she feels she needs to do, and she doesn't really give a damn about anybody else or about friendships. That's what one must expect of a genius."

Jean Erdman believes that what John Martin chiefly objected to in *American Document* was the inclusion of men in the mysterious and chaste sisterhood. The Group had been impervious, superhuman, stylized, almost ritualistic, certainly self-sufficient, and above all unsexed. Martin cherished these qualities and he drew comfort from the androgynous nature of Martha, the leader, part male, adorably but not vulnerably female. He resented change. Martha was becoming wholly female, fragile and human.

After the season at Bennington was over, Martha and Erick stayed on at the college for a few days. They took long walks around the lovely campus and indulged in long talks. It was then that the company began to realize that Martha had fallen profoundly in love, was indeed infatuated.

When *American Document* reached New York, the company danced splendidly. The piece had been pulled together; Martha was transcendent. The work was now good. John Martin agreed.

Erick was one of two male performers in *American Document* and the only male dancer among all the superb women. The other man was not a dancer but an interlocutor who spoke the comments which Martha herself had garnered from poetry, historical documents, treaties, sermons, proclamations, and her own poetic dicta, weaving the lot into an illuminating vocal chorus which verbalized this survey of American history. There were ceremonial exits and entrances of the chorus of girls, punctuating in jubilee fashion the important events. There were salutations and imprecations, a telling love passage with Martha and Erick dancing the "Song of Solomon" juxtaposed with passages from Jonathan Edwards's brimstone sermons. There was an evocation of the Indians with Martha, her hair smooth and glossed as flat as any tribal maiden's and knotted at the nape of her neck with a scarlet Navajo rag, dressed in turquoise blue, a blanket of black and white over her shoulders. In her first invocation she stood alone, her left knee drawn to her left shoulder, and, cradling her leg in her arm, she made passes in a sort of hieratic sign language with her right hand, which actually evoked the communication of the primitive with his environment, his terrors and strengths.

This was followed by a nonauthentic Indian group-dance which had never been performed on this continent before. The feet were held together, planted into the earth, feet and legs rooted into the ground and suggesting a relationship to the earth, an association with the earth, the supreme dominance of the earth, the pelvis sliding sideways, as only the Orientals and South Sea natives can move. In the exodus at the end there was a serried kneeling in banks, and rising again in canons of movement, a going away endlessly, as though an entire civilization was receding. As indeed it was.

"This is visual choral movement such as has never been seen," said Erick.

To the words of the Declaration of Independence, "We hold these truths to be self-evident," the curtain parted at the back to reveal thirteen girls standing as only Graham dancers could stand—sovereign, with aplomb, self-contained, self-mastered, sufficient—to break at last into freedom and run, bounding into the light. The hearts of those watching stopped. A very young and beautiful student, Pearl Lang, seeing this dance later for the first time, said that at that moment of revelation she "split open. . . . When I saw those girls standing there I trod clouds of glory."

Pearl had received word in Chicago that there was to be an opening in Martha's company. She had immediately left the Goodman Theater, where she had been studying, and came to New York to enlist her life in the service of Martha Graham.

In due course Pearl had to learn part of this very same dance. She was to give the Declaration as a solo walk, upstage right to downstage left, all by herself, and to use the entire statement "We hold these truths to be self-evident" as she came forward. By the time she had reached the wings she knew she was going to be a dancer and that that was all she would ever want to be.

Anyone who witnessed it could not forget the glory in the faces of the dancers, a compact block of listeners during the Emancipation Proclamation as they fell to their knees in lines, gazing in wonder and rapture on the incomparable vision of freedom and equality. The listeners went down in contrapuntal rows, their hands to their throats, and when they came up in ranks they were shaken with ecstasy.

For the end of *American Document* Erick had been given a solo. It was about the working force of our country:

"I am one man.
I am one million men.
This man has a power.
It is himself and you."

To everyone's surprise, Erick was good. As the single man and the first in Martha's group, he dominated the stage in masterly and virile fashion. Martha had used her skill and instinctive taste in giving him what he could do and nothing he couldn't. He did her proud.

The piece rounded up with a final salute as in a minstrel show and a high-kicking and jubilant exit.

And what's more, the performance in New York was successful. Martha had a popular hit for the first time, one to which all kinds of audiences could respond. In my opinion, *American Document* should have been revived for America's bicentennial celebrations. Certainly nothing of comparable worth or pertinence was presented. But inasmuch as nearly no record was kept of Graham's enormously complex ensembles, the dancers involved in the original production have expressed doubt that a revival could have been possible, or ever would be. The companies now are very much reduced in numbers. A general curtailment of the largest ensemble pieces would be needed.

Nelle Fisher made her debut as a Graham dancer in *American Document*. She was one of the heralding ponies in the minstrel processions, Nelle of the beautiful feet and the lovely bronze curls. She was remarkable throughout for her really fine balletic technique and doll-like prettiness, an outstanding variant among the thick, dark girls of the Graham troupe. Nelle was light, buoyant. Some of the other dancers achieved beauty, but Nelle was bonny and winsome.

"We were doing the 'prances' in *American Document*," Nelle recalled, "the pony entrance of the little heralds. When you lift the knee the toe must point and the body must be held very centered, and I was doing this very, very well, I thought, and I was terribly involved in being correct. Well, Martha stopped the rehearsal and she came over to me and she put a hand on my shoulder and she said, 'Now, Nelle, you're doing this well and I think you're going to be a very good dancer, but you're not going to be an exciting dancer until you do this.' And she hit me on the backside so hard that my body went into a convulsion! My hip came up, my arms flew up, my head went back, and I was in complete 'divine distortion.' I've always remembered this. I could reproduce it later without the swat."

In *American Document*, Martha used a set designed by Arch Lauterer. There were no painted flats but rather portals and frameworks and curtains at the back of the stage that could be pulled up in sections.

Graham had truly begun to think theatrically.

There were also costumes by someone other than herself, Edythe Gilfond. And for the first time there was color in the dresses.

|||||

Erick proved practically useful and enterprising. For instance, he took charge of the physical management of the productions.

"Once the scenery and props came into the studio," said Jane Dudley, "he saw to it that they got packed for the performances and tours. He was like a janitor, and he was a good one, and as there began to be added men he got all the men in the company to serve as stagehands (they were permitted to in those carefree days), and they could knock the set down and put it into crates and then set it up on arrival. And when the season's performances were over, he saw to it that all the properties and scenery were properly stored. This was an enormous help."

Erick laid out business plans. He instituted projects. Martha no longer drifted, relying on accidental invitations to perform here and there. Erick went after definite contracts, attracting collaborators, musicians, designers, and patrons for the company, and revealing himself as a quite astonishing promoter. He instilled order where all had been haphazard and impulsive.

He probably modeled his efforts on those of the master fundraiser, Lincoln Kirstein, whom he had watched with George Balanchine, promoting the American Ballet. Erick made Martha understand that if they needed real money they would have to plan, campaign, and go out and get it, and that henceforth fundraising was to be a substantial part of their endeavors. It was no longer either suitable or profitable to sit in a studio and wait modestly for help.

It was Erick who approached Katharine Cornell and arranged for her to make loans to Martha, or, rather, gifts, to pay for theater rentals, stagehands, costumes. Up to this point Martha had asked only for small loans of one or two hundred dollars, and only as advances on her own salary as a teacher. Cornell led the way with larger amounts, paying Martha's rent at the Labor Stage.

It was at this time that grants began to be available, still from private sources, but many more than had existed in the past. Erick went after them, and Erick began to get them. He was never given either credit or recompense for this work, but he was glad to do it because he loved Martha and naturally wished to further the efforts of her company—and because he realized he was learning incomparable techniques in management and fundraising which would stand him in good stead for the rest of his life.

Martha changed on an important level because of Erick. In terms of human relationships, she began to behave differently. The change was reflected in her work. Erick himself says he "got Martha off the rehearsal floor." Essentially, he made her a human being.

In the beginning Martha had concerned herself in her work with revolutionary lonely spirits, with the struggle of the individual against custom and mass restraint. Subsequently she had made studies of approaches toward devotion—aspects of the mysteries and faith. Then she had made statements about her country, an appreciation of American character and the country's democratic freedom and heritage. But now she became interested in a needful and extremely troubled man—not as a hero but as a vulnerable, impassioned, average person. Now she was thinking, and, above all, feeling, in terms of relationships: about love, hate, greed, power, lust—in short, humanity.

Her dancing became fraught with sexuality and passion. Her imagery and the characteristic impulse of her gesture grew more and more explicit. The Graham technique, always sensuous, became probably the most sensual technique ever evolved, while it remained at the same time universal—because Martha had discovered that sex is universal. The joke within the company was "you had to know who was banging who and how."*

---

*In 1969 I asked Mme. Ekaterina Furtseva, the Soviet Minister of Culture, and her assistant, Mme. Butrova, why Graham had never been asked to visit that country.

IIIII

Under Erick's inspiration, Martha essayed a satiric ballet in 1939—
Every Soul Is a Circus, with music by Paul Nordoff. The ballet is an
extraordinarily sharp and penetrating study of human relationships.
John Martin wrote that *Every Soul Is a Circus* was "hilarious and
satirical . . . deeply poetic . . . sensitive unfoldings of the processes of
a woman's mind, dealing not in outward incident but in inward experience. . . . A central figure is surrounded by other figures who are not
entities in their own right but symbols in the emotional life of the
protagonist."

In this work Martha showed crisply and with humor woman's archetypal action against—as she wrote in her program notes—"the wildly
lecherous background of instinctive human behavior" and "a woman's
inner landscape." The ballet was very funny, probably the funniest
ballet Martha ever created. Erick portrayed the Ringmaster, the epit-
ome of square-headed pomposity. (Some people unkindly suggested it
was a self-portrait.) The role of the heroine, his wife, is split between
the performer and her watching alter ego, who sits in the theater box
at the back, wearing a different hat for each phase of her emotional
drama and providing a focal point for the wife's attentive vanity. In her
highest frenzy the performer steals a look now and then to see how her
alter ego, her permanent audience, is responding.

The wife has a lover, a figment of her desire. At the end, when the
two men, master and dream lover, growing fatigued with her inconsis-
tencies, walk out on her and she is left abandoned, she literally paws
the earth in her piteous despair, even while she watches to see how her
feet look while pawing. Finally, even the spectator doffs her last hat and
leaves; the lady must thrash in absolute bored loneliness, her black hair
lashing back and forth until there ensues stillness, and then—nothing.

This was Martha's offering as a comic, light ballet. Strangely enough,
it was both.

What does the piece mean? At the conclusion of the piece was
hopeless bewilderment.

Joseph Campbell said to Martha, "There's a further step to be taken,

---

"Because we hear she's interested entirely in sex and her ballets are devoted to just
that." The Russians have never permitted Graham within iron-curtain boundaries. I
find it touching that their government has such tender concern for the sexual sensibilities of its vast people!

Ted Shawn and a very young Martha Graham in *Danse Arabe*, 1921.

TOP: **Ruth St. Denis teaching at Mariarden, her school in New Hampshire. Martha Graham is seated in the front row; Charles Weidman is standing at the far left.**

BOTTOM: **In *Tanagra*, premiered during Martha Graham's first season in 1926, at the Forty-eighth Street Theater.**

TOP: **Ruth St. Denis in *Incense*.**

BOTTOM: **Ruth St. Denis in *Radha*, 1906-8, from German postcards. There were no instantaneous photographs at this time—St. Denis had to hold the pose at least four seconds. The skirt was stretched into points, not by centrifugal force as it appeared to be, but by threads.**

TOP: **Ted Shawn and Ruth St. Denis, husband and wife.**

BOTTOM: **Ted Shawn in *Death of Adonis*, taken in the gardens of Lolita Armour (1923).**

OPPOSITE: **Ruth St. Denis and Ted Shawn.**

Martha Graham at Sarah Lawrence College, 1937.

Martha Graham as the Chosen One in Massine's version of
Le Sacre du Printemps **at the League of Composers' concert, 1930.**

Martha Graham at
the McMillin Theater,
Columbia University,
c. 1935.

OPPOSITE: **Martha
Graham in
Lamentation.**

LEFT: **Louis Horst and Martha Graham at Bennington College, Vermont, in the summer of 1935.**

BELOW: **Cartoon by Aline Fruhauf of Louis Horst with one of his favorite dachshunds.**

BOTTOM: **Louis Horst next to a bust of himself by Elena Kepalas.**

TOP: **Charles Weidman and Doris Humphrey in *New Dance*.**

BOTTOM: **José Limón in his own Mexican suite—*Danzas Mexicanas*.**

TOP AND BOTTOM:
Primitive Mysteries.
Martha Graham,
below, with Dorothy
Bird.

OPPOSITE: **Martha**
Graham.

TOP: **Martha Graham and Erick Hawkins, 1938.**

BOTTOM: **Martha Graham in *Frontier*.**

OPPOSITE TOP: **Martha Graham in *American Document* ("The Puritan" love duet with Erick Hawkins), 1938.**

OPPOSITE BOTTOM: ***Every Soul Is a Circus*, 1940.** Left to right: Marjorie Mazia, Sophie Maslow, Merce Cunningham, Freda Flyer, Ethel Butler.

Letter to the World. **Martha Graham is kneeling.**

© Arnold Eagle

Letter to the World.

Of course, I prayed
And did God care?
He cared as much
As on the air
A bird had stamped her foot
And cried, "Give me."
—Emily Dickinson

TOP: **Group photograph, taken at Bennington in 1941. From left: Erick Hawkins, Doris Humphrey, Charles Weidman, Martha Graham and Louis Horst.**

BOTTOM: **Graham and de Mille at the Hurok Christmas party celebrating Marian Anderson's tenth anniversary with Hurok. December 1945.**

OPPOSITE TOP AND BOTTOM: *Appalachian Spring.* **At top: Martha Graham, Merce Cunningham (wearing hat), May O'Donnell, and Erick Hawkins.**

TOP AND BOTTOM:
***Deaths and
Entrances.*** Below,
**Martha Graham
with Erick Hawkins
and John Butler.**

OPPOSITE: **Martha
Graham, 1964.**

TOP: *Dark Meadow.*

BOTTOM: **Yuriko Kimura in *Cave of the Heart.***

OPPOSITE: ***Seraphic Dialogue*, Ethel Winter, Bertram Ross, Carol Payne, Ellen Graff, 1960.**

TOP: **Left, Bethsabee de Rothschild; right, Joseph Campbell.**

BOTTOM: **Edith J. R. Isaacs.**

OPPOSITE: **Martha Graham in *Letter to the World*.**

TOP: **Martha Graham in** *Episodes*, **Part 1. Martha said, "In my... black dress, with its abstraction of the ruched collar, I had the security of feeling beautiful every time I appeared in it on stage."**

BOTTOM: **Mary Hinkson in** *Diversion of Angels*, **c. 1966.**

OPPOSITE: **Martha Graham in** *American Document*, **1938.**

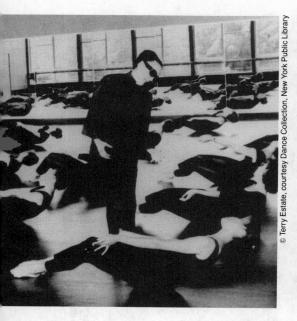

TOP LEFT: **Martha teaching a class at Connecticut College, 1950s.**

TOP RIGHT: **Drawing of Martha Graham by Milton Johnson,** *Gesture Study of Martha Graham in Studio,* **1959.**

BOTTOM: **The final issue of** *Dance Observer,* **with Horst's graduation picture on the cover, January 1964.**

OPPOSITE: **Martha Graham rehearsing** *Circe* **with Mary Hinkson and Bertram Ross, 1963.**

DANCE OBSERVER

VOLUME THIRTY-ONE, NUMBER ONE   JANUARY, 1964

Dr. Clarence B. Hilberry, (left) President of Wayne State University, after conferring
The Honorary Degrees of Doctor of Humanities upon Louis Horst and Martha Graham

30c

© Martha Swope

© Martha Swope

TOP: **Martha Graham and Paul Taylor in *Clytemnestra*, 1960.**

BOTTOM: **Pearl Lang in *Appalachian Spring*.**

OPPOSITE TOP: **One of Martha's treasures: her Chinese bed.**

OPPOSITE BOTTOM: **Left, Mario Delamo in *Phaedra*; right, Janet Eilber as Cassandra in *Clytemnestra*.**

Martha Graham.

where you go past bafflement, in which you commit yourself fully to love."

All Martha answered was, "If I were to take that step I would lose my art." (Ruth St. Denis had declared, "If I really give myself to any man I shall stop being an artist.")

Martha was terrified of taking that step.

Merce Cunningham made his first appearance in Graham's company as the puckish diversionary third in the basic triangle of wife, husband, and lover. The role capitalizes on his quality of what ballet dancers call *ballon*. He did not jump like a ballet dancer, by using his feet to full extension and soft pliés, but he could certainly get off the ground, and he went into the air with exquisite ebullience. The flower he carried later figured in an intense conversation in which the woman and her master hand the flower, the symbol of frivolous dalliance, back and forth solemnly between them. So silly! So true! The climactic trio between the woman and her two lovers is brilliantly suggestive, a study of a woman who is a silly flirt divided between her amours, erotic and ludicrous, a miracle of style.

It is in the scenes depicting relationships between men and women—passionate, disturbed, or blissfully yielding—that Graham reigns supreme, with, on occasion, enough sardonic irony to suggest Colette. (I have to use literary comparisons because there is no one in dance against whom Graham can be measured.)

Graham's dances are always, quite naturally, composed from a woman's point of view.

Every Soul Is a Circus foreshadows, although satirically, her recurrent theme—that her destiny was to live alone, to work alone, not to share happiness as people usually do. Her next works developed this idea, and the idea that her life must be dedicated to art, absolutely, totally, mercilessly. And this was surely curious, because at this very period she was finding complete love for the first time.

|||||

Lincoln Kirstein was rich and had access to great wealth and great sources of wealth. One could accordingly expect that as his enthusiasm waxed for Martha he would certainly help her. It seemed that at last she had found the patron whom she so desperately needed.

Three years after she met him I asked her, "Has he given you much?"

"Not a penny," she said. "However, he's around the whole time."

He was around, counseling and criticizing, writing, praising, and court-ing, but he gave not a cent and he opened no doors. He did give Erick: he released him from his continuing contract with Ballet Caravan.

At some point in this period—Martha couldn't remember just when—Ted Shawn came to her quite humbly and in friendship and asked her to choreograph a dance for him. She was taken aback. It must have cost his pride much, after all he had said against her and her way of doing things, to beg her help. But he did just that.

Martha felt constrained, however, to refuse. She knew all his weak-nesses and she knew his possible strengths, and they were not her strengths. She also knew he would never understand anything she was trying to convey. So as gently as she could she said no, that she thought any collaboration unwise. This refusal required from her as great tact as she was ever called upon to use. Whether or not Ted understood why she did it, she could only guess.

y 1940 Martha was composing expressly for her new male soloist, Erick Hawkins. She presented him in *El Penitente*, a trilogy in the American Indian style of *Primitive Mysteries*. Graham was the Madonna; the Christ figure was danced by the young Merce Cunningham; and Erick Hawkins was the Penitent, bare to the waist and flagellating himself in the approved Catholic Indian manner, which gave him the chance to display his strong points. The dance was a moderate success. *El Penitente* caused Martha anguish, "heartbreak," says Pearl Lang. It never was a real hit, and Martha believed it should have been. She subsequently gave her role to Pearl Lang.

The same season also brought *Letter to the World*, a study of Emily Dickinson and her poetry. This ballet was in no way a chronology of Dickinson's factual life, but rather a history of her spiritual progress, a biopsy of her emotional adventures. It progressed through youth to the encounter with a loved one, then to the realization that love was forbidden her and that she would transgress in having it—the bitter renunciation and acceptance of her fate as a poet—and finally to the domination of her soul. The ballet developed as a mystic morality play in which the different facets of Dickinson's character and the phases of the influences that pressed against her are personified verbally through her verse, and visually through the dances. It is subtle, and in some instances difficult to follow, but cohesive and powerful, and in its final cumulative statement profoundly moving.

The role of the poet was taken by two women, the one who danced—Martha Graham—and the one who spoke. The ballet began with an extensive interaction between the two figures, the dancing Emily and the speaking Emily, walking, searching, feeling, and at last finding and confronting each other. Finally the speaking Emily said, "I am nobody, who are you?" The two figures were not dressed alike, but they were dressed in the same manner; the speaker wore a lavender and blue silk skirt, the dancer a chartreuse one with a fluted felt collar. The dance was in moonlight, and the soft, elusive, tentative gestures of the running figures were such an evocation of gardens at night, of unexpected, wonderful events, unknown and unseen, shadowy dramas, as had rarely been called up in a theater. The dancing Emily entered in a veil, walking in the night.

My River runs to thee—
Blue Sea! Wilt welcome me?
My River waits reply—
Oh Sea—look graciously—
I'll fetch thee Brooks
From spotted nooks—
Say—Sea—Take *Me!*

The poet said this, and Martha in a tiny whisper of a blue veil ran across the stage. Tonight—freedom. From the beginning the two figures were identified and locked together as one.

The lover, the Dark Beloved (identity unknown in Dickinson's real life), was portrayed by Hawkins. He was not only her lover; he symbolized the attraction and power of the outer world.

The wayward, elfin spirit of Dickinson's frolicsome wit was danced by Merce Cunningham of the surprising bounding lightness. The austere and superb Jane Dudley completed the leading quartet with her remorseless portrait of the Ancestress, the New England conscience—

the postponeless creature, who forbade Emily to have love and happiness.

This ballet was the first statement that Graham had made of a lone figure not as an outcast from society or as a counterforce to social pressure but as a chosen sacrificial victim, the artist as self-immolater who gives up everything in ordinary life to find the lonely goals which are the essence of truth. "This is my letter to the world," says Dickinson's voice, and the heroine sits down quietly on her garden bench, dressed in white, to wait through eternity for whatever may come. Alone.

Letter was tried out on August 11, 1940, at Bennington College, where it had a qualified success. For the second performance the composer, Hunter Johnson, reshaped the score, which had been originally set for solo piano. But it was Louis Horst who finally cut up the music and thoroughly re-edited it. The choreography itself was drastically changed, too.

Choosing the girl to speak Emily Dickinson's poetry was difficult. Martha had first selected a Southern actress who was a friend of the composer. This lady was a beauty who looked very like the film star Vilma Banky; but she couldn't dance and was therefore seated motionless, center stage, in a period skirt and hairdo, while all the dancers, including the star, clad in nondescript, abstract get-ups, slipped and writhed around her. The actress was dead center, always there, immovable, and a beauty. It was she, therefore, who held the stage and the audience's attention. At the end of the first evening Martha knew the piece was unbalanced by the casting.

Back in New York she fired the actress and ordered new costumes for everyone, which suggested period clothes in cut and texture. Edythe Gilfond, the designer, obliged with lovely clothes that were expensive and looked it. And she employed color.

Then the hunt began for a speaking Emily who could also dance. An actress who had done solo recitals in London was considered and even rehearsed, her leg on the barre to induce strain while she read the lines, "There is a pain—so utter— / It swallows substance up—." Martha then slapped the performer with her hands, but the girl still was not sufficiently convincing, even with the stretching and the beating.

Jean Erdman, who had majored in acting at Sarah Lawrence College, was finally chosen for the speaking part. Martha had a written scenario, with entrances, positions, and dynamics carefully worked out, but the exact gestures she left entirely to Jean, who, since she was a member of the Graham Group and herself interested in choreography, was able to fill in the gaps very nicely. Jean's inventions are part of the texture of *Letter* as it is performed today.*

The work still stands as a masterpiece, as fresh as it was at its inception. The love duets and the great solo passages for Martha herself, the sacrificial solos, are stupendous, and without peer.

John Martin wrote the day after the opening in New York in 1941:

When Martha Graham presented *Letter to the World* last summer at the Bennington Festival she was counseled in these columns to leave it behind her in the hills of Vermont as an ambitious but thankless experiment. It is a pleasure this morning to eat those words. . . . Miss Graham's faith in her basic purpose and in her method of approach to it has been completely vindicated in the second version which she set forth last week at the Mansfield Theatre. Imperfect though it still is, it must rank as potentially one of the most beautiful creations yet to be revealed in American dance.

Martin found Hawkins dull, as the Dark Beloved:

Surely a woman so alert to life as Emily could not have evolved for so important a function a symbol so stuffy as Miss Graham has here written and as Erick Hawkins plays.

But Martha kept working and so did Erick.

Martin amended his views further some months later, in his season's résumé.

It is not only the greatest achievement thus far in the career of one of the most distinguished artists of our time, but it opens up new territory for the dance that must inevitably affect the field at large. . . . The idea of making a biographical portrait in terms of choreography is one to intimidate the most courageous artist, and Miss Graham did not reach her goal without detours and difficulties. What is important, however, is that she reached it, and her picture of Emily Dickinson's mind is a miracle of intuition, not to speak of the tools of the theatre by which it is brought to realization.

*While rehearsing in Washington, D.C., where they were performing in an open auditorium in public gardens surrounding a great fountain, Jean tried out her microphone. On the lip of the fountain sat a solid band of little children, mainly black. They were listening solemnly, kicking their feet against the stone as Jean continued testing: "I am nobody, I am nobody." She walked to the other side of the stage: "I am nobody." Finally a very little boy piped up: "Say, lady, you got to be *somebody*."

More than forty years later, Howard Moss wrote that "in Graham's dances, self-possession and rebirth are the hard victories wrung from anguish and obsession."

In this supreme theater piece, it seems to me, there are some possible flaws. The dances of the chorus, for instance, the cotillions and social exchanges, appear on first viewing remarkably stilted and artificial. On the other hand, it must be remembered that they are dances seen in retrospect and through a veil of grief, and possibly this warping was exactly what was intended, for they are as desiccated as dried flower petals. And there is Martha's humor, which in this ballet occasionally verges on the coy. Whereas Emily Dickinson is dry and pointed, with a kind of maidenly reticence, the figure Martha depicts in her portrayal gets slightly show-offish and cute, like someone overfamiliar and prankish, someone joking at a party. Her essays here at lightness lapse into mere pertness and are fun simply because they are contrasted with the awfulness before and after. But notwithstanding any possible quibbles, *Letter to the World* remains after forty-four years unmatched, unique. It still floods the heart.

"It is almost flawless," said Joseph Campbell. "The loveliest, the most moving theater piece of [all] her work."

Punch and the Judy, with music by Robert McBride and scenery by Arch Lauterer, was an exuberant romp dealing with the classic marital turmoils of the marionettes Punch and Judy (the first theatrical entertainment Martha had ever seen). Punch is depicted as a pompous egotist with straying fancies, and Judy as his exasperated, self-pitying, fantasizing wife. Pearl Lang made her debut as a soloist in the role of Pretty Polly, the husband's light-o'-love. Erick was extraordinarily effective as the husband, and Martha permitted herself to indulge in farcical comedy, to killing effect.

Punch and the Judy had its premiere at Bennington in August 1941. Later that year in New York Walter Terry, the dance critic for the *Herald Tribune,* wrote:

In *Punch and the Judy,* built upon a jazzy score by Robert McBride, Martha Graham is dealing with the "squabble and scuffle" of married life and she handles her theme with devastating truthfulness and roaring humor. Miss Graham, who can be as funny as Beatrice Lillie when she so desires, is wonderful as the wife who is driven, at one point, by her irritating husband to soar off into a romantic dream-world on the back of Pegasus and who, at another time, indulges in multiple and hilarious flirtings with a soldier, a scout and a highwayman by way of getting back at her spouse for his amorous digression with one called Pretty Polly. Erick Hawkins has one of his most engaging roles as the bumptious husband.

Martha did not revive this attractive work, not trusting replacements, particularly in her own role, which called for a mastery of comedy and a flair for satire. Martha could be a truly extraordinary comedienne, but she did not permit herself often to be one, to our great deprivation.

Punch and the Judy was the fifth piece that Martha Graham composed under the influence and stimulation of Erick Hawkins. These plays mirrored a love affair, and they might have been embarrassing if Martha had been any less of an artist, any less able to transfigure her passion into general terms.

In *Letter to the World* she had laid down the blueprint of her attitude toward herself. From now on Graham's recurrent theme was to be just that—the need for total isolation, for the fighting free of emotional adhesions, for the voluntary selection of the dark isolation where the individual spirit investigates and waits and prays. The reward can be enlightenment; the price must be lifelong suffering. In a sense this is what Christ advocated. But in Graham there is no moral command; it is purely aesthetic. Can beauty flourish in such cruel circumstances? It can. But must it have these circumstances to make itself known? Martha gave her life trying to answer this question.

It was Erick and Erick's love which made possible these extraordinary statements and revelations, and it was his stimulation and catholicity of interests that whetted her interests and jolted her out of the old ruts of self-invented isolation or self-bewitchment. And it had to be Erick who would force the final choice. In the practical terms of daily life, it meant that Erick was gaining mounting power within the company.

Louis's position in relation to the Graham company now was ambiguous and vague. He was acknowledged to be the senior adviser and critic, and his opinion was always asked. Whether or not his advice was now taken cannot be said. Martha tended to follow his taste, but he no longer played for her or conducted her orchestras; other, younger musicians did this. He devoted most of his time to teaching at the Neighborhood Playhouse and to lecturing at the YMHA. It was the consensus that he was certainly not now and had not been for a long time her lover. He seemed reconciled to the situation, but he was outspokenly bitter about Erick and he infected his friends with his acrid resentment. He had a new young lover, Nina Fonaroff, Martha's pupil and disciple, and she was devoted to him. Nobody ever thought that he made any mistake about the two women's comparative artistic worth or that his interest in and devotion to Martha had deviated a fraction from what it had originally been. But he cared for Nina tenderly. He must have been thirty years her senior.

Yet Louis still was Martha's taskmaster and he still, to an important extent, exerted the ultimate discipline.

Several times during the rehearsal periods at Bennington, Martha tended to neglect and postpone the work on her solos, and if they were in disarray, the piece as a whole could not be assembled properly. So Louis had taken over control—once during *Letter to the World,* once during *Punch and the Judy,* and several times during *Deaths and Entrances.* Jane Dudley reported that Louis said to Martha after one rehearsal, "These girls look like spooks. Throw that entire bit away." So she did. He commanded her to dismiss the girls for three days or more (they were enchanted to have an unexpected vacation in this lovely summer spot), and then, locking himself in the studio with Martha and barring the way to any visitors, they got at it. Food was sent in from time to time as they wrestled with problems until they had solved them. But it was Louis who took charge and who saw that the problems were solved.

However, Martha now loved another man and her true alliance was to him.

n December 1941 Martha was to go to Cuba. For her trip she purchased a splendid John-Frederics hat of folded violet velvet, very large, strikingly beautiful, and obviously costly. I remember it well; it was her first extravagant acquisition.

There was another occurrence on the trip that was memorable.

Walter Prude, the young manager of Graham's troupe, said that Martha was in a very good mood during this trip, gracious, charming, and ebullient. That was because Erick was in a good mood and she was with Erick. One day, however, something annoyed her and she went into one of her tempestuous sulks. Withdrawing from the company, she sat dumpily in a train station in her beautiful violet velvet hat, the brim pointing haughtily upward. Erick said he would speak to her, so after waiting awhile for her rage to spend itself, he sat down quietly beside her. Prude said he could see the hat gradually change its angle and come down to an agreeable and cozy position, and when she finally spoke again to her group she was dulcet. Erick had real power over her.

The company was touring the southern United States en route to Cuba. The news came through at Way Cross, Georgia, that Pearl Harbor had been bombed.

Sophie Maslow recounted:

Jean Erdman and David Campbell of Hawaii were in the company at that time and tried vainly at every station to phone home. And then when we got to Miami and were supposed to board a boat for Cuba, we had to wait through the day to find out if we had permission to proceed. I remember we went to the beach and to a little café for lunch and heard Roosevelt on the radio declare war. Nobody said anything, and we waited through the day and they let us get on the boat at night. Martha was terrified of water, a fear compounded by her terror of torpedoes. I remember speaking with some of the sailors about how one never knew where the submarines might be, and they said, "Oh, in the west, not here." Of course, later we found out that there were German submarines in those very waters. But we went to Cuba, and when we got there we were greeted with great joy—although I don't remember it as being a very successful trip. It was sponsored by the Pro-Arte group and Mrs. Alonso [the mother-in-law of Alicia Alonso]. The audience was made up entirely of the most frivolous balletomanes. They were used to pink tutus and twinkle toes. Martha was extremely nervous about the Latin-American attitude toward women and womanliness. She was extremely jittery and unsteady on the first night, losing her balance and wobbling. The only serious aspect to the audiences' minds, she believed, was their Catholicism, and they did not take kindly to a graphic depiction of the Virgin and the Christ figure in *El Penitente*. *Lamentation* was a smash hit because of their avid concern with death and kindred subjects.

The company got home safely, to learn about the war draft and the departure of their young men. Erick was spared because of his acute nearsightedness. Many others in the company went, including Walter Prude, who later became my husband.

|||||

When Martha had been creating *Letter to the World* at Bennington in 1940, she had also been thinking about the dance that three years later was to become *Deaths and Entrances*. One evening in the sitting room at Bennington which she and Erick shared with Jean Erdman and her husband, Joe Campbell, Martha spoke of these mysterious sisters, the Brontës, and their kinship to the wild spirits of the moors, the *sidh* of Celtic folklore, the fairy folk.

"Martha," said Joe Campbell, "when you talk about fairy folk you are really entering the world of the unconscious, and these creatures that come out of the fairy hills are manifestations of the psyche. You are now tapping the unconscious memories of the race."

Martha's eyes opened wide like the eyes of a young student just getting a new idea.

"Tell me," she said, and Campbell, who taught mythology and the Greek classics, explained. And Martha, in his words, "went to town." Graham had entered a new era of development.

Martha's work since the 1920s had penetrated the Freudian psychology and the romantic psychology of human nature, the impulses that are rooted in early childhood and are carried all through one's life, to inform, terrorize, and inspire. But now she began to explore the great atavistic memories of the race and clan as well, which also help to inform, terrorize, and inspire.

She had first been brought to Jung by Erick Hawkins, but then further instructed by Joseph Campbell and Isamu Noguchi, who helped to open the doors to this greater and wiser wisdom. She read extensively, and she was also beginning to study Eastern philosophies and symbolism. Once she called Campbell backstage and said to him, "Wait till I get up on the Kundalini!" The Kundalini is the Hindu system of control of all emotional dynamics and spiritual energy which motivates both physical and mental activity. The Jungian theories, together with the deeply spiritual concept of the Kundalini, which had been worked through to a manifest and practical system, seemed to bring enlightenment to Martha. It gave her a handle for her aesthetic manipulation, which was, of course, movement in space, which, while it must progress because it is art, blindly and primarily guided by instinct, now became, with her new understanding, purposeful and revelatory. The finished dance, the achieved bodily movement, clearly took place in a greater scheme. Martha and Martha's pupils thereafter derived strength from this understanding. Frankly and practically speaking, the work was often incomprehensible to her audience. At first, that is; with further viewing they, too, seemed to develop "the third eye."

Every class began with the class seated cross-legged in Yoga position, performing deep-breathing exercises that were centered very low in the pelvis. This is what Ruth St. Denis had done in her dance *The Yogi*, and what she did in all her practice classes. But St. Denis knew nothing of the Kundalini theories. Graham carried the idea further.

Pearl Lang explains:

The breath in the body goes way down from the genitals up through the waist, through the throat, and through the top of the head, and then down again. These exercises are repeated each day. In the next development the head goes all the way back and the gaze is turned upward. The back arches and then the energy returns. The dancer works always from the base of the spine all the way up through the center of the body, the navel, the heart, the mouth, the head. Graham carried it further, so that not an arm was lifted without the rising energy of the breath, on the life impulse. Only after the energy has risen to its highest level does the arm lift, very like the bud of a blossom opening. The force comes through the center of the body and finally bursts out. The process can be lyric and soft, or fierce. She has taken a spiritual idea and made it physical.*

Martha had absorbed from Ruth St. Denis a deep respect and sympathy for the ways and point of view of India. But the real Hindu thinking was still unknown to her, until Carl Jung gave her the insight she needed and she was able to seize on its vitalities and use them. She became a blazing acolyte. She felt that her dances now represented amplifications of both her art and her consciousness.

Deaths and Entrances has been called the perfect Graham ballet, and, as with all her work, it means different things to different people. It is the story of three sisters. They are assumed to be the Brontës— Charlotte, Emily, and Anne. But Graham's characters (played originally by Jane Dudley, Martha, and Sophie Maslow) were in no way like the historical Brontë girls. Within the company it was considered that these three characters were in truth Martha and her own two sisters. All Graham's major characters have elements of herself, but these characters were deeply and clinically analogous. The ballet, then, is a tripartite portrait of Martha—a triptych.

It involved mythology on several levels. First, the study of the Brontës, Martha taking the role of Emily and Erick taking the role of the brother, Branwell, who was also, in the ballet, Emily's lover. On a second level it is the study of the three Graham sisters, called "the

*See pp. 429–431 of the Appendices for a further explanation of Kundalini.

Remembered Children" in the program—Martha, Mary, and Geordie (played originally by Pearl Lang, Nina Fonaroff, and Ethel Butler)— and their interrelations as sisters: the closed world of sisterhood, girlhood, and womanhood, and the conflict with the demands of the outside world and the impingements of general society. On a third level it is the most astonishing revelation of the forces at war in Martha, between private passion and dedication to art, the forming and forging of the true artist.

The characters of the sisters were split into three adults and three children, permitting the young and the old versions of the sisters to contemplate one another across time. In this ballet Graham splinters time and reassembles it. Heathcliff, called here "the Dark Beloved," who was in some aspects the austere father figure (Martha's own father?), cut through all the sequences when he and the child Emily stand staring at each other.

Erick in his first entrance as Heathcliff (who was entitled by Martha on the music score "the Lord of the Moor") walks masterfully, rapidly, and very purposefully but, most surprisingly, backward. (Martha takes full cognizance of people who spend their energies moving backward.) At the adult Emily's (Martha's) first encounter with the Dark Beloved, she falls flat on her back. Critics remonstrated, calling such behavior ridiculous, but Martha countered that sudden perceptions of love *can* be ridiculous, and certainly they are awesome. One does fall down at the feet of the beloved object. She once said in a thank-you speech, "I stand here in sweet terror, as when confronted by love."

Mark Ryder later observed, "Her eye for sure, significant, truthful movement was unmatched." Patricia Birch said this, too, as did Dorothy Bird and Sallie Wilson.

The ballet had its premiere on December 26, 1943. John Martin wrote: "At first seeing, it is perfectly safe to say that not a single spectator can honestly report that he knows what the work is all about, though he must acknowledge that it is gripping and emotionally moving." He then went on to explain that *Deaths and Entrances* was actually meant to be "un-understandable" through "the usual organs of understanding," and that it "slips in sensory perceptions." There was no objectivity in imagery that could register on the intellect.

In a 1984 interview, Anna Kisselgoff quotes Graham as saying that "the work is 'not a mirroring of my life,' but speaks 'to anyone who has a family.' " It is a "modern psychological portrait . . . of women unable to free themselves of themselves to follow their hearts' desires. The most powerful solo goes to Emily, the Brontë who could write: 'And visions rise, and change, that kill me with desire.' Originally, Graham cast herself as Emily. 'Emily was the dominant one,' she says, 'the fantasizer. Charlotte was seemingly the dominant one. But Emily was seeking a humanity and a wideness of approach and experience to life that Charlotte was against.' "

IIIII

Whether Martha was conscious of it or not, these dance dramas, which everyone called avant-garde and psychological, were at bottom morality plays wherein separate aspects of human character are personified. But in Graham there was no attempt to illustrate a Christian ethic, as was the case in medieval theater. Graham's dance dramas probed hidden psychological relationships. Martha may very well not have been aware of the source; she certainly used her inventions freshly and spontaneously. The medieval theater is there nonetheless, as it is part of Martha's atavistic heritage. This in turn was to be replaced by the heroic classical myths. The allegorical, moral fragments were to give way to the grand racial archetypes of ancient legend: the gods, the spirits, the ghosts, the kings.

Very frequently I, among others, having a literal and rather old-fashioned taste in dramatic convention, did not understand Martha's symbolism and splintered time-sense. But I took faith and kept on going back. Martha clarified her pieces with repetition, simplified them, made them more explicit. I, and others, became more sensitive.

In *Deaths and Entrances* Martha used many props—large, ceremonial chess pieces, a chalice, a seashell, a scarf, a fan. The props became part of the gesture. (Once, while I was walking with John Martin, we passed a junk shop choked with clutter. "Ah," said Martin. "Thank God Martha never saw this!") The props in *Deaths and Entrances* are so important that they become almost personages. The interplay between the symbolic objects and the symbolic characters is constant and mysterious: the older women play with phallic symbols, the children with toys, vases, and shells, the beloved knickknacks of a Victorian household. Patricia Birch later said:

I helped revive *Deaths and Entrances* with Bertram [Ross] and Mary [Hinkson], and Martha came in to look at it. We hoped that we were setting something that could be accepted. There was one section in which the three little girls are left alone because everyone else has gone off to the ball. The choreographic detail had been devised largely by the three first dancers, Pearl Lang, Nina Fonaroff, and Ethel Butler. They run in and out and take an object up—here a seashell, there the chess piece and all the things that children should not play with. We all thought that these objects were heavily symbolic, and they became mysterious and pretentious. Martha said nothing. She just sat and watched, and then she said, "I only have one thing to say to any of you: All the grown-ups have just gone and these simply are objects that you are forbidden to touch." The dancers understood instantly. I think she was remembering back to the things she had known in her own home in Santa Barbara. . . . That lady goes for more truth than anyone I have ever known.

The dancers were never told in rehearsal what they were representing, or even, in many cases, who they were supposed to be. It seemed very strange, but Martha, Pearl Lang believed, didn't want them to have preconceived ideas of how to move or what to express. She wanted them to move as bidden and to express only the movement indicated, nothing else.

Jane Dudley recalls:

She would improvise whole passages, and Sophie Maslow and I followed behind her as best we could and picked up from what she said, any hints or clues. Then, after that, it was our responsibility to work on it by ourselves, clean it up, and finalize it as to the exact version of arms and hands, etc. She didn't always tell us what it was about, but sometimes you just knew or felt what was needed from the atmosphere in the rehearsals. We all knew together, at the same moment, what it was about.

I was given a prop—in my case it was a scarf—and told to relate to it. It was much the same with *Letter to the World*. Martha had not told me much about the Ancestress, just given me the general outlines of character and composition. I dug all the details up myself from American primitive paintings and from early memories of my own childhood.

It had been the same with *American Document*. Martha outlined the pattern, inventing it on the spot, and Jane Dudley and the two other girls imitated her, standing behind her, mimicking, mimicking; then she left and they fixed the gestures so that they would be all alike and move together. But the actual structure of the pattern was completed, according to Jane Dudley, in about three minutes and by Martha alone.

The music for *Deaths and Entrances* was again by Hunter Johnson. "But," claimed Erick, "he was too neurotic to orchestrate his own work." (He did, however, orchestrate *Letter to the World* in a way Erick had felt was never adequate for their needs.) Erick subsequently asked several composers to have a try at scoring *Deaths and Entrances*, but none was successful.

Deaths and Entrances did not come together easily as a finished work—indeed, which of Graham's ballets had? It clarified itself with considerable agony. On February 15, 1943, I wrote to Walter Prude, now my fiancé and a soldier away in camp, about Martha while she was working on it. "She's a great woman and I'm frightfully worried about her. All the time she was with me she was moving restlessly in her chair as though she were in pain or in some sort of distress, and she kept sighing as though she suddenly had trouble in breathing. I think she is on the brink of collapse." On April 28 I wrote: "Perhaps it's the new composition she is struggling with at the moment. I think also it might be change of life. [Martha was now forty-nine years old.] It might be personal emotional trouble. Martha didn't explain. She said most yearningly, 'I must get on the beam.'" ("On the beam" was part of the new slang of aviation radar, and hearing Martha use it amused me enormously. I thought it very jazzy of her.)

Alas, it was more than the ballet that was troubling her. Martha was in great turmoil in her relationship with Erick. Erick was contemplating co-stardom. And Erick was perhaps contemplating marriage. Martha was frightened.

This, of course, was the classic conflict, according to Pearl Lang. Erick was the only person Martha ever completely loved, but Martha herself denied the fact emphatically at the time, and maintained an absolutely prophylactic semblance of chastity and reticence. She lived in a small apartment west of Sixth Avenue and Erick lived nearby, but he definitely lived apart. No sign of his living habits or personal belongings was ever visible in her house. Erick confided to José Limón that Martha insisted that he keep all his belongings—razor, pajamas, etc.— put away so that when Louis or anyone else came to visit, she had no evidence whatever in her flat of living with a man. Erick never was permitted to leave even a sweater lying about, because they both knew that Louis was bitterly jealous and grieved, and Martha valued Louis too greatly as a critic and a support to drive him away. She would never invite any friend or business associate—Gertrude Macy, the company manager, for instance—to meet her at home. I was not asked in until 1947, and once only, for supper with mutual friends. Erick was nowhere about, yet it was obvious to every woman in the group that Martha and Erick were deeply involved. The relationship had been recognized way back in the Ballet Caravan days in Bennington in 1936, when Martha had singled him out for praise with sufficient exuberance so that the Caravan dancers took it for granted that they were lovers, as did the girls in her own Group.

In my April 28 letter to Walter I wrote: "I told Martha that you said you would have been in love with her if it hadn't been for Erick! 'He's quite, quite wrong,' she said, looking straight at me."

I remember this conversation well. I was walking Martha home to Sixth Avenue from her studio on Fifth Avenue and Thirteenth Street over the Fifth Avenue Moving Picture House. We had come to the Portuguese Cemetery, which consists of about nine graves that are a century and a half old in a tiny, pie-shaped triangle wedged between crumbling buildings. We stopped while we spoke. Martha was extraordinarily emphatic.

" 'Erick runs my company but he doesn't run me. Make no mistake about that.' So perhaps we've been wonderfully wrong or maybe she's slipping out. Anyhow, all I can say is thank God there is a continent between the two of you.

"Lewis Isaacs, Mrs. Edith Isaacs's son, Martha's lawyer, says there's nothing between Martha and Erick and that she's distraught that people insist on thinking there is."

Late in 1943 a friend of Walter's, a pianist, then a member of the armed forces, who was a great admirer of Graham, came to New York on leave before being sent overseas and renewed his friendship with her. Like all young men, he fell in love with her. But this one, Craig Barton, was serious.

Barton was a Southern gentleman, a Texan, with gallant, old-fashioned manners and enormous charm, young, eager, and with the instinct always to be thoughtful of women and very careful of their comfort and sensitivities. He had a diamond-blue gaze and engaging laugh-wrinkles around the eyes, soft, sensual lips, and a slurred caressing accent. His humor was enchanting. Martha, like every other female, found herself sensitive to his charm and to his extraordinary thoughtfulness. For his part, Barton considered her a goddess, and one of the most greatly gifted humans he had ever encountered.

Their meetings were passionate. Briefly they became lovers. Craig left for the war deeply enamored, and Martha was caught in the emotion. They corresponded, but Martha made no clarifying statement about Erick.

Indeed she could not. She loved Erick. But as for Craig, Martha said to me, "It was the only time I did anything equivocal. I was out of control and bewildered." Craig, too, was bewildered. Up to this time he had always been strongly homosexual.

||||

I had once offered Erick the position of partnering me in some recitals. I had small hope of acceptance, inasmuch as he was Graham's associate and anything additional or less worthy would have seemed to him unsuitable. She was the greatest—he must not associate with anyone else's work. He was polite but, as expected, negative. I did offer to pay, though. Apparently in time Erick thought better of the proposition. In January 1943, at the first audition for *Oklahoma!*, Erick Hawkins appeared, voluntarily and unbidden. He had heard, he said, that there were some small parts with a few lines, and he'd like one. I knew what he meant. He meant that he would like some regular money. He, like all the moderns, despised Broadway in all its aspects. But in view of the Graham company's financial predicament I forgave the scorn and was eager to help him.

"This is Martha Graham's partner," I said to the co-producer, Theresa Helburn, to the composer, Richard Rodgers, and to the director, Rouben Mamoulian. (Mamoulian had worked with Martha at the Eastman School of Music in Rochester in 1925. He now murmured, "Ah, Martha!")

"I vouch for Hawkins's dancing," I said. "Let him read."

"Here," said Jerry Whyte, the stage manager, handing Erick the script. "Read the first lines of the script, Curly's lines. Omit the song."

"Why omit anything?"

"But you don't know the tune," said Whyte reasonably.

"I'll make up my own tune," said Erick.

"Listen," said Whyte patiently, "just begin here—'Hi, Aunt Eller!—there. The composer is sitting in front of you. He knows the tune. You don't."

"I'll sing my tune," said Erick. And he did:

"'There's a bright, golden haze on the mead-er.
'There's a bright, golden haze on the mead-er.
'The corn is as high as an elephant's eye . . .'"

Richard Rodgers had handled the melody better.
After the first verse, Whyte interrupted. "That's enough. Now speak
the lines."
Hawkins stated flatly, "There are two more verses. I'll sing them all."
Rodgers rose suddenly and left the stage.
Hawkins sang the song through to a row of unmoving faces. He read
the intervening lines and then, with a hard, manly grin, started on the
next song, "The Surrey with the Fringe on Top."
"I'll have that now," said Whyte, snatching the script from Erick's
hands. "I think we get the idea."
"Well," said Hawkins, coming up to me with his really beautiful
smile and extending a forthright hand, "I did my best. You can't do
more than that."
"Erick," I said, leading him out, "don't you ever do that again.
When you're told by a Broadway stage manager what to do, you do just
that, nothing else."
"Oh, well," said Erick, "no harm trying."
"Martha's partner?" said Mamoulian with genuine bewilderment.
Rodgers returned without comment.
"Next!" said Jerry Whyte, handing a trembling young man a script.
"Skip the song. Be sure to skip the song. Just read the lines."
On April 28, 1943, I wrote to Walter Prude: "Erick I could not
accept as understudy mainly because Marc Platt, the dancing lead
(Curley in the ballet), took a violent dislike to him and refused to
cooperate, giving his reason, sly dog, that he was afraid that Erick would
drop him and hurt his foot again. (Marc had already suffered a bad
sprain from the work and had been forced to dance the opening night
on an anesthetized leg.) That argument is practically unanswerable.
'Hire him if you want to,' said Marc, 'but I have no physical confidence
in him and will be uneasy the whole time.' I was fearfully sorry, because
it meant fifty bucks a week all summer for Erick, only to stand by, and
that meant fifty bucks for Martha."

IIIII

Every summer, routinely, Martha went west to visit her mother. These
last few summers Erick accompanied her partway, and they had time

together en route, sojourning in the desert, sleeping out under the stars, and camping among the sagebrush and rocks, in wastes of stellar loneliness. The hours with Erick were for Martha a total verification of life. In the Far West, alone, whether indoors or out, they lived very simply and far from all of the turmoils and complications that bedeviled them in New York. Here there was no such thing as status, no such thing as greater or lesser, no tension between professional needs and private desires. Here they were just two human beings, a man and a woman, who truly loved each other and needed each other. According to Martha, they fulfilled each other. This period had a mystic aureole around it.

She once spoke of it, almost with awe, to John Butler. Inasmuch as Martha was discreet about her personal life, it was hard to know exactly what she felt, what Erick felt, and what had transpired; but from hints and scattered revelations dropped from time to time, it must be assumed that these periods were altogether happy. On later trips Martha lived with Erick in a lean-to on a mountainside. They cooked their meals over an open fire. I think it safe to assume that these episodes were idyllic.

But in New York, Erick and Martha still lived separately.

And the company still resented him.

‖‖‖

In the summer of 1944, while Martha was working on a new ballet, *Herodiade,* a film was released that impressed all naturalists, anthropologists, and, above all, mythologists. It was a remarkable newsreel concerning a Burmese priestess who lived in a small mountain village and who had been born of a line of religious devotees, bred to a single life purpose: when there were few male children, the priestess was to go alone into the high mountains and there find and confront a cobra. The priestess, sitting before the reptile in a mutual hypnotic state, performed the ceremony of leaning forward over the snake's head and kissing him three times at the nape of the neck, where the eyeglass pattern began on his hood. Cameramen with telescopic lenses installed safely in trees accompanied her and photographed her in slow motion. The snake's thrusts are so rapid and deadly that even the slow-motion camera fails to catch them completely. But the evidence of the strikes was on the woman's dress, which was soaking wet with venom as the reptile ejaculated. She held her own. She outsnaked the snake and managed to implant the sacred kisses and then depart untouched and alive as the snake retired, in, I imagine, considerable confusion. Male babies were born in the village to other women.

Martha, in common with thousands of amazed people, was thunderstruck. Out of this extraordinary newsreel she transfigured material into the deadly dance between Herodias and her mirror, between Herodias and her tiring woman, staring at each other, weaving about, interweaving, but hardly touching, Herodias facing an enemy, Herodias facing death: Martha facing old age.

She wrote to Walter Prude that at last she had determined how to dress her hair and that she was going to wear it in the headdress of a cobra, with the hood spread.

Of course, it is death that the woman is flirting with.

Herodias was the mother of Salome, whose enticement of her father, King Herod (the husband of Herodias), gained her the head of John the Baptist. A study of Herodias therefore becomes a study of the loss of seductiveness and power through age and the apprehension of youth, with its usurpation of the queen's power.

Herodiade "fractured" (their word) the girls of her company, for they felt it to be Martha's menopausal dance, her farewell to youth. She was now fifty.

|||||

In 1944 Erick persuaded Elizabeth Sprague Coolidge to subsidize a commission for two new Graham ballets—*Herodiade* and *Appalachian Spring*—to be given their premieres at the Library of Congress as part of its concert series on October 30. These were the first large grants Erick obtained for Martha. At that time there were no national or state endowments. All such enterprises had to be privately organized. Paul Hindemith was commissioned to compose the music for *Herodiade*, and Aaron Copland for *Appalachian Spring*. Noguchi designed the sets for both.

Martha spoke of her work with the great German composer in a 1985 interview:

This was during the war and he was up at Yale and couldn't travel. So I went up to see him, talk to him. I'd never met him. . . . He looked at me the whole time he sat at the piano and played. He never took his eyes off me. . . . By the time I got home the phone was ringing. It was Mrs. Hindemith. She said, "Are you all right? I think we were too strong for you." I said, "You almost were. I almost fainted, I felt so weak." It was the energy of the man. . . .

He had said, "It [the score] will be there at noon on Wednesday." I said, "Well, if it's a day or two later, an hour or two later, you just let me know." He said, "It will be there at noon on Wednesday." At noon on Wednesday the door knock came and he gave me the score. I said how moved I was, and said, "Oh, what will happen if I fail?" He said, "Then I will write you another piece."

They didn't like what I did to his music, Mrs. Hindemith particularly. She said, "Where are the bottles of perfume that you're supposed to be passing in front of? Where is the leopard on the stage?" She said, "You didn't consult the composer at all about this." I said, "Why, it never occurred to me to consult the composer about the choreography." Well, this upset her no end.

It frequently happens that masters in music, a totally abstract art, are childishly literal in their approach to other means of expression.

Appalachian Spring dealt with a pioneer frontier marriage, a simple, straightforward (well, as straightforward as Graham can be) folk festival. The characters were the young bride, the young groom, the older woman who was the adviser and protector, and the preacher, a brimstone frontier evangelist who prophesied doom and hellfire to all who did not agree with him. He was followed and supported—one might say ornamented—by a group of devout young spinsters worshiping and providing a certain element of comedy. The treatment of the lovers and their taking over of a new house and a new farm is superbly simple and moving.

Appalachian Spring is a love letter, a dance of hope, budding, fresh, and beautiful. Martha danced, as John Martin said, "like a sixteen-year-old," giving a performance altogether fragrant. And to Erick, as the bridegroom, she presented this role as a pledge of her devotion.

He was stiff, as he always was. His part has been danced since with equal manliness and more ebullience and suppleness, and also more subtlety. But Erick was the first and Martha's true love, and Martha responded to him in a way both rosy and blooming.

Merce Cunningham played the raging, inflamed preacher, a role he did not care for. In his own solo (which he himself choreographed) it has been suggested that he showed more anger than was needed. In explaining the part of the preacher to Robert Cohan when he replaced Merce Cunningham, Martha said he must be ninety-nine percent sex and one percent religion: a real popular spellbinder, a magnetic man who had power over women—like, Bertram Ross suggests, Frank Sinatra. A man who knows his own magic and uses it deliberately. Martha explained that he should be awesome, even frightening, and always compelling. May O'Donnell was the mother figure, the seasoned frontier woman who has lived through much and stands by to help the bride start a new life.

In the final moments, the bride and groom are left alone, and she sits on her porch and looks out at the evening. He places his hand on her shoulder in a gesture of such serene possession and regal domination as has rarely been seen in the theater.

The one flaw in this work—and it is minor though provoking—is that the adoring females around the preacher, dressed alike in slightly musical-comedy fashion, are treated comically; therefore, they demean the importance of the man, and he, of course, although an alien figure because a bigot, and not sympathetic to our way of thinking, is nevertheless serious. This strange slippage of styles is perhaps due to the quality of later performers. When Martha rehearsed the first group, she would not permit any triviality, any sense of cuteness or pertness, to vitiate the ecstatic spontaneity. She had made a study of evangelical worship. As her girls fell on their knees together she raised her hand heavenward and, lifting her face, shouted, "I've got Jesus by the foot!" This kind of rapt ecstasy and exaggerated expression was rhapsodic, not cute, but it is not at all what one gets from the group today.

Appalachian Spring is perhaps the most dearly loved ballet in the Graham repertory. The score is now a classic, and the set by Noguchi a theatrical landmark.

IIIII

Throughout the war Martha wrote to her soldiers, members of her troupe who had gone, her students, her friends. She wrote faithfully and cheerfully. Among those to whom she wrote was Walter Prude, whom I had married in 1943. He sent her letters on to me, and in a letter dated May 1, 1944, I wrote to him, "I must get my tickets for Martha. I think undoubtedly her work is going to be the most important event in the theater this winter."

Throughout the war, as before, I had clung to Martha as to a beloved older sister. I asked her advice, I asked her reaffirmation, and she gave it steadily and wonderfully. She had introduced me to her manager and she had seen us through our courtship and pitifully brief married time together before Walter left for the war. When he was suddenly shipped overseas for the duration, Martha came to my studio immediately, running down the block.

"We must now love him very much," she had said. She was always willing to talk to me on the phone in the evening hours of terror and bereavement.

Martha seldom entertained, because she couldn't spare the time, but she was thoughtful about sending telegrams and letters on special occasions. In material matters she was a giving person, not a taking one, and her kindnesses and generosities showed themselves in little ways, tiny courtesies, gift pretties. When she came to dinner or even on a casual meeting she brought small tokens, and later lovely things she'd picked up on her travels. After she'd been in Japan they were always tied up in Japanese kerchiefs, *furoshiki*. It must be noted, however, that she always found it easier to be the generous one, which is in reality inverse selfishness and a form of pride.

Anything I could do to help Martha, I did. But what I did for her was as nothing compared with the wisdom and loving care and fortitude she gave me, especially during this period. She came to all my shows and held my hand through the openings; she talked to me about the work afterward with perceiving grace. Martha was on hand subsequently for the big Broadway openings, and always spoke intelligently and warmly and kindly. There were also notes and letters as pretty as poems, all breathing good feeling and energy.

Martha gave me advice about whom to have as a dresser backstage, what to pay her, where to get my clothes made, what to pay for them, how to obtain help from the Salvation Army—all manner of shortcuts and aids which she had discovered. I asked her about everything.

"Don't listen to that girl," she said to me once about a dancer. "She has a bad eye, like a wrong horse." Or once when I encountered Antony Tudor head-on and turned aside—I considered him my enemy at the time—she said, "Stand your ground, don't move, don't you dare move. Make *him* go out of *his* way." And she grabbed my reluctant arm and proceeded straight ahead like a soldier, with me quaking beside her. (Incidentally, the man did not step aside. He grabbed me and kissed me and said, "I will *not* have you cutting me!")

And I always told Martha about my emotional problems, and her advice was always toward life, toward activity, toward engaging. "Never tell anyone he has no talent. That you may not say. That you do not know. That is the one absolute prohibition laid down." (Oh, my, the ballet teachers who have not heeded that!) She had faith that human character was strong enough to withstand anything, except lethargy; that marked the onset of decay and death.

The greatest thing she ever said to me was in 1943 after the opening of *Oklahoma!*, when I suddenly had unexpected, flamboyant success for a work I thought was only fairly good, after years of neglect for work I thought was fine. I was bewildered and worried that my entire scale of values was untrustworthy. I talked to Martha. I remember the conversation well. It was in a Schrafft's restaurant over a soda. I confessed that I had a burning desire to be excellent but no faith that I could be. Martha said to me, very quietly, "There is a vitality, a life force, an energy, a quickening that is translated through you into action, and because there is only one of you in all of time, this expression is unique. And if you block it, it will never exist through any other medium and it will be lost. The world will not have it. It is not your business to determine how good it is nor how valuable nor how it compares with other expressions. It is your business to keep it yours clearly and directly, to keep the channel open. You do not even have to believe in yourself or your work. You have to keep yourself open and aware to the urges that motivate you. Keep the channel open. As for you, Agnes, you have a peculiar and unusual gift, and you have so far used about one-third of your talent."

"But," I said, "when I see my work I take for granted what other people value in it. I see only its ineptitude, inorganic flaws, and crudities. I am not pleased or satisfied."

"No artist is pleased."

"But then there is no satisfaction?"

"No satisfaction whatever at any time," she cried out passionately. "There is only a queer divine dissatisfaction, a blessed unrest that keeps us marching and makes us more alive than the others."

The most practical gift she ever gave me was sometime later, and it was her studio.

In the late summer of 1953, I leased Martha Graham's school building in order to rehearse the new company I was forming. Martha had no need of the studio at the moment since it was her vacation month, and the rooms stood empty. But I learned, to my dismay, that certain of the smaller rooms had been reserved and promised to members of her company, Pearl Lang among them, for their private practice, and these she gave free to the girls to help them in their work. My pride was somewhat injured by the realization that Martha would give her rooms free to these young soloists but made me pay full rent. And my husband, with connubial loyalty, reported his indignation at the transaction to his old friend, Craig, who was now acting as Martha's personal manager. Martha and he went into consultation and made me a present of the entire school, rent free, for four weeks. It was an enormous move to make and an act of very real generosity.

Her spiritual and emotional support was incalculable and unfailing.

‖‖‖

In 1945, when the war in Europe ended, my husband, Walter Prude, had been gone two and one half years. I went to London on June 14, after V-E Day but before V-J Day, to make a motion picture. I was waiting there without news of Walter when one night, to my absolute dumbfoundment, he suddenly appeared at my apartment door. I absented myself from work for two weeks without permission (but with no great loss to the production). This unexpected visit was permitted him because he had been ordered to the Eastern Theater of war, to continue to fight the Japanese. The visit therefore constituted our farewell before a very long and dangerous separation. Martha wrote to me there on July 17, from Bennington: "So he came. Is he as wonderful as ever?" She went on to say that the Chávez music had at last arrived and that she didn't like it very much, and closed with the news that she might be with Hurok and that the contracts were being drawn up.

I had promoted the idea that Martha sign with Sol Hurok by taking Hurok's first assistant, Mae Froman, to one of Graham's concerts. I also ballyhooed Martha as though she were a combination of all the great dancers I had ever seen. Mae Froman caught fire from me and told Hurok, who offered to manage Martha and subsequently signed her up. This was a big business step for her.

‖‖‖

The opening of *Carousel*, for which I had done all the dances, had occurred on April 17, 1945, at the Majestic Theater. Louis Horst was present on a ticket from Pearl Lang. He told me he thought I was an extremely good choreographer, and I nearly dropped in the aisle.

The golden period for Graham in the early forties was an astonishing revelation to me, forlorn as I was, adrift, waiting for life to resume, not knowing how to hope, not knowing what to hope for. The war ended abruptly and Walter was shipped home expeditiously, leaving me in London for a further five-month stint on the wretched picture! I was, after his brief London visit, very pregnant. I was finally allowed to go home and rejoin my bridegroom. Life resumed with a vengeance.

The daily implementation of Martha's endeavor was, as it must be with all great and complex things, rather grubby.

"Don't you ever get depressed?" I once asked her.

"All the time," she replied brightly. "But I never tell." I believe she thought herself a stoic. And earlier, when I was first starting, I said, "Martha, how does one get up in the morning? How does one start the day with no one to tell you how to plan?" She replied succinctly, "We all face this. You must make a schedule of your day's work for every hour, all day long, from the moment you wake to the moment you fall asleep, and you must stick to it whether it seems to make sense or not. Stick to it carefully. The momentum will help you." So I did, and she was quite right.

The revolution in dancing and the theater was accomplished by courage, of course, but also by hourly walking, trudging, practicing, sitting in studios, rolling on the floor, dressing, undressing, stretching, walking, eating in the Automat, walking, stretching, back bending, and finally dropping to rest.

In 1976, when the President of the United States hung the Medal of Freedom around Martha's neck, it was not for a single act of valor or a single dance. It was for the days and hours and years of walking, stretching, rolling, thinking, praying, and dropping to rest.

And for being steadfast.

Martha was our North Star.

In January 1946, Graham produced an astonishing work, *Dark Meadow*, to music by the Mexican composer Carlos Chávez. *Dark Meadow* is a study of seemingly primitive ritual with vigorous dances for the group.

The list of characters more or less indicates the substance and point of departure for the action. "One Who Seeks," that is, Martha, the protagonist; "He Who Summons," her lover, Erick, little more than a catalyst; the "Earth Mother," roughly the figure of Persephone; and "They Who Dance Together," the members of the community. The chorus made an emotional background and intensified all the phases of Martha's passage toward self-realization and power.

At the end, Martha, the heroine, finds herself alone, and Noguchi's strange, phalliclike cactus form at the back of the stage bursts into flower, or rather buds out in Noguchi's blooms. It was a dance of sacrifice in which the artist strips herself of everything to achieve her fulfillment. I took a psychoanalyst, Florence Powdermaker, to a performance, and she sat at the end with tears streaming down her cheeks, her head in her hands, and said, "Oh, unnecessary, unneeded! This is not the price. Is there no one who can teach Martha this? She does not need to give her life for perception. The suffering! The suffering!" The doctor had to sit awhile and compose herself.

The technical demands of the dance are extremely difficult, for both the soloists and the group. The ensemble numbers demanded and attained a virtuosity seldom asked of any dancer except a leading soloist. The boys had to enter on their knees, with their arms outstretched and supporting the full weight of the girls, who crouched in bunched positions, very like the fetal postures used in Indian burials, knees to chest and head lowered forward to knees. The girls sat on the boys' chests and stretched out their arms. The boys approached and retreated, always on their knees. (This was Mark Ryder's dreaded knee exercise, which he said cost him unending pain and which Martha could do with ease.)

These dances lie within Martha's most wonderful choreographic intent and invention; they represent the absolute best of her style. She composed them quickly. There are several witnesses to the effect that she accomplished long passages in a single evening.

Erick was cast as the lover—He Who Summons—and nobody has ever replaced him in the role for strength and impact. The action was primitive and vaguely suggestive of the American Southwest, which is the land where Erick was born and where his mind and heart return for sources of strength. Erick thinks of himself as part Indian, a primitive, and he was just this in *Dark Meadow*.

John Martin wrote of *Dark Meadow:*

[The music] is utterly without theatrical or choreographic quality, pure paper-and-ink music, and long stretches of it sound like so many pages out of Czerny. . . .

That Miss Graham has been able to make a dance composition against it is inexplicable. . . . There are . . . four monolithic objects (all beautifully designed by Isamu Noguchi) which . . . seem rather to be used simply for their effectiveness as theatre devices. . . . As a piece of abstract theatre, it is thoroughly fascinating, however bewildering. It is full of suspense and surprise and, for the conservative-minded, shock. . . . Whatever substantial favor it may win with the public undoubtedly will stem from that, but it is likely to be slight.

But after handing in his copy, while having a cup of midnight coffee, Martin suddenly realized what the ballet meant and was stricken with remorse. He followed up his review with a Sunday article reversing all his judgments, and he very handsomely paid tribute to a new masterpiece. Martin could be big about such matters.

What is the ballet about? No critic has brought this point out, but in a sense *Dark Meadow* was Martha's first version of *Le Sacre du Printemps*. The dedicated victim, the Chosen One, is the artist: the sacrifice of worldly pleasure for realization is the vernal rebirth. This is the message the work seemed to convey to us, but thirty years later a sensitive and intelligent critic, Tobi Tobias, read it differently:

The scene is one of Isamu Noguchi's portentous landscapes—stone markers in a deep void. Almost arrogant in his energy, the man displays himself to his destined partner. Their mating is encouraged by passages . . . of exquisite couplings for a small chorus, They Who Dance Together, but the principals' consummation is a different matter—more troubled, more violent and perhaps more ecstatic. . . . The ensemble remains nothing but the personification of primal desires. He Who Summons, having played his part in the woman's history, rolls away into the wings like a dust ball, but She Who Seeks is left to inhabit the center of the stage alone, seemingly at the threshold of discovery.

Dark Meadow is frequently described as a fertility ritual. The view is easy to support, but to understand *Dark Meadow* simply as a wash of lovely anthropology is to miss its strange personal edge. I suspect Graham's subtext is autobiographical, but the seeker is herself, the woman who is an artist. The erotic love, she seems to tell us, the force that makes the world go round, plays a significant, even catalytic part in her self-realization, but not the principal one.

The mystery of the expression of abstract art is that it can mean quite different or supplemental things to different people—indeed, the artist's original intention may be definitely altered without loss of power. And yet Graham's work is by no means wholly abstract. There is strong emotion throughout it, recognizable human emotion, and it is this specific emotionalism and vision that marks Graham's creations and sets them apart from so many other abstract modern works, which seem by comparison almost bloodless.

And yet Martha never explained specifically what she meant. She made it clear to herself, and probably to Louis Horst, but when she felt she had achieved what she wanted, she stopped talking. Any watcher could furnish his own footnotes.

Dorothy Bird had been in the audience in 1943 at the premiere of *Salem Shore*, a solo about an abandoned woman waiting for the return of her lover. There was a ramp at the back of the stage, symbolizing, most probably, the widow's walk. So far, so good. And in the foreground lay a tangle of sea thorn with which Martha played and posed—symbolizing what? Everyone was forced to guess. Dorothy Bird, Muriel Stewart, and several of the Graham faithfuls held a mid-aisle conference. One thought it must surely be her wedding ring; another thought that it was sex. Somebody else said it symbolized Christ's crown of thorns. Bird voted for nothing specific. "I know what those roots mean. They represent a beautiful toy, a thing for Martha to play with and place in different positions and come through this way and that way. She loves to play with beautiful abstract forms. It's nothing more."

They decided to ask Martha directly.

To every question she smiled like the Cheshire Cat and said, "Hmmm." And nothing else. More she would not vouchsafe. The device was pretty enough, and they might see in it what they liked. She had done her part.

|||||

Touring on one-night stands was difficult and galling, exhausting and tedious. Martha tried to instill discipline. She herself was always carefully accoutered and sat quietly, mostly reading, sometimes making notes and planning. She asked that the girls wear skirts, but after a while she relaxed and let them wear in transit whatever they liked—the boys, too—until arrival, when she insisted that the girls be properly dressed in skirts, their hair fixed, and the boys wear ties. When they went out socially she wanted the girls in nice clothes, and she liked them to wear white gloves to all parties—cotton, if necessary, but clean. Erick did very little on the bus, sometimes reading, sometimes gossiping with the others. He drove them absolutely frantic by slapping a seat belt against his knee for long intervals. He made jokes continually. Erick was funnier on the bus than on the stage. He always thought he was wonderfully funny, and occasionally offstage he was. They would have yelled at any other member of the company, but out of loyalty to their leader they tolerated him. John Butler shared dressing rooms with Erick on these tours; nobody else would, flatly refusing the close exposure. Martha persuaded John to do this, and out of love for her he complied, but he found it an ordeal.

In wartime these trips were grinding, harder than they used to be. It was Louis who had always found out on arrival in a town where the best restaurant was and how long it stayed open after the show so that the dancers could have something to eat, because they could not eat beforehand. Louis was no longer along to hurry the performance by speeding tempi in order to ensure their midnight meals. It was Louis who would delay the buses' morning departure until after a full breakfast. He was their guardian and comforter. Louis had always been fun. They didn't have much fun these days, for Louis had been banished. He was back in New York teaching at the Neighborhood Playhouse, being cared for by Nina, and flirting with strangers.

Those long, long one-night stands grew longer and harder as time went on, and the engagements got more plentiful: the tours, the arriving late, the going to the theater, the unpacking, the ironing of the costumes with the help of one or two hired local women, the concert, the midnight snack, the unpacking of the single personal suitcase, the exhausted sleep, the early-morning departure, the repetition. Martha used to do a great deal of the ironing herself. She was, said Pat Birch, an "expert ironer." And the girls used to help. (They would not now be permitted to, under present union rulings.) "The nightly program was accordingly," said Pat, "two dances onstage and two dances ironing." (Pat once burned the sleeve off of Erick's *Circus* jacket.) While she ironed, Martha talked in a very relaxed and informative way, mainly about love and life. She often spoke of Craig Barton, her Texan friend and adoring admirer, who was away on occupation duty in India.

In 1946, when the men came home from the war, male students flocked to Martha's studio, some of them working under the GI Bill of Rights. This is when she began to recruit distinguished males into her company—including Stuart Hodes and Robert Cohan. She was surrounded by men, buttressed by them on every side; but Erick was still the king, still dominant, and still stimulating her to fine work.

Martha had always been neat and attractive, and now that there were men around she always made them feel that she was there for them, and for each one exclusively and individually. Martha was as immaculate as a surgeon, even in rehearsals, and as chic as a *vendeuse* in a robe that had cost $8.95 and been sewn by herself. You may be sure the men responded.

This was a good, rich period for Martha: rich in achievement, in recognition, and in experience. Invitations from all over the world poured in, although she could accept very few. Her seasons in New York were triumphs; her seasons in Chicago, Los Angeles, San Francisco, Dallas—wherever thinking, knowledgeable people gathered—were brilliant. Erick continued to labor to get engagements, money, commissions, support for the company. The bus trips stretched out, grindingly difficult, wearing on the girls and boys, but profitable in returns of fame and recognition. Martha never made enough money to repay her debts, which were now enormous. She had scenery to contend with, and an orchestra, and a sizable group of dancers, and a working staff of technicians, and a staff of office helpers, largely under the direction of Erick. Katharine Cornell, always Martha's champion, gave her the very nearly fulltime help of her business manager, Gertrude Macy; and her husband, Guthrie McClintic, gave his co-producer, Stanley Gilkey.

|||||

Martha had written to Craig Barton steadily throughout the period of his basic training and his occupation duty, as she had written to all her soldier friends. When he returned from India it was with the expectation of a resumption of their relationship. But this did not transpire. Martha was in love with Erick, and that became clear. Craig developed into Martha's devoted slave. He worked for her on salary, took charge of all her personal affairs, and was her representative in all business concerns. He enlisted a young Texan, Leroy Leatherman, as his assistant.

I continued to help as I could, and I also quite selfishly wished to avail myself of some very splendid dancers, hiring Martha's company members when they asked me and when they obtained permission from her: Dorothy Bird for *Horray for What!* (1937), Nelle Fisher, Anita Alvarez, and Merce Cunningham for *One Touch of Venus,* Pearl Lang for *Carousel,* John Butler for *Oklahoma!,* Anita Alvarez for *Gentlemen Prefer Blondes,* Stuart Hodes for *Paint Your Wagon,* and Patricia Birch for many TV programs. These dancers gave splendid, even stellar, performances in my shows while never stinting on any of Martha's rehearsing. They would rush to Martha every available moment. How their bodies withstood the strain is a marvel. Martha advised them to use the cab rides for sleeping!

In 1946, through my urgings, Erick had finally been engaged as understudy for the two leads in *Oklahoma!,* Curly and Jud. He was required only to phone in every night half an hour before curtain time and ascertain if the dancers were capable of performing or if he would be needed. If he was not needed he was then free for the evening, and he would receive a small weekly salary for this. He did look fine onstage, and the two lead dancers were reassuringly healthy and unlikely to need replacing often. But we had to rehearse the roles, so we tried.

"Here," I said, "you put your arms out and you catch Laurie."

"Why do I put my arms out?" I was eight months pregnant at this point and I hoped the rehearsal would be brief.

"Because," I said, "Laurie is going to take a flying leap at you shoulder-high, and if you don't catch her she'll break her coccyx."

"But the reason?"

"The reason is choreographic. Do it." (Does the second flutist ask "Why E flat?") And the reason was obvious enough. His betrothed was flying to his breast. If he caught her, she soared. If he didn't catch her, he was a bad bet as a bridegroom. But Erick wanted a long, aesthetic analysis, on union time.

Late one evening, when I had gone to Martha's studio for girl talk, undoubtedly to be straightened out about some personal matter and was waiting in the outer office until her rehearsal finished—she permitted no visitors or guests at rehearsals—I had found myself vis-à-vis Erick, who was also waiting, and I had made my proposition to him.

"Well," he said, "regular money would be nice."

"It won't be more than fifty dollars a week," I warned.

"Yes. Well, okay. But I'm determined to make my own dances. I'm going to succeed no matter what. The last attempt didn't come off." All the time he was speaking he sat stabbing at the desk blotter with a pen, stab, stab, stab, "Martha gets good results with me, somehow or other, so if she can, I can."

"Erick," I had said in plain astonishment, "I respect your decision to work out your own things, to find your own way, but when you say 'somehow or other' you are, you know, referring to the earnest and loving efforts of the greatest living choreographer. It doesn't follow that anyone else can achieve the same results."

"Well"—stab, stab, stab, eyes on blotter—"I'm going to do it."

He did take the job I offered, however reluctantly, yet Martha knew that as a man he had to find his independent strength. She refused to recognize the chasm of difference that existed between their talents. One night at a ballet performance she stepped out with me for a lemonade at a drugstore counter and voiced her intentions, beating her fists on the marble counter.

"He will succeed, and I will make"—her voice rose—"I will *make* the New York critics accept him."

"Martha, you can't do that. Erick has to do that for himself."

"I won't have it. I will make them."

("Look out for Teddy," said poor Miss Ruth. "Go to his concerts. Be kind to him.")

Martha did not "make" the critics accept Erick. One did not "make" John Martin do anything. But Erick began demanding equal space on the program, an equal number of solos, and later equal billing. The Graham company was aghast at this, and so was the management, Sol Hurok.

There was one business lunch that endured for three hours, at the end of which Hawkins stalked out in a rage, voicing an ultimatum. Martha sat drawn and silent; the executives were also speechless, out of sheer embarrassment. Walter Prude, who now worked for Hurok, was there and called Martha later on the phone. He tried to use gentleness and reason. He explained that he had to sell the troupe and that Hawkins's name did not mean a damn.

"I will decide whose name is to be in what size type," she snapped. "I will not discuss Erick." And she hung up.

Hurok, one of the two biggest management companies in the Western hemisphere, was not pleased. The only other American dancer Hurok had ever handled was also a handful, Isadora Duncan. Evidently Americans were difficult.

Erick's press, in spite of all Martha's efforts, remained cold.

Martha still rehearsed, doggedly, frenetically, tirelessly, month in, month out, as the year turned, and the next; and the next. Her real joy was still, as before, in the work. She still had ideas enough, intent enough, fervor enough. She had the strength to keep going without the slightest slackening; she still suggested, explained, exhorted, commanded. And she still hit. But now she combatted men.

Erick, of course, was the chief antagonist. But there were others. Some of the boys were abashed by her tantrums and cowed like the girls. Some bridled and fought back—not hitting, however. I never heard of a man striking her. But there were often ringing exchanges, with hot retorts. Once or twice a boy stalked out in a rage, and then she would patter barefooted after him, catching him by the sleeve at the elevator, and in a little-girl voice softly falter, "It's because I care, because I love you so much." Irresistible confession! It was flirtation in the grand manner.

She was always forgiven. "Martha is spoiled rotten," Louis Horst said to me once. "She has a temper tantrum when she doesn't get what she wants!" And she was now behaving to the public and to critics with great arrogance in regard to Erick Hawkins—with disastrous results. Once she hit Craig Barton hard in the face—the beloved, the gentle, the well-trusted Craig. He went white to the lips and stomped out of the studio, coming back, however, after some time, to resume business discussions. Once, Lee Leatherman recounts, he told Martha something that enraged her, and then felt her on his back as he turned to leave. He put out his arms suddenly to keep her hands from his eyes, loosening her hold and dislodging her. She referred to this episode thereafter as "the time Lee struck me to the ground."

Stuart Hodes had been a fighter pilot who went to study with Martha on the GI Bill of Rights. Prior to the war, Hodes had led a rather carefree, casual existence in Brooklyn—"innocent," he says, "of all aesthetics." And he had no idea of how distinguished Martha was or why she was a figure to venerate. And so when she lost her temper he quite spontaneously lost his. Because he was a man, forthright and extremely vigorous, Martha liked it. She liked the clashing of tempers. She apologized. He, too, rather enjoyed the spats, and he for one admired and trusted Erick. As the other pounding board, he sympathized with him.

It was different when she made her assault at the moment of stage entry. John Butler recounts that once as they stood together in the wings waiting to begin a performance, she spoke sharply to him: "Tonight I want you to hate me." This was in *Appalachian Spring,* and he was playing the denouncing minister. She hit him hard, hard enough to hurt. Of course he bridled.

"But, you know," he said, "I understood that role for the first time. I did hate her, and I was marvelous that night."

At other times Martha said to Butler in mid-performance, right in the process of achieving an effect, "John, shut your mouth." He shut his mouth like a trap, and he was affronted, as any performer would be, but it gave an edge to the performance and that is what she wanted; she cared not a rap for his feelings.

This brings up a very interesting point: whether it is necessary or desirable to engage the personal emotions of a performing artist. My uncle, Cecil B. DeMille, often harassed his actors, even insulting them publicly to the point of tears and collapse, until it was a marvel they didn't walk off his set. Cecil always said that no lady could be an actress, because she had learned too much control. In passing I must remark that he very rarely obtained anything like good acting by his violent methods. Martha, on the other hand, was able to turn savagery into temperament and achieve something akin to inspiration. But it is a risky technique to employ. Great actors have their own methods of working toward the hot core of energy, and those methods very rarely involve personal rancor.

The story was quite different with the girls. Any of them Martha insulted or slapped had to forgive and endure if the relationship was to continue. Most girls were intimidated by Martha, and those who did not become afraid suffered wounds. A girl who flared up at Martha did so only once; it was final. They were constrained to stay with her by several considerations, including poverty and lack of outside opportunity. It was always easier for the boys to get jobs, as good male dancers were scarce.

Erick's exacerbating presence did not make any of these conflicts easier. Martha was often right, and her suggestions and orders could be inspirational. But Erick was often just stubborn and arrogant, and very rough.

Nina Fonaroff, Martha's pupil and a member of the company, and Louis Horst's new young lover, happened to be Erick's oldest friend in the Group. Nina was there when he was in spate. She resented him as dangerous in rehearsal, she has said, and occasionally even hurtful to Martha, dropping her, letting her hit her head on the floor, and saying by way of explanation, "She wasn't where she was supposed to be." He would not yield a foot of space; he would not move. Once, in Washington, D.C., when rehearsing *Appalachian Spring,* Nina was standing on her hands with her feet up against the fence. Erick pranced with his full weight on her fingers.

"They shouldn't have been there," he snapped at her as she nursed a hand that was all but broken.

In *Punch and the Judy* Nina played a child asleep on a bench. Erick was directed to throw her into the wings and go to sleep himself in her place. He always threw her so hard that she asked two people to wait, ready to catch her. His lack of status in the classes and in the actual structure of the company was compensated for by brute temper.

Erick may have been uneasy and self-conscious in his relationships, but he also understood very well the power he had—Martha was in love with him. He was ambitious, like a willful animal, setting his teeth and plunging ahead. He bruised many people, and gave himself an awful mauling in the process as well, but he felt he couldn't afford to care. He put the company's bad feelings down to jealousy, and a good part of it undoubtedly was. It was nonetheless real, for this reason. If he could not imitate Martha's genius, he would imitate her human weaknesses, her arrogance, and he never ceased to try. And always, always he tried desperately to follow her into her creative world.

Her world? A world of glass where every step was pain and danger was the medium. It was cold there, with no indulgence and no pretense, and it was merciless. What was cozening to most people disqualified its denizens. Human friendship was not an element. This was the world of ideas. Poor Erick thought he could join, but, failing the key which is the vision, he was forever barred. With the vision all things were possible; not otherwise.

It would be forty more years—in the eighties—before Erick Hawkins would begin to receive the recognition and audience response he sought. To watch the final fruition of such an extremely difficult dedication is an extraordinary phenomenon. Hawkins is now called one of the true American originals and, by those who respond to his work, a master. This must crown his life, but what an austere and thorny trail he trod for so many, many years before he was finally hailed! I believe he suffered for a long time.

||||

The person who was still there, beside him, still teaching, was Louis. How could Louis talk to Martha about mutual work with Erick present? "Louis did," said Pearl, "when he had certain quick reactions. Of course, when it involved Martha personally he would not speak until Erick had gone. Louis would always say what was diplomatic to say when everybody was around and the full truth only when alone." And Martha still relied on him. The work they shared still brought them happiness and love. And although she was made somewhat self-conscious, even timid, by him, and although she used to send Ethel Butler to fetch him, to beg him to come, in collaboration they were one again.

||||

Joseph Campbell, deep in theology and its modern interpretations, worked with Martha on Jung's theories and discoveries. Campbell explains:

It wasn't in *Deaths and Entrances* that her psychological concepts matured, but in her Greek pieces. The collective unconscious of Jung is the dynamic of the human body, the energies of the memory. Whereas Freud's subconscious is the consequence of individual traumatic experience, Jung's collective unconscious is racial and generic; therefore Freud's subconscious is biographical and Jung's unconscious is biological. In Freudian analysis one tries to find out what happened in an individual life; Jung opens the structure of the psyche to race memory, the common treasure which we all inherit. For Jung [and for Campbell] this is the basis of art; it is our common magic. . . . The more you know of myth and psychology the more you foresee. Myth comes from below the level of consciousness.

Martha spoke to Campbell about "the moment of recognition when we first talked about this." She perceived clearly that one must open up to instinct, that one must return to intuition. Scientists claim that at the bottom of every great discovery there is a lucky guess, even in medicine. In many a baffling case one doctor will advise, "Try this. It makes no sense, but try it," and he saves the patient's life. The experts then spend the next ten years figuring out why.

Campbell thought this to be the real gift of Germany, this respect for the dynamic of the body. This is the gift of the Middle Ages, of Parsifal, of Wagner's "Ring," of Grimm's Fairy Tales, this fusing of mythology, psychology, and art. "And," said Campbell, "the more you know of myth or of psychology, the more you perceive. I have told many creative artists about my beliefs very often. They are intrigued, but very few can translate this theoretical material into art. Martha truly is the only one who can transform the material into a masterpiece with her perception. Here psychological linkings are worked through her own experiences to emerge fresh and living. She never, never quotes undigested ideas that she has heard in someone else's voice."

The new ideas, the new jargon of psychotherapy, was like wine to most creative imaginations, intoxicating and enticing artists to do all sorts of extravagances. But very few got beyond the jargon. Like the others, Martha was intrigued, but she was never misled. Of course, she did not know as much as any working analyst, but her instincts were surer and more profound. I think she went beyond the psychologists in creative perception. In a strange way she was their leader.

Martha was never psychoanalyzed. She merely talked conversationally to Mrs. Frances Wickes, the lay analyst and writer who had been Jung's mistress and who was a devout apostle of the master. Wickes was the author of *The Inner World of Childhood* (1927), *The Inner World of Man* (1938), *Receive the Gale* (1946), and *The Inner World of Choice* (1963), among others. Here was a personality of boundless richness and replenishment.

In a letter to Wickes, Martha expressed her admiration of Jung, and alluded to her gratitude to Erick for having made possible her relationship with Frances.

Frances Wickes refused to analyze Martha: "She told me she didn't wish to analyze me, that an analysis would destroy my mystery and power." It is unlikely that Mrs. Wickes or any trained analyst ever said anything like that to a patient. More probably this was Martha's excuse for not submitting to the discipline and risk of opening up her psyche to real probing. She flinched. Erick, however, did not flinch. Erick was a student and a scholar. He was dogged and he was brave. Martha sent him to Mrs. Wickes and he worked seriously with her. He went back to the source, to the Greek myths, which since his student days had been his particular province. It was Erick's joy and privilege to teach Martha.

Cave of the Heart (1946), to music by Samuel Barber, was based on the myth of Medea. This was Graham's second experiment in Greek mythology (the first having been the 1933 *Tragic Patterns*) and it was a deep exploration of Jungian psychology. It was horrifying and revealing, a study of jealousy in which the central figure literally eats her own vitals and, at the end, when she has killed off her rival in an extremely painful manner, finds herself entrapped in an armor of flamelike spikes from which she cannot escape but must live consumed.

This is what it meant to me, but to one of its creators, Isamu Noguchi, the intent was quite different. In a 1986 interview for *Ballet Review* Noguchi said:

We start with the snake. The snake is water. It is the passage from which the gods evolve. One finds it, according to my friend, Bucky Fuller, in all water-born cultures. . . . The water spiral is the perfect example. Martha didn't ask me to make a snake pad from which Medea would emerge. These are objects that I make that derive from a depiction of an emotional state. . . . One finds the worship of the snake from the American Indian all the way to the Greeks. So I used the snake. In *Cave of the Heart,* Medea dances with a red cloth in her mouth. She is dancing with the snake in her mouth. Then she spews it out of her mouth like blood.

About the terminal prop, the final cage, the spiked aureole, he said:

I thought of it as the sun because Medea was the daughter of the sun. She returned to her origins. . . . It has to do with fire and water. The dragon is the storm. It is the rain. It is the elements. It goes back to the river, to birth. . . . The volcanic pad that Medea mounts at the end of the dance wearing her flaming nimbus dress is where she disappears. She disappears behind it, and when the lights come up it looks as if she's sinking beyond the horizon like a sunset. The volcanic pad is the volcano, the house, birth. It's the way you go back to life. The five stones leading to the volcano are islands in Greece. They represent the place of passage.

And I thought Medea had done something childish, like eating her own spleen, and in the end it had been like an Elizabethan villain "catched in her own device." But I was too simplistic!

Again, perhaps Martha meant something altogether different from any of this. Maybe Martha fooled Noguchi, fooled all of us. This I know: she was concerned with jealousy and its attendant destructions.

Jason was played by Erick, and the young, second wife, a small, childlike, sexless creature, was superbly danced by the Japanese girl Yuriko. (Martha was the first to incorporate Japanese and other Orientals into her group—and Blacks, long before others did. Two of her leading female soloists were to be Blacks: Mary Hinkson and Matt Turney.)

For *Cave of the Heart* Martha perfected quickly many passages of extraordinary choreography. Mark Ryder thought this dance was an expression of a consuming jealousy of Erick's new love, a passing but anguishing fancy. Whether or not it was, *Cave* was a revelation of terrible distress and a portrait of unalleviated jealous hatred.

"Show me how low a person will go," Martha often said. "Let me see the depths to which she is capable: the heights will take care of themselves." Martha had a deep instinctual need to root out the dark side of any nature. She was cynical and sophisticated and bitterly wise. She gave full value to evil.

And this was obviously a dark time for Martha.

Errand into the Maze (1947), to music of Gian-Carlo Menotti, was her third ballet based on Greek myth, this time the story of Ariadne and Theseus. At the center is the Minotaur, the mythical monster, half man, half bull, who lived in the depth of a labyrinthine cave and destroyed all those who ventured into his lair. Ariadne unwound a ball of string as she descended into the cave, in order to be able to retrace her path to the surface world. Her confrontation with the beast, the dark unknown of the subconscious, is mortal. As Mark Ryder has said, "One must be raped by one's subconscious in order to produce living ideas." This coupling, as in many of Graham's sexual encounters, had nothing to do with love. It was a penetration and a using, fierce and terrible, for survival purposes alone.

Forty years after *Errand into the Maze* had first been performed, Anna Kisselgoff wrote, "It is this chord of recognition of universal desires and repressions that Miss Graham hits with unsurpassed truth in her work and brings to the surface." The Minotaur, the creature of fear, was designated by a half mask and a fixed stance of arms, hooked over a shoulder yoke and bound thereto, a device which rendered him inhuman, fearsome, and, at the same time, quite helpless. It is no accident that this is the manner in which slaves were traditionally trussed to be transported distances. The decor, by Noguchi, consisted of a white rope, marking Ariadne's path, and a door frame like whitened bones, symbolizing both the entrance to the nether regions and the emergent outlet to life and freedom. Erick was the original bullman and he was superb—a brute, pathetic, tragic, and terrible; harnessed, floundering about, and destroying all he touched. He was replaced by Mark Ryder.

Graham's next ballet, *Night Journey* (1947) to music by William Schuman, was based on the story of Oedipus and Jocasta. It is a ballet dealing with unrelieved misery, and was performed on props and contrivances of the most uncomfortable nature that Noguchi could assemble. Martha wanted a bed. Noguchi did not want to give her a bed. He provided instead the abstract figures of a man and a woman lying facing each other; Jocasta and Oedipus rolling on top of this couple presented the appearance of stacked cadavers in a concentration camp. It was to most eyes an uninviting marriage couch. The ballet, reflecting Graham during this period, is comprised of mighty and desperate ideas, frantic cries for identification. At this moment Martha was at the apex of her creative powers, and just then her lover had begun to attempt to identify himself, to claim parity with her in her own company, on her own stage. In short, to threaten her very essence. About Hawkins in his 1947 ballet *Stephen Acrobat,* Walter Terry had been less than kind:

Stephen Acrobat, a new dance work with choreography by Erick Hawkins, last evening was given the first of what one hopes will be but few performances. . . . [Hawkins] exploits little and devises nothing at all. As a long-term member of the Graham company, one would suppose that he could create something sensible even if he were not essentially a choreographer, but *Stephen Acrobat* is devoid of sense, of appreciable pattern.

He was not her equal, certainly he was not even comparable, yet she loved him. She was in peril of yielding. She was in grave peril of not yielding. The statements are there in her dance, Martha's anguished voice for all of us to recognize, the statements of a woman who was also a very great artist and who found herself threatened with corruption.

Her next work was *Diversion of Angels,* to music of Norman Dello Joio, and it was designed to take as long to perform as it took for the sun to come up over the desert. The original set Noguchi planned represented the sand and the rocks of the western American desert. The rocks were designed to slide upstage toward the back wall and then, at the end of the ballet, as the dancers leaped across the space, to lift upward. This was supposed to create the illusion that the point of view had tilted—that the back wall was now the ground over which the dancers were flying. The effect was not wholly successful, however, and ultimately Noguchi gave the set to Balanchine, who later used it with great success in his *Orpheus.*

The Bennington Dance Festival, which had shut down during the war, had re-established itself during the summer of 1948 with a festival at New London, Connecticut. There, *Diversion of Angels* received its premiere.

Diversion was an antidote to what Martha had been doing, a work of pure beauty and joy. This is a lyric ballet about the loveliness of youth, its pleasure and playfulness, the quick joy and quick sadness of being in love for the first time. First called *Wilderness Stair,* it was a poem of sensuous delight, without plot or story. Here was all bright beauty, unshadowed by doubt, guilt, hidden evil, or any of the usual Graham *arrière-pensées;* here, new creatures took over at the beginning of the world, and the stage was illuminated by promise. This work breathes serene peace; past anguish is not remembered.

The choreographic design was matchless. José Limón, sitting beside me, said, "Simply and plainly the work of a master choreographer."

There was a crucial incident at Connecticut College during the mounting of this work. Erick and Louis Horst quarreled onstage in front of the company. Erick made cruel and humiliating remarks, and Martha sided with him. Nina Fonaroff rushed up from New York and convinced Louis that he must finally break away from Martha and get out. Martha permitted him to go. Their long-lasting tie was finally ruptured.

When their Connecticut performances were over, Martha and Erick proceeded west to Santa Fe, Martha's potent land. There they were married.

All their friends were taken by surprise. Martha later remarked to Martha Hill that she "had to post her bond with society," by which she meant, Hill gathered, that she wished "to set her record straight." But why? She never had before. Martha frequently used elliptical and mysterious sentences which seemed cryptic on examination but which at the moment were quite satisfactory to her listener, and, I daresay, to herself. Did she mean that she wished to be a properly wedded woman? Did she mean that she wished public respect for her conduct? Did she mean that she wished to declare herself absolutely as Erick's love and commit her life to him? Nobody ever questioned her arcane remarks, and no one can say exactly why she finally married him. Pearl Lang thinks it was the Catholic in her, "because even though she's a Protestant, Martha is really Catholic."

Of Louis Horst's reaction we have no knowledge. Those who were close to Louis thought that the shock and the grief over this event was the most profound of his life.

Mrs. Morgenthau gave the couple a small and very pleasant party upon their return to New York in the fall of 1948. All Martha's friends wished her well. But her friends also knew the present jealousies and actions, the temperamental, differing, divergent imaginations. These two natures did not complement each other; rather, they canceled each other out. Friends watched and held their breath. The bride and bridegroom settled in near her studio, where they had in fact been living together secretly for years.

Martha and Erick were intensely in love. Martha confided to Bertram Ross, who had just begun studying with her, that her marriage was a going affair, and that unlike many other marriages which were in name only, hers was hot and passionate. But as the months passed, it became apparent to all in the company that a life-and-death struggle was being acted out before their eyes.

On tour in San Francisco, Martha gathered the company together before a performance and tongue-lashed all of them, including Erick, who was standing beside her. "You must give everything to your work," she said. *"Everything.* It must be all you care about. You must give all, even if it means losing your husband." And with that she stalked offstage. On the long bus trips between performances, she and Erick sat separately, barely speaking, and, what is more, they frequently had separate rooms. The signs of trouble were augmenting, and those who cared suffered deep anxiety.

"Our marriage is a living thing, a give and take, what a marriage should be," she had said. "But it is so difficult to make it work."

Martha and Erick's marriage had begun to shred almost immediately, tragically; soon it was held together only by a professional arrangement, and that too was festering. There were episodes of dreadful cruelty and suffering. Erick was being balked by Martha in his major ambition—not willingly, but because he simply could not keep up with her. That he aspired to was a matter of his conceit and his bad sense of proportion. Erick was torn with jealousy, and Martha with pity and frustration. She could not curb and maim her own gifts to serve him, as Miss Ruth had done with Ted. But neither could she eliminate his own ambition. And so he began to retaliate in the most primitive and brutal manner: he flirted outrageously with younger women, flaunting his preferences before her. And as any bereft woman must, Martha grieved from wounded vanity and loneliness.

And she tried to serve him with all her strength and talent.

In 1945 Erick composed his first solo for himself, *John Brown*. Despite the fact that Martha gave the dance a superb mounting, it was not a success.

In 1950 she composed for him a solo based on Lear, to music by Vincent Persichetti, which she called *Eye of Anguish*. She attempted something of extreme subtlety, and she went to infinite trouble, revising it four times.

Some have thought that Erick himself was responsible for part of this choreography, the way Merce Cunningham had been for some of his, and other soloists were beginning to be for their own solos in Graham's ballets. But Pearl Lang insists that the company would not have collaborated on any of Erick's choreography. Martha created this work herself, flawed as it was, and she labored over it.

Louis thought the choreography was plainly no good. *The Angst of Eyewash*, he called it.

Martha read prodigiously, and she took fire. Her notebooks are choked with quotations from Shakespeare, Milton, and Coleridge, and the ideas they suggest:

> "the mad Lear is in one sense the
> man of letters: his imagination is
> wholly alert, & whatever the disorders
> present, he has the searching &
> synthesizing insight of a poet.

He may not seem quite safe.
But the good poet never is.
And the entirely safe man is
never the good poet."

Suffering in tragedy not
an end—but a product
& a means—
          thru it comes wisdom
          & if not redemption,
          a renewed grasp
          upon the laws of
          redemption.

Coleridge
     "The howlings of convulsed
     nature would seem converted
     into the voices of conscious
     humanity."
     anodyne for pain caused
     by conduct of
     daughters

At fifty-six, Martha seemed obsessed by Lear's madness—by the study of madness, the study of age. And also by the contemplation of death—by the seemingly mad characters, such as the fool, who lives in the realm of the imagination, and symbolism, as contrasted with Lear, who was truly unhinged. Also by the relation between the physical storms and wretched events, and inner anguish. Martha thought deep and hard and wrestled with these problems, and they are mighty ones.

But to what end? The ballet was not good.

It never came together. It was a success neither by Martha's own standards nor, indeed, by the public's standards. *Eye of Anguish* contained moments of enormous invention—for instance, the introduction of the king sitting in a tube of knitted material (very like *Lamentation*), here containing not only the body of an old man but those of his two daughters, quarreling and fighting inside the containing shell for the possession of the father, crawling over each other like maggots over a scrap of meat which is working with decay.

Since the 1950s, audiences have grown in understanding. If this ballet were to be revived now, it might be a success. More probably, the protagonist would be clearer if played by someone other than Erick.

The opening of *Eye of Anguish* at the Forty-sixth Street Theater, New York, on January 22 was patently not a success. It was, in fact, a dreadful fiasco, and Erick's disappointment was accordingly acute. He truly thought it was going to bring him recognition and glory at last. After the premiere he walked the streets all night. By morning Martha was almost out of her mind with worry. The next afternoon when she went to the theater to rehearse *Deaths and Entrances*, the Brontë ballet—and it was an orchestra rehearsal in full costume—she failed to make her appearance on cue, and when she was sought in the dressing room she was found weeping inconsolably. Jean Rosenthal went to Pearl Lang, who was onstage in costume, and said, "Go to her. Pull her together. This is *The Perils of Pauline*. I can't do a thing with her. I don't know whether or not she'll come on the stage tonight."

Pearl went to Martha's dressing room. "Martha," she said, "he's not worth one of your tears. You are the greater artist. You are carrying our flag." Martha raised her ruined face and with streaming eyes said softly, "But I love him."

Lear got a universally bad press, and Erick continued to earn unfriendly and censorious reference. Except, miracle of miracles, from Louis Horst in *Dance Observer*. Louis did not praise, but he maintained scrupulous fairness, and he gave Erick space equal to that given anyone else.

Martha felt very strongly that she had made a grave mistake in allowing Erick to flounder through his own choreography unaided. She had learned to leave the girls alone. They could muddle through in good order; in some instances they could turn out crackerjack work that fitted in with hers superbly. But Erick really didn't know how. She had refused to recognize this fact and she had left him absolutely alone, treating him as an equal, or at least as an experienced disciple, which he plainly was not. She felt, in a way, that she had abandoned him.

||||||

Mrs. Isaacs and Mrs. Morgenthau had helped Martha financially as best they could, Mrs. Isaacs in particular. And Katharine Cornell had made lavish and frequent gifts. It was a substantial endowment she gave, but it could not possibly keep pace with mounting costs, now including union demands.

Miraculously, during the war, Bethsabee de Rothschild had come to work Martha's salvation. Bethsabee was a member of the European banking family which for two hundred and fifty years had been instrumental in raising up (and demolishing) royal dynasties by guaranteeing and lending money to governments, or, contrariwise, by withholding and diverting crucial funds. They were also philanthropic and always abidingly staunch religionists. Bethsabee's great-uncle, Baron Edmond de Rothschild, although an anti-Zionist, had financed a Jewish colonization of Palestine as early as 1880, and he spent the next fifty years helping to build up an agricultural and industrial base for the Israel-to-be. Bethsabee's cousin, the present Baron Edmund de Rothschild, runs the empire his grandfather had built. Her elder brother, named Guy, who inherited the French banking house, his father's title, and his business position, is also president of the United Jewish Appeal in France. Her elder sister, Jacqueline, was married to Gregor Piatigorsky, the world-famous cellist. Jacqueline was herself a chess master, a tennis champion, and a sculptress. Bethsabee's English cousins are the leading fundraisers for Israel in Britain.

Bethsabee was born in England and raised as a French national in France. She studied biology in Paris at the Sorbonne and in New York City at Columbia University, to which she fled at the fall of France. She returned to London during the war and enlisted under Charles de Gaulle in the Free French army, for which she carried out survival missions, reputedly of considerable danger.

Established in nearly every country, the Rothschild family was sadly affected by the war, and various members of the family perished— among others, the wife of Philippe de Rothschild, who was tortured to death by the Nazis despite her Catholicism.

Bethsabee was briefly married to Donald Bloomingdale, of the New York department-store family. To him she bore a child who died, which led her not to futile grieving but to scientific research into the causes of the tragedy. The baby's death was followed agonizingly by divorce and the death from a drug overdose of her husband. These bitter griefs Bethsabee was able to transmute into work and charity. The foundation she was later to found in Israel was for "the arts and sciences." She gave equally to both fields, concerning herself with the scientific projects of the country and actively supporting them, even as she actively supported two dance companies in Tel Aviv, the Batsheva and the Bat-Dor, and one theater.

Yet strangely enough, Bethsabee de Rothschild, in spite of her background, in spite of the superb environment with which her mother had surrounded her, and although she had grown up with supreme masterpieces on the walls of her house, really didn't care about fine art; she wasn't especially drawn to art or theater in general. She supported it, but what she really knew, and what she was really expert in, was science. It is thought that if she had given her time and attention undividedly to medicine and experiments in medical research, she would have made a world name for herself. In any case, the one artistic enterprise in which she was truly interested was the Graham dance theater. She was wholeheartedly in love with it. (Later she sponsored many different kinds of art enterprises in Israel.)

During the war, the Graham company had become aware of Bethsabee de Rothschild. She took technique classes in Graham's Fifth Avenue school. She was not very good, but that made no difference. She went on tour with them, observing and helping as best she could in trivial ways. She was not a member of the company and held no formal position, but she began to be present at all performances and on the trains. An extremely shy woman, retiring, sweet, she was obviously besotted with Martha's work, ideas, and purposes.

It was in Chicago that the company first really noticed her. She had, it seemed, in some unexplained way joined the show. The small, compact Bethsabee, with her engaging lisp, which amounted to a delightful speech impediment, and her ineradicable French "r," her slightly protuberant eyes, became Martha's great patron, as Ludwig of Bavaria had been Wagner's. She laid her faith, and at least a large part of her fortune, at Martha's feet.

She gave Martha presents, and to everyone's surprise, Martha, who had been so generous in giving but so reluctant in accepting, agreed to take them.

Bethsabee began picking up the very real deficits at the end of each Graham season, and quietly paying Martha's outstanding current debts. She became a monetary bulwark, as Katharine Cornell and Edith Isaacs had never been able to be. The Rothschild fortune was vast, in the Arabian Nights tradition, and although recently threatened by anti-Semitism, it had survived, thanks to the astonishing acumen of its caretakers.

Under Bethsabee's patronage, Martha began to look like a star. Martha had always loved fine things. She took real female delight in beautiful materials and good workmanship and expensive cut. No doubt she would always have preferred patronizing Bergdorf Goodman for any trifle or dress, but she had had to be content with Klein's on Union Square. Now Bethsabee allowed her at last to express a taste that had been innate, if long dormant. On Saturdays the two women went off shopping, did girl stuff, and Bethsabee saw that Martha had, for the first time, fine clothes, dresses from Bergdorf's or Saks, hats from John-Frederics, and blouses from Léron. And later, necklaces from Cartier.

Louis had always been by preference unpretentious and folksy, avoiding social contacts and despising the paraphernalia and perquisites of concert giving, avoiding the parties after the show, the committees that preceded celebrations, overtly and verbally denouncing them in a kind of inverse snobbery. But Martha began to enjoy all this as her right. She liked going around in limousines and meeting social and civic leaders. She liked being pointed out and having these small luxuries come her way.

From this time on Martha had regular New York seasons, commissioned scores, sets (usually by Noguchi), and costumes. And she began to pay her dancers for performing.

She liked all this, and she also liked mysteries, and in 1949 she was legitimately able to indulge her folly to the full. Craig Barton arranged for her to become "Miss Hush" for the March of Dimes. "Miss Hush" broadcast regularly from an unknown location, and a prize was awarded to whoever recognized the voice. This was fun for Martha, and netted her a nice amount of publicity when her identity was finally disclosed. The broadcasts were organized and aired from her own house.

|||||

In 1950, five years after the war's end, Bethsabee thought that Martha should be shown off in Bethsabee's hometown, Paris. ANTA (the American National Theater and Academy) had been sending Americans abroad, but not Martha, because of her large company and her demanding stage requirements. Bethsabee said that she would furnish everything needed and that after Paris they would broach the stronghold of ballet, London. Some of Martha's faithful patrons may have contributed as well, but Bethsabee undertook to pay the bulk of the expenses. As projected, they amounted to $80,000, unprecedented expenses in the dance world at that time.

In the spring of 1950 Martha reviewed her costumes and found them sadly inadequate for a Paris showing. She tore every one of them apart, the company's entire wardrobe, and set all the girls to work, recutting, resewing, refitting. Whenever they weren't on the floor exercising, they were on the floor with dresses spread over their knees, stitching and pinning. There never was any "will you?" It was taken for granted by Martha that everybody did everything he or she could do for the common purpose. They sewed right through the spring.

Martha's going to Europe for the first time with her troupe meant a great deal to the entire dance community of New York. I, for one, felt it was of such enormous importance that the United States be represented in its most vigorous and splendid aspect that I raised a small purse for her, simply by telephoning all the people I knew in the theater profession whom I thought were interested. Although the amount was small, it was cash, and at that point there was no such thing as tax exemption, because Martha was not incorporated as a nonprofit institution. My sister, Margaret, who worked in the garment industry as a leading executive, persuaded one of the fine designers she knew, Vera Maxwell, to give Martha outfits, and Sally Victor to make her hats. Others contributed costly accessories and shoes so that Martha could go accoutered like a royal bride. We felt very sincerely that Martha was carrying our banner and we wished her to walk proud.

The problem seemed to be the choice of the program for the opening nights in Paris and London. Erick began to show muscle.

As a married couple, Martha and Erick now went out together, but not equally. Martha was the star—no question about that. Erick, in the time-honored pattern, backed up on his wounded vanity and hurt male instincts, dug in his heels, and gave most terrible battle. He determined that when they went to Europe he would have his due. He would, he swore, be equal.

Craig Barton, now Martha's secretary, helped in all matters of personal representation, even though he had never managed a box office or a theater. But Gert Macy undertook to teach him how. These are technical jobs and require considerable skill, but Craig was able and Gert was a veteran and willing to help him. Martha hoped Craig would manage the company for the European trip in June 1950, but she wanted the O.K. of her sponsors, and she sent Barton to Kansas City, where Katharine Cornell was playing on a long cross-country tour. There Cornell and Gert Macy interviewed Craig exhaustively, with the idea of putting the entire Parisian enterprise into his care. He passed the test with honors. His Dallas friend Leroy Leatherman would accompany him, and although Cornell thought it a superfluous expense, Martha and Bethsabee won the argument, and Lee went along.

In May, Craig went to Paris to interview the European manager, Anatole Heller, and survey the preparations. There he made the acquaintance of Bethsabee's mother, the Baroness de Rothschild, and charmed her completely. He charmed and dazzled all women with his southern gallantry and humor. He then continued on to London.

In May 1950 I was also in London, readying *Carousel* at the Drury Lane Theatre. Craig took me to lunch in the adjacent Covent Garden market. He asked not one question about *Carousel* (which was a big enough opening). Rather, we spent our entire time together talking about Martha's plans.

I said enthusiastically to him, "I have considered what program she must do on her opening night."

And he replied cooly and firmly, "The opening night concert has already been determined." Then Craig gave me the order of the evening. Sure enough, *Eye of Anguish* was in the middle of it, with Erick starring. I was appalled.

"No, no, no! She is inviting failure," I all but shouted. "A betrayal of all she has stood for, of all she has lived and fought for, of the girls and Louis and what they sacrificed for!" I felt frantic. "She is our leader and now she is risking the lot for a love affair, just like any besotted old man for a chorus girl. It's heartbreaking of her. She mustn't do it. Stop her." I banged my fist on the table. "I will tell the press of London not to come to the opening night but to come the second night, and they will listen to me because I have a name here." Craig went white.

"You will do nothing of the sort. You will help Martha in every way you can and in the way she wants, exactly in the way she wants. You will be her friend. You will be a good girl." He was beside himself. "You will do as we say."

Meanwhile, Martha was having stormy sessions in New York. Her body had begun to fail.

Martha was fifty-six and arthritic, her wonderful instrument—her trained animal body, quick to every bidding, supple, elastic, strong, resiliant—now faulty, now untrue. She lashed at the technique. She drove her knees, her thighs, her back. She flogged herself. To no use. The harder she pushed, the harder she strained, the weaker she got. The pain was awful. Martha paid that no mind, but there were things she found she could no longer do. She was indeed growing old. Every athlete faces this moment, but Martha was supposed to be a goddess.

At this point Erick again began to tease and torture, praising the younger girls, the pretty ones, the bouncy ones, the ones who never tired, holding them up to Martha's attention and to his own, and extolling their beauty.

The plain fact is that Martha was scared. She was scared of the French trip, of the new exposures which would attract worldwide press coverage, of the opportunity and the challenge and the mortal hazards. She was going to be touted as America's best and she was fearful that she would appear to be a has-been, a plain, old-fashioned disappointment, to the unpredictable French and the unprepared Londoners.

A week before the departure for France, Gert Macy arrived at Martha's Fifth Avenue studio. The studio was on the second floor, and Gert was dismayed to hear the sound of screaming all the way down in the lobby, where people were gathering for the movie theater. She raced up the stairs and down the hall; the strident noises were becoming more intense as she approached the studio doors. She burst into the room to find Martha and Erick, alone and embattled, shouting at each other.

Martha was hitting, kicking, biting, and screaming, mouthing invectives of the vilest and most ferocious nature. Erick had her by the arms, pinned against the wall, trying to hold her quiet and keep her from clawing him. Somehow in the scuffle she was thrown to the ground. (Gert always said she thought any damage was psychological, not muscular, that Martha had not really sustained any bodily injury at all, but that she wished to be hurt by Erick.) In any case, when Gert separated them Martha was limping badly. She may have been bruised on the knee, but she was not screaming with pain so much as with fury. Somehow Gert got her into another room and then sent for a doctor. Injured or not, Martha claimed she could hardly walk, having strained all of the tendons in the knee and leg. She was on crutches for days afterward, barely able to move.

Her company continued to rehearse, with grim apprehension. No one spoke to Erick about what had occurred. No doubt he felt he had behaved with every justification, and he very well may have.

They enplaned in an unhappy mood. Martha used a cane. A shocked Bethsabee met them at the Paris airport and took them in her limousine to the Rothschild mansion on the rue du Faubourg St. Honoré, where her mother, the baroness, awaited them. Martha entered the great portals of the courtyard and was enclosed in the luxury of this matchless fortune and two hundred years of French elegance.

The desperate preparations continued. Now Lee Leatherman proved his usefulness, becoming Martha's lackey, manservant, and squire, running and fetching, finding what had been forgotten, doing all possible errands to make life easier for her. She had need of these comforts because the demands of her profession, and her personal exigencies, were merciless.

All the while she practiced without remission, limping through rehearsals, marking the knee walks and knee swoops, but still gripping with the hurt muscle. The stage was raked,* and this caused her extra pain.

Bethsabee took care of the publicity, which was in the grand manner. She gave a tremendous champagne party attended by the press and *tout-Paris* at the Plaza-Athénée Hotel, one of the most elaborate showplaces in the city. The dance writer Pierre Tugal reported that the gala "outranked such affairs of many a season. Martha won all with her modest presence and disarming wit." Privately she was shaking with nerves.

The date approached: the postponeless date, beyond which one could not think, a dividing bulwark, like a royal wedding, a coronation, an execution. Then the date was upon them, and the night had come.

The intellectuals, the theater and dance world, and notables from all over the Continent gathered. The Baroness de Rothschild and Bethsabee, the Countess de Noailles, Boris Kochno (the last close friend of Diaghilev), the couturier Jacques Fath, the composers Poulenc, Sauguet, Auric. The house was filled to the last seat. Bethsabee and the baroness, who was a very powerful woman, had seen to that; and Martha's reputation was clearly and simply the best the United States had to offer.

She had not been to Europe since her early Denishawn days. Paris waited. Europe waited. The theater and the overflowing audience waited. And still they could not begin. The curtain was held. Mrs. Roosevelt, the guest of honor, was late!

Erick stormed, "Don't hold the curtain for that woman—for any woman!" Mrs. Roosevelt was regarded in Europe as a kind of saint, and Craig would not dream of beginning without our First Lady in her seat. Finally the program did start, with *Errand into the Maze*, based on the

---

*In the eighteenth and early nineteenth centuries, the pit—what we call the orchestra—was built with no rise at the rear, and consequently patrons in the rear seats had only a poor and partial view of the proceedings. To remedy this, the stages themselves were tilted up on a slant from the footlights to the backdrop. This is known as a "rake." It causes great difficulties for dancers trained on a flat surface or unaccustomed to dancing on a tilted plane. Pirouettes or turns are particularly troublesome to execute, as the basic axis of the body has to be adjusted accordingly. It is, of course, equally difficult for someone trained to use raked stages to get used to dancing on flat ones.

story of Ariadne and the Minotaur, danced by Graham and Hawkins: that austere and terrifying struggle depicting a woman battling the fear of sex. And in Paris!

The Parisian theater audience is a strange one. They like what is outré; what is special, exotic, or novel; or, more often, what is shocking. What is simply sound dramatically or stringently perfect, or what is essentially intellectual, they find difficult to accept, and they tend to reject these qualities in the performing arts. Their reputation for having been the most advanced audience in the dance world was self-promulgated and had no basis in fact. Bear in mind that their ballet was the most corrupt and reactionary in Europe, and that they had themselves at this time no modern dance of any sort whatever, and did not understand what little they had seen. They like what is chic, and they have become the great central clearinghouse for all the dressmakers of the world. Their dance, on the other hand, and their attitude toward dancing, is as regrettable now as it was in 1950. Bethsabee de Rothschild, however, was a figure to listen to and her mother even more so. For this reason Bethsabee's own circle welcomed Graham. But it was, of course, a closed group. The general public was wary, and Martha did not conquer them with *Errand into the Maze*.

During the intermission Erick accosted Craig. "Tell them they must not use cameras. Tell them they will be thrown out if they use flash bulbs."

"I will do no such thing," said Craig. "How can I make such an announcement to a group of people who have come from Scandinavia, Spain, Eastern Europe, and Italy to do Martha honor?" Erick continued to fume. He then stamped onstage and performed *Eye of Anguish* to stony silence. In this, it must be admitted, the audience concurred with American taste. Erick came off shaking.

"A succès de scandale!" he called. "Nijinsky had such a reception with his *Sacre du Printemps.*" Not true! There had been some boos for Erick, but there was not a riot as there had been with *Le Sacre*. And *Eye* was not a succès de scandale; it was here, as in New York, a cold failure.

Next came the Medea ballet, *Cave of the Heart.* This contained Martha's lengthy and frenetic solo of devouring jealous passion. It was a dance of such animal anger and frustration as to defy sense and sensibilities. It almost evoked disgust. And it was done on the knees, long pas de bourrée on the knees, including a passage of quivering, carnivorous rage in which Martha would half squat, half kneel, and

vibrate the knees in and out like a hungry insect in spasms of eviscera-
tion and digestion—an effect which made the blood run cold. It was,
of course, fearfully difficult muscularly, and it took a terrible toil on the
body, even with healthy knees, and Martha's were damaged.

"Omit this step," the group had begged. Don't get on your knees.
Get on the other knee if you must, but never go down on both of them,
not with the full weight."

But Martha wished to make her effect on Paris. She wanted Erick
to admire her and her art, to have him glory in her. She intended to
conquer her failing body. Down she went, down and down, and she had
to be carried off the stage. It had been an act of self-immolation.

But she kept on dancing. The evening was not yet done. In the
program's fourth and last work, a very weary Martha, a hurt Martha,
an angry and humiliated Erick, and an exhausted audience experienced
a piece of froth, *Every Soul Is a Circus*, from 1939, to Nordoff's score,
which, under better conditions and surrounded by better programming, would undoubtedly have intrigued and delighted them. But the
audience found themselves too tired to respond intelligently. The lack
of response broke Erick's nerves and made him reckless.

Bertram Ross says that he was standing in the wings that night and
he saw Erick throw Martha unnaturally high on one of her jumping lifts
and bring her down sharply on her bad leg, which crumbled with the
shock. "After that night," he said, "she couldn't use the knee."

The long, long evening ended with another large party given by
Bethsabee at her mother's mansion, attended by Martha valiantly and
graciously, and by Erick grimly. Friends and idolators were full of
praise.

The entire company was invited to the party, but they were cau-
tioned to dress in their very best, so they took time at the theater to
make themselves clean, dry, and handsome, arriving just as all the
Parisian guests were leaving. There was still food for the troupe, however, and Bethsabee was welcoming, if distracted. She had Martha to
take care of, and Martha was in a state of near collapse, Erick having
gone to his room in black silence. The dancers ate heartily and gaped
at the museum-quality treasures in every room. On leaving, they were
astonished at being stopped by the butler and his head servants and
politely but thoroughly searched, their handbags and their purses, lest
they purloin something. On that unhappy note they departed and went
to bed to wait for what they knew would be a demolishing press.

In fact, the press varied between bewilderment and brutality. Art

Buchwald, writing in the Paris *Herald Tribune,* spoke for the French public at large: "It was the first time we saw Miss Graham and it was an impressive but highly confusing experience." Paris didn't really like Graham, in spite of a few expert critiques.

There was not one laudatory notice about Erick. Ignoring the fact that *Eye of Anguish* was built around Erick and that he was the protagonist, Baird Hastings in *Dance Magazine* reported "Helen McGehee [Erick's partner] was truly brilliant." Not a word about Erick.

About the program in general, the local Paris press was harsh.

André Warnod in *Le Figaro* reported: "At the end of the evening, one could not stand any more symbolism and metaphysics; one would have liked, by contrast, to see the French cancan or the ballet from *Faust."*

Pierre Tugal, one of the leading Paris critics, wrote:

With respect to the works exhibited, it cannot be denied that compared with the type of dance to which Paris is accustomed, these are as difficult for the average viewer to absorb as a crossword puzzle, accustomed as they are to pretty spectacles, which do not demand much from either intellect or emotion. With *Eye of Anguish,* therefore, the majority of the audience began to take a more defensive position, which became accentuated with *Cave of the Heart* and especially with *Every Soul Is a Circus.*

But there were also a few praising voices:

All the members of the company possess the great technical range created by the genius of Martha Graham . . . by her extreme technique, which fills space with unexpected forms and seems to give her rhythmic response to the most diverse pulsations of her emotions, through the many forms that she succeeds in giving to her body, by her way of making the ground participate—like any other prop—in her dancing, and, above all, she succeeds in communicating to us the entire range of human emotions, from the most tragic to the most comic, with a new vocabulary that we are surprised to understand without having had to study it.

Maurice Pourchet wrote in *Les Arts:*

Well, I marvel at the first program, and I am delighted by the reception it was accorded. Yet almost everything could have disconcerted our Parisian public: the profound novelty of the movements, the extremely intimate and subtle nature of the rhythmic continuity, the occasional mixture of advanced symbolism and tragic and caricatured elements, the conception of art pushed beyond the pretty, into the realm of Daumier, Goya, Bosch, the astonishing Cartesian qualities, the reduction of the decor to the plastic natural style of Ossip Zadkine and Henry Moore. . . . In spite of all this, and in spite of a certain suppleness, the mastery and faith of Martha Graham and her collaborators, such as Erick Hawkins, Helen McGehee, Pearl Lang, and Stuart Hodes, the cohesion of the varied sections, the knowledge with which the scenic space is utilized, the great qualities of the music, the distinguished character of the costumes, made this perhaps the most wonderful success I have ever witnessed.

Nevertheless, the general public and the majority of the press were impervious to Martha's appeal.

Martha couldn't dance the next day. Indeed, she could hardly walk. They rearranged the program entirely so that she would not have to perform: two works danced by Erick, Pearl Lang dancing *El Penitente*, and ending with *Diversion of Angels*. It was not a bad program, but it had no core, because it had no star: it did not have Martha. Throughout the second performance Martha stood backstage, leaning on her cane, a really terrible figure of watchful, even vengeful, fury. They heard her talking loudly to herself as she limped back and forth, and every few seconds she'd bang the cane on the ground like a divining rod. "Yuk!" she called out with a full guttural cry of horror and disgust. The dancers could hear this from the stage, and, understandably, it shook their nerves. The banging and calling did not cease all evening.

The company did not appear again. Nobody was buying tickets, and they had lost heart. That second excruciating night closed the season, and Bethsabee wrote checks.

They staggered to London. Erick and Martha took up their abode at the Ritz Hotel and lived in style and misery. All the company was nerve-frazzled. Could she dance? Would she? One of Martha's dancers went to an orthopedist and showed him everything that Martha had to do. He studied the matter carefully and said, "I think Miss Graham can do all this if she will use reasonable precaution." Martha demanded to see the orthopedist personally and went through the exercises herself in his office, with teeth clenched: lift, strain, grind, right on the wounded knee. Pearl Lang said to me, "She could have used the other knee. She could have shifted her weight. She could have adjusted. She would not." She tortured the same hurt member, in the same way, full force.

At the end of the ordeal, the doctor said, "Well?"

"I'm in torture," Martha replied.

The company lived in a hotel in Bloomsbury. One morning in the dining hall the phone rang; it was for May O'Donnell. It was John Martin, visiting London, who'd heard the news about Martha's French press. "If Martha is unable to dance, don't open," he warned. "Cancel. Be sure about this. Make no mistake. Don't take any chances."

Appalachian Spring was on the opening-night program, and it should have been a happy choice. But Martha's role in this ballet contains knee swoops from great lifts and swings in the bridegroom's arms, down to the floor and into a backbend, again and again. "Don't do these," begged the group. "London has never seen the dance. They won't know what they're missing. It's beautiful enough without." At dress rehearsal Martha fired herself up like a war-horse and fell on the damaged knee again. She couldn't dance on opening night.

The next night Erick left her—he left the theater and left the hotel.

In the middle of the night he threw something against the windows of the room that Pat Birch and Pearl Lang were sharing in the Bloomsbury hotel. They went to the windows and there stood Erick in the street.

"I've left the company and I've left Martha," he said. "I have no money. Can you throw me down some?"

They managed to scrape together some money, tied it in a handkerchief, and threw it down. He disappeared into the night.

This London season was to have been a tremendous opportunity for Erick, as, indeed, Paris was to have been. Martha had given him the key to two golden citadels, to enter with royal kindness and attention, and he had decided to break with his wife and with this way of life, to throw away the whole opportunity, and to risk everything alone. It was an act of desperation and also of great bravery. One must remember this always.

Erick must have felt that if he did not make a clean break for freedom right then, he was lost. So he left Martha to find himself and his identity, abandoning an aging, hurt woman in a foreign country. She was left alone with her shocked and frightened girls, a ravaged repertory, and a damaged body.

During the company's stay in London, Ethel Winter went to see

Laurence Olivier in Christopher Fry's *Venus Observed*. Looking across the theater, she saw Erick sitting there, looking "very old and tired." Erick later stated that he left Martha "for grave aesthetic and moral decisions. It was an act of probity." It was a tough one.

Martha abandoned the season, abandoned the company, and ran away. She ran home.

A year later she spoke to Mrs. Wickes of a "feeling of guilt, a sense of lasting mistake." She always thereafter referred to this season's dissolution as "the accident."

The ever-faithful and caring Bethsabee took over like a nurse. Martha was as helpless as a dismembered animal. Bethsabee brought her back to America and then set about finding the proper doctor for her knee. And very difficult it was, for at that time there were few doctors who specialized in helping what amounted to a sports casualty. But Bethsabee located one in Texas and took Martha to him. He put her on a very strong course of weight lifting and physical therapy. Then Bethsabee took Martha west to her mother in Santa Barbara and the haven of maternal arms.

When she left Martha, Bethsabee said, "Whenever you are ready— if you are ever ready—to come back and try again, I will have the means to see that you do. Don't ever worry about that."

Martha went into mourning for her ruined marriage, for her damaged career, for her lost pride, for her aging body.

Martha was unable to work. She was unable to teach. She saw almost no one. On her return to New York from the grisly European trip and the following month in California, she relied on a few friends, especially John Butler.

He was working alone in the Graham studio late one night. He knew that Erick had been there also. Erick had removed all his things from Martha's flat, and although he continued to practice in the studio, he had no communication with Martha. After work, John dressed and put out the light. As he walked across the floor in the dark, he sensed that there was someone present. And then he made out a shape on the floorboards and went over to it. Martha was lying there, face downward, weeping silently into the wood. She didn't move. He knelt beside her, and very gently he touched her.

"Martha," he whispered. She convulsed in her withdrawal, rigid, and then she hit him hard, straight from the shoulder, and punished him away. He left her.

Sometimes she called him at two-thirty in the morning.

"Don't let me lie and think. Come to me. Take me out."

They walked the streets of Greenwich Village.

They went to all-night movies, the "B" pictures that played in the early hours. He said he thought they saw every bad movie that had ever been made.

"Don't let me see the sun come up alone," she whimpered.

He moved to Sheridan Square so that he could be close at hand when she called.

She was inconsolable. She began to drink. Geordie, her little sister, came to her, but Geordie herself drank fairly consistently and was not much help toward establishing equilibrium.

One evening, on Fire Island, John went with them along the boardwalk and a storm came up: black night, sheets of lightning, thunder. Suddenly there was an enormous flash, which instantaneously revealed that at Martha's feet was a wide, jagged gap where the boardwalk planks were missing. She had all but plunged to her destruction, and would have but for John, who grabbed her back.

"Oh," she wailed, "you had the chance . . . you had the chance! It was nearly over! You should have let me go!"

Martha seemed at this point to be courting suicide.

|||||

Yet six months after the European debacle, in January 1951, she was back on the stage of Carnegie Hall dancing *Judith*, a long solo to music of William Schuman, with the New York Philharmonic. The ballet (set by Isamu Noguchi, costumes by Martha Graham), which had been commissioned by the Louisville (Kentucky) Orchestra and first performed there a year earlier, was an annihilating piece about rage and revenge.

It is based on the ancient story from the Apocrypha of Judith, the heroine-patriot who lures the enemy of Israel, Holofernes, to her tent, seduces him, gets him drunk, feeds him luxuriously, and, while he is sleeping off the repast, drives a nail through his head. It can be readily seen how this mode of dispatching a former lover suited Martha's present mood.

The story as Martha tells it is explicit enough, but the composer, William Schuman, said that when she gave him the commission she said nothing about the subject, and he worked on something else entirely, not knowing for certain what Martha was going to do with the music. On first seeing the ballet, he must have been mightily surprised—an experience many composers have known with Martha.

Martha eventually did three versions of the story of Judith (she combined the Judith legend, from the Apocrypha, with that of Deborah and Sisera, from the Book of Judges, iv:4-v). The second, to music by Mordecai Seter, had its premiere in Tel Aviv in October 1962, at the Habima Theater. The third, to music by Edgard Varèse, was first shown in April 1980, with Peggy Lyman in the starring role. She was good, but not good enough.

Martha had restudied the legends of Judith and the prophetess Deborah. The widow Judith was persuaded by the elders of her tribe to forsake her mourning, adorn herself with gold ornaments and jewels, and destroy the enemy while seeking to woo him. Joseph Campbell and Pearl Lang, who was something of a Hebrew scholar, went to the Hebrew sources and spelled out for Martha the difference between the King James text and the ancient Hebrew scripture. In the "Song of Deborah" in the King James version, Deborah gets a Caananite to bring Sisera into her tent; he asks for water: "she brought forth butter in a lordly dish. She put her hand to the nail and her right hand to the workmen's hammer; . . . she smote off his head, when she had pierced and stricken through his temples, and sent a nail through his skull. At her feet he bowed . . . and where he bowed, there he fell down dead."

Pearl explained: "That's the King James version. But in Hebrew it is 'between her legs he fell down dead.' Another connotation entirely, which Martha seized on.

"Martha said, 'I surmised that, but as the King James version didn't say it specifically, I dared not choreograph it. I'm glad to have corroboration.' "

Pearl added later, "She choreographed the sexual killing, the woman destroying the male in the sexual act. That's an integral part of her image."

Martha had once said to me, "Men and women who are really in love can never be gentle or kind with each other."

"An element of destructive savagery is very, very close to Martha," continued Pearl, "even in happier times. But that's part of her greatness, in a funny way. It's part of what finds a bell in us that begins to ring when we watch. A truly violent streak exists in her, and because she's a dancer she explores it for action. She knows that there is something in every human being that somehow needs to recognize this savagery, while at the same time recoiling from it. She is giving us an experience that we certainly will not get going to the ballet."

Martha told of members of the audience who had been so disturbed, so outraged, by her searching revelations that they rose in anger and dismay and stormed out of the theater. She had revealed to them hidden sensitivities, hidden nerves, unconscious energies and forces, lusts and rages, which they were not used to dealing with, and they were unwilling to face these emotions.

At the Carnegie Hall performance of *Judith* in 1951, the enormous audience rose and cheered.

"It was not that I was that good," Martha explained to me deprecatingly, "or that the piece was that good, but that I had sustained a road accident and I guess the audience loved me and they wished me to know that they were glad I had somehow survived."

It was more than that, of course. Martha took *Judith* to Berlin in September 1957 and danced it at the opening ceremony of the Congress Hall. The critical reaction was tremendous. I personally saw Mary Wigman weeping, with her star dancer, Dore Hoyer, half fainting against her and close to collapsing from the emotional onslaught of what they had witnessed.

At performance end on the night of the New York premiere, John Butler found Martha in her dressing room sobbing bitterly. She had received a triumphant expression of love from the audience; it was outgoing and vociferous. It should have comforted her to the bottom of her soul. But she was disconsolate. "Look," she said, and showed John a book of poems. Erick had come to the theater secretly, entered the dressing room, left the book there, opened to their favorite and most intimate poem, and departed without a word. The message was very clear, and her heart was wrung.

Erick continued to use the Graham school rehearsal halls and was constantly underfoot, which was awkward and painful. I'm sure he felt that having spent half of his time organizing the school, he had every right to use the space. Obviously, he could afford to go nowhere else.

Martha could not be hurt by ordinary methods; many an attacker had found his weapon against her broken and blunted in his hands. There were only three points where Martha could be wounded: her body, which age would surely destroy; her mind; and her sex, which was the key root to her dynamic organization. Touch this and you had reached her, reached home, reached the mortal core. It was right here that Erick had hurt her profoundly.

Of course, he himself had been hurt, too, but he had been hurt because he followed the classic male pattern. Women can espouse a mate more gifted than themselves; they have done so often and have lived well enough. But men cannot marry women with greater gifts and greater power without depletion of their own personalities, and to the woman such a union brings lifelong suffering. If the woman's power is derived from lineage, as in a royal marriage, the consort can with some discipline adjust, because the situation is clearly none of the woman's contrivance. He can accept it with grace also if the situation derives from money inherited from other men. In this case the woman may be forgiven and the resources used. But if the woman's power derives from her own activities she will not be forgiven, and the man cannot exist as an entity. Yet the hero-woman, like the rest of us, needs love. Up to now our culture has made a place for this contingency only rarely, and the women who brave the dilemma today, in our own time, are among the first to try. Many are martyrs.

Martha suffered raw anguish. Her young lover, her husband, had walked out on her. She was able to transmute the experience without collapsing totally only by persuading herself that it was her own voluntary sacrifice in the interest of artistic integrity and that by refusing to yield to his ego she had saved her art. Did she believe that if she had yielded she would have saved the marriage? She had been in the process of yielding when he left. Erick did not want only Martha's love. This he could have had; this, indeed, he did have. Erick wanted Martha's power and Martha's position. This blunt fact, however, she later chose to disregard; and when she referred to the experience, as she did indirectly in her work, it was as a ceremonial giving up of personal desires in service to an aesthetic goal. Verbally, she referred to the breakup as an "accident." In this way she was able to endure the almost intolerable humiliation and the ensuing loneliness, and in this way alone. The truth was that if Martha had yielded to Erick she would have destroyed herself and damaged him. He saved them both by walking out. Martha had the resurgence of spirit and energy to absorb the episode and to transcend it—an almost superhuman achievement for a woman at the age of fifty-six. Her enormous creativity enabled her to do this. But she carried the wounds, and they showed in her work and in her attitude toward other people.

Externally, however, her life began to take a turn for the better. Certainly she began living with more affluence.

Martha had always maintained a stringent monetary economy, and everyone supposed that she had chosen to for aesthetic reasons. I believe she had not. For after visiting Bethsabee de Rothschild and seeing what real wealth could mean in the way of comfort, Martha began acting with what some of her friends termed delusions of grandeur. Her whole style of living changed.

She insisted on a Japanese cook and a housemaid. She took club cars everywhere and would go nowhere without an escort, who acted also as an equerry and footman. It could be argued that Martha had cause for this, that she was not just being grand. She was increasingly and steadily in pain, crippled by arthritis; but, *mirabile dictu*, except for that one weekend in Paris she had never stooped to using a cane. And she never wore glasses in public, never, although her eyesight was fast deteriorating, like the eyesight of many aging people. How she managed to conduct rehearsals without glasses nobody could ever explain. And she was, besides, not infrequently unsteadied by alcohol.

She began to be treated like a royal princess. She found it a most comfortable and attractive way of living, and she became used to it. It must be remembered that Martha had grown up as a rich girl. Bethsabee, who had done so much, crowned her generosity with a prince's gift: she bought for Martha's use a small house at 316 East Sixty-third Street, between Second and Third avenues, three stories high with a garden, an unheard-of luxury in New York City. Out of this building they made studios—the very large one and two smaller—as well as two small kitchens, dressing rooms, and rest space. (The building had previously been a school for training little children. All the accommodations were accordingly small-scale: very low benches, washbasins, and toilets. Because of lack of funds, only the toilets and basins have been replaced. To this day, the space is still inconvenient and cramped.)

The large studios were on the ground floor, and were sunny, airy, and spacious—for this is where the money went. The walls were lined with mirrors and furnished only with low benches and pianos.

Here Martha was to have her school and her rehearsals—for life, although the real estate remained in Bethsabee's name.

The intricate daily routine of the school ground on. Craig Barton was general overseer; Lee Leatherman was in active charge of the school, which never closed, except for three months annually in the summer.

Martha's little sister, Geordie, was unfortunately in charge of the enrollment and of the school's funds and books. Martha had seemingly never disturbed her sister Mary; Mary had led quite an independent life. But she disturbed Geordie. Geordie was still in the shadow of her big sister, and, like any young sibling, she still resented it. She developed intensely neurotic symptoms about the situation. Remember, Martha had said to one of her colleagues, "All that is the matter with Geordie is that Martha Graham is her sister." And she added to an admirer, Arthur Todd, "Geordie finds it difficult being the sister of a genius!" This, of course, was unchangeable, and Geordie suffered very much.

Geordie's unhappy marriage to Winthrop Sargeant only intensified her feelings of inadequacy and failure. Away from Sargeant, she was reputed to have shown considerable wit and sprightliness, even to have published a couple of stories which earned good notices, but for the most part she lived in the shadows and became a kind of fretful dormouse. Martha was always fiercely protective of her, and fought for and shielded the hapless younger woman. Martha maintained her in her unkempt ministrations, suffering all the needless incumbent bothers patiently. The school continued as ostensibly the last word in sophistication.

In a letter dated June 25, 1953, Martha told her friend Frances Wickes about a spat with Geordie. Martha had come to see that Geordie could be dangerous.

Martha used to treat her little sister, Geordie, like her special charge and care, holding her on her lap even when they were both aging women, crooning over her, comforting and cozening her, grooming her, fussing over her appearance for auditions and public showings. In very truth, Geordie as long as she lived was her dependent baby. And she would not tolerate one word of criticism, though Geordie had need of disciplining, for she was in grave danger of giving up, of losing hold, of slipping away into passivity.

Among Martha's friends and supporters, Mrs. Isaacs and Mrs. Morgenthau stood by faithfully. Mrs. Isaacs was stimulating to Martha as a friend, but they could not have been in any sense intimate; Mrs. Isaacs's life was already complete. Mrs. Morgenthau, I think, was not stimulating, although she was intelligent and certainly devoted and faithful. And Katharine Cornell plainly worshiped Martha. She was herself, because of her position, intriguing.

Bethsabee was the closest of these to Martha. She adored Martha and seemed content—not happy, certainly, but content—to give what she could: enormous sums of money, boundless time, unfading friendship, understanding, faith, service in the cause of this splendid career. Martha loved Bethsabee tenderly and was deeply grateful for the unending generosity, while at the same time occasionally fretful under the dragging adoration. Martha craved a challenging mind and temperament. She found it in Mrs. Wickes, an intellectual giant, fifteen years Martha's senior, elderly and fragile but always revivifying and strengthening. Martha had never met a mind like hers, so rounded, experienced, trained, knowledgeable in all the sciences that Martha found nourishing. Hers was a personality of boundless richness.

Many patients become attached to their doctors, and if Martha was not formally a patient of Frances Wickes's, she was dependent on her, seeing her at least once a week when they were in the same city. When Martha was away, she wrote and wrote.

Martha was at the mercy of these latest passions, which tore at her. With Erick she had learned what it was like not to be lonely, and now she was defenseless against the memory, like a wounded soldier tearing open his bandages to see how the scars were healing. Each examination drew fresh blood, and all the time the victim boasted a steady cure. Nor did the suffering ever diminish, even with the years. Over these years her agony was spelled out in letters to Frances Wickes. What a painful, cruel pilgrimage this was, back from the slaughter ground!

Martha's letters told, in a most revelatory way, of her new ideas for dances and the various stages of their development. There was only very occasionally a reference to dreams, which, of course, was Wickes's great subject, since she was a Jungian.

Martha wrote continuously of her inability to sleep, and some of the letters are headed "6:30 A.M." or "Dawn" or "Midnight." The letters were all written when Martha was away from New York, out west or during the tours of Europe, the Near East, and the Far East, in times of such strenuousness as can hardly be imagined by a nonprofessional reader. They cover a period of thirteen years. When Martha was in New York she apparently saw Mrs. Wickes as often as she could manage. They had long talks in the evening after work, in Frances's quiet, comfortable rooms high above the skyline, rooms filled with flowers and memorabilia. Martha permitted nothing to interfere with these sessions. She spoke repeatedly of the warmth, the hospitality, the nourishment and beneficence of these rooms. Martha venerated the caliber of Wickes's mind and the scope of her learning, and for the woman herself she had the tenderest concern.

The letters were all addressed to "Mrs. Wickes" or "Dear One" or "Dear Lady" (Martha never used the first name familiarly), although they were always signed "With love" or "Devoted love, Martha."

Martha had always been reticent, even downright cautious, about taking anyone into her confidence or talking openly. With the confessions to Frances Wickes came black blood, impure grief, self-castigation, remorse, and yearning.

Martha fastened on to her older friend passionately, hungrily, needfully. Repeated statements of her yearning to see her, her need to be with her, her counting the days until they could meet once more and have a drink (Martha was quite frank about drink—or so Frances Wickes believed), have several drinks and settle down to share their hearts.

Erick was, in the meantime, coming back to watch her classes, and he brought her e. e. cummings's poems as a token of how beautiful he thought her work was, both in the classroom and in the recent *Judith*. She described this exchange in a letter to Mrs. Wickes as "exquisite torture," but she concluded her letter by thanking Mrs. Wickes for standing by her so faithfully and so well, and saying that she had experienced a real spiritual uplift in her pain.

|||||

At Hunter College, only a few blocks from the newly located Graham school, on January 19, 1952, two years after Erick and Martha had separated, Erick gave his first solo concert.

Martha sent for John Butler. "Stay with me," she begged him. She wanted John to walk up and down the streets with her so that she could pass Hunter College and project her presence to Erick, who was inside, working. Finally, on the night of the performance, she said, "We will go. We must go."

She, John, and Bethsabee arrived half an hour early and sat there silently. They acknowledged no one, and Martha kept her head down, but their presence was, of course, known. She sat throughout the concert without moving, without making a sound, barely seeing. It was a poor concert; all of Erick's pieces were derivative and built on his wife's work.

He continued to give concerts, which were blasted by the press and ill-attended. Martha continued to monitor alone, and sitting at the back. It was a long time before she could go backstage and speak to him. When she finally did, she said, "You are free. You have killed the Minotaur. You have conquered the riddle of the Sphinx." What Erick had conquered at that point, as far as most of the American public was concerned, was nothing at all.

In 1956 he acquired a dancing partner, Barbara Tucker, a girl of considerable charm and beauty and skill. And he acquired a musician, Lucia Dlugoszewski, who could put bottles and little pieces of tin and scraps of iron on the strings of her piano and make astonishing and not unpleasing sounds. And he dressed himself in extraordinary and sometimes wonderfully suggestive costumes (always with a great deal of bare Hawkins). He began to make a reputation for himself as a lecturer at colleges, and he held many seminars. His audiences, though limited, were enthusiastic. Certainly he was not without important admirers. Acclaimed painters, such as Robert Motherwell, thought highly of him.

In a letter to Craig Barton dated January 21, 1952, I wrote:

We keep in very close touch with Martha. She and Bethsabee are more or less inseparable but I like Bethsabee so I don't mind and Martha and I just call up and chat for hours on end. She is beginning to crawl out from under, though Erick continues to be a trial. He is still in her studio wasting students and he is giving dance recitals which nobody I know attends. . . . Martha is once more sassy and pert and capable of falling into passions of rage about new ideas. All these I take to be signs of complete recovery. She told Walter she was getting a divorce this summer. There has been a good deal of talk about a spring season but I don't know whether or not it will materialize. Her people are scattered. She has, of course, no money except what Bethsabee gives her but I feel the real problem is replacing Erick as a partner. Before this idea her spirit quails.

On August 1, 1952, Martha was in Santa Fe, New Mexico, and now her letters to Frances Wickes revealed specific distress, frantic anguish at the prospect of discussing business terms with Erick in relation to their divorce, the monies owing him for his years of service to the company. She found it almost impossible to face the business residue of the break, and she remembered with real remorse how she had run out on the company in London and left them stranded. But although she was suffering very much, her mind was not clouded by death wishes as it had been the year before. It was obvious she was now facing facts and beginning to learn stoicism and endurance, points of view and emotions that were brand-new to Martha. She hoped with faith to be able to bear whatever was in store. She remarked with real poignancy that hope was a "corroding" thing.

When, on her return in the autumn, Erick finally presented his accounts, he sent a letter asking for two hundred and fifty dollars, which was, of course, immediately given him. This minuscule sum seems pathetic considering his work and faithfulness. But it was on sums like these that dancers lived.

In certain ways Martha had wished to make him suffer. Bethsabee stepped into the picture at this point and told him he should not write to Martha anymore and that Martha would give him a divorce as soon as it was practically possible for her to do so.

Erick wrote a one-sentence note to Bethsabee in Paris, thanking her for her letter. Martha concluded that she herself had bungled the situation badly.

Erick, of course, thought he was due a share of the income from the school and its activities because of the years he had spent building it up. He had much justice on his side, and Martha knew it. The episode strikes one as needlessly harsh. Martha said once to Glen Tetley, "I am responsible for Erick. I created him and I am responsible. I have a financial obligation to him. When people separate, it's not always the husband who pays alimony. Sometimes the wife has to pay."

The real payment for Martha was in human grief and remorse, daylong and every night.

How much Erick suffered is not known. One thing is certain: he believed he had earned the money with years of hard work.

When Martha visited her mother in Santa Barbara she had always stayed with her in the old house, but after her stepfather died her mother went to live in the El Mirasol Hotel, and Martha went there also. She permitted herself to take naps, to rest, and to laze about the garden, an indulgence unheard of in her normal life, and she luxuriated in the abandonment to leisure. Her joy in small delights which most human beings know daily is touching.

Over the next two years her letters to Frances Wickes date from Santa Fe, from Santa Barbara, from wherever she was—from whenever Martha was separated from Frances Wickes. Her letters told of her need for Erick, of the difficulty of getting through a summer without him because he gave her a sense of immediacy, of not having to think before she spoke or acted. She wound up reaffirming how she longed to get back to the talks and the quiet drinks in Mrs. Wickes's study, in the company of the books, the marvelous memorabilia, and the cat. She even, in one case, ended by saying she blessed her difficulties because they had brought her into the care of the analyst.

|||||

All the while the creative work held strong and fresh and never at any point reflected the decay. Marvelous to behold! Most wonderful to share! Her company stood by her in awe. They cherished her as much as she would let them, and they bent their hearts in pity.

|||||

It was obvious that Martha had to choose a new partner, which was not easy to do. The role of prince consort in this female brigade was a hazardous one, because of Martha's domination and because of the jealousy of the others. The name that leapt to everyone's mind was José Limón, a splendid soloist, an important personality, and one of the finest human beings who ever graced the dance profession. He had been an important member of the Humphrey-Weidman company in the thirties, but that company was now disbanded. Weidman was doing only scattered choreography, and Doris, owing to grave arthritis of the hips, had retired from active performing. A virtual invalid, she lent her editing talent to José. So José now composed his own dances with the active guidance of Doris. Somehow it was made known to him that Martha was considering asking him to be her partner, and he went to Doris for advice, as he always did on professional matters. Doris was wise and had known Martha since girlhood.

"Be careful," she warned him. "Be very careful. Martha transforms the people she works with, particularly the men. She is Circe. You will be her creature. Do you wish this?" He did not. So word was conveyed back to Martha that José was unwilling. Thereafter, whenever his name was mentioned as a possible replacement for Erick, Martha railed against him—not that she disliked José or held him in poor respect, but she wouldn't hear of him as a partner, bridling at the mention of his name.

But the problem remained: she had to have someone. So she decided to have several, and they were indeed an astonishing and remarkable group. Merce Cunningham had left the company in 1945, lured away by the composer John Cage and by Lincoln Kirstein to independent choreographing for Ballet Society. But there now appeared some excellent male dancers to partner Martha and to take the male leads in some of her ballets: John Butler (whom she had begun using as a dance partner before her marital breakup), Stuart Hodes, Paul Taylor, Mark Ryder, Bertram Ross, and Robert Cohan. And these young men were seeded among the ballets (*Letter to the World, Every Soul Is a Circus, Deaths and Entrances, El Penitente, Appalachian Spring, Cave of the Heart*). She had to explain to them what the original intention had been, as well as the meanings of the gestures, although this tired her emotionally in that it involved the recapitulation of old woes, tendernesses, and ardors so ineffably connected with Erick. As long as she retained the old works—and they were masterpieces not to be discarded—the pain recurred.

Among the first reconstructions was the 1947 *Night Journey* which contained the role of Oedipus, one of Erick's strongest parts. Martha cast Bertram Ross in the role. An undeniable problem was the age difference between her and Ross, who was considerably younger than Erick. Bertram recalls discussing it with Martha, sitting in Harlow's coffee shop directly across the street from the Fifth Avenue studio. (It was to Harlow's that Martha used to send Bertram for her "ambrosias"—the mixture of orange juice, vanilla ice cream, and raw eggs she liked to drink for energy. She received physical energy from the ambrosias; spiritual strength, zest, and excitement came from Bertram.) At their meeting to discuss the part, Martha emphasized that she didn't want to do anything that would be embarrassing. She did not want to dance as an older woman with a younger lover. She had to find a partner who would be suitable. "And," Ross explained later, "since I was the most dramatic member of the new company, she felt I could hold my own opposite her despite my age, just as Erick had done. She asked me if I'd be willing to attempt this, with the understanding that if she felt it was inappropriate or offensive in any way it would be scrapped. I said I was willing, and we got to work."

Next, Martha had to face the image of Erick and his costume. She decided to remake the costume entirely. Erick had worn a little hip-length cape, but she gave Bertram yards and yards of double-knit jersey, flaming red, and they spent two unsatisfactory days pinning it together, trying to make something entirely new. Then Bertram was sent into a room alone to find out what he could do with all that yardage, and he discovered he could produce some extraordinary effects. So Martha handed the jumbled mass of fabric over to Linda Hodes, who was good with a needle. But since Martha's own costume was initially (it varied frequently before a final design was decided upon) in shades of white, off-white, and mustard, Bertram felt, quite sensibly, that

with Oedipus in half a bolt of flaming red jersey, one would not see anything else. [So] when I did my first performance, my costume was made of a fabric that ranged from black to pale gray and white. It looked like a sky, and I remember as Martha and I took a cab to the theater for opening night—having just finished my costume two seconds before—the sun was setting and Martha said, "Look at the sky: it looks like my dress." Then she asked me if I was tired. She had said she didn't want me standing for a fitting right before I had to perform, but that's exactly what had happened. I stood on top of a desk while Martha pinned bronze braid squiggles all over my briefs, then gave it to someone [Linda] to sew.

Bertram was excellent in the role. This represented a step toward freedom for Martha.

In March 1954, Martha attempted London again.

The response from audience and press was not good, although this was to be expected. London is conservative and faithful, but slow to form its response. Marie Rambert, who like Ninette de Valois managed a ballet company, and who, together with Ninette, was responsible for the renaissance of English ballet, used to mock Martha—without, I might add, having seen her—but after this London performance Rambert shut herself in Martha's dressing room and wept so hard that Craig Barton did not know what to do with her. Rambert was a white-haired woman at this point, but she had seen dancers as important as Nijinsky (with whom she had been personally in love) and Isadora Duncan (whom she had revered), and she simply collapsed before the Graham experience. This extravagance of emotion was typical of the Polish Mim (as she was always called), though it was quite gruesome to hear her sobs ring through the walls.

In the audience at the London performance was Robin Howard, a huge (six-foot-six) man with massive shoulders and no legs, just wire below the thighs. His legs had been shot away during the war. This giant propelled himself on two hand crutches and two prostheses.

That night, he later told me, his life changed; and to a certain extent, so did the company's:

. . . I was completely bowled over. It was one of the greatest—perhaps *the* greatest—theatrical evenings in my life, and I changed my entire program for the next fortnight and saw every performance. I vowed that I would never look at dance again until I brought the Graham company back to London.

I discovered that not only had hardly anyone here heard of her before, not only was she having very bad audiences (I'm one of about five thousand people who now claim to have been amongst the only twelve in the stalls [orchestra] at the second performance), not only was the press very stupid (except, of course, for Dicky Buckle, who suddenly saw the light halfway through Martha's season; his second article admitted, "I was all wrong, this is great"); I further discovered that no one was entertaining the company at all. As I happened to have been a pub keeper and owned a couple of restaurants at that time, I invited the entire company, including Martha, to a party. I asked if they would prefer a normal dinner or an Elizabethan banquet. She chose the banquet and we put Martha in the Queen's chair. Of course, she played a beautiful monarch. I invited the only people from the ballet world who had been at her performance. (Most remarkably, one of them was Beryl Grey, the ballerina.) The dinner was fun, in Tudor costume and served in Elizabethan style, and Martha enjoyed it. In this way I got to know her slightly. She seemed surprised that I, a completely unknown person, was paying attention to her.

During this trip, Martha was working to complete *Ardent Song* to music of Alan Hovhaness. The rehearsals were chaotic. Martha was uncertain, playing with costumes, postponing, changing, leaving gaps to be filled later, and finally telling Pearl Lang, who danced the role of Dawn, to improvise. When Pearl had done so, Martha said, "That's fine. Do it." On opening night, to her deep dismay, Pearl found she could remember nothing of what she had done at the last rehearsal. She went on the stage and danced blindly. She was aware that what she did was effective and good and that she had made an excellent impression, but how, in what way, she could not recall. The entire episode remains a dark blot to her. Martha dismissed it from her mind, but it was a sure indication of the unregulated, undisciplined, chaotic condition Martha was now in. It was as though she were coming unraveled.

Nevertheless, Martha did get the revised work onto the London stage quite successfully, while maintaining a full repertory and dancing herself every night—an incredible feat considering the demands made upon her, and considering her age.

The day before *Ardent Song* opened, Martha had spasms of indecision and fright, and announced her intention of not opening the work, but Gertrude Macy said she simply had to, that she must. And so the night of the performance she sat on the floor of the stage with Yuriko's little daughter, Susan, in her lap, and watched it without seeming to be present. It went all right. When they opened in London the bar stewards from the ship sent them a telegram (the company used to gather in the bar to play shipboard games, but not to drink), and the ship's doctor attended the performance. The audiences were amazed at the technique and range of movement of the dancers, at the beauty of their bodies, and at their simplicity and honesty, as well as at their very great skill.

On April 11, 1954, in Copenhagen, Martha found herself recognized not as a dancer but as a choreographer, and this upset her. She had never thought of herself as a choreographer, but this was how she was being acclaimed, and she realized that though she had planted one kind of seed and hoped for a certain crop, she was getting something entirely different. She was amazed, and she set about readjusting her entire psychological approach to her work.

From Copenhagen they went to Brussels, the American ambassador to Belgium having phoned to say that skipping Brussels would be considered an international slight—the first formal notice the U.S. State Department had ever taken of her.

Then she progressed to Germany and to Switzerland. Accompanied by Gert Macy, Martha was entertained at supper by Carl Jung and his wife. This courtesy was arranged by Frances Wickes. The great man came to Martha's concert and was vastly impressed. He talked to her afterward in impeccable English.

"How was he?" demanded all the dancers eagerly the next day. "What did he say?"

"Oh, he was cute," answered Martha, and she chuckled. "He's very, very attractive."

This reply was certainly not the one anticipated. Unfortunately, the exigencies of Martha's tour forced her to hurry away the next day; otherwise we might have an added footnote to Jungian theory.

Bethsabee had promised her father that she would never spend a penny of Rothschild money in Germany as long as she lived, and so she could not help Martha there. Martha found other sources of finance. When she reached Berlin, Mary Wigman was as exuberant and emotional as Rambert had been in London, throwing herself on the ground and kissing Martha's feet. Her demonstration was homage indeed, coming from the high priestess and leader of the entire European modern movement, and it was a remarkably generous act from a rival. It puts one in mind of Martha's cool and unenthusiastic response to Wigman's 1930 debut in New York City. But Wigman was openhearted and direct, and she recognized supreme value when she saw it.

|||||

When Martha got home from the European tour she settled into her traditional routine, turning out masterpieces in addition to teaching and training the dancers, and mounting the works. Her long-maturing ballet to music by Norman Dello Joio, first presented as the solo *The Triumph of Saint Joan* in 1951, emerged on May 8, 1955, in a completely revised version called *Seraphic Dialogue*. A note in the program read:

Seraphic Dialogue is a drama about Joan of Arc at the moment of her exaltation. In a dialogue with Saint Michael, Saint Catherine, and Saint Margaret, whose voices had guided her toward her destiny, she looks back upon herself as a maiden, a warrior, and a martyr, and, transfigured, is taken up to her place of honor.

In this piece, personifications of three aspects of Joan's character sit at the side of the stage in long, different-colored cloaks. The great window at the back contains Saint Michael, Saint Margaret, and Saint Catherine. At the end, the martyred saint is enclosed within the window's stained-glass portraits.

This use of attendant figures in cloaks reminds one of the angels, one in a blue cloak, one in a red, sitting opposite Ruth St. Denis's Madonna in her latter-day church service. And there is a hint of the same revelation and mystery in Graham's piece. No artistic creation is absolutely new, any more than a human personality is totally new but rather the amalgam of the parents and the play of new life on the old. This is the essence of growth, and there can be only a disruption of natural forces when a brand-new mutation explodes into being. The result is generally monstrous. In *Seraphic Dialogue*, as in other works, Martha owed much to Miss Ruth. But Martha went way beyond Miss Ruth. Martha achieved a knife edge, a black thrust; she gave a live vibrancy to martyrdom and sainthood. She knew through, she valued, she evaluated pain. She was at the root of intensity.

Verily, Martha did the impossible: she produced onstage a sense of beatitude. Bertram Ross's performance as Saint Michael approached holiness.

Noguchi's inspired setting of interlocking metal rods suggesting a stained-glass window is loftily beautiful and worthy of the ideal it sealed.

Now, in Martha's work as in her life, the burning was accomplished, and the agony.

And now Martha set out to conquer the world. But not England. She had tried England, and the results had been disastrous. The tight little isle had resisted her. Following the 1954 tour, Martha sent a notice to the British press that she was not coming back.

Robin Howard had never presumed on his brief acquaintance with Martha in London to start a correspondence with her, although he plainly worshiped her. He recounted:

I suddenly saw in the newspaper that she was doing a world tour but not coming to England, and I asked why and was told she'd been such a financial failure and her sponsor had lost so much money that no one was prepared to finance her again. I thought this ridiculous, so I got in touch immediately with the American embassy. "I don't know where to start to fight this, but she must come." Now, I was a nobody in the dance world. I just went and watched. By trade I was a pub keeper. At that time, happily, I had more money than I needed, and I had friends who sometimes listened to me, and I felt strongly about this.

As luck would have it, George Harewood [the Earl of Harewood] was the director of the Edinburgh Festival at that time, and I knew him quite well. I went to him. "Look," I said, "if Martha Graham comes over next year, will you help her at the Edinburgh Festival?" He said, "Of course." Then we got down to costing the project, and I was told to be prepared to lose around 80,000 pounds, or even more. So I rang up George again and I said, "Look, this is getting a bit much for me. If I take the whole of the first 10,000, will you share the second 10,000 and anything after it?" And he said, "Yes," on the telephone. Just like that. He'd never been a dance fan, but he does like to support anything worthwhile.

Robin Howard was a man of family and substance who owned enormous commercial properties. His fortune was large, and he gave a substantial part of it to Martha Graham by selling hotels and various other properties, because, as he said, "She was the greatest artist I have ever witnessed, one of the greatest artists living today in any field whatever. I decided to pledge my personal fortune to her. I wanted my countrymen to welcome her back in honor."

Martha returned to London in September 1963, and this time she was a success. Robin recalled:

I was so naive, it never occurred to me to have a contract. I trusted Craig Barton, and he trusted me, and that was that, so he didn't bother me. . . . On the last night, Martha said, "Robin, you don't seem to realize that we've done something extraordinary: we've completed the entire season without any contract. We really ought to have one." . . . So she signed one on the last night. I think that says a lot about Craig. [And, may we add, a lot about Robin Howard! He paid the entire deficit.] Marie Rambert came to me. "Mr. Howard, I don't know who you are or why you've done it, but don't stop now."

And all I could say was, "Don't stop *what*, Madam?"

And Rambert said, "We must have this training for British dancers. Martha Graham is pleased with you at the moment. Will you ask her if we can?"

Howard suggested to Martha, "If I can arrange for the expenses of it, will you allow British dancers into your school?"

She replied, "I'll give free tuition."

Robin continued: "That Christmas, the first of the British students arrived at the Graham school in New York. But we had chosen too well, and they all got jobs in New York and were unwilling to come back home, and so the project didn't help England one bit. I decided I had to start classes at home, which Martha very generously helped me to do."

"The people who really got it all started," Bertram Ross commented, "before there was a 'Graham School' in London, before there was even a studio, were Mary Hinkson and Ethel Winter, who taught classes in three or four different places a day. It was a murderous schedule, but it laid the foundations for the school."

These Graham classes developed into the first school of contemporary dance in the British Isles, The Place. There had hitherto been no modern dancing at all in Great Britain: nothing German, nothing Austrian, nothing Scandinavian, nothing. Now there was a Graham school, headed by Jane Dudley and taught by accredited teachers.

|||||

In 1955 Louis Horst suffered a severe heart attack, and Martha went to his side immediately. They were never to be intimately close again, but she had suddenly realized that he was mortal and very precious, and she was stricken with concern for his age, his feebleness, and his loneliness. Once more they became close friends and comforters, and he was deeply reinforced by the fact that she had come to him at this time of peril and was continuing now as a sustaining presence. He had always been her first critic and her first adviser, but she had seen little of him in the last decade and had listened to other voices. Now, at least, they spoke once again on their own deep level.

After the heart attack, Doris Rudko, his student assistant, described how falteringly he walked, "as though he had been out of the world and had to start walking again." But Louis had recurrent dizzy spells and once suffered a blackout while strolling in Central Park. He grew huffy and sarcastic when he was sympathized with, and he scoffed at all offers of help.

Martha was worried about his living alone and persuaded him to come uptown to a better apartment, clean and new, air-conditioned, with doormen. But Louis hankered after his old Eleventh Street lair, and he was lonely for the Romanoff Pharmacy across the street where he could get good coffee. And for the delicatessen opposite, which he had frequented for forty years, and where he used to meet his cronies and pupils before proceeding into the decayed dining room of the Albert Hotel to have drinks and poor food, and also the conversation, the gossip Louis loved. In the new quarters he had no friends close by.

There was nobody to meet him or talk to him casually. He lived there like a stranger. The small room was more expensive than what he had been used to, but he could afford it. He had saved some money. It was an austere cell with none of his lovely pictures on the walls and no Navajo mementos, no kachina dolls, nothing. He said they belonged to his past and he was living in the present and if possible the future. He wanted nothing to remind him of the past. The walls were absolutely bare and as plain as a hospital room. He lived an ascetic and prophylactic existence. And he ate out of tins, seldom cooking. His pupils fretted about him, but they simply could not take him on as a full-time responsibility, nor would Louis have allowed it. Martha had wanted him near her so that she could watch over him, but she was terribly busy. So was Nina Fonaroff. Louis lived alone.

But Martha was close again, practically and emotionally, and Louis did feel that he had once more recovered his best friend and his dear love. Martha could lay her bruised and battered spirit on his strong, steadfast belief, on his unvaryingly high standards, and come to rest. And Louis knew that he mattered.

And he did. But he could not draw comfort from her presence for long. In December 1955 Martha was off again in her search for far-flung glory, in her tireless service to her country's cultural missions, in Europe, Scandinavia, the Near East, Asia, the Far East, China, Hong Kong, and Japan. But no Iron Curtain countries except Rumania, and never Russia; nor South America and Australia. Wherever she did go she was hailed. Wherever she went there were students who had worked with her, Japanese and Koreans who had studied at her school in New York and had traveled home and had set up working cells, like Communist propagandists. Her seeds had gone all over the world.

She was, however, very particular about who claimed her. On arriving in Japan she was greeted by Michio Ito, who had staged her first appearances in the *Greenwich Village Follies*. Now he came to her, ebullient, smiling, with arms filled with flowers. "For my pupil, Martha Graham," he said. She took the bouquet in stony silence and threw it in his face. Martha was not going to recognize Ito as her teacher. He was old and obviously loving, but that made no difference to her. The point was she had not been his pupil. Not at any time.

On these overseas tours Martha traveled not only as the head of the company and the chief dancer, the absolute dancer, but as the head manager or drillmaster of rehearsal; the head technical manager; the head coordinator; the head public-relations officer; and the chief of state. It had very soon become clear that she was received, if not by the U.S. State Department then by everyone else, with high protocol, not because she was one of the world's great creative artists but because she was a national figure and judged the best our country had to offer. As a result she felt it incumbent upon her, her veritable duty as a United States citizen, to see as much as she could, to meet people the embassies asked her to meet, to go to the schools they advised her to visit, to do whatever lay within her power toward improving international relations.

The greatest artists and thinkers—Martin Buber in Israel, for instance—saluted her. She was, in fact, as she admitted to me once in a tipsy moment, "a national treasure," and she bore it all willingly and with grace.

There were also the usual company troubles, aggravated by their location and isolation. ANTA had failed to send the signed contracts to Tokyo. A dancer (female) brawled with another, bit her, was quelled by Martha with a jug of cold water ("a paper cup of water" said Bertram Ross), then put her fist through a glass window and declared she was paralyzed. Martha sat up with her all night, persuaded her she was not paralyzed, got her to walk and even to dance, but the parents were sent for. To Martha's horror they were not a bit surprised. It seems they had known their daughter was mentally unbalanced when they had sent her off on this difficult trip. A delegation of young yellow-robed Buddhist monks wanted to see the show and staged a sit-down strike. The house was sold out, and all entertainment was forbidden by their order. Nevertheless, they sat on the steps of the theater until they were let in for free. They remained giggling throughout the show, which Martha took as a mark of admiration. (Whether or not they were later disciplined for disobedience is not known.)

Leroy Leatherman wrote to Frances Wickes from Rangoon on December 13, 1956: "An American . . . said that the [Graham] company's deepest significance was that 'for the first time an American had come to the East with love, with nothing else in mind. . . . Miss Graham is the best thing America has ever done for the East. . . . There has not been one soul [before] who came with love.' "

"We must learn to respect our differences, the difference in cultural interests," Chester Bowles, American ambassador to India from 1951 to 1953 and from 1963 to 1968, quoted Martha as saying.

||||||

Martha spared herself nothing. Why she did not have frequent collapses is inexplicable. Paul Taylor reported of the 1956 tour that "Though the rest of us wilt with the heat and sometimes drop from dysentery, she never misses a performance." Bertram Ross protests Taylor's statement indignantly: "I never missed a performance with her from 1949 to 1973."

And all the time she was lonely, ailing, and despondent, although universally admired. But it wasn't fun. The joy was gone. It was a rose-strewn, palm-bedecked, garlanded Via Dolorosa.

The entire hive revolved around and existed through the creative activities of the queen. It was not eggs she was laying—it was ideas, day after day, through the nights, for weeks, for years without surcease. The group nurtured her, protected her, but they could not share. They existed only because of the continued functioning of her imagination. She did this alone.

Louis was old and failing. Erick was no longer there. She had no one to talk to except Frances Wickes, no one whose advice would help or reassure. For her it was to be the loneliness of the long-distance runner, the polar explorer, the astronaut.

She was able to endure the lonely role because she considered the imaginative search as a religious experience. She felt herself to be the vessel for power—a power that lay within her mind. All her disciplines—the training of her body, the almost Jesuitical daily attention toward maintenance and cleansing, the sharpening of her faculties—were used to enable her to press closer and closer to what was there but never consciously known: the atavistic memories, the recognitions, the instincts, the linking with all forms of life. Poets have guessed at this, and saints in ecstasy; but they seldom know it consistently and repeatedly. Yet Martha did frequently, and seemingly without a lessening of clarity. This was Martha's métier; this was why she existed, why she got up in the morning and ate and flexed her knees.

But the strain was formidable, and it might have warped her over the borderline of control but for the great healthy factory of functioning humans she had set up around her, with its constant demands on her practical attention. And but for two comforts: her little sister, Geordie, bereft, widowed now, directionless, who clung to her like a child, her only one, and who was an alcoholic; and but for Martha's own drinking. There was whiskey—all day, and every night.

A bitter, drunken woman, now in her late sixties, Martha was still the first creative voice in our theater. The works kept coming—clear, profound, and true, and full of new theatrical inventions and delights.

Sophie Maslow said: "She does not have in her life, nor did she ever have, what other women have in the way of shared love, shared responsibility, shared growth, but maybe she gets the same fulfillment in life in her artistic growth, her artistic status." Certainly in her later years the position she had was matchless.

The spectacle of this woman's achievement, year after year! She was sober one year, she wasn't sober the next; it didn't seem to matter to the work. She'd been mean to this girl, she'd been brutal to that one. And to herself. Then again, she would be wonderfully kind and generous. She was not a happy woman in any ordinary sense. She was happy only when she was working. Then she was as healthy as any of them— healthier, perhaps.

Martha was something brand new in the world of art. Hitherto artists had died young, like everyone else. Many of them had done what they had set out to do and then died before there was a chance for them to fade artistically or decay morally. In this they were fortunate. With prolonged effort there comes a dreadful fatigue and a consequent lessening of vitality. (This is one reason why, I believe, older people today seem less respectable than they used to be. They take to drink or folly; they divorce; they commit petty or grand larceny; they corrupt. Formerly they died young and were mourned, but they were respected.

Now they hang around getting into trouble. It takes such vigilance, such effort, to stay worthy! Many of us run out of energy. Children once respected their parents, were glad to, took pride in the fact and professed their devotion. Now a general disbelief and disrespect between the generations is prevalent. And the young people are in many ways right, alas, because parents are not so honorable as before.)

So it has been with artists. There are exceptions, of course. Some painters—more painters than any other species, I should say—have achieved right up to their deaths, in their eighties or nineties, with no diminution of their output: Leonardo, Michelangelo, Monet, Renoir, Picasso. And some musicians: Haydn, for instance, and Verdi, who composed *Falstaff* and *Otello* when he was in his seventies, after a lapse of more than twenty years. And a few writers: Goethe wrote great lyric verse in his seventies; Tolstoy wrote *Resurrection* between the ages of sixty-one and seventy-two, and his religious essays when he was over ninety.

Martha had been aware that she was older than any of the other pupils at Denishawn, that she was only a few years younger than the head of the school, Ted Shawn. She was conscious of being older than most of her colleagues when she went on the stage. When she began to teach, she knew she was fifteen years older than her girls, but even while she was standing beside them and dancing publicly with them, she insisted on out-dancing, out-running, out-performing every other woman on the stage, every other woman in her profession. She was forty when she began to establish her name.

She was reluctant to accept replacements for herself in big works, maintaining stubbornly that she was able to do her own roles better than anyone. And she would do them as long as she could be carried on the stage. No one dared gainsay her. She had an instinctive distrust of all young rivals.

Roth Gilbert, her pianist, said: "If this is what it means to grow old I want to die now. Old age has become ugly, and maturing seems to be unacceptable."

Every leader in every field knows the condition of being hated and distrusted. Leaders may be venerated; they are seldom loved. Along with dominance comes jealousy and anger; and in the world of dance, where neuroticism, uncertainty, frenetic ambition, compulsion, and blind hopelessness contend for mastery, these inflamed emotions predominate. It is to be expected. It must be endured. Time will erase the hideous fevers, and the leaders know this. The quality of work is all that matters.

It is so in all closed circles: in colleges and universities; in business offices; in the armed forces, certainly, where it is a means of survival; and, I daresay, in government, of which I have no personal knowledge. There is ambition and therefore fear and jealousy, and the resulting gossip, betrayal, terror, and bitterness—a never-ending struggle among the young for living space, for ground in which to put down roots, while the dominant figure struggles always to maintain superiority.

In the case of kings—and, more especially, of powerful queens—the struggle itself was often made the basis of power, and the queen ruled by never establishing a clear order. In these cases a difference of opinion amounted to high treason and involved the forfeiture of one's head or one's entrails, according to rank. In the world of art the emotions are as violent, if the stakes are less bloody, and from this writhing maggot pile comes a sinister, dark liveliness that can be zest to certain personalities. Here there is never security but constant risk and fear, and competition is maintained, not only by personal need but by the leader's mischievous projection.

Gertrude Shurr said: "Wherever Martha is, there is always turmoil and trouble. She cannot abide tranquility. She equates agitation with life energy." Martha had set Merce against Erick, Bertram Ross against Glen Tetley, both against Paul Taylor, and she did this deliberately.

Martha never would state her age. Craig Barton told me that on her passport was stamped that according to her mother's memory Martha had been born in such-and-such a year, and the State Department allowed this noncommunicative document to stand as her guarantee of identity. It carried her everywhere in the world and served as the only basis of knowledge for her business staff. She talked about events of the past but always vaguely and without dates. She was *not* going to grow old. She was a goddess and immortal. Mrs. Wickes warned her. Martha dared not listen.

Martha's paranoia was growing. Her very true power as a dancer, her magic, may have paled with time and fatigue; her power as a woman, never. She came to rely on the lethal energy of this working compost, this false, frantic excitement engendered by troubles, and she derived a sense of potency, of power as a unique catalyst. Her life wisdom, the quietness of her soul, the loftiness of her ideas were put aside too often as she drank this fateful brew. She presided over it; in many ways she concocted it, like a witch's broth, and inhaled the hideous aroma. During this period, she often supped with Hecate.

||||

Holding her company together became the motivating force of Martha's existence. Lacking the money to bind the dancers under legal contract, she had to hold them by devotion alone, by belief and loyalty, and this grew harder with time. At the age of sixty-four she was in her fortieth year of achievement, and she still asked that the dancers give their time, their bodies, and their minds, unreserved and whole. For the most part they complied, but it was by an act of mesmerism.

Martha wooed them, seduced them, wove a magic web around them, and she could never rest from doing this. Men and women alike fell under her spell, the men almost abjectly. I don't believe Martha was in love with any of them personally. She was in love with their talents and their usefulness, and she approached them with her siren song. Or, alternatively, she bullied and threatened them with frightful warnings, holding on to her creatures with primitive and wicked tenaciousness: they were not to take jobs elsewhere or to form independent professional relationships, even among themselves. And yet they had to, for Martha simply could not pay them enough to keep them alive. She recognized this fact, but she nonetheless resented their independence. She retained Bertram Ross to teach and demonstrate for her at the Graham studio, at the Neighborhood Playhouse, and at the Juilliard School; these last two paid him directly, thus assuring his availability to her at all times.

The dancers still returned regularly to do as she wished, to help her with her seasons, to teach, to study, to rehearse; and for these duties they put in hours every day in her studio at her bidding. Working with Martha became an article of faith, like patriotism; the followers were asked to believe that her work was the most important, that they would vitiate their own work by mixing it with lesser commercial enterprises, that they should, in short, keep themselves unadulterated and available for her. If they went hungry, *tant pis*. If it were argued that they gave her their lives, Martha's reply would have been that she gave hers and more, that without her they would have been nothing.

Martha accordingly thought of the pupils as her tools; their essence, their character were to her material for art, like color or clay. And the loss of a girl for whatever reason was inconvenient and maddening and, of course, unnecessary.

When Jean Erdman told Martha that she was going to have to leave the company for reasons of personal expansion and development, as well as material need, Martha cried out, "What are you doing to me?" And when Jean actually pulled out, with much heart searching, Martha refused to speak to her for two years. She seldom went to see the students' concerts. The men grew even more quickly restive, and, finding a demand for their work, they left sooner than the women, to Martha's anguish—an anguish she made abundantly clear.

Was her attitude unnatural? Martha lived for and off the Group. Martha was the Group; the Group was Martha. It was as if her own body were betraying her, as her arthritic legs and hands had begun to do. She hardened with resistance. Also, she was an aging woman and therefore fearful. She of all people was experiencing the terror of growing helplessness, the mounting weakness, aggravated by the awareness of young talents, vigorous, struggling for position all around her. She had been trained all of her life to hold her own. She defended boldly. She attacked.

One speaks of the School of Botticelli, the School of Rubens. Did their apprentices try to strike out on their own? Were they hobbled from doing so by a dominating personality using direct intimidation? Were they enticed to try independence by dreams of enrichment or by practical needs of feeding and housing? Very few became immortal themselves; some did.

There was, however, this difference. If a young painter leaves the atelier of his master, he is regretted and his talent is missed, but the work he has done is left behind intact. If a dancer leaves a group, not only are his trained body and talent lost, but the knowledge and memory of the work itself. The masterpiece is ravaged; it goes with him.

When one has disciplined oneself, deprived oneself, cauterized oneself for one's art, as Martha had done unremittingly the whole of her life, to be then told that the idea for which she had sacrificed was only one of several theories and not indeed holy and unique was intolerable; her very identity was centered on this point. The discipline makes for a cast of mind which breeds passion and power, certainly, but also a certain loss of objectivity, and with it humor. A man does not go to the stake seeing the opposing point of view.

"Perfect integrity is perfect selfishness," said Martha. She was willing to die for her art. It followed that faithful students must be willing also to die for her art, and not theirs.

They were not, as it turned out.

So she kept training new boys and resenting the loss of old ones. But as she needed the old ones, she forgave them, and they were invited back and came willingly enough, but always with the understanding that the door was to be left ajar behind them.

It was different with the women. Many of the women remained content to teach Martha's technique, to serve in her company, to proselytize. Most of the original students opened their own schools, but it was to teach Graham technique or slight variations thereof. They were Graham dancers, and few ever threw off the mantle. Nevertheless, some few had the courage and the energy to go out on their own and try.

The sad line of defectors was long, as with any voluntary organization, but in Martha's case these perfectly natural transitions took on the import of betrayals.

The earliest to leave was her angel girl, Anna Sokolow. She left in 1939 because Martha deliberately interfered with her creativity, scorning her interest in jazz (her husband was Alex North, the modern-jazz composer). Being a true revolutionary, Anna finally broke from the thrall, with bitterness and criticism on both sides. The Graham company and Martha viewed her thereafter with a wary eye, but Anna always thought of Martha as a "gawd." Anna departed with Louis's understanding and support and began composing dances on her own. Then she went to Mexico City, where, at the invitation of the minister of culture, Carlos Merida, she established a modern dance school and theater. When Anna returned to the United States it was not to be with Graham. She never went back to the Graham company, either as a guest artist or teacher.

Dorothy Bird, another of Martha's original troupe who left her in 1937, explained her apparent treachery: "The reason I left her was because if anybody asked me a question I would say, 'Martha thinks . . .' or 'Martha does. . . .' And there was a great big hole where Dorothy was. I was sensible enough at last to recognize this. I had to leave. It took me almost a lifetime to find out why. I believed in her with an almost religious fervor." (Dorothy refused two paying jobs with me because she thought I was either satirizing Martha's work or copying it. I certainly wasn't doing the first, and was doing the second only subconsciously.)

Nina Fonaroff remained for years as a faithful member of the teaching staff, replacing Martha and teaching the Graham classes at Sarah

Lawrence when Martha went on tour. Although Nina was loyal and devoted, like the others she yearned for additional training and so studied ballet with Muriel Stuart.

Merce Cunningham proved the most difficult to replace. Why he left Graham in 1945 was never stated publicly, but surely it was because he felt he must find his own way and the loyalties to Martha were constraining. He came deeply under the influence of the avant-garde composer John Cage. "I wanted Dada, not Mama," said Merce when he left Martha's company. Cunningham's departure was a body blow to Martha's organization.

The most traumatic departure had been, of course, Erick's. But years later Martha said to the Group, "If I can get over the loss of Erick Hawkins, I can get over the loss of anyone. No one is irreplaceable. I have learned that." And she added, "Don't you ever forget it."

John Butler, one of the dancers to take over Erick's roles, never wholly belonged to Martha. He danced intermittently and choreographed for other companies and for his own group. Stuart Hodes, Mark Ryder, Bertram Ross, Robert Cohan, Paul Taylor, Glen Tetley, and later William Carter came and went, most returning on occasion as guest artists for leading solos. Bertram Ross remained constant.

The task of maintaining and replenishing the company involved personal memory. It was emotionally all but unendurable to Martha. But, as it transpired, the work clarified with her explanations; the dances were subtly altered, became sharper and more distinct. Several of the young succeeding leading male dancers had much greater technique than Erick ever did, and more pliable personalities, and they brought to the roles an added strength and color.

Indeed, when new girls replaced Martha in her own roles we were given clues to the intended meaning of the ballets which might otherwise seem obscure.

Mary Hinkson and Bertram Ross remained throughout, stalwart and steadfast. And Martha's little sister, Geordie, now financially totally dependent on Martha, continued to run the school in a mussy and half-inebriated fashion, to the despair of those concerned.

Glen Tetley, not steadfast but forgiven for particular reasons (notably his ability to jump even better than Merce), had first caught Martha's attention in the late forties. Martha was eager to have him because he had a ballet foot and bounded like a deer, with springy, straight, beautiful legs, taking to the air effortlessly. He was of the air.

Tetley interrupted his studies at Franklin and Marshall to serve in the war. Upon his release from the navy in 1945 he started taking medical courses at New York University and at the same time began studying ballet with Helene Platova, Margaret Craske, and Antony Tudor. He practiced wholeheartedly, for he wanted to dance. Tetley was old to start dancing, but he was so gifted, so naturally able, that, like Igor Youskevitch and Harald Kreutzberg, both of whom started late, he rose to the top of his profession in a matter of three or four years. He began to study harder—ballet from Platova and modern dance from Hanya Holm, who took him in as a protégé, permitting him free sleeping room in her studio and free tutelage in all her classes. He also took lessons at N.Y.U. from Martha Hill, and through her, in 1947, he met Martha Graham.

Without any preamble Martha made a direct approach. "Come over at seven o'clock at night to the school at 611 Fifth Avenue when classes are over." As Glen tells it, "I was mesmerized. In the office when I arrived it was very dark. She kept her eyes down. She spoke very slowly, softly, and she said, 'I want you to come and study with me. I want you to be a member of my company.' Well, this was astounding to me."

Martha was, in Tetley's words, "a remarkable combination of goddess and courtesan." He added:

When I was a young dancer, like all young dancers I was terrified in the presence of Martha. It seemed to be overwhelming. It was clear that she was intuitive, that she seemed to know far more about you than you wanted anyone to know.

I have always been enamored of Martha. When I think back on the early days when I first saw her company, I thought I was seeing a revelation. Time stopped for me. I could not believe what I was seeing. Those works are engraved on my brain, my mind, my heart. I've never forgotten, never, the atmosphere on stage, the lighting . . . the use of props, the use of costume . . . the strongest, simplest, most powerful theater I think I've ever seen.

So when she invited me to join the company I was terribly torn. I had no money, and Hanya had been incredibly generous to me. . . . She was jealous of Martha and would barely speak to her.

But Tetley, although torn, was loyal. His first duty obviously was to Hanya, and because of all he owed her, Tetley reluctantly declined Martha's offer. He did, however, secretly and without Hanya's knowledge, study with Graham. Hanya placed him on Broadway in several of her shows, and he assisted her in *Kiss Me, Kate* (1948) and *Out of This World* (1950), which I directed. There followed an extraordinary period of work with Ballet Theatre and with Robert Joffrey. Glen was a leading dancer in Joffrey's first touring company, dancing eight performances a week and traveling by bus. When he returned from touring in 1958 he was so exhausted with ballet that he went straight to the Graham school, found Geordie at the office desk, and said, "Geordie, I've come home. I want to be taken back."

Then followed a wonderful period of blessed study and rehearsal. Glen recounted:

When I used to come to that morning class, it seemed the most beautiful space in the world. It was quiet in there. In some perfect way you brought your whole life in with you . . . it had a physical, spiritual balance. It was inspiring . . . like prayer. Everything was opening up, releasing you . . . not like a ballet class at all. I had gotten so bogged down . . . with too much performance. . . . "There's something in you," Martha said to me. "It's changing and I see it. I see it growing." This made me very happy . . . I took three classes a day, some in the morning with Martha. I had injured my left knee from dancing too hard and it was swollen like a hot-water bottle. I couldn't do a grand plié, and Martha . . . not only made me believe in dancing again but she gave me back my technique. . . . She said, "You mustn't think that the plié is an exercise for the knee: it's a total bodily function." And the moment I took my mind off the knee and started using the whole body all my trouble stopped.

Martha later said she didn't know where *Clytemnestra* came from. The music was by an Egyptian composer, Halim El-Dabh; the settings were by Noguchi; the costumes by Martha and Helen McGehee. She said to me, "It has no antecedents, no roots. It is like an orchid blooming in the air, a parasite on my own life."

I believe the key is in the last scene of the work, the vision of the dead, guilty queen, lost and roaming forever through Hades, striking herself repeatedly with funeral branches. It is poetic, it is beautiful, and it is tragic. It haunts us lastingly. And just there, I believe, is where the ballet came from. Martha was enduring the bitterest of all human emotions: remorse.

Clytemnestra was composed in 1958, a full-length ballet. It explores, with ample comments from various interfering gods, the tragic story of Clytemnestra, the unfaithful queen of Agamemnon. During her husband's long absence in the Trojan War, and with the conniving help of the cuckolding rival, Aegisthus, she plots and then executes the king's murder immediately upon his return. The king's two children, Orestes and Electra, kill Aegisthus and their treacherous mother, Clytemnestra, in revenge.

Bertram Ross told me:

Rehearsals were going wonderfully well. In the beginning she [Martha] was on top of everything and the work was wonderfully stimulating. She had strong images. We were working on the rape of Troy when suddenly she had to stop choreographing and go to Germany to perform *Judith* (her original solo) at the opening of the Ben Franklin Hall in Berlin. She really had been on a roll, but the rhythm of creation was snapped by the German trip, never to be picked up again. Bob Cohan had suddenly left the company because he had been cast as the villain Aegisthus. He explained to me that knowing how Martha worked, that she created the same situation in real life as in her plays, he didn't want Martha thinking of him as a villain.

Martha had not wanted to play repertory at the Adelphi but hoped to open *Clytemnestra* like a Broadway show and run it for as long as it could bring in audiences. This proved impractical at the Adelphi, although *Clytemnestra* was a recognized success.

Anna Kisselgoff wrote of *Clytemnestra* in 1984:

Here is the ritual drama acted out to its fullest. The story of the Oresteia, transposed to a nearly wordless pageant, takes on a full ceremonial cast in Miss Graham's treatment. The tale is familiar. How it is told, and how it will affect us, is all that matters. . . . Miss Graham's 1958 masterpiece uses cinematic techniques of flashback and her own narrative devices in which one person plays several characters or one character is depicted by more than one person. . . . The action, or rather vision, is a projection of Clytemnestra's mind. This is typical Graham. A towering figure, in a moment of crisis, looks back upon the crucial moments of her life. . . . By the time we have sorted out the characters in the first act, Miss Graham is ready to tell her story in relatively linear terms in the next two acts. Even so, the beauty of her chronology is that it is never pat, there is always time for an eruption from those wonderful grotesque Furies, hurtling their distorted bodies through the air.

Jean Rosenthal was responsible for the lighting, and it was a work of art and has been so characterized by other master electricians—Thomas Skelton, for one. Bertram Ross, who played Orestes, spoke of the times he stood onstage and watched the lights travel up the columns on either side of the proscenium arch, the poles of lights right to the roof: "It was like a dance, fading in, fading out. You could not really see the changes. It was very musical—like choreography, matchless." This "matchless" work was achieved by a woman who was mortally ill. Jean Rosenthal had cancer.

In the same season Martha also created *Embattled Garden,* a study of Lilith, Adam and Eve, and the snake in the Garden of Eden, to music of Carlos Surinach. A program note reads: "Love, it has been said, does not obey the rules of love but yields to some more ancient and ruder law. The Garden of Eden seems always to be threatened by the Stranger's knowledge of the world outside and by the old knowledge of those like Lilith (according to legend, Adam's wife before Eve) who lived there first."

Noguchi's design for *Embattled Garden* called for, by way of flooring, a raked platform, steeply tipped, containing large holes. One of the wry uses Martha found for this prop was the abrupt manner in which the men, growing weary of the women's vagaries and whinings, simply dropped them down the holes, a conclusive way of terminating any domestic argument.

Yuriko played Eve, and Glen Tetley was cast as the snake, a replacement for the defecting Robert Cohan.

With about a quarter of the ballet remaining to be composed, Martha seemed to meet a block. She left the work in the rehearsal hands of the performers.

Glen Tetley recounted the sorry story:

One night she came in and she leaned against the back wall of the studio. She didn't speak to us. The ballet started, with Yuriko sitting, combing her hair. I was up in a Noguchi tree as the serpent. I did a huge jump down into the Garden of Eden and all but raped the girl, and the ballet started. Martha watched about four minutes of this and started to scream with mounting force and vehemence—"No, no, no, NO, NO!" And we all stopped and she said, "I *will* not have sentimentality on *my* stage." And she pointed her finger at Yuriko. She said, "You are sentimental. You don't know about the Garden of Eden. There was no sentiment there. You give me that comb, and Glen, you get back up in that tree, and *I'll* do Eve and we'll start the ballet over."

Martha was in her street clothes, and she took Yuriko's place. Her hair was in a big bun. I was timid about doing such rough movement with her, but I jumped down, and she came to me and before I could grab her she grabbed me around the body and thrust her pelvis up against me, and literally driving me we scuttled across the floor. Her hair came down; she stood up with finality and said, *"That* is the Garden of Eden."

On the whole, however, notwithstanding this satisfactory rape, Martha was largely absent from rehearsals. She practically disowned the work, not attending the lighting rehearsal, nor even the full dress rehearsal. Both Yuriko and Glen called Bertram Ross before they premiered, Yuriko in tears, saying, "You're the only one close enough to Martha to speak to her. Beg her to cancel." Glen felt totally abandoned, and he was furious. He thought Martha had deserted him purposefully to get him so angry that she would force a good performance out of him.

Anna Kisselgoff wrote of *Embattled Garden* in 1984:

. . . "Embattled" is the key word in the title. Miss Graham gives an eternal story an original twist. Lilith and the serpent are the intruders in this domestic bliss, conspiring to disrupt the relationship of the other pair. Miss Graham turns this situation into a sly suburban soap opera with hints of wife-swapping. . . . Comedy has not been Miss Graham's forte, but here she hits home runs by turning the silliness of human foibles into moral verities.

Around this time, Glen Tetley recounts,

One night Martha asked Paul Taylor and me to stay after classes and rehearsal. She was dressed in a beautiful kimono and she came in and closed the door and said, "I want you both to go over and place your right hand on the barre and I want you to take second position and I want you to do a slow grand plié. I'm asking you to put your right hand on the barre because I have to watch your left side. The left side is the heart side, and I can only see from the heart side. The carriage of your head is very important. It must be lifted almost as if something were elevating your ears and you released the animal brain back here, so that your movement is totally strong and male. There was a period of dance when the woman was put on the pedestal and the male was denigrated to this position of looking up at her all the time. No, I want you to be animal and male." I was dazzled by this. She finished and did her Oriental bow and turned quietly and walked about six feet away, and I thought, "The goddess! The mother of God! Yes!" And Paul Taylor said, steadily and quietly, "What a pile of shit!"
Martha stopped dead in her tracks and then she continued out. I said,

"Paul, how can you say that?" and he replied, "Well, that's what it is. Why can't she just say keep your back straight and your chin up?"

There had begun to be rifts in the magic spell.

|||||

It was after the season at the Adelphi that Bethsabee wanted to bring the first full-length modern dance company to Israel to open at the Habima Theater and run it as one would a play for a week—exactly what had been Martha's original intent.

One night before departing, Glen Tetley went to the Sixty-third Street studio to work on his role and found Martha alone, packing costumes, tired, mussy, disheveled, the first time he had ever seen her in an unkempt condition—the only time on record that she has been so discovered.

"If you want to get things done right you have to do them yourself," she said, brushing back a wisp of fallen hair and rolling her sleeves higher. "Craig Barton has done nothing and Bethsabee [who was serving not only as Martha's treasury, but as her wardrobe mistress] has not helped. I have to do it all. Every bit of it. I am making out the customs lists, the inventories, I'm packing the trunks. I'm choreographing. I'm having to construct the costumes." She was just throwing things around. She would run into the little kitchen and grab a piece of cheese and munch on it.

"I'll help," said Glen, taking off his coat. Up to that point, he said, he had thought of her as a goddess. Now he fell in love with her afresh, as a hard-working, simple woman. After the long stint with the trunks and the lists, they went into the rehearsal room and finished off a hunk of choreography. It was after midnight.

Martha said, "I'm getting infirm. I'm getting arthritic and I have to accept it. I have these terrible hands. But I'm not going to hide them; I'm going to use them." Martha's hands had become gnarled stumps that she could neither open freely nor close tight. She could hold a pen only by inserting it with the left hand into her right knuckle. She made no excuses for the infirmity. She deliberately forced these hands on the audience when, at the beginning of *Clytemnestra,* she walked downstage and thrust them out. That was her first movement. And so superbly did she do it that many thought it a stylized gesture, displaying the tools of the murderer. While preparing the role she had a barre and a mirror placed in her apartment, and she said to Glen Tetley, "I hate looking at myself but I am going to, every morning for an hour. I'm going to look at myself as I am."

Martha took two programs to Israel: I: *Clytemnestra;* II: *Seraphic Dialogue, Embattled Garden, Night Journey.* Since Glen Tetley was in only *Embattled Garden,* Martha asked him if he would be a spear-carrier in *Clytemnestra.* He refused, but later yielded, agreeing to do the walk-on if his face could be covered.

Clytemnestra had been a very difficult ballet for her to conceive and realize, and was extremely difficult to dance. She thereafter spoke of being in a state of great restlessness, even sleeplessness when it was on the program, and always before a performance she had a night of dreams with a sense of ominous foreboding; she seemed to suffer a kind of pain, to be like a snake shedding its skin. She knew great apprehension and dread and in this broth of uncertainty and misery, in this stressful mood, she readied herself for the three-hour performance requiring every atom of intensity and energy that she was capable of summoning, going to the theater hours before curtain-rise to prepare herself.

It was during the performances in Haifa that she wrote to Mrs. Wickes that she felt a stirring within herself of a new work. She was gestating something entirely different while enduring the birth pangs of this immense tragedy.

||||

Erick Hawkins went on doggedly giving concerts, in spite of poor press and little public response. He tended to be obtuse. For example, his publicity release for his new work, *Here and Now with Watchers* (1957), contained this explanation:

We have tried to be here and we have tried to be now, something every poet really tries . . . only then is there hope for that subtle shape in time which is movement rhythm and not translation of some other kind of rhythm. . . .
The dancers created to rediscover sources of immediacy in pure movement, movement without a story, that communicates to a watcher the pleasure of a kinesthetic sensation. To achieve this the choreography employs the device of allowing no more than two dancers on the stage at any one time and with this economy and concentration emphasizing the intensity of movement itself.

To many watchers he apparently did no such thing.
In October 1965, John Martin wrote in *The New York Times:*

Hawkins seems very much of a hot weather choreographer. His movements stretch out with lazy languor, the mood is cloudless, the atmosphere bland, yet nothing in a very positive sense actually happens.

Martha still grieved. We do not know whether or not she saw Erick. She herself continued to compose like a force of nature.

I n 1956 the director Nathan Kroll had approached Martha with the idea of making a documentary film on her techniques. Kroll had been wonderfully successful in making similar films with Pablo Casals, Andrés Segovia, Jascha Heifetz, Joan Sutherland, and Luciano Pavarotti, as well as a ninety-minute documentary on Helen Hayes, but Martha was reluctant, even apprehensive of going near a camera, and she kept refusing.

When Kroll first broached the subject, she immediately called Louis Horst, who knew Kroll as a violinist. Louis responded somewhat tartly, "Don't bother me with nonsense. He's a good artist. If he wants to do something, do it. Help him." But Martha was still hesitant.

After about a year and a half of discussion, making plans, breaking plans, postponing, Kroll had persuaded Martha to collaborate to the extent that she would permit her technique to be photographed, with her star dancers performing class exercises, and she would comment. She herself was not to dance. Her voice only would be recorded, with films of her as she spoke. This was to be the first authentic statement she had made which could be broadcast and perpetuated, and it was from every point of view important. As an educational tool it would prove invaluable.

Kroll then set about raising the money to make the film. It would take $20,000—not much for a film, but a considerable sum for him to lay his hands on. He did so in conjunction with John White, Channel Thirteen's first president, who was at Case Western Reserve University in Cleveland, and then with WQED in Pittsburgh, one of two national educational TV stations functioning in the United States at that time, before moving to New York. White agreed to put up the bulk of the money. Nathan's wife, Lucy Kroll, mortgaged their house. They got to work.*

As soon as Martha was with the cameramen and the equipment, she changed from a reluctant doubter into the most avid student. She wanted to know everything about the camera lens. She looked through it. She planned shots. She took instruction. She made innovative suggestions. She was a wonderful, eager collaborator, a pupil, an artist. The work progressed brilliantly, and they began to get footage that was truly miraculous, the first of its kind, a successful capturing of movement on film, preserving its full value.

The film was done at last, and they were all well pleased. It was now time to photograph Martha speaking. Immediately she lost her professionalism. She lost all interest in the results. She lost her skill—even the skills she had known the whole of her adult life and had practiced more brilliantly than anyone else. She was like a beginner stricken with stage fright, rendered inept.

Once again, as in the frightful first abortive season in London in 1950, Martha faced exposure. She was as frightened of films as Isadora had been. Isadora had frankly refused ever in her life to face a camera. Martha knew of the living difference between three-dimensional gesture and the power of presence and the life force, and the strange, disassociated world, almost submarine, that film, for all its great technique, imposed. Although she had been willing to take advice and act on the suggestion of experts, changing, correcting, altering the work itself, when it came to her own participation Martha felt stripped of

*The first Graham documentaries, *A Dancer's World* and *Appalachian Spring*, were funded by Channel Thirteen. The third Graham film, *Night Journey*, was paid for by Bethsabee de Rothschild.

protection. With a living audience she knew she had magic, and she could rely on the love and excitement of the unseen, waiting faces, the tremendous group power. This was always a source for Martha both of comfort and of vital strength. But a camera was a dead machine. The operators might encourage her to pretend she was talking to a friend, or talking to a student, or talking to an audience. She believed nothing of the sort, and she was fearful. The moment the cameras were placed, she hung onto the barre, clung to the walls. She couldn't think what to do with her hands, with her robes, with her feet. Her face grew lined with tension. She finally did what she had done in London. She bolted. She went into the dressing room and locked the door.

The entire crew waited. The last bit of money was at stake on this final footage, and the crew was working on overtime. They were sorry that she was having hysterics, and perhaps they sympathized, but they also counted up their earnings as the clock ticked. She would not come out of her hiding place.

Lee Leatherman got down on the floor and put his mouth to the crack under the door and begged, pleaded with her, explained what they were going to do, explained why they must proceed, how much the delay was costing. Not a sound. Lee begged "like a puppy," said Nathan Kroll. Lucy Kroll was beside him. Martha outwaited them. They finally folded up their paraphernalia, shook hands with Lee, and departed. Nathan Kroll left in absolute despair, two years of effort and $20,000 wasted. Craig went home, Lee went home. Then Martha came out and stole away to her apartment.

This was the second time in Martha's life that she had gone into a total funk and simply run from the bullets. Great artists seldom do this, no matter what the cost. Martha did.

Kroll was left with a magnificent remnant. Lee and Craig were helpless. They kept repeating, "She says she won't; she says she can't possibly." So Kroll went to Bethsabee de Rothschild and asked her to put up the money to finish the film. He set up a screen at Bethsabee's house and ran the footage for her, and she was enchanted and impressed. But Martha remained adamant. Kroll then sent for John Houseman, who had worked with Martha in the thirties and whom she respected. On seeing the film, he said to Kroll, "Nathan, do you realize what you have? You have got some of the most beautiful dance film I have ever seen in my whole life."

After a great deal of persuasion, Houseman agreed to go to Martha. He cozened her and petted her and soothed her and persuaded her that she could risk this, if a way were found to make it comfortable and safe for her. The men put their heads together and decided to have Martha in a dressing room, sitting at a dressing table, making up, with her familiar paraphernalia in her hands to give her something to do. (Imagine Martha, the greatest inventor of movement in the world, having to have props put into her hands to keep her from looking self-conscious!) Bethsabee gave $10,000, enough to finish the film. Nathan hired a studio, they mocked up a dressing room, and Martha talked to the mirror—the audience in the mirror, herself in the mirror. She powdered her nose and stuck Jocasta's great gold pins through her hair and put on Jocasta's gold collar and bracelets. And then, her dresser having brought in her robes, Martha ended her little speech, left the dressing table, crossed the room, and stood at the door ready to enter the stage and face the lights and the audience. It was effective and beautiful. Martha had made a record of her work which was worthy.

The film had its premiere in Pittsburgh, Martha's birthplace, or near enough to claim part of the glory. Martha attended, and the evening was a triumph.

After the success of *A Dancer's World,* as the film was called, in Pittsburgh, Leland Hasard, the head of WQED and an executive of Pittsburgh Plate Glass (and also an amateur medieval scholar of considerable erudition) took fire and agreed to help with the financing of two more films: *Appalachian Spring,* danced by Martha and Stuart Hodes, and *Night Journey,* with Martha and Bertram Ross.

The films were beautifully made. Nathan Kroll was a musician, and he had studied the scores with an expert eye. He had also consulted with Louis Horst, who had conducted the first performance of *Appalachian Spring* and translated all of Aaron Copland's wishes exactly. Kroll understood the music, and so he was able to phrase and cut the film as both the composer and the choreographer wished. When Nathan had gone to Louis for his initial analysis of camera angles in relation to the score, he'd offered to pay for Horst's time, at which Louis, quite characteristically, laughed in scorn. "You are a musician and an artist," he said. "Don't be silly. Naturally, I will not charge you."

|||||

In 1959 George Balanchine asked Graham to compose a work for his New York City Ballet. He suggested that each of them utilize six pieces by Webern, the two sets to be played in sequence, Balanchine's, which he confidently hoped would be the stronger of the two, following

Graham's. It was a most unexpected, even bizarre, request, considering Balanchine's well-known scorn for the modern dance and Lincoln Kirstein's inveterate hatred of it. It must be borne in mind, however, that in the theater Graham was now the hottest avant-garde news. There is no question that Balanchine and Kirstein believed they had control of the situation.

Martha chose a dramatic subject: Mary, Queen of Scots, and her mortal struggle with Elizabeth of England. Balanchine's sections consisted of abstract pieces, danced in Karinska's nondescript shifts. The two parts were linked by a pretty scenic device, but otherwise were unconnected, except that they shared the same composer.

When she was finished, Graham showed her work to Balanchine and Kirstein, dancing the lead herself, whereupon Balanchine insisted that she perform with her company, with Bertram Ross as Bothwell, and Akiko Kanda, Helen McGehee, Linda Hodes, Gene McDonald, and Richard Kuch in supporting roles. Balanchine added, "I want that woman [Graham] to come and teach my dancers how to move." She considered very soberly before agreeing to the performance. The teaching invitation was not unpleasant: it was a gigantic step for her—to dance in a ballet company with a strange cast trained in an alien technique. As it turned out, however, she used mostly her own company, with only a few City Ballet dancers. Opposite her as the English queen was the young Sallie Wilson, with two ballet boys, Paul Nickel and William Carter, flanking her, holding standards.

The undertaking represented an adventure with many hazards. To begin with there was the music. Webern's "Six Pieces" is difficult, unmelodic, undramatic, each piece seemingly unrelated to the others.

"This is impossible!" Martha exclaimed at one early rehearsal, according to William Carter. "She raised her fist and *bam!*, thrust it on the piano. The whole studio reverberated with the sound, and I thought 'God! That woman has power that I didn't even know existed.' "

She continued, "This music wasn't made for dance, wasn't intended for dance, and it should never be used for dance." She overcame her dislike because she had to, having agreed to the project, but it was very hard.

She read a great deal of history in preparing the role of Mary, and her notebooks are full of quotes from Stefan Zweig's biography of the ill-fated queen: "Mary prepared for her exit from life, as one prepares for a festival, a triumph, a grand ceremony. . . . With an unmoved countenance Mary entered the hall . . . she mounted the two steps to the scaffold. Thus, proudly, when a girl of fifteen, she had ascended the throne of France. . . . . On no one (however much the books & reports may lie about the matter) can the execution of a human being produce a romantic & touching impression. Always death by the executioner's axe must be a horrible spectacle of slaughter—"

Martha used the two queens vis-à-vis, which is contrary to historical fact (half the length of England always separated them). Her queens were mounted on small platforms on either side of the stage, their ceremonial gowns displayed on great structures, farthingales and hoops capable of standing alone like shells, out of which the dancing queens could slide and perform freely, giving themselves passionately to the moment and leaving the entire regalia of their august protocol empty behind them. The dramatic climax was achieved when the royal women engaged in a kind of early-style tennis match, rigidly facing front and playing obliquely off the adjacent figure in a highly stylized manner reminiscent of a Japanese Nōh drama. On each wave of each racket, each indication that the shuttlecock had fluttered between them, hung the fate of kingdoms.

Either Antony Tudor, Martha's colleague on the Juilliard School faculty, or her medical doctor, Amos B. Cobert, who was also Sallie Wilson's doctor, had advised Martha to cast Wilson as Elizabeth. Two years earlier she had come to New York City Ballet from Ballet Theater, which had temporarily suspended activities after a fire had destroyed the bulk of their company's costumes and music. As Sallie had no modern technique, Balanchine sent her to Graham for special rehearsals.

Sallie Wilson recalled:

On Sunday I rang the doorbell and I waited a long time, and then I heard through the door a pushing sound. The door opened and there she was, alone, in her black practice gown, and she said, "You're Sallie Wilson?" And I followed her without another word down a long hall to a huge empty studio with low tables, about four inches from the floor. Sitting down on one of those, she sat next to me and stared and stared at me in silence for a long time. And she then said softly, "I am terrified of you." And I didn't know what she meant, and I didn't know what to say. But she started talking quietly, in a hushed voice, about Queen Elizabeth and Mary Stuart and talked and talked and put me at ease. She evoked images for me, fascinating and dramatic. Then she said, "Would you like to try some movement?" I had never danced barefoot. I had on a pair of old toe shoes, but the floor was too slippery so I took them off.

What she was terrified of was that I wouldn't be able to do anything that she gave me and that she would have to modify her movement to what she thought a ballet dancer could do, although I begged her, implored her, to show me exactly what she wanted and let me try. But she kept trying to accommodate me. One day I heard a gasp, and someone said, "Look at the articulation in her back!" Magic words! Bert Ross immediately started teaching me spirals down to the floor. Everyone relaxed. I was one of them. I imagine my training with Tudor had been very pure. I was trained to work with a choreographer who would give the exact style of what he wanted. I think I could work with Graham easily because I tried to see exactly what she was asking me to do without any preconceived idea. And that's why dancers today are hard to work with. They'll do it their way, the way they learned it in class, and it has nothing to do with the choreographer's idea.

The Webern music was difficult but not obscure to me. I could understand what she was doing to the music. She helped me as a dramatic dancer. She contributed to the weight of my movement. For instance, she showed me how to throw my skirt and sit with finality. I had one of the most beautiful entrances in show business. I was seated hidden in a column on a throne at the back of the column, facing away from the audience. Through the whole first half I held my costume close so that none of it would show from the front. Then, on cue, the executioner turned my throne around so that my gold costume fell open, and I made only one small hand gesture, which was powerful because nothing else on stage moved. The executioner gave me his shoulder as support and I stood up and descended a long flight of stairs, sideways, facing the audience, like an escalator, step by step, and when I reached the bottom, then and only then I started my first contraction. This style was nonrealistic, ritualistic, almost like the Grand Kabuki, particularly in the tennis match. Whenever we faced the audience, all movement stopped and held, the facial expression was frozen, no emotion was directed toward the other actor, and the effect was deadly.

One day we halted rehearsal early and Martha took me to the costumer's atelier to see what was going on. Barbara Karinska (probably the most famous costume executive in the world) had made the foundation, boned from the crotch to the chin, and it was authentic all right, but I couldn't move. Tears came to my eyes; I was in an iron maiden. Martha just sat there and smiled and said, "Oh, Madame Karinska, that's just incredible! It is authentic. Sallie, dear, do some of your movements." And, of course, I couldn't. Then she said, patting Karinska's hand, "You've done a beautiful job, Madame Karinska." And we packed up and left.

She gathered the whole company together and in sepulchral tones announced, "Catastrophe! This is awful. We must all pray." And there was a minute of silence while we concentrated. And she said to Helen McGehee and Ethel Winter, "Let's go look. We must have an old costume."

And we found one of those beautiful jersey things with the legs wrapped up so it always covered no matter how high you kick. Madame Karinska copied this. Attached at the hips was brocade with jewels on it suggesting a farthingale, but not heavy, beautifully balanced. Its light horsehair collar weighed nothing. It was so finely constructed and so flat that I didn't even know that it was on my neck. The dress was made of fourteen-carat-gold-sprayed jersey with not a bone in it, costing one thousand dollars—at that time an enormous sum. And I had a crown that was made of boning that floated. It was the lightest costume that I have ever seen, and it had absolutely the feeling of the period. And that's Martha's genius, no one else's, absolutely unbelievable. And Karinska thought she herself had designed it. That's also Martha's genius. Martha contrived she should, not wishing to negate her. Martha was in black, and there was the suggestion of the iron construction of a farthingale that stood by itself made of heavy buckram. Inside she had on a little white nightgown. Later, for her execution, she put on a blood-red overdress. [This was historically accurate.]

Episodes had its premiere on May 14, 1959, at the City Center. When Martha appeared onstage the entire audience rose, which was unexpected at the beginning of a ballet. It rose again at the end. Balanchine was rewarded with nothing like this for his part of the production.

At the conclusion of the first evening, Martha and John Butler waited for the thanks of the management in the dressing room she had shared with Melissa Hayden. The dressing table was littered with all of Melissa's make-up and pair after pair of pointe shoes, their ribbons dangling and their toes darned; and overhead hung the inverted tutus, their fluffy, flowerlike corollas forming a small canopy. Martha and John waited in vain, for neither Kirstein nor Balanchine came back to say a word. Not one. John took Martha out for a lonely supper. This exact behavior was repeated at the end of the run, when Martha had been given an ovation onstage. Their dresser, Ducky, an old Cockney, called Martha "Miss Show Biz." "I sure am glad someone has come into this theater at last who knows what the stage is for," he said. Messrs. Balanchine and Kirstein remained tacit. Not a word from the bosses. It was unprecedented conduct.

But the management requested her section the next year. Martha repeated it, using Wilson's growing mastery of Graham technique, and Wilson herself claims she was much better in the role the second year.

Martha gave Wilson a very beautiful Japanese carved bead, signed by the artist and containing a golden capsule on a golden chain. Wilson recalled, "She was understanding and wonderful to me. And I must say I was a very good pupil."*

Wilson says she was not nervous at the opening performance:

I remember great excitement, a great sense of the importance of the moment, but I was calm and cool. My foot was sure on the stage. Nor was Martha nervous. Not that I would ever know. She was marvelous to play with. It was my business to match her intensity, which, of course, I could not approximate. But there was nothing to be nervous about. I was very happy then. It never occurred to me to destroy myself with nerves. Although the ballet was devised so that Mary was the dominant figure even though the victim, and the second girl was Elizabeth, you didn't evaluate that. The only important thing was what we were doing, and it was my job to stand against her and fight her. I gave that my entire attention and heart.

Jane Dudley had said the same about her own experience onstage with Graham:

You never felt that, great as she was, she ever upstaged you, or that there was a lack of relationship between you and her while she was onstage with you. There was therefore no sense of nervousness or anxiety or unnatural responsibility. Everything settled into place because, I believe, the stage was where Martha was at home. That was her proper sphere of action.

Graham's performance as Mary Stuart was indeed superb, from the very beginning of the introduction to the moment when she placed her own head as a gift on the block; but all the time her feet were in very great pain from arthritis. She could hardly stand or walk and yet she danced.

|||||

She never considered a piece finished, and she called rehearsal the day after each premiere and redid and altered and changed. Sometimes she did this onstage following an opening.

*Later Sallie performed in Glen Tetley's *Sargasso,* which was largely Graham move-ment. Martha went to the first performance and visited backstage afterward, limping badly and leaning heavily on her doctor's arm. She said, loud enough for everyone to hear, "Oh, Sallie, I'm so glad to have had a piece of you." "She was darling. I grew enormously under her," said Sallie.

Performing with Martha in *Episodes* was a changing experience for William Carter. He was holding Elizabeth's standard, and only two feet away from Martha Graham—the woman he had heard about all his life. He had been told about Graham by Carmalita Maracci, with whom he had studied in California. He said, "As you know, Carmalita was gifted verbally. For years she talked about this woman, about her fierceness, her passion, her creativity, her devotion, her dedication, until Graham came to represent to me a genius of the first order, someone who backed with her life all her belief in dance, who never compromised, who was that unique thing: a dedicated artist. When I finally found myself next to this woman it was like a dream, because simply and plainly I worshiped her." The feeling intensified with exposure and practice.

During the rehearsals Carter had ample opportunity to study Martha. Over the years she had not learned to curb her temper one bit. One is forced to conclude she didn't wish to. Carter went on:

The other standard bearer, Rusty [Paul] Nickel, was late for the dress rehearsal on the day of the performance, and Martha came up to him and rammed him with her hand, pulled him to her so that his face was opposite hers, inches away, and she said, "If you're late once more to this rehearsal, I'll *kill* you!" and she went "Hah!"—making a sound that I'd never heard before.

I thought to myself, "My God! That's a brutality that's so primitive, so far back, I don't even know where it comes from, the eons of history that go back to a primitive fierceness like that. And she could kill." I understand. I too have a bad temper. Once she took me aside and she said, "Look, I don't ever want to see you display that kind of fierceness in my studio again." She looked me hard in the eyes and said, "I have a temper that could make you look like an amateur. But the point is, young man, and I want you to understand this, a temper is a good thing, but you have to know how to use it and use it to your advantage, certainly not by wasting it like that." I don't think she ever wasted a gesture or an action. I think everything she did was motivated by a tenacity to do what she wanted to do. Nothing was spontaneous or without motivation to her own advantage.

I think that of all the people I've known in my life, she represented the most distinct contradiction, an absolute, unbelievable opposition—great strength and power of love and generosity, and an ability to annihilate. These passions didn't show at the same time but consecutively.

Yet Bill Carter loved her.

Martha believed in Bill. She wanted him to dance Erick's old roles in *Letter to the World* and later in *Appalachian Spring.* He tells of reviving *Appalachian Spring* in 1973, after an absence of thirteen years. (Bertram Ross had done the role of the husband in England, but never in America.) Bill learned Erick's dances from film and then auditioned for Martha:

We were alone in the studio with the pianist, and she came in and I began the dance which had been Erick's. I remember distinctly how her head sank into both her hands, and she just put her hands over her face and she shook her head. She shook her head with her head bowed. And after she had composed herself she said, "Excuse me, darling. I had no idea that this would affect me the way it does, but, you see, I was very much in love with the man who did that dance, and to see it again now is something I can't bear." And she left. I got word from her later that she would like to compose another dance for me to substitute for the original so intimately associated with Erick.

Three days later at rehearsal she said, "Now, let's hear the music." She started listening to the music, and I remember she rose. She was crippled, although not to the extent she became later. She listened with fierceness. Her whole body seemed to change. Then she said, "Let's begin like this." And she entered from the piano to the center of the floor, transformed. She was no longer crippled, and she *danced.* And this is the truth. She danced the whole first section, my solo, absolutely new. It had never been done. She just did it at that moment. Unbelievable! And incredibly beautiful, musical, forceful, meaningful. She edited it the next day and it was finished in three days. But she never again moved as she had done that time. After that first day she would suggest things verbally and use her upper body and her torso, but she couldn't really rise from the chair.

In common with most young men who came into contact with her, Carter was purely enchanted, and he turned to Martha at moments of anguish, of which he had not a few; and she succored him in an almost biblical sense. He joined the Graham company in 1973.

Once in a rehearsal [for *Mendicants of Evening*] she took my face in her hands and told me that I would be great. At that particular time, shortly after my mother had had a grave stroke, I was in agony as to whether to stay in New York or go to California. I told Martha that I felt that there was no need for me to be in New York. I had terrible doubts, terrible misgivings, terrible uncertainties, as to the necessity of my being in New York at all when there was someone I loved deeply, with all my heart, in great need and alone. Martha put her hands on my face and said to me, "You don't realize what your gifts are! You don't understand. You have talent that is one in ten million. I know you have the possibilities to be a great dancer. Believe me," she said. "I know." She gave me the courage to stay.

She'd call me in the middle of the night to give me courage. . . . She phoned for my sake. But at the same time, since I was a part of her company, and since at that time she had big plans for me, she did wish to strengthen me; had I not been someone who she felt was going to be useful to her, she possibly might not have been so generous; her compassion, her love and her willingness might not have been so available, her caring, her calling up at 4:00 A.M., or letting me call when I felt I would have to reach out to someone.

Not only did she give me the courage to stay, but she gave me the money to go to California on four different weekends. To go and come back, go and come back, four different times. But I'm not stupid. Her whole life attests to the fact that she always acts with self-interest. In the meantime, we are bewitched.

Obviously, those Martha enthralled were not all lovers, not even close friends, and many were not in her profession but rather were artists in allied lines of work. Among these was Horton Foote, the playwright, a modest, unassuming, charming Texan who lived a retiring and private life with his wife and four children. In the course of his progress he won two Oscars and two Writer's Guild awards and other notable prizes. During their Neighborhood Playhouse collaborations he plainly grew to worship Martha. He told about first meeting her during the war:

I've never known anything quite like it, and I've met a lot of wonderful performers in my life. . . . She made you feel as if you could take on the world. . . . I've never been so charmed in my life. She acted as though it were a great privilege to work with me. With me! Imagine! . . . She could have had anything I had. . . . I've never fallen so totally for anybody in my life. On what level I still don't know. If she had said, "Walk across the desert in bare feet on burning coals," I'd have said, "Indeed, I will." . . . And if she had said, "Come tonight and bring your pajamas and don't bore me," . . . I would have loved it, I think. I think I would have. . . . I might have been a little frightened of that.

In the production I did with Martha at the Playhouse, Jean Rosenthal took care of the lighting, and Martha spared herself absolutely nothing in effort or time, although it was a single private performance for students with just a few invited professionals.

After rehearsals we would get on a bus and we would ride together downtown to our homes. She would talk to me as if she'd known me forever.

Horton and Martha worked together for over ten years. "In a memorial meeting for Stark Young, Martha got up without a note, with nothing in her hand, the theater was packed, and she held this theater spellbound for about fifty minutes. It was unforgettable."

||||

Three of Martha's pieces were filmed by John Butler in the color studios of *The Bell Telephone Hour* in Brooklyn. Martha had refused to go before the cameras or let any of her work be filmed unless Butler took charge. He finally consented to do three—*Cortege of Eagles, Seraphic Dialogue,* and *Acrobats of God*—only if Martha refrained from drinking, which she did. She was cold sober throughout. They finished on a Saturday night. The filming had been arduous. She gathered all the technicians, cameramen, electricians, and grips and told them her chief gratitude went to John, who had performed so splendidly, with such knowledge and expertise, in his capacity as film director. She vowed she would be eternally grateful. John accompanied her to her dressing room and she thanked him again personally. Then she invited him to come to her the following day, which was a Sunday. She was giving a birthday party in the garden. John said he loved her dearly, but that he was exhausted and longed to turn into a vegetable. He hoped to go to the country and simply collapse. She drew back her hand and clouted him across the face, hard, a direct blow, then turned on her heel and slammed the door.

Martha had to be the principle friend, the central, vital, focal point in anyone's life. She had to be reassured of this and the slightest, the most reasonable rebuff maddened her.

||||

By the early 1960s, Martha had reached a kind of plateau. She was regularly turning out good works. They were not landmark pieces, and they did not make history, either in her personal progress or in her métier, but they were good. In these years there were always new pieces, as well as several major revivals. Among them, three dances deserve special attention.

Acrobats of God, to music by Carlos Surinach, had its premiere on April 27, 1960.

A note in the program read: "This is Martha Graham's fanfare for dance as an art . . . a celebration in honor of the trials and tribulations, the disciplines, denials, stringencies, glories and delights of a dancer's world . . . and of the world of the artist."

A celebration? Rather, a savage satire on the choreographer's aesthetic experiences. Martha was, of course, the choreographer. Her régisseur, who carried a bullwhip, was danced by David Wood. The performers entered like circus animals and practiced on a Noguchi barre which was formed very like the fender guarding a Victorian hearth, but one which had gone through a mangle and was bent, uptilted, curved. It was broad enough to walk on, sit on, lie on, and could be used for charming and piquant designs. There were also Paul Klee–like mobiles, one of which was a kind of fire screen on a flexible arm which Martha could draw in front of herself and hide behind, and which she did conceal herself behind every time the dancers asked for her help, at which points she simply withdrew and blotted herself out. So much for Graham's views on the choreographer.

Phaedra, to music by Robert Starer, had its premiere on March 5, 1962. The familiar story of the young queen, the young lover, and the jealous husband is a study intrinsically of lust. It enabled Martha to do some rather extraordinarily provocative solos and pas de deux, and rollings around on a Noguchi bed that looked very much like the couch of nails upon which certain saints chose to mortify their flesh. The set consisted of symbols, and the little figure of Venus as a butterfly pinned to the wall, which at the moment of consummation opened two very large and pretty wings and revealed a tiny female in its center in a split, both legs extended in midair, straight out to the sides, constituted probably the most explicit and graphic sexual symbol that had ever been revealed on a decent stage. It was at the same time remarkable as design and powerful as a motif. The little goddess hung on the wall like the heart of an orchid, open, distended, vulnerable, and her meaning was perfectly clear to all.

This ballet had the unique distinction of being denounced in Congress as lewd. Edna Kelley of New York and Peter Freylinghuysen of New Jersey, members of the House of Representatives, rose to their feet and deplored Graham's taste and morals and the fact that she was receiving state money for sending pornography abroad! This outburst did not harm or curtail Graham; on the contrary, it filled her houses. The public rushed to see what they fondly hoped would be prurient. They were, of course, disappointed, because the art revealed was disciplined and chaste. But those who knew how to read symbols were astonished.

I sent my son and his girl, both sixteen. They had neither of them seen much ballet, and no modern work at all, and their eyes were uncorrupted. They saw just what was there, with no aesthetic adhesions. "These are Greek myths," I had explained by way of preparation, "which you know, here retold in terms of our contemporary life and psychology."*

The children were so overwhelmed that they walked the fifty blocks home, hand-in-hand, shaken to the core.

The young understood perfectly. Martha had changed their whole frame of reference. They grew up knowing her language and responded immediately.

Many years have passed since then, and it is the same as before. "Everywhere," said Martha, "it's the young who support me."

|||||

Secular Games, also to music by Robert Starer, had its premiere on August 17, 1962. It is chiefly for the men, and a fine, invigorating romp it is, unlike anything else Martha had done. The performance had the vintage crop of Martha's beautiful boys. There never had been such a collection of male dancers before, and none since.

|||||

In 1963 Martha and Bethsabee began to plan and initiate a new Israeli dance company, the Batsheva. It was to be a native company, with Israeli dancers and with Martha as the key artist.

Bethsabee was spending a good part of her time, and of her great fortune, in Israel. It was in the tradition of the de Rothschild family that no member ever earn money in this country of origin. They brought money, they spent money, but they did not take money out— not in any form. Bethsabee's mother refused to visit her in Israel until she could be entertained in a suitable house, so Bethsabee built a new house in Afika, a suburb of Tel Aviv, which not only satisfied her

---

*Martha's Greek studies titillated the dance world and fascinated and influenced many professionals, but they also appealed very deeply to Greek scholars, literary figures, scientists, and savants. I was in her dressing room once after an evening of excruciating Greek tumult and disaster when Thornton Wilder burst in, accompanied by his sister. "What a tremendous evening! What a great and glorious experience!" he said, kissing Martha. "Oh, Martha, you have revealed so much! You have shown so much. You understand so much. It's a very great experience to share your theater with you."

mother but contained a complete and enchanting wing just for Martha. The house was several years in the construction, but when finished it was a local marvel, situated on a high hill where the prevailing breezes kept it always cooler than most of the surrounding sites, even in the hot season; and in Bethsabee's house there was always air conditioning. The gardens were delightful and were Martha's great joy, containing all the flowers she had known as a child in Santa Barbara.

Bethsabee was kindness itself as a hostess, answering Martha's every need while ensuring her privacy. Accordingly, Martha was able to continue her work without hindrance. But it was to Frances Wickes she turned for comfort. On December 23, 1962, Martha wrote to her, "How I wish I were there when you mount the lion of inspiration!"

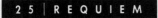

Now came the time of the dying of all the old
companions, sad and bleak to endure, however inevitable.

Doris Humphrey had been the first of the original
friends to go. She had been afflicted with arthritis for years,
and the disease had damaged and twisted her hips to the
point where she could no longer dance. Indeed, she could
no longer walk without limping badly. This had stopped all
her public appearances, but it did not cause her to cease
working, teaching, coaching, or attending the various
boards on which she served faithfully and steadfastly with
energy and wisdom, lending her experience and counsel to
all who needed it. She was respected throughout her profession and deeply cherished by her family. In July of 1958
cancer was discovered and her condition worsened rapidly.
On December 29 of that year she died, at the age of
sixty-three.

John Martin wrote a very beautiful and moving tribute
to her in *The New York Times,* and the entire dance world
bowed its head in recognition:

. . . Though she looked at the past (including her own) with perspective and a fine Yankee humor, her sights were set on developing to the full the opportunities of the present and making tangible the promises of the future.

She was of keen mind and high spirit. Mysteries existed for her only to be explored and explained, and nothing daunted her. . . .

. . . Having fought all her life for the creation, the development, the acceptance of the American modern dance, it was a foregone conclusion that she would continue to fight to the last moment of her power to do so. She was one of the half dozen women of great vision and total dedication who succeeded in giving entity to what was really a new art, if any art worthy of the name can ever be said to be new. . . . Of those handful of pioneers, none was of stronger mind or more indomitable purpose.

At the time of the publication of Humphrey's posthumously published *The Art of Making Dances*, Martin made the statement:

Doris Humphrey is an enduring part of the dance in America, as the granite under the soil is enduring. We can turn nowhere in the art without finding her.

June Rhodes, Miss Ruth's business manager and Doris's associate, now a very old woman, wrote me at the time of Doris's death: "She was a superb teacher and a wonderful friend, aware of all the problems, conflicts, and varying emotions that were common to her students. Her goodness, kindness, and loving understanding as well as tolerance and guidance gave her students more than dance training—it gave them a pattern for behavior, selfless and courageous."

Doris Humphrey's going made no real difference in Martha's life, except that Doris had been a substantial part of that hierarchy which had influenced the modern dance world since Martha had been a young woman. Doris had been Martha's coequal and her one true rival, but, according to Doris's friends, Martha's acknowledged supremacy in the field caused Doris agonies of jealousy and was in large measure responsible for bringing her low and augmenting her illness. The superseding fame of Doris's pupil José Limón furnished the coup de grâce. Yet José loved and revered Doris, and when she died he and his wife were in attendance at her bedside.

Irene Lewisohn had died in 1944, and the well-beloved Edith Isaacs in 1956, after crippling bouts of arthritis and a stroke. In the last agonizing years, Martha had helped Edith develop limited motion control and was instrumental in keeping her walking. The Neighborhood Playhouse quartet was fast disappearing. Mrs. Morgenthau was to die on April 9, 1964.

Ted Shawn and Ruth St. Denis continued, on superficial, pleasant, even cordial terms with Martha. They did not like her work and said so, but personally they were quite affable. In 1959 Martha had given a beautiful reception in her studio for Miss Ruth's eightieth birthday. The hostess was graciousness itself, Ted beamed, Miss Ruth was royal. And there was Louis, also present, on the sidelines, silent and sardonic. Louis Horst's face was, as they say, a picture.

There were now few of the old guard left to run the Neighborhood Playhouse school, and Mrs. Morgenthau and Louis faithfully held the fort alone—and these days he was often distressed with various physical malaises. Martha had long ceased to be an integral part of the institution. But Louis went, and he also ran his magazine, *Dance Observer*, and his tart criticism and vigorous discernment never abated.

Louis had also taught at the Juilliard School of Music from the inception of its dance department in 1952. He and Doris Humphrey (and later José Limón) were advisers and worked there together. Louis taught dance composition to everybody in the school, even ballet students, and his was a very important role on their advisory board and in their curriculum. He used to travel way uptown to 135th Street every week for his classes, no matter what his health.

The truth is that we were all getting old, but Louis was getting very much older than the rest of us. He was bitter, very, very bitter, particularly about Erick, who had displaced him as Martha's lover. Erick was fifteen years younger than Martha, and Martha was ten years younger than Louis.

Louis used to dodder slowly up University Place, frail and creaky, on his way to the Albert Hotel, where he lived after his Eleventh Street studio had been torn down and before Martha moved him up to East Sixty-third Street. Occasionally I would meet him. We would have a warm greeting, and he would invite me for lunch, always pleasant in the dilapidated Albert Hotel dining room, with its stamped-leather walls. There he would sit, a great fat man, his stomach separating him from the table and his mouth open over his snaggleteeth. He would drawl and mumble in a plaintive and almost winning manner: "You'd think I wouldn't be attractive"—and indeed he wasn't—"old as I am and ailing, but I seem irresistible. I can't keep the girls away from me. I can't bar any door to the little pink toes. They keep coming; they keep coming."

I didn't dare comment.

"Ahaaa." He would grin with delight, and look really like the cartoon of some dreadful old beast. By now his breathing was almost impractical. He whined constantly—a manner of speaking only, with no intention of complaint. "I've lost all my appetites; all my senses are fading. There is only one left, and that is my desire for food, and that I will indulge." And with that, he would order something inadvisable. "What is my attraction? What can it be?"

Well, he was kind, he was intelligent, he was interested and concerned. He was pathetic now, and he was alone, for Nina Fonaroff no longer shared his room. He taught regularly. He gave a few lectures and he fiddled a bit with music, but he did not play any longer.

And then, in 1963, came the episode at Wayne State University in Detroit. Martha Hill and Ruth Murray had arranged for Louis to get an honorary degree. He had never received one before.

He had been given the Capezio Award and other trade honors, but a bona fide academic recognition had eluded him, and his German heart hungered after academic honors. Wayne State offered to give him a doctorate, providing that Martha would accept one at the same ceremony. She acquiesced—whether happily or reluctantly it is not known. It was arranged that Martha would take Louis out there. The plan was for her to meet him at Grand Central Station.

On the day, she didn't come. He waited and waited. He then phoned Craig. Craig found her. She was at home, sodden with drink and not dressed. Somehow Craig got her dressed and partially sobered up, and took her to the station. They had missed the train, so they had to take one in the early-morning hours, Louis drooping with fatigue. They arrived in Michigan too late for the car that was to bring them to Detroit. Martha hired another, but when they got to the auditorium the audience was streaming out. Louis was constrained to get his honorary degree in an empty building, with only two or three members of the faculty present and Martha silent beside him. There was no honor; there was no festivity; there was no celebration.

The citation reads, in part: "As musician, artistic advisor, teacher, editor, critic and author, Louis Horst has influenced immeasurably the careers of leading modern dancers who have set out on new paths of creativeness. . . . The breadth and depth of his knowledge of music literature, his skill as a composer for dance, and his insistence on principles of artistic integrity helped Martha Graham during the years of their association to reach her present eminence. . . . His inspired teaching has had a direct bearing on the quality of choreography in this country."

When he returned from Detroit, Louis was cruelly spent, haggard with fatigue, and obviously suffering. He attended his classes and taught with his assistant, Doris Rudko, but he had frequent recourse to his nitroglycerine pills for his heart, and he was shaky and feeble.

On January 12, 1964, his eightieth birthday, Martha gave him a reception, to which all the modern-dance world was invited, and we all came and did him honor. It was a lovely party in her large studio, and there was a throne on a dais, decorated with flowers. Bertram Ross attended to producing the decorations he considered most suitable for a harem party: Louis was enthroned before a beaded curtain made entirely of gumdrops that Bertram had painstakingly strung together—a real labor of love.

Louis was sickening unto death, but he continued to teach. "I don't want to retire," he told me. "Well, look at Doris—she was able to teach, and she could hardly get from class to class. As long as I can get to a class I can teach, because my mind is still . . . big enough." He edited *Dance Observer* from his cell-like bedroom.

In their last conversation, Louis told Harry Bernstein, his assistant editor, that he had saved some money, the fruit of his life's work. He had amassed a small estate. He was very smug; it amounted to $34,000!

About a week after the birthday party, he and Doris Rudko completed a class together. Doris dropped Louis at his apartment and watched him go in through the doors, but she was worried. He had been taking nitroglycerine in the cab. "Louis, I'll see you into your house. Let me come with you." "No, no," he said, and waved her off. "I'm perfectly all right." And the doorman took his arm, so she went on her way.

But directly after the cab left, Louis collapsed and fell to the floor of the foyer, and the doorman summoned an ambulance and notified Martha Graham. This attack was Louis's second, and it was extremely serious. Martha took charge of him, with Nina Fonaroff in attendance. Doris Rudko saw him only once again, when she brought him the last issue of *Dance Observer*, and together they put the magazine to bed more or less on his hospital pallet.

Martha came often to see him in the hospital, once wearing a lovely mauve gown, which delighted him and which he said made her look nineteen again. Martha, Nina said, talked to him almost in baby talk and scolded him as if he were a naughty little boy, for getting ill, for weakening. One of his adoring pupils arrived with flowers, looking very lovely. "Ah," said Louis, very feebly, hardly able to make himself heard, "a night of madness!" And he tried to wink at her. Poor darling, his eyes were dim. She wept as she left the flowers in his hands.

He was getting a little better and was due to go home. Suddenly he suffered a stroke and became partially paralyzed and lost his speech. And so he died, on January 23, 1964, one hour after midnight.

IIIII

Martha stated in *The New York Times*, January 29, 1964: "His sympathy and understanding, but primarily his faith, gave me a landscape to move in. Without it, I should certainly have been lost. . . . He was the great influence in American dance, and those who have been touched by his thoughts are the richer for it. To many dancers he has been father, priest, confessor, and I'm proud and honored to have been among the first."

He had said, "I gave her discipline. I was the tail to her kite, because she was a wild one. I gave her what she needed: ballast. I was her thread to earth."

Lincoln Kirstein said, quite correctly, about Horst, "He believed in art without compromise. . . . The real value of Louis was that he gave a morality to choreography."

Louis had been photographed in his robes when receiving the honorary degree at Wayne State, and the photograph had been considered for the cover of *Dance Observer* for January 1964. Louis hesitated because he did not wish to seem either vain or pushy, but he was awfully proud and pleased: he who had not graduated from high school—who had, in cold fact, not entered high school—was now a Doctor of Music. So it was decided to use this very dignified and handsome photo of Louis in cap and gown holding his diploma as the cover of the February 1964 issue. It duly appeared. It was posthumous, and this was to be the last issue ever to be published of *Dance Observer*.

The night of Louis's death, Martha telephoned me and talked for hours—not about Louis, but about this and that, anything, just to keep talking. She apparently felt she had to make contact. The next day Martha (or, as Ron Protas suggests, Nina Fornaroff) went to Louis's room, retrieved Martha's letters, and stole or destroyed them.

Martha Graham had become the best-known concert dancer in America, one of the best known in the world, the leader of the modern movement, the acknowledged leader of the modern theater, recognized internationally and revered everywhere. But in spite of the spate of awards, honors, and monetary gifts, the mounting financial cost of the company overwhelmed her.

Theatrical costs in America had grown excessive, owing to union demands. Now nothing could be done for little money or done simply. The group of young women who had given their entire lives to Martha's art left, to be replaced by young men and women who wished to be treated as professionals and given, from the start, fair wages for a fair day's work. They were no longer semireligious devotees, like Nelle Fisher, who accepted fifteen or twenty dollars a year and "almost wished not to be paid because it was a sisterhood," or Pearl Lang, who turned back her pay to Louis because she got so much out of the experience she did not think she should be reimbursed. The dancers now wished to be paid. Bertram Ross said that although "Martha managed by word and manner to make you feel guilty if you asked to be paid for your work—she sometimes made the girls cry," they still wanted to be paid. The stagehands were not about to abate their terms because Graham did not have money. Martha's budget could not sustain the increasing demands of the craft unions. The stagehands' bills at the end of every season were catastrophic and necessitated urgent meetings of boards and sorrowful writings of checks.

These conditions were not particular to Martha; they were common to every dancer in the United States. All the soloists and concert dancers were in a lifelong struggle for bare subsistence and for the continuity of their work. As a necessary consequence, many of them attempted arrangements for joint appearances, and as financial protection many other soloists permitted their work to be performed by the big ballet companies.

Not Martha. She consistently refused. Ballet Theater was willing to give her a very thoughtful and careful production of *Appalachian Spring*, sending the leading dancers to her studio to be trained for months. Yet she knew that if she yielded up her pieces she would not have complete control, and that meant possible deviation. Although deviation and change are inherent in live performance—and, in fact, are not necessarily deteriorating—Martha would not countenance it.

Martha looked upon sharing the stage or the evening's time with a lesser artist as compromise, and since she considered every other dancer lesser, it meant that she had to pursue a lonely and exposed role, bearing the entire financial strain herself. She was asked often to join her colleagues, and once or twice she nearly agreed, teasing and flirting until the very last moment and then withdrawing, to the dismay of all concerned.

Bethsabee had been a grand patron, but she kept Martha on a tight string, giving her money for rent but not for taxis, money for scenery but not for cartage or storage, for music but not for copying: in short, not giving enough to set Martha free. Martha and her troupe were always forced to scramble. And yet Martha would not compromise.

Not only did she insist on keeping control of her own work, but she had a horror of not being at the head of the profession, of not having the last word in the creative voice of the time. And this is why, basically, she feared growing old. She knew that taste went in cycles and that various stars came in and went out of vogue. She longed to work, but to do so she had need of other bodies, and these were becoming increasingly expensive. She strained at the leash frantically because she couldn't get onto the floor herself.

She should not have been frantic. She should have recognized that her work was good, that good is good and knows no period or age, that what was truly sound once will always be truly sound, as long as human nature persists.

As she got older and more fragile she realized that time was running out and that whatever was to be done must be done immediately. She became frightened. She began to destroy. She drank. She kept dancing.

Bethsabee had been faithfully generous for years, but there began to be a limit to her gifts, in favor of her Tel Aviv school and theater. Established permanently in Israel, she now gave the bulk of her fortune to Israeli enterprises, especially the Batsheva Dance Company. It had become increasingly difficult for her to siphon off a large portion of her monies to an American enterprise. She still paid Martha's personal rent, however, and she still made presents. But she could no longer underwrite entire seasons and tours.

Nevertheless, Martha did not find herself bereft. In 1966 two young men approached Craig Barton, who was running the Graham school and company—that is, in essence the de Rothschild Foundation in New York.

Ben Garbor had been a dancer in the company of Robin Gregory; he had known Mary Hinkson at the University of Wisconsin, and he had studied at the Graham school, but he had never known Graham. At one point a bout of despondency had led him to the verge of suicide. Then he saw *Errand into the Maze,* and the message of this ballet, with its clear picture of facing the unknowable, the most feared, the horror of the dark places of the soul and the emergence into understanding and power, was so strong that he felt the ballet had actually stayed his hand and saved his life. He vowed that if ever he could help Graham he would spare nothing to do so. He became the friend of Bill Kennedy, who was the curator for the art collection of Lila Acheson Wallace, the publisher of *Reader's Digest.* He and Kennedy had amassed over the years, as their personal property, many remarkable works of art and other practical proofs of their success, including several houses in various parts of the world and two Rolls-Royces.

Garbor and Kennedy wanted to make a movie of *Errand into the Maze* in the deserts of Arizona or New Mexico, and they wished to discuss their plans with Martha personally. But they were blocked by Craig Barton and Lee Leatherman, who together were a kind of Cerberus guarding her privacy. It was Mary Hinkson who begged Craig to open the door, explaining that Garbor only wanted to help generously. Craig relented, and Garbor and Kennedy had their interview with Martha. Nothing came of the project, but the two men became enamored of Martha and began giving lavishly, generously, without stint, both money and time.

They decided to glamorize their heroine. They saw to it that she had wonderful clothes by the best designers. It was probably they who persuaded Halston to design for her. They virtually took over her appearance.

In time she began wearing either long black suede or white kid gloves. The gloves hid her shame, her twisted hands. Her gloves were immaculate, expensive, noticeable. One never said "How sad," but rather "How chic!"

Garbor and Kennedy took her to Jacqueline Kennedy's coiffeur who was a dear friend of Garbor's. Garbor began making her up for the stage and for all her public appearances, and then decided that she must have her face lifted. So she went to California and had the operation, the first of several. Martha never again looked like a young woman, but she did reveal an incredible distillation of herself—delicate, wrinkle-free, refined, ethereal, hollow-cheeked, waxen—a deity, in fact; and she presented an angel's appearance before the world.

Remarkably soon, Garbor and Kennedy had assumed all the escort duties that had formerly devolved upon Craig Barton and Lee Leatherman. They invited Martha up to their lovely house at Cross River, Connecticut, for rest periods and visits. They took her everywhere.

Ben Garbor accompanied her on tour in 1966, to the west. The entire company was scheduled to travel in a great bus, but Garbor thought this was unsuitable for Martha Graham, so he borrowed a limousine from Huntington Hartford for him and Graham and one or two other personal attendants, while the company went on the bus. He acted on the tour as her personal maid, her make-up supervisor, her equerry. When he returned, according to Mary Hinkson, he had developed a very marked facial tic.

Garbor's greatest achievement, however, was that during the trip and for a period afterward in 1966 he actually got Martha to stop drinking. Alas, this happy situation did not endure.

Then her promoters decided that she must get to meet the "in" people. Martha began for the first time in her life to associate not with the great artists of her time but with the successful—the successful in show biz and the successful in café society. And she was, of course, so exotic, so strange, and so bewitching that she became an instant success.

The two men then undertook to raise money. An auction was held, and they donated one of their Rolls-Royces. At last they approached Lila Acheson Wallace, the great patron, and persuaded her to become Martha's benefactor. They persuaded her lawyer, Barnabas McHenry, to set up a new financial structure for Martha's foundation and to head her board of directors.

Martha had very little time or energy left for communion with the folks she used to know and draw strength and comfort from. But no one moaned about the quality of her work. That still was extraordinary.

And did all this activity compensate for the fact that there was no love in her life? That she was a lonely, aging woman?

No, it did not. She drank.

Once, during this period, Lee Leatheman took Martha to lunch at Moriarty's on Sixth Avenue, and there told her the plot of his new novel: the story of an actress who had sacrificed everything for her work and wound up finding her lovers, her son, her husband all estranged and alien, and herself alone. Martha stared at him, then burst into tears and wept most dreadfully. "Who told you?" she asked. "How did you know?" "You did," said Lee, "I watched you." And she fled from the restaurant.

Martha, however unwillingly, was now forced to think of replacing herself in certain ballets. It had become too difficult for her to dance three pieces in one program, and as early as 1950 or 1951 Pearl Lang started doing *El Penitente* as an opening number. She performed with Erick and Merce, who was replaced by John Butler, and she carried the piece on all the long tours and then in the seasons in New York at the Ziegfeld Theater. Later Ethel Winter replaced Martha in *Salem Shore*. Martha did not care particularly about these two works. They were not important to her. But when it came to replacing herself in *Appalachian Spring*, her signature creation, she suffered, and yet she felt constrained to give it up because of its extreme difficulty and the way it taxed her fading body. It had been her gift to Erick. But she found certain dances quite beyond her strength and attempted to introduce Pearl into the leading role. This was done so reluctantly, however, that Pearl never got a rehearsal; as there were no films, she was constrained to reproduce the role entirely from memory, which was barely possible because she had originally been one of the four young women who sat on the bench

watching Martha perform her great solo dances every night. The day
of the first performance, Martha called the company together in her
dressing room. She gave no advice and no encouragement. She said to
everybody assembled, "This is the hardest day of my life." Pearl really
did not know how to continue. By dancing she seemed to be doing
Martha's bidding, but she also seemed to be dealing a death blow. Pearl
commented, "It was a terrible thing to say to me, considering the
energy that difficult piece takes." In London Martha announced Pearl
as dancing in it, and the critics, including Clive Barnes, came to see
her perform it, but Martha went on in her place and slipped Pearl in
in an unannounced performance. Pearl always went on in agony and
Martha always watched in the wings.

When Pearl at last replaced Martha in *Clytemnestra* apparently she
was very good* and Martha suffered again. Pearl's husband went to the
theater and was deeply impressed; he rushed back to Martha saying,
"Martha, this role is no longer entirely yours. The piece holds with
somebody else in it. It's a glorious work and it will live forever." The
remark turned the knife in her heart even deeper. The minute the
young man went out of the theater he realized what he had said and
was remorseful.

Mary Hinkson performed *Clytemnestra* as well as *Deaths and Entrances*. Pearl commented: "I know we all got closer to the weight that
is needed in these roles than what I see today. But dancing in front of
Martha was terrible, simply awful."

Martha had always evinced this paranoid retention of her roles, this
dominance through them. Back in the thirties she had given a program
the better part of which was performed by the company: Martha only
danced three times that evening. The next day she came into the studio
and addressed the group: "Well, I've learned my lesson: people really
want to see me dance and they've come to see me, and it's no good

---

*Clive Barnes's headline for his May 7, 1973, *New York Times* article was "Pearl
Lang Is Superb as Clytemnestra." He wrote: "The major event of the dance weekend
was probably Pearl Lang's debut in Miss Graham's "Clytemnestra" on Saturday.

"As Clytemnestra, Miss Lang has the most poignant sense of tragedy. She dances
magnificently . . . without perhaps the doom-dark stricken quality of Graham herself,
but there is a lovely fierceness here. She is a heroine who walks through the Oresteia
with a sense of anger as well as guilt."

Byron Belt wrote in the *Long Island Press* on May 7, 1973: "Miss Lang is the
supreme interpreter of the poetic Graham roles and her face is one of haunting
beauty."

if I give too much importance to the part the company plays in the program." Jane Dudley added wryly and rather bitterly, "It didn't make us feel we were worth very much."

||||||

Mrs. Wickes was still Martha's beloved, close friend and adviser, and, in effect, her doctor—certainly her emotional and spiritual counselor. One would have thought that the least Wickes was due was candor, and Martha must have known that if she were to derive full benefit from the relationship she should be totally honest.

But Martha did not tell her the extent of her drinking. Possibly Martha did not admit the craving even to herself.

Craig Barton was well aware of it, however, and deplored it. He tried to hide the bottles, and whenever possible he destroyed them. But a real alcoholic cannot be curbed in such a manner, and Martha had become just that.

She often told things as she wished or imagined them to be. Also, by Martha's own repeated admissions she was "devious." Martha's deviousness with Mrs. Wickes as well as with everyone else was made transparently clear when Craig Barton discovered that although Mrs. Wickes knew that Martha drank (Martha had written about this quite pleasantly and casually) she had no idea that Martha was an alcoholic in the medical sense. It was Craig who disabused Mrs. Wickes of her innocence in the matter. Martha, like any true alcoholic, had lied debonairly and unscrupulously.

Frances Wickes's first reaction to the news was anger and indignation. She accused Craig of maligning a helpless woman. The reaction of Gertrude Macy and Jean Rosenthal was the same. They would not believe him. And yet years before Martha had had a company, Louis Horst had told many people that Martha was reliant on her daily dosage of Irish whiskey. She confessed to Bertram Ross that she frequently vomited up her breakfast. On her last trip with Louis Horst and Bertram, to a formal lunch at the Neighborhood Playhouse, she threw up in the cab and sent the men on ahead while she cleaned up. When Mrs. Wickes finally accepted the fact of Martha's addiction, she called her up and apparently talked to her so severely that she provoked a temporary reform. At the next rehearsal Martha was on time, sober, and ready. But most of the company members, who had been used to seeing her straggle in hours late and in no condition to work, were absent, and when they finally showed up Martha tongue-lashed them bitterly.

Bertram Ross asked her, "Do you know what day this is?"

"Yes," she said, "it is Easter Sunday." Nevertheless, since she was ready, she expected them to be.

Martha was now drunk on most occasions. There were days when she did not leave her apartment, and at those times when she went to the studio she sat with glazed eyes, not seeing the dancers, not caring what they did—a remnant of herself. Bethsabee began to lose her incredible patience and refused to continue to give financial help. Martha refused to be interested. Why should she be? Martha had given up.

At a lecture-demonstration at Philharmonic Hall for a sold-out house, Martha walked onstage and after a few sentences revealed herself as quite incapable of lucidity, and thereafter, to everyone's shocked dismay, she rambled and repeated herself. When she went to Harvard to receive an honorary doctorate in 1966, Craig accompanied her, and Martha staggered and almost fell in the academic procession. This caused Craig such acute distress that he suffered his first heart attack.

During this dreadful period, Martha was obsessed, logically enough, with the thought of death. She used to call up Bertram Ross and ask him if he was willing to undertake the enormous responsibility of taking over the company, of being security for her ideas and style, the preservation of her way of doing things. That was one of her messages to him. The other was that he ought to die at the height of his youth and beauty, that he must not wait to grow old. "Die while you're still beautiful," she would say, and hang up. This phone call often came in the middle of the night and left him with that thought to go to sleep on.

She told him one night that she was going back to Israel, but Bertram said, "I thought you hated it there. What do you want to go there for?"

"Oh," said Martha very sadly, "it's better than sitting around here waiting for imminent death."

Since 1963, Bertram Ross had been co-artistic director of the company with Lee Leatherman. In 1967 they planned Martha's next appearances in Europe, which were to consist of short seasons limited to London and Lisbon.

It was a very unhappy tour for all concerned. Martha was, according to Lee, "drunk throughout the rehearsal period," and only an emergency call to Frances Wickes (now in a nursing home in New Hampshire, where the poor lady lay desperately ill) and her subsequent telephone sessions with Martha were able to pull Martha into shape.

But the very damaged and disarrayed star rose to the occasion, as she usually did, permitting the London performances to be an absolute triumph. The press was ecstatic.

Her patron Robin Howard had been extravagantly rich, but he began selling off his hotels, his restaurants, various valuable but expendable possessions, and all of the proceeds he gave to Martha. She never mentioned his name publicly; she never thanked him publicly. At the end of the 1966 season, this time at Covent Garden, no less, and after a tumultuous response from the audience, the curtain went up and Martha Graham stood on the great stage, a tiny solo figure, clad in a Halston robe of solid sequins. She glittered like a Christmas candle. When she began to speak, Howard moved forward to hear. She ended a long speech with the statement that she "would never have had this great experience if it had not been for one man." (Everyone who knew the situation believed she was at last going to thank Robin Howard.) "If it were not for his help and support, I would not be here today." And she concluded, "If it were not for Halston." Howard wept.

Clytemnestra followed, in Lisbon, in the great bullring there,* the arena of mortality, where so many fighters, young, hopeful, and valiant, had met their deaths. Here Martha enacted the full three parts of the ancient tale of betrayal, unfaithfulness, infidelity, punishment, retribution, and grief. She and her company danced in the gathering dark, before multitudes who had watched the last throes of so many in that very spot, had seen them tread out the dread measures on sand caked with blood. And in the dusk the cry went out, the salute to the bullfighter, to the brave bulls: *Olé! Olé!,* ringing against a sky now hooded with night. These people understood agony, terror, remorse. Martha endured the cry. It was, she said, "the culminating moment of my life and career."

|||||

On February 21, 1967, Martha unveiled *Cortege of Eagles,* the story of Hecuba, the bereft, monumental mother grieving for her dead. It is, for many of us, the last word on war. This is the grief for all the young—not remorse this time, but grief, the full knowledge of the world's futility and wickedness. It is infinitely mournful and touching,

*Memories of this occasion conflict. Bertram Ross remembers the performance as taking place in a vast enclosed hall, not in the bullring. All agree that the audience was huge, low-paying, and vocally enthusiastic.

and it boasts some of Noguchi's finest effects, notably the whirling, striped shields in the fatal duel between Hector and Achilles.*

Martha had learned true grief; it was all around her.

Jean Rosenthal had been excused from the hospital to do the lighting, but the effort was too much for her. She was now mortally weak with cancer. She returned to the hospital and died.

With every personal loss Martha's terror mounted.

Martha had now become morbidly sensitive to any possible threat to her position, to her power, to her privileges, and looked upon rebuffs, even the most natural and the most reasonable, as a direct questioning of her rights. This was unhealthy and unnatural, although characteristic of alcoholics. It was rooted in fear and it dominated her instincts.

|||||

Martha danced Hecuba superbly, but there was a growing agitation in the dance world to persuade her to retire, against which she set her entire will and energy. She raged, but she raged futilely. Her body was going, whether or not she would accept the fact. Other people faded and died—but not Martha. Mrs. Wickes gently told her "Martha, you are not a goddess. You are human. You are not immortal."

"I thought she meant I would die," Pearl Lang reported Martha as saying. "I never thought she meant I would grow old and infirm." That Martha wouldn't have. The body that had been her perfect machine and tool, the body she had perfected and worshiped!

"I dread the misuse of the body," Martha told Alan Kriegsman of the *Washington Post* in May 1984. "As a dancer, you take that body and you train it, almost like a little animal—you discipline it, care for it, feed it, and you adore it. It's a symbol of your life; it is your life."

Yet pressure continued to get Martha to retire. This was reinforced by increasingly frequent episodes of a calamitous nature. During her last season in New York at the Ziegfeld Theater, when she had insisted on doing repeated performances of *Clytemnestra,* she had shown signs of great strain. Nathan Kroll went to the performance one night, taking guests, and because he was a musician and a performer himself he was sensitive to the atmosphere. He realized during the performance that crisis was imminent. He broke into a sweat and sat forward in his seat

---

*Bertram Ross explained that Noguchi furnished a number of props for Martha to play with, including the striped shields, and that Bertram, in experimenting, devised the whirling of these shields so that they resembled the wheels of a great war chariot.

in extreme apprehension. Sure enough, in one of Martha's great falls, she went to the earth with her usual mastery but was unable to rise again and struggled for a second or two helplessly on the ground. Nathan shut his eyes and stopped breathing. Bertram Ross, who was dancing with her, swooped her up, performed a remarkable step, and laid her on the nearest Noguchi support. The audience had noticed nothing, and they broke into their usual cheers at the performance's conclusion, but Nathan was shaking. He rushed backstage and found her dressing-room door locked. He beat on it, demanding to be let in, until Lee did in fact admit him.

Lee was a wreck. "This is the end. We've had it this time. She can't go on this way. This is public exposure of the worst and most demeaning sort. Catastrophe!"

Martha remained silent and bitter. Nathan got on his knees beside her. "Martha, you can stop doing this one terribly demanding role. The audience has seen it. You can give yourself a rest from this. You can rest from all dancing for a time. Get your strength back."

"I'd rather die," she said. "I would die if I stopped. I cannot go on without dancing. You all know that." She had said the same to Lucy Kroll. "The love I receive from the faceless audience I cannot live without."

And she did go on. But always there were around her what Nathan Kroll called "human props," dancers who could support, pick up, carry, lift, boost. She was no longer capable of going out onstage alone and doing those feats expected of her. Martha was now just over seventy, and she was acutely arthritic. What she was asking of her body was unconscionable, beyond reach. But it was Martha's body, and she asked it.

She had been captivating to all men. Now what was she? Demoniac and frightening. She was well aware of this, and she loathed it. There were no sufficient compensations in old love letters or old press notices.

Certainly old age is a diminishing and a stifling. It is also a changing, and there can be joy in what the young furnish: the pupils, the followers, the discipline. Every teacher has known this. And with age certainly can come a calming of the frenetic zeal of egomania, to be replaced by an enlargement of interest, a spreading of emotional needs very real and valid. Apparently Martha knew nothing of this. She did not take joy in her devoted young pupils or her foster children. Maybe somewhere, subconsciously, she felt that this could degenerate into a form of laziness, that she must still do it all by herself, out of herself.

So that when young, beautiful soloists gathered around, Martha spat on them.

The first one to come out in print about Graham's unfitness for public dancing was Doris Hering in *Dance Magazine* (May 1967). The text Martha objected to was:

"The future of the dance lies . . . in the continuation of the line of dancers, who, trained, skilled, are not afraid." [Doris Hering, April 1939.] This statement might apply to a good deal of Miss Graham's dancing now. Since dancing is in essence an art of risks, risks against gravity, risks against ordered measure, risks against inertia, it should not also be one of risks having to do with uncertainty of performance.

Hering was covering Martha's March 9–26, 1967, City Center season. Martha cut her dead and never spoke to her again. The second charge was more shocking. A widely known dance soloist burst into Martha's dressing room after a performance of *Clytemnestra* and said to her bluntly, without preamble, "Martha, you have reached the point where you can no longer do these great roles. I think I should replace you. It's plainly obvious that physically it's just not in you anymore. I am ready at this point to give up my own career and take on yours." Martha turned to stone. She made no reply. To characterize the dancer's remark as chutzpah gives it too much dignity. It was plain cruelty.

The third admonition was serious, and Martha felt it had to be answered. It was from Clive Barnes, the English critic who had replaced John Martin at *The New York Times*. Barnes deplored Martha's present performing caliber and advised her in an article in the *Times*, even commanded her, to leave the stage.

Martha was wild with anger. A few days after the appearance of this article she was due to receive the Handel Medallion, the highest artistic distinction that New York City can confer. She went to the Brooklyn Academy of Music to get it, arriving late and intoxicated. She accepted the honor onstage from Dore Schary and then proceeded to make a long, rambling, and incoherent speech, defying Barnes, and, in effect, the whole world, and declaring that she would dance as long as she pleased. In the middle of this diatribe Nancy Hanks, the head of the National Endowment for the Arts, got up and walked out.

Later that year, on July 1, 1967, Craig Barton died of a stroke, complicated by heart disease, in Oklahoma. Martha was deeply grieved.

"Oh, how I miss that man!" she said, sighing, several times to me later. At the time of his death she talked to me for hours—not about Craig, but about other things.

But the lights had already gone out; Mrs. Wickes had died two months before, on May 28.

Now began the terrible descent. Lee Leatherman said to me at this time, "I don't know why she gets up in the morning, why she gets dressed, why she goes to the studio, why she eats, why she sees anybody. I don't know how she gets through the day. I don't know what keeps her going."

Nothing did. She didn't keep going. She barely existed. Martha went into hell.

She had given up hope. She was losing all her old friends, her beloveds. At length she lost all concern even for the work itself. She could no longer dance. For some time she became withdrawn. She shut herself up in her apartment, refusing to go near the school. She drank, or people believed she drank. When occasionally she went to the rehearsals, she would sit with her eyes rolled back to the whites, not speaking or moving, and then she would jump to her feet and demonstrate quite remarkable new steps, or hobble through them as her poor feet and legs permitted, before she lapsed once again into indifference. Some days she didn't even bother to dress herself decently. There were times when she was improperly clothed and exposed herself as though she wished to violate the last remnants of her sexuality and fastidiousness.

There were long stretches when she allowed the company to flounder in their rehearsals. Bertram Ross commented:

Martha's lack of interest in pieces she was not in started long ago. I thought the company the most remarkable in the world. I loved them all. This was the period before we had a rehearsal director. We rehearsed ourselves. We were all very disciplined. We signed up for space and directed one another. I rehearsed our parts. Very often Martha would walk in on a rehearsal and turn out the lights and ask us all to leave. "But Martha, we have so much to do, we need to rehearse."

"I want the building quiet." She knew she ought to be rehearsing herself and so she wouldn't let us rehearse. Very often pieces like *Seraphic Dialogue* went onstage without Martha ever having looked at it. But we all knew Martha's intent, having trained and taken daily classes with her.

Martha would watch with grim satisfaction as her dancers failed to achieve her standard, or what she had taught them to expect. Very rarely, she would appear at the last moment and set them right, and then she would retire again, sardonically, as though she had taught them a lesson.

Martha gave no help in the re-creation of *Herodiade,* which she permitted Ethel Winter to perform on March 15, 1963. As a record to work from, Ethel had fifteen minutes of silent film for a twenty-four-minute work. Ethel said that Martha gave her no working rehearsals, but did give her two helpful images: "to move as though I were being chased by a cat; to move as though a cat were following me." Martha seemed to feel this instruction was adequate.

In *Part Real—Part Dream,* created in 1965, Martha had draped a robe about Mary Hinkson and then said, "Try what you can do." Mary danced a little. "Okay, that's it. Repeat." But Mary had improvised and had forgotten what she'd done. Martha was furious. Mary meekly asked what she should do next. "You do it, girl," Martha snapped. "You're inside that robe, not me." This was the only time Mary remembers that Martha had not seemed to care. She seemed half dazed, sitting on the bench.

Lee Leatherman had obtained Martha's permission for *Diversion of Angels* to be done at the Juilliard School by the students. She did not go to see the performance, but she withdrew the right to repeat it.

Bertram Ross says that when Martha entered the rehearsal hall these days, usually late, and stood at the door making coy and incomprehensible sounds, playful, indistinct, they knew that the session would be wasted. He knew that they should have just quietly gotten up and left, but they did nothing of the sort. And maybe they were wise, because not infrequently, even in this confused condition, Martha was able to deliver herself of astonishing matters. But not always.

|||||

Craig Barton and Gert Macy had earlier asked Robin Howard to put forward a plan for the future. Howard proposed that if Martha wanted her work to continue as a creative entity, she should consider inviting Bertram Ross or some of the others to do pieces for the English group, but in her true style. What he suggested, however, was not acceptable to Martha because at that time she didn't want any of the work to survive if she couldn't herself dance.

Revivals forced Martha to relive old experiences, all but unbearable to her, and to accept new personalities in her own place, a form of suicide. And she further found no delight in creating new pieces for others to perform. "The only reason I became a choreographer was so that I could have parts I wanted," she said.

After Craig's death, Bethsabee asked Robin Howard to take over the business direction of the company. But his duties to The Place precluded his taking on any extra responsibilities. He did, however, give generously of his time, and for the better part of a year he commuted between New York and London, bearing all the travel expenses himself.

The company was in disarray, the organization tottering. Bertram Ross and Mary Hinkson tried to hold the school together and with Lee's help even succeeded in organizing studio performances, rigging up lights and using what costumes were ready to hand, that is, smart practice robes, simple indications of costumes. They had only new pupils to work with, not of Graham caliber by any means, but Bert and Mary chiefly wanted to keep the works before the consciousness of the public. They now had to pay the boys to perform, and the boys were not very good. Martha, however, did not know this, for she did not bother to come to any of the performances. She was often sick, and frequently in the hospital at this time. The members of the old group took jobs elsewhere and scattered all over the world. The Graham company was unraveling. Geordie was still running the school and was proving less and less capable, but about Geordie, Martha would not hear one word of disparagement.

Patricia Birch at last went to John Houseman and begged him to chair the board and establish some sort of order. Houseman felt strongly that he was not familiar enough with the repertory or the workings of the present organization, nor sufficiently involved, to warrant his taking over the direction, and he was loath to try. But in response to the company's entreaty, he very reluctantly agreed. Someone had to be responsible who knew something about the theater, something about Martha and her intention, and something about the working methods of the Graham dancers. Houseman qualified on all counts. Also, he loved her.

It devolved on him, therefore, to get Martha off the stage permanently, and at the same time to preserve the works. "It was her artistic obligation to herself and to her company to let younger women replace her in the great dancing roles which she had created for herself over the years but which it was still emotionally impossible for her to accept could be danced by anyone else."

Houseman went to call on Martha in her Sixty-third Street flat. He described the encounter in his book, *Final Dress:*

I had the feeling, as I always did when I was alone with her, of being in the presence of greatness—a greatness frayed, at this moment, by rage and despair. She knew why I was there, and she must have hated the sight of me. Yet, for our first hour together, she was her usual seductive, manipulative female self. . . .

"There is no reality in this piece except the inner reality of feeling eternal in all of us." So she had written in her published notebooks about one of her works. And this is what she felt now. It was not a question of ability or quality, nor even a matter of vanity. (She knew that in her day no one compared with her and that nobody would for years to come.) I believe she was convinced that without her presence these intensely personal creations of hers would cease to exist or, rather, that they would lose their "reality" if they were separated from her own physical and spiritual identity and the personality that had made them famous.

When I spoke to her of the repertory and of the irreparable loss it would be to the world if it were not kept alive, I had the impression that, in her present mood, she would just as soon pull the temple down about her head and perish in the rubble!

John found it almost impossible to proceed against such historic indifference. She didn't give a damn what happened to the Graham school or the repertory, since she hadn't the time or energy to fight. He halted his efforts.

The decisive blow occurred soon after, in a business meeting with Barnabas McHenry, Lila Acheson Wallace's lawyer, who stated flatly that Martha would have to stop performing herself if Mrs. Wallace were to continue giving money.

This was, in effect, the coup de grâce, and Martha went down under it as though she had been poleaxed. "I never wanted to choreograph," she had always said, and she repeated this to John Houseman. "I only wanted to dance. I only have my being and entity in dancing. It is all in life that has meaning for me."

Her repertory, however, was not in reality hers alone to save or destroy; it represented a joint fabrication involving the life effort and devotion of many people. If the dancers had given her their youth, it was with the understanding that she should be the immaculate guardian of their dreams, and that she would be their warranty that they had not thrown their lives away. She therefore had not the right to jettison all at will, no matter how deeply she felt, and although it was born of her inspiration and the product of her genius, bearing the hallmark of her name, there was a moral obligation involved. Too many people had also worked too long—fifty years, in fact. Martha's repertory was in great part a communal achievement like a cathedral.

|||||

A week later, on May 25, 1968, in *A Time of Snow,* the story of Eloise and Abelard in their old age, as the aged nun Eloise, Martha gave her last performance. She was seventy-two years old. She could barely walk. As the old lovers lie dead, the young ones miraculously rise and embrace, and are enfolded in the funeral cerements that are now suddenly rose-colored, and a very young, modern, contemporary girl places a bunch of flowers on the burial stone in homage. Martha departed from the dance stage; youth lay entombed behind, honored and immortal.

The year she danced for the last time, 1968, was just a year after Craig had died and the year Mrs. Wickes died.

A t long last, Martha's faithful, sturdy, ill-used body gave out. She collapsed and was taken to Doctors Hospital under the care, not of her own doctor, but of Mrs. Wallace's physician.

We were told her sickness was terminal—that she was for it. Cirrhosis of the liver, we were told. And it may have been, with complications. Publicly the doctors claimed the cause was arthritis of the hands and diverticulitis, and it was that, too. At bottom it was despair.

She was allowed a few guests.

I went to the hospital, unheralded, with a large box of early spring flowers. I had to wait, of course, but I felt that had I phoned she would quite simply have refused me entry. I was finally ushered in. "I'll stay only ten minutes," I whispered to the private nurse on duty. "Not more."

Martha's room was unusually large and fronted the East River. She lay on a hospital bed covered with a light fur rug of some costly pelt. Vases of fruit blossoms stood about. There was a chaise longue and a private bathroom; it was a hospital room of considerable luxury. Martha, I had been told, ordered her cuisine from the outside.

She moved her head slightly as I approached. She had permitted herself finally to grow gray at the temples, and the silvering softened her face and enhanced her femininity in a very gentling and humanizing way. She looked lovely, and not very ill. But she was weak. I thought she had not paid attention to anything I said and that my compliments and encouragements had fallen on deaf ears. Apparently not, for later she quoted to companions what I had said, that the graying hair made her look more attractive and that she was wise to accept age. Then her voice took on the old ring: "The hell I will," she said. But that afternoon she had said little. "What's on your mind, girl!" she asked quite sharply, her voice high but slightly burred and laryngeal.

"Martha, dear, I'll talk to you when you're better. I just wanted to see you."

"I have diverticulitis," she said.

Had everyone, then, lied to me? Or had she herself been told the truth; that she was dying of alcoholism?

But at least right now she was making real sense, quietly and succinctly, for the first time in years.

I left after about seven minutes. I kissed her forehead; she didn't care. She was bored with me. Nothing I did interested her. Her girls came to see her and she was more interested in them, but not much more. Mary Hinkson and Bertram Ross visited her to report on the group, and once when a young man named Ron Protas came and no nurse was available, he carried her to the bathroom. She was miserable at his seeing her so weak and helpless. She had no strength left for anything except survival. Because she intended to survive, and she intended to be as comfortable as possible while she made the effort.

She was not comfortable. One day she could not get her breath. Again no nurse answered the bell. She was losing consciousness just as Ron Protas entered, dropped his flowers, and fetched the oxygen tank and mask. She had been told she was mortally ill, and she felt that she truly was. She said to Protas, "Get these tubes out of me. Put me on my feet. I will not die lying down. I will not die lying down." And then she began gasping for air. As soon as Protas saw that she was safe, he ran for professional help.

The truth is that Takako Asakawa had given her air on several occasions, but Martha remembers only Ron Protas's crucial service; she grew to feel very poignantly that the rest of the company had deserted her and that Ron was the only one who had stood by her in her hour of need.

Ron Protas was a young man who had been a law student at Columbia, had done some photography, and claimed to have done publicity work for Marlene Dietrich. Two years before Martha's hospitalization, he had begun to hang around the Graham company. He was in and out of favor with Martha for several months, but was not treated too seriously by anyone. At one point he was known jocosely as "Martha's little boy," because he followed her around so faithfully. Ron Protas would appear backstage at the Brooklyn Academy of Music and keep trying to get near Martha. He fiddled about photographing the dancers—Mary Hinkson, Ethel Winter, Takako, Matt Turney—as they took curtain calls. He brought flowers. Martha, however, found him something of a nuisance and did not wish to talk to him. Finally the stage manager, William Batchelder, took him by the arm and was ushering him out of the theater when Ben Garbor happened by and said, "Let him stay. He's perfectly harmless."

Protas was not a man of any theatrical experience or background, and he had not the training for an executive position in dance management. But obviously he was interested, and equally obviously he intended to get a position. In any case, it was he who was present in the room during one time when Martha was in dire need, and it was to him she now turned in her distress. From that fateful moment on, Protas was a constant attendant at her bedside.

Now began the crystalline vigils, the cold taking of stock. The doctors told her flatly that if she drank she would die. This time she believed them. She did not touch a drop of alcohol thereafter.

She recovered, as she intended she should. When she was released from the hospital she was taken by Ben Garbor and Bill Kennedy to their house in Connecticut and nursed most tenderly back to health. But in 1972 she collapsed a second time and was returned to the hospital. Apparently Protas was not with her at this point. On her release she went home to New York and began to knit her life together very slowly, very tentatively. She had been in mortal straits.

Now Protas reappeared and steadily and faithfully gave her succor. She needed to be cared for like a baby, and she turned to him as to a savior. From the day of the oxygen salvation, Protas made it his business to become indispensable to Martha, life-giving, life-sustaining, to stand between her and every other human being, to be everything to her—her nurse, her dresser, her housekeeper (she now had a fulltime Irish maid and cook, but he supervised). He became her business manager, her adviser, her counselor, her advocate—more than Louis had been, more than Erick, but everything each had been in his own way. Protas was all.

Martha was now quite helpless physically. She accepted the sustenance he gave her with deep gratitude. At the same time she maintained that she alone made the decisions and that she was still the absolute boss.

Protas then set about slowly and deliberately separating her and her school from everyone else who had any power.

To the dismay of her staff, he began giving advice on casting; they felt he did not know enough to do this. He did it anyway. He gave advice on rehearsals, on the maintenance of the school, on the personnel of the school (except he was never to say a word against Geordie), and on all of Martha's business dealings.

She remained aloof in her flat on East Sixty-third Street, near the school, making plans with Ron, Lee Leatherman hovering by helplessly and knowing that everything he did was being supervised and criticized and condemned by Ron. The school had been getting along as best it could under the direction of Bertram Ross and Mary Hinkson, with Lee Leatherman acting as administrator and reporting to the board. Geordie still kept the school's books, such as they were.

A year later, I called on Martha at her home.

It was a bleak, foul day of wet February snow and cold mist, with filthy gutters running over; underfoot was a wet brown paste that sucked on one's boots, wheels sprayed black slush, and the air was heavy and black and cold, clouding the lungs—the sky very low overhead stretched and moist and lead again.

I had passed through a plain but decent foyer, and took a self-service elevator to an ordinary middle-income apartment. And then I entered a chamber of light.

The dominating feature of the room was an antique Chinese bed, high balustraded, canopied in carved ebony: a bower of lacelike, entwining carved wood, very dark but delicate and mysterious. When Martha sat in it (which she did not do that afternoon) she must have seemed enshrined, surrounded by an aureole of the fantasies and delights of a cunning craft. The rest of the furniture was closer to home: low, faintly Louis XVI in style, simple, and discreetly upholstered in expensive eggshell silk. The walls of the room were covered with shelves of glass, backlit as in a museum, and on these airy pedestals rested a treasure of carved rock, porcelain, and blown glass—Egyptian, Greek, Israeli, Chinese (no Western pieces)—all beautiful, all delicate, most of them very old.

On one wall was a fine Alexander Calder painting, a gift of the artist, who thought she might want to sell it and use the money for the company. Martha had become so fond of the picture that she would not part with it.

Filling every cranny and corner were tropical green plants in tubs— gigantic philodendrons, feathery palms, tree ferns—so that one seemed to be in a hothouse-cum-jewel case, burgeoning greens and translucent blooming glass, cool, radiant. And in the middle was the fairy empress, erect as ever, slender, her sleek body clad in a fashionable big-patterned garment, her hair again dyed black and piled high and poufed out like Rose Kennedy's, a most stylish and princessly person.

We had tea seated on the eggshell-silk divan, and Martha's hand was again steady. I began questioning her about her youth. She looked me straight in the eye. She knew I was not being completely candid.

"You know," she said in that slightly laryngeal voice, "I'm going to do my own autobiography."

"Marvelous! Fine! My God, it will be an immortal book!"

"It isn't that I mind telling you my age," said Martha breathlessly. "I don't mind that at all. It's just that I get confused about dates." In the course of two hours she mentioned neither her age nor any dates at all.

She held up her hands, knotted and distorted with arthritis, like the witches' hands that Arthur Rackham used to draw, the hands that turned into twigs. "I'm going to have these operated on if the doctor will let me . . . but the rest of my body is clean, no arthritis at all." This was patently not true. I'd seen her entering the John Hancock Theater in Boston on the arm of Ron Protas; she had been hardly able to walk. And I knew from her company that there were days when she was incapable of teaching and lay racked and pinned with the disease. Brave girl! She threw her head back like a dancer and said valiantly, "There's nothing wrong with my body, and you can damn well guess my age. I'm not going to help your curiosity."

During our two-hour talk Martha asked me nothing about my work or my life. She always had in the past, but not now. It's true I had not come to talk about me. Still, we had been almost sisters, or so I had fondly thought.

At the end of the interview her real sister, Geordie, came in, a Dickensian, battered little person, looking wet and frowsty, a small, old, not-quite-bright neighborhood lady whom one sees regularly at the supermarket but tries not to get involved with. Geordie was entangled with a very wet small dog, and they stood trying to extricate themselves from the leash and dripping onto the polished floor. The Ming princess helped Geordie off with her damp-smelling furs and unwound the leash. Geordie had come to dinner. She no longer lived there, as I had supposed.

"I couldn't live with anyone," said Martha to me hastily. "Only a husband."

At this point Ron Protas entered with a small bunch of flowers. Our tête-à-tête was over. Conversation became terminal. I had not come to see Ron, but he was there.

IIIII

Martha got well, in her own way, in her own time, and without alcohol. Martha rose from the dead, and verily she was changed now; and, as John Houseman said, she wished a clean slate, an absolutely fresh start, with no holdovers from the past, no reminders, no debts. She wanted new people, new ideas, new projects.

Martha began to distrust all her old collaborators—Mary, Bertram, Lee—everyone but Ron. Did she distrust Ron? Who can say? She needed him. She had said, "I need him. There is nothing further to be said." And Ron saw that he was always on hand, always present. He held a microphone to her lips at every rehearsal, he supported her as she walked, he brought her tea and comforts, he tucked her in at night and turned on the electric blanket, and he took care that she never had an interview or a conversation that he did not monitor. He also took care of her mail. So Martha could not be reached except with his permission. All this was with her consent.

The intricacies of the ensuing period were ugly, and there was much suffering. The severing of ties always involves bloodletting, and in this instance blood flowed bountifully, and with it hatred.

Martha later referred to this time as a dark passage in her life when she was sick, and to the preceding years as trauma, as though she had suffered from a disease. She erased it.

What happened was evil, or so her associates thought.

In her bewilderment and helplessness, Martha was growing more and more paranoid. Ron may not have encouraged this, but he did nothing to stop it. One by one Martha and Ron rid themselves of all the faithful workers and the board members—relentlessly, brutally, and finally. It was almost Russian in its thoroughness. No quarter was given and no respect paid to any memories. Onlookers were amazed and even considerably frightened. She or Ron, or she together with Ron, cleaned out the entire Graham organization.

Since 1971, Mary Hinkson and Bertram Ross had been billed as associate directors, and they continued to dance the leads in Martha's ballets. They were mounting the ballets and controlling them, working, as always, for very little pay. Now, suddenly, Linda Hodes, the ex-wife of Stuart Hodes, was put in charge of the repertory dances. She was inexact, they thought, and approximate, even disputing with Bertram Ross parts that he himself had created. He had to prove her wrong with the use of films, but film did not exist in all cases, and so the works were reconstructed imprecisely. According to Ross, Linda did not know the difference or did not particularly care. The casts were mostly new. Martha, in common with all choreographers, remembered her works unreliably. Who could possibly remember an entire composition, let alone an entire repertory? The original executants and co-creators remembered more, but also only partially; they remembered their own solo bits, their particular responsibilities. This is the way very great works lose sharp definition and die into legend.

Bertram Ross had for a long time been close to Martha, and Martha, he had thought, had depended on him. He told me that he called himself her "fantasy lover," her "skin." Whether Martha physically desired him is not known. Being a lusty woman, perhaps she did. He was very, very beautiful. But he was not interested in women, and he had made that clear. Martha had responded by inventing for him in various ballets every kind of tortured death in the calendar of horrors, and these he was forced to enact on the stage with her fervid participation. She beheaded him, stabbed him, poisoned him, beat him, castrated him, but on Bertram Ross the human man she dared not lay a finger.

And she tortured him in rehearsals, literally hurt him physically. Once, when rehearsing *Circe,* as he was lying in the boat, stomach down, his body curved along the shape of the ship's bottom:

She stood behind me, grabbing my head by the hair and snapping my head back. There was a terrible crack in the spine. I thought my neck had been broken, and I saw colored spots. And then she threw me face downward, smashing my teeth, and then laughed and went and sat down, and then said, "No man can ever be that cruel to another man. Only a woman could do that." One of the other dancers said, "You know, Bertram, she's lucky. Had that been anybody else he would have socked her." I really believed something physical had happened to me. Was she worried about that? Nope. She just laughed and said, "It takes a woman to be that cruel." Her ideas about love are very strange. . . . I think there was something she never got settled between herself and her father. [And, the reader must add, between herself and Erick, and other men who frustrated her consistently throughout her life. The men she deliberately chose!]

Ross had been very nervous in his role of Oedipus in *Night Journey*, because he had to lift Martha and handle her. He felt as though she were precious porcelain and that he might shatter her. He used to practice on Linda Hodes, and when he had perfected the lifts with her, he felt more able to attempt Martha's body. But he downright refused to do a good many of Erick's lifts, because they were brutal. One eliminated effect was to fall with his full weight and press on her shoulders while she sat enthroned. He stood three feet behind her and just fell forward. She took the whole brunt of the sudden descending weight and the blow without breathing, but he didn't like the image of it and saw no reason why Oedipus should be brutish or appear to be trying to break his queen's back. Erick had also pinched her and was unduly familiar, because he regarded the queen as his booty; but Bertram thought it excessive and objectionable. Martha, however, apparently wanted brutality. She corrected one of the later interpreters: "No, no, that's not what Erick did. He kicked me. He always kicked me." And she demanded violent kicking. Martha wanted the violence, the brutality, and the antagonism. She wanted nothing less.

But with Bertram the man she had to content herself with a pleasant, loving, and fruitful relationship and a minimum of brutality.

In July 1972 Martha accused Lee Leatherman, her company manager of fifteen years, of mishandling the company funds. He was not a trained accountant, but he was honest and had worked faithfully and long. Several witnesses have attested that he demanded an audit, and the books were found to balance perfectly. But he'd had enough. As a matter of fact, he had been talking for some time against Martha. Martha knew this, and she was quite ready to hasten his departure. More important, so was Ron. Martha's accusations persisted and Lee, with the encouragement of Louis Goodkind, the company lawyer, threatened to sue her if she did not desist. So she did desist. He left.

The company books balanced, but the school books were under the care of Geordie, and Martha refused to have these audited. They subsequently disappeared, all of them. Geordie had been more than careless. Several times she had passed out in a drunken stupor on the desk, with cash amounting to hundreds of dollars lying about. Martha would not have one word spoken against her little sister. Geordie was, however, bundled off to a sanitarium and was found to be suffering not only from alcoholism but from cancer. She went to Arizona, where Martha maintained her in relative peace and security. Geordie always claimed that her alcoholism had caused the remission of her cancer.

When Lee Leatherman left, she demanded that members of the company sign a letter pledging allegiance to her, in preference to Leatherman, just as, said Bertram Ross, "in the days of the Nazis."

Martha's board of directors showed signs of restiveness and acute unease. Martha decided to weed out the dissenters. On March 31, 1971, she had written to Harold Taylor, a member of her board, excusing herself for her absence from a meeting and thanking him for his services. She now sent a second letter to him, dated December 11, 1972.

Taylor's answer came on January 5, 1973:

I don't understand your letter of December 11th 1972 or your remarks about having lost a dear friend at the last Board meeting and that you now want to have people around you who believe in you and will not "undermine [your] endeavors for any reason on earth."

Are friends to be defined as sycophants who never ask questions, sit like children in a posture of perpetual adoration, and have no concern for helping you with the practical matters of organizing dance companies and dance schools? It may be that you have escaped one disease only to fall into the arms of another one, as deadly to the human spirit as the former was to the body and mind.

Their association was terminated.

This exchange was one of several Martha had with members of the board, all of like tenor and all with the same unhappy denouement.

In November 1973 Martha accused Gert Macy of mishandling her funds and bungling the work with the theater staff. She made the accusation in front of the entire stage crew while Gert stood there and stared at her. Gert walked out.

Martha fired Ross Gilbert, the pianist, claiming that he was trying to control the classes and change the teaching.

And then, at this dreadful period of post-prostration and Protas ascendance, this period of low tide and seeping distress, she and Ron suddenly claimed that Bertram Ross and Mary Hinkson were stealing the Graham company from her. Bertram decided he had better pull out and leave while he was still sane. And he wrote her a loving but final letter and made his departure on October 10, 1973. Martha accepted the verdict and thanked him for his honesty. Bertram's departure was in good order and fairly mild.

Not so with Mary Hinkson, who was now in charge of the work. Also in 1973, Ron quarreled with her violently over the renewal of her contract. He claimed she wanted an exorbitant salary and that she was holding up all the negotiations and the start of the new season by refusing to sign. Bill Carter was in the room one day working with Mary when Martha came storming in. She went straight up to Mary and demanded in a really fearsome voice, "How dare you? How dare you not sign the contract? How dare you hold up all our negotiations?" The two women withdrew to the next room, which happened to be the kitchen, and there the screaming crescendoed until Mary left, tears streaming, her clothes gathered up and bundled into a small bag. And clutching this, she fled the school forever. After all the long years of faithful service and excellent performance, to be berated like a naughty schoolgirl because she asked to be paid what she thought was adequate! She left embittered and angry.

She staggered to the nearest pay phone and called her husband.

"I've left," she said, sobbing.

He replied quietly, "I'm breaking out the champagne."

In a letter dated January 25, 1984, Harold Taylor explained to me:

It was as if Martha had just awakened from a long, deep sleep, startled by a sudden fear—death, failure, loss of friends, lack of money, and she then began flailing about. She accused Lee of everything but sodomy, fired him overnight. . . . Something did have to be done back then, the first being for Martha to shake loose from her illness, then the reorganization, with additional help from new people. . . . A simple pattern, squeeze the juice out of your friends and allies and companions of the road, then throw the skins out, get some new juicy ones. . . .

But by God she's done it, with Protas as partner! Maybe she'll mellow in her 90's.

The dreadful winnowing process continued through the next two years: soloist after soloist, collaborator after collaborator, all were separated away. There was always a good reason given for dismissal, but Martha had ears for only one side of any question, and she became enraged by contradiction. She demanded loyalty, which all people want and some people insist upon. But Martha confused loyalty with obedience, and there is a profound difference. From her disciples she wanted the subjectivity and docility of children, and this cannot be exacted from mature, independent spirits. When she pressed, it was with tyrannical insistence, and the objects of her domination regretfully were forced to leave.

These days they left with anger.

She had distrusted her colleagues. Now her colleagues were gone. But she distrusted their revenge.

At a subsequent performance in New York, the house was full of Pinkerton men in full uniform to protect her from "the attacks of Bertram Ross." Gertrude Macy (she had not yet been fired at this point) was astonished. She sent for Ron. "Did you order these men?" "We think Kissinger is in the house," he first said, but then admitted, "It's to protect Martha from Ross."

"There is a small army in full uniform out front. Who's paying for them? How much do they cost?" Ron never answered her.

When Martha subsequently went to France and her new ballet *Lucifer,* created for Rudolf Nureyev and given its premiere at the Uris Theater, New York, on June 19, 1975, was booed by the audience, she quickly organized the company into a series of curtain calls. At the first the whole company joined hands and stood perfectly still, facing the booing and waiting for the curtain to descend. On the second call Martha was alone. There were a few boos, which diminished. On the third call the stage was empty. The curtain remained up for three or four seconds and descended in silence. Then Martha faced the company.

"Don't let this worry you," she said. "It does not represent the reaction of the French public. They're good people. This is a claque hired by Bertram Ross and Mary Hinkson." When Bertram and Mary heard this story they were astonished.

Martha found the energy to say this, just as though she were a younger woman starting a career. She found the energy to make herself hated. This was the manner of her predicted demise! She had a new broom in her hand and she was using it terribly. She then proceeded to ride it.

She was truly alone now. She found new students, new disciples, new stars, new friends. They were not the same as the old ones, possibly not as staunch, not as intelligent, perhaps, not as intrinsically fine; but they were enthusiastic and full of energy. Marvel of marvels, she, the key figure, still could create.

She had, in effect, died. The past was ashes. She was to be totally reborn. She was the rising phoenix.

Throughout the filming of *A Dancer's World* Lucy Kroll had been urging Martha to publish some of her writings. To this suggestion Martha had replied negatively. She insisted that she could not speak publicly, and she maintained that she certainly could not write. But neither Lucy nor anybody else believed her. Lucy argued that Martha had produced over a hundred dance pieces, most of them with literary scenarios and overtones, and certainly with intellectual meaning. Lucy had heard Martha speak to her company and had been struck by her extraordinary command of language, the fresh use of expression and choice of words. If Martha had done all this, Lucy argued, there must be some tangible evidence, some notes, and she continued to beg. Finally, in 1965, after months, indeed years, of harassment, Martha bethought herself of her notebooks, stored in the basement of her apartment house. She took Lucy down; they opened a trunk that was filled with fifty closely written stenographer's pads in Martha's large, forceful Palmer method hand. It was a treasure-trove and Martha agreed to deliver them, unexpurgated, the whole lot of them, into Lucy's keeping. Lucy then obtained the collaboration of a remarkable editor, Hiram Hayden.

Eight years later, in 1973, the notebooks were reproduced and published in a very fine and exact edition of Martha's working text. They reveal her random thoughts; her reasons, convictions, stray loose quotations; whatever she put down that would illuminate her way in finding new compositions. The book has an excellent introduction by Nancy Wilson Ross.

Hiram Hayden had started with Crown Publishers, then he went to Atheneum, then to Random House, and finally to Harcourt Brace Jovanovich. Lucy's contract for Martha's book stipulated that she could move where Hiram moved. So finally *The Notebooks of Martha Graham* was published by Harcourt.

In reading through the notebooks, one is struck by the large and catholic approach of Martha's intelligence, almost encyclopedic in its scope, and the inclusiveness of her reading. She read poetry, fiction, history, and criticism; she was versed in English literature from Chaucer to Edith Sitwell. She spoke but one language, yet she studied in translation from others, and she quoted frequently from Goethe, Schiller, and Jacques Maritain, as well as from the classics, including Caesar. She studied psychology, sociology, and anthropology. She learned what she could of mythology. And always she returned to etymology, to the close contemplation of action and its relation to language.

The use of symbols throughout the *Notebooks* is provocative and highly theatrical, if what is emotionally charged and innovative is theatrical. She was fascinated by the double imagery found in all religions: the power of light and the power of darkness as one force, good and evil as opposite faces of the same intrinsic energy, the basis of man as a doppelgänger, the shadow self which took possession and fused with one's intentions so that one went through life as a twin linked to its opposite. The only true opposite to energy and goodness, she believed, was negation, nullity. She was haunted by the hold of basic animal passions, in other words, evil or satanism.

From *The Notebooks of Martha Graham:*

"Apollo, Admetus, Heracles, are varying names for one divine being, a Power of light & life—

And since in primitive religions the Power of light & life is at the same time the Power of darkness & death, Thanatos or Death, who seems in the play the enemy of all three, is in reality their double"

"Mythology, religion, folklore & fairy tales, all of which represent the dreams of yesterday."   Freud's contribution to Psychiatry

"When I question myself, he writes, concerning the love of my neighbor, my brother, and turn inward upon my own spirit . . . there comes to me . . . the suggestion of something . . . utterly unlike all that is commonly meant by loving one's brother . . . not altruism . . . not kindly feeling, nor out-ward looking sympathy . . . but something different from all these . . . something almost awful in its range—yes & in its rage, in its rage & fire in its scope & height & depth . . . something growing up . . . within my separate & isolated lonely being, within the deep dark of my own consciousness . . . flowering in my own heart, my own self . . . so that indeed I could not be myself without this, this strange, mysterious, awful finding of my brother's very life *within* my own—. . . this terrible blinding discovery of him in me and me in him."
Stanley Mellor (Liberation)

"A laugh was laughed
The earth was split
The sun is up
A red rift in the sky"
Johannes R. Becher

It is sinister—terrifying—beautiful—joyous—

"For love that will gaze an eagle blind"
Trollope—Barchester Towers

"Miseria honorato"
(honor-covered misery)
—Panofsky—

"Terrible frivolities of Hell"

She is obsessed by the images of woman.

Magdalene thru the ages—
always available—
never possessed—

Thus the woman is the original seeress, the lady of the wisdom-bringing waters of the depths, of the murmuring springs and fountains, for the "original utterance of seerdom is the language of water." But the woman also understands the rustling of the trees & all the signs of nature, with whose life she is so closely bound up.

Notes for "Imaginary Gardens," from which her ballet *One More Gaudy Night* derived:

A Pavilion—or summer house . . .
What is an "imaginary garden"?
It is a place more wondrous than any actually beheld garden—
There are no limits to the flowers or trees grown there
or
the possibilities of behavior there.
This concept and the idea of "Love Letter" could combine.

She is obsessed by madness, hence her preoccupation with Lear, and the place of madmen or prophesier as revealed in ancient literature.

"If man be a messenger of man why should a madman be a messenger of God?"

"Such ecstasy, then, is an exalted form of contemplation"

"caught up to God"
(caught up to their vision)

"The ravishing of sinners for their correction" Dante

"There is no chance;
And what seems hazard in our eyes
Arises from the deepest source."
                    Schiller (Wallenstein)

What Martha didn't allow for in her scheme of spiritual organization as depicted in the *Notebooks* were the human traits: organization, control, discipline, generosity, kindness, and the one exclusively human trait—humor. This is a remarkable lapse. But the void becomes apparent as one reads. Yet Martha had humor, and a saving sense of irony.
Martha's notes not only form an annotated explanation of many of

her more obscure allusions, symbols, and ideas, enabling the viewer to pierce the net of her intricate symbolism; further, they could be used as the basis for a play, or a historical treatise, or a novel. They are rich with suggestion.

The book is unique: a compendium of ideas and stimulus for any creative imagination.

Martha decided she would try something she had hitherto never granted herself. She was a pre-eminent coquette, and she now played the coquette with her public. She must have realized that there was a practical reason for employing the skill, and she went at it with elegance and finesse. She decided to become a superstar. She put her mind and energies to the project, and, as always with Martha, she outdistanced all others.

She dyed her hair black again, sometimes jet black and glossy, later with auburn highlights. It didn't look dyed, but it was, and by the very best coiffeurs. In her frequently lifted and smoothed face, worked on by the very best plastic surgeons, the still-young eyes remained superb. The face was now more gaunt than ever, masklike, colorless, matte, her high cheekbones outlining the skull, her immortality.

Did she wear glasses to read? I was told by Bertram Ross that her growing loss of sight amounted to partial blindness and that she was quite helpless in judging stage lights. He

said that she had once addressed a pink scarf left on a chair by Mary
Hinkson, saying, "You needn't wait any longer, Mary. I think we won't
get to your part until later." Mary had left the rehearsal room and there
was nothing there but a length of material.

Yet I never saw Martha in glasses. Maybe she had contact lenses,
but she could not have adjusted these with her crippled hands. Soon
she was being dressed by Halston. Her taste had always been impeccable, but now she was stylish. He gave her the very best he had, and it
was smart and sumptuous. Her poor feet were shod by Capezio in little
satin shoes or slippers of gold kid as soft as gloves. Her gnarled, broken
hands were hidden by gloves or voluminous sleeves. She added jewelry
from Van Cleef & Arpels—modern, superb, a few pieces of great cost,
the gifts of her friends Ben Garbor and Bill Kennedy. The jewelry, she
said, was to be only a life loan and would go back to the donors on her
death.

She looked like a little Oriental deity, a little goddess, an empress,
like a miniature Japanese doll. She was tiny and costly, rare and superb.
And very remote. How unlike the plain girl we used to know, with the
thunder in her head!

Although it went against a lifetime habit, she would now accept
luxuries, if the gifts were made to her for the purpose of dressing her
up to achieve some designated business end.

Was the Martha we knew still present? She was. Still there, if
disguised. Every so often Martha's New England conscience took command and ordered a curtailment of vanities, but less and less as time
went on, her new counselors being tireless in their urging of the material displays of success.

She was behaving differently. In 1974 she was seen backstage at the
ballet, kissing the hands of Rudolf Nureyev, the great ballet star, after
his performance in *Apollo* (Balanchine) and *Le Corsaire*. This gracious
act was startling, because *Corsaire* was the purest example of nineteenth-century balletic extravagance, the merest technical superficial-
ity, against which she had set her life. Passing people stopped in
amazement to see her pay such homage.

In 1974 Martha went back to London, and this was the first appearance there of the company without her starring lead. The season was
presaged by a series of lengthy press conferences held at Covent Garden, at which Martha faced a formidable battery of critics. And Martha, the star, was plainly intimidated. She faced them modestly,
decorously, and humbly, and she won their hearts. As a prelude to the

meeting she had endured a transoceanic flight, an arrival that morning at 6:00 A.M., and the dreadful difficulties of jetlag and sleeplessness; yet she handled the press exquisitely. Robin Howard, who had once more put up large sums for the season, was vindicated.

The season was a triumph.

The Graham company went on to Paris. Martha was not well, but she spared herself nothing, remaining spartan and cruel with her own weaknesses. Martha was now eighty. Age was not to be coddled or forgiven. Age was to be treated as a regrettable circumstance and an inexcusable weakness. When she found that she had an abscessed jaw from a bad tooth, she continued until she all but collapsed and was sent from La Rochelle to Paris in the care of Ron Protas. The doctors in Paris were astonished that she had been able to keep upright under such excruciating pain. After extensive dental surgery, she hastened back to the company, fearing to let them out of her sight. And she was right, for although her company was always adoring, they were, since she had fired the older, experienced faithfuls, essentially young and unseasoned. When she was with the new group and directing them, as when she had been on the stage, they could together attain a peak that was almost orgiastic. Indeed, some thought they might have been sibyls hovering over the Delphic flame. But when left to their own governance, they showed that they were children, plainly cowed by the situation. They lost their morale, and the quality of performance deteriorated markedly. Martha's return was always like a blood transfusion.

The current business manager, Lillian Libman, tried to protect Martha's fragile health, but the old habits prevailed. Martha often asked for cheaper rooms for herself, cheaper service, cheaper conveyances, and she would take no money for personal clothing or luxuries, as superstar yielded on tour to practical caretaker. Garbor and Kennedy were not along to goad her into spending. Libman finally pressed on her some leftover francs, amounting to about two thousand dollars, begging Martha to spend the sum in Paris on herself. But although Martha yearned for beautiful French clothes, she spent only a thousand, returning the extra francs to the company. She knew too well the company's need for cash, all the time.

But she also knew that the company needed a new aspect. She needed stars to replace herself. She tabled Puritan restraint.

Martha cajoled Rudolf Nureyev into dancing with her company a year later, in 1975; in June of that year she had composed *Lucifer* for him, and in December *The Scarlet Letter*, based on Hawthorne, for which she had long made notes. This introduced him to a new world while she herself entered into a new kind of relationship: that of producer with someone else as star. She championed Nureyev. She even wrote a letter to *The New York Times* defending him when he had been taken to task for unbecoming conduct.

Nureyev's inclusion and preferment threw her company out of balance, but his name sold tickets. Having never previously given weight to such considerations, she now believed she had to. For his part, Nureyev revered Martha, and he persuaded Margot Fonteyn, the star of the Royal Ballet, to appear with him in *Lucifer* at a benefit Martha was giving for her own company and in a new ballet Martha had designed for both of them, accommodating her own technique to their balletic style.

In 1978 Martha engaged Liza Minnelli, the musical-comedy star, to take the speaking part in *The Owl and the Pussycat* (Yuriko Kimura was the dancing lead), to music by Carlos Surinach and with a set by Ming Cho Lee. It was a charming and light work, and full of Martha's best fantasy, rather in the style of *Every Soul Is a Circus*, but lacking the satiric bite of the old comedy. Liza Minnelli was vivacious, pretty, charming, but had no real weight and none of the acrid force that Martha's satire needed. (She was later replaced by Janet Eilber, who was somewhat better because she was trained in Martha's style and Martha's point of view.) Fonteyn, Nureyev, and Minnelli were performers more foreign to Martha's way of doing things than could ever be imagined, but she agreed to accept them, and since they were eager for the honor, she worked for them and with them. She claimed she had merely grown with the times. Her devoted adherents thought otherwise.

"What has happened to Martha?" asked her friends. Martha was now appearing in full-page advertisements with Rudolf Nureyev and Margot Fonteyn, advocating Blackglama mink, for which she received a mink coat and the school a donation. She was attending theatrical openings and charity balls, and even, God save us, discothèques!

"Is it necessary?" asked her adherents; and some few had the temerity to remonstrate. Martha was called "tacky," but given the fame of the people involved, surely it could be considered "haute tacky." To all demurrers Martha was short, if not rude. "They are helping me get money which I badly need. The dancers will no longer work for nothing. Costumes cost, sets cost, musicians cost, and, God knows, stagehands cost. Will you give me money?"

"The people who carp are the ones who haven't done anything themselves," Martha was quoted by Anna Kisselgoff as saying. "They want to attach themselves to a legend. They want the legend to remain safe for them and predictable, something they can follow. But they have made one fatal mistake: They have confused honesty with self-indulgence."

Martha was now racked and bound with arthritis, and suffered real duress without surcease, as well as the frustration and exhaustion of incapacity, and in 1982 another malady was added to her agonizing disabilities. She had finished two new pieces for her spring program which were, the company agreed, extremely fine. She was laboring on a duet between Yuriko Kimura and Takako Asakawa which would not resolve itself into a satisfactory pattern or come clear and pointed. Martha struggled with it futilely and fretted over it day and night, until Pearl Lang begged her to let it go for the moment, to let time work out the problems, as it frequently does, and to be content with the quantity of new material she had ready for the public. The company was satisfied, so why wasn't she? But Martha never before had withdrawn a piece unfinished, had never before admitted failure. This would be the first time to give up on creating. Yet finally, in utter exhaustion and frustration, Martha did just that.

"That day," said Pearl Lang, "she broke out in shingles, which flayed her for two subsequent years." Sleep was all but impossible. She had to have medical assistance and was often carried into the theater for performances and helped on the stage for her final bow and carried off again. In 1984 she had a nurse living with her to administer shots during the night.

Her household was organized like a clinic. But to the public, and to any except her most intimate friends, not one word of complaint or explanation was vouchsafed, not a moan. How Martha got into the gloves which encased her hands, how she got into her clothes or into her special shoes, incapable of easing her agony, no one knows. These remain Martha's bedroom secrets. This stalwart woman went right on conducting rehearsals, giving interviews, making TV appearances, all but incapacitated, with no alcohol to mask the anguish, not a drop.

In an article by Anna Kisselgoff in *The New York Times Magazine* of February 19, 1984, Martha described her day:

"I get up at 6:30 A.M. and then I go back to sleep unless I have an appointment," she explains. Mornings are kept free for doctors, dentists, press interviews. . . . After lunch, Graham is driven to her school. . . . Graham choreographs or rehearses her dancers for six hours. The first three hours are in the early afternoon. Afterward, she deals with costumes and related matters, returning home at 5 to rest. "Soup and Sanka" tide her over until she returns to the school—after students have vacated the studio—to rehearse her company. A night person, Graham is apt to rehearse the dancers from 8 to 10 P.M. or 11. At 11:30, at home, she likes to take care of her paperwork. . . . "I can't sleep very much so I like to watch old movies on television—if I'm really fortunate, an animal picture until 1 A.M."

Martha was now in command of a big industry. The funds that passed through her hands amounted to hundreds of thousands of dollars—even, on occasion, a million or over. Her payroll was complicated, with a sizable roster of employees, the tax system highly involved. The school was complex and proliferating, and all the properties owned by the school and the Graham Foundation occupied large amounts of storage space and required expert and constant care. The monies for these manifold industries had to be raised by one person: herself. There were helpers, of course, but it was Martha's presence, Martha's name, Martha's personality that procured the funds, and this meant constant interviewing, consultations, examinations with corporation presidents, foundation heads. No wonder she had no private life anymore. She had always to be available and ready for interviews, and she always had to look healthy and, above all, effective.

The heads of corporations are very powerful and often charming men, but they are seldom refreshing or stimulating to an artist. Martha was obliged to talk to these personalities for hours, repeating her facts, marshaling her arguments, alert, knowing full well that she was under almost medical examination to prove herself able to carry on her work, to guarantee that their gifts of money would be well spent on her worn, very old genius and her extremely frail body. Consequently there was little time to give to her own diversion or replenishment, or to casual intercourse with friends. In fact, there was no time.

|||||

From the inception of the National Endowment for the Arts in 1965, Martha Graham had been given grants as large as the funds permitted. In the first year she was granted $10,000. I was a member of that first National Endowment board, so that it was my privilege and joy to make the presentation and request in her behalf. She was immediately voted the money with acclamation and the expressed regret that it could not be more. Her share was not quite as large as that given American Ballet Theatre, which maintained a much larger roster of dancers and company staff, and had greater needs and a wider scope. Thereafter, each year, Martha got an increasingly bigger grant as the monies in the public till augmented and the recognition of her company's worth permeated every phase of our national artistic consciousness.

In 1983 Graham submitted a request for $1 million for the purpose of establishing a foundation to perpetuate her ideas and works, and to record on film all her choreographies in an authoritative version, which she would personally edit and supervise. Ron Protas drew up the request and signed the petition. To her stunned dismay it was turned down. There was the added saving grace of a proviso that she should receive $250,000, one-quarter the amount requested.

Martha took the refusal as a direct attack on her integrity and reputation, an affront of major proportion, and for about two weeks was in a state bordering on collapse.

Protas turned frantically in every direction for help. He was frightened for her, for her state of mind and physical well-being. He was scared for the reputation of the school, and he was appalled that for the first time in her life she had been directly rebuffed, and that with this refusal, which he feared would be taken as an indication of loss of status and quality, he would find it impossible to raise monies from the other big charitable organizations. He feared a ganging up of power; he feared blacklisting against Graham, and also against himself.

It is true that there was considerable bitterness about Ron Protas, and it was widespread. This he had courted deliberately, abetted by Graham. Whether he had anything or not to do with the government's rejection cannot be proven, but he was nervous. Her spirits dragged and her heart was sore beset. She haughtily refused the small grant. "I will not take a bribe," she sneered.

Her ultimate answer to all of this came in January 1984, when she stood on the stage of the Paris Opéra holding the hand of its ballet company's director, Rudolf Nureyev, was kissed on the cheek by Jack Lang, the French Minister of Culture, while he hung around her neck the ribbon of a Chevalier de la Légion d'Honneur, by order of the President of the Republic of France. He said, "The entire world of dance is honored by this nomination."

The press was splendid and intelligent, and Martha was hailed as a heroine. Marcel Michel wrote, "Graham entered into the American myth. . . . The fight Miss Graham fought was nothing less than one against the colonization of America by European classic dance."

She was photographed by the international press, and her picture was shown around the world.

Victory after all these years!

|||||

For the opening night of the 1984 New York season at the New York State Theatre, Martha delivered a brand-new version of Stravinsky's *The Rite of Spring,* an extraordinary work, savage in its ferocity, with Terese Capucilli as the Chosen Maiden. This was not the statement of a weak or wounded person, or of an old lady. This was a fighting challenge. The audience was more or less stunned. New patterns were introduced, wherein feet and legs employed extraordinarily compelling rhythms of almost hypnotic persuasion. It was a flawed work, but it had the makings of a really phenomenal statement. At the curtain close, before a standing, shouting house, Martha waited onstage with the whole company, a very small little person with her crown of shining black hair, the great lustrous eyes hooded and observant. She was taking it all in gravely, clad in molten gold and black.

Halston paid for the entirety of *The Rite of Spring,* a considerable financial undertaking. Halston was responsible for the construction of the set, designed by Ron Protas, and the execution of the costumes, which Halston himself designed.

The press for that season was copious, constant, and overwhelming. I think it safe to say that no choreographer ever received more press coverage. One might have thought from the sheer bulk of it that someone like Graham had never danced here before, or that she had returned from the dead. The press ran the gamut, from ultimate praise to extreme condemnation.

Tobi Tobias wrote in *New York* magazine of *The Rite of Spring*:

If one did not know the choreographer, one would simply be awed by the imagery and the authority of this work. It is more satisfying still to recognize it as a synthesis of many aspects of Graham's investigations into dance, theater, and universal stories, and one can't help rejoicing in the personal triumph, to have created, at 90, a work fit to take its place among one's best.

Arlene Croce, on the other hand, in her most acrid and carping voice, wrote of this work in *The New Yorker:*

The results are still as trifling as we had every reason to fear they would be, and they are inauthentic beside. . . . That it is devoid of content will not disturb people whose knowledge of Graham's work begins with her Halston period. Older pieces on the program do not show it up, since there's scarcely anything left of them. It used to be that only those in which Graham herself formerly danced were being misrepresented. Now, because of lobotomized performing, we're losing works like *Seraphic Dialogue* and *Embattled Garden*, works that Graham never appeared in.

Deborah Jowitt of the *Village Voice* took a moderate position:

Graham reduces the emotions to their most basic level: "I WANT!" The dancers appear to be howling this with their bodies all the time, as they grab each other, stroke their hands down one another's body, hurl themselves in frustrated anguish onto one of the Noguchi structures when the desired partner is unavailable. There is no movement to show us how they normally behave together. They emote in a vacuum, voluptuous and unknowable.

Similarly, Tobi Tobias wrote:

As with the first *Phaedra*, the combination of portentous form and malicious content is unnerving, at times even a little foolish. Graham's theater, with its heroic figures, scarlet passions, and grand gestures, is already at odds with today's laconic sensibility. Even her great Greek works of the forties, though not dated, are presently unfashionable. When a lesser effort retains the familiar lofty tone and reduces the action to the level of pornography, we are bound to wonder what all the fuss is about: Surely the three of them could have worked something out.

In July 1984, the National Endowment reaffirmed its grant to Graham of $250,000 to be used for filming, and Martha changed her mind about accepting the government's money, because, according to Anna Kisselgoff, "of new concepts and techniques in documenting dances on film." The plan was to make the films at the University of California in Los Angeles, under the auspices of the dance school there. Kisselgoff described the project in her *New York Times Magazine* article of February 19, 1984: "Graham's own project calls for her voice-over narration on three films of each dance: one in costume and with full production values, one in tights to clarify the technique and one with Graham explaining the dramatic impulse and motivation behind the movement."

I said to Martha, "I hope the Endowment is ashamed of itself."

"Well," she answered, "I taught them a lesson. They never said they were ashamed, but, being a government agency, they can't. However, they've done something to rectify the mistake."

This had been Martha's point of view throughout. Whoever flouted her was making a bad mistake. This was the attitude she had kept toward Sol Hurok, who had managed her at one point, lost $15,000 on the first tour, persisted gallantly nonetheless, lost much more on the second, and then told her he couldn't go on. She thought $15,000 a trifle to pay for the privilege of presenting the greatest American dancer, and I'm inclined to agree with her. But he was not, in spite of his boasts, an art patron; he was an art dealer, and he dealt in art for money. Fame, too, of course, but always money; and since that was lacking, he terminated the contract. Martha found other management and despised Hurok ever after.

In the summer of 1984 Martha advertised auditions open to everyone, including students not her own, something that she had never done before. But the dancers who were accepted were required to take an intensive training course, five hours a day, and then to set about learning the Graham repertory. In late July I was told that the company was industriously at work and that Martha had started a new ballet (at ninety years of age and helpless with arthritis!). She was about to embark on a brief tour of Denmark and Italy, and then return to the American West for another. She was, of course, going to accompany the performers, go with them every step of the way, share everything, speak everywhere, and do such a job of public relations as few twenty-five-year-old moving-picture stars would subject themselves to.

On the American tour, in August, in Tempe, Arizona, Gertrude Shurr, who was living there after a bad bout of tuberculosis, reported that Martha appeared every night for a bow at the end of the evening, to which she looked forward like any ingénue, was beautifully made up, wore a different Halston gown at each appearance, and lived for these brief salutations and acknowledgments. She was accompanied on the tour by a hairdresser, a nurse, a maid, and, of course, Ron Protas, as well as the entire entourage of the company. Her weight was down now to skeletal subsistence. She had almost given up eating even fish, although, according to Anna Kisselgoff, she took what she called a "placid fish," like sole; but she would not touch a "valiant fish," like salmon—"too heroic." She nourished herself mostly on egg dishes like an ascetic, frugally and carefully, a life regimen policed to the smallest detail by Ron Protas. She was saving every ounce of her strength for the one brief exposure in which she gloried. And most of the night afterward, every night, she sat up in bed dictating into a tape recorder her notes on new dances, on the forthcoming winter's program. And every morning at dawn she was up, beginning transactions which would move the ideas into direct action.

In the summer of 1985 Martha accepted a post on the National Council on the Arts, the advisory body to the National Endowment, the first such position she had ever agreed to hold, the first time on record that she had served the public directly. In Washington she was treated like a minor deity and was attended with profound interest, some wonder, and always deference. Her comments were, as might have been expected, very snappy. They were lively, pertinent, knowledgeable. And they were very funny. The members of the board were shaken up. They were delighted. She made the trip to Washington without mishap and in the care of Protas. (Each trip, a royal progress, cost her five hundred dollars.) This marked the initial phase of Martha Graham as public servant.

The school was now running smoothly, headed by Linda Hodes and Diane Gray. The classes were beautifully organized and administered. Scores of young students from different countries were taken in, indoctrinated, and processed. It was slick, it was expert, and it was wonderfully productive. Some of the old girls returned to teach, and they proved inspirational to the new young students. One time Martha herself taught a class, her advent carefully prepared by Protas with forewarnings. She arrived and addressed the students, walking to her chair unaided; she turned when she reached it and said to the class, "Be seated." They went to the floor. Then she sat. She then explained that it was Diane Gray's class but that she would occasionally interrupt for comments.

"You must point your toes," she said, "so hard, you feel it in your *teeth.*" And she bared her magnificent, long, strong, white, and telling incisors. The class shivered in response. She took the two-hour class seated, paying attention to everything, Ron always in attendance these days and always fully dressed with jacket, collar, and tie, even on the most torrid August days. It might have been heat-prostration weather outside (being a dancing school there was no air conditioning); Ron was dressed like a stockbroker.

A story Martha often told in class (and it is repeated in instruction by most of her teachers) is that when two wolves fight and one wolf is clearly winning, the weaker, subdued wolf suddenly stops fighting and turns toward his opponent his unprotected neck, presenting a stretched jugular vein in complete vulnerable subjection. The conqueror does not kill but leaves quietly. Whether or not this is accurate zoological fact I cannot say, but none of the pupils who heard the story forgot it, nor did any of the teachers; and the turning of the head and baring of the throat is a memorable gesture of surrender, and a beautiful one used often in her work. It is a pity that Martha did not think about its meaning for herself.

Marian Seldes, the actress and her one-time pupil, recalled, "she waits for the moment to bow, and when she does I well remember the curtain call she taught us, showing the audience the nape of the neck. Vulnerability learned from the invincible Martha."

I n the 1980s, the life effort of Martha and her assistants was bent on preserving her work: the school, the dances, and the training. And the current strength of Ron Protas went toward keeping Martha.

In an attempt to bottle her creations, Ron Protas and Linda Hodes began to put on film and tape and in taped interviews the details of Martha's entire technique, as well as her creations. In spite of their watchfulness, Martha broke out of the constraints.

"I am more interested in achievement than in archives," she said, and she meant it.

But the others knew that only in archives was there real control. And revenue.

Martha's work was generic and had changed the art of dance and that of the theater in general. Hitherto anyone who wished to could help himself to her discoveries and inventions; whether consciously or not, one could not help doing so. "The wonderful thing about Martha in her good days was her generosity," said Glen Tetley to me. "So many people stole Martha's unique personal vocabulary, consciously or unconsciously, and performed it in concerts. I have never once heard Martha say, 'So-and-so has used my choreography.' "

Martha herself used to claim, "There is no such thing as Martha Graham technique. It is variable, expanding, alive. It must not be thought of as fixed."

Now, under the guidance of Ron Protas, there was an attempt to charge royalties for all usage, not only of composed dances, but of actual technique: an impossible project. Everyone who had taken classes from Martha for the last fifty years had gone away and taught her exercises and style. One might as well try to stop a principle in chemistry, or mathematics, or medicine; one might as well try to state the effect of a great painter's genius. But the effort, mighty elaborate and busy, was being made to do just this: encase Martha, the worker, in a casket worthy of Cellini. But closed.

In order to preserve her true style, her old girls came back to teach. Anna Kisselgoff, writing in *The New York Times*, quotes Jane Dudley:

For everyone in that room who danced in the company from 1935 to 1946, the experience of working with Martha had been one of the highest moments in their lives.

So when the Graham management asked for help in reconstructing "Primitive Mysteries" and forgotten Graham works, Miss Dudley sprang into action. "I was on the telephone for hours," she said. "The call went out and everyone I could reach rose to the occasion."

Pearl Lang came often and occasionally danced a lead, as did Jean Erdman. Dorothy Bird had taught but had to stop for family reasons. Many were too bitter to return; many were not asked. The school was as highly organized as West Point.

Martha's name appeared seven times in the first paragraph of the 1984 school bulletin. There were accompanying photographs of Martha in her prime—and few of the company. Martha Graham as a young woman, Martha Graham as a young dancer, Martha Graham as the immortal leader of an art, Martha Graham everlasting. In the years since, and with the developing individuality and strength of the dancers, there has been a lessening of insistence on the founder's personality and a growing attention to the others. This, I feel, is healthy and desirable, but at the beginning it was alarming. There were Martha Graham tote bags sold at the school, Martha Graham sweat shirts.

Every program and announcement bore the assurance that the Graham technique had been designated and registered as an official trademark.

MARTHA GRAHAM SCHOOL

OF

CONTEMPORARY DANCE

MARTHA GRAHAM, ARTISTIC DIRECTOR

DIANE GRAY, DIRECTOR

*The Martha Graham School of Contemporary Dance
is the official School of the Martha Graham Dance Company and only
authorized school where the serious dance student may learn the
Martha Graham Technique.* ™
*The School's programs in Martha Graham Technique are fully
accredited by the National Association of Schools
of Dance. Training in the Graham Technique
is conducted in two programs . . .*

The presentation hinted of Lourdes, all the externals and trappings were being enshrined and worshiped. And sold. This was called "public relations."

Martha was not a young woman. She was old, badly crippled, and depleted, with one of the most extraordinary minds of this century, the valor of a warrior, and the untiring instinct of an animal. Under the artifice, the spun-sugar fabrication, the pretense, was there still throbbing and pulsing the tiny untamable animal? The living genius? It is so pitifully easy to be caught and trapped! It can be killed, and no one the wiser! Under the wax mask, under the mummy wrappings, there could be nothing but mummy dust. Martha released living ideas. They thrive. They are free. They have their own direction and trajectory, and they cannot be caught and held. This is the power of great ideas. This is the power of original thought.

With dancing, even more than in music, changes are part of the living process. But Martha wouldn't have it, not being willing to trust the taste of others. All right, acceptable, if she herself made changes, and she always did; she considered it part of growth. But it had to be her way or not at all. Otherwise, if it was not her way, she preferred destruction. And this is exactly what she risked getting.

There was initially the basic change in Martha as a creator. This was the working of time and could not be avoided or helped. She thought as well as she ever did, but she was physically not able. All her wonderful inventions were originally spun out of a vigorous, healthy, powerful body in prime condition, at the top of its technical efficiency. The ideas and the expression of the ideas were formed together and were spun out simultaneously, unconsciously, as she moved. And there seemed no end to the variations, changes, and discoveries. Martha was prodigiously strong in her thirties and forties. She did not spare herself. She asked of herself the ultimate, and the dances had not only new patterns and often new germinal ideas but new techniques, of greater variation probably than any other choreographer's. Balanchine repeated all the time. So did Ashton. So did, in large measure, Tudor. But Graham, in the early days, did not. Within her framework she did not repeat. But as her body began to fail her, as her flexibility dwindled to nothing, finally, as she found she was confined to a chair, the inventions diminished. She began relying on what she knew would work. Most choreographers do, but forty years earlier. The miracle is that Graham was forced to face this eventuality after such a long, unmatched period of creativity and agile effort.

And did her old dances change in their reproductions since the early brave days?

Yes. One change was in us, her audience; we now looked for different things. When we first saw Graham's works we were so struck by the force of her ideas and the fresh aesthetics of the style that limitations were overlooked. After fifty years, the ideas remained striking and sound, if no longer startling, but the style, although pure, seemed crippled. It was internal and vertical, rooted to a single spot; the dance neither moved nor traveled transversely. There were none of the variations of steps and floor patterns that are the stuff of all Western folk dances and therefore ballet. There were no linkings, no exchanges, no enchaînements, Graham's dancing having been designed for the solo figure, or a soloist and a partner, or soloists and an antiphonal chorus, but never for a communal group; equal figures did not weave or exchange or move anywhere except inwardly, seldom outward. And there was incorporated none of the commonday vernacular steps like skipping, which rest the mind and are familiar and comforting.

This was particularly evident in her 1984 *Rite of Spring*, which introduced new and beautiful rhythmic patterns but little or no traveling motion. The mind panted to get loose, to get free, and to, for God's sake, go.

As early as 1943, John Martin recognized this limitation in Graham's work. He wrote:

> Curiously enough, Miss Graham has outdistanced her own technique as she has advanced into deeper territory, and there it stands, when the group performs it, declaring baldly that it has become not only familiar but frequently arbitrary and ineffectual. In her superb personal performance everything—technical vocabulary, movement, compositional pattern—is transfigured, but no such transformation can be expected from an ensemble.

Martha had given her first solo concert in 1926. Since then, a great deal of modern technique has been absorbed into the regular ballet dancer's training, including the complete use of the torso and arms and thighs, which makes possible a great deal of new technique. This would have been unheard of at the beginning of the century. In similar manner the modern dance, even Martha Graham's stringent regimen, has absorbed a sizable amount of orthodox ballet training. When the Juilliard School of Music opened their dance department, several leading dancers, both ballet and modern, were asked to be on the faculty. Graham, of course, was one of them, and she consented. This was the first time she had been brought into working proximity with ballet artists of great caliber. She taught in the room next to Antony Tudor and Margaret Craske, one of the finest ballet instructors in the world. She saw and understood with her extraordinary perception the true value of the classic technique. Probably it was at this point that she began to add the turnout and port de bras of the classic school to her curriculum and her regular vocabulary of gesture. Having found balletic training for the foot unmatched in producing jumpers, Martha began to permit the inclusion of ballet preparations. She remained, however, somewhat dubious and reluctant, until her technique was at length recognized as part of our culture. She in turn could accept without fear of contamination ballet jumps, ballet turns, ballet port de bras. The result is a much wider technique for the average dancer and a general strengthening of the body.

A second change has been in the physical conditions of performance, which have grown vastly more expensive but less luxurious. The original Graham girls worked for nothing and their costumes cost little, and so Martha could afford unlimited numbers of people. It was all relatively easy. The dancers often went hungry, of course, but they were there, working.

For economic reasons, there had been a gradual reduction in the numbers of dancers in the large group pieces, and therefore in the actual texture and shape of the choreography. The diminution began in about 1940, the third year of *American Document*. The ballet originally included some superb group numbers, which were later replaced with a reduced company, Martha having been constrained to make do with fewer dancers. The group dances accordingly lost much of their majestical counterpoint. For similar mundane reasons Martha was not ever able to revive several other of her glorious early works.

The erosion of time and usage worked further changes. From the beginning she kept changing the choreography of the 1940 *Letter to the World*. The long film that exists today is of the third version, while the notes are of quite another. Films were never made of her last great tragic solos, and the exact ending today only approximates what was there originally. Since Martha would let no one watch her in her solo rehearsals, and since only Pearl Lang participated in the choreographic process of Martha's solos, no notes were kept, and tremendous sections of the ballet are unrecorded. Now many of them have been fixed and recorded, but on other bodies and in other times, and, as a consequence, vital changes have worked their way into the very texture of the movement. Martha herself saw no need for notes, because, as Pearl Lang says, "Martha thought she would live forever, and that there never would be an occasion when she could not perform. She certainly didn't intend there to be." Of course, Martha, in common with every other fallible human being, also forgot, and, God knows, Martha altered.

There have been manifold changes in the costumes, largely because the fashion designer Halston took charge of the Graham company's wardrobe. Through the costumes he redesigned or re-edited the aspect of very nearly all the ballets currently performed. It is true that the costumes became more opulent than hitherto; they were probably better made (Anna Sokolow went onstage in safety pins), and they were stylish. They were smart the way a Saks Fifth Avenue window was smart. Halston made them chic; before, they were classic. They were then not stylish, nor were they rich; they were dead right for what they served.

Halston did what he did as a service to Martha, but also as a service to himself, since he was a contemporary designer who had never before ventured into the theater, and he obviously wished to enlarge his activity. Such editing was brand-new in Martha's experience. Martha had had great patrons in the past—the Lewisohns, Bethsabee de Roth-schild, Katharine Cornell, Lila Acheson Wallace; but none of them ever put their names on anything of hers, or interfered in any way. Halston was the first to do so. His thumb mark was on every ballet. He altered the entire pictorial aspect of her theater.

Then there was the question of the lighting, once so fastidiously and exquisitely designed by Jean Rosenthal, with her symphonic approach. In the later years the lighting was often overbright, and in some instances it was quite garish. This, some of the dancers felt, was due to Martha's growing loss of sight. She kept calling for brighter and brighter lights, which is a tendency of the aging. Jean Rosenthal had died of cancer in 1969. With her gone, the last restraints on Martha's lighting disappeared. Some of the lighting be-came a caricature of what Jean had left, and the stage managers were in despair. They developed, it seemed, three lighting plans: one for when Martha was out front, one for when she was in the wings, and one for when she was not paying strict attention and in no position to judge: then they could return to the original. But this last did not happen often. It was consistent with Martha's character, as with the general tendency of the old, to refuse to recognize the fault as any blemish in her own abilities.

In the same degree, the costumes grew bolder and more glitzy—not only more noticeable to the audience, but, what is to the point, more visible to Martha herself. She began to ask that the dancers in her classes wear practice leotards and tights of gold fabric, so that (she did not say, but they knew) she could see them and recognize instantly what they were doing. The hard fact was that the restrained decencies of the old costumes became a memory of her youth.*

For *Acts of Light* in 1981, a very beautiful ballet, Halston dressed

---

*However, at one time in *Primitive Mysteries* the girls suddenly appeared with a white ruffle at the bottom of their skirts, the white fanciness ameliorating the stark black execution robe. In New Mexico the churches of the Indian people have no glazed windows, no tiled floors; the Stations of the Cross have only painted numbers, no pictures; a table serves as an altar; the worshipers kneel in the dark. I remember on one homemade *santos,* hanging on the crude cross, blood and tears had been carefully painted by someone with little skill but with a great knowledge of blood. And He was dressed, the Holy One, this little Christ, in a pink satin frock, the best the Indians could afford. By His side hung a party favor, a pink paper candy basket.

No ruffles.

I believe that later the ruffles were eliminated.

the performers in golden tissue which almost reduced the work to a cosmetic display. The men throughout the programs seemed more naked than they ever had been before. Indeed, Halston's attention to the well-groomed buttock amounted almost to a fetish. Martha's gorgeous movement overcame these silly handicaps.

Her *Rite* was an example of a fine idea that nearly foundered in a welter of material, until finally the sacrificial victim appeared to die, not from cosmic necessity nor archetypal doom, but from a surfeit of yardage.

Howard Moss wrote of the *Rite* in the *New York Review of Books:*

Graham, who had years of making do with homemade and last-minute costumes, has a weakness for grand theatrical effects. They are more congenial to Greek tragedy than to primordial rites. In *Clytemnestra,* the red floor covering suddenly becoming the Queen's cloak after Agamemnon's murder is a stunning dramatic device, but Graham has become too much given to robes and props in general. There is something childishly puppet-theaterlike in her addiction to sweeping yards of material. Halston's support and interest in the company may have increased a tendency to rely on costumed effects, but it shouldn't be blamed on him—the tendency was there before he was associated with the company.

I could accept Martha's love of symbol when it was used for good reason, but not when it was mere ostentation. One recalls with a certain wistfulness Martha's early dictum that no costume was to cost more than one dollar; and one looks back on Martha's statement made in the thirties about her own personal austere dress. Martha's feeling for fine clothes and expensive accouterments was fun for her as a human woman. God knows, she deserved it, and if she enjoyed it, we love her for it, but it should not have touched her theater or her stage, which was her church.

These, however, were all relatively trivial details. What went to the root, what was the essence of deviation, was the fact that the dancers had not the power or the savagery of the early executors. They became therefore a transference of surface intent.

The girls and boys no longer had the eyes to see exactly what was there; and, what was more difficult, they no longer had the bodies and the dynamics to execute what Martha wanted. The dancers became slimmer, more slight, possibly more technically able; but they were also less thinking, less well read, less prepared for Graham's methods of communication. It was evident that she talked to totally ignorant youngsters, as ignorant as ballet dancers, with no interest in reading, in studying, in finding out. And while their bodies grew more facile, possibly prettier, more virtuosic, their understanding remained stunted. Also, they grew lazier. The big impulses and centered contractions take a toll of the bodily energies. Most were not willing to spend those energies. They wished to learn a role in two weeks, and they had to learn the role mainly from tapes and fragmentary films. In short, they failed to learn the role. They learned a passing reflection, without viscera. The driving, sparking impact was lost, the heart impulse eradicated. What they produced were pleasing patterns—in short, nothing. The tragic part is that they did not know that the life pulse had departed. They believed in all sincerity they were re-creating her vital dance. There can be no substitution for sincerity and lifetime dedication, as there is no substitute for genius. The mark of original purpose was missing.

Graham's original girls were superb—Bessie Schönberg, Evelyn Sabin, Martha Hill, Gertrude Shurr, Anna Sokolov, Nelle Fisher, Dorothy Bird, Bonnie Bird, Sophie Maslow, May O'Donnell, Jane Dudley, Anita Alvarez, Pearl Lang—as were the second group—Yuriko, Ethel Butler, Ethel Winter, Jean Erdman, Patricia Birch, Nina Fonaroff, Matt Turney, Mary Hinkson. And the unforgettable group of men— Erick Hawkins, and after him Merce Cunningham, David Campbell, John Butler, Stuart Hodes, Glen Tetley, Bertram Ross, Paul Taylor, Mark Ryder, William Carter. They cannot be replaced, because they were great individuals and because they were fired in the original furnace. Bertram Ross, for instance, has never been approached in his playing of Saint Michael in *Seraphic Dialogue,* or Mark Ryder in *Errand into the Maze,* or John Butler in *Appalachian Spring,* or William Carter in the same role.

In brief, the feeling of Graham's performance had altered.

This was not entirely the dancers' doing, or Martha's, either. All dancers of the new generation, ballet as well as modern, were shaped by a new attitude: an attitude of business. Formerly they starved to dance. The unions got them a decent living—good. But the effect of the unions was to limit the dancers' enthusiasm and their involvement, and the participation and sharing of their employers. Since time was the dancers' stock-in-trade, the stuff of their bargaining, it had become costly, and too much had to be done too fast. Dancers could no longer take time, could no longer give time, yet it is axiomatic that an artist cannot consider time. He gives. That is the essence of his service. The mystery and the power lie outside of practical considerations and outside of computer programming. If Martha's life meant anything at all, it proved this point, and this simple truth is what the contemporary dancer overlooks. No, Martha's girls and boys no longer took the stage with the majesty and passion that the early pupils did. Simply and briefly, their lives were not at stake. It had all become possible, even comfortable. The divine hazard was missing.

"Did you see Martha's season?" I asked John Butler in 1984.

"I could not bear to. My heart would break. I performed those dances. I loved those dances as my life; they are part of my life. Now I see them done by others. Such beautiful bodies, and so skilled! But there's nobody home. They've all gone away."

The original group shared their faith with an enthusiasm and a belief that was communicable, the very stuff of theatrical exchange, the reason why the theater is an art—to some people, a great art and of prime importance. Graham's early converts would have died for her and for her ideas. When they reached through to an audience, they lifted those people out of themselves. The people who attend the present performances do not feel they are in the presence of an experience that cannot be had in any other place in the world. The young dancers who saw Graham in the great days never were the same after; they altered their direction. Martha herself burned with the grace of heaven. She had the *feu sacré*. She ignited.

Pearl Lang waxed passionate:

Martha had in her the sense of historic weight. Her great roles belong to the world's mythology.

Martha walked onstage with her entire experience, her learning, her enormous reading, her living capabilities, and the sense of eternity and time that, for instance, Clytemnestra has to project, or that sense of eternity before Jocasta commits suicide in her walk from the back of the stage to the front, and, dear God, if you don't see yourself a thousand years before projected into a thousand years hence, you haven't got the size of it or the importance. These kids today have no idea. They think everything is here and now.

Mary Austin* told me that in all American Indian ceremonials there was a moment when the ritual ceased to be formal and became potent,

*Mary Austin (1868–1934), the distinguished American author, was the great authority on, and apologist for, the Southwestern American Indian, his arts and culture.

became magic, and the participants knew the god had entered and they felt his presence and were changed. "Never," Mrs. Austin said to me, "let the god be absent from your theater."

When Martha departed from her stage, the god departed, and the works were left lifeless husks.

But not forever.

|||||

Now that Martha was gone from the stage, others expanded.

In 1984 it became apparent that Terese Capucilli had developed into a big dance personality. She was a performer of prodigious physical prowess and generous personality, of burning passion, with the impact of an unsheathed weapon. This slight girl delivered herself of the kind of performance that made an enduring impact on the beholder. She was of radiant star quality, and in three of the leading roles which she danced in the 1984 season—in *Seraphic Dialogue, Errand into the Maze,* and *The Rite of Spring,* she proved her right to be classed as a major dancer and a worthy successor to the roles Martha had bequeathed her. This had not happened before, even with the early loyal and faithful adherents. The other performers were not dynamically large enough, intense enough, or interesting enough. Capucilli was.

Appalachian Spring was one of Martha's signature pieces. Whenever anyone else stepped into her role in this ballet, no matter who it was, the dancer seemed like a little girl in her mother's clothes. Suddenly the little girls began to assert themselves as themselves and as grown-ups. Jeanne Ruddy and Yuriko Kimura made new claims on conviction. Ruddy's exquisite last gesture, establishing horizon, peace and homeland, Kimura's joyous lifts like the shouting assertions of youth brought new dimensions to the role. And they were at home in the old patterns, which had become their own and were done freely. This had not been so before.

This was particularly true of the solo *Frontier.* Martha had a compelling wonder, approaching awe, concerning distance, the power of space. Peggy Lyman and Carol Langly had exuberance, youthful excitement in meeting the role's challenges. Langly matched herself eagerly against nature, as though she were hurling her body into the flow of primal force. Martha achieved mystery and dominion, Carol Langly, life. When Langly sat spread-legged on the earth, her whole body seemed to kiss the ground, to receive vitality from and regenerate the earth. Without changing a gesture, she brought a new face to this fifty-year-old classic, proving that Martha herself had the largeness of spirit to permit new growth and the emergence of other personalities.

In her 1987 gala Martha treated the audience to a revealing experience. She ran an old film of herself dancing *Frontier* with a recorded synchronized score, and an audience who had never seen her perform, or at least imperfectly remembered the original performance, suddenly beheld what she had been, what she had had to give. There was all the energy, the vitality of the younger woman, but also a larger dimension, the awe of destiny without aggression, with an acceptance, a tolerance, a gentleness, almost a submission to the realization of her situation.

The company never had a personality to match Martha's, but in 1987 she added three Russian stars, Maya Plisetskaya in St. Denis's *Incense,* who demonstrated that while this dance is basically only a curiosity, a star is a star; St. Denis we were told was great, Plisetskaya was great. And in *Appalachian Spring* Martha presented Rudolf Nureyev as the preacher and Mikhail Baryshnikov as the husbandman dancing opposite Terese Capucilli in Martha's role of the bride. Nureyev simplified the technique by eliminating much of the knee work, which was considered sissy of him by the true Grahamites, but was, notwithstanding, fierce, dominating, and demoniac. Baryshnikov was youthful, bonny, and heartwinning. Terese Capucilli matched the two men in strength and passion.

The audience crackled with excitement and broke, as the curtain fell, into shouts and cries. A good representation of Martha's old group was present and left the auditorium with radiant faces. "Like the good old days," they said as they embraced happily. "The glory is back."

Nor would the new revivifiers be the clones of Martha Graham. They would be different people, as they made visible what she had to say. The important thing was that the vehicle be preserved, the structure through which they were to work, Martha's literature. The performer is helpless without great tools. The music of Chopin played by a beginner is a different musical experience from Chopin played by Arthur Rubinstein. On the other hand, Chopin played by a beginner is still Chopin and still an experience to cherish. And we do have Chopin. It waits.

But who was I to say what Martha would do next? She would never be slight or external.

She continued to be herself, composing and directing and bringing to our stage her unmatched instinct, her impeccable taste, her boldness. And bringing her wonder at the human heart.

On February 29, 1986, I made a speech at the Martha Graham School. As I waited in the anteroom to begin, Martha came in to where I was sitting just before lecture time. She came in very quietly. She was wrapped in a superb mink coat and was dressed simply but extremely elegantly in a pants suit of black velvet, with, around her neck, a marvelous rope of American Indian turquoise combined with cylindrical tubes of silver. It was extremely beautiful and probably very, very valuable. "A present," she said with a smile. "From Ron Protas, of course." Her hair was now dark auburn and was dressed out on the sides like that of a Hopi bride—a squash-blossom coiffure, great coiled loops that stood out from her head. The back hair was folded very like an obi, satin smooth and wondrously elegant. Whether it was partly wig or all Martha's hair could not be told, but it was superbly ornamental. She herself was transparent, lustrous. She seemed to give out light, very pale, her lips pale pink, her eyes made up, but subtly, large and shining. She spoke in a soft, husky voice.

"I am elderly. Well, I am old, and if I dress my age I will look older than God's aunt, and I don't want to look that old. In fact, I refuse to, so I choose to be flamboyant."

She sat during my lecture, unmoving. Whether she listened to any of it or used the time to plan a new dance I cannot say. We talked afterward. She said nothing about the lecture. Throughout our conversation her voice was very, very soft, so that I had to strain to hear her in the general hubbub of post-lecture conversation. She told me that Pan Am gave the company an airplane every year to go to Europe. Otherwise they could not make their annual journeys to the Continent. Pan Am never asked anything in return, making the trip a public-relations service.

She talked about her work in Washington with the National Endowment for the Arts. She didn't like the Endowment work much because she really wasn't used. They never asked her advice but merely asked her to vote on a fait accompli. And she said to them, "I will not be brought down here to ratify what you do. If you wish my advice, ask for it and I will give it. But listen to it."

She did not inquire about my life. She did ask after Walter, my husband, and when I explained he wasn't well she said, "I must come down to see him." So I begged, "Will you come to dinner one night?" And she said, "Yes, later, when I'm not rehearsing. After the season." I did not think she really would come, and she didn't.

As I left the remote encounter with this pale, lustrous deity, I was remembering the exuberant, giggling young woman who had poked her umbrella through the shattered roof of my old jalopy and sheltered me as we proceeded ostentatiously and dry through a rainstorm toward an otherwise unmemorable dance concert.

|||||

Martha had always wanted romantic love. It is very likely she felt more than ready for a grand passion. Many people do, but few, and certainly very few artists, are capable of serving or sustaining such an emotion. Part of Martha's nature longed to be mastered, to be guided and directed; part, and probably the controlling part, took charge and changed the world. Louis controlled her, but she separated from that relationship. Thereafter she chose men she could dominate, and if they objected, the union terminated. If they didn't object, it terminated.

She wanted friends and acolytes. They were to her like proxy children, but they grew up and departed. Her intimate co-equels died. Martha could not be equal.

Her family was all gone, all dead except for her little sister, Geordie, nearly ninety, frail and very ailing, a whiner and a constant care.*

Martha was alone.

What then did she have beside worldwide glory?

What had she done in her long, hard life?

She had discovered a new way of moving that was beautiful and significant, and her discoveries and inventions amounted to a new speech: she had enlarged our language.

She had given us more than two hundred compositions in this new language and many of them were lasting works of art.

The poet Richard Howe had written in 1967: "Miss Graham's dance dramas are the most convincing representations I know of of the vastness of the unconscious," where, as Edwin Denby once said, "Folly is at home, easy to watch, and hard to take."

She had founded a school known throughout the world.

She had trained a large cadre of disciples who looked upon dancing

---

*On October 11, 1988, Georgie, the third and last of the Graham sisters, died in Tucson, Arizona, aged eighty-eight. She died alone. She had lived alone for some years. She had been fragile, ailing, bored (she used to sit in the supermarket to watch the people as they shopped), dependent, dragging on Martha, but at the same time lending her a point of emotional need on which to center. Poor little Geordie! Poor hapless Geordie! At the time of her sister's death, Martha was in the midst of her fall season. She absented herself from the theater that sad night.

not as entertainment but as a means of high communication. She had furthered, reaffirmed, and solidified the work begun by Isadora Duncan, to re-establish dancing among the major arts, as the servitor of religious and intellectual purpose, and, as a corollary, to establish its practitioners as serious artists.

|||||

Martha was now alone. She was going to die alone, as she had lived alone, without children, without adopted children in spite of her many brilliant, adoring pupils, without a lover or a husband, without, God help us, old friends. She would remain alone with her work, the alter self, the presence, the aureole—penumbra which overshadowed her life, larger, greater than her daily personality, her very meaning, never leaving, always with her. Most artists know this loneliness, as do great scientists, dedicated workers, this readiness, this waiting to be penetrated, to be possessed and used, this perception which gave Martha verification. Martha more than most, but every artist on occasion.

And is not every one of us, artist or laborer, alone, masking our hungers and fears with ambition or passion or greed, wrapping, muffling our needs in relationships, without ever making contact? Unable to speak, ever dumb, sealed off, as though a good part of our nature were paralyzed, without once knowing the clear moment of being essential, of being axial?

And what matter if she neglected friendships, or used friendships? What matter compared to this?

Was she bad, as Louis Horst had said? No, she was incorruptible by the standards of her ideal. Only that.

Still, when Martha entered the studio, crippled, immobilized, there was, waiting for her as always before, the love of her life, the Promise. It was always there, the stuff of her métier. Her Purpose.

Space. She stood in the center of creation. Space and her brain. She had only to move, to put out a hand, and it began.

Creative energy, multiplication, expansion, form, energy.

Citadels of energy,
evanescent sculptures of spatial dynamics,
Architecture of air,
Civilizations, histories of incorporeal identity.
They weren't there.

They were always there.

She had but to put her hand out and she would start the great process.

The unseen machinery would begin.

In the beginning was the word.

Before that, movement.

Her homeland.

Her calling.

Her joy.

APPENDICES

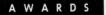
AWARDS

1932 Guggenheim Fellow
1950 Guggenheim Fellow
1956 *Dance Magazine* Award
1959 Eisenhower Appointee Advisory Member, National Cultural Center
1960 Capezio Award
1963 Wayne State University, Detroit, Michigan: Honorary Doctor of Humanities
1965 Laurel Leaf of the Composers' Alliance
1966 Aspen Award in Humanities, given to "the individual anywhere in the world who has made the greatest advancement of the humanities." Martha's comment on the award was "that it was given to a woman—that it was given to a dancer—marks a great step forward in the thinking of America."
1966 Harvard University, Boston, Massachusetts: Honorary Doctor of Arts
1968 Brandeis University, Waltham, Massachusetts: Creative Arts Award
1968 Family of Man Award
1970 Distinguished Service to Arts Award, National Institute of Arts and Letters
1970 Handel Medallion, City of New York
1971 Yale University, New Haven, Connecticut, Honorary Doctor of Fine Arts
1971 Wesleyan University Middletown, Connecticut, Honorary Doctor of Fine Arts
1973 New York State Council on Arts Award
1976 Medal of Freedom, presented by President Gerald R. Ford, who officially proclaimed Martha a "national treasure."
1979 Washington, D.C.: Kennedy Center Honors Award
1979 Royal Medal, Jordan
1981 Samuel H. Scripps American Dance Festival Award
1982 Meadows School of the Arts, Southern Methodist University, Dallas, Texas: The Algur H. Meadows Award for Excellence in the Arts
1983 Bryn Mawr College, Bryn Mawr, Pennsylvania: The M. Carey Thomas Prize, awarded to "American women of eminent achievement."
1983 New York: Artpark Award
1984 Florence, Italy: Golden Florin Award
1984 Knight of the French Legion of Honor
1985 Carina Ari Medal, presented to Martha by Princess Christina of Sweden.
1985 Paris, France: Grand Vermeil Medal

1985	President Reagan's National Medal of Arts
1986	International Alliance of Theatrical Stage Employees Local One's Local One Centennial Award. (This will not be awarded again until the year 2086.)
1986	Honorary Citizen of Tennessee Award, Chattanooga
1987	Premio Porselli Award, Reggio Emilia, Italy
1988	Certificate of Appreciation, Tucson, Arizona
1989	City of Bari Award, Bari, Italy
1989	Seal of the City of Pittsburgh, Pennsylvania
1989	City of Boston Award, Boston, Massachusetts
1990	Order of the Precious Butterfly with Diamond, Emperor Akihito, Tokyo, Japan
1991	Lifetime Achievement Award, Council of Fashion Designers of America

(These notes on Kundalini Yoga are based on a taped explanation of the subject by Joseph Campbell, in the possession of the author.)

Kundalini Yoga, Joseph Campbell has explained, maintains that there are seven psychological centers in the body, known either as *padmas* (lotuses) or as *chakras* (wheels); they are distributed along the spine. With the arrival of energy into each of these centers, a transformation of consciousness takes place. Kundalini means "the coiled-up one," the serpent. In India the serpent is a symbol of energy and vital power. Because it sheds its skin and becomes, in effect, reborn, it is a symbol for regeneration and all kindred ideas. Energy in India is always regarded as feminine, as a female: the Shakti, the Goddess. Accordingly, myth has it that there is a tiny female serpent, as big around as "a boar's bristle," coiled at the base of the spine. In normal living, it is dormant. The aim of Kundalini Yoga breathing is to arouse this coiled-up serpent, this energy, and bring it up the spine so that it can animate all the organs and spiritual powers of the body, which are also lying dormant. As the energy attains successive physical and spiritual levels, one experiences ideas and feelings that instantaneously reveal a new, complete, and startlingly clear perspective of life. It is not difficult to reach this stage of heightened awareness: it has been present all the time, waiting to be awakened. Kundalini is one of India's greatest gifts to the world, an extraordinary concept that envisages the organization of spiritual energy.

The first *chakra* or level is at the base of the spine; when this stage is reached, the individual is simply hanging on to life like a child—not dying, but barely holding on. Many people never get beyond this.

The second *chakra* is at the level of the genitals. The thinking of a person awakened to this level is completely Freudian—everything is related to sex. This is adolescence.

The third *chakra* is at the navel. (Indian thinking is always very physical.) Avidity and aggressiveness becomes apparent. The attack on life, the desire to control life, the immense urge for power in an individual who has reached this stage recalls Adlerian rather than Freudian Psychology. These are the levels of life on which animals live, as well as many human beings: simply hanging on to life, generating life, and claiming a personal share of life. Popular religions are devoted to fostering these unspiritual and worldly hopes. We pray for long life, health, wealth, and fertility; for food and for happiness.

The fourth *chakra* is at the level of the heart. When the coiled-up energy reaches this far, there is an awakening of spiritual life. The individual realizes that he and everything in the universe are but manifestations of primal force. This is the moment of awakening, and it is on this level that art functions, the art of political and didactic thought. The most vivid image, that which best represents Kundalini Yoga at this level, is the Star of David: the upward point of the triangle represents the claims of spiritual life; the downward point represents the claims of the material and physical world. Art is the claim of the world informed by the spirit, the transformation of nature into and by art. In most Indian dance forms the female dancer bends forward slightly; her movements seem to come from that part of the body in which the heart is situated—from the fourth *chakra.*

There are three *chakras* in the pelvic area. These are known as the animal levels. The awakening lies in the center of the body, where one finds the beating pulse, the beating heart, and the pulsing, beating rhythms of breathing.

Once this awakening of the spirit has taken place, people become zealous to know and understand more of the spirit: to rid themselves of the weight and downward pull of the lower animal centers. Ascetic effort, discipline, the trials of the work done in the dance studio, are all part of this *Beshunta* or cleansing level, *chakra* five; *Beshunta* is at the level of the larynx, the place from which we speak. No animal can work on this level.

Beyond this, above it, are the sixth and seventh *chakras.* These are the levels of mystical religious rapture. By the time one has reached the sixth *chakra* the psyche has, so to speak, been cleansed of its materialism, has lost its downward-pulling weight. The mystic inward eye that is depicted on the forehead of both gods and humans in Hindu painting opens, and one finally receives the blinding radiance and flash of the vision of God. This envisioned God will appear as He to whom you personally have been devoted: the ultimate mystery is transcendent—there is no hard-and-fast, definite image. All imaginings of God are in terms of the local tradition, and it is this image one will receive when the third, the inner, eye opens. This God is the final and ultimate object of love.

The ecstatic energy we experience on reaching the second *chakra,* the sexual center, is only a foretaste of the ultimate, sublime experience of the love of God. It is the emotion expressed by Dante in the *Divine Comedy* when he comes to the realization that Beatrice, his beloved and his guide through Paradise, is not a sexual object but a revelation of the divine love of God. It is through this love that one is led to the ultimate reward: Heaven; to the image of your own personal God. Here, on this sixth level, one receives an understanding of the ultimate mystery of Yoga, of all mysticism: that of identification with God. This may be regarded as heresy among some "popular" religions, but it is the truth in which every mystic believes: "I and my beloved are one." It is what Jesus is reported to have said in the early Gnostic *Gospel According to Saint Thomas:* "I and my father are one." It is a belief Buddha must also have held.

As energy uncoils ever higher up the spine, new ecstasies are reached at each level. But the rapture of the seventh *chakra,* which is located in the crown of the head, surpasses that of all others. It surpasses the rapture that is art.

This is the Kundalini.

||||

The theory and beliefs of Kundalini were well known to Hindu scholars and sages, but remained unknown to other peoples for almost four thousand years. In 1924, Sir John Woodruffe (who wrote under the name of Arthur Avalon), a scholar and voracious reader of Hindu mystical texts, translated and published a book called *The Serpent Power*, which discussed the Kundalini. The ideas proved revelatory.

Tantra, an Indian religious movement that came to the fore primarily in the sixth century A.D., influenced Buddhism, Janism, and Hinduism. It shows us a way to reach and to understand the spiritual meaning inherent in everyday life. Throughout history there have been religious movements in India that have tended to distance themselves from reality, to make themselves remote. Tantra was a movement in opposition, a teaching that showed the way *into* life, that allowed the circumstances of physical life to become the discipline of one's own religious life. Tantra teaches us to recognize God in everyday things. The movement had an enormous influence on the religious life of India.

Kundalini Yoga is part of this Tantric body of thought.

THE DANCES

Martha Graham and Concert Group (also programmed as Martha Graham and Dance Group)

Title	Date, Place of Premiere	Composer	Decor	Costumes	Lighting
1. *Chorale* (Martha Graham and trio)	Apr. 18, 1926 48th St. Theatre, N.Y.	César Franck		Martha Graham (M.G.)	Martha Graham (M.G.)
2. *Novelette* (solo, Martha Graham)	Apr. 18, 1926 48th St. Theatre, N.Y.	Robert Schumann		M.G.	M.G.
3. *Tanze* (trio)	Apr. 18, 1926 48th St. Theatre, N.Y.	Franz Schubert		M.G.	M.G.
4. *Intermezzo* (solo, Martha Graham)	Apr. 18, 1926 48th St. Theatre, N.Y.	Johannes Brahms		M.G.	M.G.
5. *Maid with the Flaxen Hair* (solo, Martha Graham)	Apr. 18, 1926 48th St. Theatre, N.Y.	Claude Debussy		M.G.	M.G.
6. *Arabesque No. 1* (trio)	Apr. 18, 1926 48th St. Theatre, N.Y.	Claude Debussy		M.G.	M.G.
7. *Clair de Lune* (Martha Graham and trio)	Apr. 18, 1926 48th St. Theatre, N.Y.	Claude Debussy		M.G.	M.G.
8. *Danse Languide* (trio)	Apr. 18, 1926 48th St. Theatre, N.Y.	Alexander Scriabin		M.G.	M.G.
9. *Désir* (solo, Martha Graham)	Apr. 18, 1926 48th St. Theatre, N.Y.	Alexander Scriabin		M.G.	M.G.
10. *Deux Valses Sentimentales* (solo, Martha Graham)	Apr. 18, 1926 48th St. Theatre, N.Y.	Maurice Ravel		M.G.	M.G.

Title	Date, Place of Premiere	Composer	Decor	Costumes	Lighting
11. *Masques* (solo, Martha Graham)	Apr. 18, 1926 48th St. Theatre, N.Y.	Louis Horst		M.G.	M.G.
12. *Trois Gnossiennes: Gnossienne, Frieze, Tanagra* (Martha Graham and trio)	Apr. 18, 1926 48th St. Theatre, N.Y.	Erik Satie		M.G.	M.G.
13. *From a XIIth-Century Tapestry*, later retitled *A Florentine Madonna* (solo, Martha Graham)	Apr. 18, 1926 48th St. Theatre, N.Y.	Sergei Rachmaninoff		Earle Franke	M.G.
14. *A Study in Lacquer* (solo, Martha Graham)	Apr. 18, 1926 48th St. Theatre, N.Y.	Marcel Bernheim		M.G.	M.G.
15. *The Three Gopi Maidens* (trio) Excerpted from "The Flute of Krishna"	Apr. 18, 1926 48th St. Theatre, N.Y.	Cyril Scott		Norman Edwards	M.G.
16. *Danse Rococo* (solo, Martha Graham)	Apr. 18, 1926 48th St. Theatre, N.Y.	Maurice Ravel		Earle Franke	M.G.
17. *The Marionette Show* (solo, Martha Graham)	Apr. 18, 1926 48th St. Theatre, N.Y.	Eugene Goossens		M.G.	M.G.
18. *Portrait—After Beltram—Masses*, later retitled *Gypsy Portrait* (solo, Martha Graham)	Apr. 18, 1926 48th St. Theatre, N.Y.	Manuel de Falla		M.G.	M.G.
19. *The Flute of Krishna* (dance and film)	May 1926, Kilbourn Hall, Rochester, N.Y., Eastman-Kodak Studio	Cyril Scott		Norman Edwards	M.G.

Title	Date, Place of Premiere	Composer	Decor	Costumes	Lighting
20. *Prelude from "Alceste"* (Martha Graham and trio)	May 27, 1926 Kilbourn Hall, Rochester, N.Y.	C. W. von Gluck		Norman Edwards	M.G.
21. *Scéne Javanaise* (Martha Graham and trio)	May 27, 1926 Kilbourn Hall, Rochester, N.Y.	Louis Horst		Norman Edwards	M.G.
22. *Danza Degli Angeli* (trio)	May 27, 1926 Kilbourn Hall, Rochester, N.Y.	Ermanno Wolf-Ferrari		Norman Edwards	M.G.
23. *Bas Relief* (trio)	May 27, 1926 Kilbourn Hall, Rochester, N.Y.	Cyril Scott		Norman Edwards	M.G.
24. *Ribands* (duet, Evelyn Sabin and Betty MacDonald)	Aug. 20, 1926 Mariarden, Peterboro, N.H.	Frédéric Chopin		Norman Edwards	M.G.
25. *Scherzo* (trio)	Nov. 28, 1926 Klaw Theatre, N.Y.	Felix Mendelssohn		M.G.	M.G.
26. *Baal Shem* (Martha Graham and trio)	Nov. 28, 1926 Klaw Theatre, N.Y.	Ernest Bloch		M.G.	M.G.
27. *La Soirée dans Grenade* (solo, Martha Graham)	Nov. 28, 1926 Klaw Theatre, N.Y.	Claude Debussy		M.G.	M.G.
28. *Alt-Wien* (duet, Evelyn Sabin and Betty MacDonald)	Nov. 28, 1926 Klaw Theatre, N.Y.	Leopold Godowsky (arr. by Louis Horst)		M.G.	M.G.
29. *Three Poems of the East* (Martha Graham and trio)	Nov. 28, 1926 Klaw Theatre, N.Y.	Louis Horst		M.G.	M.G.

Title	Date, Place of Premiere	Composer	Decor	Costumes	Lighting
30. *Peasant Sketches* (solo, Martha Graham)	Feb. 27, 1927 Guild Theatre, N.Y.	Vladimir Rebikov, Alexandre Tansman, P. I. Tchaikovsky		M.G.	M.G.
31. *Tunisia* (solo, Martha Graham)	Feb. 27, 1927 Guild Theatre, N.Y.	Eduard Poldini		M.G.	M.G.
32. *Lucrezia* (solo, Martha Graham)	Feb. 27, 1927 Guild Theatre, N.Y.	Claude Debussy		M.G.	M.G.
33. *La Canción* (solo, Martha Graham)	Feb. 27, 1927 Guild Theatre, N.Y.	René Defossez		M.G.	M.G.
34. *Arabesque No. 1*, revised (group)	Aug. 2, 1927 Anderson-Milton School, N.Y.	Claude Debussy		M.G.	M.G.
35. *Valse Caprice* (solo, Louise Gotto)	Aug. 2, 1927 Anderson-Milton School, N.Y.	Cyril Scott		M.G.	M.G.
36. *Spires* (trio)	Oct. 16, 1927 The Little Theatre, N.Y.	J. S. Bach		M.G.	M.G.
37. *Adagio* (solo, Martha Graham)	Oct. 16, 1927 The Little Theatre, N.Y.	G. F. Handel		M.G.	M.G.
38. *Fragilité* (solo, Martha Graham)	Oct. 16, 1927 The Little Theatre, N.Y.	Alexander Scriabin		M.G.	M.G.
39. *Lugubre* (trio)	Oct. 16, 1927 The Little Theatre, N.Y.	Alexander Scriabin		M.G.	M.G.

Title	Date, Place of Premiere	Composer	Decor	Costumes	Lighting
40. *Poème Ailé* (solo, Martha Graham)	Oct. 16, 1927 The Little Theatre, N.Y.	Alexander Scriabin		M.G.	M.G.
41. *Tanzstück* (trio)	Oct. 16, 1927 The Little Theatre, N.Y.	Paul Hindemith		M.G.	M.G.
42. *Revolt* (solo, Martha Graham)	Oct. 16, 1927 The Little Theatre, N.Y.	Arthur Honegger		M.G.	M.G.
43. *Esquisse Antique* (trio)	Oct. 16, 1927 The Little Theatre, N.Y.	Désiré-Emile Inghelbrecht		M.G.	M.G.
44. *Ronde* (trio)	Oct. 16, 1927 The Little Theatre, N.Y.	Rhené-Baton		M.G.	M.G.
45. *Scherza* (solo, Martha Graham)	Dec. 10, 1927 Cornell University, Ithaca, N.Y.	Robert Schumann		M.G.	M.G.
46. *Chinese Poem* (solo, Martha Graham)	Feb. 12, 1928 Civic Repertory Theatre, N.Y.	Louis Horst		M.G.	M.G.
47. *Trouvères* (solo, Martha Graham)	Apr. 22, 1928 The Little Theatre, N.Y.	Charles Koechlin		M.G.	M.G.
48. *Immigrant: Steerage, Strike* (solo, Martha Graham)	Apr. 22, 1928 The Little Theatre, N.Y.	Josip Slavenski		M.G.	M.G.

Title	Date, Place of Premiere	Composer	Decor	Costumes	Lighting
49. *Poems of 1917: Song Behind the Lines, Dance of Death* (solo, Martha Graham)	Apr. 22, 1928 The Little Theatre, N.Y.	Leo Ornstein		M.G.	M.G.
50. *Fragments: Tragedy, Comedy* (solo, Martha Graham)	Apr. 22, 1928 The Little Theatre, N.Y.	Louis Horst		M.G.	M.G.
51. *Resonances: Matins, Gamelin, Tocsin* (solo, Martha Graham)	Apr. 22, 1928 The Little Theatre, N.Y.	Gian Francesco Malipiero		M.G.	M.G.
52. *Dance* (solo, Martha Graham) "Strong Free Joyous Action": Nietzsche	Jan. 20, 1929 Booth Theatre, N.Y.	Arthur Honegger		M.G.	M.G.
53. *Three Florentine Verses* (solo, Martha Graham)	Jan. 20, 1929 Booth Theatre, N.Y.	Domenico Zipoli		M.G.	M.G.
54. *Four Insincerities: Petulance, Remorse, Politeness, Vivacity* (solo, Martha Graham)	Jan. 20, 1929 Booth Theatre, N.Y.	Sergei Prokofiev		M.G.	M.G.
55. *Cants Magics: Farewell, Greeting* (solo, Martha Graham)	Jan. 20, 1929 Booth Theatre, N.Y.	Fédérico Mompou		M.G.	M.G.
56. *Two Variations: Country Lane, City Street* (solo, Martha Graham	Jan. 20, 1929 Booth Theatre, N.Y.	Alexander Gretchanioff		M.G.	M.G.

Title	Date, Place of Premiere	Composer	Decor	Costumes	Lighting
57. *Figure of a Saint* (solo, Martha Graham)	Jan. 24, 1929 Millbrook, N.Y.	G. F. Handel		M.G.	M.G.
58. *Resurrection* (solo, Martha Graham)	March 3, 1929 Booth Theatre, N.Y.	Tibor Harsányi		M.G.	M.G.
59. *Adolescence* (solo, Martha Graham)	March 3, 1929 Booth Theatre, N.Y.	Paul Hindemith		M.G.	M.G.
60. *Danza* (solo, Martha Graham)	March 3, 1929 Booth Theatre, N.Y.	Darius Milhaud		M.G.	M.G.
Martha Graham and Dance Group					
61. *Vision of the Apocalypse: Theme and Variations* (group)	Apr. 14, 1929 Booth Theatre, N.Y.	Herman Reutter		M.G.	M.G.
62. *Moment Rustica* (group)	Apr. 14, 1929 Booth Theatre, N.Y.	Francis Poulenc		M.G.	M.G.
63. *Sketches from the People: Monotony, Supplication, Requiem* (group)	Apr. 14, 1929 Booth Theatre, N.Y.	Julien Krein		M.G.	M.G.
64. *Heretic* (Martha Graham and group)	Apr. 14, 1929 Booth Theatre, N.Y.	Old Breton Song—de Sivry		M.G.	M.G.
65. *Prelude to a Dance*, retitled *Salutation* (group)	Jan. 8, 1930 Maxine Elliott's Theatre, N.Y.	Arthur Honegger		M.G.	M.G.
66. *Two Chants: Futility, Ecstatic Song* (solo, Martha Graham)	Jan. 8, 1930 Maxine Elliott's Theatre, N.Y.	Ernst Krenek		M.G.	M.G.

Title	Date, Place of Premiere	Composer	Decor	Costumes	Lighting
67. *Lamentation* (solo, Martha Graham)	Jan. 8, 1930 Maxine Elliott's Theatre, N.Y.	Zoltan Kodály		M.G.	M.G.
68. *Project in Movement for a Divine Comedy* (Martha Graham and group)	Jan. 8, 1930 Maxine Elliott's Theatre, N.Y.	Silence		M.G.	M.G.
69. *Harlequinade* (solo, Martha Graham)	Jan. 8, 1930 Maxine Elliott's Theatre, N.Y.	Ernst Toch		M.G.	M.G.
70. *Two Primitive Canticles* (solo, Martha Graham)	Feb. 2, 1931 Craig Theatre, N.Y.	Heitor Villa-Lobos		M.G.	M.G.
71. *Primitive Mysteries: Hymn to the Virgin, Crucifixus, Hosanna* (Martha Graham and group)	Feb. 2, 1931 Craig Theatre, N.Y.	Louis Horst		M.G.	M.G.
72. *Rhapsodics: Song, Interlude, Dance* (solo, Martha Graham)	Feb. 2, 1931 Craig Theatre, N.Y.	Bela Bartók			M.G.
73. *Bacchanale* (Martha Graham and group)	Feb. 2, 1931 Craig Theatre, N.Y.	Wallingford Riegger		M.G.	M.G.
74. *Dolorosa* (solo, Martha Graham)	Feb. 2, 1931 Craig Theatre, N.Y.	Heitor Villa-Lobos		M.G.	M.G.
75. *Dithyrambic* (solo, Martha Graham)	Dec. 6, 1931 Martin Beck Theatre, N.Y.	Aaron Copland		M.G.	M.G.

Title	Date, Place of Premiere	Composer	Decor	Costumes	Lighting
76. *Serenade* (solo, Martha Graham)	Dec. 6, 1931 Martin Beck Theatre, N.Y.	Arnold Schönberg		M.G.	M.G.
77. *Incantation* (Martha Graham and group)	Dec. 6, 1931 Martin Beck Theatre, N.Y.	Heitor Villa-Lobos		M.G.	M.G.
78. *Ceremonials* (Martha Graham and group)	Feb. 28, 1932 Guild Theatre, N.Y.	Lehman Engel		M.G.	M.G.
79. *Offering* (solo, Martha Graham)	June 2, 1932 Lydia Mendelssohn Theatre, Ann Arbor, Mich.	Heitor Villa-Lobos		M.G.	M.G.
80. *Ecstatic Dance* (solo, Martha Graham)	June 2, 1932 Lydia Mendelssohn Theatre, Ann Arbor, Mich.	Tibor Harsányi		M.G.	M.G.
81. *Bacchanale No. 2* (solo, Martha Graham)	June 2, 1932 Lydia Mendelssohn Theatre, Ann Arbor, Mich.	Wallingford Riegger		M.G.	M.G.
82. *Prelude* (solo, Martha Graham)	Nov. 20, 1932 Guild Theatre, N.Y.	Carlos Chavez		M.G.	M.G.
83. *Dance Songs* (solo, Martha Graham)	Nov. 20, 1932 Guild Theatre, N.Y.	Imre Weisshaus		M.G.	M.G.
84. *Chorus of Youth—Companions* (group)	Nov. 20, 1932 Guild Theatre, N.Y.	Louis Horst		M.G.	M.G.

Title	Date, Place of Premiere	Composer	Decor	Costumes	Lighting
85. *Tragic Patterns* (Martha Graham and group)	Feb. 20, 1933 Fuld Hall, Newark, N.J.	Louis Horst		M.G.	M.G.
86. *Elegiac* (solo, Martha Graham)	May 4, 1933 Guild Theatre, N.Y.	Paul Hindemith		M.G.	M.G.
87. *Ekstasis* (solo, Martha Graham)	May 4, 1933 Guild Theatre, N.Y.	Lehman Engel		M.G.	M.G.
88. *Dance Prelude* (solo, Martha Graham)	Nov. 19, 1933 Guild Theatre, N.Y.	Nikolas Lopatnikoff		M.G.	M.G.
89. *Frenetic Rhythms* (solo, Martha Graham)	Nov. 19, 1933 Guild Theatre, N.Y.	Wallingford Riegger		M.G.	M.G.
90. *Transitions* (solo, Martha Graham)	Feb. 18, 1934 Guild Theatre, N.Y.	Lehman Engel		M.G.	M.G.
91. *Phantasy: Prelude, Musette, Gavotte* (solo, Martha Graham)	Feb. 18, 1934 Guild Theatre, N.Y.	Arnold Schönberg		M.G.	M.G.
92. *Celebration* (group)	Feb. 25, 1934 Guild Theatre, N.Y.	Louis Horst		M.G.	M.G.
93. *Four Casual Developments* (group)	Feb. 25, 1934 Guild Theatre, N.Y.	Henry Cowell		M.G.	M.G.
94. *Integrales* (group)	Apr. 22, 1934 Alvin Theatre, N.Y.	Edgard Varèse		M.G.	M.G.
95. *Dance in Four Parts: Quest, Derision, Dream, Sportive Tragedy* (solo, Martha Graham)	Nov. 11, 1934 Guild Theatre, N.Y.	George Antheil		M.G.	M.G.

Title	Date, Place of Premiere	Composer	Decor	Costumes	Lighting
96. *American Provincials: Act of Piety, Act of Judgment* (Martha Graham and group)	Nov. 11, 1934 Guild Theatre, N.Y.	Louis Horst		M.G.	M.G.
97. *Praeludium* (solo, Martha Graham)	Feb. 10, 1935 Guild Theatre, N.Y.	Paul Nordoff		M.G. costumes redesigned in 1938 by Edythe Gilfond	M.G.
98. *Course* (Martha Graham and group)	Feb. 10, 1935 Guild Theatre, N.Y.	George Antheil		M.G.	M.G.
99. *Perspectives:* 1. *Frontier* (solo, Martha Graham); 2. *Marching Song* (Martha Graham and group)	Apr. 28, 1935 Guild Theatre, N.Y.	Louis Horst	Isamu Noguchi	M.G.	M.G.
100. *Panorama* (Martha Graham and group)	Aug. 14, 1935 Vermont State Armory, Bennington, Vt.	Norman Lloyd	Arch Lauterer Alexander Calder (mobiles)	M.G.	Arch Lauterer
101. *Formal Dance,* subsequently retitled *Praeludium No. 2* (solo, Martha Graham)	Nov. 10, 1935 Guild Theatre, N.Y.	David Diamond		M.G.	M.G.
102. *Imperial Gesture* (solo, Martha Graham)	Nov. 10, 1935 Guild Theatre, N.Y.	Lehman Engel		M.G.	M.G.
103. *Horizons* (Martha Graham and group)	Feb. 23, 1936 Guild Theatre, N.Y.	Louis Horst	Alexander Calder	M.G.	M.G.

Title	Date, Place of Premiere	Composer	Decor	Costumes	Lighting
104. *Salutation* (solo, Martha Graham)	Apr. 7, 1936 Philharmonic Auditorium, Los Angeles, Ca.	Lehman Engel		M.G.	M.G.
105. *Chronicle* (Martha Graham and group)	Dec. 20, 1936 Guild Theatre, N.Y.	Wallingford Riegger	Isamu Noguchi	M.G.	M.G.
106. *Opening Dance* (solo, Martha Graham)	July 30, 1937 Vermont State Armory, Bennington, Vt.	Norman Lloyd		M.G.	Arch Lauterer
107. *Immediate Tragedy* (solo, Martha Graham)	July 30, 1937 Vermont State Armory, Bennington, Vt.	Henry Cowell		M.G.	Arch Lauterer
108. *Deep Song* (solo, Martha Graham)	Dec. 19, 1937 Guild Theatre, N.Y.	Henry Cowell		Edythe Gilfond	M.G.
109. *American Lyric* (Martha Graham and group)	Dec. 26, 1937 Guild Theatre, N.Y.	Alex North		Edythe Gilfond	M.G.
110. *American Document* (Martha Graham, Erick Hawkins, and group)	Aug. 6, 1938 Vermont State Armory, Bennington, Vt.	Ray Green	Arch Lauterer	Edythe Gilfond	Arch Lauterer
111. *Columbiad* (solo, Martha Graham)	Dec. 27, 1939 St. James Theatre, N.Y.	Louis Horst	Philip Stapp	Edythe Gilfond	Philip Stapp

Title	Date, Place of Premiere	Composer	Décor	Costumes	Lighting
112. *Every Soul Is a Circus* (Martha Graham and group) Title: Vachel Lindsay	Dec. 27, 1939 St. James Theatre, N.Y.	Paul Nordoff	Philip Stapp	Edythe Gilfond	Philip Stapp
113. *El Penitente* (Martha Graham, Erick Hawkins, and Merce Cunningham)	Aug. 11, 1940 Bennington College Theatre, Bennington, Vt.	Louis Horst	Arch Lauterer (subsequently redesigned by Isamu Noguchi)	Edythe Gilfond	Arch Lauterer
114. *Letter to the World* (Martha Graham and group) Title: Emily Dickinson	Aug. 11, 1940 Bennington College Theatre, Bennington, Vt.	Hunter Johnson		Edythe Gilfond	M.C.
Martha Graham and Company					
115. *Punch and the Judy* (Martha Graham and Company)	Aug. 10, 1941 Bennington College Theatre, Bennington, Vt.	Robert McBride	Arch Lauterer	Charlotte Trowbridge	Arch Lauterer
116. *Land Be Bright* (Martha Graham and Company)	Mar. 14, 1942 Chicago Civic Opera House, Chicago, Ill.	Arthur Kreutz	Charlotte Trowbridge	Charlotte Trowbridge	Arch Lauterer
117. *Salem Shore* (solo, Martha Graham)	Dec. 26, 1943 46th Street Theatre, N.Y.	Paul Nordoff	Arch Lauterer	Edythe Gilfond	Jean Rosenthal
118. *Deaths and Entrances* (Martha Graham and Company) Title: Dylan Thomas	Dec. 26, 1943 46th Street Theatre, N.Y.	Hunter Johnson	Arch Lauterer	Edythe Gilfond	Jean Rosenthal

Title	Date, Place of Premiere	Composer	Decor	Costumes	Lighting
119. *Imagined Wing* (Company)	Oct. 30, 1944 Library of Congress, Washington, D.C.	Darius Milhaud	Isamu Noguchi	Edythe Gilfond	Jean Rosenthal
120. *Herodiade* (Martha Graham and May O'Donnell) Title: Stéphane Mallarmé (originally titled *Mirror Before Me*)	Oct. 30, 1944 Library of Congress, Washington, D.C.	Paul Hindemith	Isamu Noguchi	Edythe Gilfond	Jean Rosenthal
121. *Appalachian Spring* (Martha Graham and Company) Title: Hart Crane	Oct. 30, 1944 Library of Congress, Washington, D.C.	Aaron Copland	Isamu Noguchi	Edythe Gilfond	Jean Rosenthal
122. *Dark Meadow* (Martha Graham and Company)	Jan. 23, 1946 Plymouth Theatre, N.Y.	Carlos Chávez	Isamu Noguchi	Edythe Gilfond	Jean Rosenthal
123. *Cave of the Heart,* (Martha Graham and Company) originally titled *Serpent Heart*	May 10, 1946 McMillin Theatre, Columbia Univ., N.Y.	Samuel Barber	Isamu Noguchi	Edythe Gilfond	Jean Rosenthal
124. *Errand into the Maze* (Martha Graham and Mark Ryder) Title: Ben Belitt	Feb. 27, 1947 Ziegfeld Theater, N.Y.	Gian-Carlo Menotti	Isamu Noguchi	M.G.	Jean Rosenthal

Title	Date, Place of Premiere	Composer	Decor	Costumes	Lighting
125. Night Journey (Martha Graham and Company)	May 3, 1947 Cambridge High and Latin School, Cambridge, Mass.	William Schuman	Isamu Noguchi	M.G.	Jean Rosenthal
126. Diversion of Angels (Company) Title: Ben Belitt (titled—at first performance only, Wilderness Stair)	Aug. 13, 1948 Palmer Aud., Connecticut College, New London, Conn.	Norman Dello Joio	Isamu Noguchi	M.G.	Jean Rosenthal
127. Judith (solo, Martha Graham)	Jan. 4, 1950 Columbia Auditorium, Louisville, Ky.	William Schuman	Isamu Noguchi	M.G.	Jean Rosenthal
128. Eye of Anguish (Erick Hawkins and Company)	Jan. 22, 1950 46th St. Theatre, N.Y.	Vincent Persichetti	Henry Kurth	Fred Cunning	Jean Rosenthal
129. Gospel of Eve (solo, Martha Graham)	Jan. 22, 1950 46th St. Theatre, N.Y.	Paul Nordoff	Oliver Smith	Miles White	Jean Rosenthal
130. The Triumph of St. Joan (solo, Martha Graham)	Dec. 5, 1951 Columbia Auditorium, Louisville, Ky.	Norman Dello Joio	Frederick Kiesler	M.G.	Jean Rosenthal
131. Canticle for Innocent Comedians (group) Title: Ben Belitt	Apr. 22, 1952 Juilliard School of Music, N.Y.	Thomas Ribbink	Frederick Kiesler	M.G.	Jean Rosenthal
132. Voyage (Martha Graham and Company)	May 17, 1953 Alvin Theatre, N.Y.	William Schuman	Isamu Noguchi	Edythe Gilfond	Jean Rosenthal

Title	Date, Place of Premiere	Composer	Decor	Costumes	Lighting
133. *Ardent Song* (Company)	Mar. 18, 1954 Saville Theatre, London	Alan Hovhaness		M.G.	Jean Rosenthal
134. *Seraphic Dialogue* (Company)	May 8, 1955 ANTA Theatre, N.Y.	Norman Dello Joio	Isamu Noguchi	M.G.	Jean Rosenthal
135. *A Dancer's World* (film)	1957	Cameron McCosh	Producer and Director: Nathan Kroll, Camera: Peter Glushanok		Jean Rosenthal
136. *Clytemnestra* (Martha Graham and Company)	Apr. 1, 1958 Adelphi Theatre, N.Y.	Halim El-Dabh	Isamu Noguchi	M.G., Helen McGehee	Jean Rosenthal
137. *Embattled Garden* (Company)	Apr. 3, 1958 Adelphi Theatre, N.Y.	Carlos Surinach	Isamu Noguchi	M.G.	Jean Rosenthal
138. *Episodes: Part I* (Martha Graham, Sallie Wilson, and Company)	May 14, 1959 New York City Center, N.Y.	Anton Webern	David Hays	Barbara Karinska, Cecil Beaton	David Hays
139. *Appalachian Spring* (film) (Martha Graham and Dance Company)	1959	Aaron Copland	Isamu Noguchi	Producer and Director: Nathan Kroll, Camera: Peter Glushanok	
140. *Night Journey* (film) (Martha Graham and Dance Company)	1960	William Schuman	Isamu Noguchi	Producer: Nathan Kroll Director: Alexander Hammid	Photographer: Stanley Meredith
141. *Acrobats of God* (Martha Graham and Dance Company)	Apr. 27, 1960 54th St. Theatre, N.Y.	Carlos Surinach	Isamu Noguchi	M.G.	Jean Rosenthal

Title	Date, Place of Premiere	Composer	Decor	Costumes	Lighting
142. *Alcestis* (Martha Graham and Dance Company)	Apr. 29, 1960 54th St. Theatre, N.Y.	Vivian Fine	Isamu Noguchi	M.G.	Jean Rosenthal
143. *Visionary Recital* (Martha Graham and Dance Company); revised as *Samson Agoniste* without Martha Graham, 1962	Apr. 16, 1961 54th St. Theatre, N.Y.	Robert Starer	Rouben Ter-Arutunian	M.G.	Rouben Ter-Arutunian
144. *One More Gaudy Night* (Company) Title: William Shakespeare	Apr. 20, 1961 54th St. Theatre, N.Y.	Halim El-Dabh	Jean Rosenthal	M.G.	Jean Rosenthal
145. *Phaedra* (Martha Graham and Dance Company)	March 5, 1962 Broadway Theatre, N.Y.	Robert Starer	Isamu Noguchi	M.G.	Jean Rosenthal
146. *A Look at Lightning* (Company) Title: Ben Belitt	March 5, 1962 Broadway Theatre, N.Y.	Halim El-Dabh	Ming Cho Lee	M.G.	Jean Rosenthal
147. *Secular Games* (Company)	Aug. 17, 1962 Palmer Aud., Connecticut College, New London, Conn.	Robert Starer	Marion Kinsella	M.G.	Jean Rosenthal
148. *Legend of Judith* (Martha Graham and Dance Company)	Oct. 25, 1962 Habima Theatre, Tel Aviv, Israel	Mordecai Seter	Dani Karavan	M.G.	Jean Rosenthal

Title	Date, Place of Premiere	Composer	Decor	Costumes	Lighting
149. *Circe* (Company)	Sept. 6, 1963 Prince of Wales Theatre, London	Alan Hovhaness	Isamu Noguchi	M.G.	Jean Rosenthal
150. *The Witch of Endor* (Martha Graham and Company)	Nov. 2, 1965 54th St. Theatre, N.Y.	William Schuman	Ming Cho Lee	M.G.	Jean Rosenthal
151. *Part Real—Part Dream* (Company)	Nov. 3, 1965 54th St. Theatre, N.Y.	Mordecai Seter	Dani Karavan	M.G.	Jean Rosenthal
152. *Cortege of Eagles* (Martha Graham and Dance Company)	Feb. 21, 1967 Mark Hellinger Theatre, N.Y.	Eugene Lester	Isamu Noguchi	M.G.	Jean Rosenthal
153. *Dancing—Ground* (Company)	Feb. 24, 1967 Mark Hellinger Theatre, N.Y.	Ned Rorem	Jean Rosenthal	M.G.	Jean Rosenthal
154. *A Time of Snow* (Martha Graham and Dance Company)	May 25, 1968 George Abbott Theatre, N.Y.	Norman Dello Joio	Rouben Ter-Arutunian	M.G.	Rouben Ter-Arutunian
155. *The Plain of Prayer* (Company)	May 29, 1968 George Abbott Theatre, N.Y.	Eugene Lester	Jean Rosenthal	M.G.	Jean Rosenthal
156. *The Lady of the House of Sleep* (Martha Graham and Dance Company)	May 30, 1968 George Abbott Theatre, N.Y.	Robert Starer	Ming Cho Lee	M.G.	Jean Rosenthal
157. *The Archaic Hours* (Company)	Apr. 11, 1969 New York City Center, N.Y.	Eugene Lester	Marion Kinsella	M.G.	Jean Rosenthal

Title	Date, Place of Premiere	Composer	Decor	Costumes	Lighting
Martha Graham Dance Company					
158. *Mendicants of Evening* (Company) Title: St.-John Perse	May 2, 1973 Alvin Theatre, N.Y.	David Walker	Fangor	M.G.	William H. Batchelder
159. *Myth of a Voyage* (Company)	May 3, 1973 Alvin Theatre, N.Y.	Alan Hovhaness	Ming Cho Lee (Associate Designer: Patricia Woodbridge)	M.G.	William H. Batchelder
160. *Holy Jungle* (Company)	Apr. 30, 1974 Mark Hellinger Theatre, N.Y.	Robert Starer	Dani Karavan	M.G.	William H. Batchelder
161. *Jacob's Dream* (Company)	July 1974 Jerusalem, Israel	Mordecai Seter	Dani Karavan	M.G.	
162. *Lucifer* (Margot Fonteyn, Rudolph Nureyev, and Martha Graham Dance Company)	June 19, 1975 Uris Theatre, N.Y.	Halim El-Dabh	Leandro Locsin	Halston	Ronald Bates
163. *Adorations* (Company)	Dec. 8, 1975 Mark Hellinger Theatre, N.Y.	Donald Frost	Leandro Locsin	Halston	Ronald Bates
164. *Point of Crossing* (Company) Based on "Jacob's Dream"	Dec. 8, 1975 Mark Hellinger Theatre, N.Y.	Mordecai Seter	Leandro Locsin	M.G.	Ronald Bates
165. *The Scarlet Letter* (Company) Title: Nathaniel Hawthorne	Dec. 22, 1975 Mark Hellinger Theatre, N.Y.	Hunter Johnson	Marisol	Halston	Ronald Bates

Title	Date, Place of Premiere	Composer	Decor	Costumes	Lighting
166. O Thou Desire Who Art About to Sing (duet) Title: St.-John Perse	May 17, 1977 Lunt-Fontanne Theatre, N.Y.	Meyer Kupferman	Marisol	M.G.	Nicholas Cernovitch
167. Shadows (Company)	May 24, 1977 Lunt-Fontanne Theatre, N.Y.	Gian-Carlo Menotti	Frederick Kiesler	Halston	Nicholas Cernovitch
168. The Owl and the Pussycat (Company) Title: Edward Lear	June 26, 1978 Metropolitan Opera House, N.Y.	Carlos Surinach	Ming Cho Lee	Halston	Gilbert Hemsley, Jr.
169. Ecuatorial (Company)	June 27, 1978 Metropolitan Opera House, N.Y.	Edgard Varèse	Marisol	Marisol, Halston	Gilbert Hemsley, Jr.
170. Flute of Pan (Company)	June 28, 1978 Metropolitan Opera House, N.Y.	Traditional	Leandro Locsin	Halston	Gilbert Hemsley, Jr.
171. Frescoes (Company)	December 9, 1979 Metropolitan Museum of Art, N.Y.	Samuel Barber			
172. Episodes, reconstructed, reworked (Company)	July 24, 1979 Covent Garden, London, England	Anton Webern	David Hays	Halston	
173. Frescoes (Company)	Apr. 22, 1980 Metropolitan Opera House, N.Y.	Samuel Barber		Halston	Gilbert Hemsley, Jr.
174. Judith reworked (Company)	Apr. 29, 1980 Metropolitan Opera House, N.Y.	Edgard Varèse	Isamu Noguchi	Halston	

Title	Date, Place of Premiere	Composer	Decor	Costumes	Lighting
175. "Acts of Light" (Company) Title: Emily Dickinson	Feb. 26, 1981 City Center, N.Y.	Carl Nielsen		Halston	Beverly Emmons
176. Dances of the Golden Hall (Company)	June 9, 1982 City Center, N.Y.	Andrzej Panufnik		Halston	Beverly Emmons
177. Andromache's Lament (Company)	June 23, 1982 City Center, N.Y.	Samuel Barber		Halston	Beverly Emmons
178. Phaedra's Dream (Company)	July 1, 1983 Herod Atticus Theatre, Athens, Greece	George Crumb	Isamu Noguchi	Halston	
179. The Rite of Spring (Company)	Feb. 28, 1984 State Theater, N.Y.	Igor Stravinsky	Ron Protas	Halston	Tom Skelton
180. Song (Company)	Apr. 2, 1984 State Theater, N.Y.	Traditional		Halston	Tom Skelton
181. Temptations of the Moon (Company)	May 27, 1986 City Center, N.Y.	Béla Bartók		Halston	Tom Skelton
182. Tangled Night (Company)	June 4, 1986 City Center, N.Y.	Klaus Egge	Ming Cho Lee	Halston	Tom Skelton
183. Untitled (Company)	Oct. 13, 1987 City Center, N.Y.	Igor Stravinsky		Halston	Tom Skelton
184. Celebration (reconstruction) (Company)	1987 City Center, N.Y.	Louis Horst		M.G.	Beverly Emmons
185. Persephone (Company)	Oct. 13, 1987 City Center, N.Y.	Igor Stravinsky		Halston	Thomas Skelton

Title	Date, Place of Premiere	Composer	Decor	Costumes	Lighting
186. *Letter to the World* (reconstruction) (Company)	1988 City Center, N.Y.	Hunter Johnson	Arch Lauterer	Halston	David Finley
187. *Night Chant* (Company)	Oct. 13, 1988 City Center, N.Y.	R. Carlos Nakai	Isamu Noguchi	M.G. and Halston	David Finley
188. *Deep Song* (reconstruction) (Company)	1988 City Center, N.Y.	Henry Cowell		M.G.	David Finley
189. *American Document* (Company)	Oct. 3, 1989 City Center, N.Y.	John Corigliano		M.G.	David Finley
190. *Steps in the Street* (reconstruction) (Company)	1989 City Center, N.Y.	Wallingford Riegger		M.G.	David Finley
191. *Maple Leaf Rag* (Company)	Oct. 2, 1990 City Center, N.Y.	Scott Joplin		Calvin Klein	David Finley

Dorothy Bird	Mary Hinkson	Gertrude Shurr
John Butler	Stuart Hodes	Anna Sokolow
Merce Cunningham	Pearl Lang	Paul Taylor
Jane Dudley	Sophie Maslow	Glen Tetley
Jean Erdman	May O'Donnell	Ethel Winter
Erick Hawkins	Bertram Ross	Bethsabee de Rothschild
Martha Hill	Mark Ryder	

DOROTHY BIRD

Dorothy Bird was born on Vancouver Island, British Columbia, and had a blissful, happy childhood, running wild in lovely country by the sea. She decided to study dancing after being kissed by Anna Pavlova as a very small child. In 1930 her mother took her to the Cornish School of Fine and Applied Arts in Seattle, where Martha Graham taught her, becoming in a sense both spiritually and artistically her mother. Dorothy said that Graham gave her "a skill that carried me through my entire life."

Bird danced in and demonstrated for the Martha Graham Group for seven years, then went on Broadway and worked with Agnes de Mille, Helen Tamiris, and Jack Cole; she later changed back to the modern dance idiom and worked in the José Limón Trio under the direction of Doris Humphrey; returning once more to Broadway, she worked with Eugene Loring, Jerome Robbins, Anna Sokolow, and Herbert Ross. Surprisingly, she taught modern movement under George Balanchine at the School of American Ballet. She taught at the Neighborhood Playhouse School for twenty-five years, preparing young professionals for careers in the theater.

Dorothy Bird returned to the Graham School to teach, stage, or coach whenever requested by Martha. She said, "I loved her at the beginning with my whole heart, and I always will."

JOHN BUTLER

John Butler was born in Memphis, Tennessee, in 1920, and raised in Greenwood, Mississippi. When he was eighteen he saw Martha Graham's photograph, looked her up in the New York telephone directory, and made his way to her studio on Fifth Avenue and Thirteenth Street. He appeared in Martha Graham's company from

1945-55, but was at the same time experimenting in the commercial theater, dancing in *Oklahoma!*, which earned him his living. Also in the late forties and fifties he began tentatively to work for television, starting with Gian-Carlo Menotti's *The Consul* (1947), *Amahl and the Night Visitors* (1951), and *The Unicorn, the Gorgon and the Manticore* (1956). He continued with *Omnibus*, and then in *Seven Lively Arts, A Lamp Unto My Feet, The Bell Telephone Hour, The Kate Smith Evening Hour,* and bits for Steve Allen and Ed Sullivan. He probably knew more about television and its problems than any other choreographer at that time. His first company, the John Butler Dance Theatre, included Carmen de Lavallade, Glen Tetley, Mary Hinkson, and Arthur Mitchell. In 1958 Butler was named dance director of the Spoleto Festival of Two Worlds, Menotti's music festival in Spoleto, Italy. In 1959 his company was the first dance troupe to appear at the Newport Jazz Festival, performing *Portrait of Billie*, based on the tragic life of the blues singer Billie Holiday.

Butler collected, with considerable discernment, paintings of real worth, which he has had to sell off from time to time in order to finance his dance adventures. He now collects African and South Pacific paintings, drawings, and sculptures. He regularly visits the Netherlands Dance Theatre, the Polish National Ballet, Ballet West, La Scala Ballet in Milan, and various Canadian and American companies—mostly outside New York—all of which produce his works.

MERCE CUNNINGHAM

Merce Cunningham was born in Centralia, Washington, and received his first formal dance and theater training at the Cornish School of Fine and Applied Arts in Seattle. He was with Martha Graham from 1939-45. He gave his first New York solo concert with the composer John Cage in April 1944.

Cunningham formed his own group in 1952, and took them to Black Mountain College in North Carolina. His dancers included Carolyn Brown, Remy Charlip, Viola Farber, and Paul Taylor, with John Cage as music director. In 1964 they embarked on a six-month tour of Europe and the Far East. From 1954-64 Robert Rauschenberg was the company's resident designer. The Merce Cunningham Dance Group has throughout its history been guided by artists of established renown, and the company's early ground-breaking pieces were followed by further experiments of all kinds in all media.

The Cunningham company has now logged well over a million miles of touring, performing in three hundred different cities in thirty-five countries on five continents. In 1987 their travels culminated in an intensive nine-month world tour.

Cunningham has choreographed two works for the New York City Ballet, *The Seasons* (John Cage-Isamu Noguchi, 1947), and a version of *Summerspace* (Morton Feldman-Robert Rauschenberg, 1958; NYCB version, 1966). His works have been included in the repertories of numerous ballet and modern dance companies, among them the Boston Ballet; the Pennsylvania Ballet; Ballet Rambert (London); the Cullberg-balletten, Stockholm; the Théâtre de Silence, France; the GRCOP (the experimental wing of the Paris Opéra Ballet); and the New Dance Ensemble.

Cunningham has an enthusiastic following. He has received many awards, including two Guggenheim Fellowships for choreography in 1954 and 1959; the *Dance Maga-*

zine Award, 1960; the Medal for the Society for the Advancement of Dancing in Sweden, 1964; the Gold Medal for Choreographic Invention at the Fourth International Festival of Dance in Paris, 1966; an honorary doctorate of letters from the University of Illinois, 1972; and the New York State Award, 1975. He was made a Commander of the Order of Arts and Letters by the French Minister of Culture in 1982, and in 1983 received the mayor of New York's Award of Honor for Arts and Culture. In 1984 he was inducted as an honorary member into the American Academy and Institute of Arts and Letters. In June 1985 he received a MacArthur Foundation Fellowship and that December was the recipient of the Kennedy Center Honors at the White House.

JANE DUDLEY

Jane Dudley, born in New York City, began her professional dance training with Ruth Doing, then progressed to the Mary Wigman School of New York, directed by Hanya Holm, and in time became a member of her senior demonstration group. She was a soloist with the Martha Graham Dance Company from 1937–44, and between 1942–54 was a dancer and choreographer with the Dance Trio, which included Sophie Maslow and William Bales. The Trio performed extensively throughout the United States. Dudley was a teaching assistant to Martha Graham at the Neighborhood Playhouse between 1938–46, and in 1948–52 a charter member of the New London Summer School of Dance, together with Martha Graham, Doris Humphrey, José Limón, Sophie Maslow, and William Bales. In 1968–70, by invitation of Martha Graham, she was artistic director of the Batsheva Dance Company in Israel. In 1971 she was appointed vice-principal and director of contemporary dance studies for the London School of Contemporary Dance, known as The Place.

The *Times* of London reported, November 16, 1977, on her reconstructions of her early great solos:

. . . the sharpest, brightest, shortest, most imaginative and original work on the program was a forty-year-old solo, 'Harmonic Breakdown', which Jane Dudley has revived. In five minutes it offers a more real choreographic invention and tells you more about human nature than all the rest put together.

Jane Dudley is a remarkably fine technician and an excellent choreographer, who has given us a score or more of fine works, mainly solos. Her later group pieces, performed with her students, are in the Graham tradition but display free invention and the stamp of her own personality.

JEAN ERDMAN

Jean Erdman was born in Hawaii and grew up there; she came to New York to go to Sarah Lawrence College when she met and began to study with Martha Graham. She joined the Graham company in 1938, leaving in 1942 to open her own studio and develop her own choreographic work. When needed, she returned to home base and appeared in Graham's works. The Jean Erdman Theater gave a yearly season in Manhattan, toured the United States and was the guest company in residence each summer at the Summer Arts Festival at the University of Colorado in Boulder from 1949–56. In 1954 she became the first American dancer to tour the Orient after World War II. From 1962–67 she developed and toured *The Coach with the Six Insides,* an adaptation of James Joyce's *Finnegans Wake* that won both the Obie and the Vernon Rice awards. It will be remembered that her mythologist-husband, Joseph Campbell, wrote a "translation" of this, entitled *A Skeleton Key to* Finnegans Wake, that gained him world renown. Erdman choreographed a number of Broadway productions, and in 1972 founded with her husband the Theater of the Open Eye. She has appeared at the Athens Festival Myth and Man Symposium, sponsored jointly by the Greek government and the American Embassy, and the International Carl G. Jung and the Humanities Symposium, sponsored by Hofstra University. In 1986, at the time of writing, she was in the process of creating a video archive of her entire dance repertory.

ERICK HAWKINS

Erick Hawkins was born in Colorado and educated in Kansas City and at Harvard. He joined the Graham company in 1936 and remained with it until 1951, before starting to pursue what proved to be a difficult career of solo concerts with a small group.

At first neither critically nor popularly successful, he has at last won through to solid acclaim and is now hailed as a true dance radical, one of the great revolutionary pioneers: original and independent. He received grants from the government, from the state, and from many private sources, and began touring the United States, visiting colleges throughout the country, where he spoke frequently. Erick always spoke very well, thoughtfully and forcibly. He has a substantial audience of enthusiastic followers.

Hawkins's publicity brochure gives a simple analysis of his style and purpose:

At the core of Hawkins' style is a unique collaboration with contemporary composers, artists, sculptors and designers. He has worked with artists such as Helen Frankenthaler, Isamu Noguchi, Stanley Boxer, Ralph Lee and Ralph Dorazio; and probably commissioned more American composers than any other choreographer, among them Virgil Thomson, Alan Hovhaness, Wallingford Riegger, Ross Lee Finney, Lou Harrison, Michio Mamiya, Ge Gan-Ru, and Lucia Dlugoszewski.

The critics have been magnanimous and vociferous in their praise.

"Hawkins is one of the most individual and inventive choreographers of our time," said Alan Kriegsman of the *Washington Post* in 1972.

"He is one of the most creative minds of our time: innovative, visionary, a poet" (Robert Sabin, editor-in-chief of *Musical America,* associate editor of *Dance Observer*).

Hawkins's brochure also states:

There are two very important aspects of his work to commend Hawkins. The first is his musicality, and, as a natural development of that, his close choreographic collaboration with the composer Lucia Dlugoszewski, who provides him with percussive music of unobtrusive originality. The second notable aspect of Erick Hawkins is his own personal dance style. It aims at ease rather than virtuosity and at its best it has a slow-motion, weighty grace that is impressively individual. . . .

In 1988 the Volvo Corporation commissioned Hawkins's *God the Reveler,* for which they paid $70,000, and for which he received the Samuel Scripps Award, amounting to $25,000, given by the American Dance Festival in North Carolina. He has claimed among his accomplishments that of never bringing a negative idea to the stage: "I deliberately avoided violence in both technique and content . . . because of its destructiveness to the human spirit. I really think negativity destroys our precious, creative brain cells."

MARTHA HILL

Martha Hill was born in East Palestine, Ohio. She was a member of the Graham company between 1929 and 1931, then became director of dance at the University of Oregon; a member of the faculty of the Lincoln School of Teachers' College; director, Bennington School of the Dance (1934–39)—the school later became Bennington School of the Arts, and Hill remained there until 1942. She was director of dance at New York University from 1930 to 1951, and was on the Advisory Commission of the School of Performing Arts in New York. Hill was founder of the Connecticut College School of the Dance and American Dance Festival (1948) and director of the Dance Department at the Juilliard School of Music from its founding in 1951. She has been its Artistic Director Emeritus since 1985.

Martha Hill was awarded an Honorary Doctorate of Humane Letters by Adelphi University in 1965, and since then has received honorary doctorates from Mount Holyoke College (Doctor of Letters), Bennington College (Doctor of Humane Letters), and, in 1987, from the Juilliard School (Doctor of Fine Arts).

MARY HINKSON

Mary Hinkson was born in Wisconsin, went to the State University there, and majored in dance. She was principal dancer with the Martha Graham Company for a twenty-one-year period—from 1952–73—receiving acclaim for major roles in *Deaths and Entrances, Cave of the Heart, Clytemnestra,* and *Circe,* which was created for her in 1963. In addition, Miss Hinkson was principal dancer with Glen Tetley's Contemporary Dance Company and the New York City Opera Ballet under the direction of John Butler. She has also appeared with American Ballet Theatre; the New York City Ballet; the Royal Danish Ballet; and the Joffrey Ballet. She has established an international reputation as a teacher, and teaches regular workshops each year in New York City.

As a sideline, she successfully manages her late husband's remarkable bakery.

STUART HODES

Stuart Hodes joined the Martha Graham Dance Company after service in the U. S. Army Air Corps during World War II. He was with the Graham company from 1947–58, and during that time appeared in a number of Broadway shows. His debut concert of his own works was held at the 92nd Street Y in 1950. After leaving Graham, he continued to dance in Broadway shows until 1964, when he joined the Rebekah Harkness Foundation and choreographed four ballets for her company. In 1968 he founded The Ballet Team, a young-audience company. In 1970–72 he served on the New York State Council of the Arts, organizing aid to cultural institutional programs in dance. From 1972–83 he chaired the dance program at New York University, meanwhile creating ballets for several different companies. In 1980 he received an NEA Choreographic Fellowship, and in 1982 was a member of the first American dance study team to visit China. From 1983–85 he was the executive director of The Kitchen Center for Video, Music, Dance, Performance, and Film in New York. From 1987 to the present he has been associate professor and dance coordinator of the Borough of Manhattan Community College.

Stuart Hodes is an able administrator, an eager proselytizer for dance, and a good, solid choreographer, who has composed a number of excellent works.

PEARL LANG

Pearl Lang was born and raised in Chicago, where she worked at the Goodman Theater. She joined the Graham company in 1941 and danced with Miss Graham until 1952, appearing in later years as a guest artist with that company. She has followed Graham in some of her greatest roles.

She formed her own company in 1952 and began to choreograph, receiving two Guggenheim Fellowships and numerous citations. She has toured in the United States, Canada, Italy, and Israel, and her works have been performed by the Boston Ballet, the Dance Repertory Theater of Utah, the Dutch National Ballet, and the Batsheva Dance Company of Israel. Aside from various university residencies, she taught at the Yale University School of Drama for thirteen years, as well as at the Neighborhood Playhouse School of the Theater. She is a senior instructor in technique and dance composition at the Martha Graham School. At present she is finishing a film based on *The Possessed—The Dybbuk,* a full evening's dance drama.

Pearl Lang is generally considered one of the leading modern dancers, and is acclaimed everywhere for her beauty and the mastery of her dancing.

SOPHIE MASLOW

Sophie Maslow was born in New York and entered the Martha Graham School as a student and apprentice. She began to compose her own dances when still in the Graham company and while dancing in Louis Horst's lecture-demonstrations, so that her work grew quite naturally out of what she had been doing with Graham. In 1942 the *Dance Observer* presented Jane Dudley, Sophie Maslow, and William Bales of the Humphrey-Weidman group, performing as the Dudley-Maslow-Bales Trio. This was highly successful, but the three agreed to limit their concert dates and what touring they could arrange to those periods that did not conflict with Graham's engagements and rehearsals. The Trio was dissolved in 1954.

Her ballets include *Champion*, based on a story by Ring Lardner, with music by Samuel Matlowsky (1948); *The Village I Knew*, based on the stories of Shalom Aleichem, with music by Samuel Matlowsky and Gregory Tucker that included Yiddish folksongs (1951); *Prologue*, based on the Prologue to Boccaccio's *Decameron*, with music by Carl Orff and Manuel de Falla (1959); *The Dybbuk*, based on Anski's play, with music by Robert Starer (1964); and *Voices*, with music by Robert Schumann *(Kreisleriana)* (1980), In 1984 she was awarded an honorary doctorate from Skidmore College.

MAY O'DONNELL

May O'Donnell was born in Sacramento, California. In her work with Martha Graham, she created the role of the Pioneer Woman in *Appalachian Spring*, "She of the Ground" in *Dark Meadow*, the Chorus in *Cave of the Heart*, and the Attendant in *Herodiade*. *Herodiade* was created as a duet, with Martha in the title role. May claims to have done the choreography for these roles, and she may have in some part, but Martha always retained the guiding hand and was the editor. O'Donnell had already created *Of Pioneer Women* in 1937, and a one-woman show, *So Proudly We Hail*, in 1940, before she joined Martha. In 1943 she continued her own creations with *Suspension*, and had begun a collaboration with the composer Ray Green that lasted fifty years. She has her own concert dance company and continues to give recitals of great distinction.

BERTRAM ROSS

Bertram Ross was born and raised in Brooklyn, New York. After serving in World War II, he began dancing at the Martha Graham School of Dance under the GI Bill of Rights. From there he went to Connecticut College, where the Bennington faculty took him on scholarship as their first male dance student. He joined the Dudley-Maslow-Bales Trio for a short tour, upon completion of which Martha Graham asked him to join her own company.

He was Martha Graham's partner and the co-director of her company for nearly twenty-five years, and has earned a place of immortality in the world of modern dance. Mr. Ross created over thirty-five leading roles in the Graham repertory. He is indelibly connected with the roles of Saint Michael in *Seraphic Dialogue*, Agamemnon and Orestes in *Clytemnestra*, Adam in *Embattled Garden*, Oedipus in *Night Journey*, and, perhaps most of all, with the Preacher in *Appalachian Spring*. He quotes Miss Graham: "I am a thief and I am not ashamed. I steal from the best, wherever it happens to be—Plato, Picasso, and Bertram Ross." Mr. Ross has been appearing for the last five seasons in an evening of solo performances of dance/theater portraits that include Raymond Duncan, Gordon Craig, Ted Shawn, Uncle Vanya, and Noah. Within the last several years he has also been appearing in a critically acclaimed theater/cabaret act with John Wallowitsch; he can presently be seen in Amy Greenfield's film *Antigone,* in which he plays the dual roles of Oedipus and Creon. He teaches at the Mary Anthony Dance Studio, the Clark Center of Performing Arts and the Peridance School in New York City.

MARK RYDER

Mark Ryder was born in 1921 in Chicago, raised and educated in New York City, and studied at the Neighborhood Playhouse, where in 1940 Martha Graham saw him and subsequently took him into her company. He was in the original cast of seven of her greatest works. He left the Graham company in 1949, and in 1950 founded the Dance Drama Duo with Emily Frankel, for which, in addition to their own choreography, they commissioned work by Valerie Bettis, Todd Bolender, Sophie Maslow, Zachary Solov, and Charles Weidman. Transcontinental tours were annual until 1958, after which Ryder was put in charge of the dance program at the Jewish Community Center of Cleveland, and served on the dance faculty at Goddard College in Vermont. From 1974 until his retirement in 1988 he was an associate professor of the dance department of the University of Maryland at College Park, Maryland.

GERTRUDE SHURR

Gertrude Shurr was born in Riga, Latvia, the younger sister of Lester and Louis Shurr, well known and highly successful theatrical agents. Gertrude was a Denishawn pupil in New York, and her concert career began with solo performances of the early Denishawn dances interpolated into a musical act developed from the production of the moving-picture prologues of that day. In 1927 she became a member of the first Humphrey-Weidman Concert Company, and stayed with them until 1929, performing in their premiere in New York. Subsequently she began a lifetime association with Martha Graham as a student, as a teacher, as a member of her company, and, from 1929 to the present, as a rehearsal coach. She participated in Martha Graham's first 1937 transcontinental tour of the United States. She taught at the Neighborhood Playhouse School from 1932–38; at the San Francisco State College, 1939–40; the University of Oregon, 1940–41; Mills College of Education, 1956; Utah State University, 1956–67; the American Negro Theater, 1945–47; the New York City Art Workshop, 1947–51; and at the High School of Performing Arts in New York, 1957–73. Miss Shurr and her lifetime associate May O'Donnell maintained the Studio of Modern Dance in New York City and San Francisco.

Poor health has kept her from active work for long periods. She lives in Utah in the summer and in Tucson, Arizona, in the winter, but holds herself free to advise and help reconstruct whenever Martha summons.

ANNA SOKOLOW

Anna Sokolow was born in Hartford, Connecticut, and grew up and was educated in New York City. She studied at the Neighborhood Playhouse with Martha Graham and Louis Horst, whose assistant she became, remaining with him for nine years. She joined the Graham company in 1928, and stayed with them until 1939, when she was invited to Mexico by the minister of fine arts, Carlos Merida, to perform with her own company. She stayed in Mexico for six months of the year for ten years, with a small company of Mexican dancers called La Paloma Azul, which is now associated with the Mexican National Academy of Dance. In 1953 she was invited to Israel by the American Fund for Israel Institutions, to work with Inbal, a Yemenite company of dancers under the direction of Sara Levi-Tanai. She formed her own company, the Lyric Theater Company, in Tel Aviv in 1962. She has been associated with the Juilliard School as guest choreographer and teacher of choreographers since 1959. During the 1950s she was invited to Switzerland, Sweden, and Holland as a teacher and choreographer.

Anna Sokolow was winner of the *Dance Magazine* Award in 1962. She has done many successful stints on Broadway, and is known chiefly for choreography, which is imaginative, sensitive, sound, and enduring.

PAUL TAYLOR

Paul Taylor was born in Pennsylvania, raised in and around Washington, D.C., and studied painting at Syracuse University, where he was on the college swimming team, before coming to New York City to begin dance studies. His dance teachers included Margaret Craske, Martha Graham, and Antony Tudor. He was a soloist with the Martha Graham Dance Company from 1955–62, at the same time giving dance concerts of his own in the United States and Europe. He danced with the New York City Ballet as guest artist in George Balanchine's *Episodes*.

Paul Taylor was elected Chevalier de l'Ordre des Arts et des Lettres by the French government in 1969, and in June 1984 elevated to the rank of Officier. He has received the Festival of Nations International Award for Choreography. He received honorary doctorates of fine arts from Connecticut College, Duke University, and Syracuse University, and in 1985 was honored by the MacArthur Foundation Fellowship for outstanding talent. His *Private Domain*, published in 1987 by Alfred A. Knopf, is highly successful and has appeared in paperback.

Taylor is generally considered one of the leaders of modern dance, and his seasons in New York last for weeks and are invariably sold out.

GLEN TETLEY

Glen Tetley was born in Cleveland, Ohio, on February 3, 1926. He did a stretch in the U.S. Navy. and on release completed premedical training at New York University, then switched to dancing, both modern and ballet. The dual influences manifested themselves in Tetley's choreography. "I have always existed in both worlds and have never felt them to be anything but one world," he once said.

Tetley toured Europe in 1955 with John Butler's American Dance Theater, and appeared in several of Butler's televised works. In 1956 and 1957 he was a dancer with the Joffrey Ballet, and was a member of the Martha Graham Dance Company during the 1958–59 seasons. He danced under Butler's direction at the first Two Worlds Festival in Spoleto, Italy, in 1958–59. In 1960 Tetley joined American Ballet Theatre for its Broadway season and tour of Europe and the Soviet Union. Then he worked alone for a year, studying and composing. On May 5, 1962, he gave the first concert of his own pieces at the Fashion Institute of Technology in New York. He went to Holland in 1962 as guest choreographer and dancer with the Netherlands Dance Theatre, became associated with England's Ballet Rambert and the Stuttgart Ballet of West Germany, choreographing several pieces for them. After the untimely death of John Cranko in 1973, he was invited to take over the direction of that company, an astonishing honor for an American. He also mounted several pieces for England's Royal Ballet.

The one quality Tetley's ballets have in common is his willingness to experiment; each of his ballets has marked individuality and considerable daring.

In 1981 Tetley received the Queen Elizabeth II Coronation Award from England's Royal Academy of Dancing. His work for the Royal Danish Ballet won him the 1982 Prix d'Italia Rai Prize, and at the Edinburgh Festival of 1983 he was presented with the Tennant-Caledonian Award.

Tetley's 1986 production of *Alice,* based on the biographies of the Reverend Charles Dodgson (Lewis Carroll) and the child Alice Liddell Hargreaves, formed the basis of an imaginative and sensitive work that has received international and far-reaching acclaim.

Glen Tetley ranks as one of the outstanding choreographers of our time, and he works equally well with dancers of all techniques and all nationalities.

ETHEL WINTER

Ethel Winter was born in Wrentham, Massachusetts. She studied at Bennington College and was a member of the Martha Graham Dance Company, 1944–69. She was the first dancer to perform Graham's solo roles in *Salem Shore, Herodiade, Night Journey,* and *Frontier,* and was acclaimed for the roles of the Bride in *Appalachian Spring,* Joan of Arc in *Seraphic Dialogue,* and Aphrodite in *Phaedra.* She has appeared in Broadway productions, TV, and summer stock, and between 1962 and 1968 directed and choreographed for her own dance company. In 1964 she was a guest choreographer and teacher with the Batsheva Dance Company in Israel, and in 1965 a guest teacher and lecturer in London. She was director of the Martha Graham School for Contemporary Dance from 1973–74.

Miss Winter was on the faculty at Bennington College; Adelphi University; Neighborhood Playhouse School of Theater; the High School of Performing Arts in New York; Repertory Dance Theater of Utah; Long Beach Summer School; University of Hawaii; American Dance Festival; Duke University; Southern Methodist University in Dallas; Florida State at Tallahassee; Skidmore College; guest teacher for the English

Dance Theater, 1984–85; and guest teacher for International Ballet Competition, Jackson, Miss., 1986. She remains on the faculty of the Martha Graham School of Contemporary Dance and the Dance Faculty of the Juilliard School.

BETHSABEE DE ROTHSCHILD

Since settling in Tel Aviv in 1958, Bethsabee (Batsheva) de Rothschild has devoted all her time and a great part of her vast fortune to furthering the Bat Dor Dance Company, comprised of Israeli dancers and starring Jeanette Ordman. The group is largely Graham-trained or Graham-derived, and its choreographers embraced most of the outstanding moderns. It has become one of the showpieces of the country, and has earned a considerable international reputation.

Bethsabee de Rothschild concerns herself equally with her scientific foundation, the Bethsabee de Rothschild Foundation for the Advancement of Science in Israel, Inc. (New York, 1958) and with the Batsheva de Rothschild Fund for the Advancement of Science and Technology (Israel, 1965). To quote from her brochure:

The Batsheva seminars is the foundation's longest running program and has not changed significantly in purpose or character since the first seminar, which introduced the first new field in molecular genetics. . . . The Batsheva seminar program is intended to generate interest and foster knowledge about the advances being made in new scientific areas which could develop into important opportunities for research. (Under this there are studies in biology, health sciences, marine sciences, plant sciences, geology, chemistry, physics, science administration.)

Grants for young scientists: [This] was the first funding program in Israel to help scientists get started on independent research at the beginning of their careers.

Grants for immigrants: Two major funding programs that no longer operate are grants and aid for immigrant scientists and the Batsheva Fellows. The first of these was a significant aid in the absorption of scientists from abroad who had begun working at an Israeli institute and intended to make their stay permanent.

Project for the promotion and encouragement of science writers and journalists.

Science teachers training projects allotted high school science teachers one year of financial support to execute a research project at a recognized institute.

Advance studies grant program (1975) gave immigrant scientists from the U.S.S.R. the opportunity to spend a term of research for study in institutions outside Israel.

Program for visiting scientists (1971–77), brought a leading expert in the topic of the previous Batsheva seminar to Israel for lectures and consultation.

More recently, the Israeli government has enlarged and developed de Rothschild's plans, in many instances following along the trails she blazed. But she was the pioneer, and Israel calls her blessed.

1 ENTER THE DANCERS

p. 4: *have failed of effect.:* Reprinted in *Dance Magazine,* April 1955, p. 31.

p. 8: *in his autobiography!):* Fokine: Memoirs of a Ballet Master, translated by Vitale Fokine, Edited by Anatole Chujoy (Boston: Little, Brown, 1961), pp. 256–58.

2 BEGINNINGS

p. 15: *". . . I had no privation.":* "Martha Graham Reflects on Her Art and Life in Dance": Anna Kisselgoff interview in *The New York Times,* March 31, 1985.

p. 17: *". . . to fear it myself.":* Anna Kisselgoff interview in *The New York Times Magazine,* February 19, 1984.

p. 17: *". . . relations were always strained.":* Letter to the author from Winthrop Sargeant.

p. 21: *" '. . . hung in the middle.' ":* Anna Kisselgoff interview in *The New York Times,* March 31, 1985.

p. 23: *The decisiveness of it!:* Ted Shawn, autobiographical audio tapes made for the Dance Collection, Library of the Performing Arts at Lincoln Center, January 1969.

3 RUTHIE DENNIS

p. 26: *". . . of a folk.":* San Francisco *Examiner,* November 26, 1917; quoted in *Isadora Speaks,* edited and with an introduction by Franklin Rosemount (San Francisco: City Lights Books, 1981), p. 47.

p. 27: *said one witness.:* Mary Hunter, a contemporary of the author's, who was present.

p. 27: *second-row center seats:* All quotations and anecdotes credited to June Rhodes are from letters to the author, 1959–72.

p. 28: *" 'the dance of the redeemed.' ":* Ruth St. Denis: An Unfinished Life (New York: Harper & Bros., 1939), pp. 117–118; hereafter referred to as *UL.*

p. 29: *". . . loved Father,":* UL, p. 3.

p. 31: *". . . a kind of dancing ritualist,":* *UL,* p. 57.

p. 33: *". . . of the universe.":* "Martha Graham returns to Her Roots." Article by Jack Anderson, *The New York Times,* May 25, 1986.

p. 33: *". . . all my audiences.":* *UL,* p. 97.

p. 35: *". . . still to come.":* *UL,* p. 140.

p. 36: *". . . so zealously . . .":* *UL,* p. 102.

p. 37: *. . . his words were true.:* *UL,* p. 123.

p. 38: *". . . of perfect beauty.":* Quoted in *UL,* p. 136.

p. 38: *". . . about himself.":* *UL,* pp. 157–58.

p. 38: *". . . agreed with Mother.":* *UL,* p. 164.

p. 39: *". . . a roaring lion.":* Quoted in Suzanne Shelton, *Divine Dancer: A Biography of Ruth St. Denis* (New York: Doubleday, 1981), p. 123.

p. 39: *June further declares.:* Letters to the author from June Rhodes.

p. 40: *". . . pouting and tantrums.":* Letters to the author from June Rhodes.

4 DENISHAWN

p. 44: *in one-piece bathing suits.:* Recalled by Mary Neely Warrington, an early pupil of Denishawn and a contemporary of Martha Graham.

p. 44: *". . . of Japanese technique.":* *UL,* p. 144.

p. 44: *". . . except, perhaps, the Japanese.":* Rosemount, p. 52.

p. 45: *". . . the trend of a whole art.":* John Martin in the Capezio Award testimonial booklet. Published in *Dance Magazine,* April 1955.

p. 47: *". . . basis of teaching genius.":* Mary Neely Warrington conversation.

5 THE PUPIL MARTHA

p. 52: All quotations from Ted Shawn are from his autobiographical tapes made for the Dance Collection in 1969. In reading these notes it must be kept in mind that they were made at a time when he was bitter about what he considered his professional neglect.

p. 53: *Betty Horst.):* Jane Sherman, *The Drama of Denishawn Dance* (Middletown, Conn.: Wesleyan University Press, 1979), p. 24.

p. 53: *Andreas Pavley and Serge Oukrainsky:* These two dancers came to America from Russia with Anna Pavlova and her Russian ballet troupe in 1911. They settled in Chicago and formed their own company, worked extensively in the Chicago Opera, and toured in vaudeville. Serge Oukrainsky was one of the very few male dancers who performed on full pointe, sometimes in bare feet, which is a remarkable tour de force.

p. 54: *". . . the makings of a real artist.":* *UL,* p. 198.

p. 58: *". . . give it her own coloring.":* *UL,* p. 187.

p. 58: *". . . most appealing dancer.":* Letter from June Rhodes, December 26, 1971.

p. 58: *". . . strength of character?":* *UL,* p. 204.

p. 59: *in these domestic comforts.:* Charles Weidman conversation.

p. 59: *manager as well.:* In the Russian Imperial Ballet companies one became a teacher only after thirty years of intensive work—nine years after having entered the school as a student one was accepted into the corps de ballet, then rose through the ranks of first soloist, second soloist, coryphée—perhaps fifteen years later attaining the rank of prima ballerina. Denishawn moved with greater dispatch.

p. 59: *and settled on Grand Street:* "In that period after I came back and got rid of the big house facing Westlake Park, and kept only the Sixth Street house and the tennis court studio, Martha and I were the only teachers. I taught all the professionals and Martha taught the children and the night classes with these girls who were stenographers and clerks. . . . In a way it was a rather happy period, although I was going through emotional hell. So Martha went on with me into Grand Avenue [sic] as an assistant teacher there." Ted Shawn tape, January 28, 1969.

p. 60: *the Greek Theater in Berkeley.:* UL, p. 43.

p. 61: *". . . never told anyone.":* June Rhodes letter, December 11, 1973.

p. 63: *". . . markets of the world.":* UL, p. 171.

p. 65: *". . . my early life.":* Anna Kisselgoff, *The New York Times,* February 19, 1984.

p. 65: *". . . into a kind of courage.":* Tobi Tobias, *Dance Magazine,* March 1984.

p. 70: *". . . in tears and unhappy.":* Letter to the author from June Rhodes.

p. 71: *". . . a mild form of dishonesty.":* UL, p. 191

p. 74: *Denishawn had ended.:* James Sherman and Barton Mumaw, *Barton Mumaw, Dancer* (Brooklyn, N. Y.: Dance Horizons, 1986), p. 65.

6 FIRST CONCERT

p. 83: *". . . they wish me to stop.":* Martha Graham lecture, New York, April 15, 1974.

p. 84: *". . . it should have vibrancy.":* McCandlish Phillips in *The New York Times.*

7 FORMING TECHNIQUES

p. 89: *cannot be lyrical.:* John Martin, *The New York Times,* April 15, 1929.

p. 91: *for three years.:* The notes about Graham and details of her early classes are derived from interviews and conversations with Gertrude Shurr, Martha Hill, Anna Sokolow, Nelle Fisher, Pearl Lang, Dorothy Bird, and Sophie Maslow.

p. 98: *". . . and a shock.":* Anna Kisselgoff, *The New York Times,* February 19, 1984.

p. 99: *". . . it is visceral.":* Martha Graham lecture, New York, April 15, 1974.

p. 102: *her published notebooks,: The Notebooks of Martha Graham,* with an introduction by Nancy Wilson Ross (New York: Harcourt Brace and Jovanovich, 1973).

p. 104: *". . . and so . . . did the lion.":* Martha Graham lecture, New York, April 15, 1974.

p. 108: *embryonic movement phrase.:* Said in a taped interview with the author.

8 NEIGHBORHOOD PLAYHOUSE

p. 114: *". . . starve for beauty."*: *The New Yorker*, April 30, 1927.

p. 117: *"a tough cookie."*: Dorothy Bird told this to the author.

p. 118: *of Jean de Reszke:* Polish singer (1874–1944) who changed his voice from baritone to tenor and achieved enormous success throughout Europe and America.

p. 118: *". . . saw Martha Graham dance."*: Marian Seldes, *The New York Times*, section 2, p. 1, October 4, 1987.

9 THE GROUP

p. 141: *". . . governed by music."*: In *Martha Graham: The Early Years*. Edited and with a Foreword by Merl Armitage (Los Angeles: Merle Armitage, 1937; rpt. New York: Da Capo Press, 1978), p. 37.

p. 141: *a breath association:* Letter to Dr. Frances Wickes.

p. 146: *so we go lonely.:* W. Somerset Maugham, *The Moon and Sixpence*, pp. 149–50.

10 RITES OF PASSAGE

p. 153: *choreographic assignments.:* This episode is related by Michel Fokine in his *Memoirs of a Ballet Master*, pp. 201–215.

p. 155: *". . . over the whole . . ."*: Laura Shapiro, *Newsweek*, November 16, 1987.

11 SUNDAY-NIGHT RECITALS

p. 161: *and talked,:* For background material on this period, see Allen Churchill, *The Improper Bohemians: A Re-Creation of Greenwich Village in Its Heyday* (New York: E. P. Dutton, 1959).

p. 163: *issue of* Dance Magazine.: It appears on pp. 28–29.

12 THE MYSTERIES

p. 185: *as I remembered it.:* Agnes de Mille, *Dance to the Piper* (Boston: Little, Brown, 1952). The textual difference between this version and the description of the incident as it appeared in my book is a matter of editing. The present version is what I originally wrote.

13 PERSONAL LIFE

p. 201: *". . . against nature."*: Letter from Martha Graham to Dr. Frances Wickes, January 21, 1952.

p. 201: *". . . between the sexes."*: Alan Kriegsman, *Washington Post*, May 1984.

p. 211: *choreographic movement.:* Harold C. Schonberg, "Isamu Noguchi: A Kind of Throwback," *The New York Times Magazine,* April 14, 1968.

p. 211: *". . . like in a hospital.":* Harold C. Schonberg, "Isamu Noguchi: A Kind of Throwback," *The New York Times Magazine,* April 14, 1968.

15 FRONTIER

p. 220: *". . . a sculptor herself.":* Robert Tracy, "Noguchi: Collaborating with Graham," *Ballet Review,* Winter 1986.

p. 221: *". . . her individual expression.":* Lincoln Kirstein, quoted in Armitage, p. 32.

p. 223: *any external means.:* John Martin, quoted in Armitage, pp. 21–22.

16 ERICK AND MARTHA

p. 227: *". . . used to watch me. . . .":* Pierre Vladimiroff was a member of the Russian Imperial Ballet appearing at the Maryinsky Theater, St. Petersburg, and later of Diaghilev's Ballets Russes. In 1928–31 he joined Anna Pavlova's touring company and became her partner. He later became a faculty member of the School of American Ballet (founded 1934).

p. 238: *". . . of the protagonist.":* John Martin, *The New York Times,* January 23, 1943.

17 LETTER TO THE WORLD

p. 244: *as Erick Hawkins plays.:* John Martin, *The New York Times,* January 26, 1941

p. 244: *brought to realization.:* John Martin, *The New York Times,* June 1, 1941.

p. 245: *". . . anguish and obsession.":* Howard Moss, *The New York Review of Books,* April 26, 1984.

p. 246: *as the bumptious husband.:* Walter Terry, New York *Herald Tribune,* February 27, 1941.

18 THE WAR

p. 252: *". . . sensory perceptions.":* John Martin, *The New York Times,* January 23, 1944.

p. 253: *" '. . . that Charlotte was against.' ":* Anna Kisselgoff, *The New York Times,* February 19, 1984.

p. 260: *was thunderstruck.:* The effect of this film on Martha and her use of it in the dance were told to me by Joseph Campbell.

p. 261: *upset her no end.:* Anna Kisselgoff, *The New York Times,* March 31, 1985.

19 POTENT LAND

p. 268: *to be slight.:* John Martin, *The New York Times,* January 24, 1946.

p. 269: *the principal one.:* Tobi Tobias, *New York* magazine, June 14, 1982.

p. 280: *the place of passage.:* Robert Tracy, "Noguchi: Collaborating with Graham," *Ballet Review,* Winter 1986.

p. 281: "*. . . brings to the surface.*": Anna Kisselgoff, *The New York Times,* March 4, 1987.

p. 282: *appreciable pattern.:* Walter Terry, New York *Herald Tribune,* March 9, 1947.

20 PARIS

p. 294: "*. . . disarming wit.*": Pierre Tugal was a Russian immigrant who became one of the leading critics of Paris. A bibliophile who collected archives on the dance, in 1932 he helped organize the International Choreographic Competition, held in Paris, at which Kurt Jooss won first prize with his *Green Table,* and launched his extraordinary international career.

22 WORLD TOUR

p. 324: "*. . . never misses a performance.*": Paul Taylor, *Private Domain,* p. 66.

23 QUEEN BEE

p. 335: *through the air.:* Anna Kisselgoff, *The New York Times,* March 9, 1984.

p. 337: "*. . . moral verities.*": Anna Kisselgoff, *The New York Times,* March 3, 1984.

24 *EPISODES*

p. 345: *the ill-fated queen:* Stefan Zweig, *Mary Queen of Scotland and the Isles,* p. 352.

25 REQUIEM

p. 358: *. . . indomitable purpose.:* John Martin, *The New York Times,* January 11, 1959.

p. 358: *without finding her.:* Ibid.

26 DECRESCENDO

p. 371: *Howard wept.:* Nina Fonaroff told this story to those members of the company who were not present.

p. 374: *uncertainty of performance.:* Doris Hering, *Dance Magazine,* May 1967.

p. 378: *in the rubble!:* John Houseman, *Final Dress,* pp. 438–40.

29 PHOENIX

p. 401: *". . . with self-indulgence.":* "Martha Graham: Still Charting the Graph of the Heart": Anna Kisselgoff interview in *The New York Times,* May 15, 1977.

p. 404: *among one's best.:* Tobi Tobias, *New York* magazine, March 19, 1984.

p. 405: *never appeared in.:* Arlene Croce, *The New Yorker,* March 26, 1984.

p. 405: *voluptuous and unknowable.:* Deborah Jowitt, *Village Voice,* March 13, 1984.

p. 408: *". . . the invincible Martha.":* Marian Seldes, *The New York Times,* October 4, 1987.

30 THE WAY

p. 410: *". . . to the occasion.":* Anna Kisselgoff, *The New York Times,* June 10, 1977.

p. 416: *with the company.:* Howard Moss, *New York Review of Books,* April 26, 1984.

p. 422: *". . . of the unconscious,":* *New York Times Book Review.* Opera and Plays by Gertrude Stein, reviewed by Richard Howe, May 24, 1987.

Armitage, Merle. *Martha Graham: The Early Years*. New York: Da Capo Press, 1937.

Buckle, Richard. *Diaghilev*. New York: Atheneum, 1979.

Clarke, Mary. *Dancers of Mercury: The Story of Ballet Rambert*. London: Adam & Charles Black, 1962.

Cohen, Selma Jeanne, ed. *Doris Humphrey: An Artist First*. Connecticut: Wesleyan University Press, 1965.

Crowley, Alice Lewisohn. *The Neighborhood Playhouse*. New York: Theatre Arts Books, 1959.

Desti, Mary. *Isadora Duncan's End*. London, Victor Gollancz, Ltd., 1929.

Duncan, Irma. *Duncan Dancer: An Autobiography*. Connecticut: Wesleyan University Press, 1965.

———, Isadora. *My Life*. New York: Boni and Liveright, 1927.

Fokine, M. *Memoirs of a Ballet Master*. Edited by Anatole Chujoy, translated by Vitale Fokine. Boston: Little, Brown, 1960.

Houseman, John. *Final Dress*. New York: Simon and Schuster, 1983.

Humphrey, Doris. *The Art of Making Dances*. Toronto: Rinehart & Co., 1959.

Kendall, Elizabeth. *Where She Danced*. New York: Alfred A. Knopf, 1979.

McDonagh, Don. *Martha Graham: A Biography*. New York: Praeger Publishers, Inc., 1973.

MacDougall, Allan Ross. *Isadora: A Revolutionary in Art and Love*. New York: Thomas Nelson & Sons, 1960.

Magriel, Paul, ed. *Isadora Duncan*. New York: Henry Holt & Co., 1947.

———. *Nijinsky*. New York: Henry Holt & Co., 1946.

Maugham, W. Somerset. *The Moon and Sixpence*. London: Doubleday Doran & Co., 1919.

Nijinsky, Romola. *Nijinsky*. London: Victor Gollancz, Ltd., 1933.

Rambert, Dame Marie. *Quicksilver*. New York: Saint Martin's Press, 1972.

Rosemont, Franklin, ed. *Isadora Speaks*. San Francisco: City Lights Books, 1981.

St. Denis, Ruth. *An Unfinished Life*. New York: Harper & Brothers, 1939.

Sargeant, Winthrop. *In Spite of Myself: A Personal Memoir*. New York: Doubleday & Co., 1970.

Shawn, Ted, and Poole, Gray. *One Thousand and One Night Stands*. New York: Doubleday & Co., 1960.

Shelton, Suzanne. *Divine Dancer: A Biography of Ruth St. Denis*. New York: Doubleday & Co., 1981.

Sokolova, Lydia. *Dancing for Diaghilev*. Edited by Richard Buckle. New York: Macmillan, 1961.

Steegmuller, Francis, ed. *Your Isadora*. New York: Random House, 1974.

Stodelle, Ernestine. *Deep Song: The Dance Story of Martha Graham*. New York: Schirmer Books, 1984.

Taylor, Paul. *Private Domain*. New York: Alfred A. Knopf, 1987.

Terry, Walter. *Isadora Duncan: Her Life, Her Art, Her Legacy*. New York: Dodd, Mead & Co., 1963.

———. *The "More Living Life" of Ruth St. Denis*. New York: Dodd, Mead & Co., 1969.

Wald, Lillian (R. L. Duffus). *Neighbor and Crusader*. New York: Macmillan, 1938.

———. *Angel of Henry Street*. New York: Julian Messeur, 1948.

Zweig, Stefan. *Mary Queen of Scotland and the Isles*. New York: Viking Press, 1935.

Capucilli, Terese, 53n, 222n, 404, 419, 420
Carmer, Carl, 120, 169
Carnegie Hall, 80, 81, 92, 146, 210, 302, 304
Carnegie Institute of Technology, 7
Carousel (Rodgers and Hammerstein), 265, 272, 292
Carter, Leslie, 30
Carter, William:
  dancing of, 332, 345, 350–352, 417
  on Martha, 345, 351, 351–352, 390
Cartier, 290
Casals, Pablo, 341
Case Western Reserve University, 342
castanets, 49
Cave of the Heart, 279–80, 295–96, 297, 313
  Noguchi on, 279–80
  scenario of, 280
Celtic mythology, 250
censorship, 168–69, 202
Central European dance, 11, 69, 121
Ceremonials, 185–86
Cézanne, Paul, 174
Chaminade, Cécile, 46
changements, 129
Channel Thirteen, 342
Chaplin, Charlie, 175
charity, organized, 114
Chatsworth Hotel, 65
Chatterton, Ruth, 49
Chaucer, Geoffrey, 91, 393
Chávez, Carlos, 265, 267
Chicago, Ill., 4–5, 10, 53, 84, 114, 127, 234, 289
Chicago Summer Opera, 199
Chief, The (train), 175
Childs restaurants, 130, 131
China, 322
Chinese dancing, 47, 165
Chopin, Frédéric, 9, 94, 420
choreography, Graham, see Graham choreography
Choric Dance for an Antique Greek Tragedy, 190–91
Christensen, Harold, 228
Christensen, Lew, 228
Christian Science, 29, 31, 35, 36, 46, 61, 201
Circe, 386–87
City College of New York, 114

Civilisation, 56
Civil War, Spanish, 222–23
Civil War, U.S., 28, 29, 197
Clair, Ina, 49
Clark, Kenneth, 56
Cleveland Symphony Orchestra, 123
Clurman, Harold, 118
Clytemnestra, 334–36, 338–39, 371, 372–74, 416
  Lang in, 368
  reviews of, 335, 368n
  scenario of, 334–35
Cobert, Amos B., 346
Cohan, Robert, 261, 313, 332, 335, 336
Cohen, Harriet, 121
Cole, Jack, 73
Coleridge, Samuel Taylor, 143–44, 285–86
Colette, 239
College of Physicians and Surgeons (Baltimore), 16
Color Harmony, 78
Columbia Concerts, 169
Columbia Encyclopedia, 29n–30n
Columbia University, 120, 168, 288, 382
Comédie des Quinze, 189
Communists, 87, 161, 193
Compositions in Dance Form, 83
Concert Dancers' League, 168–69
Concurrence, 163
Congress, U.S., 114, 354
Congress Hall, 304
Connecticut College for Women, 108, 282–83
Coolidge, Elizabeth Sprague, 260
Copeland, George, 64
Copenhagen, 316
Copland, Aaron, 184, 207, 260, 344
Coralli, Jean, viii
Cornell, Katharine, 118
  career of, 188–89, 291
  on Martha, x, 189
  Martha supported by, 188–90, 223–24, 237, 272, 287, 289, 307, 415
Cornish, Nellie, 128, 130
Cornish School of Fine and Applied Arts, 128, 130, 199, 204
Corsaire, Le, 398
Cortege of Eagles, 353, 371–72
Cossack dancing, 47
Costume Institute (Metropolitan Museum), 115

costumes:
  ballet, 43, 348
  bodies revealed by, 88, 90, 94, 415
  choreographic movement of, 47–48, 90, 347
  color in, 236, 243
  designing of, 32, 48, 77, 85, 90, 115n, 153, 156
  fabric selection and, 48, 77, 88, 90, 180, 189, 208–9, 231, 313, 348, 349
  historical accuracy in, 347–48
  Martha on, 209
  Martha's design of, 48, 53, 56, 77, 85, 88, 90, 149, 151, 178–80, 182, 183, 189, 208–9, 220, 231, 302, 313–14, 334, 348
  museum collections of, 115
  rehearsal, 43, 77, 81, 93–94, 112, 128–29, 158, 174, 213, 214, 337, 415
  of St. Denis, 32, 33, 36, 41, 47–48, 53, 60, 63, 209
  of Shawn, 41, 47, 48, 49
  see also Halston; Karinska, Barbara
court dancing, 76, 107
Covent Garden, 292, 371, 398
Cowell, Henry, 207
Craig, Gordon, 115
Craig Theatre, 177–83
Craske, Margaret, 333, 413
criticism, dance, 83, 87, 155n, 212
  Martha's influence on, 212
  music and art criticism compared with, 212
  teaching of, 168, 204, 205
  see also specific critics
Croce, Arlene, 404–5
Crown Publishers, 393
"Crucifixus," 177, 178–79
Cuba, 248–49
cummings, e. e., 309
Cumnock School of Expression, 23–24, 50
Cunard, Lady, 8
Cunningham, Merce, 109, 205, 210, 328, 417
  biography of, 457–58
  Cage and, 312, 332
  choreography of, 312
  dancing of, 239, 241, 242, 261, 272, 285, 367
Curie, Marie, 36
Czechoslovakia, 230

Dabh, Halim El-, 334
Dalcrozian Eurythmics, 28, 153
Daly, Augustin, 30
dance:
  Americans vs. Europeans in, 166
  attitude toward males in, 28, 74
  as celebration of life, ix, 35–36, 103, 132
  Christian proscription of, 182
  funding for, 205, 374, 402–3, 405–6, 407, 421
  gesture and expression in, 22, 27, 28, 30, 33, 34, 44, 47–48, 79, 88, 104, 134–35, 143–44, 208
  gravity and, 78, 89n, 100, 374
  hierarchies and tradition in, 161
  history of, viii, xii, 49, 101–2, 126, 168
  Horst on, 107, 108, 111, 174–75
  Humphrey on, 78
  machinery imitation in, 89
  Martha on, viii–x, 84, 96, 102–3, 132, 134, 207, 213, 214
  modern vs. nineteenth-century character of, x, 101–2, 206
  movement of costumes in, 47–48, 90, 347
  music performances compared with, 94
  physical distortion in, 47, 135, 236
  re-creation of, viii, 8, 26, 53n, 154–55, 410
  revolutionary American developments in, 25–28, 35
  romantic forms in, 128
  social attitudes toward, 160–61
  structure and architecture of, 78
  talent and greatness in, 158–59
  visual character of, viii, 78
  see also ballet; modern dance
dance forms, 107, 128, 216
Dance Horizons, 63
Dance Magazine, 4, 163, 297, 374
Dance Observer, 164–65, 195, 287, 359, 360, 361, 362
Dance of Job, A, 65
Dance Repertory Theater, 172–73, 176
  dissolution of, 176
  founding of, 172
  Primitive Mysteries produced for, 177–84
  rehearsal conditions at, 180–81
Dancer's World, A, 341–44, 392
Dance to the Piper (de Mille), 185–86

Graham, Martha (*cont.*)
passion and recklessness of, 21, 23,
52–53, 57, 87, 201, 202, 237, 350
perfectionism of, xi, 57–58, 136–37,
401
performance preparation by, 209,
338–39
personality of, 11, 13, 14, 52, 57, 58,
130, 151
personal power of, 112, 123, 127,
131–32, 202, 221, 328–29, 345
personal sacrifices of, ix, x, 81
pets of, 173, 174, 175, 186
philosophy study of, 250–51
photographs of, 53, 197, 400, 404, 410
physical appearance of, 13–14, 20, 52,
58, 67, 81, 88, 93, 128–29, 182, 366,
384, 397, 421
physical deterioration of, 292–93,
299–300, 324, 330, 338–39, 349,
372–76, 379–83, 399, 401, 411
physical therapy used by, 298–99, 300
physique of, 16, 96, 99–100
pithy sayings of, 102–3, 120, 134
poetic instincts of, 54, 102–3, 193, 212
political stance of, 223–24
poverty of, vii, 9, 18, 53, 79, 80–82, 84,
87, 92, 122, 157, 172, 173, 198, 223
pre-performance hysterics of, 147, 150,
179–80, 181, 185–86, 287
press reviews of, 82–83, 87, 122, 183,
190–91, 222–23, 232–33, 244,
296–98; *see also specific critics*
privacy guarded by, x–xi, xii, 196, 202,
255–56, 259, 309, 366
program notes of, 212n, 238, 317, 336,
353–54
program notes omitted by, 212
prolific output of, 86, 90, 392
prominent eyes of, 13, 151, 216, 397,
404
provocative mind of, xii, 393
psychological interests of, 278–79,
393–95
public service of, 322–23, 407, 421
rare artistic compromises of, 190–91
reading tastes of, 193, 200, 202, 250,
285–86, 345–46, 393–95
receptions and parties for, 283, 296,
315
rehearsal clothes of, 77, 81, 93, 112,
128–29, 174, 213, 214, 337

religious beliefs of, 179, 201, 283
religious upbringing of, 17
as reluctant choreographer, x, 378
remorse felt by, 311, 334, 368
retirement urged upon, 372–74, 377–78
role replacements for, 327, 332,
367–69, 377–78, 419–20
royalties charged by, 79n, 410
scenarios composed by, 140, 177–79,
238, 242–43, 251–52; *see also
specific titles*
scores commissioned by, 140, 207n,
260–61, 290
Scotch-Irish antecedents of, 15, 140
sculpted image of, 210
self-absorption of, 21, 149, 151, 198
self-analysis of, ix, 157–58, 246, 378
self-assurance of, 54, 85, 157–58
selfless attachment to work by, ix–x, 52,
57–58, 80, 93, 325–27, 330
sensuality of, 237, 386
sentimentality scorned by, 336–37
servants of, 306, 383, 406
sexual attitudes of, 23, 65, 68, 87,
201–2, 237, 238n
shyness of, 52, 58, 188, 190, 216
society and fashion contacts of, 290,
306, 366–67, 397–98, 400
solo dancing of, 138, 147, 152–53,
156–58, 167, 179, 182, 184, 220,
242, 244–45, 247, 295–96, 367–68
speaking voice and manner of, xi, xii,
13, 14, 102–3, 151, 163–64, 213–17,
255, 283, 333, 342, 346, 421
speeches of, 99, 353, 371
spiritual and reverential attitude of,
ix–x, 96, 132, 213–17
spiritual vibration achieved by, 179,
182
split-kick technique of, 100, 144
stage bows of, 97, 337, 390, 401, 406,
408
stage magnetism of, 64, 88, 123, 129,
179, 182, 220–21
standing ovations for, 348, 404
stature of, xii, 13, 16, 99, 149, 157,
182, 371, 398, 404
stoicism and endurance of, 310–11, 399
storytelling of, 407–8
street clothes of, 13, 18, 81, 112, 122,
209, 248, 289–90, 291, 361, 384,
398

student devotion to, 125, 126–28, 130,
131–32, 138–39, 150–51, 213
studios of, 91–92, 112, 176, 185, 199,
210, 256, 264–65, 293, 306
stylishness of, 81, 122, 209, 248, 271,
289–90, 291, 366, 385, 398
success and fame predicted by, 157–58
superstardom of, 397–401
teaching assistants of, 117, 119, 214,
329, 331–32
teaching of, 59, 64, 67, 76–77, 79–80,
81–85, 91–104, 112, 113, 117, 118,
124–25, 127–35, 157–58, 170, 199,
204–6, 213–17
teaching theories of, 117
technical prowess of, 96, 100, 133, 184,
220, 234, 268
thoughtfulness of, 262–64, 351–52
total dedication of, ix–x, 52, 136–39,
239, 284, 325–26, 339, 350
touch communication by, 215, 337,
350, 351
touring of, 68, 150, 206, 214–15,
270–72, 284, 290–300, 308, 314–17,
319–20, 322–24, 366, 370–71
turmoil and trouble surrounding, 105,
139, 145–48, 275–77, 323, 328
unhappiness of, 58, 59, 67, 85, 87, 194,
326
vacations of, 188, 259, 311
vegetarianism of, 81
as vessel of higher force, ix–x, 325–26
violent behavior of, 146, 147, 274–76,
293, 301, 303–4, 322, 350, 353,
386–87
on virginity, 23, 65
vulnerability of, 304–5, 308
water feared by, 150, 249
weeping of, 147, 301, 304, 367
White House performance of, 221–22
wit and gaiety of, 104, 151
working methods of, 82, 84–85, 117,
130, 132, 135–41, 198, 213–17, 254
world influence of, 322, 363
Graham, Mary (sister), 16, 24, 58–59,
199, 251, 252
death of, 202
illnesses of, 18, 20, 202
independent life of, 81, 307
marriage of, 202
physical appearance and personality of,
20–21, 51

Graham, William (brother), 16
Graham choreography, 434–54
of 1920s, 86–91, 167, 434–40
of 1930s, 167, 177–84, 185, 190–91,
219–21, 222–23, 440–46
of 1940s, 241–47, 249, 251–55,
260–62, 279–292, 446–48
of 1950s, 147, 285–87, 302–4, 309,
317–318, 334–39, 344–50, 448–49
of 1960s, 353–56, 371–72, 376, 379,
449–51
of 1970s, 390, 399–400, 452–53
of 1980s, 401, 404–5, 453–54
audience demands made by, 101
barefoot dancing in, 158, 180
body postures in, 96–98, 179, 184, 215,
220, 234, 347
ceremonial content in, 177–78, 185,
233–34
Congressional denunciation of, 354
design and construction of, 140–41,
251
early examples of, 77, 82–85
efforts to save, 377–79, 386, 409–10
emotional impact of, 88, 89, 90, 99,
179, 182–83, 187, 188, 222–23, 234,
268, 304, 314, 355
emotion through gesture in, 134–35,
140
expressive strength of, 87, 99, 220
falls in, 89, 100–101, 184, 196, 216,
252, 373
feminine and personal point of view in,
99–100, 233, 237, 238
films of, 167, 341–44, 353, 386, 409,
414
grief-stricken postures in, 89–90, 179
group contribution to, 136–37, 285
group movement in, 89, 179, 190, 213,
234–35, 245, 268
hand positions in, 88, 97, 98, 347
Hawkins's effect on, 231–32, 237–38,
241, 246, 271
historical heritage themes in, 220–21,
222–23, 232–36, 237
humor in, 238, 245–46, 337
innovations in, 88, 90, 184, 206–8,
212–13
kneeling and sitting positions in, 53,
90, 96–97, 184, 234, 235, 268,
295–96
literary comparisons with, 221, 239

Graham choreography (*cont.*)
loss of, 91, 167, 235, 405
male/female relations depicted in,
231–32, 233–34, 237, 238, 239,
245–46, 261–62, 295
Martha's exclusive hold on, 364–65
Martha's personal life reflected in, 246,
251–53, 260, 261
as morality plays, 253
music for, 139, 140–41, 177, 184,
207–8, 220, 238, 243, 245, 255,
260–61, 264, 267, 280–81, 283,
302–3, 317, 336, 344, 345, 354, 400;
see also specific composers
for New York City Ballet, 344–50
notation of, 167
open mouth in, 88
Oriental influences in, 53, 77, 178, 210,
234
percussive vs. melodic music for, 207–8
pleading positions in, 101
program notes for, 212*n*, 238, 317,
336, 353–54
props used in, 253–54, 280, 336, 372
psychological content of, 253, 278–81,
303–4
reconstruction of, 221, 235, 253–54,
313, 332, 376, 377, 386, 410
recurring themes in, 239, 246
religious and mythical subjects of, 17,
88, 89–90, 177–84, 191, 221,
250–53, 259–60, 277–81, 302–4,
317, 334–37, 354–55
satire and irony in, 238, 239, 246, 337,
354
scenarios for 140, 177–79, 238, 242–43,
251–52; *see also specific titles*
scenic devices and stage sets for,
210–12, 219–20, 236, 245, 253, 280,
281; *see also* Noguchi, Isamu
selection process in, 136–38
sexual content in, 237, 238*n*, 280–81,
295, 303–4, 354
social comment in, 86–87, 89, 90,
222–23, 238–39, 243
speaking parts in, 242, 243, 400
spiral falls in, 89
theater dancing influenced by, vii, 88
titles chosen for, 212
young people attracted to, 355
see also specific titles
"Graham Crackers," 133, 135

Graham Foundation, 367, 402
Graham technique, x, 95–104
animal sensuality in, 103
arm movements in, 97, 98, 103, 133
ballet compared with, vii, 90–91, 95,
99, 101–2, 144, 206, 208, 347, 413
basic root positions in, 96–97, 102, 213
breathing and, 97–99, 220, 250–51
contraction and release in, 97–99, 101,
215, 216, 347
counting of musical beats and, 99, 105
difficulty of, xi, 86, 96, 100–101,
133–34, 135, 215–16, 230, 268, 339
"divine distortion" in, 135, 236
documentary films of, 167, 341–44,
353, 386, 409
evolution of, 84, 132–34, 135–40
exercises in, 94–95, 96, 101, 103–4,
230
experimental beginnings of, 82, 83–85
floor used in, 53, 82, 90, 94, 100, 184,
234
Grand Kabuki compared with, vii, 347
head positions in, 103
innovations in, 94–95, 101–2, 129,
132–34, 206–8
jerks and spasms in, 98–99, 135
knee positions in, 96, 132–33, 213,
234, 235, 268, 299
leg positions in, 53, 94–95, 96, 97, 98,
100, 129, 144, 234, 404
mannerisms in, 97, 100, 144
Martha as exponent of, 135, 182
Martha on, 410
medical problems caused by, 101, 133,
268
pelvis use in, 96, 97–98, 132, 234
percussive force in, 98, 215
philosophy and aesthetics of, 213–17
physical and psychological essence of,
207
sensuousness of, 237
spinal positions in, 96–97, 102–3
split-kicks in, 100, 144
torso use in, 96–97, 100–101, 133, 220
warm-up and preparation for, 94–95,
96, 250–51
Gramont, Duchesse de, 8
Grand Kabuki, viii, 347
Grauman, Sid, 63
Grauman's Egyptian Theater, 57
Grauman's theaters, 55, 57, 63

Joyce, James, 91, 205
Judith, 302–4, 309, 335
    scenario of, 302–3
Juilliard Foundation, 108
Juilliard School of Music, 147, 189, 329, 346, 359, 376, 413
jumps, 95, 99, 101, 134, 154, 155, 239, 332, 413
Jung, Carl, 142, 250, 251, 277–78, 279, 309
    Martha and, 316
Junger, Esther, 162, 205

Kanda, Akiko, 346
Kandinsky, Wassily, 84
Kansas City, Mo., 45, 226, 291
Karinska, Barbara, 345, 347–48
Karsavina, Tamara, 6
"Kashmiri Song," 69
Keats, John, 26
Kelley, Edna, 354
Kelly, Myra, 113
Kennedy, Jacqueline, 366
Kennedy, Rose, 384
Kennedy, William, 365–67
    support and promotion of Martha by, 366–67, 398
Keppel, Alice, 34
Kern, Jerome, 171
kimonos, 48, 49, 214, 337
Kimura, Yuriko, 107, 280, 315–16, 336–37, 400, 401, 417, 419
King James Bible, 303
King Lear (Shakespeare), 285–86
Kirstein, Lincoln, 221, 224, 227–29, 239–40, 312, 348, 362
    Balanchine and, 227–28, 236, 345, 348
    Ballet Caravan founded by, 224, 227, 228, 240
    fundraising of, 236
    Hawkins and, 224, 227, 228, 229, 236, 240
    Martha and, 229, 239–40, 345
    modern dance disliked by, 228–29, 345
    physical appearance and personality of, 229
    writing of, 227–28, 240
Kisselgoff, Anna, 252
    on Martha, 98, 281, 335, 337, 401–2, 405, 406, 410
Kissinger, Henry, 390
Kiss Me, Kate (Porter), 334

Klee, Paul, 106, 193, 210, 354
Klein's, 289
Knaths, Otto Karl, 106
knee-flexes, 95, 132–33, 213, 268
knee pads, 133
knees, crooked, 96
knee squats, 47, 100, 184
Kochno, Boris, 294
Kodály, Zoltán, 89, 207
Kollwitz, Käthe, 106
Kolodney, William, 170
Koslov, Theodore, 3, 186
Krenek, Ernst, 207
Kreutzberg, Harald, 106, 121, 165, 190, 226, 227, 333
Krevitsky, Nik, 106
Kriegsman, Alan, 201, 372
Kroll, Lucy, 342, 343, 373, 392–93
Kroll, Nathan, 341–44, 372–73
Kuch, Richard, 345
Kundalini Yoga, 250–51, 429–31

Laban, Rudolf von, 69, 97
Labor Stage, 189, 237
La Brea tar pits, 24
Lady Chatterley's Lover (Lawrence), 169, 202
Lakmé (Delibes), 32
Lamentation, 89–90, 167, 212, 222, 249
Lamp Unto My Feet, A, 74n–75n
Lang, Jack, 403
Lang, Pearl, 100, 108, 131, 200, 264, 299, 363, 401
    biography of, 461
    choreography of, 109, 137, 315
    on dance, 108, 217
    dancing of, 234, 241, 245, 252, 254, 273, 298, 367–68, 410
    on Hawkins, 285, 287
    Hebrew study of, 303
    on Horst, 109, 110, 277
    on Martha, 100, 136–38, 241, 251, 254, 255, 283, 287, 298–299, 303–4, 368, 372, 414, 418
    reviews of, 368n
    solo concerts of, 109
Langly, Carol, 419–20
Lauterer, Arch, 171, 204–5
    set design of, 210, 236, 245
Lawrence, D. H., 169, 202
Lawrence, Pauline, 58, 63, 70, 78, 162
Lawton, Dorothy, 167

Mann, Joseph, 170
Mansfield Theatre, 244
Maracci, Carmalita, 350
March of Dimes, 290
Marin, John, 106
marionettes, 245
Maritain, Jacques, 393
Market, Russell, 190
Marks Levine, 166
"Marseillaise, The," 27
Martha Graham Dance Company, 33–34,
    411; see also Martha Graham Group
Martha Graham Group, 104, 124–25,
    126–40, 186–87
  absolute devotion required of, 149, 151,
    329–30, 353, 388, 390
  ballet dancers compared with, 92–93,
    347
  character and quality of dancers in,
    92–93, 104–5, 138, 219, 416–17
  chorus costumes of, 149
  contemporary vs. original dancers in,
    416–17
  costumes sewn by, 104, 180, 290–91,
    313–14
  creative involvement of, 136–37, 285
  dancers' pride in, 149, 151
  defections from, 312, 330, 331–32, 335,
    336
  Eastern tours of, 308, 322–23
  European trips of, 290–300, 314–17
  evolutionary changes in, 411–19
  first men in, 230, 233, 235
  formation of, 92, 127
  funding for, 236–37, 260, 367, 402–4
  Hawkins resented by, 230, 231–32,
    274, 276–77, 285, 328
  Hawkins's position in, 230–32, 236–37,
    246, 256, 260, 274, 276–77
  husbands and lovers and, 105, 135–36
  Israeli trip of, 338–39
  labor unions and, 364, 417
  maintenance and replacement in, 331,
    332, 363, 406
  male roles in, 312–14, 355
  Martha's combative behavior with,
    274–76
  Martha's hold on, 329–31
  Martha's identification with, 329–30
  medical problems of, 101, 133
  men recruited for, 271
  minorities in, 280

original dancers in, 92–93, 127, 417–18
outside earnings of dancers in, 128,
    129–30, 131, 272, 329
payment of dancers in, 290, 329,
    363–64, 377
production costs of, 290, 320, 363–65,
    400, 413
Radio City Music Hall appearance of,
    190–91
regular seasons established for, 290
replacement of Martha's roles in, 327,
    332, 367–69, 377–78, 419–20
street clothes worn by, 209–10, 270,
    297
touring of, 206, 214–15, 270–72,
    290–300, 319–20, 322–24, 366,
    370–71
weeding out process in, 104
World's Fair appearance of, 230–31
world tour of, 319–20, 322–24
Martha Graham School of Contemporary
    Dance, 306–7, 311, 320, 322, 329,
    365, 402, 411, 421
  administration of, 309, 332, 334, 377,
    383, 387
  London branch of, 321, 376–77, 407
  public relations of, 410–11
  see also Graham, Martha, teaching of
Martin, John, 83, 163, 164, 212
  dance reviews of, 71, 89, 183, 218,
    232–33, 238, 244, 252, 261, 268–69
  on Hawkins, 339–40
  on Horst, 4, 45, 110
  on Humphrey, 357–58
  judgments reversed by, 270
  on Martha, 89, 136, 173, 183, 187,
    222–23, 233, 244, 253, 261, 268,
    299, 413
  Martha and, 232–33, 299
  physical appearance and personality of,
    87
  teaching of, 168, 204, 205
Martin, Louise, 205
Mary, Queen of Scots, 345–49
Masks of God, The (Campbell), 205
Maslow, Sophie, 95, 106, 109, 131, 231
  biography of, 461
  dancing of, 251, 254, 417
  on Martha, 95, 123, 134, 138, 231,
    326
Mason Opera House, 21, 24, 27
Mass, Catholic, 17, 19

Wickes, Frances, 323
  death of, 375, 379
  intellect and personality of, 278–79,
    309, 379
  Martha's relationship with, 278–279,
    300, 307, 308–9, 311–12, 316, 325,
    328, 339, 356, 369, 370, 372
Wigman, Mary, 11, 69, 154, 165, 304
  American visits of, 121, 163, 169, 317
  choreography of, 97, 98
  Martha acclaimed by, 316–17
  Martha compared with, 98, 316–17
wigs, 56, 57
Wilder, Thornton, 120, 171, 355n
Wilderness Stair, 282
Williams College, 203
Wilson, Sallie:
  on Martha, 252, 346–47
  Queen Elizabeth role of, 345, 346–49
Wind, Edgar, 13
windshield wiper, invention of, 189
Winter, Ethel, 299–300, 321, 348, 367,
    376, 417
  biography of, 465–66
Winter Garden Theater, 11, 68
Wintergarten (Berlin), 71
Wisconsin, University of, 365
women's rights, 26, 36–37
Women's Wear Daily, 183
Wood, David, 354
Woodford, Charles, 63
Woodward, Joanne, 120

Works Progress Administration (W.P.A.),
    192
World's Fair of 1939, 230–31
World War I, 58
World War II, 165, 166, 249, 257, 265,
    271, 287, 288, 289, 314
WQED, 342, 344
Writer's Guild, 352

Xochitl, 57, 63, 67–68

Yale University, 260
Yeats, William Butler, ix
Yoga, 250–51
Yogi, The, 95–96, 251
Young, Stark, 120, 122, 183, 353
Young Men's Hebrew Association
    (YMHA), 157, 158, 167, 170, 246
Youskevitch, Igor, 333
Yuriko, see Kimura, Yuriko

zapateado, 47, 121
Zaza (Breton and Simon), 30
Zemach, Benjamin, 124
Zemach, Naum, 124n
Zen Buddhism, 210, 323
Ziegfeld Follies, 49, 70
Ziegfeld Theatre, 367, 372–73
Zimbalist, Efram, Jr., 120
Zuñi pueblo, 175–76
Zweig, Stefan, 345–46